Beggars, Iconoclasts, and Civic Patriots

Beggars, Iconoclasts, and Civic Patriots

THE POLITICAL CULTURE
OF THE DUTCH REVOLT

Peter Arnade

CORNELL UNIVERSITY PRESS *Ithaca and London*

Copyright © 2008 by Cornell University

All rights reserved. Except for brief quotations in a review, this book, or parts thereof, must not be reproduced in any form without permission in writing from the publisher. For information, address Cornell University Press, Sage House, 512 East State Street, Ithaca, New York 14850.

First published 2008 by Cornell University Press
First printing, Cornell Paperbacks, 2008

Printed in the United States of America

Library of Congress Cataloging-in-Publication Data
Arnade, Peter J.
  Beggars, iconoclasts, and civic patriots: the political culture of the Dutch Revolt / Peter Arnade.
    p. cm.
  Includes bibliographical references and index.
  ISBN 978-0-8014-4681-8 (cloth : alk. paper) — ISBN 978-0-8014-7496-5 (pbk. : alk. paper)
  1. Netherlands—Politics and government—1556–1648. 2. Political culture—Netherlands—History—16th century. I. Title.
  DH187.5.A76 2008
  949.2′03—dc22   2008013718

Cornell University Press strives to use environmentally responsible suppliers and materials to the fullest extent possible in the publishing of its books. Such materials include vegetable-based, low-VOC inks and acid-free papers that are recycled, totally chlorine-free, or partly composed of nonwood fibers. For further information, visit our website at www.cornellpress.cornell.edu.

Cloth printing   10 9 8 7 6 5 4 3 2 1
Paperback printing   10 9 8 7 6 5 4 3 2 1

Contents

	Preface	vii
	Acknowledgments	xi
	Abbreviations	xiii
	Introduction	1
1	Princely Triumphs: The Consecration of Burgundian Political Authority	12
2	Faithful to the King: Associations of Dissent	50
3	Vivent les Gueux! Iconoclasm, Inversion, and the Problem of Authority	90
4	Time, Space, and the City: Iconoclasm in Ypres, Ghent, and Antwerp	125
5	A New Idolatry: Alba as Avenger and Usurper of Royal Authority	166
6	Spanish Furies: Sieges, Sacks, and the City Defiant	212
7	Father of the Fatherland: William of Orange as Civic Patriot	260
8	Abjuration and Assassination: The Dilemma of Authority	304
	Epilogue	328
	Bibliographic Note	335
	Index	337

Preface

The Dutch Revolt has long been granted canonical status. Already by the end of the sixteenth century before its outcome was predictable, learned contemporaries like Emanuel van Meteren and Pieter Bor were publishing the first books of their general histories about the conflict. By the seventeenth century, the Revolt had become a handy reference point in other European struggles against monarchical authority. In 1649 radical English parliamentarians in conflict with their king, Charles I, pointed to the success of the United Provinces of the Netherlands. Eighteenth- and nineteenth-century writers acclaimed the Dutch Revolt widely as instrumental in the shaping of the modern political state. In 1788 on the eve of the French Revolution, Friedrich Schiller, the German playwright and poet, hailed the Revolt as the sixteenth century's watershed event because it pitted freedom against tyranny in ways others might emulate. Eighteenth-century French and American revolutionaries also embraced the Dutch Revolt, not so much with Schiller's poetic enthusiasm as with a sober, Whiggish recognition of its cornerstone principles of constitutional rights. In 1781 John Adams described the American Revolution as a "transcript" of the Revolt and the United Provinces. Even the fiercest critics of the Dutch Revolt's supposed political fruits touted its centrality in the lineage of modern political revolutions. In *Capital* (1867), Karl Marx viewed the Revolt as the historical incubator of the industrial bourgeoisie—and all the ills of capitalist inequalities and colonial exploitation that followed their political ascendancy.

Few of these men comprehended the Revolt's complex history well, a task that awaited nineteenth-century historians. These masterworks were divided between Protestant-inspired historians like Guillaume Groen van Prinsterer or the American John Lothrop Motley, who in soaring prose recounted the triumph over Spanish tyranny, and the liberal nationalists, like Johannes van Vloten, Robert Fruin, or Petrus Johannes Blok, who interpreted the upheaval as the wellspring of popular sovereignty and freedom of conscience. These studies were written with the conviction, gusto, and vigorous prose of true believers, marking them as products of the age of nationalism. They were tempered considerably by the more exacting historical methods of twentieth-century students who pursued the Revolt with the rigorous methods of social scientists, exploring local circumstances in archivally rich case studies, and scouting out social factors, economic exigencies, and religious ideals and realities. As the grand metanarratives of the nineteenth century with their supercharged religious conviction or nationalist brio were cast aside, historians concentrated on the causes and consequences of the Revolt's major chapters. They abandoned the well-trodden ground of political narrative in search of the deep structures that provoked key social groups to revolt, highlighting the role of urbanization, representative bodies, and civic traditions of dissent in creating a political climate based on a defense of custom and of local rights. The international dimension of the Revolt is also now acknowledged, for the provinces of the Low Countries represented just one part of Habsburg Spain's vast possessions. As contemporaries knew, the many tiers of the Revolt were intimately linked to conflicts and concerns elsewhere, neighboring France and Germany most pertinently, but also the Mediterranean world, where conflicts between the Ottomans and Spain often determined the degree to which Philip II could give sustained attention to the troubles in the Netherlands.

The harvest of these studies has been an exhaustive inventory of the political, social, and economic triggers of the troubles, and an assessment of how the unsettled religious landscape of the sixteenth-century Low Countries, where a Catholic monarch, determined to ensure that his lands not succumb to the religious violence that beset his father's German territories nor replicate the turmoil in France, struggled mightily against a seemingly irrepressible Protestantism. But for all this research's empirical richness, it has left us curiously unable to understand the Revolt's distinctive character. Important as urbanization, commercialization, radical Calvinism, class tensions, and noble self-interest were, none alone explains the genesis or progress of the Revolt, and none explains how it was that diverse—and often mutually antagonistic—groups propelled the conflict forward. Even the most committed student of the Revolt's political thought, Ernst Kossmann, has hesitated to argue that the rebels were fully enacting, or even clearly anticipating, political ideals that would come to be associated with the "age of democratic revolutions" to follow. Thus while the Dutch Revolt has retained its privileged status in the pantheon of early modern European rebellions, there is no consensus about which ingredients were unique or its precise legacy to other upheavals. Its protagonists were too diverse, their motivations and goals too hybrid, for easy explanation.

In this book I revisit the Revolt's political events and chronology, not as tales of Herculean struggles or for narrative's sake. Instead, I am interested in how protagonists of the Revolt flourished in one of early modern Europe's most vibrant public realms. It is this book's premise that the real political legacy of the Revolt lies not exclusively in the high texts of the theorists or in the institutions and formal political bodies where politics were officially enacted, but in the political culture the conflict birthed. The pulse of the Revolt was its public dramatization—the acts, words, observations, and cultural representations that were the upheaval's daily bread and its popular voice. For it is in the public spaces and through the vernacular sources that theory met practice and the Revolt was wagered and fought. Noblemen protesting state centralization and religious policy; Calvinists advocating public recognition of their faith; rural and urban craftsmen, shopkeepers, laborers, and middling professionals drawn to civic populism and, if Calvinist, often to iconoclasm; and urban magistrates zealous to protect local turf and legal right—it was these people who made the Revolt. They did so by occupying and claiming the public domain and seizing popular media, in the process creating a polyphonic language of rebellion and a vernacular political culture that constitutes the Revolt's most novel feature.

An approach to the Revolt that pursues its symbolization and ritual scripts takes us out of the calculus of categories and causes by which the Revolt can be assessed and pursues instead its very enactment, not as static set pieces, but as a process by which its advocates created a voice and vocabulary for themselves. It allows us to see the principal actors *as* actors: people staking public claims that were not just translations of a priori ideas—a Calvinist sermon or a formal political treatise—but original wagers realized in the performance of the act itself. It also reinforces the idea that the Revolt possesses its own unique ingredients, and that the best vantage point from which to harvest its political meaning is through the strategies by which its advocates championed their causes. This book returns to the iconic high moments of the Dutch Revolt to come to grips with its vernacular language, and to capture the political dramas and cultural conceits around which people rallied, found political voice, and forged a rebellion whose jigsaw complexity and remarkable outcome still engages and confounds us today.

Acknowledgments

Many years ago, while researching late-medieval Flanders, I encountered Marcus van Vaernewijck's stirring chronicle of Ghent between 1566 and 1569. At the time, I needed only a few references, but Van Vaernewijck's lapidary account of Ghent's iconoclasm riots and the city's strain under the Duke of Alba's occupation seized my attention, and some years later, I returned to it. Little did I know that the end result of my curiosity would be this book. My research began with work on the iconoclasm riots of 1566, thanks to a summer grant from the American Philosophical Society. A National Endowment for the Humanities fellowship gave me an invaluable year to dig deeper and broaden my subject, and a membership in the School of Historical Studies at the Institute for Advanced Study allowed me to finish the study. California State University San Marcos helped make these grants possible, and I thank the Department of History and the Office of the Dean for their support.

Over the decade I have spent on the subject of the Dutch Revolt, I have profited from a community of European and North American scholars whose generosity and intellectual camaraderie is unparalleled. The scholars in medieval and early modern history at the Universiteit Gent have been the best of colleagues. I am especially grateful to Walter Prevenier, Marc Boone, Hilde de Ridder-Symoens, Anne-Laure van Bruaene, Jelle Haemers, and Jan Dumolyn, all of whom responded to my e-mail, pointed me to documents, read early drafts of my work, and provided digital reproductions of sources. The participants of the UCLA Center for Seventeenth- and Eighteenth-Century Studies and the William Andrews Clark Memorial Library conference on the Dutch Revolt in October 2005 enriched my understanding of the Revolt by complicating its terrain, and in this regard I thank Marc Boone, Alastair Duke, Henk van Nierop, Anne-Laure van Bruaene, Catherine Secretan, Mark Meadow, René van Stipriaan, Judith Pollmann, Guido Marnef, James Tracy, Yolanda Rodríguez Pérez, Wayne te Brake, Peter Riell, and Margaret Jacob. For help with sources and queries, I thank Geoffrey Parker, David Lagomarsino, Walter Simons, Charles van den Heuvel, and Daniel Horst. While a member of the School of Historical Studies at the Institute for Advanced Study at Princeton, I profited from the ideal setting in which to think and write, and I thank Jonathan Israel and Benjamin Schmidt for sustained conversations about the early modern Low Countries and elsewhere, Caroline Walker Bynum for her weekly medieval table and our discussions about religious images and iconoclasm, Richard Kagan for his reading of several draft chapters and help with Spanish materials, and the intellectual and social camaraderie of Martha Newman, Karl Shoemaker, Herman Bennett, Geoffrey Hosking, James Hankins, Felice Lipshitz, Joseph Patrouch, Mario Biagioli, Raymond Jonas, Matthew Stanley, Florin Curta, Cordula Grewe, and Katherine Tachau, among others. Steven Hahn, Stephanie McCurry, Tom Passananti, and Kristen Lauter provided memorable camaraderie and abiding friendship as I dashed to finish this book. Richard Trexler taught me much about ritual and urban life, and his intellectual zest will be much missed. Martha Howell read several drafts even when she had no time, and offered invaluable advice about how to reshape it. Anton van der Lem read a penultimate version with rigor and care, and shared his scholarship with me. Alastair Duke and Henk van Nierop helped with research from the outset, humbling me with their scholarly generosity by sharing their unsurpassed knowledge of sixteenth-century Netherlands and the Revolt with me. Judith Pollmann offered invaluable feedback and trenchant criticism in a final draft of this work. Aimee Lee Cheek spent hours improving my errant prose, and for her help, and her and Bill Cheek's sparkling friendship, I am deeply grateful. The anonymous readers for Cornell University Press offered invaluable advice, and I thank them for their astute reports. For her sharp copyediting that sparred me errors and brightened my prose, I am grateful to Katy Meigs. For his commitment to this book and his sage editorial help, I thank John G. Ackerman, the director of Cornell University Press.

I would like to thank the professional staff at the many libraries and archives where I did my work, especially the Algemeen Rijksarchief and Koninklijke Bibliotheek van België in Brussels; the Koninklijke Bibliotheek in The Hague; the Universiteitsbibliotheek and its Bijzondere Collecties in Leiden; the Universiteitsbibliotheek in Gent—its department of manuscripts and rare books in particular; and the Stadsarchief Gent and Stadsarchief Antwerpen. All research has been done in original sources and languages, but where solid English translations already exist, I have cited them. I have used in particular Alastair Duke's translations of key sections of the Wouter Jacobsz. diary available under "sources in translation" at the Dutch Revolt website: http://dutchrevolt.leidenuniv.nl. All other translations are my own.

Friends and family have buoyed me through the years of writing this book. I thank Elizabeth Colwill for the rich world of scholarship and partnership we share, and for her model embrace of scholarship, pedagogy, politics, and family. Our children, Liam and Julia, are my favorite rebels and iconoclasts, so it is fitting that I dedicate this book to them.

Abbreviations

Archives d'Orange-Nassau	G. Groen van Prinsterer, ed., *Archives ou correspondance inédite de la maison d'Orange-Nassau*, 23 vols. (Leiden, 1835–1915)
Bor, *Oorsprongk*	Pieter Bor, *Oorsprongk, begin en vervolgh der Nederlandsche oorlogen, beroerten, en borgerlyke oneenigheden*, 4 vols. (Amsterdam, 1679–1684)
BT Van Vaernewijck	Marcus van Vaernewijck, *Van die beroerlicke tijden in die Nederlanden en voornamelijk in Ghendt, 1566–68*, ed., Ferd. Vanderhaeghen, 5 vols. (Ghent, 1872)
Corr. Granvelle	E. Poullet and C. Piot, eds., *Correspondance du Cardinal de Granvelle 1565–1586*, 12 vols. (Brussels, 1878–97)
Corr. Philippe II	L. P. Gachard, ed., *Correspondance de Philippe II sur les affaires des Pays-Bas*, 5 vols. (Brussels, 1848–79)
Corr. Taciturne	L. P. Gachard, ed., *Correspondance de Guillaume le Taciturne*, 6 vols. (Brussels, 1847–66)
Dagboek Jacobsz.	I. H. van Eeghen, ed., *Dagboek van Broeder Wouter Jacobsz.*, 2 vols. (Groningen, 1959–60)
Epistolario Alba	Duke of Berwick y de Alba, ed., *Epistolario de III Duque de Alba, Don Fernando Alvarez de Toledo*, 3 vols. (Madrid, 1952)
GB	E. T. Kuiper and P. Leendertz Jr. eds., *Het Geuzenliedboeken naar de oude drukken uit de nalatenschap van E. T. Kuiper* (Zutphen, 1924–25)
Kroniek Van Haecht	Rob. van Roosbroeck, ed., *De Kroniek van Godevaert van Haecht over de troebelen van 1565 tot 1574 te Antwerpen en elders*, 2 vols. (Antwerp, 1929)
NG	J. van Vloten, ed., *Nederlandsche Geschiedzangen*, 2 vols. (Amsterdam, 1864)
RvB	Algemeen Rijksarchief Brussels, Raad van Beroerte
SAG	Stadsarchief Gent

Texts Revolt   E. H. Kossmann and A. F. Mellink, eds., *Texts concerning the Revolt of the Netherlands* (Cambridge, 1974)

Troubles religieux   Ed. de Coussemaker, ed., *Troubles religieux du XVIe siècle dans la Flandre Maritime, 1560–70*, 4 vols. (Bruges, 1876)

Beggars, Iconoclasts, and Civic Patriots

INTRODUCTION

The commonwealth of the United Provinces so wore its independence on its sleeve that an English observer in the mid-seventeenth century quipped, "Tell them of Monarchy but in jest, and they will cut your throat in earnest."[1] But monarchy had enjoyed a secured lodging in the political anatomy of the Burgundian and Habsburg Netherlands. Sixteenth-century inhabitants of the Low Countries, even during the most violent years of the Dutch Revolt, would have been surprised to learn that their heirs would be deemed hostile to the lordship of Emperor Charles V and King Philip II. The Dutch Revolt did not so much deny the principle of monarchy as insist that sovereignty in the Low Countries was regionally divided according to local titles of rule. Even before the outbreak of conflict, elites were quick to remind Charles V and Philip II that they governed in the Low Countries by the same amalgamation of dukedoms and countships as had their fifteenth-century Burgundian predecessors. At stake was not princely sovereignty, but rather its alignment with the other great spheres of political power in the Burgundian Netherlands: the cities and their privileges, and the regional representative bodies, the Estates, and their authority. As Charles V groused to his brother Ferdinand in 1531, "Everyone in the Low Countries demands privileges that are contrary to my sovereignty, as if I were their companion and not their lord."[2]

When, wearied by war and racked with gout, Charles V finally abdicated his possessions at a ceremony held in the Burgundian Coudenberg Palace in Brussels on October 25, 1555, the event served as an opportunity to celebrate lordship's relationship to its subjects, the churchmen, *grands seigneurs*, and politically enfranchised townsmen who made up the States General. Emotions were high, and more than one source reported tears shed by

---

1. *The Dutch Drawn to the Life* (London, 1664), 39; in general, see Wyger R. E. Velema, "'That a Republic Is Better Than a Monarchy': Anti-Monarchism in Early Modern Dutch Political Thought," in *Republicanism: A Shared European Heritage*, ed. Martin van Gelderen and Quentin Skinner, 2 vols. (Cambridge, 2001), 1:9–25.

2. Quoted in James Tracy, *Emperor Charles V: Impresario of War* (Cambridge, 2002), 53.

the emperor himself and his audience.³ Arrangers orchestrated the ceremony as a moment of political gravitas, of elegiac tributes to princely accomplishments. A dashing young William of Orange, the Netherlands' greatest nobleman, who had been raised in the orbit of Charles since his youth, helped the aged ruler take his seat in a richly appointed armchair. It was a well-attended and tightly scripted occasion, taking place in the presence of senior Habsburg officials and an audience of around one thousand, comprising deputies of the States General of the Netherlands, knights of the prestigious Order of the Golden Fleece, members of the Council of State and Privy Council, and foreign ambassadors. We owe to the graphic artist Frans Hogenberg a public record of the event, a print that shows a neatly arranged great hall, hung generously with tapestry sets of the Golden Fleece and of the biblical Gideon, and an audience standing in dutiful attention before Charles V and Philip II.⁴ Despite the fact that in a political testament to his young son Philip in 1539 Charles had warned that the Low Countries were a troublesome place of "divisions and factions, riots and uprisings" populated with "unappreciative and unruly people," at this event in 1555 he offered no harsh appraisal of his often contentious subjects, though he did counsel dutiful respect for their new lord, Philip II.⁵ The pensionary of the City of Antwerp, representing the Estates of Brabant, followed Charles's formal adieu with praise for his wise and just government—warm words from a province that would be among the most difficult for the emperor's son, and that routinely chafed at enforcing the government's heresy edicts.⁶ This highly orchestrated political ceremony had as its overriding purpose to celebrate the deeds of its famed sovereign and to confirm the lordship of his successor.

Just twenty-six years later, on July 26, 1581, an entirely different public mood prompted the States General to issue the famous *Plakkaat van Verlatinghe*.⁷ No fanfare accompanied this edict of abjuration by which Charles's son Philip II was vacated of his lordship on the grounds that he had failed to uphold the traditional rights and privileges to which he had sworn fealty. By then absence of public celebration—despite the impact of the abjura-

---

3. The sources concerning Charles's abdication and his retreat to the Jeronymite monastery of Saint Yuste in Castile are collected in L. P. Gachard, ed., *Retraite et mort de Charles-Quint au monastère de Yuste*, 3 vols. (Brussels, 1854). A summary of the abdication ceremony, with extracts from a variety of official and civic accounts, is in ibid., 1:80–105.

4. For all its grandeur, the abdication took place inside the grand Coudenberg Palace in the royal district of Brussels, performed before a hand-picked audience. The Catholic observer of public life in Brussels, Jan de Pottre, member of the mercerers' guild, mentioned it only in passing. See Baron de St. Genois, ed., *Dagboek van Jan de Pottre* (1861), 13.

5. See Charles's letter to Philip dated November 5, 1539, in Manuel Fernández Alvárez, ed., *Corpus Documental de Carlos V*, 5 vols. (Salamanca, 1973–81), 2:36.

6. Nor was there any mention of Charles having scaled back regional and urban privileges, most famously after the Ghent rebellion of 1539 but also against 's-Hertogenbosch in 1525 and Brussels and Utrecht in 1528. See Gachard, *Retraite et mort de Charles-Quint*, 1:93.

7. See N. Mout, *Plakkaat van Verlatinge 1581* (The Hague, 1971) for a critical edition of this text.

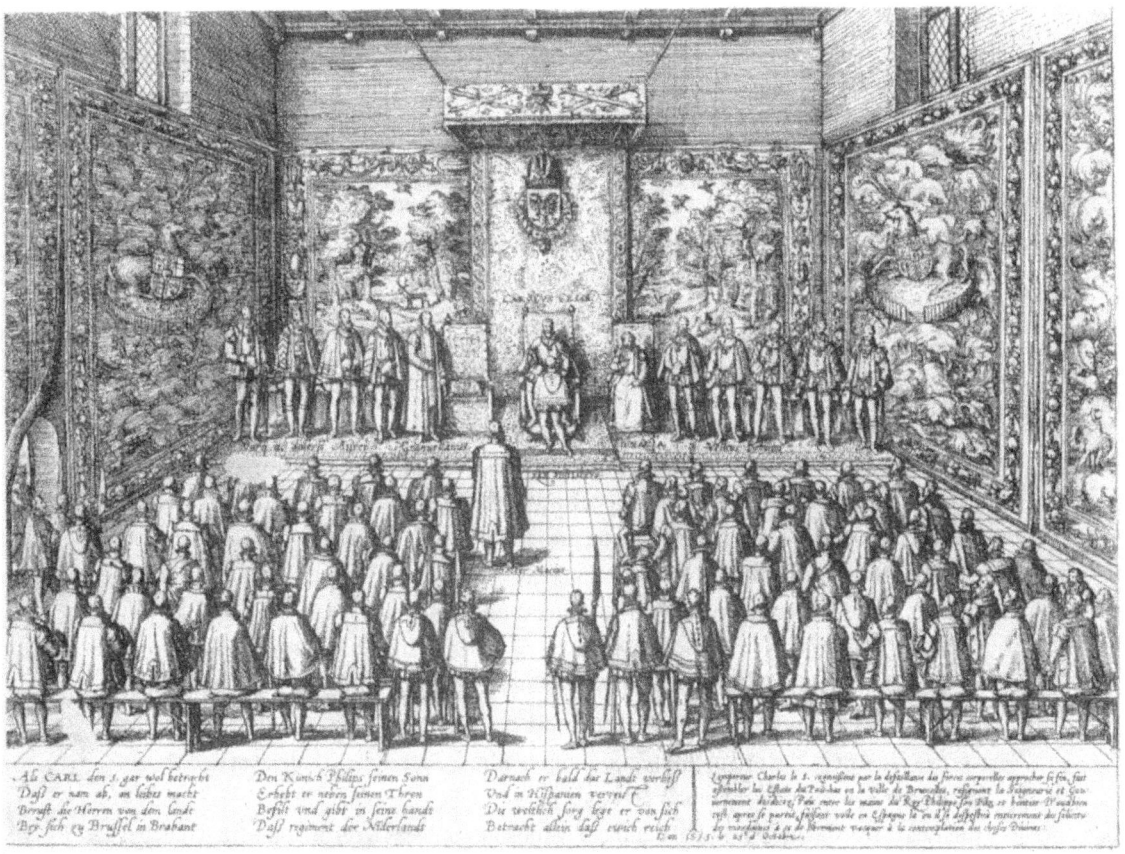

The Abdication of Charles V before the States General at the Coudenberg Palace in Brussels. Frans Hogenberg, 1555. Courtesy of the private collection of Karel Kinds.

tion—came as no surprise. The war against Philip's policies had trudged on for what seemed to contemporaries an eternity, pursued since 1568 by an ever-changing coalition of townspeople, regional Estates, and provincial noblemen. Much had transpired over these thirteen years. The conceptual ground for the rejection of Philip II had been laid by the mid-1570s in Holland and Zeeland, bastions of the Revolt, where the notion of rule with strong parliamentary and constitutional moorings had become a feature of political thinking.[8] Those directly opposed to such a political scheme, such as the great aristocrats of the southern territories of Artois, Hainault, and Walloon Flanders, had reconciled

---

8. Johan Decavele has argued that by August 1579 Calvinist Ghent also was ready to renounce Philip II's sovereignty. See his "De mislukking van Oranjes 'democratische' politiek in Vlaanderen," *Bijdragen en Mededelingen betreffende de Geschiedenis der Nederlanden* 99 (1984): 626–50.

themselves to Spain in 1579. In 1580 the States General of those provinces still in revolt had accepted—not without worries—a new lord, the French king Henry III's brother François de Valois, Duke of Anjou, as Philip's replacement.[9] But no matter what province went in what direction, the repudiation of a king's titles of lordship was everywhere controversial. For that reason, the language of the Abjuration of 1581 was legalistic and cautious, prepared by a committee of highly trained jurists who concentrated on the king's transgressions and not on the value of princely rule itself. Yet, for all their care, the Abjuration's authors could not obscure the fact that Europe's most powerful monarch was denuded of his titles of sovereignty by the very heirs of the delegates who had gathered in 1555 to bid farewell to Charles V and acclaim Philip as his successor.

These two political renunciations—one voluntary, the other imposed—bookend this study of the political culture of the Revolt of the Netherlands. More is at stake than the obvious irony that the father's concession became the son's albatross. The two events function not merely as political opposites, but also as cultural barometers of their era, carefully crafted ritual events whose content can be pressed to extract political clues about the representation of sovereign authority in the sixteenth-century Low Countries. As contrary political acts, the abdication and abjuration cast the States General in opposite roles—as audience in 1555, and as protagonist in 1581. The conceptual gulf between the two events is no easy knot to unravel. The explanation is located not merely in the body of political theory tested in these politically terse decades that resulted in invocations of popular sovereignty, but also in the urban politics and popular religious violence that carried the Revolt forward and gave it vernacular color.

Charles V's abdication was not cut from wholly new cloth; in form, it borrowed generously from fifteenth-century Burgundian precedents, even while embracing a stricter concern for public presentation than previous rulers had imposed. It was at once a grand ceremonial staging and a closed event, one thoroughly orchestrated in a safe royal space not prone to the spontaneity of the public square or the city street. Yet its scripted formalities could not hide certain strains already surfacing well before any overt onset of political crisis. The event culminated when the reserved Philip II faced the assembled States delegates to announce that, owing to his meager command of French, his speech would be read by Antoine Perrenot de Granvelle, bishop of Arras. Such an admission on Philip's part immediately distanced him from the intimate ties of language and camaraderie that bound together the provincial elites and court nobility, and the choice of Granvelle, the future target of the noblemen's wrath, as his spokesman, carried with it latent tensions that would soon become apparent.

---

9. Mack P. Holt, *The Duke of Anjou and the Politique Struggle during the Wars of Religion* (Cambridge, 1986), 128–40; and Frédéric Duquenne, *L'entreprise du Duc d'Anjou aux Pays-Bas de 1580 à 1584: Les responsabilités d'un échec à partager* (Paris, 1998).

The Abjuration of 1581 was also cautiously aired, but it reflected the hothouse political climate of a time when fractures among the provinces were deep—Hainault, Artois, Walloon Flanders, Namur, Luxemburg, and Limburg were reconciled with the king—and the future of those in revolt still uncertain.[10] More pertinently, the passage of a decade and a half of political and religious convulsions after the collapse of Habsburg authority in the Low Countries and the great iconoclasm riots of 1566 had complicated both the proper configuration of royal authority and its public representation. Indeed, like the Abdication of 1555, the Abjuration of 1581 had a rote formality to it—a strategy to avoid inflaming a tense political environment. Yet its inherent public dimension became obvious when the Abjuration required the removal of the Habsburg coat of arms from public buildings and of Philip II's name or portrait from all legal instruments and from coinage. Its most exacting requirement was a new oath that public officials and civic militia companies had to swear, renouncing Philip's sovereignty and releasing themselves from legal obligation to the now discredited lord. The oath proved to be the Abjuration's most public problem. The power of this ritual act was one contemporaries knew intimately—oaths secured agreements and sealed charters of privileges—making its undoing all the more dramatic.[11]

The sixteenth-century Low Countries were northern Europe's most urbanized zone, home to great commercial centers and vibrant small towns. By the time of Charles V's abdication, the Low Countries had a population of about three million, with two-thirds of the Netherlanders settled in the provinces of Brabant, Flanders, and Holland, where half of the inhabitants were townspeople. The metropolis of Antwerp bustled with some one hundred thousand inhabitants in 1560, and cities like Douai, Lille, Ghent, Bruges, Brussels, Mechelen, Amsterdam, Leiden, and Haarlem, among others, had populations that ranged from fourteen thousand to forty-five thousand. It was home also to some of Europe's highest literacy rates and its most developed system of lay secondary schools; the Guild of Saint Ambrose in sixteenth-century Antwerp alone registered 372 schoolmasters. In Low Country cities lived men and women well versed in the world of print and readership, with centuries of local political concern for the *gemeente*, or the public's local rights and privileges and the effort to achieve the appropriate balance between these zealously guarded rights and the prerogatives of lordship and the state.[12]

---

10. For the reconciliation of these provinces, see C. H. Th. Bussemaker, *De afscheiding der Waalsche Gewesten van de Generale Unie* (Haarlem, 1895).

11. The value of the oath was the subject of a popular pamphlet prepared in favor of the abjuration. *Politicq Onderwijs* was published in Mechelen in 1582. It is translated in full in Martin van Gelderen, ed., *The Dutch Revolt* (Cambridge, 1993), 165–226. Many Lutherans and even some Calvinists had misgivings about taking a public oath releasing them from their former allegiance to Philip II. See Geoffrey Parker, *The Dutch Revolt* (Ithaca, 1977), 200.

12. On literacy and secondary and university education, see Hilde de Ridder-Symoens, "Education and

The Low Countries boasted one of early modern Europe's most extensive civic spheres, a vernacular world of commerce and urban bustle, factional politics and local culture, with the sensibility of the street, marketplace, and public square. It fostered the aspirations and pretensions of urban political elites who staffed local aldermanic bodies and who celebrated and socialized together in urban sodalities such as the militia companies or the vibrant chambers of rhetoric, which were lay literary societies.[13] As that inveterate defender of monarchy, Jean Bodin, acknowledged in the sixteenth century, a civic public realm was already established. Kings who did not recognize the power and extent of this terrain risked imperiling their lordship. This world existed independent of full sovereign reach, a civic "public domain" where, in the words the 1606 English edition of Bodin's *Les Six Livres de la République*, there flourished citizens and

> their markets, their churches, their walks, ways, lawes, decrees, judgements, voices, customs, theaters, wal[l]s, publik buildings, common pastures, lands, and treasure; and in briefe, rewards, punishments, su[i]tes, and contracts: all which I say are common unto the citizens together, or by use and profit; or publick for everyman to use, or both together.[14]

I posit that the Dutch Revolt was one of the first European early modern upheavals waged in what Heinz Schilling has described as a hot zone of "civic republicanism," a world of corporatism, urban rights, and checks on sovereign authority.[15] There was no

---

Literacy in the Burgundian-Habsburg Netherlands," *Canadian Journal of Netherlandic Studies*, no. 16 (Spring 1995): 6–21. On rates of urbanization and population, see Jan de Vries, *European Urbanization, 1500–1800* (London, 1984), 116–18, 168; on the urban dimensions behind the Revolt, see Guido Marnef, "The Towns and the Revolt," in *The Origins and Development of the Dutch Revolt*, ed. Graham Darby (New York, 2001), 85–106.

13. On the shooting companies, see Theo Reintges, *Ursprung und Wesen der spätmittelalterlichen Schützengilden* (Bonn, 1963), and M. Carasso-Kok and J. Levy-Van Halm, eds., *Schutters in Holland: Kracht en zenuwen van de stad* (Zwolle-Haarlem, 1988). The literature on the chambers of rhetoric is vast, but two recent works offer the fullest social and cultural analysis: Anne-Laure van Bruaene, *Om beters wille: Rederijkerskamers en de stedelijke cultuur in de Zuidelijke Nederlanden (1400–1650)* (Amsterdam, 2008), and Arjan van Dixhoorn, "Lustige geesten. Rederijkers en hun kamers in het publieke leven, van de Noordelijke Nederlanden in de vijftiende, zestiende en zeventiende eeuw" (PhD diss., Free University, Amsterdam, 2004).

14. Cited in Jeffrey K. Sawyer, *Printed Poison: Pamphlet Propaganda, Faction Politics, and the Public Sphere in Early Seventeenth-Century France* (Berkeley, 1990), 21, from Jean Bodin, *The Six Bookes of a Commonweale*, ed. Kenneth D. McRae (Cambridge, 1961), 11, a facsimile edition of the 1606 original translation.

15. Like scholars of the French Revolution Mona Ozouf, Lynn Hunt, and François Furet, who pried the study of the Revolution away from modernization theories and the paralysis of structuralist categorizations to focus on language, symbolization, and cultural strategies of revolutionary politics, in this book I attend to political culture as an envelope of ritual action and discursive strategies and argue that they were the essential ingredients of the Revolt itself. See Keith Michael Baker, *Inventing the French Revolution* (Cambridge, 1990), esp. 4–10 for a conceptual overview of the political culture model, and especially the impact of

The Low Countries in the Sixteenth Century

more enduring and symbolically resonant figure in the Netherlands than the male *poorter*, or citizen.[16] Whether guildsman or urban patrician, wage laborer or merchant, the townsman was the primary ingredient of political identity in the urban Netherlands, and in the city, the space that guaranteed specific legal and economic rights. So engrained was this formulation of the political self that the late-medieval and early modern lords of the Netherlands constantly confronted the sting of urban protest and rebellions against policies that treaded too heavily on the prerogatives of citizenship.[17] When Charles V appointed his sister Mary of Hungary as regent of the Netherlands in 1531, she complained that it was like having a rope put around her neck, and twenty-four years later when her brother abdicated his titles of rule in Brussels, she grumbled that the Netherlands was nearly impossible to govern, "for this country does not render the obedience that is due a monarch."[18] She was hardly alone among princes, regents, and governors-general in this sentiment, for all had to spar with provincial Estates and urban magistrates over perceived state intrusions on the civic realm.

This book is about the vernacular world of the Dutch Revolt between 1563 and 1585 and the process of identity formation secured in its public realm. Structurally, it resembles a triptych: one wing concerned with the cultural forerunners of the Revolt in the Burgundian era of the fifteenth and early sixteenth centuries, and the emergence of religious and political dissent from that heritage; a central panel offering a fine-grained analysis of the transformative "wonder year" of 1566 that ushered in full-scale religious and political turmoil; and a final wing that charts how Spanish Habsburg efforts after 1568 inspired republican-tinged sentiment about a common fatherland in defense of popular sovereignty and its long-standing privileges among the disjointed territories of the Low Countries. It is a study of how the act of rebellion forged a political identity and the rituals and symbols that were its tools. The Dutch Revolt was launched in 1563 as a set of grievances lodged

---

François Furet, *Interpreting the French Revolution*, trans. Elborg Forster (Cambridge, 1981), published originally in French as *Penser la Révolution française* (Paris, 1978). Equally as fundamental as Furet's work was Lynn Hunt's *Politics, Culture, and Class in the French Revolution* (Berkeley, 1984). See her appraisal of her book's impact in the preface to its twentieth-anniversary edition (2004). On the Revolution's political ritual as a crucible in which sovereignty was transferred from monarch to nation, see Mona Ozouf, *La fête révolutionnaire* (Paris, 1976).

16. For the legal and cultural category of Dutch citizenship, particularly for the Dutch Golden Age, see Maarten Prak, "Burghers, Citizens, and Popular Politics in the Dutch Republic," *Eighteenth-Century Studies* 30, no. 4 (Summer 1997): 443–48.

17. For pre-Revolt traditions of urban revolt in general, see W. P. Blockmans, "Alternatives to Monarchical Centralization: The Great Tradition of Revolt of Flanders and Brabant," in *Republiken und Republikanismus im Europa der frühen Neuzeit*, ed. H. G. Koenigsberger (Munich, 1988), 145–54; Marc Boone and Maarten Prak, "Rulers, Patricians, and Burghers: The Great and Little Traditions of Urban Revolt in the Low Countries (12th–18th Centuries)," in *A Miracle Mirrored: The Dutch Republic in European Perspective*, ed. David Lucassen (Cambridge, 1995), 99–134.

18. Charles Weiss, ed., *Papiers d'état du Cardinal de Granvelle*, 9 vols. (Paris, 1841–52), 4:474.

by the nobility in the Habsburg Netherlands against incursions into their spheres of privilege and against the strict religious persecution of Protestants. Already under duress, Habsburg political authority collapsed during the sprawling iconoclastic riots of 1566 and a short-lived Calvinist military campaign. The turmoil intensified into outright war by 1568, after which endemic factional violence and regional variation colored its future course. The conflict was waged most intensely in its first decades, but waxed and waned for eighty years. Benchmarks included the repudiation of Philip II's sovereignty by the States General of the Netherlands in 1581; the death of William of Orange in 1584; Spanish reconquest of southern territories, including Flanders and Brabant by 1585; the twelve-year truce from 1609 to 1621 between Spain and the United Provinces; and final recognition of the sovereign authority of the United Provinces by Philip IV's government in 1648.

It is in the fifteenth century that tensions between the civic and princely spheres of the Habsburg Netherlands come fully into relief. The dukes of Burgundy were master ceremonialists and astute students of the public realm over which they ruled. In an effort to secure their lordship in a composite state strained by the centrifugal pull of regional and civic traditions, the Burgundian dukes turned to the power of state ceremony to bolster their monarchical ambitions, and made liturgical and classical motifs essential to its content. In chapter 1 I explore how state ritual grew both more prolix and authoritarian as the Burgundian state developed over the course of the fifteenth century, a strategy accompanied by a parallel effort by both state authorities and urban elites to supervise more vigorously urban public life. When Protestantism and efforts to extirpate it swelled in the third decade of the sixteenth century, this regulatory campaign intensified. Prior tensions between civic prerogatives and royal ambitions offer a perspective for understanding the deterioration of state power in the 1560s, and present a cultural context for the first great wave of dissent by the Netherlands' nobility and key urban magistrates against state policies in religion, law, and governance.

In chapter 2 I explore how dissenting noblemen and Calvinists in town and countryside aired their grievances dramatically by tapping into traditional forms of social protest and festive behavior that had existed for decades. This swell of discontent peaked with the formation of the Order of the Compromise and the adoption of its members' satirical insignia as "beggars." The Beggars were not alone in invoking ritual inversion in that weighty year. Cut from a wholly different social cloth, the men and women who fomented the iconoclasm riots of late summer and fall 1566 were inspired by their Calvinist commitments. Chapters 3 and 4 offer detailed considerations of the iconoclasts' violence as enacted in countless cities and small villages across the Netherlands, particularly Flanders and Brabant. In my consideration of Flanders' Westkwartier (West Quarter) and its surrounding areas in chapter 3, and of the prominent cities of Ypres, Antwerp, and Ghent in chapter 4, I explore the plural causes of iconoclasm, and how rites of degradation enacted by Calvinist laborers, craftsmen, and middling professionals, among others, were rife with themes of inversion: of spaces, times, images, and all the material representations of Catholic liturgy and worship. By concentrating on iconoclasm's actors and their acts, I hope to avoid the checkmate of Low Country historians of the Reformation and social history when they squared off over the primacy of economic or theological factors that provoked iconoclasts to action.[19] But I hope as well that a renewed focus on the social and local dimensions of this kind of religious violence will advance the literature on Reformation iconoclasm more generally.[20]

It is my contention that the *annus mirabilis* of 1566 was the great accelerator of the Dutch Revolt's political culture, and the incubator of what transpired thereafter. Chapter 5 takes up how Fernando Alvarez de Toledo, the Duke of Alba, conceptualized his governorship when he arrived in Brussels in August 1567 in the aftermath of the iconoclasm riots, and how his subsequent campaign to punish treasonous nobility and heretics transformed the political and ritual landscape. The chapter explores the critical elements of Alba's policy of exemplary punishment for the sins of the wonder year: his campaign to reestablish Habsburg authority by a strategy of military occupation and high profile arrests and executions. With these policies, Alba trampled upon civic political and legal rights dear to Low Country political culture and gave the cause of the Dutch Revolt renewed vigor.

Chapter 6 charts the direction in the Revolt's political culture in reaction to Alba's policies. Turmoil in Holland, Zeeland, and Brabant in 1572 and the bitter warfare between their cities and Alba's Army of Flanders supercharged an ethos of civic heroism, a period of impassioned rhetoric among advocates of the Revolt about the selfless fight of imperiled citizen-soldiers against a cruel tyranny. In the artwork, pamphlets, chronicles, and ballads that recounted this story was embedded the third great trope of the Dutch Revolt: the urban patriot defending city and *patria* on behalf of a father prince.[21]

Chapter 7 tackles the symbolic cargo William of Orange took on as the Revolt matured. As the most important *grand seigneur*, Orange became the savior prince to whom re-

---

19. The suspicion of overly ambitious economic readings of the 1566 iconoclasm riots is a response to Erich Kuttner's 1941 *Het Hongerjaar 1566*, published posthumously in Dutch in 1949 and reissued in 1997 in its German original, with an introduction by Maximilian Ingenthron as *Das Hungerjahr 1566: Eine Studie zur Geschichte des niederländischen Frühproletariats und seiner Revolution* (Mannheim, 1997).

20. Olivier Christin, *Une révolution symbolique: L'iconoclasme Huguenot et la reconstruction catholique* (Paris, 1991); and Lee Palmer Wandel, *Voracious Idols and Violent Hands* (Cambridge, 1994).

21. The Revolt's Party of the Patriots was the first major political affiliation in an early modern upheaval to rally around an emotionally laden term that became popular in the language of political resistance in the seventeenth century from England to the territories of the German empire. Invoked in the German empire in the early sixteenth century, the designation patriot later became essential to political concepts of duty and resistance in the seventeenth century. See Robert von Friedeberg, "The Making of Patriots: Love of Fatherland and Negotiating Monarchy in Seventeenth-Century Germany," *Journal of Modern History* 77 (December 2005): 881–916.

dounded the paternal imagery that Philip II had forfeited, and the fraternal associations that the king had never possessed. The Prince and his Nassau brothers were comrades in arms, the perfect models of heroic self-sacrifice on behalf of the fatherland—a term that presupposed a territorial unity for the Netherlands and stirred a collective emotional rootedness of place. After the revolt of 1572, however, the figure of the citizen-patriot became inseparable from heady talk about the fatherland, a ratcheting up of an awareness of a cultural identity as Netherlanders.[22] As Alastair Duke has observed, the ever-shifting political borders of the late-medieval and early modern Netherlands, and the territories' strong regional inflections, made such expressions of a coherent political identity weak and partial, more a cultural projection than a social reality.[23] No standard nomenclature for describing this region of Europe existed. By 1557, maps of the Low Countries appeared that gave cartographic expression to the region. Not coincidentally, an affective attachment to the Netherlands as a territory steadily emerged among those in opposition to Habsburg political and religious policies.[24] By 1568, with Orange and his allies in exile, such sentiment about the fatherland became a touchstone for fomenting opposition to the king and his policies. It proved one of the strongest cultural legacies of these central years of the Revolt, at once confirming the markedly civic vocabulary of Netherlands political life and offering to the new United Provinces a clear model of political identity, a "fatherland" for a commonwealth where localism and regionalism were still the order of the day.

Chapters 8 and 9 conclude the book with a consideration of the renunciation of Philip II's sovereignty in 1581, particularly the dilemma of how to represent publicly a refurbished vision of lordship, in the guise of the Duke of Anjou, to a populace wearied after the iconoclasm riots and horrific urban warfare of the 1570s. In the violence and losses of this phase of the Dutch Revolt are found the seeds of the new United Provinces, whose birthplace might have been the late sixteenth century, and whose great epoch was the seventeenth century, but whose politics bore the legacy of the late-medieval Burgundian Netherlands, and the ongoing political and cultural tensions that bedeviled its rulers.

22. S. Groenveld, "'Natie' en 'patria' bij zestiende-eeuwse Nederlanders," *Netherlandsch Archievenblad* 84 (1980): 372–84.

23. Alastair Duke, "The Elusive Netherlands: The Question of National Identity in the Early Modern Low Countries on the Eve of the Revolt," *Bijdragen en Mededelingen betreffende de Geschiedenis der Nederlanden* 119 (2004): 10–38. See also Robert Stein, "The Multiplicity of a Unity in the Low Countries," in *The Ideology of Burgundy: The Promotion of National Consciousness, 1364–1565*, ed. D'A. J. D. Boulton and Jan Veenstra (Leiden, 2006), 223–86. On cartographic depictions of the Low Countries, see Paul Regan, "Cartography, Chorography and Patriotic Sentiment in the Sixteenth-Century Low Countries," in *Public Opinion and Changing Identities in the Early Modern Netherlands*, ed. Judith Pollmann and Andrew Spicer (Leiden, 2007), 49–68.

24. Duke, "Elusive Netherlands," 36.

CHAPTER 1 PRINCELY TRIUMPHS
THE CONSECRATION OF BURGUNDIAN
POLITICAL AUTHORITY

The propensity of Netherlanders to contest princely authority already made itself amply felt during the reign of Charles the Bold, the last Valois Duke of Burgundy. Charles ruled from 1467 to 1477, a decade of intractable turmoil in the cities of the Low Countries and constant sparring with the French king, Louis XI.[1] Charles was still count of Charolais when his future rival gained the French crown in 1461, but he knew the new king well. As dauphin, Louis had been residing at the Burgundian residence at Genappe near Brussels when he learned that his father Charles VII, from whom he was estranged, had died. When Louis rushed back to France, he did so in the company of his former Burgundian hosts. Both Charles and his father, Duke Philip the Good, were at the cathedral at Rheims on August 15 when Louis was proclaimed "rex Christianissimus" at the *sacre*, the coronation ceremony of the French monarchy. Charles witnessed the archbishop of Rheims anoint the French king with sacred oils from the holy ampulla in a rite whose prayers, psalms, communion, and mass were a full-throated religious acclamation.[2] Of all the royal coronation ceremonies in northwestern Europe, France's was the least burdened with constitutional obligations, with the em-

---

1. For Charles's rule, see Richard Vaughan, *Charles the Bold: the Last Valois Duke of Burgundy* (New York, 1973); J. Bartier, *Charles le Téméraire* (Brussels, 1970); Werner Paravicini, *Karl der Kühne: Das Ende des Hauses Burgund* (Zurich, 1976). On the duke's cultural world, see Edward Tabri, *Political Culture in the Early Northern Renaissance in the Court of Charles the Bold, Duke of Burgundy, 1467–77* (New York, 2005). In general on the Burgundian Netherlands, see Wim Blockmans and Walter Prevenier, *The Promised Lands: The Low Countries under Burgundian Rule, 1369–1530*, ed. Edward Peters, trans. Elizabeth Fackelman (Philadelphia, 1999). For his nickname "le Téméraire", see J. M. Cauchies, *Louis XI et Charles le Hardi, de Péronne à Nancy, 1468–1477: Le conflit* (Brussels, 1996), 47–59.

2. The classic study of the liturgical dimensions of French and English monarchs, particularly their curative powers, in the medieval era and beyond is Marc Bloch, *Les rois thaumaturges: Étude sur le caractère surnaturel attribué à la puissance royale particulièrement en France et en Angleterre* (Strasbourg, 1924), and on acclamations and their ceremonial motifs, Ernst Kantorowicz, *Laudes Regiae: A Study in Liturgical Acclamation and Medieval Ruler Worship* (Berkeley, 1946). On the French coronation ceremony and its evolution, see Richard A. Jackson, *Vive le Roi! A History of the French Coronation from Charles V to Charles X* (Chapel Hill, 1984), esp. 36–38 on Louis XI, and Aimé Bonnefin, *Sacre des rois de France* (Limoges, 1982).

phasis instead on the king as the sacred protector of church and kingdom. It was a message reinforced by the Te Deum that followed the coronation and by the elaborate entry ceremony the new king made into Paris at the month's end, accompanied by both Duke Philip the Good, lavishly dressed in black velvet and a ruby-encrusted hat, and by Charles, outfitted in crimson velvet.[3]

The Burgundian party's sacerdotal splendor was the source of much comment. These two weeks of royal ceremony in which Charles played a key role must have seemed like halcyon days some six years later, during his own wrenching succession to his father's titles of rule. After the period of mourning for the deceased duke ended in late June 1467, Charles prepared for his accession to the various titles of his Low Country territories, where his lordship was distributed, as was his father's, among a welter of different countships and dukedoms. As observers noted, Philip the Good had led a Burgundian train to Louis XI's coronation at Rheims that was larger and more splendid than that of the heir to the French crown himself. But the inaugural protocols for the dukes of Burgundy little resembled the splendor of the French *sacre*. In lieu of prayers, consecrated oil, and liturgical anointments, Charles got a handful of urban grief, starting in Ghent with his entry on June 28, 1467, as the new count of Flanders. There, a miscalculation in timing got Charles ensnared in a raucous uprising led by pilgrims returning from the annual translation of the relics of the popular Saint Lieven, and the new count had to endure insults from the very people he expected to proclaim his lordship. If this humiliation were not enough, trouble broke out elsewhere, the legacy of past quarrels between city regimes and his father over local political rights, urban taxation, and state centralization. With the old Duke Philip dead, the powerhouse province of Brabant and its Estates immediately began discussions about a way to force concessions from Charles as a precondition for accepting his lordship, and even debated among themselves offering sovereignty to another prince if their demands were not met. Although this did not happen, Charles's inaugural visit to Mechelen on July 3 sparked protracted internal turmoil that engulfed the city in a wave of violence soon after his departure, and Antwerp openly quarreled with the new duke on the eve of his September 5 entry into the city.[4]

The city of Liège, however, proved the greatest irritant to Charles's first year as ruler. Townspeople there had pushed so far that by August 1467, a mere two months after

---

3. On the Parisian entry ceremony and Louis XI, see Lawrence Bryant, *The King and the City in the Parisian Royal Entry Ceremony: Politics, Ritual and Art in the Renaissance* (Geneva, 1986), 89; and on Louis XI's coronation and entry ceremony into Paris in general and Philip the Good's and Charles's central role in it, Joseph Calmette, *Le grand règne de Louis XI* (Paris, 1938), 10–14, and an anonymous contemporary account in Bernard Guenée and Françoise Lehoux, eds., *Les entrées royales françaises de 1328 à 1515* (Paris, 1969), 86–95.

4. See Peter Arnade, "Secular Charisma, Sacred Power: Rites of Rebellion in the Ghent Entry of 1467," *Handelingen der Maatschappij voor Geschiedenis en Oudheidkunde te Gent* 45 (1992): 69–94; on Charles's urban woes in the opening years of his reign, see Vaughan, *Charles the Bold*, 1–40.

Philip's death, Charles prepared anew for war against this troublesome city. Liège was seat of a bishopric and a strategically located border principality, whose official autonomy from direct rule made it stand out among the other Low Country provinces fighting governmental centralization. No sooner had Charles been inaugurated as the new Burgundian lord than Liège erupted in defiant protest against the hand-picked Burgundian bishop, Louis de Bourbon, in office since 1456. This trouble was firmly rooted in previous unrest, most recently that of 1465, when the aged Philip had to confront an open rebellion and had imposed a punitive settlement on the city. Radical elements in Liège, aggrieved by Philip's actions, gained the upper hand after his death; they captured and executed the mayor of Dinant and threatened the bishop, who had fled with a well-armed escort to nearby Huy.[5] The fighting was fierce and dirty, fueled by visceral hatreds accumulated from this controversy and by the pungent residue of past conflicts. On November 12, 1467, the resistance crumbled, and Liège yielded to Burgundian troops. As the walls and gates of the city were being dismantled, as houses were being looted, as citizens were being assaulted, a delegation of 340 citizens performed an *amende honorable* before the duke, a penitential ritual in which the defeated kneel in their undergarments before a triumphant duke to beg his forgiveness.[6] Peace was granted, but at a steep price: Charles confiscated the city's prized charters of rights and privileges. It is all the more amazing, then, that less than a year later, in September 1468, the Liègois would revolt anew as returning exiles stirred up trouble yet again. This time, Charles dispensed with any attempt at reconciliation. When the city was recaptured on October 30, 1468, soldiers were given a free hand to loot it. Even the churches were turned inside out, though Charles later required that the ecclesiastical loot be inventoried and returned.[7]

Anything of value in Liège was ripe for plunder, with one notable exception. The duke intervened personally to protect the relics of St. Lambert, housed in the bishop's cathedral.[8] According to court chronicler Olivier de La Marche, Charles had prayed to the relics

5. Vaughan, *Charles the Bold*, 21.

6. For the uses of the *amende honorable* elsewhere, see Peter Arnade, *Realms of Ritual: Burgundian Ceremony and Civic Life in Late Medieval Ghent* (Ithaca, 1996), 119–20; and for the southern Low Countries more generally, Elodie Lecuppre-Desjardin, *La ville des cérémonies: Essai sur la communication politique dans les anciens Pays-Bas bourguignons* (Turnhout, 2004), 302–11.

7. Blockmans and Prevenier, *Promised Lands*, 180–81. Compelling accounts of the two Liège uprisings and the destruction of the city are Henrici de Merica, *Compendiosa Historia de Cladibus Leodiensium*, in *Documents relatifs aux Troubles du Pays de Liège sous les princes-évêques Louis de Bourbon et Jean de Horne, 1455–1505*, ed. P. F. de Ram (Brussels, 1844), 135–83, and T. Pauli, *Historia de Cladibus Leodiensium*, in ibid., 188–232, esp. 223–24 on the ransacking of religious houses and the final sack of the city.

8. Marc Boone, "Urban Space in Late Medieval Flanders," *Journal of Interdisciplinary History* 32, no. 4 (Spring 2002): 639; A. Marchandisse, I. Vrancken-Pirson, and J. L. Kupper, "La destruction de la ville de Liège et sa reconstruction," in *Destruction et reconstruction de villes, du Moyen Âge à nos jours/Verwoesting en wederopbouw van steden, van middeleeuwen tot heden*, Crédit Communal/Gemeentekrediet, no. 100 (Brussels, 1999): 69–96.

before the siege, and in the wake of victory rushed to save them from the hands of looters, leaving his battle standard in the cathedral's nave as a talismanic symbol of his protection.[9] Although the rebels had defiantly marched beneath the saint's banner in their first campaign of 1467, the relics were the property of the cathedral, and by extension, of the Burgundian bishop Louis de Bourbon, cousin of Charles the Bold, whose appointment had caused this last, great cycle of violence. In 1471 Charles donated to the cathedral a beautifully wrought gold statue executed by the Lille goldsmith Gérard Loyet that had been commissioned four years earlier. The still extant votive portrait consists of two statuettes resting on a silver pedestal. A fully armored Saint George stands above a kneeling Charles the Bold, one hand tipping his helmet, the other resting on the duke's left shoulder. Charles too is armed, but unlike the saint, he is bare-headed, while his helmet lies in front of the cushion on which he kneels. The duke holds a hexagonal reliquary, while on his breastplate is the collar of the most prestigious confraternity, the Order of the Golden Fleece. Charles and Saint George are presented as distinct, yet their faces are alike, as if the two were interchangeable.

After Liège's 1467 revolt, Charles had confiscated a public bronze column called the Perron, symbol of Liège's autonomy, and had it transferred as war booty to Bruges, where it was put on display to record the city's exemplary punishment.[10] Robbed of its greatest political symbol, the city also suffered the dismantlement of its walls and gates, the surest physical markers of its urban space. After the second insurrection of 1468 everything was fair game; the city was looted of its material possessions just as it had been deprived a year earlier of its emblem of independence and its physical barriers. The votive statue was the one trophy Charles bequeathed to the denuded city, but it carried a potent resonance. It would be easy to interpret the gesture as an expiatory offering, as many historians have done since the sixteenth century.[11] But whatever conciliatory intentions Charles may have had should not obscure the fact that the offering was a showpiece for the high altar of a cathedral in a city that had lost its Perron.[12] As Hugo van der Velden has argued, the votive portrait was, more than anything else, a forthright assertion of ducal authority.[13] In the ransacked city, the votive statue was an ever-present reminder that Charles was its sa-

---

9. Olivier de La Marche, *Mémoires*, ed. Henri Beaune and J. d'Arbaumont, 4 vols. (Paris, 1883–88), 3:86–87; cf. Pauli, *Historia de Cladibus Leodiensium*, 223.

10. Boone, "Urban Space," 628; Raymond van Uytven, "Flämische Belfriede und südniederländische städtische Bauwerke im Mittelalter: Symbol und Mythos," in *Information, Kommunikation und Selbstdarstellung in mittelalterlichen Gemeinden*, ed. Alfred Havekamp (Munich, 1998), 132–45.

11. Hugo van der Velden, *The Donor's Image: Gerard Loyet and the Votive Portraits of Charles the Bold*, trans. Beverley Jackson (Turnhout, 2000), 101–5.

12. On Saint George as important Burgundian saint, see Wim Blockmans and Walter Prevenier, *The Burgundian Netherlands* (Cambridge, 1986), 175, 250.

13. Van der Velden, *Donor's Image*, 152–53.

Gold votive image of Charles the Bold with Saint George. Gérard Loyet, 1471. Charles commissioned the statue of himself holding a reliquary in Liège's cathedral at the beginning of his two campaigns against radical forces in the city. Courtesy of l'Institut Royal du Patrimoine Artistique / Koninklijk Instituut voor het Kunstpatrimonium, Brussels.

cred lord and guardian of its most precious relics, the man of war who was also master of the city after two brazen attempts to evade his authority.

The Regal and the Civic

Charles the Bold's rocky beginning as the new Duke of Burgundy, and the strategies he deployed to punish the two cycles of revolt in Liège, call attention to the kind of urban politics and cultural negotiations that sovereigns in the sixteenth-century Netherlands would have to confront. From the very beginning of his official reign, events thrust Charles into the middle of an acute tension between the urban and the sovereign spheres, between the civic defense of localism and the Burgundian dynasty's interest in royal trappings and state centralization. As prime observers and key participants in Louis XI's *sacre*, Philip and Charles were well versed in the religious language of authority that was a customary part of French coronations—and of the general conception of French kingship as sacerdotal. As Duke of Burgundy, Philip the Good was first peer of the French realm, and if the chronicler Chastellain is to be believed, he even usurped the role of the archbishop of Rheims in Louis XI's coronation ceremony, when he placed the crown upon Louis after the anointment.[14] But no matter what his actual role in this ceremony, no matter how grand his and Charles's ceremonial retinues, and no matter how dazzling their bejeweled clothing and accessories, Philip was himself no monarch, but rather duke, count, and lord over many scattered regions. Charles's decision to protect the cathedral and its precious relics during the destruction of Liège and his bestowal of the ex-voto reliquary reflects the fact that while the French monarchy's sacred lineage was well established, the same was not true of the rulers of the Burgundian Netherlands. Although religious iconography and control of the sacred were not intrinsic to the ceremonies of Burgundian lordship, the dukes recognized their usefulness and found new ways to evoke them. Their inauguration as rulers was precisely the opposite of the French Crown from which they descended: a constitutional exercise that recognized urban and provincial rights and privileges, and whose meaning was irreducibly local, repeated in one city after another rather than performed at one great ceremonial event, as in Rheims. An ex-voto statue on Liège's central altar was important because it offered something more durable—perhaps even eternal—than did the baseline political ritual.

Modern historians have echoed their late-medieval contemporaries in celebrating the Burgundian state that arose in the urban thicket of northwestern Europe in the fifteenth century. As Louis XI's coronation makes plain, the Burgundian princes were noted for their zeal for finery, public display, and courtly ceremony, all tokens of wealth and power.[15] Court chroniclers such as Georges Chastellain, Olivier de La Marche, Jean Molinet and others penned official histories of the late-medieval Burgundian court that boast of neochivalric deeds and glossy ceremonialism.[16] But such cultural pretensions were grafted on a very hard-fought policy of territorial acquisition. As the dukes warred with

---

14. Georges Chastellain, *Oeuvres*, ed. [Joseph] Kervyn de Lettenhove, 8 vols. (Brussels, 1863–66), 4:59. Chastellain's description of Philip's role is at variance with the coronation *ordines* of this French royal ceremony and Jackson, *Vive le Roi!*, argues against accepting it as truthful.

15. The best introduction to the world of the Burgundian Netherlands remains Blockmans and Prevenier, *The Burgundian Netherlands*, but see also the wide-lens overview, particularly strong on social and economic history, in D. P. Blok, W. Prevenier et al., eds., *Algemene Geschiedenis der Nederlanden*, 2nd ed., 14 vols. (Haarlem, 1977–83), esp. vols. 3–4.

16. Chastellain, *Oeuvres*; La Marche, *Mémoires*; Jean Molinet, *Chroniques*, ed. Georges Doutrepont, 3 vols. (Brussels, 1935–37).

their quarrelsome cities, as they fought their jealous adversaries, as they centralized government agencies, they stitched together a great swath of lands that stretched from the gentle, rural hills of Burgundy to the polders, marshlands, dikes, rich farmlands, and even richer cities of Brabant, Flanders, Holland, Zeeland, and other Dutch-speaking provinces of the north. Burgundian rule birthed a cultural and political syncretism in the Low Countries that melded together an ambitious, Francophone court with the heritage of centuries of urban life and its commercial, artisanal, cultural, and social rhythms.

At the heart of this stood the dukes, their entourages, and their courts, as the charismatic center of a political network of intense rivalries, territorial ambitions, easy patronage, and complex client relations.[17] As they struggled to command authority and expand their rule, the Valois princes bathed themselves in luxuriant display, offering up fabulous parades, grand banquets, mythological joust cycles, and costly festivals to celebrate their persons and personas. To an earlier generation of historians, including the masterful Johan Huizinga, this great splendor was an Indian summer of late-medieval chivalry, set in a postplague world of hypersymbolism and intensely etched sentiments, where forms overrode content to produce an unsettling abundance.[18] More recent historians have tempered such a viewpoint with an ethnographic appreciation for the work of court ritual. They have argued for the strategic economy of Burgundian ceremonialism, explored its urban audience, and suggested its role in dramatizing and sealing power in a world in which authority—as Charles the Bold learned in Ghent, Liège, and elsewhere—might be claimed but was never quite secure.[19] Attention has rightly been cast on the greatest court celebrations: stunning banquets such as the Feast of the Pheasant in Lille in 1454, great marriage celebrations such as Charles the Bold's to Margaret of York in Bruges in 1468, the romance-drenched joust cycles, the *pas d'armes*, and the sumptuous entry ceremonies of the dukes and duchesses.[20] Artists, from painters and poets to cooks, were mobilized

---

17. On the patronage networks and clientage networks, see Wim Blockmans, "Corruptie, patronage, makelaardij en venaliteit als symptomen van een ontluikende staatsvorming in de Bourgondisch-Habsburgse Nederlanden," *Tijdschrift voor Sociale Geschiedenis* 11 (1985): 231–47.

18. Johan Huizinga, *Herfsttij der middeleeuwen* (1919) and the most recent English translation by Rodney J. Payton and Ulrich Mammtizsch, *The Autumn of the Middle Ages* (Chicago, 1996). On Huizinga, his legacy, and the complicated textual history of the many translations of his original work, see Edward Peters and Walter Simons, "The New Huizinga and the Old Middle Ages," *Speculum* 74 (1999): 587–620.

19. This literature is both a tribute to Huizinga's masterwork and a thoroughgoing correction to his early twentieth-century functionalism. See, for a sampling, Blockmans and Prevenier, *Burgundian Netherlands*; Arnade, *Realms of Ritual*; Lecuppre-Desjardin, *Villes des cérémonies*; Hugo Soly, "Plechtige intochten in de steden van de Zuidelijke Nederlanden tijdens de overgang van middeleeuwen naar nieuwe tijd: Communicatie, propaganda, spektakel," *Tijdschrift voor Geschiedenis* 97, no. 3 (1984): 341–61. On Holland and Zeeland, including the pre-Burgundian fourteenth century, especially on the itineraries of the count of Holland, Zeeland, and Hainault, see J. G. Smit, *Vorst en onderdanen: Studies over Holland en Zeeland in de late middeleeuwen* (Louvain, 1995).

20. One of the first studies of Burgundian ceremonialism still remains useful today: Otto Cartellieri, *The Court of Burgundy*, trans. Malcolm Letts (New York, 1979; orig., 1929).

to create a surfeit of sensations. The finest cloth, the sweetest music, the most chivalric ethos, the most sumptuous food—these pleasures flattered the political and cultural elitism of the urban and court nobility.[21]

Like most premodern sovereigns, the fifteenth-century Burgundian dukes were master image makers, harnessing public performance and patronizing art to make visible their authority and secure their place in the public eye.[22] As the dukes negotiated, fought, and expanded their territories, they secured the framework for the Burgundian Netherlands, one of early modern Europe's most important concentrations of wealth, commerce, and cities. Because it spanned the fifteenth and early sixteenth centuries, the Burgundian state affords an opportunity to track a political dynasty in its very act of creation, as its members cobbled together new territories and eliminated old threats. Because the lands acquired contained some of Europe's biggest cities, because these urban centers had long-standing political traditions of local rule, and because Burgundian overlordship was constantly challenged, the dukes strove constantly to enlarge their public profiles. Princely authority in the Burgundian Netherlands was not centralized, but resided in a grab-bag of titles that the sovereign held in separate counties—Duke of Brabant, Count of Flanders, Count of Holland, and so forth. Crisply defined legal charters defined this authority. But no matter how secure these titles were, the dukes lacked the unifying political and cultural weight of monarchical authority.

That the Valois and Habsburg princes desired a legitimacy more universal and emotionally potent than provincial lordship is fundamental for understanding their enormous investment in self-presentation, for seeing why, as during Louis XI's coronation and Parisian entry ceremony, they upstaged the king in clothing and retinue. In 1473 these cultural and political ambitions inspired Charles the Bold's high-profile attempt to secure a royal title, continuing a push begun by his father to elevate one or more of his principalities to the status of a kingdom. At a famous meeting with the Holy Roman Emperor, Frederick III at Trier, beginning on September 30 of that year, Charles and his advisors openly sought the office of "king of the Romans." Charles had entered Trier wearing an ermine-trimmed gold mantle and surround by one thousand lavishly outfitted men. This had set in motion a week of sartorial display that elicited the comments of observers. Apart from Charles's agreement to marry his daughter Mary to Maximilian of Austria, the Trier meeting did not produce the crown Charles sought. Nevertheless, he was so enthralled with the royal project that he commissioned his goldsmith Gérard Loyet, maker of the Liège

---

21. Francis Salet, "La fête de la Toison d'Or et le marriage de Charles le Téméraire: Bruges, Mai-Juillet 1468," Annales de la Société d'Emulation de Bruges 106 (1969): 5–16; Agathe Lafortune-Martel, *Fête noble en Bourgogne au XV siècle: Le banquet du Faisan, 1454* (Montreal, 1984).

22. On royal ceremonialism, for a sampling see Sergio Bertelli, *The King's Body: Sacred Rituals of Power in Medieval and Early Modern Europe*, trans. R. Burr Litchfield (University Park, 2001); János M. Bak, ed., *Coronations: Medieval and Early Modern Monarchic Ritual* (Berkeley, 1990); and the comparative essays in David Cannadine and Simon Price, eds., *Rituals of Royalty: Power and Ceremonial in Traditional Societies* (Cambridge, 1987).

votive statue, to create a royal scepter and redesign his crown for the office of king.[23] However many lordly titles Charles possessed, they mattered little to him in his zeal to have the kind of ritual authority wielded by the French, English, and German monarchs.

The Burgundians' cultivation of sacred idioms and religious devotions and their quest for royalty were their response to a political landscape characterized by stubborn pockets of localism and no single title of rulership over their expanding domains. Burgundian expansion in the later half of the fifteenth century was accompanied by a transformation of public ceremonialism, to include sacred associations and imagery, then royal and eventually imperial allusions, especially in the Habsburg Burgundian era of the early sixteenth century. The means of articulating authority grew too. Ceremonies became more fanciful and complicated, involving great set pieces such as triumphal arches and *tableaux vivants*, while the medium of print allowed the publication of booklets, or *livrets*, to memorialize weddings, funerals, and royal entries. As the case of Liège makes clear, these developments in state ceremony took place not merely for the sake of internal developments at court or because of the intense political rivalries among the rulers of northwestern Europe. They were part of a more general Burgundian strategy to manage their urban subjects, whose challenges to state rule were a constant irritant and a practical check on princely rule. Over the course of the late-fifteenth and early sixteenth centuries, the image of the Burgundian lord was not only expanded, it was linked to his command over the urban sphere. Accordingly, townspeople fell under increasing supervision by state officials and urban elites, who more strictly monitored their public behaviors and political practices. Within this regulatory environment, the early arrival of Protestantism in the Low Countries by 1520 presented regional, state, and ecclesiastical authorities with the new threat of heresy, alongside old worries about urban public life and its social and political excesses.[24] The rise in Burgundian ceremonialism, its increased sacralization, the heightened supervision of the urban public realm, and the sudden outburst of Protestantism in the 1520s are all developments that historians have typically explored as discrete phenomena. Yet it is their orchestration and interplay that more than anything else helps us

---

23. A detailed description and analysis is in Petra Ehm, *Burgund und das Reich: Spätmittelalterliche Außenpolitik am Beispiel der Regierung Karls des Kühnen (1465–1477)* (Paris, 2002), esp. 132–68.

24. For a general cultural theory that sees a process of elite identity formation as part of the campaign to regulate urban social and festive behavior, see Herman Pleij, *De sneeuwpoppen van 1511: Literatuur en stadscultuur tussen middeleeuwen en moderne tijd* (Amsterdam, 1988). While indebted to Norbert Elias's work on the civilizing process, Pleij also sees the widening between elite and popular behaviors that Robert Muchembled charted for northern France in his *Culture populaire et culture des élites*. The arrival of Protestantism has not been linked to the general literature on the growth of urban social regulation or Burgundian state ceremony. For a general account of the growth of the Reformation in the Low Countries, see Alastair Duke, *Reformation and Revolt in the Low Countries* (London, 1990), as well as J. G. de Hoop Scheffer, *Geschiedenis der kerkhervorming in Nederland van haar onstaan tot 1531*, 2 vols. (Amsterdam, 1873), and Johan Decavele, *De Dageraad van de Reformatie in Vlaanderen*, 2 vols. (Brussels, 1975).

to see the strands out of which the political culture of the sixteenth-century Burgundian Netherlands was woven on the eve of the Dutch Revolt.

Sacred Appropriations

If boosting their profile became essential to Burgundian rulers, they did not do so in a vacuum, or merely for fellow court insiders, but rather acted within an urban realm rich in its own public life. It was not merely that the Low Countries had such a dense tissue of urban life, but also that the compact geography meant that cities and towns were located within tightly clustered nodes of interaction, stamping Netherlandish public life with special inflections that Burgundian dukes ignored at their own peril.[25] Urban cultural life in the Low Countries flourished not only within individual city walls, but proliferated through networks and zones of regional interactions—cultural economies of circulation that mirrored the market ethos and marketplace realities of urban centers.[26] In the fifteenth century, the two most prominent urban social confraternities, the military guilds of archers and crossbowmen (*schuttersgilden*), and the drama and poetry troupes dubbed "the chambers of rhetoric" (*rederijkerskamers*), set the groundwork for mapping out zones of urban cultural interactions. On a regular basis, these societies sponsored shooting and theater competitions, respectively, in which scores of cities competed over several days at elaborately staged ceremonies held in a preselected city.[27] At such events, hundreds of participants crisscrossed borders to compete. Prizes were awarded to the best entry ceremony or the finest athletic or verse-writing display. These celebrations, therefore, were exercises in economies of exchange, while their participants were assigned valuations of status replete with metaphors of circulation and worth. They were also, in no small measure, essential to building up supralocal cultural identities. The dukes of Burgundy were keenly aware of the cultural work of these urban associations, and even enrolled in some as members, and at very select times appeared alongside other men in an urban competition, as Philip the Good did at the enormous contest sponsored by the Saint George crossbowmen

---

25. For urban density and population figures, see De Vries, *European Urbanization*, 116–18, 168.

26. For a recognition of this cultural orbit, see Anne-Laure van Bruaene, "Harmonie et honneur en jeu: Les compétitions dramatiques et symboliques entre les villes flamandes et brabançonnes aux quinzième et seizième siècles," in *Le verbe, l'image et les représentations de la société urbaine au Moyen Age. Actes du colloque international tenu à Marche-en-Famenne du 24 au 27 Octobre 2001*, ed. Marc Boone et al. (Antwerp-Apeldoorn, 2002), 227–38, and her "'A wonderfull tryumfe, for the wynning of a pryse': Guilds, Ritual, Theater, and the Urban Network in the Southern Low Countries, ca. 1450–1650," *Renaissance Quarterly* 59 (2006): 374–405.

27. I explored these confraternities and their economies of exchange in Arnade, *Realms of Ritual*, 65–94. See also Reintges, *Ursprung und Wesen*. For the rhetoricians, see J. J. Mak, *De rederijkers* (Amsterdam, 1944). For the sixteenth century, see Gary K. Waite, *Reformers on Stage: Popular Drama and Religious Propaganda in the Low Countries of Charles V, 1515–1556* (Toronto, 2000), and especially Van Bruaene, *Om beters wille*.

in Ghent in 1440.²⁸ Later observers would have judged this Burgundian policy wise. In 1574, during one of the most trying years of the Dutch Revolt, the governor of Veere in Zeeland, Johan Junius de Jonghe, enthusiastically proclaimed that any sense of general Netherlandish identity was the result of the cultural ethos the *schutters* and *rederijkers* cultivated in their regional competitions:

> For who does not know that the provinces of these Netherlands have always derived the greatest advantage from being united with each other? Had this union not been the origin of the old custom they have always observed, of assembling towns and provinces for the meeting of the archers and crossbowmen and bearers of other old-fashioned arms, which they call the *landjuweel*? Why else have the towns and provinces always met for public repasts and plays by order of the authorities unless it were to demonstrate the great unity of these provinces, as Greece showed her unity in the meeting of the Olympic Games?²⁹

But if these two well-known urban sodalities helped to develop a sense of urban identity that was at once local and situated in regional networks, the same can be said for aspects of Low Country popular religion. Here too the Burgundian princes paid close attention, knowing full well that shrewd interventions into the wider religious sphere would be critical to massaging their image—and increasing its sacred associations. But if religious devotions became sources of Burgundian patronage, the inherited ecclesiastical framework was institutionally inadequate. The whole of the Habsburg Netherlands in the mid-sixteenth century still had only five bishoprics, administered either by the archbishoprics of Rheims or Cologne: Utrecht in the north and Tournai, Arras, Cambrai, and Liège in the south. Already by the late middle ages, this administrative system was rife with problems. The dioceses did not line up in any rational way with the principalities and their borders as they developed; there was no match between diocesan structure and language spoken; and the surge of urbanization over the centuries saw no concurrent effort to add new bishoprics.³⁰ As Walter Simons has observed, this arrangement only heightened the already established distance between senior and upper clergy and lay people, allowing an institutional gap through which popular religious initiatives could gain momentum before catching the eye of a bishop or archbishop.³¹

Low Country cities were the engines of a rich devotional life that by the late middle ages

28. Arnade, *Realms of Ritual*, 84–91.

29. An English translation in *Texts Revolt*, 123. For a consideration of the original, see Martin van Gelderen, *The Political Thought of the Dutch Revolt, 1550–1590* (Cambridge, 1992), 130–33.

30. M. Dierickx, *L'Érection des nouveaux diocèses aux Pays-Bas, 1559–1570* (Brussels, 1967), provides a complete background to the reorganization of ecclesiastical administration under Phillip II.

31. Walter Simons, *Cities of Ladies: Beguine Communities in the Medieval Low Countries, 1200–1565* (Philadelphia, 2001), 19.

featured the greatest variety of clerical and religious expression.[32] Towns boasted handsomely endowed parish churches, a panoply of religious orders and houses, semireligious orders such as the celebrated Beguines and Beghards, and scores of urban confraternities whose members served as patrons of altars, liturgies, and art. As elsewhere, processions were central to the religious calendar because of their public visibility and the social ordering they enacted.[33] The Low Countries had their own variation in which prominent social cohorts—town aldermen, clergy, religious orders, guild leaders, ward captains, militiamen, and confraternities—marched in front of important municipal buildings and landmarks and around prominent walls. *Ommegang*, the middle Dutch word for a going around, was the term often employed to describe a procession, a perfect distillation of its ambulatory purpose. Also, as elsewhere, the most important processions were those linked to either local devotions or central liturgical moments in the religious calendar, be it a patron saint's feast day, Corpus Christi, or the Assumption of the Virgin.[34]

The urban *schutters* and *rederijkers* were not alone in promoting intraurban exchanges. Certain processions in any given locale involved devotees from other cities, most notably, the annual September 14th devotion to the Virgin Mary in the southern episcopal seat of Tournai. There, scores of cities from across Artois, Hainault, Brabant, and Flanders responded to formal invitations to send delegations to honor the city's Virgin.[35] The annual procession doubled as local commemoration of a miraculous recovery from an eleventh-century plague and as an opportunity for all the cities within its episcopate to pay honor to the Virgin, the city, and its elite confraternity with gifts. In the fifteenth century, the procession began to accommodate sacred theater too, and gained popularity as an ever-widening circle of cities sent delegates. In this mix of civic diplomacy and sacred celebration was also the hand of the Burgundian dukes in their capacity as counts of Flanders. The Burgundian duke annually donated a robe for the Virgin to wear during the proces-

32. J. van Herwaarden and R. de Keyser, "Het gelovige volk in de late middeleeuwen," in *Algemene Geschiedenis der Nederlanden*, ed. D. P. Blok, W. Prevenier, et al. 2nd ed. (Haarlem, 1980), 4:405–20; Ludo Milis, "De devotionele praktijk in de laatmiddeleeuwse Nederlanden," in *Hoofsheid en devotie in de middeleeuwse maatschappij: De Nederlanden van de 12de tot de 15de eeuw* (Ghent, 1981), 13–145. See also J. Toussaert, *Le sentiment religieux en Flandre à la fin du Moyen Age* (Paris, 1960), the first attempt, with uneven results, to explore lay religious expression in the Low Countries with Annalist-inspired methodology.

33. Pioneering studies of lay urban devotions include Natalie Z. Davis, "Some Tasks and Themes in the Study of Popular Religion," in *The Pursuit of Holiness*, ed. C. Trinkhaus and Heiko Oberman (Leiden, 1974), 307–36; Richard C. Trexler, "Ritual Behavior in Renaissance Florence: The Setting," *Medievalia et Humanistica*, n.s. 4 (1973): 125–44; J. Bossy, "Holiness and Society," *Past and Present* 75 (1977): 119–37; and Robert Scribner, "Ritual and Popular Religion in Catholic Germany at the Time of the Reformation," *Journal of Ecclesiastical History* 35 (1987): 47–77.

34. Still useful is Frans de Potter, "Schets eener geschiedenis der gemeentefeesten in Vlaanderen," *Annales de la société des Beaux-Arts et de literature de Gand* 12 (1870): 41–188.

35. Alfred Cauchie, *La grande procession de Tournai* (Louvain and Paris, 1889); Jean Dumoulin and Jacques Pycke, eds., *La grande procession de Tournai* (Tournai, 1992).

sion, supervised by the prestigious Confraternity of Notre Dame.[36] Although not as visibly dramatic as the Liège votive offering, the dress ensured an essential Burgundian frame to the otherwise intensely civic devotion.

In general, the religious policy of the dukes of Burgundy involved patronizing select devotions, strategic involvement in a handful of essential civic processions, and dramatic interventions in a city's religious culture, typically tied to punitive measures taken after political turmoil. As Elodie Lecuppre-Desjardin has observed, many of the best-known urban processions in the southern Low Countries—the procession of Our Lady in Lille, the Holy Blood procession in Bruges, and the Our Lady devotion in Brussels—trace their origin to a seigniorial act, be it the bringing back of a relic from the Holy Land, as was the case in Bruges, or the authorization of a procession in honor of a miraculous image, as was the case in Lille with a statue of the Virgin in the Church of Saint-Pierre.[37] Still, the level of ducal involvement in such celebrations varied considerably. While the Tournai Virgin received an outfit annually from the Burgundian dukes, the equally important May 3 procession of the Holy Blood in Bruges involved no direct ducal sponsorship, though occasionally guest visits did occur, as was the case when Louis de Male, Count of Flanders, attended the procession in 1379.[38] The *ommegang* of the statue of Our Lady in Brussels, celebrated annually on the Sunday before Pentecost, received appreciably more ducal attention. No doubt this was because of the centrality of Brussels as a court city and administrative center of the sprawling Burgundian territories.[39]

It was Philip the Good and Charles the Bold—the real architects of the Burgundian state—who more than their predecessors scaled up Burgundian patronage of the religious devotions. Hugo van der Velden has observed that no other fifteenth-century sovereign commissioned so many votive offerings to various shrines and churches as Charles the Bold. The prince gave portraits to Liège, Notre Dame de Boulogne, Notre Dame de Halle, Our Lady of Scheut, Our Lady of Aardenburg, Saint Adrian in Geraardsbergen, Saint

36. Jean Dumoulin, "Le culte de Notre Dame à la Cathédrale de Tournai," *Revue Diocésaine de Tournai* 15 (1963): 266–303, 332–52.

37. Lecuppre-Desjardin, *Ville des cérémonies*, 89.

38. See Thomas A. Boogaart II, *An Ethnogeography of Late Medieval Bruges: Evolution of a Corporate Milieu, 1280–1349* (New York, 2004), chap. 6, for the most comprehensive treatment of the procession.

39. A. Wauters, *L'ancien Ommeganck de Bruxelles* (Brussels, 1848); C. Dickstein-Bernard, "Détails inédits concernant l'Ommegang," *Cahiers Bruxellois* 7 (1962): 259–66. As the procession grew over time, it also acquired more ducal patronage, and the arms of the dukes of Burgundy were soon annually displayed along the route. An even more significant addition was drama, specifically the performance of a rotating cycle of seven plays, *The Seven Joys of the Virgin*, on Brussels' Great Market. Of the seven plays, only the first and last survive. For an annotated text, see W. H. Beuken, *De Eerste Bliscap van Maria en Die Sevenste bliscap van onser vrouwen* (Noorduijn-Culembourg, 1978), 55. For city boosterism in the ommegang, see Robert Stein, "Cultuur en Politiek in Brussel in de vijftiende eeuw: Wat beoogde het Brusselse stadsbestuur bij de annexatie van de plaatselijke Ommegang," in *Op belofte van profijt: Stadsliteratuur en bugermoraal in de Nederlandse letterkunde van de middeleeuwen*, ed. Herman Pleij (Amsterdam, 1991), 228–43.

Sebastian in Linkebeek, and three gold statues, probably intended for shrines of Saint George in Lier, among others.[40] Two miracle-working Our Ladies, one at Boulogne and the other at Halle, were promoted by Philip the Good and by Charles as principal vehicles of Burgundian sacrality. Both Boulogne and Halle were popular pilgrimage sites outside the civic sphere, and as such were prime opportunities for the dukes to shape their religious quality unmediated by urban institutions.[41]

Notre Dame de Halle near Brussels was so patronized by Burgundian lords that the veneration had strong political valences. This long-standing devotion in Hainault had a venerable list of royal patrons who were members of the elite Confraternity of Notre Dame de Halle: the Holy Roman Emperor; the counts of Holland and Hainault; the king of England; and Louis of Male, the late-fourteenth century count of Flanders, among other dignitaries.[42] It also had a famous champion: the early seventeenth-century humanist Justus Lipsius, who penned the first authoritative history of the devotion to which he fervently subscribed when he returned to the south and to Catholicism late in his life, offering an ex-voto silver pen to the shrine in 1603 in thanks for his gifts as a writer extraordinaire![43] The impressive devotion of Philip the Good and Charles the Bold no doubt had to do with the history of royal patronage that Halle boasted, but also with the fact that Philip the Bold, the first Valois duke of Burgundy, had died at Halle, presumably on pilgrimage, and his entrails were interred in the church there. When Philip the Good finally acquired Hainault in 1427, one of his first acts was to commission regular masses for his grandfather's memory.[44] Gifts and visits followed; among the items are statues of the Virgin Mary, twelve silver statues of the apostles, stained-glass windows, and a painting of Philip the Good at the feet of the Blessed Virgin. The military theme evoked in the votive portraits at Notre Dame de Boulogne finds echo in the two statues of men-at-arms that Philip had placed in the chapel in Halle.[45] The durable link between Burgundian authority and Notre Dame de Halle received an added boast under the Habsburg Burgundians. Charles V even donated a cloak for the Virgin, visible in the woodcut illustration that accompanied Lipsius's book. The crowned and dressed Virgin is situated on the central altar amid several statues and votive offerings, including the twelve apostles and two silver angels that Philip the Good

40. Van der Velden, Donor's Image, 155.

41. On Notre Dame de Boulogne, see Jean Leroy, Saint-Marie de Boulogne (Montreuil-de-Mer, 1985); on Halle, see Justus Lipsius's treatise Diva Virgo Hallensis (Antwerp, 1604), written on his move back south and his reconciliation with Church and king. It was translated into Dutch by Albert van Oosterwijck as Heylighe Maghet van Halle. Hare weldaden ende Miraculen ghetrouwelijck ende ordentelijk uutgeschreven (Delft, 1605). For an overview of Burgundian patronage of both shrines, see Van der Velden, Donor's Image, 155–88.

42. Guldenboek der Broederschap van O.L. Vrouwe van Halle: Volledige tekst en begeleidende kommentaren, 2 vols. (Halle, 1989), excerpted in Van der Velden, Donor's Image, 168–69.

43. Lipsius, Diva Virgo Hallensis; Van der Velden, Donor's Image, 66.

44. Richard Vaughan, John the Fearless (London, 1966), 1.

45. Van der Velden, Donor's Image, 171–72.

Illustration of the Chapel of Notre Dame de Halle with the Virgin and the shrine's votive offerings on the altar. The chapel was a favorite place of worship for Burgundian and Habsburg princes. Justus Lipsius, *Diva Virgo Hallensis*, Antwerp, 1616. Courtesy of Bijzondere Collecties, Universiteitsbibliotheek, Universiteit Leiden.

had previously donated. When the Virgin was carried in her annual procession on the first Sunday in September, she bore the cloak given by Charles V.[46]

Notre Dame de Boulogne and Notre Dame de Halle were twin devotions essential to Burgundian authorities, the forefront of an ever-widening arc of holy objects and spaces that the dukes patronized throughout the Burgundian Netherlands. The traces of Burgundian patronage are located in the mundane financial ledgers that record their monthly pious gifts, and in devotions such as the cult of Our Lady of Seven Sorrows in the Old Church in Delft, promoted by the Dominicans.[47] Popular were the various holy mothers and the warrior saints, especially Saint George, Saint Adrian, and Saint Andrew, who flattered the chivalric-jingoistic appetites of Philip the Good, Charles the Bold, and their successors.

Devotions associated with strong Burgundian patronage were sometimes directly utilized for their religious and symbolic valences in especially difficult political struggles. In the mid-fifteenth century, Philip the Good refined his use of the highly theatrical penitential ritual of the *amende honorable*, in which a delegation, typically the well-heeled, was required to grovel in the white garb of the penitent before a Caesar-like fully armored Burgundian duke, and beg his forgiveness.[48] The most spectacular case occurred after the Ghent war of 1452–53, when patrician and guild radicals had seized the reins of power and proclaimed rebellion against an astonished Philip the Good. After Ghent's sound defeat, the aldermen and guildsmen trudged out in the rain outside the city's wall to utter their plea for forgiveness before a triumphant duke. Guild banners had been central symbols of defiance during the rebellion, and were thus required to be turned over as booty to the duke.[49] Once confiscated, the banners were taken to none other than the shrines of Notre Dame de Boulogne and Notre Dame de Halle, where they were hung.[50] Around the same time, Philip the Good donated an ex-votive portrait to Halle. The votive offering sat on Halle's altar in thanksgiving for Philip's victory, while the banners from Ghent were sacralized as emblems of civic pride alchemized into tokens of defeat.[51] Another set of the

---

46. Ibid., 177.

47. G. Verhoeven, *Devotie en Negotie: Delft als bedevaartplaats in de late middeleeuwen* (Amsterdam, 1992).

48. Arnade, *Realms of Ritual*, 119–20, and Lecuppre-Desjardin, *Ville des cérémonies*, 302–6. For other parts of Europe, England and France most notably, see J. M. Moeglin, "Pénitence publique et amende honorable au Moyen Age," *Revue Historique*, no. 604 (Oct.–Dec. 1997): 225–69, and Moeglin, "Harmiscara-Harmschar-Hachée: Le dossier des rituals d'humiliation et de soumission au Moyen Age," *Archivum Latinitatis Medii Aevi* 43 (1996): 11–65.

49. Peter Arnade, "Crowds, Banners and the Marketplace: Symbols of Defiance and Defeat during the Ghent War, 1452–53," *Journal of Medieval and Renaissance Studies* 24 (Fall 1994): 471–97. For the Ghent war, see Jelle Haemers, *De Gentse Opstand, 1449–1453: De strijd tussen rivaliserende netwerken om het stedelijke kapitaal* (Kortrijk-Heule, 2004).

50. La Marche, *Mémoires*, 2:323.

51. See Van der Velden, *Donor's Image*, 162, on the votive portrait.

same banners followed a mere eighteen months later when the *amende* was performed again at the ducal palace of Coudenberg in Brussels, again split between Boulogne and Halle.[52] The practice continued under the Habsburg successors. Justus Lipsius reports that during Maximilian's late fifteenth-century regency, the city of Brussels donated a statue to Notre Dame de Halle of an unidentified mitered man holding a sword in one hand and a cross in the other "as penalty and amende imposed on them."[53] Maximilian even had a banner taken from Venetian troops in northern Italy in 1509 sent to the shrine.[54] Notre Dame de Boulogne and Notre Dame de Halle, it seems, had become a searing memory palace where objects of defeated subjects sat alongside gifts of pious thanksgiving. The two devotions also remind us that the Burgundian dukes readily evoked their authority in the religious realm by patronizing established devotions or nurturing new ones, especially through select interventions in the urban religious calendar. While the *schutters* and *rederijkers* were key sodalities for the Burgundians to monitor, religious devotions, shrines, and processions offered to the dukes an opportunity to command sacred power, and then deploy it when necessary as part of efforts to regulate, control, and even punish urban constituents.

The Liturgy of Chivalrous Knights

As soldier-princes who constantly battled rivals like the French king or errant townspeople who defiantly tested the limits of ducal authority, the Burgundian dukes loved military affairs. Charles the Bold even perished fighting, much like a hero in a classical epic or feudal *chanson de geste*, his badly mutilated corpse barely recognizable after the battle of Nancy in 1477 against the Swiss.[55] No surprise, then, that the Burgundian princes had a passion for chivalry, seen in their literary love of romance, their elaborate tournaments and jousts, and the sumptuous narrative tapestries woven with silver and gold thread and hung in banquet halls and elsewhere, whose subjects included Gideon, Alexander the Great, and the Trojan War.[56] The chivalric ethos found powerful echo on January 3, 1430, in the establishment of the court's premier confraternity, the Order of the Golden Fleece, during the sumptuous wedding celebrations of Philip the Good and Isabel of Portugal, held in Bruges.[57] The Order of the Golden Fleece was the men's club par excellence of the

52. Arnade, "Crowds, Banners, and the Marketplace."
53. Justus Lipsius, *Die Heylighe Maghet van Halle* (Brussels, 1607), 122–23.
54. From an August 23, 1509, letter from Maximilian to his daughter Margaret, quoted in Van der Velden, *Donor's Image*, 177.
55. Blockmans and Prevenier, *Promised Lands*, 196.
56. On these tapestries, see Thomas P. Campbell, ed., *Tapestry in the Renaissance: Art and Magnificence* (New Haven, 2002), esp. 13–28.
57. F. A. de Reiffenberg, *Histoire de l'ordre de la Toison d'Or* (Brussels, 1830); Luc Hommel, *L'histoire du no-*

Burgundian and Habsburg rulers, and the famous gold collar of the Golden Fleece with the symbol of the ram became its fashionable insignia, sported by the late-medieval Valois dukes and the early modern Habsburg Burgundians in every painted portrait and statue. The establishment of the Order of the Golden Fleece meant many things: a way to imitate royal chivalric orders such as the Knights of the Garter in England, giving the dukes of Burgundy monarchical prestige, a way to create a common fund of insignia to sport in public, a way to enhance the Burgundian passion for chivalry, and a useful vehicle for acculturating sometimes autarkic regional nobility into the Burgundian political orbit.[58] As part of the Burgundian quest to widen their cultural authority, the order had a double benefit: it called attention to the dukes' chivalric prestige (explicitly not the province of their urban, nonpatrician subjects), and it sacralized their persons, thereby consecrating their power and raising their royal prestige.

The order purported to be the most private of elite clubs. At its inception, membership was limited to twenty-four noble "knights" who could trace four lines of nobility through their blood, and two-thirds of whom originally came from the county of Burgundy and the northern French and Flemish border areas.[59] But chapter meetings took place in the most important parish churches of sizable Low Country cities, and involved processions and banquets that blurred the line between public viewership and private meetings. The fact that urban churches were used for the spectacles of the Golden Fleece meetings made these affairs one of the court's most vigorous efforts to affirm the sacred aura of ducal leadership, not merely by merging chivalric and liturgical motifs, but also by locating this syncretism in elite sacred space, with the duke himself at its center.

Philip dedicated the Order of the Golden Fleece to the Burgundian patron saint, Andrew, and to the Virgin Mary, securing the alliance between holy mother and warrior male saint in shrines at Halle, Boulogne, and elsewhere.[60] The first chapter meeting was held

---

ble ordre de la Toison d'Or (Brussels, 1947); Françoise de Gruben, Les chapitres de la Toison d'Or à l'epoque bourguignonne (1430–1477) (Louvain, 1997); Pierre Cockshaw and Christiane van den Bergen-Pantens, eds., L'Ordre de la Toison d'Or de Philippe le Bon à Philippe le Beau, 1430–1505 (Brussels, 1996). On heraldry, insignia, and their ritual importance, see D'A. J. D. Boulton, "The Order of the Golden Fleece and the Creation of Burgundian National Identity," in Ideology of Burgundy, ed. D'A. J. D. Boulton and Jan Veenstra, 21–97. On the Golden Fleece in the urban sphere, see Lecuppre-Desjardin, Ville des cérémonies, 159–64; on its importance to later Burgundian imperial imagery, see Marie Tanner, The Last Descendant of Aeneas (New Haven, 1993), 146–61. On the Burgundian court's chivalric ethos, see J. Rychner, La littérature et les moeurs chevaleresques à la cour de Bourgogne (Neuchâtel, 1950).

58. On the Order of the Garter and other royal chivalric orders, see D'A. J. D. Boulton, The Knights of the Crown: The Monarchical Orders of Knighthood in Later Medieval Europe, 1325–1520 (Woodbridge, 1987); Yves Renouard, "L'Ordre de la Jarretière et l'Ordre de l'Étoile: Étude sur la genèse des ordres laïcs de chevalerie et sur le développement progressif de leur caractère national," Moyen Age 55 (1949): 281–300.

59. Blockmans and Prevenier, Promised Lands, 74.

60. Gruben, Chapitres de la Toison d'Or, 1–30. On the imperial significance of the Golden Fleece legend, which remained essential to the order, see Tanner, Last Descendant of Aeneas, 146–49.

on the feast day of Saint Andrew, November 30, 1431, at the collegiate church of Saint-Pierre in Lille, the administrative seat of the Burgundian government.[61] Over time, these festivities were held in the most important Low Country cities, drawing in an ever-growing group of knights—the membership was enlarged over time—and crowds of spectators to watch the public aspects of the four days of highly liturgical processions, feasts, and masses. Churches were festooned with the knights' banners and armorial devices—usually donated as gifts to be hung perpetually in commemoration of the event—and adorned with richly woven tapestries. For the Bruges meeting of 1432, held at the collegiate church of Saint Donatian, Philip the Good had tapestries of the Virgin Mary and her important feast days commissioned. Over time, meetings no longer always fell on the feast day of Saint Andrew, and the gifts bequeathed grew more elaborate.[62] A constant, however, was the central importance of the collar of the Golden Fleece. Composed of gold firesteel links hung with a jewel in the form of a golden ram, the collar became the order's most important public symbol. As D'Acry J. D. Boulton has argued, it formed part of a repertoire of Golden Fleece heraldry and insignia that, together with the cross of Saint Andrew and military pennons and uniforms of the Burgundian army, went far toward spurring a cultural consciousness of Burgundian political identity in the critical second half of the fifteenth century.[63]

The order reached a peak in the sixteenth century, with chapter meetings both bigger and more international under Habsburg leadership. The twenty-second meeting, held during the week of January 18, 1556, in the great parish church of Onze-Lieve-Vrouw (Our Beloved Lady) in Antwerp, was a spectacle of solemnity that appears in hindsight contrived in its evocation of unity, a false calm before the storm of political and religious violence threatening on the horizon. Philip II entered the city on January 18, but the collapse of a fire display that killed seven local inhabitants marred this rare royal visit. The chapter meeting got underway three days later, with a procession of hundreds of clergy and several hundred noblemen on horseback from Saint Michael's Abbey, where the royal party was residing, to the Onze-Lieve-Vrouwekerk. The entourage was impressive, given the small size of the central party: a mere eight knights and the king, all splendidly outfitted in crimson velvet gowns. Some knights were absent—busy with war, of course—and even more had died. The already dazzling church of some seventy altars was further embellished with eight Gideon tapestries that Philip the Good had commissioned in 1448 for a chapter meeting in Tournai, and the monumental twelve tapestry set commissioned in

---

61. See Gruben, *Chapitres de la Toison d'Or*, 93–103, for the ritual protocols of a chapter meeting. See also Olivier de La Marche, "Epistre pour tenir et celebrer la noble feste du Thoison d'Or," in *Mémoires*, 4:158–89.

62. A careful review of all the chapter meetings until 1477 is in Gruben, *Chapitres de la Toison d'Or*; the increase in gifts is clear.

63. Boulton, "Order of the Golden Fleece."

1546 by the regent Mary of Hungary to celebrate Charles V's 1535 Tunis campaign.[64] The fifteenth-century tapestries affirmed the order's foundational roots, and the unprecedented Tunis set announced the imperial flair of the new Habsburg sovereigns while harking back to Philip's father's military heroics as the master of ancient Carthage. Relics and reliquaries filled the central altar, and the choir stalls were hung with the knights' banners, including those of the many deceased. A round of masses and banquets followed, and events peaked on January 27, when ten new knights were named, including Philip II's son Carlos and none other than the king's future nemesis, William, Prince of Orange. The next day, nine others received the prestigious honor. Philip stayed in Antwerp to conduct royal business until March 3. When the king left, he donated three stained glass windows for the central choir of the Onze-Lieve-Vrouwekerk. The central pane depicted Saint Paul and Saint Andrew; to the left was a window with Philip kneeling in prayer, and to the right was another of his wife, Mary Tudor.[65]

However much the Order of the Golden Fleece grew in size, its protocol remained fixed and its membership remained the exclusive domain of the noble protégés of the court. From one perspective its chapter meetings were decidedly private, held inside parish churches and ducal palaces. Yet they also were insistently public, transpiring inside large cities and punctuated by important, formal processions to and from the parish church and ducal residence. The banquets, too, had guests. The fifteenth-century chronicler of Burgundian court life, Olivier de La Marche, noted that noble women watched from side stands (hourts), and that the duke might seat himself at a table with important local prelates and regional senior church officials, or be joined by senior ambassadors. The banquets might even include urban officials because, in La Marche's words, they typically helped to fund the occasions with gifts and financial support.[66] The festivities of the chapter meetings merged the chivalric with the sacred, centering on the duke surrounded by his most noble "knights" and scores of clergy and high church officials, in a revolving set of masses and meetings. Important townspeople sometimes were afforded access to the affair. The church and the crowds provided a frame, space, and audience for this sacred politics, while the banners and gifts were sacralized in perpetuity on the altar and in the chapel and choir.

Contract and Covenant: The Joyous Entry

Entrée Joyeuse / Blijde Inkomst: whether penned in French or Dutch, the "Joyous Entry" was the legal term for the ceremony that Low Country townspeople and court dignitaries

---

64. On the Tunis tapestries, see Hendrik J. Horn, *Jan Cornelisz Vermeyen, Painter of Charles V and His Conquest of Tunis: Paintings, Etchings, Drawings, Cartoons and Tapestries*, 2 vols. (Meppel, 1989).

65. A full overview of festivities is in Floris Prims, *Geschiedenis van Antwerpen*, 29 vols. (Antwerp, 1941), 19:1–5.

66. La Marche, "Epistre pour tenir et celebrer la noble feste," 8–10.

could agree most closely bound the city and state together.[67] The entry ceremony was at once a constitutional act and a premier public performance, the Burgundian political rite that more than any other displayed the power of its princes and the limits of their sovereign reach. As the principal venue for affirming Burgundian authority, it became the favorite ritual device of Burgundian and Habsburg rulers. But its use came at a price, since the Joyous Entry nourished civic ambitions as much as it proclaimed the prerogatives of lordship. Because of this double purpose and its elemental political power, Burgundian rulers were determined to redraw the entry ceremony's ritual contours. Their efforts are apparent by the mid-fifteenth century, when classical and biblical invocations of lordly authority became more overt. What better way to quiet urban constitutionalism than to render the princely entry more sacred and more based on classical, imperial motifs.

In the early modern Low Countries, the term Blijde Inkomst carried constitutional punch. It originally referred to the charter of rights secured by the Estates of Brabant in 1356 from Duchess Jeanne and Duke Wenceslas, which neatly codified a grab-bag of urban and duchy rights into thirty-three articles. The charter granted the towns legal priority in their relationship with the duke, with all important acts—financial, legal, and monetary most notably—requiring the stamp of urban approval. By the late sixteenth century, William of Orange and his fellow rebels against the king of Spain had recast the Blijde Inkomst as a blanket invocation of all the historical rights—real or supposed—that Low Country towns and provinces had secured, all the more sacrosanct since Charles V had unsuccessfully tried to remove a key article from the original charter that permitted Brabanters to withdraw their allegiance to their sovereign if he failed to uphold its legal stipulations.[68] That the term for the ceremonial entry in the Burgundian Netherlands was synonymous with a charter that over the course of two centuries had grown as the master symbol of perceived rights and freedoms meant that this political ritual resonated with townspeople more for what it guaranteed to them than for what it secured for the prince. A regal reception for the sovereign was assured, but more viscerally, the Joyous Entry bespoke urban rights.

---

67. For the late-medieval northern entry ceremony, see Gordon Kipling, *Enter the King: Theatre, Liturgy, and Ritual in the Medieval Civic Triumph* (Oxford, 1998); Joseph Chartrou, *Les éntrees solonnelles et triomphales à la Renaissance, 1484–1551* (Paris, 1928); Guenée and Lehoux, *Entrées royales françaises*; Bryant, *The King and the City*. For the Low Countries, see Jesse Hurlbut, "*Vive Bourgogne est nostre cry*": *Ceremonial Entries of Philip the Good and Charles the Bold (1419–1477)* (Turnhout, forthcoming); the theoretical and political overview is in Soly, "Plechtige intochten"; Lecuppre-Desjardin, *Ville des cérémonies*, 135–58; I. von Roeder-Baumbach, *Versieringen bij Blijde Inkomsten gebruikt in de Zuidelijke Nederlanden gedurende de 16e en 17e eeuw* (Antwerp, 1943); and Jan Landwehr, *Splendid Ceremonies: State Entries and Royal Funerals in the Low Countries, A Bibliography* (Leiden, 1971).

68. On the constitutional legacy of the Brabantine Joyous Entry, see Bryce D. Lyon, "Fact and Fiction in English and Belgian Constitutional Law," *Medievalia et Humanistica* 10 (1956): 82–101. On the propagandistic value of the charter to the political theory of the Dutch Revolt, see P. A. M. Geurts, "Het beroep op de Blijde Inkomste in de pamfletten uit de Tachtigjarige Oorlog," *Standen en Landen* 16 (1958): 3–15.

Since the rulership of Philip the Bold, first Valois Duke of Burgundy, the sovereigns of the Burgundian Netherlands had made use of the Joyous Entry to inaugurate their lordship in much the same fashion as their English, French, and other counterparts. What differentiated it from other Burgundian spectacles, including the chapter meetings of the Golden Fleece, was the contractual element at its heart. True, jousts depended on the financial support and spatial coordinates of the city, and even the exclusive Golden Fleece meetings allowed some townspeople to sit at the ducal banquet. But these inclusions were quietly admitted without much comment into the stylized fiction of princely display. The formal role that a Golden Fleece chapter meeting prescribed to a citizen was that of spectator and facilitator. In countless other political ceremonies, the Burgundian dukes were at pains to emphasis that their lordship was unimpeachable, and that the hierarchical division between prince and subject was as natural as that between parent and child. When subjects balked at ducal demands—as the Estates of Flanders did when they failed to support the siege of Neuss to the satisfaction of Charles the Bold in 1475 —the prince might register his contempt by using domestic metaphors that cast citizens as mere dependents. On July 12, 1475, Charles excoriated the Flemish Estates for his failed Neuss campaign and threatened: "Since you have refused to be governed by me as children by their father, you could be disinherited as an unworthy son from his father's property."[69] The Joyous Entry, by contrast, made townspeople more equal players in a two-way ceremony of contractual exchange, rooted in the old but essential feudal oaths of respective rights. The duke entered the city, and a delegation of clergy and aldermen dutifully met and lauded him; once inside the city, however, both parties swore oaths to uphold each other's rights and privileges. The heart of the Joyous Entry was a tidy legal balance between lord and subject.

Despite its legal essence, the entry ceremony also relied on a religious frame, and holy objects were essential ingredients. The profession of oaths by town magistrates and prince during the Joyous Entry required religious artifacts and officiating clergy to consecrate their words. The role played by parish churches, relics, and ecclesiastical dignitaries in the princely entry ceremony was crucial. In Dijon, the duke and townspeople swore their oaths in the abbey church of Saint Benigne, after kissing the holy objects and kneeling in prayer before the altar "richly furnished with relics."[70] In Bruges, the oath were sworn at the Church of Saint Donatian, and in Ghent, they were made official over the relics of the Holy Cross at the central parish church of Saint John.[71] At some places like

69. L. P. Gachard, ed., *Collection des documents inédits concernant l'histoire de la Belgique*, 3 vols. (Brussels, 1833–35), 1:256.

70. Bibliothèque Nationale, MS. Fr. 11507, fols. 205–9.

71. On the entry ceremony in Bruges, see James Murray, "The Liturgy of the Count's Advent in Bruges from Galbert to the Van Eycks," in *City and Spectacle in Medieval Europe*, ed. Barbara Hanawalt and Kathryn Ryerson (Minneapolis, 1992), 137–52. For Ghent, Peter Arnade, "The Emperor and the City: The Cultural Politics of the Joyous Entry in Early Sixteenth Century Ghent and Flanders," *Handelingen der Maatschappij voor Geschiedenis en Oudheidkunde te Gent* 54 (2000): 65–92.

Dijon, clergy administered the oaths; at other places, this role fell to a city official, as in Mechelen in 1467 when the city's pensionary (the town's attorney) conducted the oath before the town hall.[72]

During most of the fifteenth century the dukes of Burgundy were on the move through their territories, with no single principal residence, leading to a constant stream of urban entries. There were the momentous inaugural ones for every new duke and duchess, but also the more common routine visits which, however minor, typically involved a formal urban reception, and perhaps a banquet.[73] For the most part, these entries were modest affairs, recorded succinctly in city records by payments to the duke for gifts—typically wine—and by legal ordinances to clean the streets, tidy up house frontages, and maintain law and order.[74] Torches and tapers were carried, houses prettified and hung with tapestries, oaths administered on relics, and gifts offered. Most entries were just that: neat and economical.

Not so in 1440 in the great metropolis of Bruges. The 1430s had been turbulent times in Flanders; Philip the Good had ridden out four revolts in Ghent between 1432 and 1438, all the result of socioeconomic problems stimulated by his monetary policy.[75] In 1436 troubles exploded in Bruges too. The craft guilds agitated against their own town magistrates just as the duke concluded a failed expedition against the English at Calais, for which the Bruges militia had been mobilized. As political recriminations mounted, Philip decided to pay a visit to the city, and on May 22, 1437, he arrived fully armed with an impressive posse of men. But no ceremony, not even the perfunctory offering of gifts, greeted them. Instead, they were ambushed, and the duke was locked outside the city gates as part of his armed retinue entered the city. In the aftermath, Philip's senior official in his expedition, the Lord of L'Isle-Adam, lay dead in the street, his killers having brazenly ripped the knight of the Golden Fleece collar off his body. The rebels took twenty-two Picardian soldiers prisoner, then executed them in public.[76]

Bruges's turmoil was especially infuriating to Philip the Good. A ducal visit, even an admonitory one with an army in train, still qualified as an entry, for which the protocols required the formulaic exchanges of decorum. All that had been turned upside down when the reception was staged as a murderous trick. The most senior advisor in the duke's ret-

72. H. Coninckx, "La joyeuse entrée des seigneurs de Malines," *Bulletin du cercle archéologique, littéraire et artistique de Malines* 6 (1895): 165–308, esp. 264–68.

73. Hurlbut, "*Vive Bourgogne est nostre cry*", provides a chronological list of more than two hundred entries for Philip the Good and Charles the Bold.

74. Ibid., table 2.2, for a list of gifts for inaugural entries.

75. See Marc Boone, *Gent en de Bourgondische hertogen, ca. 1384–1453: Een sociaal-politieke studie van een staatsvormingsproces* (Brussels, 1990), 216–20, for a summary overview and analysis. See also Boone, "Urban Space and Political Conflict in Late Medieval Flanders," 634–35.

76. For a comprehensive treatment, see Jan Dumolyn, *De Brugse Opstand van 1436–1438* (Kortrijk-Heule, 1997).

inue had been killed in cold blood, and his nobility derided. The city was forced to pay dearly: an enormous indemnity of 200,000 golden riders, the arrest and execution of forty people, the sealing up of the Boeveriepoort (the gate where the riot had started), and the erection of a chapel endowed with masses to be sung in perpetuity. More spectacularly, Philip ordered the performance of the *amende honorable*, imposed on the rioters of Bruges with the greatest fanfare hitherto associated with it.[77]

City officials performed the rite on December 11, 1440, kneeling barefoot in white penitential garb before the triumphant duke as they surrendered the city keys to Philip, after which the clergy sang a Te Deum.[78] The *amende* was an expiation searing in its humiliation, especially of the urban elites, who were as much the target of the rioters' wrath as had been the duke's men. No stand-alone event, the *amende* served as prologue to a spectacular Joyous Entry, one in which, for the first significant time in the Low Countries, dramatists mounted a reception that featured twenty-four pageant stages organized around the theme of urban repentance and ducal triumphalism. The entry was thus a ceremonial corrective, turning upright that which had been so brazenly inverted. But in a larger sense, the Bruges entry shifted the terrain of the Burgundian Joyous Entry by transforming what previously had been a legal rite facilitated by religious space and objects into a kind of holy apotheosis, the duke as Messiah, his townspeople as prodigal children seeking reconciliation, the ritual itself more biblical covenant than feudal contract.[79] For the first significant time in the Low Countries, the entry ceremony was turned into a liturgical acclamation of the Burgundian duke.

Philip had entered Bruges on December 11, the third Sunday of Advent season, the time of preparation for celebrating the birth of Christ and, by implication, for preparing for his second coming in judgment. The first pageant to greet the duke after the *amende* was that of John the Baptist proclaiming the Messiah: "I am the voice of one crying in the wilderness, make straight the way of the Lord" (John 1:19–23).[80] Inside the city, the duke wound through the streets to view a series of pageants that began with Job praising God, followed by a series of Hebrew prophets, and concluding with the resurrection and transfiguration

---

77. The stipulations are found in L. Gilliodts-van Severen, ed., *Inventaire des archives de la ville de Bruges*, 5 vols. (Bruges, 1871–85), 5:136–58. Minted between 1434–1440, the golden rider was equal to twenty-four stuivers.

78. Enguerrand de Monstrelet, *La chronique d'Enguerrand de Monstrelet*, ed. Douet d'Arcq, 6 vols. (Paris, 1857–62), 5:445–46; Willem Vosterman, *Dits die Excellent Cronike van Vlaenderen* (Antwerp, 1531), fol. 106r. For the exact textual relationship of Vosterman's account to earlier manuscripts, see Dumolyn, *Brugse Opstand*, 48–49.

79. For a close treatment, see Kipling, *Enter the King*, 48–60.

80. For the account of the entry, I have followed Vosterman, who copies the *Kronyk van Vlaenderen van 380 tot 1467*, ed. Philippe Blommaert and C. P. Serrure, 2 vols. (Ghent, 1939–40), and follows the unpublished "Die maniere hoe ons gheduchtich here ende prinche ontfanghen was tot sijnder incomste binnen sine stede van Brucghe van 11sten dach van decembre anon 1140," Stadsbibliotheek Brugge, MS. 436.

of Christ. As Gordon Kipling has underscored, the Bruges pageantry staged Philip as the Christ savior and Christmas king, an association sealed by the choice of the Advent time and the pageant liturgy featuring prophets who anticipate the Messiah. So pleased was Philip with the performance that he gave back the keys to the city after he reached the Burgundian residence where the procession and narrative terminated.[81] Submission had been achieved, but happily, reconciliation too. So successful was the entry as expiation for the townspeople and apotheosis of a prince as Messiah that it served as inspiration for the 1458 entry into Ghent some five years after its war against Philip the Good: again a spectacular *amende honorable*, again the surrender of the city's keys, and again the duke entering a chastised city to be proclaimed a savior.[82]

The Bruges entry of 1440 and the Ghent one of 1458 did not recast all subsequent entries, but they did dramatically widen the symbolic repertoire available to entry planners, introducing the entry as penitential rite to the Burgundian Netherlands. In addition to their heightened theatrical grandeur, these entries were the most remarkable attempts, through public ritual, to stage the duke as a holy person, and they illustrate the degree to which Philip the Good and his advisors actively pursued the sacralization of his public person. The Advent themes, the admonitions of the prophets, the heraldic devices enveloped in a larger messianic field of symbols—these potent symbols completely obscured the constitutional tropes common in entries, and essential in inaugural ones. The consecration of the ruler was predicated on the submission of the citizens, whose errant behavior was iterated at every step of the processions and pageants.

The two Advent entries of 1440 and 1458, however novel, did not erase the entry ceremony's basic building blocks—nor did they solve the problem of urban pride, as Charles the Bold learned in his own inaugural entries of 1467. Most entries still centered on the legal dramaturgy between prince and subject, but Advent elements could now came into play, as at Dijon in 1474, when the prophets and other Biblical heroes made their appearance yet again.[83] The set designs of an entry ceremony grew more elaborate, and so too did their means of commemoration; in 1496, the city of Brussels commissioned a lavish manuscript with sixty colored drawings to memorialize the entry of Joanna of Castile there in December.[84] Bigger changes occurred in the sixteenth century, when entry pageantry

---

81. Vosterman, *Dits de Excellent Cronike*, 108v–109r.

82. On the Ghent entry, see Arnade, *Realms of Ritual*, 131–42; Jeffrey Chipps Smith, "Venit nobis pacificus Dominus: Philip the Good's Triumphal Entry into Ghent in 1458," in "*All the World's a Stage . . .*" *Art and Pageantry in the Renaissance and Baroque.* vol. 1. *Triumphal Celebrations and Rituals of Statecraft*. Papers in Art History from the Pennsylvania State University, no. 6, ed. Barbara Wisch and Susan Scott Munshower (University Park, 1990): 259–90; and Kipling, *Enter the King*, 264–80.

83. Henri Chabeuf, *L'entrée de Charles le Téméraire et les funérailles de Philippe le Bon à Dijon en Janvier en Février 1474* (Dijon, 1903).

84. Wim Blockmans and Esther Donckers, "Self-Representation of Court and City in Flanders and Brabant in the Fifteenth and Early Sixteenth Centuries," in *Showing Status: Representations of Social Positions in the Late Middle Ages*, ed. Wim Blockmans and Antheun Janse (Turnhout, 1999), 81–111.

grew even grander in scale as a response to the coming to power of the Habsburg Burgundian dynasty, especially after Charles V linked the Low Countries to the other parts of the composite empire he was amassing. Urban humanists and chambers of rhetoric played a stronger role as official planners of the ceremonies, and classical motifs including triumphal arches and imperial symbols began to crop up, thereby muting the older late-medieval constitutional forms so important in the fifteenth-century entries.

If Bruges in 1440 marked the vigorous sacralization of the entry ceremony, the sixteenth-century marriage of old and new forms is first apparent in the entry into the same city of the young Charles V in 1515, the year he gained the countship of Flanders.[85] A commission of six rhetoricians in Bruges, in conjunction with its community of foreign merchants, prepared a bedazzling show of twenty-seven pageants, eleven dedicated to the specific theme of the economic rise and sorrowful decline of the city itself, with fifteen separate pageants designed by the foreign merchants. With economic decline and urban rights informing the story of the city's eleven offerings, the rhetoricians audaciously staged Bruges as a historical Jerusalem, creating a series of tableaux vivants featuring parallel narratives of the ancient Israelites and local civic history. The Spanish, Italian, and Hanseatic merchants, conspicuously ignoring this theme, presented allegories of imperial lordship, including a Hanseatic triumphal arch, featuring the figure of Atlas helped by a lion to hold up the world, and an Italian classical arch on the Beurseplein with an attic bearing the laudatory inscription: "A Charles qui doibt dompter le monde" (To Charles who must conquer the world).[86]

The hybridization of urban symbols, Biblical allegories, and newer imperial and classical motifs grew more pronounced in subsequent entries, as Charles acquired first the kingship of Castile and Aragon in 1516, and then the office of Holy Roman Emperor in 1519. In 1520 Antwerp's rhetoricians and humanists received Charles V with an enormous spectacle that featured thirteen tableaux vivants, a colonnade of some four hundred arches, and a printed Latin commemorative booklet prepared by Peter Gillis. The sacralization of the emperor was a noticeable motif, including a final tableau of Charles as the Shepard who lovingly tends his flock. There was nothing new presented in this message, except that the pageant added the figures of Africa and Asia kneeling before the emperor, who embraced a figure of Europe, a whisper of the still very early colonial enterprises

---

85. The entry produced a lavish manuscript with thirty-three color drawings by Remy du Puys for Charles, published as a forty-page account with thirty-three woodcuts made in Paris by Gilles de Gourmont. For a facsimile edition of this livret, see Sydney Anglo, ed., *La tryumphante Entrée de Charles Prince des Espagnes en Bruges 1515* (Amsterdam, n.d.). For a discussion of the relationship between the two texts, see ibid., 7–11.

86. For a description of these motifs, see Anglo, *Tryumphante Entrée*, 13–17; Jean Jacquot, "Panorama des fêtes et cérémonies du règne: Evolution des thèmes et des styles," in *Fêtes et cérémonies au temps de Charles Quint*, ed. Jacquot (Paris, 1960), 413–91; and Blockmans and Donckers, "Self-Representation of Court and City in Flanders and Brabant," 108–11.

under way that would grow louder and carry even heavier imperial motifs in subsequent entry ceremonies Charles made elsewhere, particularly in Italy.[87]

The syncretism between Renaissance stylistics and local traditions reached maturity with the 1549 entry of Charles V and the future Philip II into Antwerp, undoubtedly the most important public ritual of lordship before the abdication of Charles V. As had become customary with Charles's entries elsewhere, especially in Italy, the pageantry was rich in triumphal arches and classical architecture, yet the content still adhered to the message of unwavering obligation between ruler and prince that the late-medieval Blijde Inkomst so powerfully encoded.[88] The history of the Joyous Entry in the Burgundian Netherlands, therefore, is one of cultural evolution and stylistic changes, shot through with the tension between the entry as legal contract and the entry as religious covenant. Its elasticity allowed planners to feature, variously, a repentant city; the city as historical Jerusalem; the city as the new Jerusalem; and the city as itself, rich in historical privileges; the prince as savior; the prince as forgiving father; the prince as triumphant imperial leader; and the prince as local count or duke. Each development—the modest entry of the first Burgundian dukes, the vigorous religious allegorization promoted by Philip the Good, the blending of the neoclassical and the biblical under Charles V—invoked new ways to vaunt princely authority without negating civic motifs. No matter how varied the entry's theme, its planners increasingly relied on sacred props, be they the modest local relics on which an oath was sworn, the clergy in procession, the church as reception hall, or the prince himself alchemized into savior. And despite stylistic changes, the center of the dramaturgy always remained the prince, at once viewed and viewer, the charismatic center around which a multitude of images and imaginations orbited.

Reverent Princes, Unruly Subjects

Beginning with the official Habsburg historiographer Remy du Puys's livret commemorating Charles V's entry into Bruges in 1515, all significant joyous entries in the Low Countries were followed by published accounts authored by well-heeled humanists, com-

---

87. The livret was published as P. Aegedius, Hypotheses sive argumenta spectaculorum quae serennis. et invictissimo Caes. Carlo . . . praeter alia multa et varia Fides et Amor celebratissimae civitatis Antverpienis . . . sunt edituri (Antwerp, 1520). See Soly, "Plechtige intochten," 348. On the classical motifs in Charles's triumphal entries, see Bonner Mitchell, The Majesty of the State: Triumphal Progresses of Foreign Sovereigns in Renaissance Italy (1494–1600) (Florence, 1986), 139–78, and Peter Burke, "Presenting and Re-presenting Charles V," in Charles V and His Time, 1500–1558, ed. Hugo Soly (Antwerp, 1999), 393–476.

88. Cornelius Grapheus, De seer wonderlijcke/schoone/Triumphelijcke Incompst van den hooghmogende Prince Philips (Antwerp, 1550); J. C. Calvete de Estrella, El felicíssimo viaje del muy alto y muy poderoso principe Don Phelippe 2 vols. (Antwerp, 1552; repr., Madrid, 1930), 2:108–217. For a reading of the entry as a ritual of negotiation, and the rhetorical tropes of its Serlian classical architecture, see Mark A. Meadow, "Ritual and Civic Identity in Philip II's 1549 Antwerp Blijde Incompst," Nederlands Kunsthistorisch Jaarboek 49 (1998): 37–68.

monly as booklets with woodcut illustrations, but sometimes in more lavish editions with colored illustrations. Whatever the format, their charge was to capture the brilliance of the entry in prose and publish the result with illustrations, typically of the ephemeral triumphal arches. Antwerp's city secretary and humanist Cornelius Grapheus prepared such a livret for the 1549 Antwerp entry, published by the printer and engraver Pieter Coecke van Aelst.[89] While not naked paeans to regal authority, these handsomely produced livrets nonetheless secured an official memory for these ceremonies compatible with the affirmation of princely authority. They clearly presented city and state interests, praised the prince and admonished him to be a good ruler, and visually reproduced the brilliantly designed arches and tableaux.

That such iconic events were increasingly tied to neatly packaged official accounts was no accident, but was the result of careful regulation. Among the many ordinances Antwerp issued in preparation to receive Charles V and his son Philip in 1549 was the decree that "no painter, sculptor, printer or any one else can print or have printed any portraits, paintings, sculptures, prints of any plays, texts, ceremonies, pageants, triumphal arches, descriptions or inscriptions (of the event)." Nor could anyone take home souvenirs from the ephemeral artwork, including from the triumphal arches.[90] Grapheus's official published livret thus was ensured no competition in the marketplace of texts and artwork for which sixteenth-century Antwerp was so renowned.[91] It was the single, authorized account, produced through a commission and legal regulation. The official ceremony was ensured a worthy custodian of its memory, and a medium—the printed booklet—whose audience was the literate public.

Regulation of social behavior and cultural production typified the cities of the southern Low Countries in the sixteenth century. It added yet another crucial layer to the effort begun in the mid-fifteenth century to burnish the Burgundian image and authority in the public realm and render the urban sphere more stable and secure.[92] Charles came to his majority in 1515 and finally reached the Burgundian dream of royal legitimacy by becom-

89. On Grapheus and van Aelst, with full literature review, see Meadow, "Ritual and Civic Identity," esp. 43.

90. For these two important ordinances dated September 19, 1549, and September 26, 1549, see P. Génard, "Index der Gebodboeken, berustende ter Secretary der stad Antwerpen, beginnende met 8 February 1489, en eindigende met het jaer 1794," in Antwerpsch Archievenblad 39 vols. (Antwerp, 1864), 1:236.

91. Werner Waterschoot, "Antwerp: Books, Publishing and Cultural Production before 1585," in Urban Achievement in Early Modern Europe, ed. Patrick O'Brien et al. (Cambridge, 2001), 233–48; J. van der Stock, ed., Antwerp: Story of a Metropolis, 16th–17th Century (Ghent, 1993).

92. The divergence between elite and nonelite cultural life in the early modern period is explored in Muchembled, Culture populaire et culture des élites, and Peter Burke, Popular Culture in Early Modern Europe (New York, 1978). For the Netherlands, with special attention to Brussels, see Pleij, Sneeuwpoppen, and Herman Pleij, Het Gilde van de Blauwe Schuit: literatuur, volksfeest en burgermoraal in de late middeleeuwen (Amsterdam, 1983), as well as the provocatively theorized study of folkloric strains in P. Vandenbroeck, Jheronimus Bosch: Tussen volksleven en stadscultuur (Berchem, 1987).

ing king of Castile and Aragon in 1516, and Holy Roman Emperor in 1519, an achievement celebrated in 1530 with his papal coronation at Bologna. As Charles gained regal titles, he everywhere scaled up his self-presentation, including in the Low Countries, drawing up an international team of writers, artists, poets, and chancery officials to craft his public image in a highly coordinated and broadly cast cultural exercise. This effort began at Charles's very birth, which occasioned a memorable baptism ceremony in Ghent on March 7, 1500 that recast the ritual parameters of royal baptism to assert more aggressively the newborn's future political worth. The newborn was treated to tableaux vivants and three triumphal arches bearing allegories of wisdom, justice, and peace as a large civic and court retinue carried him beneath a canopy along an elevated gallery from the court residence, Ten Walle, to Saint John's Church.[93] According to witnesses, citizens packed the streets to praise their future count of Flanders, while the triumphal arches were a prescient hint of great things to come and titles to wield.

In the cities of the Low Countries, Charles's ritual self-presentation was inseparable from the campaign to better regulate the urban cultural and religious sphere. This included measures by civic elites to purge the social body of behaviors deemed too plebian and those reflecting the emerging humanist concern for social and educational reform. It also comprehended state-inspired legal efforts to extirpate a fast-growing Protestant movement with general legislation against heresy. With religious iconography greatly increased in Burgundian ritual since the last century, and with German Protestantism demanding much of his attention and resources, Charles was determined to keep the Low Countries both firmly Catholic and culturally supervised.[94] Protestantism in the Low Countries presented the same religious threat it did elsewhere to Catholic rulers. But its challenges to the public representation of Burgundian sovereignty also merit attention, especially given the vigorous invocations of sacred lordship princes had cultivated since the time of Philip the Good.

This new regulatory environment was readily apparent in urban life in the third decade

---

93. SAG 400/25, fols. 261r–v, and fol. 265v for the celebrations. See also Ph. Blommaert, "Vruegdebedryven by de geboorte van Keizer Karl den Vyfden binnen Gent," *Belgisch Museum* 2 (1838): 135–38; and Rolf Strom-Olsen, "Dynastic Ritual and Politics in Early Modern Burgundy: The Baptism of Charles V," *Past and Present* 175 (2002): 34–64, which includes a hitherto unknown account of the ceremonies by Diego Ramirez de Villaescusa de Haro, a Spanish envoy to the Burgundian court. For Lieven Bautkin's description of the event, see *Die warachtighe gheschiedenisse van allen geloofweerdighe saken vanden alder overwinnelijcsten ende alder moghensten Keyser van Roomen Carolus de vijfste van dien name Coninck van Spaengnen, etc.*, transcribed in G. Everaert, "Letterkundig leven te Gent in de vijftiende eeuw: De Rederijkers" (master's thesis, University of Ghent, 1964), 116–22.

94. Two recent biographies of Charles V concentrate on the Low Countries in relation to his challenges in German territories and the Mediterranean world. See Wim Blockmans, *Emperor Charles V, 1500–1558* (Oxford, 2002), and William S. Maltby, *The Reign of Charles V* (New York, 2002).

of the sixteenth century. Consider, for example, two ordinances penned by a city clerk on the same folio page of Antwerp's book of civic ordinances (Gebodboeken) in 1535.[95] The first, issued on June 26, prohibited popular archery contests and celebrations associated with them; general public gatherings on the streets, especially with tambourines and drums; feasting or drinking during the night watch; and roaming the streets after the evening bell, even on pretext of celebrating a wedding.[96] Its spirit, to ensure sobriety, enforce curfews, prohibit street-corner congregations, even stop neighborhood versions of the wildly popular shooting contests typically handled by the great guilds of the crossbowmen and archers, fits perfectly within a broader pattern of civic and state regulation of social behavior that began in the late-fifteenth century but gained considerable ground after the 1520s, in part because Lutheranism was now a serious and growing challenge.[97] The second ordinance, issued on September 4, also exemplifies larger cultural and religious concerns. It mandated the celebration of a great procession of devotion in honor of Charles V's defeat of Barbarossa at Tunis—the subject of classical bombast in his other territories, including a series of remarkable triumphal entries throughout Italy.[98] It directed Antwerp's clergy and the elite religious confraternities to marshal the all-important holy objects and relics; citizens to clean their streets and houses; and the social confraternities, guilds, and foreign merchant companies to compete among themselves to hold the best festivities, with prizes of wine and ham.[99] The statute diverted festive energies away from the roguish play of arms, drink, and the crash-and-boom of street music prohibited in the first decree, and toward good pious cheer and the valorization of Charles and his military triumph over the infidel enemy. Curb excess, clean your house, honor God, praise the sovereign.

Contemporaries of Charles V responded to his astonishing inheritance of Habsburg Burgundian domains stretching from Spain to the Low Countries by concocting superla-

95. Stadsarchief Antwerp, Gebodboeken, with index and excerpts in Génard, "Index der Gebodboeken," 120–464. For transcriptions of a selection of documents concerning the religious troubles of the sixteenth century, see Antwerpsch Archievenblad, 2:1–68 (for period 1521–50), and ibid., "Ordonnantien van het Antwerpsch Magistraat, rakende de godsdienstige geschillen der XVIe eeuw," 2:308–472. For the June 26 and September 4, 1535, ordinances, see ibid., 1:202–3.

96. Génard, Antwerpsch Archievenblad, 1:202–3.

97. Hugo Soly, "Openbare feesten in Brabantse en Vlaamse steden, 16de–18de eeuw," Het openbaar initiatief van de gemeenten in België, Historische grondslagen, 11e Internationaal Colloquium, Handelingen Gemeentekrediet van België. Historische uitgaven, no. 65 (n.p. 1984), 614–19.

98. On this campaign and Charles's other military ventures, see Tracy, Emperor Charles V. On Charles's triumphal receptions in Italy in 1535–36, see Mitchell, Majesty of the State, 151–74.

99. Génard, Antwerpsch Archievenblad, 1:202–3, "Huysen te vercieren, straeten te reynigen, vieringen te doen door de Gulden en Ambachten, op alsulke prysen van haemelen en wynen als de Stad geven sal; natien, kooplieden en andere poorteren ook te vieren."

tives about his universal monarchy and his imperial might, rhetoric promoted by men like his grand chancellor, Mercurino Arborio di Gattinara.[100] But as vast as this Renaissance emperor's domain might be, and for all the imperial imagery his stable of artists and writers promoted, it still had a Burgundian Achilles' heel. For Charles's regnum was less a unified empire than a hodgepodge of seventy-two titles cut from the cloth of different regions, each with its own codes of law, political institutions, and cultural traditions.[101] Such heterogeneity did not stop Charles's public presentation in the Netherlands from being the richest in visual imagery of any Burgundian leader, a style honed even before he gained his key royal and imperial titles. Charles's entry ceremonies of 1515, 1520, and 1549 in Bruges and Antwerp are some of the best examples of his visual stylization and public laudation. So, too, are well-known statues and paintings such as Titian's equestrian portraits and the monumental tapestry series celebrating his Tunis campaign, as well as the lesser-known artwork sold for urban public consumption, such as the free-standing busts of Charles that apparently graced some patrician homes and guildhalls in Antwerp and other Low Country cities.[102]

Greeted at birth with a poem penned by the rhetorician Lieven Bautkin and by classical arches in 1500, inaugurated as Count of Flanders in Bruges in 1515 with paeans to imperial destiny, praised as ruler over foreign domains such as Africa and Asia in 1520 in Antwerp, and treated as emperor par excellence by citizens of the same city in 1549, Charles V reigned with a full-throttled embrace of the politics of images, both classical and plumbed from the scriptural and Catholic ceremonies of his Valois predecessors. If his great-grandfather Charles the Bold had favored votive portraits in his commissions for religious artwork, Charles V turned the urban audience into the votive offering itself, to render thanksgiving for his political deeds and his endless military campaigns. Cities such as Ghent and Antwerp ordered a steady stream of processions in praise of the emperor and his accomplishments, with as many as eight in one year in Antwerp alone.[103]

The celebration of the 1529 peace treaty of Cambrai between Charles and the French king inspired fairly typical decrees by the town fathers of Antwerp and Ghent to hold celebratory processions.[104] Each involved a carefully laid-out itinerary and mobilized urban relics and the Holy Sacrament; each required as well the participation of key social confraternities and neighborhood groups; and each awarded prizes to the societies that

---

100. See Francis Yates, *Astraea: The Imperial Theme in the Sixteenth Century* (London, 1975), and Tanner, *Last Descendant of Aeneas*, esp. 109–30.

101. For the imperial motifs, see Francis Yates, "Charles Quint et l'idée d'empire," in *Fêtes et cérémonies au temps de Charles Quint*, ed. Jean Jacquot (Paris, 1969), 59–97.

102. Van der Stock, *Antwerp*, 265.

103. The ordinances for Ghent are found in SAG, series 93 BB, Voorgeboden, 1485–1545. For Antwerp, see Génard, "Index der Gebodboeken."

104. SAG, series 93 BB, fol. 132r, and Génard, "Ordonnantien van het Antwerpsch Magistraat," 322–24.

mounted the best decorations. Of the two civic decrees, Antwerp's is fuller. The October 29, 1530 ordinance required the mobilization of the city's most important holy objects, images, and relics: the prized foreskin of Christ, the relic of the Holy Cross, the Holy Sacrament, and the statue of Our Beloved Lady in the Onze-Lieve-Vrouwekerk. The procession was dedicated in prayer "to bid our lord the emperor good welfare, health, success, and prosperity"; to spare Antwerp from the looming threat of plague and pestilence; and to forgive its good citizens for their misdeeds and sins that had surely brought the threat of pestilence to their doorsteps. This juggernaut procession thus incorporated religio-political expressions of thanksgiving to the emperor with local concerns over public health and intractable human sinfulness. Lest there be any worries about public participation, all households were required to have at least one attendee, and the guilds and confraternities were ordered to march, bearing two torches of no less than two pounds each, in the order they typically assumed in the major annual religious processions. Houses along the processional route were to be properly cleaned and embellished with candles, tapestries, images, or other religious accoutrements in honor of the Holy Sacrament and the relics. Finally, since recent processions in honor of the emperor had experienced scuffles among youth "not fearing God," social groups marching in the procession were ordered to monitor strictly their young participants to prevent a repeat of the problem.[105]

Worries about combative youth were not unique to the sixteenth century, but they partook of a more general legal effort to clean up roguish social behavior.[106] In Antwerp, the oft-repeated ordinances to hold processions in honor of Charles V required scrupulously pious behavior as well as clean streets. The dictates were sometimes more specific: to remove prostitutes from doing business anywhere along the parade route; to close shops and taverns during the procession; to insist on the presences of at least one member of each household; to ensure that people who marched alongside lay and clerical companies follow rather then precede the holy objects and official participants; and to forbid any scurrilous mocking of either political or religious authorities.[107]

105. Génard, "Ordonnantien van het Antwerpsch Magistraat," 324.
106. On Antwerp, see Soly, "Openbare feesten"; on Ghent, Arnade, *Realms of Ritual*, for the late fifteenth and early sixteenth centuries. For Oudenaarde, B. Ouvry, "Officieel ceremonieel te Oudenaarde, 1450–1600," *Handelingen van de Geschied- en Oudheidkundige Kring van Oudenaarde* 22 (1985): 25–64, and B. A. M. Ramakers, *Spelen en figuren: Toneelkunst en processiecultuur in Oudenaarde tussen middeleeuwen en moderne tijd* (Amsterdam, 1996); for Mechelen, E. van Autenboer, *Volksfeesten en rederijkers te Mechelen, 1400–1600* (Ghent, 1962). Herman Pleij has characterized these early sixteenth-century initiatives as a "civilizing process" on the part of urban elites who, out of pride and a wish to ape aristocratic behaviors that were the traditional prerogative of the court, "officialized" cultural life by distancing themselves from rough merriment. See Pleij, *Sneeuwpoppen*.
107. See Génard, "Index der Gebodboeken," 130, for the September 17, 1501, ordinance concerning prostitution, repeated several times thereafter; *Antwerpsch Archievenblad*, 1:151, for July 9, 1513, requirement

In the same vein, humanists and urban elites with a hankering for aristocratic glamour as well as budding Protestants all agreed that the urban religious devotions were vulnerable to holy irreverence. Antwerp's magistrates presented the case starkly in a decree dated June 11, 1544, concerning the Corpus Christi procession traditionally held on the Thursday after Holy Trinity; they ordered it reformed to a "procession of devotion, as many dissolute acts of playing and suchlike foolishness have happened in this procession, with wagons, children, and other spectacles, being very unfitting and tending more to vanity than to devotions and reverence for the Holy Sacrament."[108] In its very wording, the ordinance asserts that as previously conducted, Corpus Christi was irreligious, given over to rambunctious foolery. Regulations of other religious processions, religious spaces, and broader festive actions fill the pages of urban ordinance books. As processions in honor of the Burgundian emperor grew more frequent in a city like Antwerp, so too did repeated references to reining in scabrous behavior and protecting sacred spaces: no gaming on the streets; no begging, loitering, or eating in or around the Onze-Lieve-Vrouwekerk or other churches and chapels; no dicing or archery in the church's courtyard; no dancing around the chaplet during the summer festival of St. Paul and St. Peter on June 29; no gaming in the marketplace; no songs or poems to be sung in the streets or in front of churches; no slander against king, city magistrates, or clergy, and so forth.[109] Ghent's ordinances are even thicker, in part a response to its constant political upheavals, and a specific result of the quixotic revolt against Charles V in 1539 that stripped the city of its political liberties, reorganized its cultural and political life, and inspired on the part of the hand-picked aldermen in the years thereafter a fervor to regulate heavily its public life. Beside its regular processions in honor of Charles V, Ghent regulated nearly every other of its religious and festive events.[110] Gone was the bothersome Saint Lieven procession, and gone too was the participation of the troublesome weavers in the Assumption Day procession in the Seigneury of Saint Peter, the result of Charles V's 1540 peace settlement on the city.[111]

But Ghent's aldermen went further. There would be no more popular New Year's eve

---

of one attendee per household; ibid., 159, August 12, 1516, for an example of a regular caution against shops and taverns doing business, but also concerns over the order of procession; ibid., 1:154–55, for the October 14, 1514, prohibition of satirical songs, poems, and broadsheets against authorities.

108. Génard, "Index der Gebodboeken," 224. I have used the translation that appears in Guido Marnef, *Antwerp in the Age of the Reformation: Underground Protestantism in a Commercial Metropolis, 1550–1577*, trans. J. C. Grayson (Baltimore, 1996), 29.

109. For a sampling of these ordinances, see Génard, "Index der Gebodboeken," 123–24, 132, 134, 147, 154–55, 172, and 178.

110. SAG, series 93 BB, Voorgeboden, 1485–1545. A summary of the regulation of Ghent's cultural life is in Gerda Temmerman, "De feestcultuur te Gent in de periode 1515–1608," 2 vols. (master's thesis, University of Ghent, 1981).

111. Boone, "Urban Space and Political Conflict in Late Medieval Flanders," esp. 637; and Arnade, *Realms of Ritual*, 205–6.

singing—and the spontaneous begging for food on someone's doorstep—except by official city balladeers; no more donning of masks and disguises at different festive occasions; no more rowdiness in the annual carnival cycle, including throwing garbage and dead rodents at one another on Three Kings' Day on January 6; no more ritual mocking of clergy or political authorities; no more bonfires, music, or dancing on Saint John the Baptist Day, June 24; and no more embarrassing emotional behavior—"some drunk, others screaming and crying"—before the relics of Saint John on display in Saint Bavo's Cathedral (Sint-Baafs, formerly Saint John's parish church).[112] In their place would be orderly processions and officially sanctioned competitions for the best-outfitted houses, neighborhood, plays, or pageants, not undertaken by troublesome youth or drunken pilgrims, but by the lettered chambers of rhetoric and official neighborhood societies, as called for in the procession in honor of the peace treaty of Nice between Charles V and Francis I, ordered on July 5, 1538, by the city's aldermen.[113]

The concern expressed in these regulatory decrees over drinking, fighting, singing, gaming, and general impiety located troublesome behavior in the urban spaces and among certain social groups. Excess tended to run free on the street corner, in houses of prostitution, in taverns, and among pugnacious youth and unlettered adults.[114] The early sixteenth century also witnessed other concerns that meshed with the ones lodged in these legal ordinances, particularly over poverty and public begging. The reformation of poor relief in the Netherlands was one piece of a general sixteenth-century movement, undertaken by Catholics and Protestants alike to delimit begging, distinguish between the "idle" and the "deserving poor" (putting the former to work), and to prohibit vagrancy, with policies of social control centered around the worthiness of work and the moral corruptness of beggary.[115] In the Netherlands, this social reform took root between 1459 and 1461, when the three most urbanized provinces, Brabant, Flanders, and Holland, legislated against begging by anyone other than mendicants and those physically unable to work. Stricter controls and more urgent language against begging appeared by the third decade of the sixteenth century.[116]

Heresy, of course, was one evil that fueled this urgent concern about ensuring that the deserving poor were secure within the Church's fold. The conflict over religious affiliation between Charles and his Low Country inhabitants struck early in the Reformation. It

112. Temmerman, "De feestcultuur," 2:234–70, with archival transcriptions. For the Saint John decree, see SAG, series 93 DD, dated February 23, 1562, fol. 67r.

113. SAG, series 93 BB, fol. 148r.

114. For these same concerns for the fifteenth century, see Kathelijne Geerts, *De spelende mens in de Boergondische Nederlanden* (Bruges, 1987), esp. 79–93.

115. R. Jütte, *Poverty and Deviance in Early Modern Europe* (Cambridge, 1994); T. Riis, ed., *Aspects of Poverty in Early Modern Europe* (Florence, 1981).

116. Wim Blockmans and Walter Prevenier, "Poverty in Flanders and Brabant from the Fourteenth to the mid-Sixteenth Century: Sources and Problems," *Acta Historiae Neerlandicae* 10 (1978): 20–57.

pitted an emperor who had famously uttered that his "principal care is to preserve Catholicism and ensure its observance" against urban communities where the traffic in books was thick, literacy and public education unusually strong, humanism fashionable, and new evangelical ideas attractive. Lutheranism's early arrival in the Low Countries began over the next few decades to yield to other religious commitments, from martyr-minded Anabaptism to tenacious Calvinism.[117] Erasmus's comment to Thomas Wolsey in May 1519 that Luther's books and ideas were vigorously circulating in the Low Countries was no off-the-mark observation, and Habsburg authorities responded to this sudden emergence of Lutheranism by banning Protestant literature. Already in October 1520, Louvain had staged the public burning of Lutheran books, and anti-Lutheran edicts had been issued a month earlier. A measure of the seriousness of the Protestant challenge in the Low Countries is the decision by Charles to preside over a book-burning ceremony at Antwerp in July 1521 and to authorize another in Ghent during a meeting of the States General at which he also was present.[118] At the same time, Charles established a Netherlands Inquisition to wrest authority away from the episcopal courts charged with investigating the canonical offence of heresy.[119] It first victims were two Augustinian friars, Hendrik Voet and Johan van den Esschen, burned on July 1, 1523 in the marketplace in Brussels and the first Protestant martyrs in Europe.[120] One thousand three hundred executions followed between these deaths and 1566, when religious violence and iconoclasm broke loose. Many of the condemned fled, and the less fortunate meet their fate in theaters of death so spectacular that their memory helped to write the Dutch Revolt's incipient language of dissent.[121]

Urban legislation about religious behavior and festive life thus had separate origins in the fifteenth century, but they soon became entangled with poverty and heresy decrees issued by Charles V's central administration. That there were shared concerns over the social body and social and religious orthodoxy animating all three types of regulation, and

117. Alastair Duke, "Building Heaven in Hell's Despite: The Early History of the Reformation in the Towns of the Low Countries," in his *Reformation and Revolt in the Low Countries* (London, 1990), 71–100, and 73 for the quote.

118. Johan Decavele, ed., *Keizer tussen stropdragers: Karel V, 1500–1558* (Louvain, 1990), 83–84.

119. M. E. Kronenberg, *Verboden boeken en opstandige drukkers in de hervormingstijd* (Amsterdam, 1948); and Kronenberg, "Uitgaven van Luther in de Nederlanden verschenen tot 1540," *Nederlands Archief voor Kerkgeschiedenis* 40 (1953): 1–25.

120. J. Scheerder, *De Inquisitie in de Nederlanden* (Antwerp, 1944), 34–35; Alastair Duke, "The 'Inquisition' and the Repression of Religious Dissent in the Habsburg Netherlands (1521–1566)," in *L' Inquisizione: Atti del Simposio internationale*, ed. Agostino Borromeo (Vatican City, 2003), 419–44; and Aline Goosens, *Les inquisitions modernes dans les Pays-Bas méridionaux, 1520–1630*, 2 vols. (Brussels, 1997–98). Their deaths became instantly celebrated in pamphlets, including *Der actus vnd handlung der degradation vnd verprenung der Christlichen Ritter vnd merterer Augistiner orden geschehen zu Brussel*, in *Bibliotheca Reformatoria Neerlandica: Geschriften uit den tijd der hervorming in de Nederlanden*, ed. S. Cramer and F. Pijper, 10 vols. (The Hague, 1911) 8:13–19.

121. Figure in Duke, "Building Heaven in Hell's Despite," 73.

that the state's hand in drafting policy was foremost, is rendered stunningly clear in an ordinance issued in the name of Charles V on October 7, 1531, throughout his Netherlands territories. The heart of the decree was a series of regulations concerning poor relief, alms, and begging, but these stipulations were prefaced by a call for the immediate republication of the heresy placards that the government had already issued—evidence that Charles V had rightful concerns about the lack of their enforcement by hesitant urban elites.[122] The alms decree railed against the great influx of the poor into the Low Countries and their unchecked begging, "because of which they are given over to idleness, which is the root of all evil." Alms were to be limited to the mendicants, to the disabled, to lepers, and to religious pilgrims; the collection of alms was to be centralized and coordinated among the various urban charitable institutions; the children of vagrant beggars were to be enrolled in school or trained in a craft and given a proper religious education; and the deserving poor were to wear badges and be prohibited from squandering their alms in game houses or taverns.[123] The ordinance singled out taverns, hostels, and game houses as sites of drunkenness, quarrels, and general mayhem. Because of the general dissipation that Charles and his administration perceived to be encouraged by these social sites, they decreed that all festivals, carnivals, and celebrations be limited to one day.[124] Succinct in wording, the article was far reaching in purpose: to legislate a wholesale cultural reformation in the Low Countries by forcing popular cultural practices into the procrustean bed of a single, common celebration by Everyman, shorn of frolic and the layers of local rites that colored big city and small village celebrations.

However ambitious in scope, the festival decree was apparently an utter failure and remained unenforced throughout the sixteenth century, no doubt because provincial governors and urban magistrates alike deemed its goal both impractical and unpalatable.[125] The forcefulness of the ordinance's wording and the lack of its enforcement is proof positive that the sixteenth century witnessed a sort of cultural war between sovereigns, their state administrators, and their urban subjects. The conflicts were complicated and never neatly bifurcated between state interests and city folks, especially since urban elites took a strong hand in advocating the regulation of social behavior, and often for the same reasons as court administrators. But the tensions were plainly there, the result of the multipronged effort to maximize the image of state authority by enlarging the ritual field upon which it was played while circumscribing public behaviors. In the morality play of the

---

122. M. J. Lameere, ed., *Receuil des ordonnances des Pays-Bas. Deuxième Série: 1506–1700* (Brussels, 1902), 3:256–75. On the lack of enforcement of the edicts in the different territories, see Juliaan Woltjer, "Public Opinion and the Persecution of Heretics in the Netherlands, 1550–59," in *Public Opinion and Changing Identities*, ed. Judith Pollmann and Andrew Spicer, 87–106.

123. Lameere, *Recueil des ordonnances*, 3:268–70.

124. Ibid., 3:270.

125. Soly, "Openbare feesten," 618.

Habsburg Burgundian state, subjects ought to be reverent, productive, and politically docile, avoiding the crude excesses embedded in traditional festivity while steering clear of the new lure of Protestant heresy.

From the time of Philip the Good, the third Valois Duke of Burgundy, to that of the emperor Charles V, Burgundian sovereigns in the Low Countries scaled up sacred symbols and spaces of their public authority. These cultural efforts were purposeful and didactic, advocated so that the ritual authority of the Burgundian dukes might match their political and dynastic accomplishments. Charles V represented an apogee; however dispersed his titles, he stood as testament to the attainment of regal and imperial titles by the heir of the fifteenth-century Burgundian dukes. As ruler of the Seventeen Provinces of the Netherlands, as Holy Roman Emperor and head of the house of Austria, as king of Castile and Aragon, as sovereign of their American domains, Charles V had amassed more territory than any other European sovereign before his time. In 1548 he had also succeeded in detaching the Low Country provinces from his other imperial holdings in the Treaty of Augsburg, giving them stand-alone administrative status, and only a year later he persuaded all the Netherlands provincial Estates to sign the Pragmatic Sanction that recognized his successor as their prince. The practical effect of these efforts was to give the Low Countries an independent shape within his imperial conglomerate and to ensure a stable dynastic core.

All the more dramatic then was Charles's decision, soon after, to abdicate. Ailing and tired of the burdens of empire in an age of fierce warfare and insurgent Protestantism, Charles chose retirement at the Jeronymite monastery of Saint Yuste in Castile, transferring his imperial titles to his brother Ferdinand, and the remainder to his son Philip. The solemn ceremony of abdication held before the States General at the Burgundian palace in Brussels on October 25, 1555, secured one last grand public spectacle for the prematurely old ruler.[126] Ideal for a prince who favored well-crafted state ceremonies, the abdication was visually splendid and thematically shrewd in its cobbling together of heraldic and sacred references. On the afternoon of the ceremony, Charles rode a mule from the small residence in Brussels where he had lodged in preparation for retirement to the grand hall of the Coudenberg Palace, ostensibly because severe gout prohibited him from mounting a horse.[127] But the mule also evoked biblical references, particularly its association in the Old Testament with royalty (2 Samuel 18:19 and 1 Kings 1:33, 38, and 44, for example), and perhaps too with Christ's entry into Jerusalem. Once inside the palace hall, the infirm emperor donned glasses to read his abdication speech, before a room packed with Golden Fleece knights, governmental officers, and representatives from the Estates. The great hall was festooned with tapestries, most prominent the Golden Fleece history

---

126. Gachard, *Retraite et mort de Charles-Quint*.
127. Ibid., 1:80.

of Gideon. After a short speech that recounted his greatest deeds and counseled political obedience, adherence to the heresy placards, and fidelity to the church, Charles invested Philip with sovereignty over his domain in the Netherlands.[128]

A humble procession on a mule, then a chivalric adieu framed by Golden Fleece tapestries and other heraldic symbols—in this melodramatic ceremony the emperor played both the simple old ruler and the powerful heir to Burgundian chivalric splendor. His retirement at Yuste added yet a third portrait: Charles as cloistered pilgrim, the sixteenth-century emperor now the quiet cultivator of monastic tranquility. The Spanish clergy who surrounded him reported, of course, a retirement of exemplary piety. Charles heard four masses a day and met his end with flawless solemnity on September 21, 1558. "Intone psalms, prayers, and liturgies," Charles urged his deathbed confessors as he clutched a crucifix between his two hands.[129] Charles died a fervent devotee and the object of devotion, a fitting denouement to a century and a half of Burgundian engagement with sacred objects, spaces, and times that enabled liturgies of power. The new monarch, Philip II, came to power in the Low Countries well aware that Catholic sacred imagery and symbols were essential to his public presentation, and well aware too that in this land of increasing Protestant activity, he was expected to extirpate heresy at all costs, as his father had explicitly instructed him to do in a memorandum issued to him on May 4, 1543, long before the abdication.[130] The increase in the liturgical presentation of Burgundian sovereignty and the heightened policing of the public realm that we have charted encountered its most serious challenge soon after Charles's retirement, as new forms of religious and political dissent arose that threatened to undo what a century of cultural developments in political ritual had achieved. The unity of the Seventeen Provinces Charles formally achieved in the Pragmatic Sanction of 1549 might have suggested that the Low Countries had been finally stabilized and centralized under one powerful lord, but events would soon prove such an assessment wrong.

128. A summary of the ceremony, with generous excerpts of eyewitness accounts, is in ibid., 1:81–100.
129. Ibid., 1:25, 2:385.
130. A full transcription is in Jose M. March, *Niñez y juventud de Felipe II*, 2 vols. (Madrid, 1942), 2:11–22.

CHAPTER 2 FAITHFUL TO THE KING
ASSOCIATIONS OF DISSENT

In good Burgundian fashion, a stupendous public funeral marked Charles V's private death at Yuste. On December 28, 1558, in Brussels, Philip II assembled the knights of the Order of the Golden Fleece together with governmental and church officials of the Low Countries to honor the emperor's memory and proclaim the titles of rulership that he had held since his father's abdication.¹ The company marched from the Burgundian palace at Coudenberg to Saint Gudule's Church through streets hung with black cloth and packed with onlookers holding candles bearing the emperor's heraldic devices. The warmth of thousands of burning tapers cut the late December chill of this Holy Innocents' Day and bathed the elite train in a liturgical glow of light.² The funeral drew freely on a number of established ritual genres, evoking Golden Fleece chapter meetings with their solemn processions to and from great urban parish churches as well as urban *ommegangen*, especially because the event featured a pageant car, an allegorical ship of state. Observers like the Englishman Richard Clough, who recorded the event in detail, waxed poetic about the funeral's grandeur. Before the *chapelle ardente*, lit up with scores of candles, in Saint Gudule's, Clough observed the religiously saturated funeral plaint of William of Orange: "He is dead, and there is another risen up in his place greater than he ever was."³ The young prince, rich in lands and titles, himself recently selected as a knight of the Golden Fleece, had three years earlier assumed

---

1. The official *livret* of the ceremony, *La magnifique et sumptuese pompe funèbre*, was prepared by Johannes and Lucas van Deutecum and published in Antwerp in 1559. For the ceremony, see Stephanie Schrader, "'Greater Than Ever He Was': Ritual and Power in Charles V's 1558 Funeral Procession," in Reindert Falkenberg et al., eds., *Hof-, staats- en stadsceremonies: Nederlands Kunsthistorisch Jaarboek/Netherlands Yearbook for the History of Art* 49 (1998): 69–94.

2. For the religious significance of torches, candles, and other lights in ducal processions, see Élodie Lecuppre-Desjardin, "Les lumières de la ville: Recherche sur l'utilisation de la lumière dans les cérémonies bourguignonnes (XIVe–XV siècles)," *Revue Historique* 301 (2001): 24–43.

3. J. W. Burgon, *The Life and Times of Sir Thomas Gresham*, 2 vols. (New York, 1849), 2:254. A full analysis is in Schrader, "Greater Than Ever He Was."

a central role in Charles V's abdication ceremony, lending the shoulder upon which the gout-ridden emperor leaned as he walked unsteadily toward the dais.[4] Now, in the premier parish church in Brussels, one that contained the stained glass window Charles V had donated in 1537 depicting himself and his wife, Queen Isabella of Portugal, William of Orange solemnly commemorated the emperor's death and affirmed his son Philip's accession to many Low Country titles. The minutely choreographed ceremony had gone perfectly, without a hint in the two-day event of the tensions and antagonisms that would within a decade rend asunder the monarchical and aristocratic unity that the funeral promoted.

Not everyone, however, recalled the emperor's funeral with the admiration of Clough or that expressed by Johannes and Lucas van Deutecum in their official text memorializing the ceremonies, printed the next year by the famed Antwerp publisher Christopher Plantin.[5] Calvinist minister Adriaen van Haemstede of Antwerp believed the funeral piety fed on innocent blood. Author of a Dutch martyrology, Van Haemstede railed against the gruesome execution of Gilles Verdickt, caught in the same inquisitorial dragnet that had sentenced his own brother Anton, a deacon and preacher in Antwerp, to death.[6] Verdickt was burned alive at the stake in Brussels on December 24, just four days before the state funeral of Charles V. The coincidence was not accidental in the eyes of Van Haemstede, who believed that Verdickt had served as a sacrificial offering to the soul of the deceased emperor. The "spectacle of death," in Van Haemstede's words, was purposely placed as prologue to the "spectacle of the funeral ceremony." In so doing, Catholic officials had

---

4. The father figure of the Dutch Revolt, William of Orange, is the subject of a vast literature. For a short interpretive biography, see A. Th. van Deursen, *Willem van Oranje: Een biografisch portret* (Amsterdam, 1995), and A. Th. van Deursen and H. de Schepper, *Willem van Oranje: Een strijd voor vrijheid en verdraagzaamheid* (Weesp, 1984). See also K. W. Swart, *William of Orange and the Revolt of the Netherlands, 1572–84*, trans. J. C. Grayson (Aldershot, 2003). For older and broadly contextualized studies, see P. J. Blok, *Willem de Eerste, prins van Oranje*, 2 vols. (Amsterdam, 1919–20), and Felix Rachfahl, *Wilhelm von Oranien und der niederländische Aufstand*, 3 vols. (The Hague, 1906–24), especially pertinent for the first revolt of the 1560s. For the historiography of Orange, see E. O. G. Haitsma Mulier and A. E. M. Janssen, eds., *Willem van Oranje in de historie, 1584–1984: Vier eeuwen beeldvorming en geschiedschrijving* (Utrecht, 1984). The best introduction to Orange are his letters. See *Corr. Taciturne; Archives d'Orange-Nassau*, particularly vols. 1–8; and N. Japikse, ed., *Correspondentie van Willem den Eersten, prins van Oranje* (The Hague, 1934). All of Orange's enormous correspondence is now digitized into an online database of original documents available at http://www.inghist.nl/Onderzoek/Projecten/WVO.

5. Van Deutecum, *La magnifique et sumptuese pompe funèbre*.

6. Adriaen van Haemstede, *De Geschiedenisse ende den doodt der vromer Martelaren* (Arnhem, 1896), 543–44; the first edition was published in 1559 by Gilles van der Erve in Emden. On Van Haemstede, see Brad S. Gregory, *Salvation at Stake: Christian Martyrdom in Early Modern Europe* (Cambridge, 1999), 167. Van Haemstede's account is almost verbatim adapted in the edition of Jean Crespin's 1554 work, which was expanded after his death in 1572 by the Genevan minister Simon Goulaert in 1582. I have consulted the 1619 edition edited by Daniel Benoit, *Histoire des martyrs persecutez et mis à mort pour la verité de l'evangile depuis le temps des apostres jusques à present (1619)*, 3 vols. (Toulouse, 1885), 2:628–32. On the multiple editions of Crespin's martyrology, see Gregory, *Salvation at Stake*, 3–4, 189–91.

rekindled a heathen custom "to offer sacrifices and perform executions at the funeral of famous princes."[7]

In 1558 it was unthinkable that somehow the worlds of William of Orange and Van Haemstede would eventually, if somewhat warily, coalesce. At twenty-five, William was the court darling and scion of the Orange-Nassau dynasty, the richest *grand seigneur* in the Low Countries, with extensive properties in northern Brabant, Holland, Burgundy, Luxembourg, and the tiny enclave of Orange in southern France. He was Prince of Orange, Count of Nassau, Katzenelnbogen, Vianden, Dietz, Buren, Lingen, and Bergen-op-Zoom; Burgrave of Antwerp; Baron of Breda, IJsselstein, Diest, and Cuijk, and a year away from his appointment as *stadholder* (governor) of Holland, Zeeland, and Utrecht. In 1561 his marriage to Anna of Saxony, niece of the Lutheran elector Augustus of Saxony, would give him access to her dowry and help to retire debts, but would render his relationship to the Brussels court more complex.[8] Still, until this marriage, no taint of Lutheran heresy blemished the handsome and faithful knight of the Golden Fleece. Orange's orbit of court patronage, dynastic politics, and Burgundian chivalric ethos seemed safely removed from the growth of Protestantism taking root in the Low Countries.[9] His world was the Burgundian court Charles V had known, and Orange's key ceremonial role both at this funeral and at the emperor's abdication speak volumes about the favored status he enjoyed within it.

Despite the Brussels government's efforts to rout heresy, Lutheranism not only flourished, but itself was soon overshadowed by an upsurge of Anabaptism and Calvinism in the Netherlands.[10] However much Johannes and Lucas van Deutecum's *livret* represented Charles V's funeral as a portrait in state consensus, the stubborn reality of regular executions like that of Verdickt reminded Low Country inhabitants that their lands were contested grounds, increasingly home to religious splintering and fractious politics. Van Haemstede's screed, polemical though it was, points to a reality contemporaries knew well: the burning tapers and urban spaces employed to laud the deceased emperor were the same objects and sites employed for religious repression and juridical punishment—double strands of the same cultural helix. The sacred objects, spaces, and liturgies of power invoked by Charles V's predecessors in the fifteenth century were more fully developed by the mid-sixteenth century, but an unforeseen consequence of this enhancement of public lordship was how much more severe it made the clash between royal authority in the Netherlands and the Lutherans, Anabaptists, and Calvinists. Philip II inherited Charles V's ceremonial protocols and also the legacy of his father's determination not to

---

7. Van Haemstede, *De Geschiedenisse*, 544.
8. A point made by Geoffery Parker in *Dutch Revolt*, 50–51.
9. The development of the prince's religious policy and his interactions with Lutherans and Calvinists in his critical early years is the subject of H. Klink, *Opstand, politiek en religie bij Willem van Oranje: Een thematische biografie* (Heerenveen, 1998).
10. Duke, "Building Heaven in Hell's Despite," 73.

let the Low Countries go the way of the German territories, and increasingly, France. The new sovereign was intent on continuing the political centralization of the Low Countries and intensifying the fight against Protestantism. But his hard-line policies increasingly stepped on the toes of a varied company—the small but influential high nobility, or *grands seigneurs*; the more numerous lesser nobility, the *gentilshommes*; and the urban political and economic elites.[11]

Tensions mounted by the early 1560s and came to a head in 1566. In this annus mirabilis, or *wonderjaar*, the combustible mix of an aggrieved nobility, the temporary suspension of the heresy placards, widespread religious violence centered around iconoclasm, and Calvinist armed revolt shook the Low Countries.[12] Despite the Low Countries' long tradition of urban dissent, direct outcries from the nobility against princely authority had been hitherto rare. As part of their public opposition to Philip's policies, the dissenting nobles both created a party affiliation and concocted a group identity. In 1563 the most notable among them formed a league centered on a campaign to dismiss the senior minister of state, Antoine Perrenot de Granvelle. In late 1565 their midlevel brethren assembled as the Order of the Compromise, and soon thereafter, the Order of the Beggars, a fraternal protest organization, which specialized in satirical barbs and the motifs of inversion. Foremost among the list of grievances drawn up by the Compromise was concern about the excessive use of heresy placards, especially the ways they stepped on traditional legal rights guaranteed by provincial and urban privileges such as protection against the outright confiscation of a suspect's property and the right to be tried in one's home jurisdiction.

These complaints were not outright endorsements of Protestantism—the majority of the grands seigneurs and gentilshommes were still Catholic moderates—but rather expressions of concern about how best to handle the challenge of multiconfessionalism.[13]

---

11. Between 1503 and 1572, more than half of all provincial governorships were in the hands of seven noble families: Croy, Nassau, Egmont, Lalaing, Berghes, Lannoy, and Montmorency. For a political overview of the nobility of the Low Countries, see Henk van Nierop, "The Nobility and the Revolt of the Netherlands: Between Church and King, and Protestantism and Privileges," in *Reformation, Revolt, and Civil War in France and the Netherlands, 1555–1585*, ed. P. Benedict et al. (Amsterdam, 1999): 83–98. On Holland itself, see Henk van Nierop, *The Nobility of Holland: From Knights to Regents, 1500–1650*, trans. Maarten Ultee (Cambridge, 1984), esp. chap. 7 on the nobility and the Revolt. Older considerations include H. A. Enno van Gelder, "De Nederlandse adel en de Opstand tegen Spanje, 1565–1572," in *Van Beeldenstorm tot Pacificatie* (Amsterdam/Brussels, 1964), 138–69.

12. Floris Prims, *Het Wonderjaar (1566–1567)* (Antwerp, 1941), offers a basic political narrative of events, while Phyllis Mack Crew, *Calvinist Preaching and Iconoclasm in the Netherlands* (Cambridge, 1978) focuses on the development of Calvinism as a force and the relationship between ministers and iconoclasm. For the Walloon provinces in particular, see S. Deyon and A. Lottin, *Les "casseurs" de l'été 1566: L'iconoclasme dans le nord de la France* (Paris, 1981).

13. Juliaan Woltjer, "Political Moderates and Religious Moderates in the Revolt of the Netherlands," in *Reformation, Revolt and Civil War*, ed. P. Benedict et al., 185–200.

The resolutely Catholic Lamoral, Count of Egmont, one of the most prominent grands seigneurs, argued in the Council of State in October 1564 that a strict enforcement of heresy placards was impractical in the Netherlands because, unlike Spain, its territories were porous and not "bounded by oceans and mountains."[14] Calvinists, however, saw such sentiments against Philip's religious policy as a golden opportunity to widen their public exposure. Like the Netherlands nobility, they keenly grasped the power of religious time and space and traditional forms of protest, and in these years, they took to the fields and streets to proclaim their faith. To mount a public campaign rooted in protest and satire, as the nobles did, or to undertake public psalm singing, field sermons, even prison rescues, as Calvinists did, was to do more than to lodge a religious brief against governmental policies or Catholic forms of worship. It was also to press hard against Burgundian command over the public realm, and, by doing so, to go against decades of efforts to regulate it more effectively. These two strands of protest gained momentum in the early 1560s and peaked in 1566 with a twofold effect. First, Philip II had to confront two types of dissent, one forthrightly religious, the other more narrowly political. Both movements presented fundamental tests to the king's political grip over the central government in Brussels. More broadly, they also punctured holes in the Habsburg Burgundian theory and practice of sovereign representations in the public realm, dependant as they were on liturgical enactments of power that required an obedient and Catholic citizenry. Second, what practitioners of Calvinism and dissenting nobles shared in these years was the effort to make protest public and to develop a vocabulary and repertoire for its enactment. Their successes were many; manifold too were the currents they unleashed. The inversions set into play by the great nobles, the lesser seigneurs, and Calvinists would give example to those who would foment the iconoclastic riots that began in mid-August 1566. By year's end, the world had been truly turned upside down, as the party of the Beggars and the looser bands of iconoclasts redefined what authority looked like and how it was claimed and contested in the public realm. They had destabilized the political culture Philip II had inherited from past Burgundian rulers and simultaneously begun to shape their own.

Madame and the Parrot: The Disgruntled Nobility and Forms of Dissent, 1559–1564

Ominous rumblings of the political crisis of 1566 first sounded seven years earlier when Philip II decided to return to Spain, leaving his half-sister Margaret of Parma, illegitimate daughter of Charles, to rule as regent. Never comfortable in a land whose languages he did not know, Philip had reason to return to Castile: the growing threat of Ottoman supremacy in the Mediterranean began to take precedence over rival European powers, es-

---

14. J. S. Theissen and H. A. Enno van Gelder, eds., *Correspondance française de Marguerite d'Autriche, duchesse de Parme avec Philippe II*, 3 vols. (Utrecht, 1925–42), 3:462.

pecially after the Habsburg victory at Saint Quentin in nearby Picardy on August 10, 1557, had resulted in the treaty of Cateau-Cambrésis between the rival kingdoms of Spain and France.[15] Philip II departed Brussels only two years later on July 5, 1559, never to return to the Low Countries. This absence created many practical problems, not the least of which was that the Burgundian cult of rulership required physical manifestations of princely power on a semiregular basis, even if the dukes had smartly dispersed symbols of their authority in select religious sites and devotions. True, the Low Countries had grown accustomed to an absent lord now that the territories were part of a larger imperial configuration, but Charles V had spent a total of ten years of his reign there, had wisely consented to enormous public spectacles which, while rare, were intentionally packaged for a long memory, and had regularly called for processions on behalf of his various military campaigns in major cities like Antwerp. While Philip II did not abandon these ritual protocols, he showed no real inclination to nourish them either, nor to give them his own stamp, with the result that his subjects knew their ruler in the public realm better by the efforts to extirpate heresy than by other enactments of his sovereignty. Philip II's one great ceremony prior to his departure for Spain was his father's funeral in December 1559, and there the emphasis was less on his lordship than on Charles's glorious rule. Philip II was eclipsed in this ceremony just as he had been at the abdication ceremony at the Coudenberg Palace in 1555, casting the new king as a poor successor to his father, which became a standard contrast invoked in Dutch political pamphlets and elsewhere. The heavy weight of Burgundian ceremonialism could not sustain itself in the absence of a strong prince willing to perform his sovereignty.

Designating Margaret of Parma as regent provoked further problems in the representation of Philip's lordship, though here too the move was hardly unprecedented. Despite the popular convention that government was not the realm of women, Margaret had two predecessors as female regents of the Low Countries: Margaret of Austria (1507–15 and 1517–30) and the very capable Mary of Hungary (1531–55). Unlike her contemporary, Catherine de Medici, who gained the regency in France in 1560, however, Margaret of Parma could not claim the luster of the title of Queen Mother, and unlike Elizabeth in England, who boasted that she ruled with "the heart and stomach of a king," Margaret's part was that of half-sister and royal stand-in.[16] Philip had, however, appointed a strong-minded, capable advisor to Margaret. Antoine Perrenot de Granvelle was born at Be-

---

15. For a compact narrative overview, see Parker, *Dutch Revolt*, 41–46. On Philip II's cultural interest but unease in the Low Countries, Henry Kamen, *Philip of Spain* (New Haven, 1997), 77–78. In general, on the period 1561–64, see the excellent factual account, based largely on original sources, in Rachfahl, *Wilhelm von Oranien*, 2:165–344, as well as the classic account by Robert Fruin, "Het voorspel van den tachtigjarigen oorlog," in *Verspreide geschriften*, 9 vols. (The Hague, 1900–1915), 1:266–449.

16. There has been no systematic study of this string of female regents. For France, see Katherine B. Crawford, *Perilous Performances: Gender and Regency in Early Modern France* (Cambridge, 2004). On Elizabeth, see Carol Levin, *The Heart and Stomach of a King: Elizabeth I and the Politics of Sex and Power* (Philadelphia, 1994).

sançon to an established nonaristocratic family with deep ties to the Habsburg-Burgundian upper echelon. His father, Nicholas, had been a chancellor in Charles V's administration, and in this capacity had taken William of Orange under his wing when the German-raised eleven-year-old arrived at Brussels.[17] Margaret of Parma and Granvelle were an odd political coupling to carry the symbolic requirements of Habsburg rulership in the Low Countries, so necessary because of the king's absence. Philip's half-sister had almost no public profile, and her ambitious senior councilor was regarded with suspicion by the great nobility and nonclerical men of the provincial Estates. The result was that the ritual cargo of Philip's rule became particularly vulnerable, languishing in his absence in a way it had not during his father's reign.

Although she lacked a ritual profile, Margaret was no weakling, and she presided over a well-functioning central government. Three political bodies set up by Charles V in 1531 still firmly anchored the Brussels administration: the Council of State, with twelve members mostly drawn from the great noblemen of the southern Netherlands, but headed after Philip's departure by Viglius van Aytta, a jurist and nobleman from Friesland; the Council of Finance; and the Privy Council, staffed by lawyers and other professionals intended to act as a salaried, bureaucratic counterweight to the grands seigneurs whose approach to politics was familial and proprietary.[18] The noblemen, in conjunction with the urban patriciate with whom they shared ties of interest and patronage, nonetheless wielded enormous influence. Numbering about four thousand, the majority were of the middling sort, important but without governmental posts or deep resources. But the top cohort—almost all from the southern Low Countries—came from a small cluster of great families that dominated the provincial governorships and the Council of State.[19]

The nobility's presence could also be felt in the provincial Estates, the representative body found in all Seventeen Provinces, usually comprising delegates from the clergy, the middle to lower nobility, and the cities. The Estates possessed the right to assent to taxes and raise troops, and, above all, considered themselves custodians of local rights and privileges. In 1427 Philip the Good had brought several of these parliamentary bodies together with the Estates of Hainault, thereby creating the embryo of what became the States General of the Netherlands.[20] The number of regular delegates sent to this assembly was small in the beginning and limited to the original hereditary provinces of the rulers of Bur-

---

17. M. van Durme, *Antoon Perrenot, bischop van Atrecht, kardinaal van Granvelle, minister van Karel V en Philips II, 1517–1586* (Brussels, 1953).

18. M. Baelde, *De Collaterale Raden onder Karel V en Filips II, 1531–1578* (Brussels, 1965).

19. Van Nierop, "The Nobility and the Revolt of the Netherlands."

20. R. Wellens, *Les Etats Généraux des Pays-Bas, des origines à la fin du règne de Philippe le Beau (1464–1506)* (Heule, 1974); H. G. Koenigsberger, *Monarchies, States Generals and Parliaments: The Netherlands in the Fifteenth and Sixteenth Centuries* (Cambridge, 2001), 16–41. Note that Holland, Friesland, and Gelderland had no clerical representation in their provincial Estates.

gundy; by 1555, when the States convened to ratify the emperor's abdication, all of the provinces of the Netherlands except Overrijssel sent delegates (though until 1576 the non-patrimonial provinces rarely attended).[21]

With a political sphere dominated by the nobility and urban magistrates, political quarrels were common in the Burgundian Netherlands. Wrangling over domains of interest and governmental policies between the regent, the faithful Viglius, and Granvelle, on the one side, and the elite clique of Netherlandish grands seigneurs on the other, set in immediately after the king's departure. The nobility also grew increasingly restless about key political decisions now being made in Spain. But at the top of the list of issues provoking trouble were the heresy placards. Many of the nobility disliked them and disagreed with their excessive implementation. They also disagreed with Philip's unflinching commitment to their letter—for example, his insistence on capital punishment even for repentant heretics. The lower nobility expressed their distaste for the placards even more strongly, not because they were overwhelmingly Protestant—in fact the majority were Catholic—but because they were less tied to the king and to the Brussels government, and did not hold central governorships or military offices.[22] Even more critical of the placards were the urban elites. They worried about the placards' practical effects on economic life—trade in particular—and opposed their breach of traditional urban privileges, which included confiscation of the guilty party's property and the conflation of the canonical offense of heresy with *lèse majesté*.[23] What many sectors of the political class shared, from the top grands seigneurs to the middling gentilshommes and city *schepenen*, was a recognition that the Low Countries abutted territories already Protestant—German imperial cities, for example, or neighboring kingdoms like France where since 1562 royal edicts had attempted some sort of religious accommodation. They had practical concerns about the effects of the heresy placards on regional trade and commerce, deepening whatever personal distaste many had for the use of excessive punishment to combat Protestantism.

It was the public announcement in 1561 by the Brussels government and Granvelle of a plan to reorganize the ecclesiastical structure of the Seventeen Provinces by expanding the woefully inadequate numbers of bishoprics from four to eighteen that provoked a full-blown political crisis. Although agreed to by king and pope in May 1559, the plan did not provoke a stir until March 1561, when Granvelle's elevation to the archbishopric of Mechelen was made known. This ecclesiastical revamping had been first attempted by Charles V's administration, and thus was nothing new, but the formal declaration in May caught

---

21. Koenigsberger, *Monarchies, States Generals and Parliaments*, 168–71.

22. Van Nierop, "The Nobility and the Revolt of the Netherlands," 88, stresses the failure of Protestantism to gain a toehold among the high nobility, and also the fact that among the gentilshommes it was still a minority movement.

23. Alastair Duke, "Salvation by Coercion: The Controversy surrounding the 'Inquisition' in the Low Countries on the Eve of the Revolt," in *Reformation and Revolt*, 152–74.

the senior nobility and provincial Estates by surprise. They were particularly aggrieved not to have had a part in discussing the plan, and it only confirmed their suspicion that key decisions were made in Spain, not in the Council of State, and that Philip II had no intention of consulting them, nor the States General. The plan stipulated four bishops for the Walloon provinces under the archbishop of Cambrai, six in the Dutch-language southern Netherlands under the archbishop of Mechelen, and five in the north under the archbishop of Utrecht.[24] The nobility, significant parts of the clergy, and the urban patriciate balked. The nobility worried that this ecclesiastical reorganization would hamper their ability to influence appointments, and complained that the final plan for this enormous restructuring by Philip II and the pope in 1559 had transpired without their consultation. Even worse, the reorganization elevated the already suspect Granvelle to archbishop of Mechelen and primate of the Low Countries as well as guaranteeing his seniority at the Council of State, and incorporating the rich Brabant abbey of Afflighem into his archbishopric, thereby giving him a seat among the first Estate at the Estates of Brabant, the all important province where Orange held most of his property. Moreover, the planned incorporation of other abbeys and benefices in most of the new bishoprics provoked opposition from important elements of the clergy. To make matters worse, the urban patriciate openly feared what the nobility admitted among themselves: that the plan was a ruse to strengthen the Inquisition in the Netherlands, especially since two canons in each new bishopric were to hold the office of diocesan inquisitor. Granvelle and the Brussels government did, indeed, place several seasoned inquisitors in the mix of new office holders, including the bishops of Middelburg, 's-Hertogenbosch, Roermond, and Haarlem.[25] Philip II betrayed such an intention in a February 18, 1561 letter to Granvelle, in which he observed that the new bishoprics were the best mechanism to retard the growth of heresy.[26]

A noble troika took up the cudgels against the new ecclesiastical plan: the astute Orange; Lamoral, hero of the battle of Saint Quentin, from the powerful Egmont clan whose origins were in Holland but who had acquired significant properties in the south; and Philip de Montmorency, Count of Hornes, erstwhile captain of Philip II's bodyguard, with considerable experience in Castile.[27] In 1559 the three were so closely allied to the power base in Brussels that it was still unimaginable that they would become the oppositional

---

24. M. Dierickx, L'Érection des nouveaux diocèses aux Pays-Bas, 1559–70 (Brussels, 1967). Dierickx argues that the May 1559 agreement between Philip and the pope to expand greatly the number of bishoprics caused no furor until spring 1561, when its actual first steps at implementation included Granvelle's elevation to the office of archbishop of Mechelen.

25. Jonathan Israel, The Dutch Republic: Its Rise, Greatness, and Fall, 1477–1806 (Oxford, 1995), 143.

26. Archives d'Orange-Nassau, 6:278.

27. On Egmont and Hornes, see Théodore Juste, Le comte d'Egmont et le comte de Hornes (Brussels and Leipzig, 1862).

holy trinity in the political lore developed in the Dutch Revolt: William the valiant father figure, and Egmont and Hornes the martyred victims of the Duke of Alba's restoration government of 1567. Their intense opposition to Granvelle and the new ecclesiastical reorganization of the Low Countries took them irrevocably, and probably unwittingly, down this path. Whatever inchoate religious or political principles helped to cement these men's opposition—there are faint hints, inspired by his German background, that Orange already favored religious accommodation between Catholics and mainline Protestants—a more obvious motivation was sheer self-interest.[28] All three rightly suspected that Granvelle would pare back their established sphere of influence, especially that of Orange, who could not abide Granvelle's appointment as archbishop in the very province in which his most important lands were located, a fact made worse by Granvelle's elevation to a cardinal in 1561. As noblemen—courtiers, soldiers, and politicians—their prerogatives of manhood and aristocracy prompted them to distrust Granvelle and Viglius, both of nonnoble origin, with families from outlying areas. Nor would they passively defer to the illegitimate half-sister of the king.

As the political crisis mounted in Brussels, the regent and Granvelle became easy targets of disdain in the newly emerging sphere of popular political satire. By the mid-sixteenth century, the world of print in the Low Countries was vibrant—340 titles are still extant from the year 1566 alone, while the average number for the second half of the sixteenth century is 286 works a year.[29] These figures are only for those texts that have survived the centuries, and therefore can only hint at what was a larger and more varied print world, characterized by books, cheap pamphlets, ballads, and broadsheets produced either openly or under the nose of censors, and especially in Antwerp, home to more than half of all the region's printers.[30] Pamphlets in cheap octavo editions sold for as little as one or two stuivers, affordable on the daily wage of around fifteen stuivers that a journeyman mason could make in Antwerp, or even the six or seven stuivers an unskilled laborer might earn. Given the fame of the Low Countries' print industry, it is more than a little surprising that political pamphlets and related forms of popular print only took off in the 1560s.[31] In past decades, there had been a steady stream of social commentary and in-

28. On Orange's religious orientation and the influence of Protestant thinking, see Klink, *Opstand, politiek en religie*, 97–113.

29. Figures based on E. Cocks-Indestege, G. Glorieux, et al., eds., *Belgica typographica, 1541–1600*, 4 vols. (Nieuwkoop, 1968–94), and P. Valkema Blouw, ed., *Typographia Batava*, 2 vols. (Nieuwkoop, 1998), with an analysis in Alastair Duke, "Posters, Pamphlets and Prints: The Ways and Means of Disseminating Dissident Opinions on the Eve of the Dutch Revolt," *Dutch Crossing* 27 (2003): 23–44.

30. Nico J. P. van der Lof, "Boekdrukkers en hun werk," in *Het boek in Nederland in de 16de eeuw*, ed. P. van Boheemen, N. P. J. van der Lof, and E. van Meurs (The Hague, 1986), 11–20.

31. Duke, "Posters, Pamphlets and Prints," 29–30. The calculation about wages is from E. Scholliers, *De levensstandaard in de XVe en XVIe eeuw te Antwerpen* (Antwerp, 1960). Currency in the sixteenth-century Netherlands comprised a mix of coins and monies of account. The principal money of account was the

creasingly Protestant-tinged ideas, but it was the ubiquitous *rederijkers* at their civic competitions who were the main vernacular spokesmen for this mix of religious, moral, and social reflection. This growing corpus of verse and drama had long been in view of regional and state authorities, and became more troublesome once individual versions of performances, such as the Lutheran-laced plays from a competition in Ghent in 1539, began to appear in print. Rhetoricians who favored Protestantism increasingly directed criticism against Catholic religious practices, with a standard mix of Erasmian and Lutheran critiques of idolatry, the cult of the saints, relic worship, processional life, and voluntary poverty, among other topics. Virtually absent, however, was any overt political criticism; to the contrary, several famed rhetoricians, such as the Bruges factor Cornelius Everaert, penned works in honor of Charles V.[32]

Direct political criticism of Habsburg Burgundian policies through the use of broadsheets, handbills, and pamphlets was something new, a measure both of the more aggressive use of print as a vehicle of political criticism and of the severity of the crisis in the 1560s, particularly the way it ensnared the senior nobility, who traditionally had been loyal to the Burgundian dynasty even during past political crises.[33] But once cheap print came into use, its popularity accelerated. The former pensionary of Antwerp, Jacob van Wesenbeke, who was forced into exile with William of Orange in 1567, noted the role it had played in the tumultuous events of the previous year, describing the availability of "a great many colored prints, pictures, engravings, ballads, songs, and pasquils, in manuscript and in print, but also many and diverse small books, both in French and Dutch, all attacking these persecutions, inquisitions, and innovations."[34]

Granvelle and the regent were soon targets of this new genre of political criticism. Written handbills were the best way to voice criticism quickly and anonymously, and the first known to appear against Granvelle was posted in Antwerp in March 1562, besmirching him as the handmaiden of the "Spanish swine" and their dreaded Inquisition.[35] Margaret of Parma fared no better. A 1566 broadsheet circulating in Brussels shortly before July 22, 1566, dished out pure contempt for the regent on the grounds of her birth, her sex, and

---

florin or guilder, which consisted of twenty stuivers. The stuiver was originally a silver coin in the Flemish money of account, the *livre gros flamande*.

32. Gary K. Waite, *Reformers on Stage*. See also Anne-Laure van Bruaene, "Printing Plays: The Publication of the Ghent Plays of 1539 and the Reaction of the Authorities," *Dutch Crossing* 24 (2000): 265–84.

33. Van Nierop, "The Nobility and the Revolt of the Netherlands," 84, points to the crisis that enveloped the Netherlands in the wake of Charles the Bold's death in 1477, and the sixteenth-century Valois–Habsburg wars.

34. C. Rahlenbeck, ed., *Mémoires de Jacques de Wesenbeke* (Brussels and The Hague, 1859), 150. For a fuller analysis, see Duke, "Posters, Pamphlets and Prints."

35. Kervijn de Lettenhove, ed., *Relations politiques des Pays-Bas et de l'Angleterre sous le règne de Philippe II*, 11 vols. (Brussels, 1882–1900), 2:675. I thank Alastair Duke for this reference.

her spouse: "Awaken, Brabantines, a bastard should not occupy even the most minor office, so vile is it. How you suffer from a woman bastard at the head of government, wife of a traitor and enemy of our land, who is a son of the sodomitical and wicked Pier-Luigi [the father of the Margaret's husband, Octavio Farnese]!"[36]

By the time of the wonder year, visual satire was in full swing. Prints, political cartoons, single-sheet woodcuts, and other visual media emerged in the Low Countries late in the 1560s, though popular in Germany since the onset of the Reformation.[37] In 1572 a set of four engravings accompanied by short texts in Dutch and French railed against the Duke of Alba's reign (1567–73) as that of a vicious lieutenant of a larger Catholic tyranny. Even though five years had passed by then since Margaret of Parma had departed the Low Countries, one of these prints still yoked the regent and Granvelle, offering one of the most acerbic commentaries about their earlier heyday. In it, Granvelle and Margaret virtually inhabit the same physical and political space. Situated to the left of Alba and Pope Pius V, the cardinal and the regent stare blank-eyed ahead at the duke and pope—tools of a power larger than themselves. The profiles visually taper together from the trunk downward, with Alba's foot, shod in armor, atop the long fur-trimmed robe of the regent, who bears a closed, cloistered look alongside the three bearded men. Finally, the pairing of Granvelle and the regent found an echo in a ballad, another new vehicle of popular politics. Though its date of composition is unknown, it first appeared in print as part of a 1577–78 collection dubbed the *Beggars' Songs*, which enjoyed such popularity that four new editions appeared in the sixteenth century and an amazing twenty-seven in the seventeenth century. The ballad tells of "a valiant parrot" who sits near the regent's hand, "bird" being a popular slang term for clergy and used in this instance to refer to Granvelle. The parrot dutifully carries out the mandate of the regent to issue a placard ordering the silencing of God's word and the seizure of goods and estates in order to burn evildoers.[38] When the

36. *Corr. Philippe II*, 1:450–51, and *Corr. Granvelle*, 1:382.

37. A full consideration of the emergence of visual prints as polemical weapons is in Daniel R. Horst, *De Opstand in zwart-wit: Propagandaprenten uit de Nederlandse opstand, 1566–1584* (Zutphen, 2003), a comprehensive catalogue and analysis of print propaganda during the Dutch Revolt.

38. For an edition of the 1581 songbook of the Beggars, see GB, thought by the editors to be the original imprint. The Margaret of Parma ballad is found in GB, 1:123, and NG, 1:374–75, a valuable collection of early modern political and religious songs that incorporates both the Beggars' repertoire and additional material. In 1996 scholars working on a repertorium of early modern Dutch songs located a hitherto unknown 1577–78 edition of the Beggars' songbook, apparently the earliest produced, featuring a frontispiece with Philip II, a pair of clasped hands, and a Beggars' bowl and sack, that was published in Dordrecht as *Een nieu Geusen Lieden Boecxken*. It was followed by editions in 1581, 1588, and 1592. See Martine de Bruin, "Bevroren boekjes: Een geuzenliedboek van 1577–78 en andere vondsten," in *Veelderhande liedekens: studies over het Nederlandse lied tot 1600* (Louvain, 1997), 74–102, and Martine de Bruin and Johan Oosterman, eds., *Repertorium van het Nederlandse lied tot 1600*, 2 vols. (Ghent/Amsterdam, 2001). The Margaret of Parma ballad is catalogued as T4479 (subsequent ballads cited are given with the catalogue number with the reference de Bruin and Oosterman, *Repertorium*). On the reception of the *geuzenliederen* (Beggars' Ballads) and their stylistic vari-

Margaret of Parma and Cardinal Granvelle depicted in league with Alba, who receives his commission, symbolized by the sword and pots of money, from Pope Pius V. Anonymous, 1572. Courtesy of Stichting Atlas van Stolk, Rotterdam.

regent—alternately referred to as "the woman" or "Madame"—informs Granvelle that the noble protestors believe "that each should live freely in his religion," the dastardly cardinal denounces them as high-born rabble ("canaille").[39]

But as important as print, visual, and lyrical polemics became in the 1560s and thereafter, the fall of Granvelle was largely prompted by the formation of an association against him and by the satirical insignia its members fashioned. On March 11, 1563, Orange, Egmont, and Hornes demanded that Philip II dismiss Granvelle. To achieve this, they

---

ation through *contrafacta*, that is, new lyrics set to an original song's melody, see Louis Grijp, "Van geuzenlied tot Gedenck-clanck. Tweede deel: De receptie van geuzenliederen in het bijzonder in de contrafactuur," *De zeventiende eeuw* 10 (1994): 266–76, and Martine de Bruin, "Het Wilhelmus tijdens de Republiek," in *Nationale hymnen: Het Wilhelmus en zijn buren*, ed. Louis Peter Grijp (Nijmegen, 1998), 16–42.

39. NG, 1:375.

turned to traditional, confraternal behavior, using the occasion of an aristocratic banquet, redolent of Burgundian splendor, to launch a fraternal association known as the League.[40] The League offered a rallying cry for disgruntled grands seigneurs and gentilshommes opposed to Granvelle, and a type of male sodality that the great nobility knew well. The Leaguers immediately developed a party outfit, dressing their retainers in black liveries with long sleeves embroidered on both sides with a jester's head—a reference to carnival symbolism, but probably also to Granvelle's new cardinal's red hat.[41] In fact, the choice of sleeves embroidered with heads of men and foolscaps with pointed ears was a purposely ambiguous symbol; the Jesuit historian Famiano Strada, to whom we owe the fullest description of the League's birth, noted that contemporaries were not sure of its precise meaning, though they agreed that it spoofed Granvelle. The League's livery was apparently both a big success and a worry; Strada reported tailors busy with orders for the new outfit and that the regent was sufficiently concerned to send one to the king himself to alert him to the opposition to Granvelle.[42]

The anticlerical and satirical dimension of the League is not surprising, given that its new leader, the Holland nobleman Hendrik van Brederode, took to appearing in public during the anti-Granvelle campaign dressed either as a Franciscan or as a cardinal.[43] Brussels was fertile ground for such mockery, particularly of the mendicants, and the Franciscans above all. Just a few years earlier, in April 1559, the city's prestigious chamber of rhetoric, the Cornflower, had won first prize in a city competition to celebrate the peace of Cateau-Cambrésis. Its winning entry was "Barefoot Brothers," which bitingly mocked the Franciscans through the character of one Hans Goetbloet, who complains about having to deprive his children of food and drink in order to feed the mendicants, and suggests the real "barefoot brothers" are his hungry youngsters. The play was such a success it was performed again at the central marketplace a few months later. This prompted an investigation of the performers' religious orthodoxy, initiated by none other than Granvelle

---

40. L. P. Gachard, "La chute du Cardinal de Granvelle," in *Études et notices concernant l'histoire des Pays-Bas*, vol. 1 (Brussels, 1890), 107–29; Rachfahl, *Wilhelm von Oranien*, 2:288–97.

41. F. Strada, *De thien eerste boecken der Nederlandsche oorlogen* (Antwerp, 1645), 1:197–201, offers the fullest account of the League's inauguration. His work was first published in Latin as *De Bello Belgico Decas Prima ab Excessu Caroli V. imp. usque ad Initia Praefecturae Alexandri Farnesii Parmae* (Rome, 1632). Analyses of these cultural symbols are also in Henk van Nierop, "A Beggars' Banquet: The Compromise of the Nobility and the Politics of Inversion," *European Historical Quarterly* 21 (1991): 419–43, esp. 433, and Alastair Duke, "Dissent, Propaganda, and Political Organization at the Outbreak of the Revolt of the Netherlands," in *Reformation, Revolt and Civil War*, 115–32. In a letter to Philip II dated April 18, 1564, Granvelle compared the bundled arrows to what appeared on the Spanish *real*: Charles Weiss, ed., *Papiers d'état du Cardinal de Granvelle*, 9 vols. (Paris, 1841–52), 7:495.

42. Strada, *De thien eerste boecken der Nederlandsche oorlogen*, 1:198.

43. Van Nierop, "Beggars' Banquet," 433, from Alexandre Henne, ed., *Mémoires de Pontus Payen*, 2 vols. (Brussels, 1860), 1:59.

himself, which widened into an inquiry by the procurer general of the Council of Brabant.[44]

Brederode was plainly anticlerical in his satirical getup, and no wonder, given how receptive the civic climate must have been to his antics. Other League nobility such as Egmont, however, exercised more discretion and decided to replace the fool's head on their retainers' livery with a sheath of arrows bound together to denote strength and unity, particularly after Margaret of Parma loudly complained.[45] The bound arrows recalled the fasces of the classical world and had the added benefit that it had been Queen Isabella of Castile's personal device and was featured on the Spanish *real*. It also affirmed the martial ethos of the nobles, and made an allusion to the arrows of the elite urban archers guilds, staffed by townsmen of means but patronized selectively by noblemen and Burgundian sovereigns.[46] Given these powerful valences, it is no surprise that this aspect of the League's insignia later was echoed in the States General's new seal, adopted in 1578: a crowned lion with a sword in one hand, and, in the other, a bundle of seventeen arrows to represent the unified provinces.[47] But the original arrow symbolism of the League also carried anticardinalist sentiment, since it emphasized virile militarism, a quality supposedly absent in a churchman like Granvelle.

A satirical print concerning the Inquisition issued around 1566 exploits this arrow symbolism and makes a direct connection to the popular pastime of the shooting competitions held by archers and crossbowmen's guilds.[48] The print features two groups taking aim at a wooden parrot atop a pole. On the left are the noblemen, one holding a parrot already successfully won, the others shooting their "true and straight" arrows. To the right are the bumbling clergy, priests, monks, and a bishop, complaining that they have already lost the first parrot, symbol of the Inquisition, because their arrows are "short and crooked." Daniel Horst has observed that the contrast between the effective arrows of the noblemen and the ineffectual ones of the clergy resonated as a contrast between righteous and false belief, noting that a parrot was popular Netherlandish slang for clergy, a satiri-

---

44. See Willem Van Eeghem, ed., *Drie schandaleuse spelen: Brussel, 1559* (Antwerp, 1937), and the discussion in Anne-Laure van Bruaene, "Minnelijke rederijkers, schandelijke spelen: De rederijkerskamers in Brussel tussen 1400 en 1585," in *De macht van het schone woord: Literatuur in Brussel van de 14de tot de 18de eeuw*, ed. Jozef Janssens and Remco Sleiderink (Louvain, 2003), 125–39.

45. Duke, "Dissent, Propaganda, and Political Organization," 118–20, and Strada, *Thien eerste boecken der Nederlandsche oorlogen*, 1:201. The decision to alter the livery is recounted too in the deposition of Egmont after his arrest in 1567. See a French translation of the Spanish original as an appendix to Baron de Reiffenberg, ed., *Correspondance de Marguerite d'Autriche suivie des interrogatoires du Comte d'Egmont* (Brussels, 1842), 314.

46. On these military guilds and their symbolism, see Arnade, *Realms of Ritual*, 65–94.

47. S. Groenveld, H. L. P. Leeuwenberg, et al., *De kogel door de kerk? De opstand in de Nederlanden en de rol van de Unie van Utrecht, 1559–1609* (Zutphen, 1979), 145. The print was such a concern that Granvelle sent a copy to Philip II; see Duke, "Dissent, Propaganda, and Political Organization," 127.

48. Horst, *Opstand in zwart-wit*, 43–44.

A print parody of the fight over the enforcement of the heresy edicts that depicts fumbling clergy losing the battle against their noble opponents. The conflict is portrayed as a shooting competition. Anonymous, 1566. Courtesy of Rijksprentenkabinet, Rijksmusuem, Amsterdam.

cal device we saw employed in a Beggars' song.[49] Perhaps equally compelling are the gender valences of the arrow symbolism. The long, straight, and accurate arrows evoke the kind of masculine athleticism that urban viewers, accustomed to the *schutters* (bowmen) and their popular contests, would instantly recognize as contrasted with the unmanly clergy, without athletic skill and saddled with shriveling arrows. The nobles, in opposition, were privileged men of their sex; Granvelle and the clergy were bumbling churchmen in league with a bastard woman regent.

Defiant in symbolism, the League scored its ultimate political prize when Philip II recalled Granvelle from the Netherlands on December 14, 1563. Without resigning his archbishopric, Granvelle left Brussels on March 14, 1564. Members of the League feted the event at yet another banquet, this time at the residence of the Count of Mansfeld in Lux-

49. Ibid.

embourg. At the June 24, 1564 feast in honor of his son's baptism, Mansfeld offered a Burgundian-style tournament, accompanied by a masquerade. Three costumed men entered the tournament field: first, a hermit chewing on a rosary; next, a cardinal on horseback; and third, a devil whipping the cardinal's horse with fox tails. The cardinal was then ritually massacred with fist blows and lashes from fox tails, and his cardinal's robe shredded.[50] The attendees howled, gloating in the League's triumph over its archenemy. Their ceremonial adieu to Granvelle was taken from the same ritual tradition that had nourished the League's association as a fraternal order: carnivalesque imagery redolent of noble privilege, cheer, and athletic prowess.[51] As a tournament in honor of the baptism of an infant boy, the event paid homage to male noble lineage and its chivalric prerogatives. It was shaped by a religious rite of passage—the sacrament of baptism—yet it turned on the castigation of the pope's primate of the Netherlands, Cardinal Granvelle. The League nobles might chuckle at the good fun without fully realizing the ripple effects that would follow. Tellingly, they did not mobilize prints, ballads, or popular images to their cause, though these were newly available, but instead turned to older associational and satirical forms with which they were more familiar. The grands seigneurs were not full-throated critics of either the king or the religious order he aimed to preserve in the Low Countries. But by fashioning a campaign against his hand-picked primate, and by employing symbols steeped in festive mockery and anticlericalism, they modeled forms of opposition to which a broader populace might refer, as significant segments began their own forms of defiance in the early years of the 1560s. They had launched a public movement, and by doing so, opened up a Pandora's box.

Psalms, Sermons, and the Badly Burned: Calvinist Dissent

After the bishop of Arras ordered a visitation to the trade and textile center of Valenciennes in Hainault in 1555, the report to him bemoaned the erosion of faith in the city of some twelve thousand souls on the Scheldt River. Attendance at mass was irregular, unmarried cohabitation was everywhere, and, worst of all, behavior at mass and processions ran the gamut from misplaced devotional excess—clamoring to see the Eucharist, for ex-

---

50. This ritual is reported in Weiss, *Papiers d'état*, 8:76–77, 93–94. Early attention to its importance was paid by John Lothrop Motley, *The Rise of the Dutch Republic*, 3 vols. (New York, 1856), 1:344. Recent analyses are in van Nierop, "Beggars' Banquet," 433, and Duke, "Dissent, Propaganda, and Political Organization." Van Nierop pays particular attention to the symbol of the foxtails, an allusion to slyness in general, and a specific reference to Granvelle, known for this quality. They might have also been a *jeu de mots* association to Granvelle's erstwhile friend turned adversary, Simon Renard. Pontus Payen recounts that Brederode and Lumey called Granvelle "le grand renard," and Berlaymont and Viglius were "les renardaux"; see Henne, *Mémoires de Pontus Payen*, 1:59. They placed foxtails in their hats to signify that one day they would all lose their tails.

51. On early modern anticlericalism, see Burke, *Popular Culture*, 199.

ample—to bland indifference. "People stroll in the marketplace and in front of the town hall on feast days and Sundays during divine service to the great scandal of good and virtuous Christians," complained the report.[52]

To remedy Valenciennes's religious climate, the authors reprimanded the improper religious expression of the devotees and called for better trained curates. They zeroed in on the lack of rigor in Catholic observation of liturgy and counseled education and reform as the remedy. But no mention was made of Calvinism, the newest force shaping the religious landscape in Valenciennes and other cities of the mid-sixteenth century Netherlands. The Reformed religion entered tardily in the Low Countries after several decades in which Lutheranism, Anabaptism, Spiritualism, and other varieties of Protestantism had taken hold. But Calvinism soon eclipsed these other denominations as the religious countercurrent to Catholicism. Its adherents came to the Low Countries by at least two significant paths: first, from the south, as the growing Calvinist movement in France seeped across the border into key Walloon cities like Tournai and Valenciennes; and second, from exiles from Charles V's heresy placards who had developed refugee churches in England and Germany, where they encountered and adopted militant Calvinism.[53] But before either of these waves of influence took root, Calvin had already set his eye on the urban, rich Low Countries, sending his Geneva-trained disciple, Pierre Brully, who arrived in 1544 in Tournai. Brully fell into the hands of authorities within months of his mission, and was promptly executed, but he left behind the foundations of a local movement that would gain adherents from all social ranks, including the urban patriciate.[54] By the time of Philip II's departure from Brussels, southern cities like Tournai and Valenciennes were bulwarks of Reformed sentiment, boasting adherents among the artisan and merchant sectors, and to a lesser extent among the patriciate. Reformed congregations spread rapidly elsewhere, prominently in the rural textile industries of the Flemish Westkwartier in cities like Hondschoote and Armentières, but also more surreptitiously in the great old cities of Antwerp, Ypres, and Ghent, and with substantial echoes in Holland, especially Amsterdam and Enkhuizen, though not until 1566.[55] Calvinism and other forms of Protestantism were so entrenched in the Castellany of Baillieul in the Westkwartier that in a

---

52. P. Beuzart, "la Réforme dans le diocèse d'Arras en 1555 d'après un document inédit," *Bulletin de la Société de l'Histoire du Protestantisme français* 77 (1927): 468–76. On late-medieval Valenciennes, see L. Nys and A. Salamange, eds., *Valenciennes aux XIVe et XVe siècles: Art et histoire* (Valenciennes, 1996).

53. For Calvinism in relationship to other religious currents, see Andrew Pettegree, "Religion and the Revolt," in *Dutch Revolt*, ed. Darby, 67–83; and Philip Benedict, *Christ's Churches Purely Reformed: A Social History of Calvinism* (New Haven, 2002), 173–201, on the Netherlands. See also Duke, "Building Heaven in Hell's Despite."

54. Gérard Moreau, *Histoire du Protestantisme à Tournai jusqu'à la veille de la Révolution des Pays-Bas* (Paris, 1962), 83–116.

55. Marnef, *Antwerp in the Age of the Reformation*; Moreau, *Histoire du Protestantisme à Tournai*; M. Hodeigne, "Le Protestantisme à Valenciennes jusqu'à la veille de la Revolution des Pays-Bas," (master's thesis, University of Liège, 1967); Duke, "Building Heaven in Hell's Despite," and Decavele, *Dageraad*.

letter dated September 4, 1561, the Council of Flanders informed the regent that any strict enforcement of the heresy placards would result in "a terrible eruption of blood that would result in the depopulation and destruction of the area."[56]

In 1561, Viglius, president of the Council of State, singled out Valenciennes as the chief "ville mauvaise" in the Low Countries.[57] His scolding was not unfounded. Both in Valenciennes and in nearby Tournai, seat of a bishopric, Calvinists had risked their safety by staging open-air sermons and public psalm singing, the later provocatively performed inside the city walls. September 14, 1561, was Tournai's feast day of Our Lady, a devotion that regularly drew urban delegations from across the Low Countries and was of religious value to the dukes of Burgundy who annually sent a robe to outfit the statue of the virgin. The feast day's procession merged two devotions: one to the plague-saving Virgin Mary, whose statue was housed at the cathedral and whose reliquary was carried aloft, and the other to the Exaltation of the True Cross, celebrated the evening before by a train of barefoot penitents led by a cathedral priest. The religious venerations also coincided with eight days of markets and fairs, the trade and kermis (market fair and festival) atmosphere being the perfect environment for a procession that accommodated scores of outside visitors.[58]

In 1561 trouble marred the feast day of Our Lady. On the day of the procession, Calvinists hurled taunts at the celebrants. Their defiance culminated between September 29 and 30, when hundreds of Calvinists marched through Tournai's main streets loudly singing psalms.[59] Royal commissioners were dispatched from Brussels to investigate the troubles and reported "more than one hundred men, women, girls, and children who tumultuously sang the Ten Commandments and the psalms of David in French."[60] Six hundred more enthusiasts followed them. Their organizer, "a small, dark man with a short beard," led the devotees through all the principal streets of Tournai, marching uninterrupted from seven to ten p.m., pausing only to stop at the house of the bishop's vicar, the Augustinian convent, and the central marketplace, where they fanned out in groups to maximize their visual and physical presence.[61] The chronicler of religious troubles in Tournai, the fiscal procurer Pasquier de le Barre, put the number of Calvinist marchers even higher: four to five hundred on the first night, and three to four thousand on September 30.[62]

---

56. Troubles religieux, 1:82–83.

57. Geoffery Whitman Clark, "An Urban Study during the Revolt of the Netherlands, Valenciennes, 1540–1566" (PhD diss., Columbia University, 1972), 215.

58. See Susan Boynton, Jean Dumoulin, and Jacques Pycke, "Une réalité religieuse," in Grande procession de Tournai, ed. Dumoulin and Pycke, 29–34; and Catherine Dambroise and Ana Maria Jorge, "La procession: Miroir des mentalités," in Grande procession de Tournai, 72–77.

59. Moreau, Histoire du Protestantisme à Tournai, 168–69.

60. Report in Aldolphe Hocquet, Tournai et le Tournaisis au XVI siècle, au point de vue politique et social (Brussels, 1906), 307. Sixty participants were identified by name. See Archives Générales du Royaume, État et Audience, reg. 354, fols. 30r–40r.

61. Ibid.

62. Gérard Moreau, ed., Le journal d'un bourgeois de Tournai: Le second livre des chroniques de Pasquier de le Barre,

The public testimonial to their faith by the Calvinists in Tournai was the opening wedge of public Calvinist agitation in the Low Countries, a force that paralleled the dissent fomented by the grands seigneurs in the political realm and was equally rooted in defiant acts and discrete rituals. Public gatherings and psalm singing boldly defied the heresy laws issued by the Habsburg Burgundians. The expression of Protestantism was explicitly prohibited; the 1546 placard also proscribed the printing of "ballads, songs, and refrains" that were considered scandalous.[63] The psalms sung in Tournai had been rendered into French verse by Clément Marot, and were so favored by Calvin that he had them set to music and published in 1539, with a flurry of subsequent editions.[64] The Marot psalter became the mainstay of French Protestantism, available in cheap editions as well as pricey quartos, despite its condemnation by the theologians of the Sorbonne in 1543. It was enlarged in a new edition by Théodore Beza in 1551, and within a few years, psalm singing and public gatherings erupted in French cities, prompting Henri II to forbid the practice in 1558.[65] So vigorous a signature of French Calvinism were the psalms that Catholics craftily used them to lure their opponents into a trap; during the siege of Rouen in 1563, for example, a Catholic cavalry unit sang psalms as a trick to gain entrance as its men approached the city's gates.[66]

Psalm singing presented authorities in the Burgundian Netherlands with an unexpected challenge. Heretical songs and ballads had been prohibited since the 1546 placard. But these ordinances referred specifically to the scandalous verses of anonymous satirists or the Protestant-laced allegories of the chambers of rhetoric, like those from the Ghent competition of 1539.[67] City elites had been keen to crack down on public singing in general, as was the case in Ghent, where since 1549 town officials had prohibited any balladry on New Year's eve except on the part of official city singers.[68] Psalm singing was never fully anticipated in any of these song ordinances. Yet the musical versification of these cherished Old Testament treasures was just as threatening as the banned works, since the psalms consoled Calvinists in their religious dissent, urging strength in the wake of per-

---

1500–1565 (Brussels, 1975), 404–5. For the wonder-year period, see A. Pinchart, ed., *Mémoires de Pasquier de le Barre et de Nicolas Soldoyer pour servir à l'histoire de Tournai, 1565–70*, 2 vols. (Brussels, 1859–65). For a critical edition in English, see Charlie Steen, ed. and trans., *The Time of Troubles in the Low Countries: The Chronicles and Memoirs of Pasquier de le Barre of Tournai, 1559–1567* (New York, 1989).

63. Placcaet, inhoudende zeker ordonnacie, statuut ende verbod, eeerst van diversche nieuwe ghereprobeerde ende suspecte boucken, ghecondemneert by der faculteyt van Theologien der Universiteyt van Leuven, etc., June 30, 1546.

64. Orentin Douen, *Clément Marot et le psautier Huguenot: Etude historique, littéraire, musicale, et bibliographique*, 2 vols. (Amsterdam, 1967; orig., 1878). An overview of the importance of metrical psalms and community singing to the Protestant cause in northern Europe is in Andrew Pettegree, *Reformation and the Culture of Persuasion* (Cambridge, 2005), 4–75.

65. Barbara B. Diefendorf, *Beneath the Cross: Catholics and Huguenots in Sixteenth-Century Paris* (New York, 1991), 137.

66. Douen, *Clément Marot et le psautier Huguenot*, 1:14.

67. On the prohibition of the 1539 Ghent plays, see Van Bruaene, "Printing Plays."

68. SAG, Series 93 CC, fols. 99r–100r.

secution. The Old Testament symbol of David, purported author of the psalms, presented to Calvinists a model of triumph in the face of adversity, of the titanic, righteous struggle against forces larger than oneself. David was also hailed as a warrior, and the psalms offered a pugnacious symbol to the Low Country Calvinists in which to locate their struggle in a land ruled by a Goliath-like, persecuting king.[69] The psalms' general invocation of righteousness as a weapon against oppression and adversity; the militant language of God crushing the wicked (Psalms 9–10), or avenging those who "slay the widow and the stranger, and murder the fatherless" (Psalm 94); the plaint about "princes who sit and speak against me" (Psalm 119); and the praise offered to God "who trains my hand for war and my fingers for battle" (Psalm 144)—these were precisely the kind of Israelite themes that could be readily extrapolated to the contemporary experience of zealous inquisitors, formidable placards, and an inflexible Catholic king. Psalm singing was one of the earliest examples of the Low Country Calvinists' efforts to write their history in the language of Zion; it peaked with such seventeenth-century publications as the *Netherlands Anthem of Commemoration* by Adriaan Valerius, a history of the Dutch Revolt penned as a Hebraic narrative of freedom and redemption from bondage and slavery.[70] While the psalms gave insurgent Calvinists a vocabulary of optimism and consolation, they also cast obstreperous magistrates, royal officials, and even the king as Biblical tyrants.

City and state officials quickly recognized the danger inherent in the *chanteries* (public psalm singing) that Calvinists organized in city streets and on public squares. Even if the analogy between the psalms and contemporary religious struggles was more implied than explicit, confident public singing from French Calvinist psalters was seen as a threat. And the time chosen by Tournai's Calvinists to voice their convictions—the September 14 celebrations of Our Lady and the Exaltation of the Cross—was a direct repudiation of a procession that had since the late fourteenth century commanded the attention of scores of cities and the patronage of the Burgundian sovereigns. Worse, David's psalms were not the only compositions sung. Ballads railed against those who would extirpate the word of God, and implicated Catholic magistrates, inquisitors, bishops, and the regent. One ballad from Tournai appeals to "the Lord" to stop the prohibition against public psalm singing—a pregnant double entendre to God and king:

> O Seigneur true and faithful. Your orders are carried out by perverse and cruel men filled with falsehood and error. They have prohibited the psalms that all Christians

---

69. See Diefendorf, *Beneath the Cross*, 137–39, for an excellent dissection of the importance of psalms to French Calvinism; on the military metaphors, and more generally, Pettegree, *Reformation and the Culture of Persuasion*.

70. On this work, and the Hebraic analogy of Dutch Calvinism, see Simon Schama, *The Embarrassment of Riches: An Interpretation of Dutch Culture in the Golden Age* (Berkeley, 1988), 93–125, and Lea Campos Boralevi, "Classical Foundational Myths of European Republicanism: The Jewish Commonwealth," in *Republicanism*, 1:247–62.

must sing. In spite of you, they want to eradicate false heresy from our souls. They have rejected, blasphemed, and misused your celestial grace by their dishonest and false council against the will of your majesty.[71]

The ballad denounces authorities who "worship stones and wood" and inflict the "sword, fire, cord, and ax" on Calvinist psalm singers; it concludes with an appeal to the "very Christian king" to support Reformed activity in order to "maintain your renown."[72]

No such luck. On the contrary, Tournai's magistrates on September 30 denounced the night-time singing by men, women, and children and prohibited all public assemblies, blaming the disturbances on outsiders.[73] Not satisfied, the regent sent her own royal investigators, who drew up a list of sixty suspects, arrested several, executed the Calvinist pastor Jean de Lannoy (though he had not approved of the *chanteries*), forced the most important Calvinist leader Guy de Bray to flee, and proclaimed a solid victory on January 11, 1562.[74]

The commissioners who proclaimed Calvinism defeated were as wishful as had been the author of the ballad appealing for support from Philip II. Not only did psalm singing continue in Tournai, it carried on as well in Valenciennes, where it had been occurring since September 27, 1561, when hundreds had marched in the dark of evening to pause before the Franciscan and Dominican convents and the Benedictine Abbey of Saint Jean, home to the largest collection of relics in Valenciennes.[75] At the same time, in different areas of the Low Countries, there began public assemblies of Calvinists in the woods and pastures beyond city walls and thus outside the jurisdiction of urban authorities—events that were even better attended than the *chanteries*. The first so-called hedge sermon was held in the cemetery of Boeschepe in the always turbulent Flemish Westkwartier on Sunday morning, July 12, timed to coincide with mass. The participants came armed with clubs, knives, and pistols, joyously singing psalms after a sermon delivered by the minister, Ghilein Damman.[76]

---

71. Archives Générales du Royaume, Papier d'Etat, no. 354, fols. 74r–75r, transcribed in Hocquet, *Tournai et les Tournaisis*, 95–97.

72. Ibid.

73. M. Vandenbroeck, "Ordonnances publiées à Tournai dans les années 1560 à 1567, au sujet des troubles religieux qu'il y eut en cette ville," Académie Royale des Sciences, Lettres et des Beaux-Arts de Belgique, *Bulletin de la Commission Royale d'histoire* 12 (1859): 83–84. On the magistrates' explanation to the regent, see Hocquet, *Tournai et les Tournaisis*, 178–79, from Archives Générales du Royaume, Papier d'Etat, no. 354, fols. 30r–40r.

74. Hocquet, *Tournai et les Tournaisis*, 178–85, and Charlie R. Steen, *A Chronicle of Conflict: Tournai, 1559–67* (Utrecht, 1985), 37.

75. C. Rahlenbeck, "Les chanteries de Valenciennes," *Bulletin de la Commission de l'Histoire des Eglises Wallonnes* 3 (1887): 121–59. On the abbey of Saint Jean and other ecclesiastical institutions, see Simon LeBoucq, *Histoire ecclésiastique de la ville et comté de Valenciennes* (Valenciennes, 1844).

76. M. F. Backhouse, "The Official Start of Armed Resistance in the Low Countries: Boeschepe 12 July 1562," *Archiv für Reformationsgeschichte* 71 (1980): 198–213.

The government's reaction to the hedge sermons was swift. Margaret of Parma ordered the arrest of all sermon-goers the very next day. Out of the ninety-eight known attendees, sentences were issued against seventy-eight. It is hard to know what irked the Brussels government the most: the militarism implied in the bearing of arms, or the forthright evangelicalism paired against Sunday mass. Three-quarters of those charged were banished, but twelve received death sentences.[77] Still, more hedge sermons followed, especially in Tournai and Valenciennes. They were early rehearsals for the heady summer of 1566, when heresy laws would be temporarily suspended and sermons sprouted up everywhere. By December 1563, the notorious inquisitor of Flanders, Pieter Titelmans, had seen enough agitation in Tournai to declare the city "very inclined to tumult under the cover of religion." Indeed, anticlericalism was now unalloyed there. One Quintin Daubicy was arrested for attacking two clergy and shouting at full throat, "It is because of them that these are such poor times. These sodomite priests ought to burn, and it will be me who stokes their fire."[78] The magistrates issued more ordinances, most importantly the May 1, 1563 decree making hedge sermons a capital crime, but the gatherings only grew stronger.[79]

Perhaps the most notorious instance of Calvinist public defiance occurred in Valenciennes on April 27, 1562, in a daring rescue of two condemned Calvinists already bound to the stake to meet their martyrdom. The name popularly given to this event, *maubruslez*, or badly burned, satirically references death at the pyre.[80] Simon Fauveau and Philip Maillart were two deacons active in Valenciennes, apprehended after the royal inquisitor had located their names in papers seized from minister Guy de Bray. Fauveau was a master soap maker and Maillart made women's socks and slippers. Under interrogation they came off as crisp and articulate Calvinists, and apparently both had studied in Geneva.[81] Unrepentant in prison, Fauveau and Maillart were sentenced to death while magistrates equivocated about the precise date of execution because local Calvinists had threatened unrest. On March 22 admirers thronged outside the walls of the prison in which Fauveau and Maillart were held, and sang psalms. The next morning a broadsheet was found affixed against a wall on the marketplace proclaiming "those who suffer persecution for my name will be saved." Exasperated, the regent ordered the execution date set immediately. The

---

77. Ibid., 204–10.

78. M. Vandenbroeck, "Ordonnances publiées à Tournai," 90.

79. Ibid., 92–94, for transcriptions of the ordinances. See also Steen, *Chronicle of Conflict*, 225, for a summary.

80. E. Bouton, "La journée des mau-brulez," *Archives historiques et littéraires du Nord de la France et du midi de la Belgique* 3 (1833): 50–63; Rahlenbeck, "Les chanteries de Valenciennes," esp. 146–57. Most of the primary sources concerning the incident are gathered in C. Paillard, ed., *Histoire des troubles religieux de Valenciennes*, 4 vols. (Brussels, 1874–76), especially 1:55–74 and 2:154–217. See also the account in Henri d'Outreman, *Histoire de la ville et comté de Valenciennes* (Douai, 1639; repr., Marseille, 1975), esp. 200–201.

81. For their interrogations, see Paillard, *Histoire des troubles religieux*, 2:113–35.

magistrates reluctantly complied, selected the morning of April 27, and mustered a guard of sixty. A sure sign of the city's divided religious loyalties was that half of those mustered by the magistrates were known Calvinists.[82] The noble governor of Valenciennes, Jean de Glymes, the Marquis de Berghes, was no friend of the heresy placards, and made sure to absent himself, though he did leave behind his lieutenant and a few men who indifferently assisted in manning the execution scene. At 5 a.m. the stakes were ready for their victims, and though the magistrates had hoped the early morning time would discourage onlookers, a sizable crowd of men and women agitated behind the barricade erected to seal off the execution site. The magistrates appeared on the balcony of the town hall, and their clerk read aloud the death sentence, off-loading responsibility onto the royal placards enforced by Philip II and Regent Margaret of Parma.[83]

A heavy guard led the two prisoners to the stake. As had become typical of condemned Calvinists on their march to the execution site, Fauveau and Maillart sang psalms. But instead of the more common fifty-fourth psalm invoking God's salvation, Fauveau defiantly sang the ninety-fourth, a stinging indictment of the proud and an affirmation of godly wrath:

> O Lord God, to whom vengeance belongeth;
> O God, to whom vengeance belongeth, show thyself.
> Lift up thyself, thou judge of the earth:
> render a reward to the proud.[84]

The crowd erupted. A woman threw a shoe at the magistrates, a reference perhaps to the fact that one of the condemned was a cobbler and sock maker. This act introduced an artisanal symbol into this sacred drama, and the crowd responded with a hail of rocks thrown at the men guarding the execution site.[85] Sensing a riot underway, authorities quickly whisked the men back to the prison, while onlookers rushed the barricades and destroyed the stakes and wood piles. Neither Berghes's men nor the civic muster did much to stop the rioters as they ripped timber from the execution scaffold and rushed to use it as a battering ram on the prison door. The crowd arrived to rescue Fauveau and Maillart just as they were about to be privately executed. The rescuers sang psalms as they triumphantly hoisted the two deacons aloft on their shoulders.[86]

The *maubruslez* episode in Valenciennes spoke volumes about just how strong urban

---

82. Ibid., 1:63.
83. Ibid., 1:63–65. For the death sentences, see ibid., 2:186–87, 188–89.
84. Rahlenbeck, "Les chanteries de Valenciennes," 155.
85. Henri d'Outreman, *Histoire de la ville et comté de Valenciennes*, 201.
86. Bouton, "La journée des mau-brulez." For the regent's account of events, see her May 8 letter to Philip II, transcribed in Paillard, *Histoire des troubles religieux*, 2:208–17. She claimed the crowd had intended to sack the Dominican convent.

Calvinism had grown. Its adherents had overturned an execution that had involved the regent's own intervention. The condemned men had approached the stake defiantly singing a psalm that castigated the proud—a reference everyone could interpret as alluding to intransigent Catholic political and religious officials. Their rescuers had boldly converted the tools of the execution into the means of its prevention. However much the rescue was motivated by pure religious conviction, it was staged with words, gestures, and implements that implicated secular authorities and defied their power.

"Can any religion exist without public worship and ceremonies, by which it is maintained?" asked the Antwerp Calvinist Francis Junius in 1566 in a treatise to Philip II imploring the public recognition of Calvinism.[87] The field sermons with armed attendees, the psalm singing with public processions before ecclesiastical houses or in marketplaces, and the freeing of condemned prisoners—these were rites essential to securing a Calvinist public identity for a prohibited religion and its practitioners. These religious behaviors drew eclectically from diverse sources. In form, for example, psalm-singing marches emulated the great *ommegangen*, but the purpose of the later marches was to mark the space of religious dissent. The bearing of weapons at sermons and the marketplace assemblies also closely imitated traditional forms of artisanal protest in which arms-bearing and guild-flag waving men mustered in public to demonstrate force and to issue proclamations.[88] The singing of scurrilous ballads, unscripted public assemblies, the bearing of arms, and the sharp anticlericalism were public activities already under regulation, as we have seen, during the reign of Charles V. That they now transpired within the heretical idiom of Protestantism made them all the more noxious to Catholic magistrates and royal officials. The fact that these Calvinist actions were intensifying at precisely the time that the grands seigneurs' League triumphed over Granvelle made for a level of public dissent unparalleled in the Low Countries. Nor were their funds of inspiration wholly discrete. Urban Calvinists' actions were overtly religious, but they borrowed from political and festive forms; the grands seigneurs' actions were overtly political, but drew on religious and cultural symbols. Both sets of developments challenged governmental policy, if from quite distinct social locations, setting the stage for their intensification during the annus mirabilis of 1566.

Supplications: Petitioners and Beggars

Of all the Low Country inquisitors, Pieter Titelmans was surely the most despised. Dean of Ronse, Titelmans was appointed provincial inquisitor for Flanders in 1545. By 1566 he

---

87. *Texts Revolt*, 56, excerpted from the original, *Brief discours envoyé au Roy Philippe nostre sire et souverain Seigneur, pour le bien et profit de sa Maiesté, et singulierement de ses Pays-Bas.*

88. Arnade, "Crowds, Banners, and the Marketplace"; Marc Boone, "Armes, coursses, assemblees, et commocions."

had pursued heretics with such efficiency that he had racked up an amazing 1,600 cases—an average of one every three working days. No wonder that criticism of his labor was especially sharp. In Baillieul in April 1561, Titelman's life was threatened when his men attempted to apprehend suspects. In nearby Hondschoote, underground songs denounced him. Probably these were not unlike the anonymous satires aimed at him after the outbreak of religious violence in 1566, in which the satirized Titelmans would confess that "Papafucker is the sodomitical Pope who gave me my charge" to sow tyranny in Flanders.[89] Lest we conclude that such a salty spoof expressed sentiments held only by hack poets, consider the instance of a city clerk in Ghent who, in copying a directive from Titelmans, inserted next to the inquisitor's official title, "alias tyranny."[90]

Opposition to the Inquisition soared after Granvelle's departure in the spring of 1564. So too did Calvinist agitation, even in a metropolis like Antwerp, where unrest on October 3 nearly stopped yet another public execution of a Calvinist preacher, the former Carmelite monk Jan de Smet, known more elegantly as Christoffel Fabricius.[91] Betrayed by a bonnet-seller subsequently vilified with the name "Tall Margaret" in a ballad celebrating his martyrdom, Fabricius was condemned to die at the stake by a reluctant burgrave and magistrates rightly nervous about provoking Calvinist agitation. City authorities had in fact tried to avoid a death sentence; when the regent insisted, they made plans to execute Fabricius quietly in private. Margaret of Parma, however, wanted an exemplary punishment for all to see. In compliance with her wish, the central marketplace was selected. As Fabricius was bound to the stake on the morning of October 3, a riled up crowd responded with a chorus of psalms and a hail of stones. City officials beat a hasty retreat to the town hall, making sure, however, that the executioner had killed Fabricius before he could be freed from the fires. There was no successful rescue this time to match the freeing of Fauveau and Maillart in Valenciennces. Instead, Fabricius became a martyred hero celebrated in the Reformed imagination; the ballad about his fate praises his martyrdom as it denounces the "bloodthirsty" burgrave and his men who sent him to his death. This near riot was the last straw for the city magistrates, who essentially gave up enforcement of the heresy placards until forced to resume after the iconoclastic riots of 1566.[92]

---

89. Decavele, *Dageraad*, 1:24–28; *Troubles religieux*, 1:82–83, for the incident in Baillieul. For the ballad, see *De Clage vanden inquisiteur, meester Pieter Titelmanus*, Bibliotheek Universiteit Gent, MS. 278.

90. Dacavele, *Dageraad*, 1:28 n. 87.

91. For Fabricius, see the contemporary account, *Historie ende gesciedenisse van de verraderlicke ghevanghenisse der vromer ende godsaligher mannen Christophori Fabritii*, published in 1555 by a Calvinist sympathizer and reproduced in S. Cramer and F. Pijper, eds., *Bibliotheca Reformatoria Neerlandica*, 10 vols. (The Hague, 1913–14), 3:258–459, and *Antwerpsch Archievenblad*, 9:169–273. A good overview is in Guy Edward Wells, "Antwerp and the Government of Philip II, 1555–1567" (PhD diss., Cornell University, 1982), 340–44.

92. NG, 1:267–70. For the decision not to enforce the placards, see Wells, "Antwerp and the Government of Philip II," 347–48.

The great noblemen could sense that full-blown unrest was near the surface in the cities. Even the cautious Orange surprised his fellow Council of State members in December with a long plea for freedom of conscience that marked him out as now explicitly opposed to the king's religious policy, even as he maintained no public commitment to rebellion.[93] He and his fellow senior colleagues also dispatched Egmont to Spain to plead with Philip II to moderate the heresy laws and give the Council of State wider powers to govern the Low Countries. Egmont came back to Brussels claiming victory, under the illusion that Philip II had agreed to their demands. The men learned otherwise when they received copies of Philip's famous letters from his residence in the Segovia Woods dated October 17 and 20, 1565, refusing any moderation of the heresy laws, rejecting changes in power of the Council of State, and appointing the loyalist duke of Aarschot to its membership.[94]

Overconfident since their League had rid Brussels of Granvelle, the senior nobility had fumbled in their campaign to widen their political authority and scale back the hated heresy laws. The burden of opposition would soon pass to the more numerous middle nobility, with regional prestige, some resources, and several Calvinist sympathizers. Much was at stake, but because these gentilshommes lacked significant government positions and aristocratic trappings such as membership in the Order of the Golden Fleece, they had much less to lose than Orange and Egmont. Modeling themselves after their superiors, these lesser noblemen banded together, held the first of several meetings in the summer of 1565, and issued the Compromise of the Nobility in December 1565, signed by four hundred men. Searing in tone, the text of the Compromise introduced several polemical devices soon to be the mainstay of oppositional pamphlets, most notably the equation of the Inquisition with slavery, its enforcement with "the worst barbarism ever practiced by tyrants," and the mythologizing of "ancient privileges, franchises, and immunities" as the bedrock of liberty in the Netherlands.[95] But the gentilshommes also took cues from the League association of 1563 by forming a fraternal sodality of their own: the Compromise of the Nobility, and by developing forms of public dissent that were much more vigorously wagered before a public audience than the anti-Granvelle campaign had been.

The new Compromise of the Nobility opted for a dramatic public showing to inaugurate their movement. On Friday April 5, 1566, a grand retinue of two hundred of the Compromise's signatories gathered to present a petition to Margaret of Parma at the Burgundian

---

93. Rachfahl, *Wilhelm von Oranien*, 2:474–75.

94. On Egmont's diplomatic blunders in Spain, see Parker, *Dutch Revolt*, 64–66. For letters from the Segovia Woods, see *Texts Revolt*, 53–56.

95. *Texts Revolt*, 60. On the signatories of the Compromise, see G. Bonnevie-Noël, "Liste critique des signataires du Compromis des Nobles," *Vereniging voor de geschiedenis van het Belgisch protestantisme*, 5 ser., no. 3 (1968): 80–111, and the Brussels government's original tally in "Catalogue des gentilzhommes confederez," ARA Brussels, Audientie, no. 477/5, which lists 387 names.

palace in Brussels. April 5 was the Friday before Palm Sunday, the eve of the feast day of Our Lady of Seven Sorrows. Not only were confraternities dedicated to this veneration scattered throughout the cities of the Netherlands, the cult had been vigorously promoted by none other than the Dominicans—mendicants and inquisitors par excellence—and patronized by the court.[96] Our Lady of Seven Sorrows was part of a broader set of devotions to the Holy Mother, most of which received outright royal support and patronage for processions, chapels, and images. The presentation of the Compromise's petition before the religiously charged feast day weekend of Our Lady of Seven Sorrows and Palm Sunday was a risky act, the largest voicing of political dissent Brussels had yet seen and one for which an audience had been carefully sought.

Leaders of the Compromise had carefully planned the supplicatory procession. They had requested signatories to the Compromise to come to Brussels with as many horses as possible and without weapons. They had also sought an urban audience, urging citizens in Tournai, Antwerp, and Valenciennes, and elsewhere to attend, and even distributing some five thousand handbills one week prior to the event in Antwerp to solicit support. No wonder that Granvelle's faithful correspondent about Low Country affairs, Maximilian Morillon, the vicar general of Mechelen's archbishopric, fretted that the procession might involve some 1,200 people if all the lesser nobility turned out with their servants.[97] The Compromise's march mimicked the solemnity and grandeur of such great processions as the Brussels *ommegang*, or the Joyous Entry of a prince or visiting dignitary. Stylishly dressed, the noblemen entered Brussels on horseback, then in crisp order marched in a double column into the Coudenberg Palace. The manner in which they presented their official request was much like that of citizens issuing statements about urban rights and privileges during the traditional Blijde Inkomst. As such, the choice of the Friday before Psalm Sunday resonated in a second way. Christ's Passiontide entry into Jerusalem, as recorded by Matthew, was at the center of the Church's Advent liturgy, a rich fund of religious imagery seized upon by Philip the Good as early as 1458 to render his entries sacred. If the noblemen's procession anticipated Our Lady of Seven Sorrows, it looked even more to Palm Sunday weekend, coming up close upon advent celebrations in a way typically exploited by Burgundian ceremonialists for their own ritual purposes.[98] Whether intentional or not, the choice of the Friday before Palm Sunday by the nobles of the Compromise was so steeped in important religious time that their procession carried associations beyond that of a routine state visit.

96. G. Celis, *Volkskundige kalender voor het Vlaamsche land* (Ghent, 1990), 28–29, which incorrectly identifies the Friday before Palm Sunday as the feast day of Our Lady of Seven Sorrows. See also Verhoeven, *Devotie en Negotie*, 43–50.

97. For the handbill, see Duke, "Dissent, Propaganda, and Political Organization," 121, and for Morillon's comment, see *Corr. Granvelle*, 2:190, letter dated March 31, 1566.

98. Kipling, Enter the King, 22.

The master engraver of the Dutch Revolt, Frans Hogenberg, famously recorded the petition as part of the series of prints executed by his workshop chronicling the conflict and war with Spain. Born in Mechelen, Hogenberg gained his expertise in the vibrant humanist and artistic circles of Antwerp, even working for a stint for the engraver Hieronymous Cock. He fled Antwerp in the 1560s, apparently for religious reasons, and settled eventually in Cologne by 1570. There he safely issued his many engravings as separate sheets, though they later became incorporated into others' works, such as Michael Aitsinger's enormously popular *De Leone Belgico*, first printed in 1583. After Hogenberg's death in 1590, his widow and printmaker sons continued to expand his corpus.[99] His print of the petition, therefore, is not that of a witness to the ceremony, but that of a skilled graphic artist and canonizer of the Dutch Revolt's great historical moments. In Hogenberg's depiction, the physical and visual act of processional entry anchors the scene. We see the handsomely dressed noblemen—capes, doublets, and hats signs of aristocratic prestige—filing through the arched entryway, with the gateway assuming the same symbolic importance as an urban wall in the princely entry ceremony. The picture plane converges on the inner second archway, as members climb up the stairs to greet the regent.

The petition presented by the nobleman Hendrik van Brederode on behalf of the Compromise is visible through an open window, almost like a miniature box insert, in the center-right of the image. It is thus seen from afar, framed by the archway, and situated as a spatial endpoint to the sweep of moving bodies filing inside the courtyard. While heraldic symbols and allegories of rulership are engraved above each of the two archways, a smaller niche, placed exactly at the same level as the window through which we see the regent, holds the Virgin Mary, positioning her at the same level as Margaret herself. The visual confluence of the regent and the Virgin Mary implies an alliance of Catholicism, rulership, and womanhood amid a converging sea of aristocracy that marks off the political, gendered, and religious difference of these two sets of protagonists. The supplication of Brederode and the seated regent are seen in miniature, the focus more fixed on the swords, capes, and movement of the Compromise nobles into royal space.

Hogenberg perfectly captures the April 5 event as a display of aristocratic prestige and political muscle. It is curious, then, that the Compromise chose Philip of Bailleul, a lesser-known and physically handicapped nobleman from Artois, in lieu of their charismatic

---

99. Karel Kinds, *Kroniek van de opstand in de lage landen, 1555–1609: Actuele oorlogsverslaggeving uit de zestiende eeuw met 228 gravures van Frans Hogenberg* (Rekem, 1999), with the prints, a short introduction, and bibliography; F. Hogenberg, *De 80-jarige oorlog in prenten* (The Hague, 1977); and Christi M. Klinkert, *Nassau in het nieuws: Nieuwsprenten van Maurits van Nassaus militaire ondernemingen uit de periode 1590–1600* (Zutphen, 2005), 57–63, on Hogenberg's workshop. Hogenberg's legacy is not unlike that of Perrissin and Tortorel for Reformation France, for which see Philip Benedict, Lawrence B. Bryant, and Kristen B. Neuschel, "Graphic History: What Readers Knew and Were Taught in the Quarante Tableaux of Perrissin and Tortorel," *French Historical Studies* 28, no. 2 (Spring 2005): 175–229.

The aristocratic members of the Compromise of the Nobility make their dramatic entry into the Coudenberg Palace to petition Margaret of Parma to suspend the heresy placards on April 5, 1566. The success of their request led to the formation of the Order of the Beggars. Frans Hogenberg. Courtesy of the private collection of Karel Kinds.

leader, Hendrik van Brederode, to lead the procession.[100] But it was Brederode who read the plea to suspend the Inquisition and moderate the heresy laws before the regent and her Council of State. When finished, he and all the other assembled noblemen genuflected the *caracole*, an explicit military half-turn that pistol-bearing horsemen in the sixteenth century usually executed, before filing out of the palace.[101] It was at this moment, the chronicler Jacob van Wesenbeke claimed, that Charles, Count of Berlaymont, dismissively

---

100. H. A. Enno van Gelder, "Baillieul, Bronkhorst, Brederode," in his *Van beeldenstorm tot pacificatie*, 41; Van Nierop, "Beggars' Banquet," 426. On Brederode's place among Holland's senior nobility, see van Nierop, *Nobility of Holland*, 186–89.

101. Henne, *Mémoires de Pontus Payen*, 1:135.

advised the regent not to be frightened by a group of "beggars."[102] This was a remark of contempt, obviously inspired by the very act of petition, but perhaps one based on the fact that the handicapped Bailleul had led the train of noblemen.

The name stuck—and with reason, since the procession itself was orchestrated with the tension of purposely poised opposites. The fashionable display of several hundred privileged men bespoke power, but the leader of the grand retinue was a crippled noble, a reference to physical limitations and dependence, perhaps even to the lame who begged on the public streets. The procession was a forced entry into the regent's palace by the emboldened lesser nobility. Yet at the same time, their act was a petition, that is, a request contingent on the will of the recipient. In its language, the text Brederode read professed the Compromise's obedience as "good and loyal servants and faithful vassals," but warned of "disasters, disorder, sedition, revolt or bloodshed" if their entreaty was disregarded.[103] Finally, the noblemen insisted on their peaceful intentions but gave the *caracole*.[104]

The term "beggars" thus fitted the petitioners handily, even if it was uttered as a put-down. It parodied the noblemen's privilege by reference to their social opposites—a combination they had already invoked in the procession itself. Brilliantly staged and timed, the April 5 petition was also effective; on Monday April 8 the regent announced her intention to issue an official moderation the next day to suspend the placards and Inquisition until further notice. That night, the victorious *gentilshommes* of the Compromise celebrated a night of drink and cheer at the Count of Culemborg's palace. Buoyed by drink, Hendrik van Brederode stood to urge his fellow celebrants to adopt the sobriquet Beggars as their badge. Henk van Nierop has mined Pontus Payen's account of the banquet to emphasize that the carnivalesque dinner—with its toasts, oaths, and brandishing of beggars' wallets and wooden begging bowls—created a symbolic reservoir for their association. From the banquet inauguration of the new order to their ribald quality, the newly dubbed Beggars took their cues from the League of 1563, but proclaimed their message more aggressively and to a wider public. The revelers playfully deployed stock props bor-

---

102. C. Rahlenbeck, ed., *Mémoires de Jacques de Wesenbeke* (Brussels, 1859), 189, and *Kroniek Van Haecht*, 1:30. For an analysis, and for the scholarly debate over the etymology of the name "gueux," see van Nierop, "Beggars' Banquet," 419, esp. n. 4.

103. *Texts Revolt*, 64.

104. Charles Paillard, *Huit mois de la vie d'un peuple: Les Pays-Bas du premier janvier au premier septembre 1566* (Brussels, 1877), 80 n. 1, for the *caracole*, which he describes as close to a formation called the limanchon. I have been able to locate two other instances in 1566 in which the limanchon was performed: first at a public assembly of Calvinists in Tournai in July 1566 in the central marketplace; second, by a ragtag group of Calvinist soldiers from Flanders' Westkwartier in December 1566 at the abbey of Saint Nicholas of Chartreux outside Tournai before fighting forces under the command of the Baron of Rassenghien. See Alex. Pinchard, ed., *Mémoires de Pasquier de le Barre et de Nicolas Soldoyer pour servir à l'histoire de Tournai, 1565–70* 2 vols. (Brussels, 1859), 1:334, and *Troubles religieux*, 2:253.

rowed from the real and imagined practices of mendicants, as well as from other beggars, lepers, and outcasts.[105] The banquet also inaugurated a fraternal organization that mimicked royal and urban lay solidarities, especially the Order of the Golden Fleece, to which none of these midlevel nobles belonged. In lieu of the symbol of the lamb, the Beggars sported a medal bearing on one side the image of Philip II with the exclamation "Faithful to the king" and, on the other, a pair of clasped hands and a beggar's wallet with the inscription "To the point of wearing the beggars' pouch."[106] They also began to wear, in various combinations, a mendicant-like grey cloak, a begging bowl hung off the belt, a hat with miniature begging bowls and pilgrim bottles, and a moustache in the "Turkish style" that boasted a dash of exoticism and alluded to Philip's most hated enemy in the Mediterranean world. Reports in Antwerp even told of women with Beggars' earrings, and a brisk sale of miniature Beggars' bowls and medals.[107] A sixteenth-century portrait of a Beggar shows off symbols of pilgrimage, mendicancy, and martial vigor. The man stands alert; his grey mendicant outfit is embellished by a capacious pilgrim's cape. He wears a high hat and Turkish moustache, a Beggars' medal around his neck, and a Beggars' bowl and pumpkin-shaped flask off his belt. The sword in his left hand and the pistol in his right hand are prominent, underscoring the fact that although a supplicant, he is ready for action.[108]

The Order of the Beggars was an extension and elaboration of the League against Granvelle, with anticlericalism now burning hot, and inversion motifs fully pronounced. Indeed, Orange, Egmont, and Hornes had made a brief appearance at the Compromise's banquet. The regent suspected they were fully involved, but at the treason trial of Hornes in 1568, he insisted the three had paid an obligatory visit but politely refused to be seated, a position confirmed by the chronicler Pontus Payen.[109] At the heart of the Beggars' mockery was the tension between expressions of fidelity to the king and contempt for Catholic religious practice—voluntary poverty and its abuses, for example—and pretended empathy for social outcasts like the indigent and the disabled who had been under new cen-

---

105. Van Nierop, "Beggars' Banquet," with the emphasis on the banquet itself and the creation of the mock Order of Beggars. Payen's account is in Henne, *Mémoires de Pontus Payen*, 139–44. See also Magdi Tóth-Ubbens, *Verloren beelden van miserabele bedelaars* (Ghent, 1987), with a more general interest in policies and images of leprosy.

106. For the complicated history of the original Beggars medal and its subsequent variations, see Anton van der Lem, *Verbeeldingen van vrijheden: Partijtekens en nationale symboliek in de eerste decennia van de Tachtigjarige Oorlog, 1564–1584* (Utrecht, 2006), and G. van der Meer, "The Beggars' Medals Worn by the Rebellious Dutch Nobles in 1566," *The Medal* 33 (1998): 14–22.

107. *Kroniek Van Haecht*, 1:48–49.

108. Van Nierop, "Beggars' Banquet," 422, with the relevant primary sources. See also Duke, "Dissent, Propaganda, and Political Organization," which traces symbolic propaganda back to the League to oust Granvelle in 1563.

109. Henne, *Mémoires de Pontus Payen*, 141. Egmont similarly denied involvement. See Baron de Reiffenberg, ed., *Correspondance de Marguerite d'Autriche*, 346.

82 BEGGARS, ICONOCLASTS, AND CIVIC PATRIOTS

The popular Beggars' medal with Philip II on one side and the clasped hands and Beggars' wallet on the other, 1566. Courtesy of Geldmuseum, Utrecht.

tralized poor laws since at least the 1530s. In a letter to Philip II dated April 2, 1566, Margaret of Parma expressed vexation about the Beggars' double entendre: Were they good vassals playfully expressing their loyalty to the king, or were they serious troublemakers claiming allegiance to the "malheureux?"[110] That ambiguity, of course, was the very point, the petition ceremony a polysemic ritual that allowed the Beggars to imagine—even scheme—revolt while professing allegiance. It was sharpened even more by the timing of these events. The Beggars' April 5 petition to Margaret of Parma, their April 8 banquet, their donning of a livery, their marketing of signs and symbols—all this was accomplished in festive merriment around the weekend of Palm Sunday, the culmination of Lent. The solemnity and grandeur of the Friday procession and the cheerful abandon of the Monday night debauch, both made positive reference to the closing of the Lenten season and subverted its abstemiousness.

The Netherlands nobles and court officials who opposed the Beggars eventually seized on the Virgin Mary to mount a visual counterattack, though their decision to wait until late fall to do so weakened this attempt to neutralize the dissenters. The particular veneration chosen was Notre Dame de Halle, featured on a silver pilgrim's medal bearing the image of Christ as Salvator Mundi. The Duke of Aarschot and other loyalists wore the medal pinned on their hats, for which a papal indulgence was awarded.[111] As we have seen, this

110. This matter is discussed in Tóth-Ubbens, *Verloren beelden van miserabele bedelaars*, 46. For the April 3 letter, see *Corr. Philippe II*, 1:408.

111. The first mention of the Halle medal, however, was not until late fall 1566, sometime between October 27 and November 1; see *Corr. Granvelle*, 2:65, and also Strada, *Thien eerste boecken der Nederlandsche oorlogen*, 1:292–93.

A handsomely outfitted member of the Order of Beggars. Courtesy of Nationaal Archief, the Netherlands, Handschriften Derde Afdeling, 3.22.01.02, inv. nr. 1672, The Hague.

The Notre Dame de Halle medal that opponents of the Beggars sported by the fall of 1566 as part of their response to the Beggars' movement and the popularity of their symbols. Courtesy of the Geldmuseum, Utrecht.

small chapel not far from Brussels had been a favorite of Burgundian dukes. It not only housed the remains of Philip the Bold, the first Valois duke of Burgundy, but also several ex-voto gifts from Burgundian leaders, and, more tellingly, mementos from defeated subjects like the guild banners from Ghent in 1453. While the Beggars had timed their procession to coincide with the feast day of Our Lady of Seven Sorrows, Aarschot and his loyalist opponents responded by rallying around that Madonna most associated with royal power and patronage.

The triumph of the Beggars and the suspension of the Inquisition and heresy persecutions inaugurated a golden summer for the noble opposition and the southern Low Country Calvinists. Leading figures like Brederode reveled in their victory by luxuriating in their new satirical order in public. Already by April 11, Brederode and several associates made a splashy entry on horseback into Antwerp outfitted "from head to feet" in the Beggars' livery; in July, he essentially set up camp in the city.[112] In late June, Brederode rode triumphantly into Amsterdam, hailed by enthusiasts there as the great Beggar—and laying the groundwork for early July pro-Beggar revelries held at the meeting house of the archers guild that imitated the riotous good cheer of the original Brussels inaugural dinner, complete with satirical jabs at the mendicants and beer-drenched exclamations in honor of the king.[113]

112. *Kroniek Van Haecht*, 1:30; *Corr. Granvelle*, 1:354; Rahlenbeck, ed., *Mémoires de Jacques de Wesenbeke*, 234.

113. "Anteykeningen gedaen van Broer Hendrik van Biesten, Orateur van de Minnebroeders binnen Amsterdam, op de nijeuwe mare en geschiedenis, dat geschiet is binner en omtrent Amsterdam, sedert de jaere 1534 tot den jaere 1567, getrouwelijc gecomponiert," *De Dietsche Warande* 7 (1866): 532–33.

Meanwhile, hundreds of exiled Calvinists streamed back to their homeland as a result of the suspension of the placards, triggering a remarkable revival of the field sermons that had so vexed urban and state authorities a few years earlier. Underground preachers and ministers went public, while new ones arrived from England, France, Geneva, and the German territories. They were a mixed lot. For every well-trained Geneva minister with an impressive Latin name there was the apostate priest lacking polish, such as the Limburg pastor Jan van Gutekoven, popularly named "Kackhoes" (Outhouse), or the rustic evangelical, such as Sebastian Matte in the Flemish Westkwartier, a former hatmaker.[114]

Learned observers like the acute Ghent chronicler Marcus van Vaernewijck responded to the great swell in sermons with curiosity and condescension. He described "a small band of people of little morals, most outsiders who had come to work as journeymen in Ghent," who gathered safely outside the city in mid-June. The preacher delivered his sermon atop a mill ladder, urging passersby to hear God's word. A few weeks later, another delivered his sermon bareheaded in an ermine-trimmed robe on a makeshift pulpit on a small hill. He spoke in the dialect of Kortrijk, clutched a cheap psalter in his hands, and prayed that the "God might enlighten the minds of the magistrates, king, and the pope so that the Word may go forward in peace." His audience sat in rows of three, "men, women, and young girls," all with inexpensive psalm books from which they sang. There were more onlookers than participants—or so said his washwoman, who had been among those who gullible enough to marvel at the event.[115] Not just this observation but everything about Van Vaernewijck's description emphasized his learned disdain for these work-a-day evangelicals. Peopled by foreign workmen, women, and girls, led by a bumpkin preacher who spoke in a regional dialect, guided by cheap psalters, this was a congregation of unlettered provincials pathetically making appeals to pope and king. Van Vaernewijck, however, would soon revise his evaluation. The sermons accelerated, grew bigger, and drew in a wider arc of social backgrounds. He described the new preacher Nicasius van der Schuere as a sober, educated, and upright man, son of a Ghent wine merchant, whose sermon on July 3 attracted a crowd of rich and poor alike, including the Count of Batenburg. A week later, Van Vaernewijck reported, attendance at another sermon had spiked to nine thousand.[116]

The growing popularity of the hedge sermons and their social heterogeneity greatly worried urban magistrates. So did the tenacity of the sermon goers, who ignored official

---

114. For a consideration of the ministers and pastors, see Crew, *Calvinist Preaching and Iconoclasm*. On van Gutekoven, see J. Scheerder, *Beeldenstorm*, 91, and W. Bax, *Het Protestantisme in het bisdom Luik en vooral te Maastricht, 1557–1612* (The Hague, 1941), 128. On Matte, *Troubles religieux*, 4:38–40.

115. BT *Van Vaernewijck*, 1:2–3. On Van Vaernewijck's social background, public career in Ghent, and his intellectual disposition, see Koen Lamont, *Het wereldbeeld van een zestiende eeuwse Gentenaar Marcus van Vaernewijck* (Ghent, 2005).

116. BT *Van Vaernewijck*, 1:8 and 21.

proscriptions issued by various cities and braved, in the words of Van Vaernewijck, "cold and hot, rain and wind."[117] So taxed were city officials in Valenciennes that they employed three spies on July 7, 1566, to describe the sermon goers' activities and gather names.[118] What is more, the spike in hedge sermons in the summer of 1566 was not limited to the southern Netherlands. In Holland, what started as a series of sermons held within the safe confines of the Count of Culemborg's castle in early June branched out by July into a series of open-air gatherings outside Haarlem, Alkmaar, and, daringly, Amsterdam, a town so notorious for "the cruelty of the magistrates . . . that on account of the burning and slaughter of people there for their faith, was known not as Amsterdam but Murderdam."[119] However numerous Amsterdam's Calvinists, the city's Catholic burgomasters prevented sermons near the city, with the result that they took place in nearby Hoorn and Overveen. One of the most energetic of the Reformed preachers conducting these services was Jan Arentsz., a basket maker from Alkmaar, who defied the placards against public preaching by doing precisely that on July 14 in a field near Hoorn. Shortly thereafter, he gathered a large crowd outside Alkmaar, and according to the eyewitness account by the Amsterdam Calvinist merchant Laurens Jacobsz. Reael, "Among those that heard him were several clergy, who were most astonished, that this basket maker, a mere layman, should expound the Holy Scriptures so pertinently, and use such method and order in a sermon that lasted about four hours."[120] On the last day of July, services were finally held outside Amsterdam itself—a sign of the Reformed community's growing public confidence—and in August the preaching spread more widely, to Delft and Leiden among other places. This included The Hague, where attendees brazenly gathered to hear a sermon before the home of the president of the provincial court, Cornelis Suis, who had opposed their activity.[121]

Although thoroughly different from the activities of the dissenting nobles and their Order of the Beggars, the remarkable Calvinist hedge sermons of Hainault, Flanders, Brabant, and Holland had the similar goal of crafting a public profile for the Reformed movement. In doing so, they transgressed local laws proscribing their gatherings, while

---

117. Ibid., 1:56.

118. "Déposition faite le 8e du mois de Juillet 1566 par devant Couronnel et de le Val," *Bulletin de la Commission de l'Histoire des Eglises Wallonnes*, ser. 1, vol. 3 (1887): 160–88, and C. Paillard, "Les grands prêches Calvinistes de Valenciennes," *Société de l'Histoire du Protestantisme Français* 26 (1887): 33–43, 73–80.

119. G. Brandt, *Historie der Reformatie en andre kerkelycke geschiedenissen in en ontrent de Nederlanden*, 4 vols. (Amsterdam, 1671–1704), 1:314–15, which account made use of the writings of the Amsterdam merchant Laurens Jacobsz. Reael, only fragments of which have survived. See *Uittreksel uit de Amsterdamsche gedenkschriften van Laurens Jacobsz. Reael, 1542–1567*, ed. Joh. C. Breen, *Bijdragen en mededelingen van het Historisch Genootschap gevestigd te Utrecht* 17 (1896): 1–60.

120. *Uittreksel uit de Amsterdamsche gedenkschriften van Laurens Jacobsz. Reael*, 20.

121. Ibid., 22–24.

professing allegiance to the king. Such utterances of loyalty in the teeth of defiance defined the Beggars, whose motto was "Faithful to the king to the point of wearing the Beggars' pouch." For the gentilshommes, such a proclamation was, of course, an ironic ploy, a part of their anticlerical antics and a reference to their official political status as dependent vassals. The hedge sermons lacked the parodic quality of the Beggars, while still managing the same balancing act between solemn assertions of fidelity and armed demonstrations of their independent command of space, time, and place. While the sermons were held in fields, meadows, and woods, they were prefaced and concluded with public assertions over key urban spaces and places with the processional element being as ritually important as the gathering itself.

In a few instances, Calvinist ceremonialism daringly butted up against expressions of social grievances, threatening a dangerous coalescence. The Tournai magistrate and fiscal procurer Pasquier de le Barre was executed in 1568 during Alba's reign for his complicity in the iconoclastic riots of 1566. Before his capture, de le Barre had catalogued, as part of his diary of the eight tumultuous years in Tournai from 1559 to 1567, a mounting series of hedge sermons and processions by that city's Calvinists. The culmination was a July 25, 1566 armed rally at the city's central marketplace after a sermon outside the city behind the abbey of Prestz-aux-Nonnains.[122] Only two days earlier, the same marketplace had experienced a grain riot during which the house of the merchant Michel Baudelet—dubbed "the red house" by rioters since it had been built on profits from "the blood of the poor"— came under attack. Baudelet and other merchants were accused of hoarding grain and inflating its price when the commodity was unusually scarce.[123] De le Barre notes that the sermon-goers returned, marched to the marketplace in a "military formation," and, once assembled, performed the *limanchon*, a martial formation akin to the *caracole*.[124] The magistrates went further, describing the Calvinist procession as a "battle formation" that together with their marketplace assembly were "acts of manifest disobedience and public sedition."[125] The armed showing was so closely aligned to the grain riot as to make the two events shade into one another. Further, the Calvinist performance of the *limanchon* evoked the martial maneuver performed by the Compromise earlier that April in Brussels. Indeed, during the field sermons overt signs of kinship with the Beggars were not unknown. The Tournai merchant Jacques Gombault was executed in 1569 for, among other

---

122. For biographical details about de le Barre, see Pinchard, *Mémoires*, 1:xv–xxviii, including a transcription of the sentence pronounced against him by the Council of Troubles; and Steen, *Time of Troubles in the Low Countries*.

123. Pinchard, *Mémoires*, 1:115–16.

124. Ibid., 1:107, also confirmed by the Catholic chronicler Nicolas Soldoyer, whose memoirs are in ibid., 2:236–38.

125. Letter of the Tournai magistrates to Margaret of Parma, dated July 26, 1566, in ibid., 1:334–36.

crimes, wearing the "symbol of the Beggars around his neck" on his way to a hedge sermon there in 1566.[126]

By August 1566 the Netherlands was riven with religious dissent as the field sermons peaked in the south and north. Meanwhile, the Beggars flaunted their popularity while the senior nobility tried desperately to gain control of a situation they had set in motion. This effort included a meeting held between Orange, Egmont, and leaders of the Beggars on July 12 at Duffel, outside Antwerp. At the gathering, Brederode, Culemborg, and the others insisted on legal toleration for Protestants and the summoning of the States General.[127] Orange favored liberty of conscience but not yet an explicit legalization of Protestantism. Egmont was even more conservative. Orange's hope for a political reconciliation dimmed, and the "belle tragédie" he earlier predicted after receiving copies of Philip II's letters from the Segovia Woods seemed increasingly likely.[128] Orange warned his younger brother, Count Louis of Nassau, and Brederode that Calvinists were flirting too dangerously with "disobedience and sedition," but was unsuccessful in slowing down the field sermons and other Calvinist public activity.[129] Yet however much great noblemen like Orange were eager to make a social and political distinction between themselves and the Compromise, the two were increasingly conflated in the minds of more than a piqued regent and a furious king. Maximilian Morillon reported to Granvelle that when Orange entered Antwerp on July 13 to help in his capacity as burgrave to stabilize a city rocked by religious dissent, he was greeted with cheers of "Vivent les Gueux!" (Long live the Beggars!).[130] This emerging rallying cry, Morillon indignantly noted, was "now the vogue" among youth who daringly exclaimed it loudly, and no longer followed the salutation with "Vive le Roy!"[131]

Seven and a half years after Charles V's dignified funeral in Brussels and Orange's liturgical exclamation on behalf of Philip II, vows in support of the Beggars now were detached from those to the king. This political and cultural turn of events was rapid and two-pronged. First, the grands seigneurs and their League and the gentilshommes with the Compromise and the Order of the Beggars had loosened their unquestioning fidelity to the crown. Second, a robust Calvinist movement, firm in its convictions, had emerged in various urban centers. Both these associations of dissent had professed overt loyalty to royal power and respect for its cultural appurtenances. But both sets of players also reg-

---

126. Moreau, Histoire du Protestantisme à Tournai, 349; A. L. E. Verheyden, Le Conseil des Troubles (Flavion, 1981), 121.
127. Parker, Dutch Revolt, 73; Rachfahl, Wilhelm von Oranien, 2:678–80.
128. Swart, William the Silent, 13.
129. Letter of July 16, 1566, in Archives d'Orange-Nassau, 2:158–59.
130. Corr. Granvelle, 1:375. On Orange's residency in Antwerp, see Wells, "Antwerp and the Government of Philip II," 441–63.
131. Corr. Granvelle, 1:392.

istered their dissent through careful interventions in religious times and urban spaces, through the use of popular media previously unexploited for political purposes, and through ritual public acts that evoked those used in earlier traditions of collective action. The 1563 League evoked anticlericalism and the carnivalesque; the urban Calvinists mocked the Catholic religious calendar and borrowed processional motifs from the world of urban ceremonialism; the Compromise and Beggars fashioned highly strategic public associations of protest. Everything about these dissenters' deeds violated the social legislation Charles V had enacted and put pressure on the sacred practices and patronages that extended back to the fifteenth-century Burgundian dukes. These violations were sometimes more implied than explicit, but no less potent. In giving form and content to dissent in the public realm, they shook the representational universe the Burgundian–Habsburg dynasty had set firmly in place. As much as Granvelle and his colleagues implored the king to come to the Low Countries to settle matters, convinced that his political and ceremonial presence would restore public order, Philip II declined in favor of more urgent preoccupations in the Mediterranean.[132] While the ritual center of Burgundian–Habsburg authority atrophied, the public realm was soon shaken to its core by the great iconoclastic riots of late summer and fall 1566.

132. See, for example, Granvelle's direct appeal to Philip II about the value of his physical presence in a letter dated May 20, 1566, in ibid., 1:265–68.

CHAPTER 3 **VIVENT LES GUEUX!**
ICONOCLASM, INVERSION, AND THE
PROBLEM OF AUTHORITY

About Philips Moreel we know precious little, except the crime for which he was sentenced to death by hanging on May 8, 1568, by a court in Cassel. Sometime shortly after the first iconoclastic riots broke out on August 10, 1566 in Flanders' Westkwartier, an area rife with Calvinist agitation, Moreel rushed into the parish church in the community of Watou with a small group of accomplices. Brazenly, he committed "great acts of insolence and iconoclasm" by attacking the church's images and its statues, particularly the one of Saint Christopher, which he stabbed through the leg with a knife. Moreel then took an iron hammer and "other tools" and completely destroyed the center altar and a retable on the altar of Our Lady. Local parishioners gathered to watch, and implored Moreel and his companions to stop. But apparently relishing the audience, Moreel only grew bolder. He demanded beer in return for ceasing the violence, but when the upset onlookers hurriedly provided five or six jugs, Moreel left, only to return the next day and continue the destruction. After pulling down several images and dunking them upside down into the baptismal font, Moreel taunted a horrified churchwarden who had come for the baptism of a child, jeering to the man as he rushed out of the church, "Baptize the child: Vivent les Gueux!"[1]

The specter of iconoclasm had worried many, the regent included, but it began not in Brussels or Antwerp, nor Tournai or Valenciennes, as was feared, but rather in places like Watou in Flanders' Westkwartier. The first target was a small chapel dedicated to Saint Lawrence outside Steenvoorde, on August 10. Much to the government's dismay, from there the destruction spread with remarkable speed. In the weeks that followed, iconoclasm coursed through the entire Westkwartier, taking its toll on more than four hundred churches and chapels. By the third week of August, iconoclastic riots gripped the big cities of the southern Netherlands, Antwerp included, before moving steadily and surely north-

---

1. Moreel's sentence by the court of Cassel, dated May 8, 1568, is reproduced in *Troubles religieux*, 2:98–99. Neither his profession nor the exact day of the first attack is specified, though Moreel is cited again in the local bailiff's registers, ibid., 2:134.

ward, into Holland and elsewhere. By September 14, iconoclasm had reached as far north as windswept Winsum in the Groningen Ommelanden (the area surrounding the city of Groningen), covering all the major territories of the Low Countries, where images, statues, and ecclesiastical and liturgical materials were either violently cast down by small but determined crowds or removed peacefully by legal fiat, as at Culemborg or in Friesland.[2]

Although iconoclasm was as old as Karlstadt's attack in Wittenberg in 1521, although it had occurred widely in German and Swiss principalities and in England, France, and Scotland, although it had been predicted in the Netherlands, still no one could have foreseen just how extensively it would affect the Low Countries. After all, this was the land of independent-minded but conservative town magistrates, a Catholic majority, and a king who famously insisted on a hard line for these territories. Indeed, two days after the August 10 attack in Steenvoorde, Philip II reiterated to Don Luis de Requesens, then his ambassador in Rome, a point he had made a year earlier: "Thus, you can assure His Holiness, that before suffering the smallest thing that would bring prejudice to religion and service to God, I would lose all my states, and would lose even a hundred lives, if I had them, for I could never be a lord of heretics."[3]

---

2. The best overview of Low Country iconoclasm is J. Scheerder, *De Beeldenstorm* (Bussum, 1974). See also M. Dierickx, "Beeldenstorm in de Nederlanden in 1566," *Streven* 19 (1966): 1040–48; O. J. de Jong, *Beeldenstorm in de Nederlanden* (Groningen, 1964); Crew, *Calvinist Preaching and Iconoclasm*, esp. 20–38; Alastair Duke, "De Calvinisten en de 'Paapse Beeldendienst': De denkwereld van de beeldenstormers van 1566," in *Mensen van de Nieuwe Tijd: Een liber amicorum voor A. Th. van Deursen*, ed. M. Bruggeman et al. (Amsterdam, 1996), 29–45; S. Deyon and A. Lottin, *Les "casseurs" de l'été 1566: L'iconoclasme dans le nord de la France* (Paris, 1981); David Freedberg, *Iconoclasm and Painting in the Revolt of the Netherlands, 1566–1609* (New York, 1988); and Peter Arnade, "The Rage of the Canaille: Iconoclasm and the Problem of Authority in the Wonder Year of 1566," in *Fever Running in the Blood: Feelings and Representing Emotions in the Heart of the Town*, ed. Anne-Laure van Bruaene and Elodie LeCuppre-Desjardin (Turnhout, 2005), 93–111. Regionally specific studies include M. Backhouse, *Beeldenstorm en Bosgeuzen in Het Westkwartier (1566–1568): Bijdrage tot de geschiedenis van de godsdiensttroebelen der Zuidelijke Nederlanden in de XVIe eeuw* (Kortrijk, 1971); A. C. Duke and D. H. A. Kolff, "The Time of Troubles in the Country of Holland, 1566–1567," *Tijdschrift voor Geschiedenis* 82 (1969): 316–37; H. F. K. van Nierop, *Beeldenstorm en burgerlijk verzet in Amsterdam, 1566–1567* (Nijmegen, 1978).

3. *Corr. Philippe II*, 1:445–46 for Philip's quote, a reiteration of a point he had made in 1565, ibid., 1:346–47. The literature on iconoclasm during the Reformation is vast. Important contributions outside the Low Countries include John Philips, *The Reformation of Images: Destruction of Art in England, 1535–1660* (Berkeley, 1973); Eamon Duffy, *The Stripping of the Altars: Traditional Religion in England, 1400–1580* (New Haven, 1992); D. McRoberts, "Material Destruction Caused by the Scottish Reformation," in *Essays on the Scottish Reformation, 1535–1625*, ed. David McRoberts (Glasgow, 1962), 415–62; Olivier Christin, *Un Révolution symbolique: L'iconoclasme huguenot et la reconstruction catholique* (Paris, 1991); the historiographical overview in Denis Crouzet, "A propos de la plasticité de la violence réformée au temps des premières guerres de Religion," *Bulletin de la société de l'Histoire du Protestantisme français* 148 (2002): 907–51; Martin Warnke, ed., *Die Zerstörung des Kunstwerks* (Frankfurt, 1988); Mathias Müller, *Von der Kunst des calvinistischen Bildersturms* (Marburg, 1993); Lee Palmer Wandel, *Voracious Idols and Violent Hands: Iconoclasm in Zurich, Strasbourg and Basel* (Cambridge, 1994). Important considerations of the image question are in Margarete Stirm, *Die Bilderfrage in der Reformation* (Gütersloh, 1977); Carl Christensen, *Art and the Reformation in Germany*

This chapter and the next explore iconoclasm as the apogee of the wonder year, important both for the repertoire of destruction it spawned and the ways its violence echoed and interacted with the broader political turmoil of 1566. In this consideration of the Westkwartier and nearby areas where iconoclasm first started, I show how the rioters paid close attention to their targets and how their social station patterned how and why they acted as they did. In doing so, I underscore two points. First, the social and material specificity of the rioters' actions can tell us much about their critique of image worship and the Catholic mass. Through the acts of destruction fomented by men like Philips Moreel with his iron hammer and other work tools, the iconoclasts of the Westkwartier region exposed religious objects and images as so much wood, canvas, stone, alabaster, marble, metalwork, and other materials, reading these revered objects as mere concrete matter. Theirs was sacred behavior that aimed to detach the holy from its material referent, and their actions are more complex than a priori formulas of ritual desacralization or carnivalesque behaviors. As we shall see, iconoclasm in the Westkwartier and its surrounding areas drew heavily from these cultural stores, but not mechanically so, because the rioters' actions were both more concrete and more contingent than these scripts—a violent series of acts that defies easy classification.

In current understandings of sixteenth-century religious violence, we are now accustomed to viewing religious riots as contests over sacredness and its location, over the boundaries between the pure and impure; we read the violence against persons and objects as the culmination of these contestations, and not a consequence of a grain riot or bad economic times, as one school of interpretation once advocated. But if material life is no longer seen as a causative trigger to the early modern religious riot, it is also downplayed as an analytical category more generally.[4] My reading of iconoclasm asks us to return to the material and the social not as interpretive categories of causation but as references points for how iconoclasts in the Low Countries experienced their sacred commitments.[5] The artisanal ethos of the Westkwartier iconoclasts is a reminder of how religious practice is shaped by local inflections and of how larger sixteenth century debates about the precise location of the holy reverberated widely. Catholics saw images and ob-

---

(Athens, Ohio, 1980); Carlos M. N. Eire, *War against the Idols: The Reformation of Worship from Erasmus to Calvin* (Cambridge, 1986); and Joseph Leo Koerner, *The Reformation of the Image* (Chicago, 2004).

4. Natalie Zemon Davis, "The Rites of Violence: Religious Riot in Sixteenth-Century France," in her *Society and Culture in Early Modern France* (Stanford, 1975), 152–87 is the classic formulation, though not about iconoclasm, but rather the violent paroxysms between Huguenots and Catholics in France in the 1560s and the collective rituals that were their instruments. See also Mack P. Holt, "Putting Religion Back into the Wars of Religion," *French Historical Studies*, 18, no. 2 (Fall 1993): 524–51.

5. John Bossy, "Unrethinking the Sixteenth-Century Wars of Religion," in *Belief in History: Innovative Approaches to European and American Religion*, ed. Thomas Kselman (Notre Dame, 1991), 267–85, and Susan Rosa and Dale van Kley, "Religion and the Historical Discipline: A Reply to Mack Holt and Henry Heller," *French Historical Studies* 21, no. 4 (Fall 1998): 611–29.

jects as vessels of sacred matter; the iconoclasts, by contrast, acted with exuberant violence to deny this proposition, and attacked their religious targets precisely to expose the material girders behind the miracle-working objects, images, and liturgical items—the wood, glass, plaster, marble, polychrome, and other components that the heavy blows of hammers, axes, and ramming rods exposed as the "reality" of the representation. For sixteenth-century Catholics and Protestants, these very material components of religious veneration begged the question of whether the holy was present in sacred representation; this was the most urgent matter at hand, one that was fought bitterly in the heat of riot and other social arenas as much as from the pulpit or the theologian's treatise.

My second point is more general but no less urgent. Iconoclasm in the Low Countries was both a theological project and social labor, but it was something more: a heavy blow to the more than century-long quest by the Valois and Habsburg Burgundian princes to consecrate their authority through managing the sacred. Direct attacks against explicit symbols of royal authority did occur, but as we shall see, they were the exception to an otherwise scrupulous vigilance the rioters exercised with regard to representations of the sovereign and his symbols and insignia. Be that as it may, the iconoclasts' brazen destruction of a huge inventory of religious objects, images, and artifacts across the sweep of the Low Countries may have varied in form—sometimes taken down peacefully, sometimes attacked with unspoken pious resolve, and sometimes with ribald, scabrous excess—but was uniform in destabilizing the way sacred devotions and representations anchored both the religious world and public authority. In a political universe already bruised by the acts of dissent and the religious and party allegiances that emerged between 1561 and 1566, iconoclasm threatened to shatter the representational universe the Burgundians had carefully nourished.

Even more fundamentally, the riots were no sideshow to the great constitutional and theological debates of 1566, but their dynamic interlocutor. Since the first histories of the Dutch Revolt by the Antwerp-born Emanuel van Meteren and Utrecht notary Pieter Bor onward, historians have too often bracketed iconoclasm off from the great constitutional quarrels and debates over religious policy that fueled the main stage show in Brussels. To many such historians, the importance of iconoclasm lay in its consequences and less in its actual deeds because the aftershocks of the riots forced everyone—from the grands seigneurs to Philip II—to reposition themselves.[6] But attention to the actions of the iconoclasts in the Westkwartier and elsewhere suggests just as powerfully that their acts were determinative, a fusion of religious sentiment and popular action that played on the same terrain as the elite actors jockeying for influence and wielding authority in Brussels and

---

6. For example, Bor dedicated a mere ten pages of his magisterial study to the iconoclasm of 1566; see Bor, *Oorsprongk*, 1:82–92. On his and Van Meteren's inattention to iconoclasm, see Duke, "De Calvinisten en de 'Paapse Beeldendienst'," 29–30.

other great cities across the Low Countries. When Philips Moreel and his unnamed companions attacked the small church in Watou, they did so with an audience present to witness their deed as a public act and declaration of intention. What is more, Moreel chose to engage those gathered to watch him in disbelief, bartering with them for beer as he negotiated whether to continue or stop his desecration. But it is Moreel's taunt that a child should be baptized with the name "Vivent les Gueux!" that alerts us to the broader significance with which the iconoclasts intended to align their acts of destruction. No matter how minor the act of violence carried out in Watou, Moreel made sure to link it to the Beggars and the broader campaign of religious and political dissent being waged in Brussels and other metropolitan areas in 1566.

Part of the reason for scholarly inattention to the significance of time, space, and objects attacked by Low Country iconoclasts and their relationship to the era's political culture is the division among historians in the Low Countries over whether the religious violence was actually about religion—a division that mirrors more explicit historiographical quarrels with which a whole generation of historians of the French religious wars have wrestled.[7] To an earlier generation of social and economic historians, the fact that iconoclasm was launched in the center of new draperies and proto-proletarianization, where hand-to-mouth day laborers swelled the population and economic problems festered, is proof enough that this religious violence was a surrogate for economic grievances.[8] Historians of the Reformation have acknowledged that economic woes contributed to a climate of unease, but have countered that iconoclasm was exactly what it purported to be: Calvinist theology in action, with the rioters enacting scripts drafted for them by their Calvinist ministers and preachers.[9] The effect of each school of thought is to read iconoclastic acts through the prism of a predetermined cause, be it economic want or Protestant image criticism. The violence was hot and extensive, but since the causes

---

7. Best appraised in Holt, "Putting Religion Back into the Wars of Religion." The most forthright case for the role of religious inspiration and, in particular, apocalyptic thinking, as a master key to French Calvinist actions in the French religious wars is Denis Crouzet's *Les guerriers de Dieu: La violence au temps des troubles de religion, vers 1525–vers 1610*, 2 vols. (Seyssel, 1990).

8. This line of argument, best articulated by Eric Kuttner in *Hongerjaar 1566* (Amsterdam, 1949), was no historiographical sidebar, since it was adumbrated by none other than Henri Pirenne. See his "Une crise industrielle au XVI siècle: La draperie urbaine et la nouvelle draperie de Flandre," in *Histoire économique de l'Occident médiéval* (Paris, 1951): 621–53. For similar interpretations, see Emile Coornaert, *Un centre industriel d'autrefois: La draperie-sayetterie d'Hondschoote, XIV–XVII siècles* (Paris, 1930), and Herman van der Wee, "The Economy as a Factor in the Start of the Revolt of the Netherlands," *Acta Historiae Neerlandica*, 5 (Leiden, 1971), 52–67.

9. Crew, *Calvinist Preaching and Iconoclasm*; Scheerder, *Beeldenstorm*; Johan Decavele, "De reformatorische beweging te Axel en Hulst (1556–1566)," *Bijdragen voor de Geschiedenis der Nederlanden* 22 (1968–69): 1–42, is a more subtle analysis, but Decavele strongly leans toward the Reformed religious currents explored in his *Dageraard*. For a good, though dated, debate among proponents of both schools, see Dierickx, "Beeldenstorm."

had been predetermined, the actions were secondary, an inexhaustible catalogue of smashed statues, knifed paintings, decimated tabernacles, broken rood screens, cracked baptismal fonts, and pilfered chapels. Paying close attention to the acts of iconoclasts like Philips Moreel and his peers, however, allows their behaviors to shed their scholarly albatross as epiphenomena. Iconoclasts were not ventriloquists for economic grief or social complaint, nor the worker bees for the theological projects of Calvinist ministers. They were people, almost all of Reformed conviction; the majority in the Westkwartier were craftsmen and laborers who were alert to the tussles of their age, and convinced through their religious principles that the sacred representations Catholics so vigorously attended could be exposed as nothing more a mere assemblage of materials. Their sensibility was material, their means was physical destruction, and their inspiration was squarely religious. But as iconoclasts like Philips Moreel rioted to the party slogan of "Vivent les Gueux!" before crowds like the astonished parishioners of Watou, they declared a political affiliation, linking their actions to the other great events of the wonder year.

Textiles, Heresy, and Reformed Sentiment: Flanders' Westkwartier

Flanders was a county known more for its great medieval cities, their trade and commerce, and their cultural glow than for its small towns and rural hinterlands. Yet most of the county's low-lying territory was dedicated to agriculture and was dotted with small towns, especially in west and southwest Flanders. By 1566 this area known as the Westkwartier had evolved into a busy production center for rural draperies, particularly cheaper and lighter serge cloth. Home to booming small cities like Hondschoote, Armentières, Nieuwkerke, and Poperinge, it was administratively divided into seven castellanies that were de facto territorial communes, with their own laws, courts of jurisdiction, and relationship to the Count of Flanders.[10] The area had attracted thousands of workers, drawn to opportunities outside the tightly regulated drapery industries in Ypres, Ghent, Valenciennes, and elsewhere, themselves evolving to meet new demands and changing economic circumstances.[11] Small Westkwartier towns swelled in population. Hondschoote, the center of the new draperies, jumped from an estimated population of 2,500 in 1469 to 15,000 in the 1560s. There, the textile industry in serge developed in the firm hands of tradesmen, small dealers, and brokers who employed an army of workers. These were a heterogeneous group who came from surrounding areas where the big cities of Bruges

---

10. Backhouse, *Beeldenstorm en Bosgeuzen*; *Troubles religieux*, each volume of which is prefaced with general legal information about the different castellanies.

11. H. van der Wee, ed., *The Rise and Decline of Urban Industries in Italy and the Low Countries (Late Middle Ages–Early Modern Times)* (Louvain, 1988).

and Ypres had prohibited rural textiles in an effort to monopolize the industry, and from such faraway locations as Holland, Friesland, England, France, and Strasbourg. Most did not have privileged journeyman status, but toiled as day laborers eking out an existence as pieceworkers, wool combers, wool washers, and the like. Some might own their own tools, but many did not; some worked at home, others in their master's workshop.[12]

The production of lighter serge cloth, made largely from Spanish wool, helped Flanders weather economic downswings in the northwestern European textile industries. But it also placed capital in the hands of a small clique of draper-merchants, and drew on a sizable army of impecunious workers. Aggressive economic development, grossly uneven distribution of wealth, and an immigrant workforce make for a combustible mix in any circumstance. In the context of burgeoning political problems between the nobility and the Brussels government and the luxuriant spread of urban Calvinism, these social forces were all the more vexing. The Westkwartier bordered French territory and lined the West Flemish coast, across whose North Sea an exile community of Netherlands Calvinists flourished in London and in Sandwich, the latter town a particular breeding ground for those of a more radical stripe. The Westkwartier also was washed by historical currents of peasant radicalism and anticlericalism. Here one of the greatest late-medieval peasant rebellions had flared between 1323 and 1328, producing such peasant leaders as Jacob Peyt, captain of the district of Bergues, who proclaimed that he wanted to rid the land of priests and confiscate their goods.[13]

In the 1560s Calvinism gained a sure footing in the Westkwartier, preoccupying the tireless inquisitor general of Flanders, Pieter Titelmans, and prompting officials from the Council of Flanders, after an October 1561 visit to the castellany of Bailleul, to write the regent that any strict enforcement of the hated heresy placards would provoke "a terrible bloodbath that would result in the depopulation and destruction of the entire castellany."[14] As Johan Decavele has shown, the Westkwartier abounded in Protestant activity: of the 2,793 cases of heresy suspected in Flanders between 1521 and June 1566, 1,124 were located there, despite the absence of big cities.[15] In the established cities of the northern and southern Netherlands, Calvinism attracted adherents across the social spectrum, with a strong footing among the merchants, tradesmen, teachers, and guildsmen. Of the

12. This growth in Hondschoote's population was due to a long-held charter awarded by the Count of Flanders, Louis de Male, in 1374 that gave the city an early right to manufacture serge textile. See Coornaert, *Centre industriel d'autrefois*, and Emile Coornaert, "Draperies rurales, draperies urbaines," *Belgisch Tijdschrift voor Filologie en Geschiedenis* 28, no. 1 (1950): 59–96.

13. William H. TeBrake, *A Plague of Insurrection: Popular Politics and Peasant Revolt in Flanders, 1323–1328* (Philadelphia, 1993), 117. The peasant quality of the late-medieval Westkwartier inspired the well-known spoof, the Kerelslied (Song of the Hicks). See Paul Fredericq, ed., *Onze Historische Volksliederen voor de Godsdienstige Beroerten der 16de eeuw* (Ghent, 1894), 11–14.

14. For the September 4, 1561 letter, see *Troubles religieux*, 1:82–83.

15. Decavele, *Dageraad*, 2:60–207.

sixty-eight Calvinists persecuted in Antwerp between 1560 and 1566, almost half were craftsmen; fourteen were artists, writers, teachers, or worked in the publishing trade; and fifteen had employment in the trade and transport sector. These were not especially wealthy folks, but neither were they the unpropertied working poor.[16] This data reflects social trends elsewhere, especially in the southern Netherlands cities.

The Westkwartier was different, in large part because of the absence of sizable professional classes in its small cities and also because of the lopsided number of wage laborers who toiled in serge production. While the area's rural nobility was attracted to the Reformed faith, its members were not a large cohort.[17] An armed, militant field sermon held at Boeschepe on July 12, 1562 is one of our first good indicators of the social status of those for whom the Reformed message mattered enough to risk placards and Titelmans's efficient scouting. Of the sixty-six attendees identified by profession, thirty-two were farmers (a loose category that could include small landholders now working in textiles), twenty-seven were laborers or artisans, only six were merchants, and there was a lone city magistrate. Confiscation records of the convicted show most owned little or no property and had experienced downward social mobility.[18]

Amid this swelling population of country folk and laborers worked the Calvinist preachers, few of whom were schooled in the theological niceties of a Genevan academy. They were led by the indefatigable Sebastian Matte, former hatmaker from Ypres who preached around Armentières in 1563, fled to England to avoid persecution, and returned in May 1566, after the success of the Compromise, to spread the Word on his home turf. Contemporary sources describe him as a "short, fat, and bearded man about age thirty."[19] This artisan-turned-minister was joined by several former monks: Pieter Dathenus of Cassel, a Carmelite; Jacob de Buzere, an Augustinian; and Anthonis Algoet, a Dominican, all from religious houses in Ypres. Others included the former priest Pieter de Haze and Jan Lannoot, a weaver from Reningelst.[20] The summer of 1566 was to prove as electric in the Westkwartier as in the big cities of the Low Countries. Hedge sermons swelled, verbal and gestural taunts against clerics and ecclesiastical houses multiplied, and local officials worried aloud that overt violence was near at hand. A letter from officials in Veurne on July 22, 1566, to Margaret of Parma warned that the Calvinists were on the verge of "the scandalous pillage of churches, monasteries, and abbeys."[21] To be sure, Westkwartier minis-

16. Marnef, *Antwerp in the Age of the Reformation*, 71; Alastair Duke, "Building Heaven in Hell's Despite"; Pettegree, "Religion and the Revolt," 71–72.
17. Backhouse, *Beeldenstorm en Bosgeuzen*, 45–47.
18. Backhouse, "The Official Start of Armed Resistance in the Low Countries," 204–11.
19. *Troubles religieux*, 4:38–40.
20. Backhouse, *Beeldenstorm en Bosgeuzen*, 74. On these preachers and others, see Crew, *Calvinist Preaching and Iconoclasm*, esp. appendix B, 185–88.
21. July 22 letter in *Troubles religieux*, 4:74.

ters were careful to issue no direct threats against private property or political officials. As one observer from Veurne put it, "About the king they speak gently so that nobody will consider them rebellious."[22] As Phyllis Mack Crew has pointed out, ministers in the Low Countries at this time were as clearly divided about armed resistance and iconoclasm as they were varied in social background, with only ten of fifty-six active in the summer of 1566 in directly orchestrating iconoclasm.[23]

But just as in Valenciennes and Tournai, Calvinist actions in the Westkwartier had strong political echoes nonetheless. A psalm-singing incident in Ypres on July 25 is suggestive. Ypres was a special target of the militant Westkwartier Calvinists. It was home to an important concentration of religious houses and seat of a new bishopric led by Maarten van Riethoven, former inquisitor and zealous collaborator with Titelmans. Ypres also had long-standing economic rivalries with new drapery centers like Hondschoote that had led to periodic raids against its textile manufacturers and others in the area and inspired unsuccessful attempts to command the serge market.[24] Along with Bruges, its castellany the Franc, and Ghent, Ypres made up the all-important Estates of Flanders, giving it untold political importance. To the working poor converted to Calvinism, Ypres represented economic and political elitism in addition to the inquisitorial menace of a bishopric headed by an associate of Titelmans. Under the leadership of the former local Dominican Anthonis Algoet, a band of psalm-singing Calvinists marched into the city on July 25, headed for the marketplace, and stopped to sing psalms in front of the upper alderman's house, where he had gathered with the city bailiff and some of his colleagues to inspect the action.[25] This show of strength directly in front of local political and legal officers was audaciously direct, especially in a city in which political and religious privilege were interwoven.

On August 10, the feast day of Saint Lawrence, tensions finally erupted into violence. The Calvinist hatmaker-turned-minister Sebastian Matte appeared with his associate Jacob de Buzere and a group of armed devotees to hector those conducting feast day services at the chapel of Saint Lawrence outside Steenvoorde. After Matte preached an impas-

22. P. Heinderyckx, ed., *Jaerboeken van Veurne en Veurneambacht*, 4 vols. (Bruges, 1853–54), 3:12.
23. Crew, *Calvinist Preaching and Iconoclasm*, 45, and appendix B, 185–88.
24. Alphonse Vandenpeereboom, *Ypriana. Notices, études, notes et documents sur Ypres*, 7 vols. (Bruges, 1878–83), vol. 3 on the ecclesiastical terrain of Ypres; Decavele, *Dageraard*, 1:5; Emile Coornaert, *Centre industriel d'autrefois*, 30. In 1474 Bruges and Ghent assisted Ypres in a vigorous campaign against draperies in the Westkwartier; see Jelle Haemers, "'Ende hevet tvolc goede cause jeghens hemlieden te rysene': Stedelijke opstanden en staatsvorming in het graafschap Vlaanderen (1477–1492)," (PhD diss, University of Ghent, 2006), 389–90.
25. I. L. A. Diegerick, ed., *Documents du XVIe siècle concernant les troubles religieux, faisant suite à l'inventaire des chartes*, 4 vols. (Bruges, 1874–77), 1:28–29, as reported by the city's aldermen. See also the deposition of one witness to the event, who estimated about 150 marchers, in Guillaume Des Marez, ed., "Documents relatifs aux excès commis à Ypres par les iconoclastes (le 15 et 16 août 1566)," *Bulletin de la Commission Royale d'Histoire de Belgique*, 7 (1897) and 89 (1925): 3–38, 96–127, esp. 126–27.

sioned sermon, de Buzere led the attendees, once mass was over, into the chapel to smash all the statues and paintings.[26] Violence started not among those schooled in Protestant treatises on images, but as a spark ignited by a former artisan turned minister and his crowd of small-town devotees. Although we do not possess the sermons of these rural ministers, vernacular denunciations of Catholic image worship in the forms of treatises or plays were plentiful.[27] One of the most vigorous was *Der Leken Wechwyser* (The Layman's Guide) by Johannes Anastatius Veluanus. First printed at Strasbourg in 1554, it is a forthright condemnation of representations of God, the Virgin Mary, and the saints, repeating lines of arguments rehearsed at earlier times in Church history and by the near contemporaries Luther and Zwingli.[28] But perhaps even more important are the denunciations of images found in the popular plays and refrains of the rhetorician chambers. By the third quarter of the sixteenth century, and especially after a major drama competition at Ghent in 1539 yielded several plays with strong Lutheran overtones, the rhetoricians had become problematic to authorities as mouthpieces of Reformation sentiment.[29] A play written sometime in the 1530s and published on the eve of the religious violence in 1565, *Priest, Sexton and Weaver*, not only exalted the artisan weaver as the repository of evangelical sentiment but puts in his mouth a vigorous denunciation of images as pure idolatry—of no small interest to the artisans and workers flocking to the rustic Calvinist pastors in the Westkwartier and elsewhere.[30] Nor were all the songs sung at the *chanteries* Hebrew psalms, as we have already noted. An anonymous refrain from the Walloon cities of the south exclaimed, "They put robes of silk on their idols made of old wood, leaving us brethren of Christ naked and shivering"—voicing the popular Protestant critique, first articulated in earlier centuries by Saint Bernard, that images were richly outfitted while the deserving poor went wanting.[31]

26. M. Backhouse, ed., "Dokumenten betreffende de godsdienststroebelen in het Westkwartier: Jan Camerlynck en tien zijner gezellen voor de Ieperse vierschaar (1568–1569)," *Handelingen van de Koninklijke Commissie voor Geschiedenis* 138 (1972): 79–381, fol. 18v, a transcription of the trial records of radical Calvinist Jan Camerlynck and his associates who had fought a guerilla campaign in the Westkwartier in 1567 and many of whom had also participated in the iconoclastic riots a year earlier. See also M. Backhouse, "Guerilla War and Banditry in the Sixteenth Century: The Wood Beggars in the Westkwartier of Flanders (1567–68)," *Archiv für Reformationsgeschichte* 74 (1983): 232–56.

27. In some instances, we know the biblical texts about which the ministers preached. For north Holland, for example, Jan Arentsz. gave the first public sermon on Psalm 127 and Pieter Gabriel preached on Ephesians 2:8–10. See G. N. M. Vis, *Jan Arentsz: De mandenmaker van Alkmaar* (Hilversum, 1992).

28. Freedberg, *Iconoclasm and Painting*, 38–47; see also the very important consideration in Keith P. F. Moxey, "Image Criticism in the Netherlands before the Iconoclasm of 1566," *Nederlands Archief voor Kerkgeschiedenis* 87 (1977): 148–62.

29. For themes relating to the Reformation in early sixteenth-century rhetorician drama, see Waite, *Reformers on Stage*. On the 1539 rhetorician festival there, see Arnade, *Realms of Ritual*, 196–200; Waite, *Reformers on Stage*, 134–64; Van Bruaene, "Printing Plays."

30. Waite, *Reformers on Stage*, 128–30.

31. J. van Vloten, *Nederlands opstand tegen Spanje* (Haarlem, 1856), 183–84. On the image criticism and the deserving poor, see Palmer Wandel, *Voracious Idols*, 38.

Equally compelling was the public terrain prepared by the grands seigneurs, their Beggar counterparts, and the Calvinists engaged in field sermons and psalm singing. Neither prominent Reformed ministers nor the cautious Low Country nobility embraced iconoclasm after it shook the Netherlands, since it was redolent of violence, disobedience, revolt, and disrespect for law and property. To the contrary, they disavowed any responsibility for these actions, though evidence suggests that some consistories were fully involved in specific places like Tournai and Valenciennes and that a minority of ministers had actually had a direct hand.[32] A defense of iconoclasm like the one penned by Philips van Marnix, Lord of St. Aldegonde, Calvinist nobleman and future secretary to William of Orange, was rare. Even Marnix explicitly disassociated the nobility and urban Calvinists from the riots and justified the destruction as the handiwork of the will of God.[33] Egmont and Orange were aghast at widespread violence, but had left key cities, Ypres and Antwerp respectively, right before the trouble started to respond to a summons by Margaret of Parma for an urgent meeting.[34] Yet for all this aristocratic and Calvinist attempt to deny any hand in the iconoclastic riots, the parodic anticlericalism of the Beggars and the muscular demonstrations by the Reformed communities offered models of dissent that the rioters could reference. The iconoclasts were no understudies for roles already scripted for them, but neither were they provincial illiterates unaware of the larger political and religious climate within which their actions had been forged. Their violence flared brightly and widely, with the theological messages of the pastors and ministers whose sermons they attended as their inspiration. But the culture and behaviors of dissent established in the 1560s by noblemen and urban Calvinists also informed the behavior of the *beeldenstormers* (iconoclasts).

Once iconoclasm was kindled at Saint Lawrence Chapel on August 10, the rest of the Westkwartier was set ablaze. Reports required by the Duke of Alba in 1568 to the Council of Flanders from Westkwartier churches and chapels furnish a good index of the extent of the destruction across its seven castellanies. Priests and churchwardens of the region's smaller communities dutifully enumerated artwork and other belongings restored or repaired after the riots. The report filed by the churchwardens of Steenwerck in the castellany of Bailleul is typical. They were proud of their possessions: seven functioning altars in their three choirs. On the high altar sat a "beautiful, gilded" retable of Christ on the crucifix, Saint Nicholas, Saint Louis, and Saint John, patron of the church. The altar also had a tabernacle and a copper candelabrum. In the choir dedicated to the Holy Mother

---

32. Guido Marnef, "The Dynamics of Reformed Religious Militancy: The Netherlands, 1566–85," in *Reformation, Revolt and Civil War*, 23–34.

33. J. J. van Toorenenbergen, ed., *Philips van Marnix van St. Aldegonde: godsdienstige en kerkelijke geschriften*, 4 vols. (The Hague, 1871–91). The treatise *Vraye Narration et apologie des choses passées au Pays-Bas, touchant le Fait de la Religion en l'an 1566* is in ibid., 1:37–133, and on the nobility, ibid., 99.

34. Rachfahl, *Wilhelm von Oranien*, 2:718–23.

there was a tabernacle, a painting of the Virgin Mary, one of Saint Anne, another of Saint Clare, and a copper candelabrum. The chapel of Saint Vincent contained his statue, one of Saint Nicholas, another of Saint Louis, and a copper candelabrum. Behind the choir were several other altars: one dedicated to the Holy Trinity with a tabernacle and painting; a Saint Peter altar with statues of Saint Peter, Saint Fiacre, and Saint Quentin; an altar with statues of Saint George and Saint Sebastian; and altars of Saint Barbara and Saint Catherine, also with statues. In addition, the church had a baptismal font, a copper water basin, a crucifix, and two paintings of the Virgin and Saint John.[35] Other small parish churches admitted not all was yet repaired: Ekelsbeke needed a new tabernacle, while Ledringhem still awaited theirs, though its churchwardens reported all three damaged altars were now sufficiently repaired to celebrate mass.[36]

This artwork restored or replaced was not created by the great Dutch artists of the sixteenth century whose work was found in parish churches in Ghent, Antwerp, Haarlem, Leiden, or other major cities. It was probably locally made, or in the case of retables, purchased at an art marketplace, since the Netherlands specialized in premade ecclesiastical art sold to religious houses and churches during urban fairs or at year-round markets, particularly in Antwerp.[37] But the extent of the damage suggests that images—sculpted or painted—were far from the only items targeted by iconoclasts. Rather, the whole material accoutrements of the church, from clerical vestments to liturgical books and baptismal fonts, had become targets as the attackers sought to cleanse and purify interior spaces crowded with a dense variety of sacred objects.

The rioters worked fast and efficiently. From the accounts of witnesses and trial records of captured iconoclasts, it is clear that the riots were less a set of spontaneous uprisings than a series of coordinated attacks led by a band of iconoclasts under the leadership of preachers like Matte and de Buzere. The initial group of iconoclasts who attacked the Saint Lawrence chapel outside Steenvoorde was small, but their numbers grew as they continued their work. The knot of people fanned out in small clusters across the different castellanies, often joined by local people when they arrived at a town or village.[38] One group headed slightly northeast with Matte to Poperinge and the area around Veurne; another went with de Buzere to the castellany of Bailleul; yet another group crossed out of Flanders into Artois, especially the tiny enclave of the Pays de l'Alleu tucked between the two

---

35. These reports for all the castellanies are transcribed in the four volumes of *Troubles religieux*, a treasure trove of records from local Westkwartier courts and Alba's infamous Council of Troubles. For the report cited, see ibid., 1:334–35.

36. Ibid., 3:331–51 for all the parish churches of the castellany of Bergues Saint Winoc.

37. Lynn Jacobs, *Early Netherlandish Carved Altarpieces, 1380–1550: Medieval Tastes and Mass Marketing* (Cambridge, 1998); Jeremy Dupertuis Bangs, *Church Art and Architecture in the Low Countries Before 1566* (Kirksville, Missouri, 1997).

38. Scheerder, *Beeldenstorm*, offers a full chronology.

territories; all these areas served as staging grounds for more attacks in the general vicinity, including Ypres, the great prize.[39]

On the basis of trial records and property confiscations during Alba's reign, Marcel Backhouse identified 112 Westkwartier iconoclasts, including forty-seven whose profession is known. Although this identification hardly represents the sum of those involved, it offers a portrait, however imperfect, of the rioters' social composition. Nineteen worked in draperies: a draper merchant, three serge weavers, three fullers, a fuller-weaver, a linen weaver, a shearman, seven serge workers, and two men who did not own their own tools. There also were artisans and others of modest to simple means: a chairmaker, two clothmakers, a shoemaker, two innkeepers, a locksmith, two butchers, a stonecutter, four carpenters, a tilemaker, two bricklayers, two farmers, a knifemaker, a cobbler, a baker, and a peddler. There were also some small-town professionals and religious personnel: an alderman, a city messenger, a clerk, and a lay preacher and guardian of a cloister. An analysis of property holdings is difficult because of the imprecision about whether the currency listed is in Flemish or Parisian pounds (with a valuation difference of one to twelve) and also because many victims had a full year to alienate or hide holdings before confiscation. But even with these handicaps, it is clear that the wealth of those arrested was modest at best. Information about assets is available for twenty-three names, of whom thirteen had no movable or immovable property listed, either because they had time to sell them off in advance, or had none. Only three people listed immovable assets like land or houses: Pieter Liebart of Bailleul, with 125 pounds 30s and no profession listed; the carpenter Jacob Visage with 7 pounds 10s; and Caerle Weecxsteen, also without a profession listed, with 18 pounds. In terms of geography, almost all hailed from Hondschoote or the immediate environs.[40]

Despite reports of women's involvement in the riots, particularly around Ypres, all 112 of the identified iconoclasts were men, a fact suggested too in the gendered behaviors documented. An iconoclast punched the wife of Cassel's solicitor in the stomach. Rioters tore rings and pendants off young women in Armentières, and they told nuns in that city's convent of Grey Sisters that they must now marry as they overturned reliquaries and mocked their saints' bones with cries of, "Look how you have abused them!"[41] However rough this data, it strongly indicates that male artisans and workers, joined by a few minor professionals and charismatic regional preachers, were the main protagonists of Westkwartier iconoclasm. As much as serge production had changed the area, in many ways the iconoclasts still mirrored the world of rural laborers so spoofed in the fourteenth-century *Song of the Hicks* that poked fun at inhabitants of the Westkwartier: country folk eking out an

---

39. The itinerary can be pieced together based on the letters and depositions in *Troubles religieux*. A factual reconstruction is in Scheerder, *Beeldenstorm*, 18–33.

40. Backhouse, *Beeldenstorm en Bosgeuzen*, 102–11.

41. *Troubles religieux*, 2:124; J. M. Regnault and P. Vermander, "La crise iconoclaste de 1566 dans la region d'Armentières: Essai de description et d'interpretation," *Revue du Nord* 59 (1977): 221–31.

unrefined existence, buoyed occasionally by festive recreation in the form of uncouth ruckus where celebrants "jump head over heels" and make rude noises to the sound of "the big piper"—not unlike a later Brueghel kermis painting.[42]

Hounded by inquisitors, these Westkwartier rioters nevertheless displayed a sensitivity to larger political currents that belied the mockery of their lineage as mere bumpkins. The choice to inaugurate the iconoclastic riots with an attack on Saint Lawrence's Chapel outside Steenvoorde on the saint's feast day might have been coincidental, but given that this religious time mattered to both Philip II and to Lamoral, Count of Egmont and the governor of Flanders, the opposite is just as likely. In 1563, Philip II had laid the foundation for his future mausoleum and Jeronimite monastery near the small village of El Escorial in the Sierra de Guadarrama. San Lorenzo de El Escorial was ready for partial occupancy by 1566, though not completed until 1584. Philip dedicated this grand baroque complex of church, court, monastery, and library to Saint Lawrence, on whose feast day, August 10, 1557, Lamoral had led his forces to score a decisive defeat against the French at Saint Quentin.[43] The complex boasted paintings, sculptures, relics, and other artwork exalting Saint Lawrence, the Virgin Mary, and sundry other saints, as well as devotions that touted the king's Catholicism and girded El Escorial as a bulwark against northern Protestantism. Among El Escorial's historical associations, the battle of Saint Quentin was given pride of place; in late 1589, it even became the subject of a fresco in the Hall of Battles that paired it with the victory over the Muslims of Granada at Higueruela in 1431.[44]

El Escorial's foundation, ongoing construction, and dedication to Saint Lawrence was of no abiding concern to Westkwartier inhabitants. But because the feast day linked governor to king, the attack on Saint Lawrence's Chapel outside Steenvoorde was of wider importance in 1566 than simply a small town celebration interrupted by rowdy sermon goers. Even more intriguing, there was a lull of three days before any follow-up to this first burst of iconoclasm. When iconoclasm recommenced, it too was against a religious devotion with broader significance. On August 13, Jacob de Buzere preached in front of the Augustinian cloister at Bailleul. In it was housed a statue of Saint Anthony that a confraternity routinely circulated for devotion throughout Flanders, including Ghent, where different parishes shared its use. The assault on the cloister was particularly vehement; men armed with arquebusiers, hammers, and knives cast down all painted and sculpted images, Saint Anthony included, broke crosses, tore up priestly vestments, and stomped communion wafers beneath their feet.[45] No doubt the intensity was due to the fact that the Father Superior of the cloister was an inquisitor who worked closely with Titelmans. But

---

42. Fredericq, Onze Historische Volksliederen, 14.

43. Cornelia von der Osten Sacken, El Escorial: Estudio Iconológico, trans. María Dolores Abolos (Madrid, 1984).

44. Ibid., 86–89.

45. See the "Récit de Pierre Reynier, prieur de l'abbaye de St. Jean au Mont à Ypres," in Troubles religieux, 1:227–29.

the presence of the Saint Anthony statue also was provocative. The Saint Anthony veneration in Flanders and elsewhere had been criticized by no less than Erasmus, and had caught the skeptical eye of the Catholic chronicler of the wonder year, Marcus van Vaernewijck. Van Vaernewijck colorfully described the ritual fighting for the saint's possession among neighborhood youth groups and also its ceremonial reception by Ghent's aldermen when carried into town by confraternity brothers.[46] He expressed puzzlement about all this fanfare and the devotion inspired for a simple block of wood made into a saint.

Contemporaries, from urban chroniclers to the regent herself, lambasted the iconoclasts as hydra-headed "canaille" (riffraff) who indiscriminately vented their anger.[47] But the examples of the first two attacks in the Westkwartier suggest that the crowd, whatever its precise composition, engaged in no free-for-all, but instead carefully chose its targets. As iconoclasm picked up steam, so too did the use of gestures and rituals of inversion and satire, echoing those undertaken by the League and the Compromise. Studies of Reformation iconoclasm for the German and Swiss territories, particularly those by Robert Scribner and Lee Palmer Wandel, have demonstrated that sixteenth-century iconoclasm featured highly ritualized behaviors that endowed the rioters' violence with real purposefulness.[48] Iconoclasm in the Westkwartier likewise is rich in ritual idioms whose purpose is grasped by attending to the social composition of the rioters and by the nitty-gritty details of their acts of destruction.

Men at Work

Jan Gherstecooren, resident of tiny Haringe, was a typical Westkwartier iconoclast. On March 24, 1569, magistrates of nearby Hondschoote condemned him to death by hanging for his misdeeds in the summer of 1566. Gherstecooren left no property, and his verdict mentions no formal profession, suggesting that he was one of the many day laborers who worked in rural draperies. In mid-August, Gherstecooren had joined others in sacking churches in Gijverinkhove, Hoogstade, and Beveren. He brandished a club in the parish church of Gijverinkhove, "smashing and ruining several images and ornaments including a wooden statue standing above the door of the central choir, and two or three images placed upon an altar near the entrance to the church." Gherstecooren also dismounted a wooden door and used it as battering ram against an altar in the south choir,

46. BT Van Vaernewijck, 1:63–65.

47. For a good discussion of these sociological categories employed by chroniclers and early historians of the Time of Troubles, see Duke, "De Calvinisten en de 'Paapse Beeldendienst',", 29–30, and the sources listed in the footnotes; see also Deyon and Lottin, *"Casseurs" de l'été 1566*, 172–73.

48. Robert Scribner, *Popular Culture and Popular Movements* (London, 1987); Palmer Wandel, *Voracious Idols and Violent Hands*.

then smashed up the statues of the apostles standing before the rood screen, after which he joined others in pulling down the crucifix that stood above it. From there, he helped to sack the priest's house before heading off to Hoogstade and Beveren, where he continued his work with equal vigor, destroying a statue in the former and a crucifix in the latter.[49] The weapons used to inflict such damage were simple: a club, a door, and his own hands. Gherstecooren's willingness to move from one small parish church to another with a band of men extended the damage. That most iconoclasts traveled in clusters is reflected in countless sentences imposed on them. Another who engaged in such an itinerary was Jacob van Hende, a forty-four-year-old carpenter from Diksmuide later condemned to death by Hondschoote's magistrates.[50] After destroying artwork at the Augustinian abbey of Eversam, he and his fellow iconoclasts ransacked the refectory, bedding down for the night after an impromptu gorging on food and drink. From there, he went to the all-important Cistercian abbey of Ter Duinen, where he ripped up illuminated manuscripts and gold-lettered books and fed the shredded pages and parchments to the fire. Regrouping at Hondschoote, his gang headed for Adinkerke, smashed an organ, and hauled out statues and paintings hidden by the churchwardens and destroyed the objects in the middle of the nave.

Jan Gherstecooren and Jacob van Hende were typical of the 112 men identified as participants in Westkwartier iconoclasm. Neither had property listed; one worked as a carpenter; the other had no profession recorded. They carried out their actions as part of small cohorts of men of similar social profiles who used simple found objects or work tools. Beside the club that Gherstecooren wielded, or the door used as a battering ram, other weapons that appear in the records include axes, hammers, knives, and hatchets—everyday tools of the iconoclasts' work and lives. To these instruments the men added their physical strength, as they broke down doors, climbed ledges, battered rood screens and altars, chopped statues, and pulled down pictures and crucifixes with ropes and pulleys. In a way, their destruction recalled another realm of violence that periodically seized fourteenth- and fifteenth-century Flanders: the attacks of urban militias and even textile workers, often weavers, on the looms and workshops of competitors, which were violently smashed up in rivalries over turf, owing to the tightfisted urban regulation of rural production by Ypres, Ghent, and Bruges.[51] In this respect, the novelty of iconoclasm in the Westkwartier was not so much in the violence against a precious asset, but in its tar-

---

49. *Troubles religieux*, 4:198.
50. Ibid., 198–201, sentence of April 22, 1569.
51. For fifteenth-century examples, see Boone, *Gent en de Bourgondische hertogen*, 196, on the political power of the big cities, and Peter Stabel, "'Dmeeste, oirboirlixste ende proffitelixste let ende neringhe': Een kwantitatieve benadering van de lakenproductie in het laatmiddeleeuwse en vroegmoderne Vlaanderen," *Handelingen der Maatschappij voor Geschiedenis en Oudheidkunde te Gent*, 51 (1997): 113–52, esp. 142–43 on economic rivalries.

get: religious objects and Catholic sacrality itself. Nor was the iconoclasts' wrath limited to images, be they painted or sculpted. As we have seen, the beeldenstorm encompassed more than its name implied; the violence visited on images was great, but destruction was likewise inflicted on altars, rood screens, tabernacles, chalices, patens, priestly vestments, holy books, and baptismal fonts. In monasteries and cloisters, the iconoclasts ransacked refectories and sleeping quarters, stealing kitchenware and bedding and feasting on food and drink. Van Hende drank and ate heartily from the abbey of Eversam's refectory, and opted with others to pass the night there before starting his destruction afresh the next morning.

The Westkwartier iconoclasts' actions reflect both workmanlike behavior and an exultation in a temporary command over sacred objects, important religious property, space, and time. To admit such cultural forces is not, however, to deny iconoclasm's religious purpose, especially since at the head of these bands of men were the provincial ministers such as Matte. But as the violence unfolded, the social habits of these rioters molded their behaviors; they saw their religious project as a material task: to expose the concrete stuff that constituted the supposed sacrality of the holy object. Even more, their feasting and related acts of indulgence merged the carnivalesque with the anticlerical, not unlike the kind of satirical commentary that the League, the Compromise, and the Beggars had stirred up in their public campaigns.

Clearly the small bands of roving men—sometimes joined by women and children—mirrored the social profile of the ateliers in which many found employment.[52] The language of masculine labor colored iconoclasm, certainly in the Westkwartier, but also elsewhere. This is true, for example, in the north Brabantine city of Turnhout, where iconoclasm was the work of a determined but diverse group.[53] A rich set of depositions reveal that 116 people were implicated in Turnhout's religious troubles, many known Calvinists. Professions for fifty-four are recorded, with seven weavers, six joiners, five needle makers, and nine merchants numerically dominating the other professions.[54] Artisans clearly dominated this heterogeneous group. Remarkably, their image-breaking commenced as if for a day of work. They started to gather at around 4 a.m. on August 23 in Turnhout's

---

52. Coornaert, *Centre industriel d'autrefois*, on associational life in Hondschoote. Cf. Valenciennes in George Espinas, "Groupe économique, groupe religieux: Les tisserands de Valenciennes au XIV siècle," *Annales d'histoire économique et sociale* 2 (Paris): 48–63.

53. E. van Autenboer, "Uit de geschiedenis van Turnhout in de 16de eeuw: Voorbereiding, uitbarsting en gevolgen van de Beeldenstorm (1566)," *Taxandria*, n.s. 40/41 (1968–69): 1–275, with a transcription of the deposition of witnesses to image-breaking as part of a report filed to the duke of Alba; see ibid., "Informatie genomen tot Turnhout door den Drossaert van Brabant raeckende de Beltstormerye," 245–62, followed by the punishment imposed on Turnhout's iconoclasts by the Council of Troubles October 19, 1568, in ibid., 262–65.

54. "Informatie genomen tot Turnhout door den Drossaert van Brabant raeckende de Beltstormerye," 235–39.

central marketplace, but did not begin their attack until the work bell rang and daylight broke at 6 a.m.[55] In the Flemish city of Oudenaarde, all sources indicate that textile workers, day laborers, and guildsmen bulked large among its crowd of iconoclasts. In an exculpatory report to Alba, Oudenaarde's magistrates described the image-breakers as "people of little quality" and "laborers," many of whom they identified as weavers.[56] The witness Anthonis vanden Kerchove blamed the turmoil on the wage laborers who lived outside the city's walls in Pamele, Ten Baillen, and Luepeghem, describing them as "poor folk" armed with "hammers, knives, and other instruments."[57] Iconoclasm in fact began in Pamele, slightly beyond the jurisdiction of Oudenaarde's magistrates, at the chapel of Our Lady. A smith led a crowd of enthusiasts, shouting, "Come here, companions (*gezellen*), here is our work!"[58] At 's-Hertogenbosch, the sacristan of Saint John's Cathedral described the iconoclasts who struck on August 22 and 23 as mainly "guildsmen and workers," a social category reported by other witnesses who gave authorities specific names of iconoclasts and their accomplices. Such is the case with two smiths, who, according to the witness Leonard Peeterzone, brought twenty ruffians with them.[59] This social profile helps to explain why so much looting accompanied the regular destruction, and also its masculine brio, exemplified in the deposition of the tailor Gillis Henricxzone. He was drinking a tankard of beer in a local tavern after returning from a local *kermis* in the late morning of August 22 when he encountered a man who excitedly proclaimed, beer in hand, that he and others were about to attack the cathedral.[60] The drinking apparently continued. After hauling the gilded statues and other smashed items out of the cathedral and setting them ablaze, the iconoclasts sat around the large bonfire, enjoying their beer as they watched everything go up in smoke.[61]

The violence of Low Country iconoclasm was also rich in satirical gestures and rites of inversion. There was the looting—of clergy's houses, of cloisters, but also of some private houses, with food, drink, and household objects stolen. On August 22 Margaret of Parma wrote to Philip II that she feared the iconoclasts would attack figures of authority.

---

55. Deposition of burgomaster Hendrik van Roye, "Informatie genomen tot Turnhout door den Drossaert van Brabant raeckende de Beltstormerye," 250–51.

56. D. J. vander Meersch, ed., *Mémoires Justificatif du Magistrat d'Audenarde sur les troubles arrivé en cette ville, en 1566, avec de nombreuses pièces à l'appui* (Ghent, 1842), 42–44.

57. Ibid., 181–82.

58. Ibid., 172–73.

59. Prosper Cuypers van Velthoven, ed., *Documents pour servir à l'histoire des troubles religieux du XVI siècle dans le Brabant Septentrional: Bois le Duc (1566–1570)* (Brussels, 1858), with an introduction and complete transcription of *Informatie begonst te nemen binnen der stadt van 's-Hertogenbossche, den xiiien May 1567*. See ibid., 398–99 for the sacristan's list of names, and on the two smiths, ibid., 340.

60. Ibid., 464–79.

61. H. van Alfen, ed., *Kroniek eener Kloosterzuster van het voormalig Bossche Klooster "Mariënburg" over de troebelen te 's-Hertogenbosch e.e. in de jaren 1566–75* ('s-Hertogenbosch, 1931), 5–6.

She worried about a "general pillage everywhere," but especially in Brussels, even of the king's private chapel at court, or the assault or murder of royal officers and clergy with the tacit approval of Orange, Egmont, Hornes, and Hoogstraten.[62] No doubt her anger against the nobles prompted a dash of hyperbole, but her fear cannot be dismissed as entirely feigned, since twelve days of image-breaking had convinced her that iconoclasm went hand-in-hand with riotous assaults against people, property, and symbols of authority, not simply against church and chapel. That this behavior was highly ritualized, that it was done with rough-and-tumble antics, that it involved food and beer, that it was accompanied by psalm singing, that satirical insults were flung against images and clergy—all this not only bespoke heresy, but also the sort of raw festive behavior that urban magistrates and the royal court had been trying to regulate since the beginning of the sixteenth century. I have suggested that Charles V waged a parallel campaign against traditional festive behaviors and religious heresy during his reign in the Low Countries, and that in the 1560s the cluster of movements of dissent that roiled public authority tested the boundaries of the permissible. In iconoclasm, the *stormers* brought the two realms of concern palatably together, articulating their Calvinist commitments through topsy-turvy rites.

Jan de Druck was a busy iconoclast. He participated in attacks in Broxeele, Eecke, North and South Berkijn, and Ledringhem, for which he was condemned to death on October 28, 1567, by Alba's special law court, the Council of Troubles. His crimes centered on destruction of religious art and objects in parish churches in mid-August 1566: at South Berkijn, Druck helped smash a cross and destroy a statue of Saint Gilles, and wreaked similar havoc at Eecke. But he was guilty of more: in south Berkjin, he took a chasuble stored in a chest in the church's chapel of Saint Nicholas, cut it up, and boasted that it would make a fine garter. He also ransacked several altars at Ledringhem, stealing money amounting to 3 or 4 Parisian pounds and intended "for common devotion." On August 17 he seized a statue in the parish church at Broxeele, turned it upside down, and dunked its head into the baptismal font, shouting, "I am baptized! I am baptized!" Druck then smashed the font, gleefully exclaiming, "Is this the holy basin for which the papists so dearly paid?" As he moved on to other statues, altars, and even candles and candleholders, he instructed companions to head to the sexton's house, haul out all the ecclesiastical goods and ornaments and destroy them in front for others to see. Once finished, Druck and his accomplices gathered together for a good meal and drink.[63]

Druck's deeds mirror those of other individuals and small groups. At Ledringhem, on September 10, a crowd of about thirty-two seized the priest's house, eating and drinking

---

62. H. A. Enno van Gelder, ed., *Correspondance française de Marguerite d'Autriche, duchesse de Parma avec Philippe II* 3 vols. (Utrecht, 1925–42), 2:326–27.

63. *Troubles religieux*, 2:114–15.

heartily before they settled down for the night there. Refreshed, the next morning they sacked the local parish church, destroying four altars. They scattered for the balance of the day, some going to Ekelsbeke, others to Arnèke, both sets listening to sermons, only to return at nightfall, this time to the chaplain's house, where they had something to eat and pocketed four candles. Afterward, they randomly searched private houses looking for objects the churchwardens might have hidden, or domestic altars or shrines. The next morning, they continued their efforts, overturning basins of holy oil, smashing up more altars, and shredding the priest's and chaplain's books. As a parting shot, they derisively cut up the chaplain's bonnet.[64]

No doubt Druck and his associates acted out of religious conviction, perhaps egged on by an articulate Reformed preacher or minister—themselves divided over the seditiousness of iconoclasm.[65] But he did so with rites of inversion that stressed a temporary command of sacred objects and spaces through spoofs, transgressions, and mocking of symbols and sites of authority. Dunking a statue head first into a baptismal font to profane it; turning a chasuble into a garter; reshaping a chaplain's bonnet; stealing money; taking over the sacristan's, priest's and chaplain's houses and ransacking their goods, being careful to haul them out for others to see before destroying them; entering private homes; guzzling beer and devouring foodstuffs—such acts were repeated with minor variations throughout the Westkwartier, carried out to the accompaniment of solemn psalms and hearty cheer. One small-town alderman in Lavantie, located in the enclave of the Pays de l'Alleu between Artois and Flanders, was later sentenced to death for guffawing as a young girl hurled "some images" onto the floor in the parish church.[66]

In his ordinance restricting festivals issued on October 7, 1531, Charles V had cited taverns as social spaces of indecorous behavior, in need of regulation. Drinking and image-breaking went hand in hand, exemplified by the case of the 's-Hertogenbosch iconoclast who described his plans for an attack over a tankard of beer in a local tavern. Several sentences, such as the one issued on March 27, 1568, by the court of Bailleul against Vincent Oustlandt, a native of Steenbeke, specify "eating and drinking" as accompaniments to iconoclasm.[67] Sometimes, as with the case of the small-town alderman of Merville, this meant retreating to a tavern for beer and food after the destruction. At other times, it meant ransacking a monastery or cloister's refectory, or even, as was the case in Estaires, having drink brought to the parish church by the owner of the Three Kings tavern.[68] If the

---

64. Ibid., 3:104.
65. Crew, *Calvinist Preaching and Iconoclasm*, 132, and appendix B, 185–88, a list of ministers active during the wonder year, including some who participated in image-breaking.
66. *Troubles religieux*, 2:360–61. Sentence against Nicolas Salengré, June 21, 1568.
67. Ibid., 1:235.
68. Ibid., 2:363, sentence of alderman Antoine de Becque and sentence of tavern owner Charles Le Josne in ibid., 2:366–67.

Council of Troubles October 12, 1568, sentence against Gilles Bateman of Cassel is any indication, such carnivalesque indulgence sometimes carried a theological point. Bateman was particularly bold and violent, having assembled a band of iconoclasts in Cassel's marketplace and urged them on with the rallying cry, "The Beggars will kill the papists!" He had assaulted the wife of a local pensionary, spurred his armed companions to shout "Kill the papists, the bailiff, the pensionary and the aldermen!" and finally had ransacked a chapel near Estaires, stealing money from a chest to treat himself to food and spirits at a nearby tavern, boasting "saints don't need to eat or drink."[69] Several witnesses to iconoclasm in and around Ypres stressed that heavy drinking accompanied the violence. As Jan Macs put it, the iconoclasts "zeer bij dranke waren [were very full of drink]."[70] They also ransacked cloisters for food, and when they eventually depleted all the stock, they demanded that the Franciscans fetch them more bread, crying, "We have pillaged hard and now we must eat."[71] An anonymous sister from the tertiary order of Saint Francis in 's-Hertogenbosch, who penned an account of iconoclasm, was so fascinated by the binge drinking that she reasoned that the image-breakers thought they were participating in carnival.[72] So much did it smack of plebian frolic that she imagined a small revenge by God: the miraculous turning of an iconoclast's beer into blood, to his astonishment.[73]

The emphasis on drink in certain depositions, even legal sentences, may have had something to do with criminal law statues in the Low Countries, offering drunkenness as a mitigating factor in determining guilt.[74] And yet many death sentences issued by city magistrates and the Council of Troubles cited drink without offering mercy, and many chroniclers describe binge drinking without reference to the law—indications that the tavern grousing and heavy drink had less to do with the law and more to do with the rioters' own cultural world of male sociability. The iconoclasts' indulgence in drink also highlights the celebratory zest that many displayed as they pulled down and smashed holy objects and artwork. Drinking and feasting had also been central features of the political dissent over the heresy placards waged by the grands seigneurs and the gentilshommes. Such behavior played a prominent role in the inauguration of the League against Granvelle, and especially of the Order of the Beggars, whose formation at a celebratory banquet laced with much drink earlier that year had modeled tavern antics as a means of protest. The Beggars' public campaigns in late spring and the two summer months be-

---

69. Ibid., 2:123.
70. Guillaume Des Marez, ed., "Documents relatifs aux excès commis à Ypres," 11–13. Compare the comments about excessive drink in the account of iconoclasm in the Westkwartier by the Yprian corn inspector Augustijn van Hernighem in Eerste bouck van beschrijvinghe van alle geschiedenesse, 1562–72, ed., A. L. E. van Roosbroeck (Brussels, 1978), 20.
71. Des Marez, ed., "Documents relatifs aux excès commis à Ypres," 32–33.
72. Van Alfen, Kroniek eener Kloosterzuster, 5–6.
73. Ibid., 6–7.
74. L. T. Maes, Vijf eeuwen stedelijk strafrecht (Antwerp, 1947), 486.

fore iconoclasm broke loose had been also in part waged in the masculine world of the tavern, the guildhall, and the *schutters'* assemblies, like Hendrik van Brederode's beer-washed toasts to the Beggars in late June in Amsterdam, prologue to a pro-Beggars rally at the meeting house of the archers in early July.[75]

For all of iconoclasm's masculine color, observers often claimed that women and children figured prominently in the riots, either because this was a common social trope in describing seditious public behavior, or because, as select examples hint, there were real instances of their participation. The pensionary of Antwerp, Jacob van Wesenbeke, blamed the violence in Antwerp on a classic quartet of "enfans, jeusnes, garçons, et canaille (children, young people, boys, and riffraff)."[76] Van Vaernewijck's account of iconoclasm in Ghent in several instances mentions the participation of children and youth, including a fourteen- or fifteen-year-old image-breaker in Saint Jacob's parish church and children who playfully taunted statues by crying, "Say 'Vivent les Gueux!' or we will behead you!"[77] Witnesses deposed after the riots in 's-Hertogenbosch confirm that children were vigorous participants who, among other things, destroyed a cross and a baptismal font in the cathedral.[78] In Ypres, the former city treasurer, Marx de Wilde, spoke of "women, children, and youth" among the rioters. Another Yprian witness marveled at the children in Saint Peter's Church who beheaded statues with little hammers.[79] Chroniclers of iconoclasm in Amsterdam, including Laurens Jacobsz. Reael, also underscored the active role taken by youth, including stoning images on the altar in the Oudekerk.[80] That children were sometimes aware of the broader political context of their actions is made clear in the games they played in the streets. In Tournai, so bothersome were the gangs of kids squaring off as "Beggars" versus "Papists" that the town fathers passed a law on June 10, 1566, proscribing such mimicry.[81] A ten-year-old child in Amsterdam actually died in just such a game in 1573, when he was fatally hit by a rock.[82] Sometimes children profited from iconoclasm. In Turnhout, the cobbler and linen weaver Hans van Beke confessed to having brought home incense sticks for his children after the iconoclastic riots, and Hans Vervoort removed several unidentified statues from the Our Lady altar at Saint Peter's Church to give to his children as toys. In the small town of Venthie just south of Flanders'

75. Hendrik van Biesten, "Anteykeningen gedaen van Broer Hendrik van Biesten, oratuer van de Minnebroeders binnen Amsterdam, (. . .) (1534–1567)," *De Dietsche Warande* 7 (1866): 332.

76. Rahlenbeck, *Mémoires de Jacques de Wesenbeke*, 280. So present are descriptions of the young in the iconoclastic riots that in 1964, in a published lecture, O. J. de Jong floated the idea that the iconoclastic riots of 1566 were a collective protest by youth: De Jong, *Beeldenstorm*.

77. BT *Van Vaernewijck*, 1:128, 151.

78. Cuypers van Velthoven, *Documents pour servir à l'histoire des troubles*, 361.

79. Des Marez, "Documents relatifs aux excès commis à Ypres," 19, 25.

80. Van Nierop, *Beeldenstorm en burgerlijk verzet*, 38–40. On Reael's account, see "Uittreksel uit de Amsterdamsche gedenkschriften van Laurens Jacobsz. Reael."

81. M. Vandenbroeck, "Ordonnances publiées à Tournai," 96–97.

82. *Dagboek Jacobsz.*, 1:359.

Westkwartier, the town clerk, Mahieu Wastepatte, took home stone pieces of the altar for his children.[83]

Chroniclers and witnesses also insisted on the presence of women in the riots, but rarely specified names. The exception was in Ypres, where several witnesses actually confirmed individuals. A François van der Crone, for example, noted that the wife of Gillis van der Strate participated in the attack on the nunnery of Saint Clare. She stole a jar of preserves and later boasted of her deed in the fish market.[84] An anonymous sister from the tertiary order of Saint Francis at a convent and church in 's-Hertogenbosch wrote about the iconoclasts' attack:

> They went wherever they pleased and they stole the sheets and blankets from the beds in the dorter and they broke the lock on the door of our mother superior's room and took what they wanted, including new sheets, wool and linen and they were given as much food and drink as they wanted, but that was still not enough because the women carried it out of the convent by the load as well as platters, pots, cans, whatever they could lay their hands on, indeed they have stolen more from us than we could say.[85]

The two cases typify a gendered division of labor in iconoclasm, noted by more than one observer, in which men do the physical destruction and women pilfer goods. There were a few exceptions, however, to this pattern. As several witnesses in Ypres noted, the wife of Gillis Hessele, a tavern owner in Ypres, pulled down images, cut off the noses and heads of several statues, and drank alongside the men.[86] During the iconoclastic riots in Delft on August 24, women apparently led much of the wrath waged against the cloister of Saint Clare and the Franciscans, protected by an armed gauntlet of men, though their efforts were mostly rebuffed by city authorities.[87] Yet, on balance, men, buoyed by drink, monopolized the pushing, pulling, and smashing while women seized items of household use. Both men and women underscored the wastefulness of provisioning mute images, statues, and well-fed clerics, by redirecting material goods to their own physical and domestic needs. Men fed their stomachs in a carnivalesque indulgence of beer, bread, butter, and cheese; women carted off provisions for the kitchen and bedroom.

Satisfying one's hunger, hurling insults at clergy, looting parish priests' houses, carting off of the provisions of churches and chapels, and efficiently destroying sacred places and properties all suggest that the world-turned-upside-down was as attractive a source of inspiration to the iconoclasts as was Calvinist theology. So too does the particular way

---

83. Van Autenboer, "Uit de geschiedenis van Turnhout," 147, n. 34, and 258; *Troubles religieux*, 2:247.
84. Des Marez, "Documents relatifs aux excès commis à Ypres," 10–11.
85. Van Alfen, *Kroniek eener Kloosterzuster*, 6. I have used a translation prepared by Alastair Duke.
86. Des Marez, "Documents relatifs aux excès commis à Ypres," 108–9.
87. J. Soutendam, "Beeldenstormerij te Delft in August en October 1566," *Bijdragen voor Vaderlandsche Geschiedenis en Oudheidkunde* 9 (1877): 173–221, esp. 179–180.

certain statues and images were destroyed. This included classic instances of scatological desacralization: one Isabeau Blancheteste in Limburg urinated in the priest's chalice; iconoclasts in 's-Hertogenbosch did the same in priests' chests; an iconoclast in Hulst outside Antwerp threw a crucifix he had pulled down into his pig sty; and the Count of Culemborg fed the Eucharist wafer to his pet parrot.[88] Not to be outdone, Lodewyck Caenen entered a church at Buysscheure, climbed atop the altar, and turned all the statues so that their backside faced forward.[89]

Related to such behaviors was the ritual torture and destruction of ecclesiastical artwork. The day laborer Mathieu Tahoen was charged in 1572 with "cutting the nose and otherwise disfiguring many images in the parish church of Westoutre."[90] In an August 18, 1566, letter to the regent, the governor of Aire, Jean de Morbecque, lamented not merely the extent of destruction across Flanders but also its form: iconoclasts playing ball with the holy ciborium, for example, or gathering up images, paintings and crucifixes, among other items, and burning them outside chapel and church for all to see.[91] Legal records prove Morbecque's accusation, however polemical in purpose, was grounded. At Ekelsbeke, the iconoclasts neatly gathered up all broken images and burned them in the central marketplace.[92] At 's-Hertogenbosch, they lit a spectacular bonfire before Saint John's Cathedral and watched the artwork go up in flames.[93] The alderman of Cassel condemned Gadifer vander Clyte to death for, among other crimes, beheading a statue in Mechelen and then beamingly displaying it in public.[94] Mathieu Baert, a day laborer from Venthie, cut the noses off several saints.[95] And at Wormhoudt, an iconoclast performed a mock execution of Saint Nicholas, hanging him by the neck.[96]

Decaying Arms and Desecrated Tombs:
Iconoclasm and Symbols of Authority

In a broad sense, such forms of violence visited on this artwork constituted an act of desacralization, since it made mockery of the sacred power of the image, and unlike the com-

---

88. F. Lemaire and A. L. Ed. Verheyden, "Une enquête sur le Protestantisme au duché de Limbourg en 1569," *Bulletin de la Commission Royale d'Histoire* 118 (1953), 187, for Blancheteste; Van Alfen, *Kroniek eener Kloosterzuster*, 5–6, for 's-Hertogensbosch; Johan Decavele, "De Reformatorische Beweging te Axel en Hulst, 1556–1566," *Bijdragen voor de Geschiedenis der Nederlanden* 22, no. 1 (1968–69): 2–42, for the pig sty; on Culemborg, see Scheerder, *Beeldenstorm*, 85–87.
89. *Troubles religieux*, 3:254.
90. Ibid., 1:248.
91. Ibid., 2:84.
92. Ibid., 3:103.
93. Van Alfen, *Kroniek eener Kloosterzuster*, 5.
94. *Troubles religieux*, 1:98–99, and 105.
95. Ibid., 2:264.
96. Ibid., 3:97.

plete destruction of images and statues that also occurred, these particular acts partially defaced or ritually humiliated images and objects. As Robert Scribner has noted of the Reformation in Germany, these acts of derision borrowed from festive forms of inversion as their perpetrators affirmed the powerlessness of the revered item.[97] As I have stressed, inversion was a leitmotif of Low Country iconoclasm. But to understand these ritual executions and hangings only within the framework of cultural forms of inversion would be to miss an essential ingredient for the Low Countries of these ritual punishments. Since 1523 the execution of apprehended Protestants was a common occurrence in the Low Countries—and the source of intense debate and anxiety. As earlier mentioned, one thousand three hundred victims, from Lutherans to Anabaptists, were sentenced to death between 1523 and 1566, the highest number in Europe. A 1529 placard prescribed methods of execution; it legislated death by burning for the unrepentant and by the sword for those who reconciled before death, with drowning reserved for women.[98] Beheadings and gruesome burnings on account of religious conviction occurred over these critical years with enough frequency—in the 1530s above all—to be part of the religious and juridical landscape of the Habsburg Netherlands. Such executions were enormous events, even in an age when capital punishment and the spectacle of death were a given. The pain of death at the stake could be mitigated by strangling the victim prior to the fire or putting a gunpowder sack on his or her neck to hasten death.[99]

But as some chroniclers noted, Habsburg authorities sometimes insisted on its severest application, especially in the case of the despised Anabaptists. The Ghent chronicler Marcus van Vaernewijck recounts how the Spanish officer presiding over the execution of four young Anabaptists on March 30, 1568, prevented the executioner from strangling the victims before he set their pyre afire. In fact, the soldiers fed the flames to intensify the heat as the victims succumbed, and pitched extra firewood at the dying men.[100] Iconoclasts who gouged out the eyes of statues and images, beheaded them, and lit bonfires with chopped up artwork in front of churches and chapels were attempting to visit the same forms of violence on Catholic holy objects as was visited on Protestants condemned to death by the hated placards. Such actions echo the rites of violence, especially the mimicry of judicial punishment, that Huguenots and Catholics in France inflicted on one another as recounted by Natalie Davis, but with special inflections.[101] As Judith Pollmann has explored, the Netherlands never developed a vigorous Catholic party, and from the

97. Bob Scribner, "Reformation, Carnival and the World Turned Upside-Down," *Social History* 3, no. 3 (1978): 303–29.

98. Duke, "Building Heaven in Hell's Despite," 73.

99. Scheerder, *De Inquisitie in de Nederlanden*, esp. 56–84; Aline Goosens, *Les inquisitions modernes dans les Pays-Bas méridionaux, 1520–1663*, 2 vols. (Brussels, 1997–98).

100. BT Van Vaernewijck, 3:310–12.

101. Davis, "Rites of Violence," an essay that fundamentally reoriented studies of popular violence in the French Wars of Religion. For the impact of this essay, see Holt, "Putting Religion Back into the Wars of Religion," 533.

first intimations of iconoclasm, there was far less fratricidal violence between Calvinists and Catholics than in France.[102] During the wonder year, although clergy were attacked, up until the armed revolt broke out later that winter Calvinist violence was centered squarely on iconoclasm *tout court*. Images, objects, and the spaces of devotion were the most important targets for avenging the pain of punishment and execution suffered by the Reformed and other Protestant brethren. Catholic images and objects bore almost all the weight of violence in the riots of 1566, making their mockery and destruction all the more intense and all the more important as a transfer point for larger debates about the location of the holy, its representation, and its relationship to public authority.

In one instance, the connection between the iconoclastic riots of 1566 and previous inquisitorial activities was unambiguous. Bertrand Le Blas, a citizen of Tournai and resident of Wesel, where he had sought refuge, had become Tournai's first documented iconoclast back in 1554. On Christmas Day, he had entered the cathedral with the intent to disrupt mass. Unable to reach the central altar, he had turned to a smaller chapel of the church, where its curé, Jehan Laloux, was consecrating the host. At the key moment of its elevation, Le Blas had snatched the Eucharist from the curé's hand, thrown it on the ground, and stomped it to bits, declaring it "an idol." For this act he had been sentenced to death by the seneschal of Hainault, Pierre de Werchin. Le Blas had been led to the central marketplace on December 29 where his right hand and his right foot had been seared with hot pincers. Then the executioner had torn out his tongue. Le Blas had been bound to the stake and slowly burned to death with a small fire ("à petit feu") that several times had to be rekindled. For this gruesome death, Le Blas earned accolades in the Arras-born Jean Crespin's celebrated martryology.[103] Almost twelve years later, his memory was very much alive to his religious progeny, the rioters of 1566. The late seneschal Pierre de Werchin, who had condemned the martyr, had recently died and been interred in the Tournai church of Chartreaux. When iconoclasm broke out on August 23, his sepulcher was destroyed, and Jean Ruyant, a butcher, rifled through it. The seneschal's corpse had deteriorated considerably, though the left arm still had skin on it. Ruyant wrapped the arm up and brought it home with him because he wanted to burn it in his oven, doing to it what the seneschal had done to Le Blas. But his wife balked, ordering him to take the decaying body part out of their house. As Pasquier de Le Barre reports, Ruyant obliged, and threw the arm into the Scheldt River.[104] This proved a satisfying second option since it was in

---

102. Judith Pollmann, "Countering the Reformation in France and the Netherlands: Clerical Leadership and Catholic Violence, 1560–1585," *Past and Present*, no. 190 (2006): 83–120.

103. Moreau, *Histoire du Protestantisme à Tournai*, 131–32, with transcriptions of the sentence from register 13708 in série B, ADN, esp. fol. 82v. The Tournai chronicler Pasquier de la Barre offers excellent details in Pinchart, ed., *Mémoires de Pasquier de le Barre*, 1:197–98. See also the account in Jean Crespin, *Histoire des martyrs persecutez*, ed., Benoit, 2:312–15.

104. Pinchart, *Mémoires de Pasquier de le Barre*, 1:197–98. A February 1567 report of the commissioners sent to Tournai by the regent confirms this incident, but specifies that the arm in question was the right not the left. See ibid., 2:195.

this very river that Le Blas's ashes were thrown. In both his original intention to burn the arm and his actual decision to throw it in the Scheldt, Ruyant inflicted on the memory and physical remains of the seneschal the punishment that he had meted out to Le Blas almost twelve years earlier.

Historians of these iconoclastic riots have noted their conservative political character: there were no great waves of murder against clergy as in France; there was no attack on secular political symbols such as town halls or royal residences; and iconoclasts demonstrated a general caution about symbols of political authority. The Calvinist ministers themselves had been divided over the appropriateness of image-breaking, since most desperately wanted legitimacy in the eyes of the Crown.[105] As astonished as they were by the violence, some contemporaries marveled that images of God and the saints were vigorously attacked while images of secular authority that were of lesser status were not. Commenting on the Ghent cathedral of Saint Bavo (Sint-Baafs), Van Vaernewijck noted, "They [the iconoclasts] appear more cautious about the representations and statues of our temporal prince than they did about the representations and statues of our eternal, heavenly prince and God."[106] While this sensitivity to overt symbols of political authority was real enough, it would be wrong to categorize Low Country iconoclasm as merely a theological project against the Catholic Church. True, town halls and princely residences were not targets, and understandably so, since iconoclasm *was* directed against religious spaces, times, and objects. It is also true that iconoclasm was no economic protest masquerading as religious riot. To grant this, however, is not to overlook the very material grounding of the violence, given that it was directed against private property, nor to reject social grievances as a stimulus, since contemporaries like Van Vaernewijck, a man of learned, conservative tastes, admitted as much. In fact Van Vaernewijck noted that so concerned were the well-to-do and patricians in Ghent about a social revolt that on the eve of iconoclasm, August 19, they began to hide their money and valuables. And Ghent's aldermen expressed fear that the impending religious violence might shade over into a social protest. Earlier that year, on January 16, Cardinal Granvelle had written to Philip II that a crisis in grain prices would help spur a revolt.[107] And probably with a touch of exaggeration, Cornelis van Campene claimed that in the aftermath of the riots in Ghent the *beeldenstomers*

---

105. This general interpretation is stressed by Crew, *Calvinist Preaching and Iconoclasm*; Scheerder, *Beeldenstorm*; and Dierickx, "Beeldenstorm in de Nederlanden in 1566," and in general represents a reputation of Kuttner's staunchly Marxist, *Het Hongerjaar 1566* and the general school of economic historians who have stressed the riots' connection to social and economic grievances, particularly the bad times of 1565.

106. BT *Van Vaernewijck*, 1:142.

107. Victor Fris, "Notes pour servir à l'histoire des iconoclastes et des Calvinistes à Gand de 1566–1568," *Handelingen der Maatschappij van Geschied- en Oudheidkunde te Gent* 9 (1909): 14–18 for excerpts from these and other sources on the matter of social grievances; *Corr. Granvelle*, 1:86.

lamented that had they not attacked images but focused more on the goods of the well-to-do, they would have become "lords of the villages and towns."[108]

In a land regulated by heresy placards, ruled by a most Catholic king, and with a Catholic majority in the population, iconoclasm was a radical act, even if it left no great number of corpses in its wake, save those of the image-breakers themselves, later prosecuted under Alba.[109] It is easy to be skeptical of reports by Catholics like Van Campene in Ghent that the rioters masqueraded their real desire for political pillage in image-breaking. At the same time, iconoclasm, as I have argued, had direct political overtones. "Vivent les Gueux!" went the cry of many *beeldenstormers* as they desecrated images, thereby linking their efforts with those of the aristocrats' protests earlier in 1566. In some instances, such a correlation was directly inscribed in an act of violence itself. One Mathieu Bart, a day laborer in the small village of Lavantie south of Flanders, was fined for shouting his support of the Beggars while recarving the beard of an unidentified male saint in their "Turkish" style.[110] As I have already noted, children in Ghent taunted statues of the saints and the Holy Family, threatening them with public beheading if they did not exclaim "Vivent les Gueux!"[111] Iconoclasm was clearly religious work whose aftereffects, everyone has agreed, carried political implications. While it might be going too far to describe iconoclasm as a species of "popular" politics, it is equally misleading to read it as devoid of political awareness or even political goals. As one admittedly drunken rioter boasted in Bergues, "Let our lord the king and his soldiers come to our land, for they will be defeated."[112]

The disinterment of the seneschal's decaying arm in Tournai was not the only direct assault on the physical remains of a figure of authority. At the monastery of Beaupré just south of Flanders on August 20, rioters removed the freshly buried corpse of its abbot from its sepulcher. With lay sisters forced to watch, the men dragged the corpse by its feet around the church, strung it upright against a tree, beat it with switches, and dragged it out to a bonfire to burn it along with all the destroyed paintings, statues, and ecclesiastical ornaments.[113] The corpse was made to undergo public humiliation, a whipping, and an execution by fire—all references to forms of punishment inflicted on condemned Protestants as a result of Philip II's religious placards.

---

108. Frans de Potter, ed., *Dagboek van Cornelis en Philip van Campene behelzende het verhaal der merkwaardigste gebeurtenissen voorgevallen te Gent sedert het begin der godsdienstberoerten tot den 5en April 1571* (Ghent, 1870), 37.

109. Eire, *War against the Idols* notes that iconoclasm could assume a radical political dimension in such centralized states as France or Scotland when a challenge to idolatrous worship de facto became a challenge to monarchs who supported such worship.

110. *Troubles religieux*, 2:246.

111. BT Van Vaernewijck, 1:110.

112. *Troubles religieux*, 3:264.

113. Ibid., 2:198–99.

Like violence was visited on statues, tombstones, and sepulchers of important figures. As the regent herself wrote to Philip II on August 22, "In all the monasteries and cloisters they attack the sepulchers of the counts and countesses of Flanders."[114] While there is no basis to support her broad-brush suggestion that every burial site was vandalized, there were several cases of the destruction of tombs and epigraphs, especially of clergy or the urban patriciate. In depositions taken in September 1567 in the Pays de l'Alleu, for example, the wood-seller Jehan Sohier recalled widespread attacks on sepulchers during the troubles a year earlier.[115] The astute chronicler Pontus Payen described similar ravages in Tournai. The most notable occurred at the tomb of Adolf, Duke of Gueldre, a Ghent captain who had died in a 1477 skirmish with the city and was buried in the church of Saint Quentin, a point confirmed in a report on iconoclasm filed with the regent by commissioners whom she had appointed to investigate the troubles there.[116] At the Cistercian abbey of Fontenelle outside Valenciennes, during a second wave of iconoclasm in January 1567, rioters destroyed the statue of Jeanne de Valois, wife of the early fourteenth-century count of Hainault, and Anne de Bavière, a granddaughter of the same countess.[117] And even though canons of Ghent's Saint Bavo's Cathedral had removed many objects in advance of the attacks, iconoclasts managed to deface the epigraphs of important patricians, including those of the de Maech, the de Baviers and the Van de Triest families, as well as the tombstone of the last abbot of the Saint Bavo's Abbey (razed by Charles V in 1540 following a major revolt in Ghent). In Saint Jacob's parish church, on the marble sepulcher in front of the high altar, the sculpted faces of the former bailiff—the government's legal representative in the city—François van der Gracht, and his two wives were disfigured, their noses hacked off.[118]

Iconoclasts also ransacked religious spaces and religious objects associated with the sacred prestige of sovereigns. In Valenciennes, for example, the palace Salle-Le-Comte had a church of Saint Francis in which the counts and countesses of Hainault had been buried since the fourteenth century. What is more, the gates of the palace served as the traditional site at which the count of Hainault during his inaugural entry swore to uphold the city's privileges. During the iconoclastic riots, the soldier François Dartois broke paintings and statues in the king's chapel in the Salle-Le-Comte, for which he later paid with

114. Van Gelder, *Correspondance française*, 2:325–26.
115. *Troubles religieux*, 2:278–79.
116. Henne, *Mémoires de Pontus Payen*, 1:183–84; Pinchart, *Mémoires de Pasquier de le Barre*, 2:198.
117. P. L. De Robaulx de Soumoy, ed. *Histoire des troubles advenues à Valenciennes à cause des hérésies 1562–79, tirée de plusieurs écrits en 1699 par Pierre Joseph Le Boucq* (Brussels, 1864), 20–22. The chronicle is a copy of a text compiled by Jean Doudelet of Notre Dame de la Chaussée, who used reports of two contemporary tax collectors and not Le Boucq's, despite the editor's attribution. On this matter, see Félicien Machelart, "La Destruction du patrimoine artistique médiéval de Valenciennes," in *Valenciennes aux XIVe et XVe siecles*, 90, n. 5.
118. Victor Fris, "Eene treurige bladzijde in de Gentsche Kunstgeschiedenis," *Bulletin der Maatschappij van Geschied- en Oudheidkunde te Gent* 19, no. 2 (1911): 106–7.

his life.[119] More provocative targets were churches that had served as sites of the great chapter meetings of the Order of the Golden Fleece, including Ghent's Saint Bavo's Cathedral, Valenciennes' Saint Paul's Church, and Antwerp's Onze-Lieve-Vrouwekerk.[120] These were attacked as part of the general assault on Catholic churches and chapels, but no doubt rioters were well aware of their elite status. That this was so is confirmed by the iconoclasts in Ghent's Saint Bavo's Cathedral, who carefully avoided the insignia, banners, and other objects from the 1559 Golden Fleece chapter meeting. In Antwerp, by contrast, rioters damaged the heraldic device of Philip II's uncle Ferdinand, Holy Roman Emperor, and several banners from the 1561 chapter meeting in the Onze-Lieve-Vrouwekerk, and punishment against those deemed guilty was swift and severe.[121] But, if generally careful not to attack Golden Fleece insignia, the iconoclasts showed little concern for the religious artifacts of the parish churches themselves, though they too had sacralized chapter meetings of the Golden Fleece. Always the astute observer, Van Vaernewijck grasped this very point. Imagine, he wondered, what Philip II's reaction might have been had he known in 1559 when he held his chapter meeting of the Golden Fleece at Saint Bavo's Cathedral that this revered space would fall prey to such destruction.[122]

Iconoclasts occasionally destroyed objects and images associated with court officials and royalty, whether or not they were cognizant of these connections. In the Church of Our Lady just outside Oudenaarde in Pamele, a Calvinist minister urged the men to knock over the baptismal font where the local bailiff had earlier tried his best to prevent the men from entering. The crowd surged in and obliged the minister's request, destroying a font that had been used in the baptism of none other than the regent herself.[123] In Tournai's cathedral, iconoclasts cautiously avoided damaging the banners left hanging after a 1531 chapter meeting held by Charles V, but in the church of Chartreux they destroyed an image of Saint George donated by Henry VIII after his brief seizure of the city in 1513, perhaps because it commemorated his victory over the city.[124] On balance, the record suggests that direct violence against Golden Fleece banners and insignia, royal ex-voto statues, or other ecclesiastical gifts was very selective. The iconoclasts mainly exercised care in not directly attacking symbols of political authority, though the tombs of hated officials and local patricians appear to have been more regularly targeted. There were, nonetheless, contradictory attitudes occasionally expressed toward royal symbols, as was best il-

---

119. Machelart, "La destruction du patrimoine artistique," 91–92.

120. De Gruben, Les Chapitres de la Toison d'Or.

121. BT Van Vaernewijck, 1:142; Gus. van Havre, ed., Chronijck der stadt Antwerpen toegeschreven aan den notaris Geeraard Bertrijn (Antwerp, 1879), 137.

122. BT Van Vaernewijck, 1:143.

123. Vander Meersch, Mémoires Justificatif du Magistrat d'Audenarde, 172–73.

124. On the Golden Fleece insignia, see Pinchart, Mémoires de Pasquier de le Barre, 1:137, and on the Saint George image, 184.

lustrated in Ghent. At the church of the abbey of Saint Peter, much was ransacked, but iconoclasts did not touch the memorial to Charles V's sister, Isabel, one saying, according to Van Vaernewicjk, that they did not want to provoke the king's anger.[125] On the other hand, it was in this same city that a Vincent Salamon formed part of a group that destroyed a gilded statue of Charles V and Our Lady at the Keizerpoort, probably the most direct attack on the image of a Burgundian figure in the whole sweep of Low Country iconoclasm.[126]

Iconoclasm and Public Authority

Iconoclasts thus worked within a set of contradictions concerning symbols of political authority. On the one hand, they overwhelmingly avoided any direct damage to symbols of princely power, though they felt less inhibited when venting anger upon the burial epithets, tombstones, and sarcophagi of regional officials or urban patricians who, in many instances, had aligned themselves with Habsburg interests. A disinterred seneschal's arm, a patrician's tombstone—these were targeted for their secular as well as sacred prestige, and were obviously considered to carry far less dangerous consequences than any direct assault on a regal symbol. On the other hand, iconoclasts were engaged in the wholesale project of overturning sacred objects and ransacking religious institutions. These objects and sacred places were essential to Catholic worship and, by extension, to securing the legitimacy of king, aldermen, and other political officials. While in a narrow sense the iconoclasts discriminated between a Golden Fleece banner and a statue or painting, in a more important sense they were putting pressure on the very alliance between sacred space, holy object, and Burgundian authority that we have seen in play since the emergence of the Burgundian Netherlands as a political and cultural entity. As much as the iconoclasts wanted to make a distinction between sacred and secular incarnations of authority, no such clear bifurcation was possible.

For the most part iconoclasts committed their deeds illegally, without the clear support of local magistrates. Nevertheless, as more than one historian has noted, they often profited from the tacit approval of the urban shooting guilds, whose members in many instances did nothing to stop the violence.[127] In the north, iconoclasm occasionally took place with the support of regional nobility or local magistrates; in these instances, image

---

125. BT Van Vaernewijck, 1:149.

126. Ibid., 2:321. Salamon was apprehended by the bailiff of Saint Peter's on June 21, 1567, but released on September 3. See Fris, "Notes pour servir à l'histoire des iconoclastes," 103.

127. On the *schutters* and iconoclasm, see Parker, Dutch Revolt, 79–80; Duke and Kolff, "Time of Troubles," 329–32; and especially, J. C. Grayson, "The Civic Militia in the County of Holland, 1560–81: Politics and Public Order in the Dutch Revolt," *Bijdragen en Mededelingen betreffende de Geschiedenis der Nederlanden*, 95 (1980): 35–63.

destruction occurred in a supervised, orderly fashion. This happened most notably in Friesland, where urban magistrates and rural nobles supervised the removal of images and the formation of Calvinist congregations. At Leeuwarden in September 1566, for example, the town council itself directed the cleansing of churches and the establishment of Protestant worship.[128] Sometimes, as in the case of Floris van Pallant, Count of Culemborg, churches were cleared out of images at the behest of a local nobleman. Sometimes Calvinist nobility themselves undid their own ancestral venerations. Willem van Zuylen van Nijvelt had his family chapel destroyed at Aartsbergen, and Herbert van Raephorst requested the removal of two family altars from a Wassenaar church.[129] But even in the absence of such direct authorization, iconoclasm could still take place with indirect official support. In The Hague, for example, iconoclasts appealed to the president of the Court of Holland and said they had an official mandate to cleanse the churches. The president, Cornelis Suys, granted them permission, but warned them to undertake their task "without causing a commotion." With the *schutters* setting up outside, twelve men paid by the president assisted the iconoclasts in cleansing the church while outside the city other churches and chapels were similarly stripped, with two nobles of the Compromise, Ghilein Zegers van Wassenhove and Herbert van Raephorst, as active participants.[130]

In the majority of cases in which iconoclasm happened violently, fictions of authority were essential to rousing support and initiating action. Mathys Blaere of Hondschoote, for example, was sentenced to death by hanging in 1569 for having frequented the sermons of Sebastian Matte in the wonder year, and for having been in the forefront of iconoclasm in Gijverinkhove, Hoogstade, and Loo; he led his forces with the cry, "Let us freely break, I have an official commission!"[131] He was not alone. In Ypres, the rioters claimed a mandate both from Egmont, governor of Flanders, and the local bailiff.[132] That this was the case is confirmed in the clemency request a year later by the bricklayer Claeys de Back, who claimed he was duped into participating in the image-breaking because he thought he and his associates had an official mandate.[133] False letters approving iconoclasm were frequent in the castellanies of the Westkwartier. In Valenciennes, iconoclasts also claimed they had secured official permission, as did their counterparts in Ghent and The Hague, with officials in these latter two cities actually granting permission to break images.[134] Such fictive assertions of official permission demonstrate a conscious level of deception,

128. Woltjer, *Friesland in Hervormingstijd*.
129. Duke and Kolff, "Time of Troubles," 322–23.
130. Scheerder, *Beeldenstorm*, 76–78.
131. *Troubles religieux*, 4:197.
132. Diegerick, *Documents du XVI siècle*, 1:60.
133. Ibid., 1:80–81.
134. Scheerder, *Beeldenstorm*, 24; Paul Beuzart, *La Répression à Valenciennes après les troubles religieux de 1566* (Paris, 1930), 117; RvB, no. 76, a set of depositions taken in August 1567 concerning iconoclasm in Ghent, fols. 310v.

to be sure, but they also suggest that the leaders of the various cadres of image-breakers were worried about the broader political implications of their actions, and opted for a forged legal cover. His fundamental critique of Catholic image worship notwithstanding, Calvin himself never explicitly advocated acting against the authority of "idolatrous" princes or magistrates.[135] In his 1537 treatise *On Shunning of the Unlawful Rites of the Ungodly and Preserving the Purity of the Christian Religion*, Calvin did, however, take up the story in the Book of Daniel (Daniel 3, 1-29) of three Jewish officials Shadrach, Meshach, and Abednego, who were thrown into a fiery furnace for refusing to worship before a golden statue set up by Nebuchadnezzar. In a gloss on the three men's steadfast bravery and miraculous survival, Calvin observed, "It seemed easier to allow their bodies to be cruelly consumed by the flames of a fiery furnace than to please the king's eye, by bending their thigh for a little before his statue!" That the story received illustration sometime in 1552 by the Antwerp painter Pieter Aertsen makes this comment the more pertinent, especially since Calvin had praised the willingness of the three men to hold to belief at the risk of "flaming the anger of a mighty king against them."[136] If Calvin did not openly sanction flaunting royal authority on matters of idolatry, he and Aertsen raised the problem of idolatrous kingship and celebrated its rejections in a climate in which such issues mattered, in places such as the Low Countries.

Because iconoclasts had invoked fictive letters of authorization to commit image-breaking before anxious bailiffs or fired-up crowds, their apologists like Philips van Marnix, Lord of St. Aldegonde, strained after the riots to deny that iconoclasm had been a crime of sedition against magistrate and king. In his 1567 apology for the iconoclastic riots, this future secretary to William of Orange argued that since images erected in chapels and churches were privately endowed, they in no way redounded on public political authority.[137] Marnix's spirited defense matched the iconoclasts' own sense that since they largely avoided overt symbols of political authority—a symbol, that is, like the idol in the Book of Daniel—theirs was spiritual work. And yet as we have seen, a parish church, a private chapel, and public authority were not so cleanly divisible. Moreover, since Philip the Good's entry into Bruges in 1440, Burgundian and Habsburg rulers had sacralized their image through allusions to biblical kings, Nebuchadnezzar included.[138] With the exception of Ghent, it is true that iconoclasts refrained from attacking statues of

---

135. Eire, *War against the Idols*, 277.

136. Keith P. F. Moxley, "Reflections of Some Unusual Subjects in the Work of Pieter Aertsen," *Jahrbuch der Berliner Museen* 18 (1976): 57–83, quote on 72. The story of Shadrach, Meshach, and Abednego was portrayed in ten engravings of the Book of Daniel published by Hieronymus Cock, after drawings by Maarten van Heemskerck, who produced a set of Old Testament prints. See Eleanor A. Saunders, "A Commentary on Iconoclasm in Several Print Series by Maarten van Heemskerck," *Simiolus* 10 (1978–79): 59–83.

137. Philips van Marnix van Saint Aldegonde, *Vraye Narration et apologie des choses*, in *Philips van Marnix van St. Aldegonde*, 1:107–8.

138. Kipling, *Enter the King*, 264–80.

Adoration of the Lineage of Nebuchadnezzar. Pieter Aertsen, 1552. Aertsen's painting is of the story from the Book of Daniel (Daniel 3, 1–29). Courtesy of Boijmans-van-Beuningen Museum, Rotterdam.

king, counts, or regents. Yet iconoclasts did provoke the "flaming anger of a mighty king" because they inflicted their violence on the sacred instruments that helped to seal elite public authority, be it royal or civic. Both in their actions and in the riotous, satirical, and laborers' idioms they invoked, the iconoclasts of 1566 conflated festive forms, social labor, and religious convictions. More fundamentally, they voiced a religious position on the appropriateness of image-worship and the Catholic mass that engaged and dramatically transformed the religious and political quarrels that had so preoccupied the titans in Brussels and elsewhere. The elite cadre of nobles who butted heads in the 1560s against Spanish legal and religious policy in the Netherlands knew the power of the state's political culture—and its vulnerability. Their choreographed protests in the spring of 1566 mixed ribald humor, carnivalesque inversion, anticlerical parody, social satire, and hardball politics. As they drew up eloquent formal briefs against the hated placards, they seized on well-tested cultural props, mastering the procession and invoking sacred times and images. The iconoclasts in Flanders Westkwartier and elsewhere might have been far removed from these events in Brussels and other large cities. But they set off a chain reaction and laid claim to this politics of inversion. "Vivent les Gueux!" was no empty slogan. It articulated, most directly, Reformed sentiment. But it also meant precisely what it said. The rioters, be they young or old, male or female, rural villager or urban Calvinist, identified with the political world of the Beggars, and shared their taste for protest through inversion. Household and work tools in hand, the iconoclasts ritually mocked, disfigured, and pulverized religious objects and images to reveal that Catholic sacred representations were nothing more than mere heaps of material.

CHAPTER 4 TIME, SPACE, AND THE CITY ICONOCLASM IN YPRES, GHENT, AND ANTWERP

Iconoclasm began in the rough-and-tumble drapery centers of Flanders' Westkwartier and their surrounding countryside, where craftsmen and laborers embraced Calvinism, imbuing it with their local concerns. Westkwartier image-breaking, however, culminated in a matter of days in an attack on Ypres, an old cloth city and a new episcopal center. Once there, the religious violence quickly enveloped the southern Low Countries' great cities, including the metropolis of Antwerp and Flanders' chief city, Ghent, before moving steadily north. In this chapter I explore the cartography of iconoclasm in this trio of cities, and how the spaces, places, and timing of the violence differed among them. In Ypres and Antwerp, religious time and the place of civic devotions mattered most, particularly the attention iconoclasts showered on veneration of the Virgin Mary. In Ypres, iconoclasts centered their actions on the August 4 "Tuindag" procession and the Assumption Day services of August 15. Iconoclasts practiced an even more acute awareness of Assumption Day and the places of devotion in Antwerp, a bellwether in many ways for the tussle between Reformed religion, urban privilege, and Spanish Habsburg policy. Although Antwerp boasted many religious venerations, its iconoclasts paid extraordinary attention to the popular but elite devotion of Onze Lieve Vrouw (Our Beloved Lady) in the Onze-Lieve-Vrouwekerk. Ghent too experienced the violent thunder clap of iconoclasm. Yet, unlike Antwerp, it did not have an obvious sacred center, despite the importance of Saint Bavo's Cathedral. More so than in Ypres and Antwerp, strong material and political overtones colored Ghent's iconoclasm, and included the theft of goods, the mock execution of images, and the destruction of a statue of Charles V with the Virgin Mary. In Ghent, too, historical memory was determinative: iconoclasm happened in the long shadow of the revolt the city had fomented in 1539 against Charles V, and its timbre reflects the legacy of this turmoil amplified by new Calvinist sentiment. The fund of iconoclastic acts I described in the previous chapter was a repertoire of violence whose application varied considerably. Nowhere is this more evident than in these three cities, where the religious violence partook of the famous particularism so apparent in the political realm, and where the results helped to change the course of the rebellion against Habsburg authority.

Ypres and Religious Time: The Tuin Virgin

Ypres in the sixteenth century had seen better days. One of the four members of the Estates of Flanders and an old center of draperies, Ypres was still active in textiles, but its economic prestige had slipped in the wake of the production of lighter, cheaper serge cloth in the other parts of the Westkwartier. In 1485 the city could not meet the sum it owed to the Transport of Flanders, an important fourteenth-century tax levied regularly on Flanders' three great cities. Unlike Bruges or Ghent, Ypres had no secondary economic pillar, be it foreign trade or a grain staple.[1] Young workers not bound to its traditional guild system were emigrating to seek work elsewhere, including to Hondschoote. In 1506 its population hovered around 9,500, far less than the more robust Bruges and Ghent, themselves undergoing slippage.[2] In 1545 Ypres tried to experiment with serge production, importing colonies of outside workers. At the same time, its magistrates kept up a steady economic and political hectoring of the new drapery centers, a practice waged since the fourteenth century against Poperinghe, and since the fifteenth century against Bailleul and Cassel.[3] But if Ypres' economic prestige was now diminished, its political importance remained strong thanks to its seat in the Estates of Flanders. Its Catholic religious life gained luster when Ypres became a bishopric in 1559 after the ecclesiastical reorganization of the Low Countries. On November 11, 1561, the former inquisitor Maarten van Riethoven was appointed Ypres' first bishop; within months, he was collaborating with Flanders' inquisitor Pieter Titelmans, who was so much the object of Calvinist disdain.[4]

Sixteenth-century Ypres, therefore, was a city of bygone greatness but contemporary importance. The economic tensions over Ypres' attempt to colonize serge production and its new position as episcopal handmaiden to Titelmans complicated the long-standing political jealousies other Westkwartier cities harbored against this walled, privileged city. But even before Ypres gained an episcopate, it had boasted some of the Westkwartier's most important religious institutions. It had eight parish churches; the two oldest, Saint Martin's and Saint Peter's, originally marked the boundaries of the city in 1093. There

---

1. David Nicholas, *Medieval Flanders* (London 1992), 82–83.
2. H. Pirenne, "Les dénombrements de la population d'Ypres au XVe siècle (1412–1506): Contribution à l'histoire statistique sociale au moyen âge," *Vierteljahrsschrift für Sozial-und Wirtschaftsgeschichte* 1 (1903): 1–32.
3. For examples, see I. Diegerick, ed., *Inventaire chronologique et analytique des chartes et documents appartenant aux archives de la ville de Ypres*, 7 vols. (Bruges, 1853–68), 5:6, 8–13, and 30–31; Coornaert, *Centre industriel d'autrefois*, 4–7.
4. Decavele, *Dageraad*, 1:5–6. Titelmans was appointed to his position on June 2, 1545.

were also two twelfth-century establishments: the collegiate church of Saint Martin, rich in lands, revenues, and dominion over the parish churches by its Augustinian canons, and the Augustinian nunnery of Nonnenbosch, named for its location right outside the city walls in the nearby woods. The city featured many other religious houses, including very active mendicant orders, the Franciscans since 1255 and the Dominicans since 1268.[5]

As they did elsewhere in urban Europe, the Franciscans promoted the cult of the Virgin in Ypres. The veneration grew rapidly after a July and early August siege of the city in 1383 by the English forces of Henry Despenser, bishop of Norwich. Although the siege lasted weeks and included an attack by Ghent's militia, nothing was destroyed other than unwalled, outlying suburbs. Yprians attributed their good fortune to the intervention of the Virgin Mary, whose statue had been paraded on the city's ramparts during the siege. In thanksgiving, they made August 8, the penultimate day of the siege, the feast day of Onze Lieve Vrouw van Tuin (Our Lady of the Garden), but soon designated the first Sunday of August for subsequent celebrations in her honor.[6] The Franciscans were only too eager to place the Virgin's statue in a chapel in their cloister. As the original promoters of Marian worship in Ypres who had helped during the 1383 siege by opening up part of their religious house to be used as a mill when the others had been rendered unusable, they became guardians of the devotion of the Tuin Virgin. As a result, the Franciscans' reputation grew handsomely, as did their good relationship with the city's aldermen.[7] In 1385 they produced a new, more elaborate statue of the Tuin Virgin. It depicted a crowned Mary holding the Christ child in her right hand and flowers in her left in an enclosed "garden fence," a *hortus conclusus* style that had its origins in thirteenth-century France. While the *hortus conclusus* motif theologically evoked the maternity and fertility of the Virgin, its Yprian version referred more concretely to the enclosed walls around which the original statue had been carried. According to local lore, thick green hedges had blanketed the walls and provided cover for Yprian soldiers manning the ramparts.[8] Soon after 1385, an elite confraternity formed to keep up the chapel of the Tuin Virgin and manage her veneration; their responsibilities included annual gifts of cloth and jewels to bedeck the statue. At the same time, Ypres retained other Marian devotions. The belfry received a statue of the Virgin Mary, its placement confirmed in a 1377 payment to a city painter who had to spruce it up, and another Onze-Lieve-Vrouw was placed in the aldermen's council room.[9]

---

5. Alphonse Vandenpeereboom, *Ypriana*, 3:71–81, and 5:1–14, especially on the military siege.

6. Paul Trio and Walter Simons, "Achtergronden bij het ontstaan van de tuindagprocessie: Bronnen en situering," in *Ieper Tuindag: Zesde eeuwfeest*, ed. Romain Vinckier (Ypres, 1983), 107–28.

7. Trio and Simons, "Achtergronden bij het ontstaan van de tuindagprocessie."

8. Bernadette Rose, "O. L.-Vrouw van Tuine, een beeld uit het begin van de zestiende eeuw," in *Ieper Tuindag: Zesde eeuwfeest*, 181–211.

9. Vandenpeereboom, *Ypriana*, 5:10–11.

No matter how diverse Ypres' religious culture, the Tuin Virgin became its most important veneration. In 1384, a year after the siege, Ypres' magistrates permitted an annual procession in honor of Tuindag.[10] This August 8 procession elevated the memory of the siege in the civic consciousness, exalted the Franciscan-housed statue of the Tuin Virgin to whom victory was attributed, and anticipated Assumption Day, celebrated throughout Europe on August 15. In its original iteration, there was a lavish procession on August 8 alone. Over time, the feast day was set for the first Sunday of August, and inaugurated days of religious worship and civic celebration that stretched to Assumption Day itself. Competitions arose for the best praise poem in honor of the Virgin among city festive groups and rhetorician groups like the Confraternity of Alpha and Omega. Prizes included gold rings and bejeweled goblets, regularly put on public display before the festivities began. Since at least 1483, short theater pieces recounting the Virgin's life accompanied these contests, performed by members of Alpha and Omega; by the 1550s, chambers of rhetoric from elsewhere were invited to mount plays too. For the first centennial of the siege in 1483, the Alpha and Omega rhetoricians set up an open-air theater in front of the great Cloth Hall and five local societies performed plays.[11]

The Tuindag festivities grew in scope, but the veneration of the Tuin Virgin remained the unwavering anchor. Beginning in 1385, canons of the parish church of Saint Martin had chantry priests celebrate weekly masses in honor of the Virgin. But it was the statue in the Franciscan cloister whose veneration was the pivot of these religious celebrations, and it was the Franciscans who brought the Tuin Virgin to Saint Martin's on the feast day. The Tuindag procession featured an orderly train of the city's guilds, clergy, and town officials parading with the statue fashionably outfitted in damask, silk, and gold cloth and studded with pearls, diamonds, and other jewels. Subvented by the city, the procession was a boon to the arquebusier, archer, and crossbowmen guilds, whose members received annual cash payments for new costumes. They also led the procession, gathering at 6 a.m. in front of the Belfry. They were followed by torch-bearing guildsmen and their insignia, themselves followed by wagons upon which rhetoricians mounted mystery plays. Devotees thronged behind them, some barefoot, others carrying wooden crosses, including groups of young girls dressed in white and bearing candles. At the center of the processional train, the Franciscans and confraternity members of the Tuin held the statue of the Virgin aloft; they were followed by other religious confraternities, and Ypres' remaining secular and religious clergy, who carried other important venerations and relics, including the Corpus Christi borne beneath a richly appointed baldaquin. At the rear of the procession marched the city's magistrates.

---

10. There is a May 3, 1436, document from the confraternity of the Tuin Virgin that confirms this date in Diegerick, *Inventaire chronologique*, 3:306.

11. Vandenpeereboom, *Ypriana*, 5:94–117.

In its mix of religious veneration and social ordering, of mystery plays and marching aldermen, of clergy and guildsmen on display, the Tuindag procession was a typical Low Country *ommegang*. In its merging of a standard Marian devotion with a memorable event in the city's history, the Tuindag procession was also redolent of civic boosterism. With Protestantism on the rise—above all in the Westkwartier in which Ypres was situated—the procession gained new meaning in the 1560s as an affirmation of Catholic identity in a fledgling bishopric that stood as a bulwark against a growing sea of Reformed and Anabaptist conviction. That Calvinism was hatched in the new drapery centers that Yprian officials had attempted to rein in must have made it seem all the more noxious. That three of the area's most energetic Calvinist preachers, the Carmelite Pieter Dathenus, the Augustinian Jacob de Buzere, and the Dominican Anthonis Algoet all hailed originally from the city's religious houses only made matters worse to Ypres' religious officials, especially the bishop.

These apostate clergy were quick to make Ypres a special target of their attention in the weeks before iconoclasm finally broke loose. It was Algoet who led a crowd of energized, psalm-singing followers inside Ypres to the central marketplace on July 25 to confront the bailiff, the upper aldermen, and several of his colleagues.[12] This show of force occurred just days before the Tuindag procession was scheduled to occur, on August 4, the first Sunday of the month in 1566. Clearly worried that an assault on their city was imminent, the town fathers reluctantly decided to close eight of the city's principal gates and celebrate the feast day without any great fanfare and with no procession. Extra guards were posted at the city's gates, but the gates were not impassable because the aldermen, perhaps as a sign of their equivocation, had allowed wickets on each to handle some foot traffic. On the Sunday Tuindag had been scheduled to begin, a group of Calvinist enthusiasts easily penetrated the barrier and streamed into the city. When later forced to explain, the aldermen sheepishly described the crowd as armed strangers from Cassel and Poperinge who had entered the city resolved to sing psalms on the central market place. To the aldermen's amazement, despite the marchers' brazenness, they neither assaulted people nor harmed property. By nightfall, the throng left Ypres to hear sermons by de Buzere and Algoet, but then re-entered the city some two thousand strong and with de Buzere in attendance. They rushed to the Cloth Hall to sing psalms, even though local officials had already tried to secure the area.[13]

As former members of religious orders from Ypres, de Buzere and Algoet knew their city's ecclesiastical calendar perfectly. They had defiantly entered a fortified Ypres on the day of its most important religious procession, and once inside Ypres' walls they substi-

---

12. Diegerick, *Documents du XVIe siècle*, 1:28–29, part of the *Mémoire justificatif* of the aldermen. This event is confirmed in repeated sources, including F. van der Putte, ed., "Cort verhael van 't ghonne binnen de stadt van Ypres, en daer ontrent ghepasseert" *Société d'Emulation de Bruges*, ser. 2, vol. 2, 214.

13. Diegerick, *Documents du XVIe siècle*, 1:47–51.

tuted their train of psalm-singing devotees for the cancelled procession, even mimicking its itinerary by assembling in front of the Cloth Hall beneath the towering Belfry. Their entry not merely violated the decree to seal Ypres' walls; it substituted Reformed worship for the city's signature procession.

Worse was yet to come. Once iconoclasm broke loose in the Westkwartier on August 10, de Buzere, Algoet, and their followers' assault on Catholic religious time in Ypres intensified. For the Westkwartier preachers and their hammer-wielding followers, Ypres was the great prize, the region's historically dominant city and, even more important, the seat of a bishop in league with the hated inquisitor Titelmans. Little wonder that the Westkwartier's most energetic lay preacher, Sebastian Matte, made Ypres his special target. His campaign against the city began on August 14, an action yet again attuned to Catholic religious time, namely, the eve of Assumption Day.[14] No less a figure of authority than the governor of Flanders, Egmont, was in the city, answering a desperate call from its magistrates to "set the city in order from all the troubles." That very day, Egmont had appeared publicly before the Cloth Hall to order the city's gates secured and a redoubling of its forces to prevent trouble. But informed of the depredations of Matte and his associates nearby, he departed, leaving the aldermen to fend for themselves.[15] Matte was dangerously close to the city, despite Egmont's presence, preaching a kilometer away at Brielen. On August 15 proper, Matte's followers stormed the churches and cloisters surrounding Ypres: the Onze-Lieve-Vrouwekerk, the Augustinian cloister at Brielen, the cloister of the shoed Carmelites, and the cloister of Saint Clare. A split-off group, mostly from Hondschoote, raided the Augustinian Nonnenbosch, right outside the city at Zonnebeke. But they failed to gain Ypres, and Matte, frustrated, feigned illness and retreated, although he refused the entreaty of a delegation of city officials to quit his activities. The next day, the iconoclasts rushed on Ypres, thanks in no small measure to inside help, and the parish churches, chapels, and newly appointed cathedral of Saint Martin fell victim to their wrath.[16]

An anonymous Yprian chronicler spared no words in describing the iconoclasts as "sworn enemies," "hellish devils," and "raging tigers" for their violations of "the glorious feast day of the almighty Virgin and Mother of God, Mary."[17] One of the first religious institutions attacked on August 15 was the Saint Clare cloister just outside Ypres proper,

14. Summaries in Scheerder, Beeldenstorm, 28–30, and Backhouse, Beeldenstorm en Bosgeuzen, 79–80.
15. Diegerick, Documents du XVIe siècle, 1:55–56.
16. Ibid. for the aldermen's accounts. For a reconstruction of events based on the depositions of witnesses and participants, see Des Marez, "Documents relatifs aux excès commis à Ypres," and the two narratives, F. van der Putte, ed., "Cort verhael van 't ghonne binnen de stadt van Ypres," Société d'Emulation de Bruges, ser. 3, vol. 7: 293–96, and the longer version, "Cort verhael," ser. 2, vol. 2: 209–56. See also the account of the destruction in Ypres and the Westkwartier more generally in the diary of the Yprian corn inspector Augustin van Hernighem, Eerste bouck van beschrijvinghe, 20–22.
17. Van der Putte, "Cort verhael," ser. 3, vol. 7: 293.

in Sint-Jan. As the sisters later deposed to authorities, the rioters were mostly men and women from the Westkwartier who seemed bent on looting and drinking as much as on image desecration. It was night when the *beeldenstormers* raided the cellar and demanded beer. The abbess, Jehanne de Noyelles, described the crowd as inhabitants of Hondschoote. Armed with their work tools, the men destroyed everything they could get their hands on, while other rioters stole goods. The wife of a local tavern keeper filched a pot of conserves and a crystal goblet, which she later proudly displayed in Ypres' marketplace; a certain drummer took eggs; one Griete van der Waerde swiped linens from the dorter. Many witnesses stressed that the iconoclasts were thoroughly drunk.[18] This combination of image destruction, looting, and drinking intensified as the iconoclasts swept inside the city. A witness described how the crowd grew as certain Yprians joined them, splitting up into small groups, and conducting their raids on chapels and churches with the noticeable participation of "youth, women, and children."[19] Children of one draper-weaver beheaded statues in Saint Peter's with tiny hammers.[20]

As the image-breaking intensified, the iconoclasts zeroed in on Ypres' Tuin Virgin, the religious objects associated with her veneration, and the bishop. In the Franciscan cloister, iconoclasts arrived just as a group of men tried desperately to secure the chapel of the Tuin Virgin.[21] In a matter of minutes, the elite chapel and its contents were no more. In Saint Jacob's parish church, Colard van Lichtervelde witnessed an iconoclast seize wooden candleholders from the Tuindag procession and use them to smash up countless statues of saints.[22] The iconoclast Hans Tavernier visited his fury with an iron hammer upon the prominent statue of Our Lady that had long graced the front of the Cloth Hall in a niche in the Belfry. Although Tavernier was seized by city officials, they meekly released him from custody after being threatened by an angry crowd.[23]

The looting of churches, cloisters, and chapels bled into raids on private houses. To the magistrates, the social composition of the crowd—later described as "weavers, fullers, serge weavers, and serge day laborers"—accounts for why nonreligious property and goods were attacked. Had not one iconoclast, Steven Chastelain, even exclaimed, "Within three days the journeymen and poor will be as rich as the masters and the wealthy."?[24] But no residence was assaulted with more grim determination than that of the bishop of Ypres. Iconoclasts dragged books out of his residence and burned them in the kind of public bonfire usually reserved for Protestant literature. According to an anonymous chroni-

18. Des Marez, "Documents relatifs aux excès commis à Ypres," 8–16, and 99–103.
19. Ibid., 19, deposition of Marcx de Wilde, treasurer of Ypres.
20. Ibid., 25.
21. Ibid., deposition of Arnoud van Ackere, 25.
22. Ibid., 117.
23. Van der Putte, "Cort verhael," ser. 2, vol. 2: 223–25; Diegerick, *Documents du XVIe siècle*, 1:63.
24. Ibid., 62, and 214–15.

cler, the rioters had also gathered up clerical vestments from their various raids and dragged them all together to the Cloosterpoort to burn. In the heap was a jewel-studded choir cape donated by the bishop of Thérouanne, which the new bishop of Ypres had worn during his inaugural entry. A sexton who lived near the gate luckily intervened and plucked it out moments before it went up in flames.[25]

When forced later to justify their inaction in preventing iconoclasm to Habsburg authorities, the magistrates of Ypres nervously reasoned that the use of force to deter the iconoclasts would have resulted "in a great spilling of blood and a general sack and pillage of the inhabitants of this city."[26] However much this explanation smacks of self-interest, it confirms the vulnerability the magistrates felt as propertied, middle-of-the-road men in a sea of evangelical furor. No longer the great urban center it had once been, Ypres nonetheless still encapsulated economic and political privilege, and something even worse: Catholic authority. Accompanied by raids on houses, the stealing of goods, and the intense bouts of drinking and eating, iconoclasm in Ypres carried earthy, material tones, possibly even currents of revenge against this city that had waged a campaign against centers of rural textile manufacturing. But even more striking is just how closely its time frame and target paralleled the Tuindag procession and its attendant celebrations. The fury spent on Ypres happened during the Tuindag celebrations, from the day of the cancelled procession to its culmination eleven days later on August 15. Instead of the orderly display of Ypres' civic and ecclesiastical elites, instead of mystery plays and visiting pilgrims, the city got just the opposite: a violent and riotous overturning of everything the Tuindag procession represented. This was so much the case that when the procession was held anew on the first Sunday of August 1567, the Yprian Catholic Augustijn van Hernighem rejoiced, bitterly noting that times were better than the year before, "when the Beggars held their Tuindag."[27] Iconoclasm in Ypres was about many things, but none so obvious as the importance of religious time and how it shapes the cultural profile of an urban center. Tuindag celebrated the religious veneration of the Virgin linked to a heroic episode of the city's glorious medieval past, with all the city's crucial religious and secular corporations on display beneath the great Cloth Hall and Belfry. Iconoclasm impugned this sacred-cum-political pinnacle of the Yprian public calendar, leaving a fragile commune to pick up the pieces in its wake, and badly shaken magistrates who begged the regent for help in protecting the venerable city from the Calvinist juggernaut.[28]

25. Van der Putte, "Cort verhael van 't ghonne binnen de stadt van Ypres," *Société d'emulation de Bruges*, ser. 3, vol. 7: 294.
26. Diegerick, *Documents du XVIe siècle*, 1:220.
27. Van Hernighem, *Eerste bouck van beschrijvinghe*, 51.
28. Diegerick, *Documents du XVIe siècle*, 1:226–30, August 26, 1566, letter.

Antwerp and the Place of Veneration: Onze-Lieve-Vrouwekerk

However great Ypres' reputation in the Westkwartier, it was a poor regional cousin to Antwerp, the greatest metropolis in the sixteenth-century Low Countries. Boasting a population of some one hundred thousand, it was a vibrant commercial city with colonies of merchants from across Europe who trafficked in English cloth, Portuguese spices, south German copper, and silver, among other goods. It was home as well to luxury silk weaving, diamond cutting, sugar refining, glass and pottery works, and a print industry that boasted no less than 271 printers, publishers, and booksellers who churned out an array of religious works, humanist treatises, and books in natural philosophy and geography aggressively exported throughout Europe, Spain included. It was a city of artists, humanists, and educators who lived crowded alongside merchants and artisans. The city had twenty-six official guilds that ran the gamut from textiles to food to transport, and many more day laborers who worked in a variety of occupations, from the booming construction trades to the busy docks and warehouses dotting the Scheldt River. At base, Antwerp's reputation was resoundingly commercial: at the English bourse and the new bourse, and in the many permanent sales halls throughout the city, merchants, buyers, insurers, and brokers met, negotiated, bought, sold, issued bills of exchange, and bartered. The explosive growth and commercial success Antwerp underwent in the first half of the sixteenth century secured the city an international fame and a polyglot citizenry. But with economic success came all the social ills of commercial expansion and growth: widening social inequality and a built environment characterized by high rents, a housing shortage, and a geography of wealth in which the most well-to-do lived in the city's central wards while the poor crowded the outer ones, particularly the seventh on the southwestern corner and the twelfth on the northeastern side.[29]

Antwerp's cosmopolitan bustle and worldly inhabitants astonished observers, including one of its most perceptive, the long-time Florentine resident Lodovico Guicciardini, who marveled that ordinary merchants, women included, seemed to handle three or four

---

29. A valuable summary of the city's social and economic profile is in Marnef, Antwerp in the Age of Reformation, 3–13. On Antwerp's population, see J. van Roey, "De bevolking," in Antwerpen in de XVIe eeuw, ed. Watter Couvreur et al. (Antwerp, 1975), 95–108. On Antwerp's economy and its social effects, see Hugo Soly, "Sociale relaties in Antwerpen in de 16de eeuw," in Antwerpen verhaal van een metropool, 16de–17de eeuw, ed. Jan van der Stock (Ghent, 1993): 37–47, and Hugo Soly, Urbanisme en kapitalisme te Antwerpen in de 16de eeuw: De stedebouwkundige en industriële onderneming van Ghilbert van Schoonbeke (Brussels, 1977). On the print industry, see Léon Voet, "De typographische bedrijvigheid te Antwerpen in de 16de eeuw," in Antwerpen in de XVIe eeuw, 233–55, and Werner Waterschoot, "Antwerp: Books, Publishing, and Cultural Production before 1585," in Urban Achievement in Early Modern Europe: Golden Ages in Antwerp, Amsterdam, and London, ed. Patrick O'Brien et al. (Cambridge, 2001), 233–48.

languages as effortlessly as they plied their wares.[30] Surely, Guicciardini boasted, there is no other northern European city save Paris so great in stature, and none in the world that could rival Antwerp's commercial bustle. Little wonder that during the enormous rhetorician competition, or landjuweel, held in the city in 1561, trade was lionized in poetic verse, including a work entitled, "Eulogy of the Honest Merchant."[31] This city of tradesmen and laborers was also an intellectual mecca, whose tone was not dictated by the Latinate culture of a university but by a hunger for practical knowledge and a vibrant publishing world. Antwerp had numerous parochial schools teaching vernacular literacy and basic numerancy: five elite clerical schools with a Latin curriculum, and a surprising number of secular competitors that offered the same, with 372 new schoolmasters registered in the teachers' guild of Saint Ambrose between 1530 and 1600.[32] Antwerp was home to a tight cluster of educators, humanists, geographers, printers, and painters, including the great Pieter Bruegel and the no less celebrated Christophe Plantin, who rose from a French immigrant leather craftsman in 1549 to become Europe's renowned publisher of religious texts and scientific and humanist works.[33]

As with the other Low Country cities, Antwerp zealously guarded its hard-earned political privileges and harbored a fierce sense of independence. As Guicciardini put it, Antwerp was so rich in charters of liberties that though it owed fealty to the Duke of Brabant it was "almost like a free city and a republic." Over the centuries, its magistrates had secured many economic, legal, and political concessions from the dukes of Brabant, and four separate compilations of privileges were made in the sixteenth century in an attempt to canonize written charter and unwritten custom.[34] But if Antwerp's economic life encouraged a push-pull dynamism and immigrant talent, its political life was noticeably more fixed. A cohort of conservative, old-line magistrates—eighteen aldermen, two burgomasters, two treasurers, and a receiver—held the reins of government. Unlike other Netherlands cities in the south, the guilds had never succeeded in gaining a toehold in city hall, though their economic and political weight was felt in indirect ways, especially in the

---

30. Ludovico Guicciardini, *Description de la cité d'Anvers par messire Louis Guicciardini, Gentilhomme Florentin, traduction de François de Belleforest*, ed., M. Sabbe (Antwerp, 1920), 68–69, translated and excerpted from the original 1567 work, *Descrittione di tutti i Paesi Bassi, altrimenti detti Germania Inferiore*.

31. Waterschoot, "Antwerp: Books, Publishing and Cultural Production," 246. For the edited texts of this *landjuweel*, see E. Cockx-Indestege and Werner Waterschoot, eds., *Uyt Ionsten Versaemt: Het Landjuweel van 1561 te Antwerpen* (Brussels, 1994).

32. Marnef, *Antwerp in the Age of the Reformation*, 33–35.

33. L. Voet, *The Golden Compass: A History and Evaluation of the Printing and Publishing Activities of the Officiana Plantiniana at Antwerp*, 2 vols. (Amsterdam, 1969–72).

34. Wells, "Antwerp and the Government of Philip II, 1555–1567," 77–78. For a preliminary exploration of how privileges and unwritten custom, some fictional, figured as central to the Dutch Revolt, see J. J. Woltjer, "Dutch Privileges, Real and Imaginary," in *Britain and the Netherlands: Some Political Mythologies*, ed., J. S. Bromley and E. H. Kossmann (The Hague, 1975), 19–35.

city's meetings of the Broad Council.³⁵ The magistrates busied themselves with asserting traditional rights and privileges and preserving the status quo. The city toed a more conservative line than others such as 's-Hertogenbosch in the Estates of Brabant. This is no doubt because its elite had so much to lose by alienating the Brussels government to which its members had direct access through a pensionary and whose administration, since the reign of Charles V, leaned heavily on the city for credit. Yet for all their pragmatic accommodation, on matters of law, finance, and economics Antwerp's magistrates, when provoked, never desisted from taking on the central government. After all, unlike all the other provinces, Brabant did not have a provincial governor to serve as an intermediary between its regional cities and the royal government. Furthermore, it possessed the Blijde Inkomst, the most lionized medieval privilege in a land in which privileges were the sacred stuff of politics. This 1356 charter explicitly affirmed the primacy of local rights, freedoms, and privileges for Brabantine cities.³⁶

This city of privileges had a public profile that befitted its civic ambition. Apart from the new town hall built between 1561 and 1564, the Onze-Lieve-Vrouwekerk was Antwerp's most significant repository of cultural pride and religious prestige. This great parish church served as the visual center of Antwerp in numerous early modern bird's-eye view maps, even as the city underwent significant urban redesign in the early sixteenth century, including the addition of a new set of walls, the rebuilding by the contractor Gilbert van Schoobeke of the city's urban core—the Vrijdagmarkt, the Stadswaag, and the Arenbergstraat, most notably—and the construction of the Nieuwstad to the north of the old city.³⁷ In Hieronymus Cock's 1557 cityscape, the new fortifications stoutly reinforce Antwerp's urban density, with the soaring spire of the parish church standing out of the maze of houses and streets, a landmark more prominent than any other public building, including the *stadhuis* (town hall). Onze-Lieve-Vrouwekerk was a privileged and protected niche in the city's otherwise bustling and fluid center, with ordinances regularly issued against begging, gambling, ball playing, or plying wares within and against its courtyard.³⁸

The Onze-Lieve-Vrouwekerk was also the Netherlands' biggest parish church. By the late fifteenth century, its eighty-four chantry priests and thirty-one different altars handled no fewer than 245 masses per week. Despite Antwerp's urban growth, Onze-Lieve-Vrouw remained the only church in Antwerp with parish rights, denying separate incorporation

---

35. A detailed overview of these branches of government is in Wells, "Antwerp and the Government of Philip II," 18–19.
36. Wells, "Antwerp and the Government of Philip II," 38, 78, 230; Meadow, "Ritual and Civic Identity," esp. 40–41.
37. Piet Lombaerde, "Antwerp and its Golden Age: 'One of the Largest Cities in the World,' and 'One of the Best Fortified in Europe,'" in *Urban Achievement*, 99–127.
38. On these ordinances, see Génard, "Index der Gebodboeken," 123, 132, 134, 172, among others.

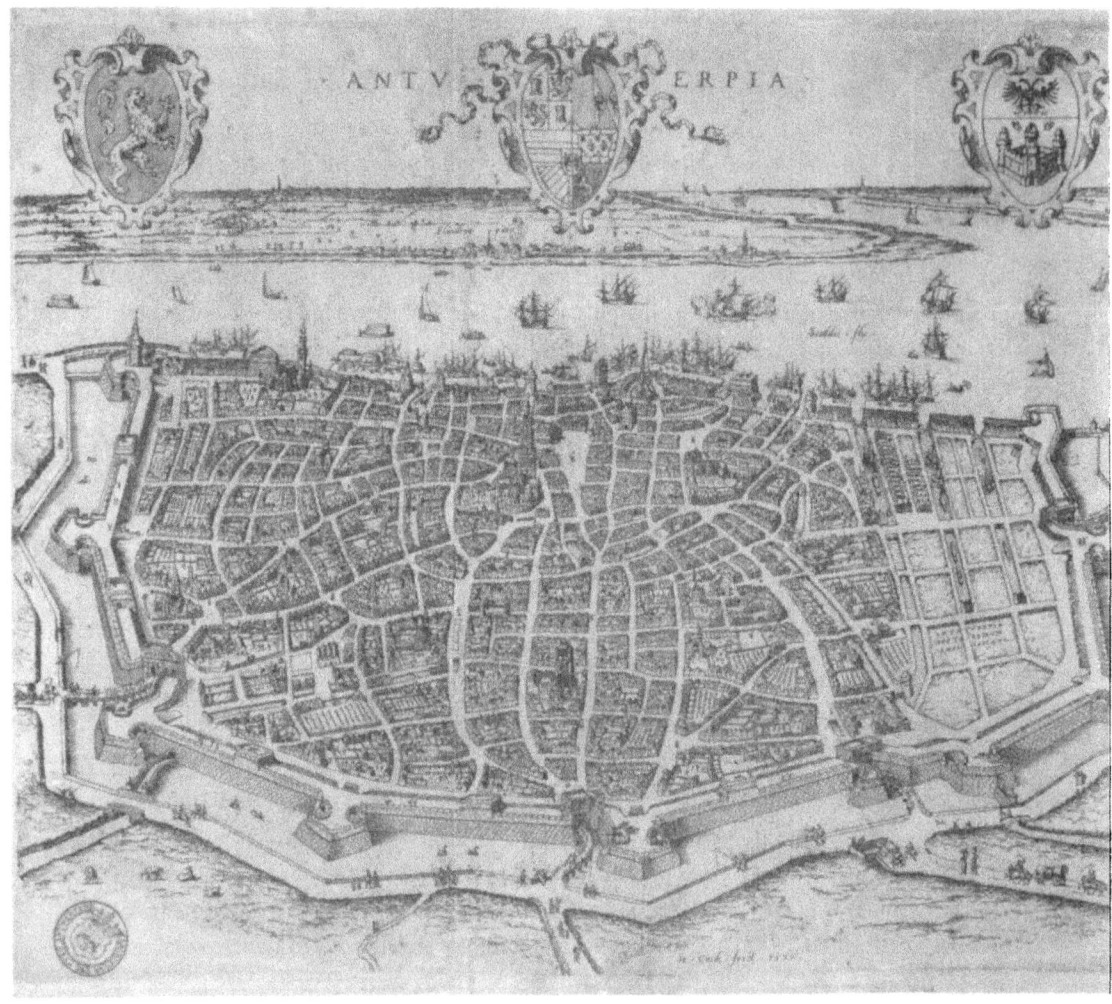

Bird's-eye view of Antwerp with its new city walls and the spire of the Onze-Lieve-Vrouwekerk dominating the skyline. Hieronymus Cock, 1557. Courtesy of Stedelijk Prentenkabinet, Antwerp.

to the churches of Saint George, Saint Walburgis, and Saint John. Even when these churches finally received parish status in 1477, the powerful canons of Our Lady reserved the right to nominate their priests and chaplains and demanded from them baptism fees, alms, and oblations.[39] The city had many other religious institutions too, including five

39. J. van den Nieuwenhuizen, "Under the Spiritual Care of the Chapter of Our Lady," in Antwerp: Twelve Centuries of History and Culture, ed. Karel van Isacker and Raymond van Uytven (Antwerp, 1986), 65–70; W. H. Vroom, De Onze-Lieve-Vrouwekerk te Antwerpen: De financiering van de bouw tot de Beeldenstorm (Antwerp, 1983); J. van Brabant, Onze-Lieve-Vrouwekathedraal van Antwerpen, Grootste gotische kerk der Nederlanden (Antwerp, 1902).

abbeys and cloisters: the original Norbertine abbey of Saint Michael, where important visiting dignitaries often resided; a Dominican cloister consecrated in 1276, whose brothers' responsibilities included weekly mass in the chapel of the aldermen's hall; the Carthusian convent of Sinte-Katherine op de Berg Sinai outside the city's wall in the Kiel area, founded in 1323; a modest Cistercian priory established in 1477; and a Franciscan convent established in 1450. Each of these religious houses was nominally independent yet accountable to Onze-Lieve-Vrouw, and each had to enter into agreements that secured parish rights for the great church, especially concerning confessions and preaching.[40]

Even though Antwerp's religious landscape diversified as the city grew, the Onze-Lieve-Vrouwekerk remained its anchor, boasting a tower of 123 meters and a nave with seven aisles by 1521. Fire devastated the church in 1533, gutting more than fifty-seven altars, yet repairs were quick and efficient. By 1566 the nave had been fully repaired and the church had seventy altars with masses performed by a cohort of chantry priests who already numbered ninety-six in 1539. Unsurprisingly, its twenty-two canons were rich, privileged sons of great families whose appointments owed much to nepotism. Many were well-educated, being *magistri artium*, with degrees in theology and law. With vicars, chaplains, and chantry priests doing all the pastoral work, the canons enjoyed the perks of their benefices, and half of them resided outside the city.[41] The church wardens handled Our Lady's all-important finances, keeping tabs on parish fees, guild offerings, gifts and bequests in addition to significant contributions received from the city, including for the church's physical upkeep. In 1535 Antwerp's magistrates laid out 155 pounds Brabant to finance its recovery from a bad fire.[42]

In spatial location, physical size, administrative privilege, and financial support, Onze-Lieve-Vrouw was the religious center of Antwerp's otherwise plural culture, monopolizing prestige to an astonishing degree even as the city grew in spatial complexity and institutional diversity. Its canons were so powerful that they successfully retarded turning their church into a cathedral as part of the 1559 ecclesiastical reorganization of the Netherlands. In 1562 the magistrates learned that two of the canons in the new bishopric would serve as inquisitors, a significant enough worry to inspire an urgent campaign to delay the planned installation of a bishop. The success of these efforts can be measured by the fact that when Filips Nigri, the bishop-designate for the city, died in January 1563, he had never entered Antwerp to claim his seat. Antwerp's magistrates openly gloated that the city, and Brabant in general, would never permit an inquisitor the likes of Titelmans

---

40. Van den Nieuwenhuizen, "Under the Spiritual Care of the Chapter of Our Lady." Guido Marnef has estimated Antwerp's total clerical population on the basis of hearth tax returns for 1480 and 1526 (three years before the city received a new parish church, Saint Andrew's) at 981 and 906 respectively, around 1 percent of the total civic population in *Antwerp in the Age of Reformation*, table 4.1, 50.

41. Vroom, *Onze-Lieve-Vrouwekerk te Antwerpen*, 17–21.

42. Ibid., 42.

in Flanders.⁴³ In a city characterized by exchange and circulation, Antwerp's religious authority was surprisingly concentrated, yet effective in the general effort to resist outside authority, be it grasping overlords or power-hunger foreign prelates.

The status of Onze-Lieve-Vrouwekerk and its canons was further heightened by its housing the city's most important religious venerations: the prized relic of the Foreskin of Christ; the chapel and painted statue of Onze-Lieve-Vrouw, Corpus Christi, and the miracle-working Our Lady of the Pole.⁴⁴ With the exception of the Pole Virgin, these venerations also formed the basis of Antwerp's most important religious processions. These *ommegangen* were conventionally lavish affairs, bearing local inflections but in form no different from their counterparts elsewhere in the Low Countries, save for the importance put on the space and place of the Onze-Lieve-Vrouwekerk. The oldest was the procession of the Circumcision, an exuberantly Catholic affirmation of Christ's physicality captured in the rare relic of the foreskin—only Rome had another significant foreskin veneration—acquired by Antwerp as a gift from its eleventh-century burgrave, Godfrey of Bouillon. Such a prestigious relic demanded important guardians, and in 1426 an elite confraternity was chartered to promote the foreskin relic. Its members included several city aldermen, and the income from the *doodgeld* (death money) of deceased members was one of the Onze-Lieve-Vrouwekerk's most important sources of incomes; its church wardens collected 94 pounds in Brabant in 1465.⁴⁵ Already by 1398, the annual Trinity Day procession of the foreskin relic combined the orderly display of religious and secular corporations with allegorical floats and short theater pieces. The procession also consecrated the opening day of the Sinxenmarkt, one of Antwerp's two annual trade fairs. No surprise then that it was the guilds that led the enormous train of devotees. The shippers, proclaimed by Guicciardini as Antwerp's oldest and most prestigious guilds, headed the craftsmen. They were followed by wagons of tableaux vivants, among whose representations figured one of the Duke of Brabant; the religious and secular clergy, the important *schutters* and lay corporations, the magistrates and other city officials, visiting prelates, and the abbot of Antwerp's oldest religious house, the abbey of Saint Michael, which claimed the right to carry the reliquary as its original possessor.⁴⁶

43. Wells, "Antwerp and the Government of Philip II," 250–67.
44. Vroom, *Onze-Lieve-Vrouwekerk te Antwerpen* 49–62; F. Prims, "De Antwerpsche Ommeganck op den vooravond van de Beeldenstormerij," in *Mededelingen van de Koninklijke Vlaamsche Academie voor Wetenschappen, Letteren en Schone Kunsten van België* 8 (1946): 5–21; Leo de Burbure, *De Antwerpsche Ommegangen in de XIVe en XVe eeuw naar gelijktijdige handschriften* (Antwerp, 1878), a valuable transcription of the extant programs for these ommegangen for the late fifteenth and early sixteenth centuries; Roland A. E. op de Beeck, *De Gilde van Onze-Lieve-Vrouwe-Lof in de Kathedraal van Antwerpen* (Antwerp, 1978); L. Phillipen, "Le culte de Notre-Dame Op 'T Stocken," *Annales de la société d'archéologie de Belgique*, 7, no. 2 (1924): 204–30. A review of the Antwerp's ommegangen can be found in Mark Meadow, "'Met geschickter ordenen': The Rhetoric of Place in Philip II's 1549 Antwerp Blijde Incompst," *Journal of the Walters Art Gallery* 57 (1999): 1–11.
45. Vroom, *Onze-Lieve-Vrouwekerk te Antwerpen*, 49–50, and 60–62.
46. De Burbure, *Antwerpsche Ommegangen*, 1–5 for 1398, and 6–11 for 1420–1494.

All the same elements found in Antwerp's oldest religious *ommegang* were replicated with minor variations in the Corpus Christi celebration, held only four days after the Circumcision procession, and the Onze-Lieve-Vrouw procession, celebrated the first Sunday after Assumption Day on August 15. Of the two, it was Onze-Lieve-Vrouw that acquired a bigger reputation and assumed more unique features.[47] But while the Onze-Lieve-Vrouw procession gained supreme prestige, it was apparently not the most popular Marian devotion in the realm of gifts and bequests. That honor went to another Onze-Lieve-Vrouwekerk devotion: Onze-Lieve-Vrouw op 't Stocxken (Our Beloved Lady of the Pole), popular because the image had worked miracles since at least 1474. As the devotion grew, it gained a chapel in 1537 maintained by the gardeners' guild. It became the most lucrative devotion for the churchwardens of Onze-Lieve-Vrouw; at its peak between 1485 and 1497 the Pole Virgin brought in over four hundred guilders a year in bequests.[48] Although miracle books do not exist for it, probably, like its counterparts in nearby Lier or 's-Hertogenbosch, Onze-Lieve-Vrouw op 't Stocxken was renowned for medical cures, a point reinforced by later early modern depictions of crutch-bearing pilgrims praying to her.[49] That an iron screen had to be installed in front of the statue in 1478 to keep devotees from damaging the Pole Virgin in their urgent supplications speaks to its popularity.[50]

Yet by the time Albrecht Dürer witnessed its splendor in 1520, the Assumption Day procession of Onze-Lieve-Vrouw was easily Antwerp's most important public religious event. The Onze-Lieve-Vrouw procession of more than two hours duration put Antwerp's officialdom on display. A retinue of smartly outfitted guildsmen, clergy, and city officials took turns carrying a lavishly clothed, bejeweled Virgin Mary, accompanied by allegorical and biblical tableaux vivants on pageant cars, for which printed programs were distributed by city officials (as was also done for the Circumcision procession).[51] Although Marian devotion was as old as Antwerp's religious history, the first *ommegang* of the statue of Onze-Lieve-Vrouw was not until 1399. As early as 1348, however, a confraternity on behalf of this Virgin had been active in the Onze-Lieve-Vrouwekerk, and it was these men who carried the statue in its first documented procession. By the late fifteenth century, this original confraternity had evolved into the prestigious Gilde van Onze-Lieve-Vrouwe-Lof.[52]

The Assumption procession involved all religious and social groups found in the Cir-

---

47. De Beeck, *Gilde van Onze-Lieve-Vrouwe-Lof*, on the Our Lady chapel and confraternity, and de Burbure, *Antwerpsche Ommegangen*, 13–20.

48. Vroom, *Onze-Lieve-Vrouwekerk te Antwerpen*, 51; Marnef, *Antwerp in the Age of Reformation*, 52–53.

49. Phillipen, "Le culte de Notre-Dame Op 'T Stocken," 316–17; the miracle book for the 's-Hertogenbosch Our Lady veneration is published by H. Hens et al., *Mirakelen van Onze Lieve Vrouw te 's-Hertogenbosch, 1381–1603* (Tilburg, 1978). For a discussion of the Lier veneration of Saint Gummarus, see Vroom, *Onze-Lieve-Vrouwekerk te Antwerpen*, 58–59.

50. Phillipen, "Le culte de Notre-Dame Op 'T Stocken," 319.

51. Prims, "Antwerpsche Ommeganck op den vooravond van de Beeldenstormerij."

52. De Beeck, *Gilde van Onze-Lieve-Vrouwe-Lof*.

cumcision *ommegang*. At Vespers the day before the procession, canons and Onze-Lieve-Vrouwe-Lof brothers removed the sumptuously dressed statue from her chapel and carried her around the central choir to the antiphon of Gaude Maria and Inviolata. The magistrates, the guilds, and the *schutters* came to pay their honor, then retired for food and drink at the town hall. At noon on Sunday, eight canons carried the statue to Kornmarkt (grain market), inaugurating the procession during which *schutters*, guildsmen (the first honor went to the shippers), and the Salve Regina and the Gilde van Onze-Lieve-Vrouwe-Lof confraternities, among others, took turns carrying Onze-Lieve-Vrouw before her return to the choir of the church, where she remained set out for a week.[53]

As with the Circumcision procession, Assumption Day involved tableaux vivants and wagon plays. In both processions, rhetoricians and other local festive groups presented biblical stories and secular allegories that by the 1560s began to broach contemporary affairs. In 1566 the four new wagon pageants struck a somber tone, repeating a theme rehearsed two years earlier: the present time. The booklet of the Assumption Day program produced by the print workshop of Hans de Laet began gloomily: "The four parts of the world at the present time / Are now full of turbulence and entanglements."[54]

Personifications of an entangled Present Time and Four Parts of the World set the allegory's tone. The representation featured Miserliness, depicted as a grasping man, and Disorderly Nature, depicted as an old woman placed above a man with a hungry dog, both hectored by an alms-seeking beggar at their side. They led a shop-of-horrors flame-throwing, smoke emitting, Tyrannical Cruelty, his horse hung with weaponry and shackles. A Cave of Discord wagon followed, featuring four devilish musicians. Discord sat in a rocky outcrop spinning the wheel of False Practice with tangled thread, while representations of Celestial Hate, False Advice, and Self-Interest sowed trouble. If to observers the world seemed hopelessly turned upside down and under the weight of violence, the next two pageant wagons promised hope. The third wagon had God's Providence as its theme; it transported the figures of Wise Counsel, Careful Investigation, and Unified Community, carrying arrows bound by olive branches and bearing the insignia of Antwerp's guilds. Through unity, proclaimed the text, discord is defeated. The last pageant car deepened this hopeful theme with its Seat of Grace allegory that pronounced God's mercy to be at hand.[55]

In the typical hybrid style of urban pageantry in the Low Countries, lofty allegory and artisanal symbols—the theme of spinning, the guild insignia—colored this jeremiad of a world gone awry and a call to seek the righteous path to redemption. If the pageantry seemed urgently dire and preachily unctuous, it was in no small measure owing to the fact

---

53. De Burbure, *Antwerpsche Ommegangen*, 17–20.
54. Prims, "Antwerpsche Ommeganck op den vooravond van de Beeldenstormerij," 15.
55. Ibid., 15–20.

that all hell had already broken loose in the Westkwartier, and that like other Low Country cities, Antwerp was facing a turning point in its season of discontent. This was the city from which the first two Protestant martyrs hailed—two apostate monks who met their unhappy fate in Brussels' central marketplace in 1523 and whose cloister was ritually cleansed and enwalled after their execution.[56] With its large German and northern European immigrant population, with its constant comings and goings of people and ideas, with its busy printing presses, Antwerp was so much an early breeding ground of Protestantism that the Duke of Alba contemptuously described it in February 1568 as a "Babylon, confusion and receptacle of all sects indifferently and as the town most frequented by pernicious people."[57]

In the 1560s, as elsewhere in the southern Netherlands, Calvinism emerged as dominant in Antwerp among the swirl of Protestant denominations, with a French Walloon congregation as active there as the Dutch-speaking one and composed of refugees fleeing fierce attempts to uproot Calvinism in Lille, Tournai, and Valenciennes.[58] Guido Marnef's research has identified sixty-eight Calvinists who were subject to persecution between 1550 and 1566, almost half of whom (48.5%) came from the crafts, with 15 percent from the trade and transport sectors and 11 percent from the applied arts. While this represents, of course, only a fraction of those who openly or secretly professed the Reformed faith, it demonstrates a heterogeneous set of adherents, in contrast to the overwhelmingly poor Anabaptists. Of the 102 Anabaptists persecuted in the same period, two-thirds were laborers and craftspeople.[59] Likewise, Anabaptists formed the majority of the 105 people executed for heresy in Antwerp between 1555 and 1567, equaling Amsterdam in the numbers of Anabaptists put to death.[60] By contrast, the conservative and

---

56. Scheerder, *Inquisitie in de Nederlanden*, 56–58.
57. *Epistolario Alba*, 2:33–34.
58. Marnef, *Antwerp in the Age of Reformation*, 63.
59. Ibid., 71, table 5.1, and 77, table 5.2. Between 1531 and 1540, Amsterdam executed at least seventy-four Anabaptists, and the Court of Holland sentenced a further twenty-three, some of whom were executed in Amsterdam; see G. Grosheide, *Bijdrage tot de Geschiedenis der Anabaptisten in Amsterdam* (Hilversum, 1938); figures are incomplete. On Dutch Anabaptism in general, see W. E. Keeney, *The Development of Dutch Anabaptist Thought and Practice, 1539–1564* (Nieuwkoop, 1968), and on its development in Antwerp, A. F. Mellink, "Antwerpen als anabaptistencentrum tot ± 1560," *Nederlands Archief voor Kerkgeschiedenis* 46 (1963–69): 155–68, and the treatment of martyrdom by Gregory, *Salvation at Stake*, 197–249, with scholarly skepticism about the religious meaning of the social demographics of professing Anabaptists.
60. Wells, "Antwerp and the Government of Philip II," 320–21. For full factual overviews of the events of Antwerp's wonder year, see Robert van Roosbroeck, *Het wonderjaar te Antwerpen (1566–1567): Inleiding tot de studie der godsdienstonlusten te Antwerpen van 1566 tot 1585* (Antwerp, 1930), and Floris Prims, *Het Wonderjaar (1566–1567)* (Antwerp, 1941), a work that relies heavily on Godevaert van Haecht's chronicle as well as the magistrates' correspondence that the author himself edited; see Floris Prims, "Het wonderjaar te Antwerpen naar de briefwisseling van magistraat en ghedeputeerden," *Bijdragen tot de Geschiedenis* 31 (1940): 1–184, 243–84.

Catholic magistrates balked at the active persecution of Calvinists, since this group typically included economically important foreign merchants. Antwerp's Calvinist community, though underground, was influential, even hosting a synod in 1562 under the noses of the disapproving magistrates. While the magistrates were not fully passive about Calvinist activity—they did try to break up psalm singing on Christmas Day in 1562—neither were they eager to take action. When they had done so under pressure, as with the execution of the minister Christoffel Fabricus in 1563, the result was exactly what they feared: a near public riot that forced them to retreat under a hail of stones to the town hall.

The emergence of the Compromise in spring 1566 complicated political matters for Antwerp's city fathers. Zealous about their privileges, and willing to take on the Flemish inquisitor Titelmans when they thought he encroached on their jurisdiction in Brabant, the magistrates were hardly rebels-in-the-making. They were worried when the Beggars' leader Hendrik van Brederode made an attention-grabbing entry into Antwerp on April 11 with his associates, fully dressed in their new liveries. Brederode played to the crowd, allegedly ate capons on Friday, and made rousing speeches denouncing the heresy placards.[61] That the magistrates feared trouble was apparent in their approach to the Circumcision procession on Trinity Sunday, June 9, and the Corpus Christi procession on June 13. As the chronicler of Antwerp's troubled times, Godevaert van Haecht, reported, they took extra steps to secure the procession, including curfews for youth and a militia reinforcement along the route. Although rumors of trouble swirled, the *ommegang* occurred without incident; four days later, more talk of trouble surrounded preparations for the Corpus Christi procession, though once again the celebration was without disturbance. However, as Granvelle's faithful correspondent Morillon noted, several guildsmen wore the Beggars' medal around their necks as they marched in these processions, a forthright assertion of political sentiment in this otherwise outwardly Catholic event.[62]

But it was the surge of hedge preaching and of assertions of Calvinists' preaching rights inside the city during the summer months of 1566 that spun events beyond the deft political hands of Antwerp's magistrates. Hedge sermons began outside the magistrates' jurisdiction on June 24, and were regularly repeated, swelling to eighteen thousand by July 18, if the English observer John Keyle's numbers are to be trusted.[63] To make matters worse, neither the guild deans nor the ward captains in the Broad Council endorsed the magistrates' measures to prohibit attendance at hedge sermons through a beefed-up city watch and the reissuance of an ordinance against lodging foreigners who were not already established merchants in the city.[64] Keyle reported that "armeur and wepones ar as fast

---

61. *Kroniek Van Haecht*, 1:30; Wells, "Antwerp and the Government of Philip II," 394.

62. *Kroniek Van Haecht*, 1:46–47; *Corr. Granvelle*, 1563–83, 1:305.

63. For an overview, see Wells, "Antwerp and the Government of Philip II," 407–9. On Keyle's estimate, see Baron Kervyn de Lettenhove, ed., *Relations politiques des Pays-Bas et de l'Angleterre sous le règne de Philippe II*, 11 vols. (Brussels, 1882–1900), 4:309–13.

64. For the June 27 council meeting, see *Antwerpsch Archievenblad*, 10:314–44.

boght upe hier as drinck is dronck up, which is fast inogh."[65] Catholics, Protestants, and everyone in-between worried that violence was imminent. Convinced that events had slipped beyond their control, the magistrates took the unusual step of asking the regent for outside help. She responded on July 13 by sending Orange, who among his many titles held the largely symbolic one of burgrave of Antwerp.[66] Brederode and his fellow associates feted Orange's arrival as if he were making a Beggars-style Blijde Inkomst, riding out to greet him, firing pistols in the air and shouting "Vivent les Gueux!" which, as the chronicler Van Haecht smartly noted, Orange himself found imprudent. The magistrates, by contrast, chose to greet him in private.[67]

Orange managed to send Brederode packing, but was unsuccessful in negotiating an end to the hedge sermons or in satisfying the Calvinists' demands for places to worship inside Antwerp. Tensions peaked as news of the outbreak of Westkwartier iconoclasm reached Antwerp. Even though the attack around Ypres on Assumption Day had rattled Antwerp's magistrates, the Onze-Lieve-Vrouwekerk canons and the Onze-Lieve-Vrouwe-Lof confraternity chose to go forward with their ambitious procession, embellished with the four new wagons and allegorical tableaux. After all, despite invidious rumors of unrest and the brazen displays of Beggars' medals on the outfits of some participants, the two June *ommegangen* had occurred without serious problems. On Sunday, August 18, to the theme of "the present time," the canons, confraternity members, guildsmen, and other religious and political cohorts carried the richly appointed Onze-Lieve-Vrouw in procession. Among the throng of onlookers were Orange and his wife, seated before the great town hall. As one observer noted, several marchers wore Beggars' insignia, most notably the all-important *schutters*. But more disturbing, anonymous onlookers hurled insults directed at Our Lady despite the fact that the greatest nobleman in the Netherlands was a visiting observer. "Little Mary, Little Mary, this is your last time!" they shouted, and rocks and other blunt objects were brazenly thrown at her. Confraternity brothers and canons quickly whisked the statue back to the Onze-Lieve-Vrouwekerk and put it under watch.[68] How relevant, after all, was the theme of discord presented in the wagon plays, but how elusive too seemed the unity they urged on Antwerp.

As in Ypres, the Assumption Day procession was the tinderbox that sparked iconoclasm in Antwerp. Notwithstanding Antwerp's many religious houses and orders, all narrative accounts of the riots—the Catholic *Chronicle of Antwerp*, the magistrates' report, the ob-

65. Kervyn de Lettenhove, Relations politiques, 4:313.
66. Prims, Wonderjaar, 118–20.
67. See Orange's account, Corr. Taciturne, 2:316–17, and Kroniek Van Haecht, 1:69–70.
68. Gus. van Havre, ed., Chronijck der stadt Antwerpen toegeschreven aan den notaris Geeraard Bertrijn (Antwerp, 1879), 130; Kroniek Van Haecht, 1:96; Rahlenbeck, Mémoires de Jacques de Wesenbeke, 283; "Verantwoording van het Antwerpsch Magistraat," Antwerpsch Archievenblad, 10:130. Besides the above sources, for iconoclasm, see also Antwerpsch Chronykje (Leiden, 1743), 90, and J. H. Hessels, ed., Abrahami Ortelii et virorum eruditorum ad eundem et ad Jacobum Colium Ortelianum Epistolae, Ecclesiae Londino-Batavae Archivum, 4 vols. (Cambridge, 1887–97), 1:37–40, the August 27 letter of Ortelius; Burgon, Life and Times of Sir Thomas Gresham, 1:137–45.

servations of the English factor Richard Clough, the Antwerp geographer Abraham Ortelius's letter, the pensionary Wesenbeke's account, and the chroniclers Geerard Betrijn and Godevaart van Haecht's excited summaries—dwell almost obsessively on the damage done inside the Onze-Lieve-Vrouwekerk. What these diverse observers shared is the sense of just how profoundly the Onze-Lieve-Vrouw statue and the Onze-Lieve-Vrouwekerk anchored religious life in Antwerp and served as its holy center.

The day after the troubled Assumption Day procession, Orange had left Antwerp, called to Brussels by the regent for an urgent meeting of the Order of the Golden Fleece to deliberate how to respond to the outbreak of iconoclastic riots in the Westkwartier. With the senior nobleman gone, disquiet intensified, this time at the Onze-Lieve-Vrouwekerk where the Virgin had been returned. On Monday afternoon after Calvinists held sermons outside the city with enormous attendance, a young man, probably no more than eighteen and apparently drunk, rushed into the church, climbed the pulpit, and delivered a mock sermon. He was stopped only when a young boatman forcibly hurled him out of the church.[69] The next day, iconoclasm broke loose, triggered by the canons' decision to return the statue of Onze-Lieve-Vrouw to its chapel after vespers rather than leaving it on central display for a few days longer, as was customary. Insults were hurled at the Virgin as the canons set her back in the chapel in the late afternoon, much to the dismay of devotees in fervent prayer. As the service proceeded, several protestors shouted, "She'll be knocked down soon." Ridiculed too was an old woman selling candles and other devotional items to worshippers. She protested the barbs aimed at the Onze-Lieve-Vrouw and doused the hecklers with water after they insulted her. The Protestant sympathizer Van Haecht estimated the crowd of Calvinists at about two hundred, while Abraham Ortelius more cautiously ascribed the trouble to a core group of around thirty. When the emboldened protestors broke into psalm singing, men dispatched by the magistrates entered to clear the church.[70] They forced most of the crowd out, but carelessly left the south door unlocked; as soon as these officials had retreated with the burgomasters to the town hall, the Calvinists rushed back in and reopened the locked front doors. With neither the magistrates nor the *schutters* there to protect the church—for better or worse, they thought it best to secure the town hall, probably fearing a riot—the iconoclasts began their work, setting furiously upon the statue of Onze-Lieve-Vrouw in the chapel. As if enacting an execution ritual, the image breakers first cut off her head, her right hand, and then her left arm before wreaking havoc on the chapel, and everything else in this richly appointed church.[71]

69. Kroniek Van Haecht, 1: 7; Van Havre, Chronijck der stadt Antwerpen, 132.
70. Kroniek Van Haecht, 1:98; Hessels, Abrahami Ortelii, 1:38–39. For a summary of events, see Scheerder, Beeldenstorm, 37–52, and the primary sources listed in n. 69, which concur on the outline of events, though varying in detail.
71. Kroniek Van Haecht, 1:97.

The attack on the church lasted until the next day, when fresh rioters entered to help pull down large-scale items. Of the seventy great altars, only three were spared. Armed with hatchets, hammers, knives, and other blunt instruments, iconoclasts chopped, hacked, pushed, and pulled, attacking not only images and statues but all the material accoutrements of Catholic worship—psalters, song books, and Bibles. Attuned to the significance of the three great religious *ommegangen*, the rioters also attacked the Holy Sacrament, crushing it beneath their feet, and the relic of the foreskin, which, if the staunchly Catholic *Chronicle of Antwerp* is to be believed, was sported as booty by the minister Herman Moded, who upset local officials by preaching a sermon at the mostly cleansed Onze-Lieve-Vrouwekerk on August 21.[72] Much like the Westkwartier iconoclasts, Antwerp's rioters divided into small bands and attacked the monastic houses, chapels, and nunneries. The destruction lasted until the next morning. Psalm singing, looting, eating, and drinking accompanied the violence; the shredded pages of ripped up religious books were so thick, wrote Van Haecht, that it reached the knees.[73]

Although legal depositions taken after the riots laconically record the damage to Antwerp's many religious institutions, the eyewitness accounts are quick to note how the Onze-Lieve-Vrouw statue served both as trigger to the riots and its prized target.[74] Given the attention iconoclasts paid to the Assumption Day Virgin, it would be easy to forget that this statue and its *ommegang* had not been Antwerp's most popular Marian devotion. This honor belonged to the miracle-working statue of Onze-Lieve-Vrouw op 't Stocxken, itself destroyed in the same riots, though its fate did not elicit the attention showered on the Onze-Lieve-Vrouw statue. Although there had been a steep decline in gifts and bequests to the Pole Virgin in the decades before the wonder year—falling off because of the robust upswing in Protestantism—she was still the object of clamorous devotion, and still screened off in 1566 because so many devotees desired to touch her.[75] Onze-Lieve-Vrouw, by contrast, was Antwerp's most official devotion, having surpassed the Circumcision procession in importance, and was now a key venue for the city's most elite religious and lay social groups. In 1566 the Virgin had received the honor of no less than the Prince of Orange and his wife as they stood at the town hall to watch the procession. As in Ypres, iconoclasm in Antwerp pressed directly on the urban religious conjunction between time and devotion, with the Assumption Day Virgin centering violence that might otherwise

72. Ibid., 1:98–100; *Antwerpsch Chronykje*, 90; Van Havre, *Chronijck der stadt Antwerpen*, 30.
73. *Kroniek Van Haecht*, 1:99.
74. For sentences and depositions of iconoclasts, Algemeen Rijksarchief Brussel, Rekenkamer, Register 111, *Registre des condamnés et bannis à cause des troubles survenues en ce pays despuis l'an 1568 à 1572*, especially fols. 6r–10r, 11r–13v, 16r–v, 18v–20r, 33r–v, and 67r–v, and *Antwerpsch Archievenblad*, 10:10–69, and, 11:4–34 for letters and ordinances of the magistrates.
75. The falling off of contributions to the Pole Virgin began in 1524 and plummeted after 1545, after which contributions stayed at ten guilders or below, in contrast to the peak years when her devotion netted the church over three hundred guilders annually. See Marnef, *Antwerp in the Age of Reformation*, table 4.1, 53.

seem indiscriminately diffuse. Although all religious houses were attacked, and some private residences too, the chapel and statue of Onze-Lieve-Vrouw so constituted the central target of the iconoclasts' wrath that their destruction preoccupied written accounts of iconoclasm in Antwerp in a way that downplayed violence inflicted on the city's other religious houses and worships.

The Onze-Lieve-Vrouwekerk was clearly the spatial center of Antwerp's iconoclastic riots. There, in the words of the English factor Richard Clough, a tight cluster of working men had made a "mervellus styr" in "the costylyst church in Europe, and have so spoylyed yt, that they have nott left a place to sytt."[76] In many respects, the destruction of this great Gothic church registered the magnitude of iconoclasm not only for Antwerp but for the Low Countries as a whole. That the attack on this church became the signature event of the iconoclastic riots of 1566 is clear in the treatment it receives from Frans Hogenberg. His workshop's print of the attack came to summarize Low Country iconoclasm in general.[77] It depicts iconoclasm underway through a cutaway view of the church's interior; men armed with axes, hammers, and large sticks are strenuously engaged in the act of destruction. A group of seven pull down statues on pedestals with ropes. Several are seen further down the nave with sharp axes. A large chest is being opened and papers and books shredded. There is a decapitated statue on the ground at center foreground. Directly outside the church men stand guard while a woman is carting off something wrapped in a blanket. To the right, we see another woman carting off goods and two men behind her carrying a basket of what appears to be linens. Another man is carrying off an enormous bundle over his shoulder, obscuring his face. Through a window into a second story to the right, men feast on food and drink.

Hogenberg's print gives visual form to the behavioral and gendered patterns of iconoclasm recounted in narrative and legal sources: men pushing, pulling, and smashing accompanied by rites of inversion, mock execution, feasting, drinking, and looting. That stealing occurred is amply documented—so much so that the Calvinist ministers themselves brought back broken relics, chalices, ciboria, crucifixes, and much more to the magistrates at the town hall and requested that the thieves be punished. The town fathers immediately set up a gallows and issued an ordinance against stealing. On August 28, with the Prince of Orange himself present, three iconoclasts were publicly hung for wrecking the coats of arms of the knights of the Golden Fleece that had hung in the Onze-Lieve-Vrouwekerk since the 1556 chapter meeting there, underscoring just how severe were the consequences of disfiguring representations of political authority.[78]

Legal investigations held after Antwerp's iconoclasm confirm the eyewitnesses' report

76. Burgon, *Life and Times of Sir Thomas Gresham*, 1:138.
77. Kinds, *Kroniek van de opstand in de lage landen*, 31.
78. "Verantwoording van het Antwerpsch Magistrat," in *Antwerpsch Archievenblad*, 10:134–35. The sentences against the three in 9:327.

Antwerp's iconoclasts attack the Onze-Lieve-Vrouwekerk in coordinated fashion. Frans Hogenberg. Courtesy of the private collection of Karel Kinds.

that while the crowd of people who surged into the Onze-Lieve-Vrouwekerk on August 20 was in the hundreds, image breaking itself was the work of a smaller group of men. Many had been apparently paid by Calvinists. Pasquier Fleurquin, a marble merchant who lived in the neighborhood of the church, had small hatchets purchased in preparation for the riots and had even rounded up volunteers. Pierre de Saint-Vaast and Jean des Maistres had hired men to break images for between three to seven stuivers—more than a day laborer could earn in a day.[79] Guido Marnef's prosopographical research has revealed that almost none of the prosecuted iconoclasts owned property, and the occupation for the majority

---

79. Scheerder, *Beeldenstorm*, 40–42; Van Roosbroeck, *Wonderjaar te Antwerpen*, 35–36; and Algemeen Rijksarchief, Rekenkamer, Register 111 *Registre des condamnés et bannis*, fols. 9r–v for Fleurquin and Saint-Vaast. See also the sentence against Lucas Hallie, fol. 8v, who also paid several men.

is unknown. The "workmanlike" quality of the destruction is perhaps due to the fact that several participants undertook it as paid labor.[80]

But even if the consistory played a directing hand in iconoclasm's organization, as seems apparent, and though a small handful of rioters were paid, it would be wrong to conclude that the riots in the Onze-Lieve-Vrouwekerk lacked intentionality. Work paid for is not perforce work uninspired, and the wage dimension of the troubles, equally found in the Westkwartier, only enhances the degree to which iconoclasm assumed a worklike quality.[81] The social dimension to Antwerp's riots was not muted either. One Hans Rykers was heard yelling during the attacks, "We have destroyed dead images, now let us attack the living!"[82] These qualities might also help to explain the explicit zeroing in on the statue of Onze-Lieve-Vrouw, her chapel, and the church. All three were signifiers of officialdom and eliteness in terms of symbol, property, space, and power. It might also explain the gendered quality of the riots. Working men set themselves upon the richly appointed statue of the Virgin, prefaced by young boys and men who showered insults at the elderly lady peddling candles, and at the devotees there to watch the statue's reinstallation. Certainly, in the Calvinist imaginary, the Catholic penchant for dressing up their statues smacked of sensual indulgence. As Philips van Marnix, Lord of St. Aldegonde put it, "Against the commandment of God, they [Catholics] have erected a multitude of beautiful images, paintings, and statues gilded and dressed up in the manner of whores from a brothel."[83] As the poor workingmen rioted, drank, ate, and looted, as they worked their way across Antwerp, they attacked not merely the material representations of Catholic worship, but the spaces and places of religious privilege. The iconoclasts and their work tools sundered more than the embroidered robe or jeweled necklace that outfitted the Virgin; they more tellingly severed the alliance between time, statue, and place that had centered Antwerp's religious culture.

Ghent: The Burden of the Past

The fact that iconoclasm partook of larger political and cultural matters, that it fulfilled Calvinist religious objectives while bearing material considerations, that for all its actors' care not to attack symbols of princely authority it nonetheless imperiled spaces and places

80. Marnef, *Antwerp in the Age of Reformation*, 89.

81. Scheerder, *Beeldenstorm*, 100, has summarized the places where certain image breakers were paid. See also Marnef, "The Dynamics of Reformed Religious Militancy," 55. Evidence that Westkwartier iconoclasts were paid is found in Algemeen Rijksarchief Brussel, Raad van Beroerte, no. 6, fols. 257v–258r, though no mention is made of the sums. See also, for example, the accusations against iconoclasts Gilles Bateman from Cassel and Jehan van Elst, who broke images at Hazebrouck, both of whom apparently offered some money (sums not disclosed) to others to help, in *Troubles religieux*, 2:123.

82. Algemeen Rijksarchief, Rekenkamer, register 111 *Registre des condamnés et bannis*, fol. 11v.

83. J. J. van Toorenenbergen, *Philips van Marnix van St. Aldegonde*, 1:76.

of political honor, that its participants ranged from comfortable members of Calvinist consistories to poor day laborers, that its behavioral forms married the carnivalesque with solemn theology—all this is evident in the August 22–23 violence in Ghent, Flanders' supreme city. However, the attack on a statue of Charles V and the Virgin at the city's Keizerpoort is proof that in contrast to other locales, iconoclasm in Ghent had overt political connotations. The city's iconoclasm is worth pursuing in some depth to unravel how new religious concerns were bound up with old cultural inclinations and political enmities, and how what might seem like a scatter-shot day and night of rioting actually reveals patterns centered on key religious institutions and spatial nodes. Ghent's radical past fundamentally influenced the shape and timbre of the iconoclast riots there. In Ypres, iconoclasm had zeroed in on the relationship between the religious calendar and civic veneration of the Virgin Mary; in Antwerp, the place of the Onze-Lieve-Vrouwekerk added a spatial quality to a similar dynamic. Iconoclasm in Ghent, by contrast, had neither a singular target nor a special time, but instead invoked behaviors associated with previous unrest, targeted religious institutions particularly hated by Calvinists, and was carried out with the memory of the failed insurrection of 1539 against Charles V—and contemporary economic woes—weighing heavily on top of the religious grievances. Fueled by contemporary religious concerns, iconoclasm in Ghent bore the imprint of the city's fractious history.

Sixteenth-century Ghent was not equal to the metropolitan bustle of Antwerp, but was nonetheless Flanders' greatest city. No longer the vital drapery center of the fourteenth century that had boasted 60,000 inhabitants, it still packed political and economic punch. With a population that Johan Dambruyne estimated was close to 42,000 in 1571, Ghent was still active in textile production, though its focus was now on cheaper, lighter cloth. The city remained the unassailable lead voice of the Estates of Flanders.[84] It also retained its all-important grain staple, an economic plum that ensured a regular flow of income as ships laden with provisions passed through the city. But Ghent had undergone significant political and cultural setbacks since its fourteenth-century era of guild radicalism and the regimes of the strongmen Jacob and Philip van Artevelde.[85]

In a satirical ballad written sometime around 1577, the city of Bruges lambastes Ghent

---

84. On sixteenth-century Ghent, see Johan Decavele and Paul van Peteghem, "Gent 'absoluut' getemd," in *Gent: apologie van een rebelse stad*, ed. Johan Decavele (Antwerp, 1989), 107–33, and for a social and economic portrait, Johan Dambruyne, *Mensen en Centen: Het 16de eeuwse Gent in demografisch en economisch perspectief* (Ghent, 2001), esp. 54 for the population and Johan Dambruyne, *Corporatieve middengroepen: Aspiraties, relaties en transformaties in de 16de-eeuwse Gentse ambachtswereld* (Ghent, 2002) for its artisanal world.

85. On the Arteveldes, see David Nicholas, *The Van Arteveldes of Ghent: The Varieties of Vendetta and the Hero in History* (Ithaca, 1988), but also Hans van Werveke, *Jacob van Artevelde* (The Hague, 1963). On the social and political landscape of fifteenth-century Ghent, see Boone, *Gent en de Bourgondische hertogen*, and on cultural life, Arnade, *Realms of Ritual*.

as a town of "noose-wearers and rioters."[86] The allusion to rebelliousness readily describes any point in Ghent's long history of political turmoil, but "noose-wearers" is a precise reference to the uprising Ghent waged in 1539 against Charles V.[87] The trouble began when Ghent's Broad Council—a political forum for representatives of the patricians, the weavers and their dependents, and the fifty-three other guilds—refused a subsidy proposed by the regent Mary of Hungary to help defray the costs of the interminable Habsburg-Valois wars. This refusal had quickly snowballed into a revolt of the city's radical guild masters. Convinced that the elite aldermen were secretly compliant with the Brussels government, worried that the city's cherished privileges had been violated, and chafing under a 1515 settlement imposed on the city by Charles V which, among other stipulations, prevented them from selecting their own deans, protesting guildsmen quickly took control of the city. In their most radical move, the rebels invited an unincorporated block of day laborers, the so-called *Creeschers* (those who cry out) into the Broad Council to be seated among the mandate reserved for the patricians. On August 28, radicals forced the city's bailiff to execute a former head dean of the fifty-three guilds, Lieven Pien, for supposedly meddling with the city's privileges. On September 3, the 1515 Calfvel (calf hide) treaty was ceremonially vitiated, and radicals now argued that a hitherto unknown privilege, the Purchase of Flanders, which guaranteed the city financial independence from its sovereign, had been withheld from public knowledge, and had some time in the recent past been whisked away.[88] An urban revolt against a late-medieval prince was risky enough, but one of such radical quality against the imperial might of Charles V was completely Quixotic. By November, the revolt reached its peak and soon thereafter began to falter. The weavers became internally divided, and the day laborers openly threatened patrician property and privilege. One Hans van Kortrijk admitted later under torture that he

---

86. NG, 1:226–28.

87. Johan Decavele, ed., *Keizer tussen stropdragers: Karel V, 1500–58* (Louvain, 1992), esp. 123–92; Victor Fris, *Histoire de Gand* (Brussels, 1913), 172–96; C. Steur, *Insurrection des Gantois sous Charles-Quint* (Brussels, 1834); Peter Arnade, "Privileges and the Political Imagination in the Ghent Revolt of 1539," in *Charles V in Context: the Making of a European Identity*, ed. Marc Boone and Marysa Demoor (Brussels, 2003), 103–24; Marc Boone, "Le dict mal s'est espandu comme peste fatale.": Karel V en Gent, stedelijke identiteit en staatsgeweld," *Handelingen der Maatschappij voor Geschiedenis en Oudheidkunde te Gent*, n.s. 53 (2000): 29–61; Dambruyne, *Corporatieve middengroepen*, 613–34.

88. For an overview of these events, see Arnade, "Privileges and the Political Imagination"; on the *Creeschers*, R. Stagier, "De Kreesers te Gent in 1530–40," in *Etudes d'histoire dédiés à la mémoire de Henri Pirenne par ses anciens élèves* (Brussels, 1937), 331–36, and a social analysis of the term and its use in Jan Dumolyn, "Marginalen of radicalen? Het vertoog over de 'roepers en krijsers' tijdens stedelijke opstanden, voornamelijk in het graafschap Vlaanderen," *Tijdschrift voor sociale en economische Geschiedenis* 2 (2005): 29–53. Many of the archival documents concerning the revolt can be found in L. P. Gachard, ed., *Relation des Troubles de Gand sous Charles Quint par un anonyme* (Brussels, 1846); the depositions of the leaders of the revolt are in SAG 214, Boek van Criminele Zaken, fols. 228r–266v, *Quahier vander oorcondscepe angaende den troublen ende emotion 1539*.

and his associates had raided religious houses to steal food and drink. In nearby Oudenaarde, where the revolt had spread, there was even a minor bout of iconoclasm.[89]

A measure of how seriously Charles V took the uprising in the city of his birth was his decision to come to Ghent from Spain to settle the matter—something Philip II did not do during the broader turmoil of the early 1560s. The emperor entered Ghent with a military train on February 14, 1540, and wasted no time in settling affairs. He issued a new civic constitution, the Caroline Concession, that stripped Ghent of all its medieval legal and political privileges and reconfigured the city's corporative and political organization, condensing the weavers and fifty-three other guilds into twenty-one corporations and confiscating all but the politically conservative shippers' and butchers' privileges and archives. The emperor also altered the city's public appearance by ordering the demolition of the venerable abbey of Saint Bavo's and its church of the Heilige Kerst (Holy Savior). The abbey's canons were transferred to the central parish church of Saint John's (Sint-Jans, now rechristened Saint Bavo's), and the ground was prepared for the construction of a military citadel in lieu of church and abbey. Charles also ordered the closure of eight city gates, the dismantling of portions of the city's walls, and the scaling back of important festivals renowned for their strong civic and guild resonances, such as the Saint Lieven procession and the Assumption Day procession of the Virgin Mary held by the weavers in the parish of Saint Peter's.[90] The emperor also imposed a spectacular *amende honorable* on May 3, 1540. Ghent's aldermen, its guild deans and lesser officials (six men from every corporation), the head dean of the weavers with fifty of his guildsmen, and fifty of the despised *Creeschers* were together forced to grovel for the emperor's forgiveness at the Burgundian palace of Ten Walle in central Ghent. The political and economic leaders dressed in fine black robes, but the day laborers wore white penitential garb and ropes around their necks like the common criminals they were deemed to be.[91] The next day, the emperor seized the city's guild and civic privileges from the archives, as well as the city's

---

89. SAG 214, fol. 225r. Dambryne, *Corporatieve middengroepen*, 628–29, and table 211, has clarified the role of the *Creeschers* in the uprising, seeing them less as independent agents than as tools of the weavers and other guilds; this is borne out by the fact that those punished after the revolt were overwhelmingly guildsmen.

90. For the Caroline Concession, see L. de Hondt and A. du Bois, eds., *Les coustumes de la ville de Gand*, 2 vols. (Brussels, 1887), 2:140–83. For the alteration of Ghent's public life, Arnade, *Realms of Ritual*, 205–6, and Boone, "Urban Space in Late Medieval Flanders," 637–38. On the construction of Ghent's citadel, and sixteenth-century citadels in the Netherlands in general, see P. Lombaerde, "Herrschaftsarchitektur: Über den Abbruch von Zitadellen und den Bau neuer Paläste in den Niederlanden," in *Italienische Renaissancebaukunst an Schelde, Maas und Niederrhein. Stadtanlagen, Zivilbauten, Wehranlagen* Jülicher Pasqualini—Symposium vom 18. bis 21 Juni 1998, ed. G. Bers und C. Doose (Jülich, 1999), 317–33. On Sint-Jans, see Paul Trio, "Volksdevotionele aspecten in de Sint-Jans en de Sint-Baafskerk (tot omstreeks 1560)," in *De Sint-Baafskathedraal in Gent van Middeleeuwen tot Barok*, ed. Bruno Bouckaert (Ghent, 2000), 13–45.

91. For an account of the ceremony, see Gachard, *Relation des Troubles*, 156.

weaponry, leaving behind a commune humiliated and denuded of its legal and political might.

The wonder year of 1566 was a generation removed from the events of 1539–40. But with the citadel now flanking the city's eastern edge, with its walls and gates still bearing the scars of destruction and closing, and with its public and political life altered—the aldermen now handpicked on May 10 instead of on August 15, Assumption Day—the events of yesteryear were hardly forgotten. Protestantism only added to Ghent's troubles. As elsewhere in the Low Countries, Protestantism had made a vigorous, early appearance in Ghent, famously articulated at its 1539 rhetorician festival, during which several chambers of rhetoric, Ghent's included, espoused openly Lutheran ideas.[92] As early as July 25, 1521, the papal nuncio had three hundred "heretical" books burned at the Friday market. The primacy of Lutheranism, however, slowly gave way to competition from Anabaptists, for whom Ghent, with its great numbers of working poor, became a major stronghold, and Calvinism, attractive to propertied guildsmen and merchants alike.[93] In the summer of 1566, the city was so beset by hedge sermons that Margaret of Parma wrote to Philip II on July 31 that Ghent was in danger of a social upheaval. She described assemblies that had swelled to between twelve and fourteen thousand armed sermon-goers, whom Marcus van Vaernewijck characterized as socially mixed and strikingly defiant.[94]

Both Van Vaernewijck and the regent worried about sermon-goers' defiant air, undoubtedly because of Ghent's reputation as the urban *enfant terrible* of the southern Netherlands. The harsh winter of 1565–66, chronic grain shortages, and economic woes in the drapery industries had also convinced an earlier generation of social historians that Ghent's iconoclasm sprang from material concerns.[95] This economic determinism seems overdrawn, especially since, as it turns out, grain prices actually had improved in the summer of 1566. Yet witnesses to Ghent's troubles had expressed a practical awareness that bad times stirred trouble, especially in this turbulent city.[96] Van Vaernewijck believed that

92. Waite, *Reformers on Stage*, 134–64; Van Bruaene, "Printing Plays."

93. J. Scheerder, "Het Lutheranisme te Gent," *Annales van de Vereniging voor de Geschiedenis van het Belgisch Protestantisme*, 4th ed., vol. 6 (1963): 304–9; Decavele, *Het eind van een rebelse droom*, 12–20. Between 1530 and 1595, 252 death sentences involving Ghentenars, most of them Anabaptists, were handed down. See A. L. E. Verheyden, *Het Gentsche Martyrologium* (1530–95) (Bruges, 1946).

94. Letter in Fris, "Notes pour servir à l'histoire des iconoclastes et des Calvinistes à Gand," 16; BT *Van Vaernewijck*, 1:1, 5, 8, 13, 26. On patrician and professional attendees, see ibid., 1:32, 47. On mocking youth, see ibid., 1:23–24. The summer hedge sermons took off starting on June 22. For eyewitness accounts, see also RvB, no. 76, fol. 287r, fol. 290v, and fol. 292r.

95. Herman van der Wee, "The Economy as a Factor in the Start of the Revolt of the Netherlands," *Acta Historiae Neerlandica*, vol. 5 (Leiden, 1971): 52–67. The most direct formulation is in Kuttner, *Het Hongerjaar*. But see also C. Verlinden, J. Craeybeckx, and E. Scholliers, "Mouvements des prix et des salaires en Belgique au XVI siècle," *Annales, Economies, Sociétés, Civilisations* 10 (1955): 185–87. For a critique of the economic thesis as too monocasual, see Dambruyne, *Corporatieve middengroepen*, 639–40.

96. Parker, *Dutch Revolt*, 76.

a depressed job market and the grain shortages of the winter and spring of 1566 spurred attendance at the hedge sermons by people who otherwise might not have done so.[97] Similarly, Margaret of Parma wrote on July 7 that "the great problem is people's poverty, a result of the cessation of trade and marketing that raises emotions and provokes them to novelties and to the pillage of the rich."[98] On July 12, Ghent's aldermen complained to the city's guild deans about the "miserable state of the current times," seeking their help to prevent the "sack and pillage" of the city. Things had gotten so bad, they wrote, that nonresident merchants now refused to come to trade, for fear of assault.[99] Van Vaernewijck reported that the poor openly threatened the rich. On July 3, one taunted a well-off woman, "You will shortly learn just how much courage the poor have!" Another two had this exchange as a well-dressed burgher passed them: The one exclaimed, "I would not want to be as rich as he." His friend inquired, "And why not?" To which the first replied, "I would not want to be killed because of my possessions."[100]

As the sermons grew and social grievances received sporadic airings, the magistrates despaired. In their later justification to the Duke of Alba for why they failed to stop iconoclasm, the aldermen pinned the blame in part on the legacy of the Ghent revolt of 1539, and especially Charles V's strict punishment.[101] Ghent was without its civic arsenal, they bemoaned, its gates and walls were in a state of disrepair, and by order of the Caroline Concession they were unable to raise a muster quickly to prevent the hedge sermons.[102] Although the aldermen obviously pressed the point to justify their inaction during the riots, their complaint was no fiction, as proved by their actions in the month prior to the iconoclastic riots. On July 21, Margaret of Parma had directed Ghent's aldermen to halt Calvinist sermon-going and to fortify the city by calling up the ward-based militia companies. The aldermen immediately summoned the guild deans to the town hall. The tone was severe: they were reminded that the Caroline Concession of 1539 prohibited illegal assemblies; they were asked to remember the devastating settlement imposed on the city because of the previous trouble; and they were urged to profess an oath of obedience to

---

97. BT Van Vaernewijck, 1:53.

98. Quoted in Fris, "Notes pour servir à l'histoire des iconoclastes et des Calvinistes à Gand," 12, n. 1.

99. Ph. Kervijn de Volkaersbeke, ed., *Verslag van 't Magistraat van Gent, nopens de godsdienstige beroerten aldaer, loopende van 30 Juny 1566 tot den 30 April 1567, gevolgd door talryke bewysstukken* (Ghent, 1850), 99–100.

100. BT Van Vaernewijck, 1:8.

101. A consideration of all draft versions of the aldermen's justification, including a transcription of the excised description of iconoclasm that did not make it into the final report, is found in Marcel Delmotte, "Sociale aspecten van het Calvinisme te Gent (1566–67)," (master's thesis, University of Ghent, 1959), 21, for the various versions of the justification, and for the excised section on iconoclasm, see the transcription in appendix 1, 169–77.

102. D. van de Casteele, ed., *Justification du magistrat de Gand concernant les troubles religieux arrivés en cette ville du 30 juin 1566 au 7 mai 1567 Annales de la Société d'Emulation de la Flandre Occidentale*, 3rd ser., vol. 4 (1869), 380.

church and king.[103] While eighteen guilds quickly promised loyalty, they did so in the vaguest language, and never mentioned any willingness to stop sermon-going. Ghent's traditionally elite guild trio, the butchers, fishmongers, and free shippers, were the only ones to promise explicit obedience.[104]

The summons did nothing to dampen enthusiasm for the hedge sermons. On July 26 and 27, the aldermen called a mixed group to the town hall—fourteen men who ranged from craftsmen to comfortable merchants—to account for their actions.[105] The most forthright defiance came from one of the richest among them. The aldermen asked Goris vanden Bogaerde, former colleague of the lower bench in 1565 and a successful cloth merchant, why he had broken the oath he swore to the 1540 Caroline Concession. Not only did Vanden Bogaerde defend his attendance at the sermon by saying he no longer held office, he more startlingly questioned whether the constitution was legally valid.[106]

Still, the aldermen persisted in the teeth of such defiance. On August 3, they divided the city into seventeen quarters, each with two superintendents (with the exception of the parish of Saint Salvador) to oversee local captains of companies of nineteen men. On August 20 the aldermen required each muster captain to confirm his men's willingness to defend the city in the name of the king against religious violence. Among the captains was the merchant, rhetorician, and chronicler Marcus van Vaernewijck, appointed to the Saint Jacob's muster.[107] All but one of the 189 captains brought responses, representing 1,767 out of their nearly 4000 men. A weak 18 percent were explicitly willing to take up arms to protect the Catholic Church against iconoclasm or any other form of attack.[108] The low positive response rate was accompanied by explicit disdain for the Catholic Church or open profession of Calvinism. Captain Jan Heyndrix, for example, refused to fight to protect priests but said his men would take up arms for their preacher.[109] Van Vaernewijck wrote that his men's attitudes ranged from apathy to overt hostility to the Church. One said he had lost his weapon when it was confiscated after the 1539 uprising and had no money to replace it. Van Vaernewijck also complained about the shabby state of the city's defenses—munitions and fortifications in particular—the result of the 1539 punishment of Ghent.[110] On the eve of iconoclasm, Ghent was a city so rent with divisions that its

---

103. SAG 94 bis, no. 8, fols. 221r–222r.

104. Delmotte, "Sociale aspecten van het Calvinisme," 27–31.

105. BT Van Vaernewijck, 1:46–47; Delmotte, "Sociale aspecten van het Calvinisme," 34–35; SAG, Keurereresolutiën, fol. 361v.

106. BT Van Vaernewijck, 1:47.

107. SAG, Keurereresolutiën, fol. 365r. A full discussion is in Delmotte, "Sociale aspecten van het Calvinisme," 38–75. See also M. Delmotte, "Het Calvinisme in de verschillende bevolkingslagen te Gent (1566–1567)," Tijdschrift voor Geschiedenis 76 (1963): 145–76.

108. See Delmotte's analysis, "Het Calvinisme in de verschillende bevolkingslagen," 152.

109. Quoted in Delmotte, "Sociale aspecten van het Calvinisme," 69, from SAG, Keurereresolutiën, fol. 371r.

110. BT Van Vaernewijck, 1:58–59.

propertied men and craftsmen who formed the traditional militia were mostly unwilling to take up arms to protest ecclesiastical property.[111]

With Ghent tense, matters were made much worse by a grain riot by angry women on August 21. Ironically, the scarcity of grain had peaked the previous winter, the result of a bad harvest and the closing of the Baltic because of war among several of its principalities; by early summer prices had returned to their normal level for wheat, rye, and corn.[112] But a minicrisis took hold in Ghent, prompted by the news of the iconoclastic riots in the Westkwartier that reached the city on August 17. Prices were at normal levels at Friday's market, but by Monday they had shot up one schilling a sack, and yet another schilling by Wednesday, sparking an uproar that included verbal and physical attacks against several merchants.[113] While the riot was obviously about grain prices—Calvinists were among the merchants attacked—contemporaries evaluated this flare-up in Ghent within the broader context of the religious troubles engulfing Flanders. Van Vaernewijck reminded his readers that Ghent was a city in which social unrest was endemic. His description of the grain riot brims with narrative tension as he intersperses the reception in Ghent of news about iconoclasm in the Westkwartier with efforts to secure the city's religious art. "Some women said they had no bread to eat," he wrote, "and that their children would perish from hunger since they were without money. As they said this, men began to remove statues made of alabaster and other materials in various churches."[114] The aldermen likewise viewed the grain riot and the concern over iconoclasm as intertwined, and explained later that they were so preoccupied with how to keep grain prices reasonable that the iconoclasts took them by complete surprise.[115] There is a good measure of truth to the aldermen's assertion—they were in fact busy with addressing the grievances of the rioters out of fear that a larger revolt was imminent. But Ghent's chroniclers Van Vaernewijck and Cornelis van Campene, as well as evidence that emerged from depositions taken after the troubles, paint a more unflattering portrait of city officials, especially of the government's officer in the city, the bailiff Adolf van Bourgondië, lord of Wakken. In their official account of the riots, the aldermen described how they spent the morning of Thursday, August 22, in session while the bailiff and his officers met separately to plan security for the next market day. Without warning, Lieven Onghena, leader of a large band of iconoclasts who had gathered at the court of the Templars, made a surprise visit to the bailiff to present an official mandate to rid the churches of idolatry. The bailiff protested and dis-

---

111. Cf. the case of Middelburg, whose magistrates admitted that many of their citizens refused to take up arms in 1566 to defend "churches, monks, and the pope." See J. van Vloten, ed., *Onderzoek van 's konings wege ingesteld omtrent de Middelburgsche beroerten van 1566 en 1567* (Utrecht, 1873), 103, 131, 156.

112. Verlinden, Craeybeckx, and Scholiers, "Mouvements des prix et des salaires en Belgique au XVI siècle."

113. BT *Van Vaernewijck*, 1:91.

114. Ibid., 1:91–92

115. Van de Casteele, *Justification du magistrat de Gand concernant les troubles*, 392–93.

patched his officer Artus Bousse and armed men to eject the iconoclasts.[116] But records of legal inquests, including the death sentence pronounced against Bousse, together with that of the always perceptive Van Vaernewijck tell the story differently. They confirm that the bailiff was indeed taken by surprise, but describe how he sent Bousse and his men to the Templars not to stop the destruction but to make sure it happened without bloodshed or stealing. Ghent's iconoclasm, in fact, got underway with the grudging approval of a city official, a scenario that repeated itself when iconoclasm befell The Hague.[117]

The result was a full day and night of image-breaking in Ghent replete with carnivalesque behaviors and violent passions. Unlike Ypres or Antwerp, neither Assumption Day nor a single veneration anchored the iconoclasts' wrath. Nor was there a clear spatial focus. Instead, Ghent's riots were as dispersed as they were intense, hitting seven parish churches, the Saint Bavo's Cathedral, twenty-five cloisters, ten hospitals, and seven chapels.[118] If there was a common thread to the violence, it was hatred of the religious houses: the Dominican cloister located at Ghent's center and the monastery and parish church of the seigneury of Saint Peter's to the city's south. In social profile and behavior too, Ghent's iconoclasm had the uproarious, artisanal, even plebian quality associated not only with the previous day's grain riot but more broadly with collective forms of urban unrest, long a feature of this city. The *beeldenstormers* had as their target Catholic religious practice, but much like the rioters in the Westkwartier, they referenced material forms of protest older than Calvinist criticism of images. Indeed, the social profile of the rioters seemed on casual glance to resemble that of the rioters of 1539, a parallel that the aldermen themselves had worried about in their earlier unsuccessful attempts to warn their fellow Ghentenars against piquing the king's anger.

Legal and narrative sources have turned up 118 names of iconoclasts, of whom sixty-four are accounted for in government records of the confiscation of property and goods.[119] The list is obviously partial, representing only those cited or apprehended. Van

---

116. Ibid., 365; for the slight variations in the draft accounts, see the excellent discussion in Delmotte, "Sociale aspecten van het Calvinisme," 141.

117. BT Van Vaernewijck, 1:104–7; cf. De Potter, *Dagboek van Cornelis en Philip van Campene*, 12. On Onghena's claim of a mandate, see the witness depositions of the pastors Jan Martins, Gillis Nijs, and Leo Bernaerts, RvB, no. 76, fols. 290r, 291r, and 293r. On Bousse's culpability, see SAG, ser. 93, no. 39, fols. 307v–310r. Bousse was accused of permitting iconoclasm in all the churches and chapels in Ghent on the condition that the men work efficiently in groups of thirty to forty.

118. For a summary of the destruction, see Victor Fris, "Eene treurige bladzijde in de Gentsche Kunstgeschiedenis," *Bulletin der Maatschappij van Geschied- en Oudheidkunde te Gent* 19, no. 2 (1911): 97–120, and Decavele, *Het eind van een rebelse droom*, 24.

119. A comprehensive and annotated list is in Delmotte, "Sociale aspecten van het Calvinisme," 249–322, in part based on earlier accountings in Fris, "Notes pour servir à l'histoire des iconoclastes et des Calvinistes à Gand," 89–105, and J. Scheerder, "Gentenaars voor den Raad van Beroerte," *Bijdrage tot de Geschiedenis en Oudheidkunde te Gent* 4 (Ghent, 1943): 131–41. A new social analysis is provided by Dambruyne,

Vaernewijck, not known for exaggeration, estimated the armed iconoclasts who gathered before the Templars at around four hundred. He described them as "mostly outsiders" who had come to work as day laborers or apprentices in Ghent and lived in the swelling workers' quarters of Muide, Saint Peter's, the Zand nearby Sint-Lievenspoort and Ekkergem, or crammed together in rental rooms around the city's center.[120] From property and legal records, Marcel Delmotte identified the domiciles of sixty-seven iconoclasts, finding six nonresidents, ten outside workers who listed Ghent as their home, and twenty from the Saint Peter's seigneury, an area where Calvinist support was high and summer hedge sermons had flourished right outside its boundaries. That these figures do not neatly line up with Van Vaernewijck's social description of the iconoclasts might have to do with the fact that most rioters fled before the strong hand of the law was asserted in 1567.[121]

Of the 118 Ghent rioters identified, the profession of seventy is known. Fifteen worked in textiles. The tanner Lieven Onghena, along with his brother Jan, a rhetorician and sometime teacher, led the iconoclasts.[122] Nineteen labored in the building trades; six in victuals, including four butchers; five in minor civic positions; and twenty-three in other lines of work, including soldiering and soap boiling. There was even a cloth merchant and young nobleman among them. Yet despite the presence of the merchant Lieven de Smedt, rich and Calvinist, or the young, impecunious nobleman Claude Goetghebuer, thirty-four of the sixty-four for whom we have records of assets owned nothing. On the basis of these facts—and supported by Van Vaernewijck's social description—Delmotte concluded that Ghent's iconoclasts were the wage laborers who crowded the city's outer ring of poor neighborhoods.[123] More recently, Johan Dambruyne has modified this assertion, pointing out that this cohort also included twenty-nine guild masters.[124] It is obvious that this group of rioters, like the Ghentenars who fomented rebellion in 1539, mixed wage laborers with better-to-do craftsmen. At the same time, it is vitally important to remember that this snapshot is but a partial portrait of those who fomented discord in Ghent, making it hard to extrapolate larger conclusions about the social occupation and economic status

---

Corporatieve middengroepen, 641–43, and appendix 33, 831–32, which lists all Gentenars implicated for either iconoclasm or Calvinism.

120. BT *Van Vaernewijck*, 1:106 for the crowd, and 1:202–3 for domiciles.

121. Delmotte, "Sociale aspecten van het Calvinisme," 216–27; Delmotte, "Het Calvinisme in de verschillende bevolkingslagen," 154.

122. On the two brothers, see BT *Van Vaernewijck*, 1:29–30; on Lieven, see the information gathered in Delmotte, "Sociale aspecten van het Calvinisme," 287–89, and Fris, "Notes pour servir à l'histoire des iconoclasts et des Calvinistes à Gand," 128–30; on Jan, see Delmotte, "Sociale aspecten van het Calvinisme," 285–87, Fris, "Notes pour servir à l'histoire des iconoclasts et des Calvinistes à Gand," 94–95, and his July 3, 1567, deposition in *Antwerpsch Archievenblad*, 9:374–77, executed August2, 1568, in Ghent.

123. Full analysis is in Delmotte, "Calvinisme in de verschillende bevolkingslagen," 158–62.

124. Dambruyne, *Corporatieve middengroepen*, 641–42.

of the rioters and the relationship of this data to religious conviction. Clearer is the noticeable difference between these iconoclasts and the 1,400–1,500 Calvinists who can be identified as active in Ghent in the wonder year. As Delmotte has pointed out, of ninety-five Calvinists who fell victim to prosecution and left property records, the overwhelming majority had significant assets, with 43.1 percent holding real property worth between one and five thousand florins. Of the seventy-four whose professions are given, the crafts and trade sectors each make up 31 percent, with another 24.3 percent in professional work, including lawyers and solicitors at the Council of Flanders (located in Ghent).[125]

However distinct professing Calvinists and rioting iconoclasts were in social standing, all evidence points to the fact that the Reformed community helped to launch image-breaking as it did in Antwerp, though its members were divided about whether the violent removal of images was advisable. On August 19, two days after news of iconoclasm in Westkwartier arrived in Ghent, Calvinists held an enormous hedge sermon outside the city walls near the Carthusian cloister at Rooigem. The attendees were even reported to have threatened the cloister and apparently only desisted from image-breaking when the Calvinist ministers themselves posted a guard. One of the ministers, Franciscus Junius, favored the removal of images only with official permission, evidence of a split found elsewhere between radicals and conservatives. These events were reported back to Ghent and prompted confraternities and churchwardens to remove costly images from certain churches, the Saint Bavo's Cathedral included. The plan for iconoclasm in Ghent was hatched at Lieven Onghena's home. On the morning of August 22, Lieven's brother Jan met with a member of the consistory, Jan Dierickx, in the inn De Mortier on the Veebrug. Dierickx alerted Onghena that men from Antwerp were on their way to Ghent. In the early afternoon, iconoclasts armed with muskets, hammers, picks, and other work tools headed to Templars while the Onghena brothers and nobleman Claude Goetghebuer went to see the bailiff.[126]

From the start, iconoclasm in Ghent was rife with satirical inversion, jabs at figures of local authority, and extra fury spent on religious institutions associated with the enforcement of the hated heresy placards, especially the Dominicans and the Benedictine Saint Peter's Abbey. In this regard, the violence in Ghent more strongly resembles the social reverberations of the Westkwartier than it did in Ypres and Antwerp, where, as we have seen, religious time and a central Onze-Lieve-Vrouw devotion mattered most. Yet iconoclasm in Ghent harbored its own internal logic, characterized more than anything else by the ever-present memories of 1539, when the city's radical politics was severely put down by Charles V himself and the city's public landscape and guild associations visibly altered. That the grain riot and worries about social revolt were a prelude to the outburst of icon-

---

125. Delmotte, "Calvinisme in de verschillende bevolkingslagen," 166–72.
126. Scheerder, *Beeldenstorm*, 42–45.

oclasm colored both the nature of the ensuing violence and how it was described by contemporaries like the aldermen and Van Vaernewijck, who characterized the rioters as mere street ruffians. While Ghent's iconoclasts engaged in all the same Calvinist-inspired destruction of religious art, their actions were heavily laced with references to the Beggars. As we shall see, Ghent's iconoclasts were quick to humiliate images and attack ecclesiastical houses with cheers of "Vivent les Gueux!" and they also feasted and drank heavily, yet another ritual association with Brederode and his peers. Iconoclasm in Ghent, in short, took on punchier, more direct political tones both as reference to the past legacy of 1539 and as reference to the party of the Beggars.

The Templars chapel slightly northwest of the city's center was the start of an arc of destruction by Ghent's iconoclasts, covering all of the city's churches, chapels, hospitals, cloisters, and other religious houses. The first to be attacked was the Augustinian church and cloister, alarmingly close to the Burgundian palace. This may have been simply because of its proximity to the Templars, but it is important to note that it was from this order that Luther hailed, and its cloister in Antwerp had produced the first two Protestant victims executed in the Low Countries. In Ghent, the Augustinians had fallen for a short period at the beginning of the 1520s under a reform impulse with Lutheran overtones. Regional church officials forced out a reform-minded abbot in 1522 and steered the cloister back into the orthodox fold, though the house remained a source of some worry to them as compared to its conservative equivalent in Bruges, home to the Spanish friar Lorenzo de Villavicencio. Perhaps iconoclasts attacked this well-established religious house first because of the memory of a reform movement quashed and its association with militant Catholicism.[127]

From this spot the iconoclasts spread out, working into the early morning hours. Van Vaernewijck watched with amazement from his doorstep, as groups of "thirty, forty, and fifty, women and youth among them, with many singing psalms" rushed about at two and three a.m., torches and work tools in hand, shouting, "Have you been here or there and destroyed this or that image?"[128] Their actions involved wry mockery and ritual disfigurement. In the Carmelite cloister, iconoclasts even attacked murals, scraping them off the wall and disfiguring eyes and faces rather than the whole portrait. At the parish church of Saint Nicholas, a teenaged boy entered an unlocked chapel of a patrician family and cut off the hands and disfigured the faces of its various statues.[129] Such actions, as David Freedberg has noted of historical iconoclasm in general, demonstrates that worshipper and iconoclast alike knew the power of an image's sensate representation. But as we have already seen in the Westkwartier and the Walloon cities, such ritual desecration

---

127. Johan Decavele, ed., *Zeven eeuwen Augustijnen: een kloostergemeenschap schrijft geschiedenis* (Ghent, 1997).
128. BT Van Vaernewijck, 1:137–38.
129. Ibid., 1:109–10, 151.

also evoked the methods of execution to which Protestant victims were subjected.[130] That the young boy attacked a patrician's chapel startled Van Vaernewijck, but it was one of many assaults in Ghent on altars and sarcophagi of local authorities or prominent families. Although the canons and church wardens of the prestigious Saint Bavo's Cathedral had removed much artwork in advance, including the epitaphs of the Bette family, those of the Van Triest, Van de Baviers, and De Maechs families were all destroyed, as was the tomb of the last abbot of the Saint Bavo's Abbey. In Saint Jacob's parish church in the heart of Calvinist-rich neighborhoods, iconoclasts did more damage than elsewhere, including gouging out the faces of the former bailiff Francis van der Gracht and his first and second wives at their sepulchers. At the Carmelite cloister, the tombstone of a former president of the Council of Flanders was thoroughly destroyed.[131]

Such outright violence directed against the memory of urban notables was accompanied by the taunting of religious statues and images to expose their fraudulent sacrality and their material reality. When a crowd of Calvinists gathered before the town hall on Assumption Day more than a week before iconoclasm broke out, Van Vaernewijck observed bands of children singing satirical ballads about clergy whose last stanza closed with the cry of Westkwartier iconoclasts: "Vivent les Gueux!"[132] No surprise then that such an exclamation should accompany the day and night of iconoclastic violence, nor that it was youth again who taunted statues at the Dominican convent to "say 'Vivent les Gueux!' or we will behead you."[133] In the church of Saint Nicholas stood a sculpted retable of Mary in her "kinderbed" (birthing bed), the infant Jesus in her arms, and Joseph beside them. The retable was an obviously popular devotion. The statues were handsomely dressed, bejeweled, and hung with roses, and had ex-voto offerings—wax replicas of arms and legs most prominent. Before beheading Joseph and destroying the whole artwork, iconoclasts taunted Mary in much the same way as had been done with the Onze-Lieve-Vrouw statue in Antwerp. Children, noted Van Vaernewijck, yelled, "You have been in bed long enough. Get out, Mary!"[134] Nearby, a young woman tried to carry a wooden statue of the local Saint Macharius in a sack over the Gravenbrug to safety, but iconoclasts snatched it from her, threw it below into the water, then shouted, "Look, look, a miracle, the fully armored saint still can swim!"[135]

---

130. David Freedberg, "The Problems of Images in Northern Europe and its Repercussions in the Netherlands," in *Hafnia: Copenhagen Papers in the History of Art* (1976): 25–45, and more significantly his *Iconoclasts and Their Motives* (Maarsen, 1985).

131. See Fris, "Eene treurige bladzijde in de Gentsche Kunstgeschiedenis" for a full tally.

132. BT *Van Vaernewijck*, 1:68.

133. Ibid., 1:127.

134. Ibid., 1:110. On this retable and others like it, see Paul Trio, *De Gentse Broederschappen (1182–1588)* (Ghent, 1990), 51–52.

135. BT *Van Vaernewijck*, 1:129. Van Vaernewijck says the image came from a cloister. I can find only one reference to Saint Macharius, namely a family chapel of the prominent Wieland family in the parish church of Saint Jacob. See Trio, *Gentse Broederschappen*, 141.

The violence against the epitaphs and sarcophagi of patrician, religious, and political elites and the violent mocking of religious tabernacles and statues indicate that image criticism could intersect with material grievances in exactly the way Van Vaernewijck had feared. But if the riots assumed the quality of a protest, their target and inspiration were no less religious. Riotous, ludic acts received their fullest airing not at Ghent's most famous parish church, but at the religious institutions most directly associated with the heresy placards and legal rights of religious privilege. In central Ghent, the Dominicans bore the brunt of the iconoclasts' vehemence, already apparent in the weeks prior to the violence; Van Vaernewijck remarked that the Calvinists regularly fired weapons above the cloister's roof and hurled insults at the Dominicans, calling them "master heretics, inquisitors, persecutors, who like cannibals devour human flesh."[136] The strong feelings no doubt had to do with the Dominicans' close association with inquisitor general Titelmans, who in 1559 awarded them with extra money—300 florins—for their unwavering cooperation in hunting Protestants.[137] When the cloister was stormed, the rioters turned the event into a pillage-cum-banquet—a triumphal celebration. They smashed images, raided the refectory and cellar, drank and ate excessively, even out of liturgical vessels, smeared butter on the walls, and all but destroyed the enormous library, with so many torn books littering the Leie River that it looked as if fresh snow had fallen.[138]

The most extensive damage to artwork occurred at the venerable Saint Peter's Abbey and parish church of Onze-Lieve-Vrouw just south of the city. Ghent's oldest monastery, and its most prominent since the razing of Saint Bavo's by Charles V in 1540, Saint Peter's Abbey was located in a seigneury that was home to at least twenty of the sixty-seven iconoclasts identifiable by domicile. It was also an area of vigorous Reformed sentiment and populated by a vast assortment of guildsmen, artisans, and wage laborers. The abbey was steeped in historical prestige, including its role as the first stop when a new count of Flanders entered Ghent on his Blijde Inkomst; the count would hear mass and swear to uphold the seigneury's privileges before entering Ghent proper.[139] The Onze-Lieve-Vrouwekerk was also Ghent's most important center of Marian devotion, home to an Assumption Day procession so popular with the politically troublesome weavers that Charles V had scaled it back in 1540. The alderman had even cancelled the procession in 1566 for fear of violence. Tellingly, celebrations in honor of Onze-Lieve-Vrouw traditionally culminated at the Onze-Lieve-Vrouwekerk on the octave of Assumption Day, August 22, the day iconoclasm hit Ghent.[140]

The abbot and lesser officials of Saint Peter's were ready for the iconoclasts when they

---

136. BT Van Vaernewijck, 1:88–89.
137. Decavele, Dageraad, 1:25.
138. BT Van Vaernewijck, 1:113–15.
139. Arnade, "The Emperor and the City."
140. Trio, Gentse Broederschappen, 79–84. A good description of the procession is in BT Van Vaernewijck, 1:60–65.

arrived, and tried desperately to buy them off. The rioters would have none of it, and set about their destruction with extra vehemence, including ransacking the wine cellar as well as the sleeping quarters. Although the abbot had wisely stored several costly sculptures, paintings, and other liturgical items in the citadel that Charles V had constructed, the bulk of the monastery's and church's artwork was destroyed, including works by Frans van den Velde and Jan de Heere, most notably de Heere's Saint Andrew retable in marble, alabaster, and ashlar.[141] For all his acute observations on Ghent's iconoclasm, Van Vaernewijck was typically a dispassionate compiler of religious objects destroyed. But the rioters' destruction in Saint Peter's bothered him especially. It was the rage of "Bacchus," despaired the chronicler, performed by mere "shoeless ruffians" who dared to destroy high art and denounce the abbot and his monks as "blood suckers" for prosecuting and imprisoning Calvinists. The artwork was especially precious and the iconoclasts particularly vulgar. The nighttime attack also made the rioters all the more frenzied, having arrived at Saint Peter's already drunk and worked up from their destruction in central Ghent, where they consumed every jug of beer or wine they could get their hands on.[142]

Iconoclasm in Ghent stretched from the afternoon of August 22 until the next morning, when the bailiff and his men finally sent the bands of rioters out of Ghent toward the religious houses and smaller parish churches of its hinterland, where they continued to vent their wrath, especially against the Premonstratian abbey of Drongen.[143] Iconoclasm took place on Thursday and the night hours of Friday morning, between two market days, the first of which had been roiled by a grain riot. That the aldermen feared yet more trouble on August 23 is evident in their decision to rid Ghent of rioters before the market started and to secure the Koornmarkt with extra men.[144] In their official report on the troubles in Ghent, the aldermen talked openly about the possibility of a social revolt, including attacks on tax booths that a century earlier religious pilgrims had smashed up during the feast day celebrating the procession of Saint Lieven's relics in June 1467.[145] Van Vaernewijck's account of iconoclasm in Ghent likewise constructs its storyline around the tensions, real and perceived, between the August 21 grain riot, the August 22 iconoclasm, and its termination on August 23 as the new market day began—the poor clamoring for food while well-fed clerics, confraternity brothers, and churchwardens fretted about how to protect precious statues and images. Looming even larger than this connection between the material and the spiritual was the legacy of the 1539 revolt against Charles V. As

---

141. Fris, "Eene treurige bladzijde in de Gentsche kunstgeschiedenis."
142. BT Van Vaernewijck, 1:129–33.
143. Delmotte, "Sociale aspecten van het Calvinisme," 160; Scheerder, Beeldenstorm, 45.
144. Delmotte, "Sociale aspecten van het Calvinisme," 165.
145. On the 1467 riot, see Arnade, "Secular Charisma, Sacred Power." On the aldermen's worry about a social revolt, see the draft version of their official justification, transcribed in Delmotte, "Sociale aspecten van het Calvinisme," esp. 175, echoed in BT Van Vaernewijck, 1:194.

we have seen, all players evoked the memory of the revolt, as they wrestled with how to stave off the iconoclastic riots. That the actual image breaking was done by diverse hands, with day laborers strongly present, proves that suspicions of a connection between the events of 1539 and of 1566 were not overdrawn; however sociologically imprecise the rioters' composition, strong parallels exist between the *dagloners* (wage laborers) of 1539 and the "shoeless ruffians" of 1566. Moreover, there was an actual generation bridge that connected the two epochs. The Calvinist cloth merchant Lieven d'Herde was banished by order of Alba's Council of Troubles on March 29, 1568, for his Calvinist activity in Ghent. He was the son of the radical dean of the weavers and leader of the 1539 revolt, who had been executed in 1540.[146] It was, however, less bloodline than urban political memory that made the events of 1566 relevant to those of 1539. The destruction of the statue of Charles V and the Virgin Mary at the Keizerpoort, a rare assault on a representation of royal authority, provides strong evidence that iconoclasts fomented their actions with 1539 in mind.[147] In no other city across the Netherlands during the various waves of iconoclasm did a representation of the emperor or of Philip II come under attack. In Ghent, however new the theological ideas and however contemporary the political circumstances, the troubled past weighed mightily upon the dizzying events of the summer of 1566. As they drank, chopped, smashed, and hacked away at images and objects, Ghent's iconoclasts cheered the Beggars and even attacked a statue of the larger-than-life emperor who had so humiliated the city after its 1539 revolt.

Time, Space, and Iconoclasm

The progression of the wonder year of 1566 had a political logic: the formation of the Compromise, the theatrical petition to mitigate the heresy placards and the formation of the Beggars, the forced relaxation of these laws, the swollen crowds at the summer hedge sermons, the paralysis of political authority, and the outbreak of iconoclasm. From the outset of troubles in the Netherlands, the League, the Compromise, and the loyalist opponents seized on supercharged symbols and times to stake out their positions. In the trio of cities I have examined, religious violence was acutely attuned to historical time and to the place and space of local devotions. From the very first incident of iconoclasm on August 10, on the feast day of Saint Lawrence in the Westkwartier, attacks often happened during religious times essential to local, regional, even state elites. In Ypres and Antwerp, Assumption Day, the August 15 celebration of the Virgin's ascension, was that special

146. On d'Herde, see RvB, no. 6, fols. 66r–69r, and BT *Van Vaernewijck*, 3:276. D'Herde fled to England with his family, only to return during the Calvinist regime in Ghent.

147. De Potter, *Dagboek van Cornelis en Philip van Campene*, 19; BT *Van Vaernewijck*, 1:149. The more loquacious Van Vaernewijck uses only the term "emperor," but Van Campene confirms that the statue was of Charles V.

time. Ypres might have been of shrinking economic importance in 1566, but it still dominated the Westkwartier's religious and political domain, and as such was a special target of the iconoclasts' wrath. Led by apostate clergy from Ypres' own religious houses, the Reformed enthusiasts inaugurated their actions with psalm singing on August 4 in the city's center—Tuindag proper in 1566—and then attacked the outskirts of the city on Assumption Day, successfully entering Ypres the following day. Once there, they destroyed the Tuin Virgin, the statue of the Virgin in the Belfry, and liturgical items such as the candle sticks used in the procession. They also gathered as a crowd beneath the Cloth Hall in a manner that imitated Tuindag worshippers. In doing so, they disturbed the city's most important religious time and a cherished historical memory—a blow both to the city's sacred significance and to its civic pride.

As in Ypres, so in Antwerp, but on a scale befitting the Low Countries' greatest city. The city's three great summer *ommegangen*, the Circumcision, Corpus Christi, and Assumption Day processions, were all occasions for increasingly overt dissent that ranged from participants' donning Beggars' insignia to the open desecration of the Onze-Lieve-Vrouw statue. When iconoclasm finally seized the city, relics or statues essential to all three old devotions were destroyed, with the most prestigious veneration, Onze-Lieve-Vrouw, providing the electric charge from which the troubles drew energy. But if iconoclasm in Antwerp shared with Ypres the provocation of a particular religious time, it differed in the heightened significance that iconoclasts attached to the Onze-Lieve-Vrouwekerk. The richly endowed church in Antwerp's center had monopolized the city's religious life, even preventing the legal independence of other urban parishes until the end of the fifteenth century. It was home to an elite chapter of canons, half of whom failed to take up residence in the city. For the Calvinists and iconoclasts, Onze-Lieve-Vrouwekerk became the key to severing the city's alliance between Catholic worship and religious authority. Although iconoclasm shook all the city's religious houses, chroniclers and commentators elevated the attack on the Onze-Lieve-Vrouwekerk to the great symbol of Antwerp's image-destruction and to Low Country iconoclasm as a whole.

Religious time mattered too in Ghent; it was not coincidental that iconoclasts wrought their most severe destruction in Saint Peter's church and monastery on August 22, the octave of the seigneury's procession of Onze-Lieve-Vrouw and a day of intense Marian devotion. But more than anywhere else, iconoclasm in Ghent wrestled with the devils of the past, particularly the 1539 revolt fomented against Charles V, and the fuzzy borders between social grievances and theological complaint. Iconoclasm in Ghent was just as religiously charged as in Ypres and Antwerp, obvious in that the Dominican cloister and the Benedictine monastery—in their differing ways institutions of enormous prestige associated with the fight against heresy—bore much of the brunt of the iconoclasts' wrath. But Ghent's iconoclasm also intimated a social ethic that contrasted richly apportioned images and liturgical goods with the working poor, suffering in a rocky economy. The space of Ghent's iconoclasm was not so concentrated as in Ypres and Antwerp, and the time that mattered was not merely Assumption Day but the whole historical memory of a city famous for its pugilistic attitude. "Vivent les Gueux!" in Ghent was a cheer that both championed the Reformed cause and the gentilshommes' fight against the heresy placards; but it also cried out its grievance against princely authority, made plain by the felling of a statue of Charles V and the Virgin. The material tones of iconoclasm in the Westkwartier were not only reflected in Ghent's riots; their political valences were sharpened.

Iconoclasm in Ypres, Antwerp, and Ghent tell us much about the outbreak of religious turmoil in Flanders and Brabant. But while the religious violence in these three great cities share many features, more than anything else they are reminders that troubles that roiled the Low Countries partook of the territories' characteristic of localism and heterogeneity. Iconoclasm in the three urban centers point out that a shared repertoire of Reformed ideas and riotous acts could result in very different patterns of enactment. What they have in common, apart from Calvinist inspiration, was a ritual kinship to the behaviors deployed by the Westkwartier iconoclasts, and a shrewd sense of how their own urban religious and political grievances could be dramatized in the heat of riot. In all three cities, no matter how distinct were the rioters from the Beggars, the *beeldenstormers* used their violence to proclaim public oaths in favor of this aristocratic cause. Such exclamations of support in favor of the Beggars, however, presented a dilemma for these noblemen, since it yoked image-breaking explicitly to the spring protests of the Compromise, and their associates. The very real distinction between these two sets of developments seemed to shrink, and could hardly be discerned from afar, especially not from a king and court in Castile. Such a gross violation of God and king required the severest of punishments and the fullest restoration of royal authority. The iconoclasts had become the most important protagonists in the Netherlands, and in the aftermath of the riots, the nature and direction of the original set of protests launched by the Compromise and the Beggars would require urgent reformulation.

CHAPTER 5 A NEW IDOLATRY
ALBA AS AVENGER AND USURPER
OF ROYAL AUTHORITY

The iconoclastic riots of the late summer and fall of 1566 shattered more than just altarpieces, tabernacles, paintings, statues, and relics. They struck the political landscape like a huge tornado, cutting a swath of destruction that many had seen coming but whose intensity no one had predicted. In the aftermath, everyone, Calvinist ministers included, denied responsibility. Even the most outspoken apologist for iconoclasm, Philips van Marnix, Lord of St. Aldegonde, ascribed image-breaking to the will of God and blamed the events on a conspiracy of priests and the rabble. Margaret of Parma's letters about the troubles reached Philip II on September 3, reportedly distressing him so much that he fell ill. The sensational news roiled Spanish Catholic sentiment, and in Madrid, Netherlanders expressed fear of appearing in public. By September 22, Philip convened his closest advisors to debate a plan to dispatch an army to the Netherlands, putting to rest quibbling between two court factions divided over the wisdom of a hard-line policy toward the Seventeen Provinces.[1]

In Brussels the religious violence likewise disrupted well-laid strategies and shifted political calculations, especially among the grands seigneurs and the Compromise. Great men of state like Egmont and Orange took stock of the events, with the former vigorously pursuing legal proceedings against iconoclasts. Outwardly respectful of the regent, they also worked to implement an agreement they had wrested from her on August 23 allowing the practice of Protestantism in places where it had been already established. Presumably, the regent intended to keep actual worship outside city walls, where it had been reluctantly permitted prior to the riots.[2] But on September 2 Orange enacted a more gen-

---

1. On the reception of the news of iconoclasm in Spain, see Kamen, *Philip of Spain*, 116; Patrick Williams, *Philip II* (New York, 2001), 121. On the formulation of Habsburg Spanish policy toward the Low Countries, and the factions and debates it entailed, see David Lagomarsino, "Court Factions and the Formulation of Spanish Policy towards the Netherlands (1559–67)," (PhD diss., Cambridge University, 1973).

2. Parker, *Dutch Revolt*, 81. On Orange's arrangement in Antwerp, see the published texts in *Antwerpsch Archievenblad*, 10:48–51, 56–58. For the effect of the August 23 accord in general, see Israel, *Dutch Republic*, 152.

erous arrangement in Antwerp—never officially endorsed by the regent—tolerating Protestant worship, Anabaptism excepted, inside the city as well. Egmont and Hornes approved similar plans quickly thereafter in Ghent and Tournai. Of the three, Orange was inspired not just by exigencies, but by the articulation, however inchoate, of a call for "liberty of conscience." He favored a *religievrede* (religious peace) between Protestants and Catholics, a pragmatic plan for coexistence that he first set in motion in Antwerp, but that he worked diligently to extend to the north at places like Breda, Utrecht, and Amsterdam. With both Lutheran sympathies and dynastic obligations to the Burgundian court, Orange famously tried to play to a moderate middle ground that was fast disappearing, as Catholic royalists and militant Calvinists polarized the conflict.[3]

Efforts to punish *beeldenstormers* and rebellious Calvinists and to achieve political reconciliation preoccupied the various political factions for nearly a year after the iconoclastic riots. In August 1567 the official toleration of Lutheran and Reformed practice came to an abrupt halt with the arrival of Fernando Alvarez de Toledo, Duke of Alba in Brussels. For all the attempts at reconciliation, the period before Alba's arrival had been beset with conflict and violence. In the fall of 1566, Calvinist insurgency had rocked the Flemish and Walloon areas, prompting its violent repression in early 1567 in Tournai, Valenciennes, and elsewhere, despite the attempt by the Beggars' inspirational leader, Van Brederode, to coordinate the Calvinist cause from Vianen. There were, however, hopeful developments. Orange had skillfully convinced the other senior nobles to advocate a religious settlement that avoided armed revolt against the crown, and Margaret of Parma had put down militant Calvinists, settling the Antwerp revolt with troops and by her own temporary residency, and had ordered magistrates to execute select rebels and iconoclasts while pursuing economic and political reconciliation.[4]

This juggling act between punishment and accommodation, however, did not sit well in Castile, and earned disapproval from none other than the king himself.[5] The winter of 1567 saw preparations underway to settle the problem of the Netherlands through a force of ten thousand under the leadership of Alba. Although Alba was not the king's first choice to lead the punitive expedition—Philip II apparently preferred the regent's less controversial husband, the Duke of Parma—he was an iron-fisted old soldier, a Castilian conservative, and court veteran whom the king trusted to carry out a hard-line settlement.[6]

---

3. K. W. Swart, "Wat bewoog Willem van Oranje de strijd tegen de Spaanse overheersing aan te binden?" *Bijdragen en Mededelingen betreffende de Geschiedenis der Nederlanden* 99 (1984): 557–58.

4. Deyon and Lottin, *Casseurs de l'été 1566*, 55–111, especially pertinent on Tournai and Valenciennes. On Antwerp, Marnef, *Antwerp in the Age of Reformation*, 105–10.

5. Lagomarsino, "Court Factions and the Formulation of Spanish Policy," 251–59.

6. The fullest treatment of Alba is William S. Maltby, *Alba: A Biography of Fernando Alvarez de Toledo, Third Duke of Alba, 1507–1582* (Berkeley, 1983), and Henry Kamen, *The Duke of Alba* (New Haven, 2004). See also Duke of Berwick y Alba, *Contribución al estudio de la persona del III Duque de Alba* (Madrid, 1919), a work by a distant twentieth-century heir, as well as the seventeenth-century Latin biography translated into Spanish:

Four months after his departure from Cartagena, Alba arrived in Brussels, on August 22, 1567, bearing the title of captain general. His six-year rule in the Netherlands marked the most turbulent period of the Dutch Revolt, a calcification of political, religious, and cultural enmity so deep that it made any resolution of the conflict remote. Accounts of this period have enumerated its political and military events: the establishment of the infamous Council of Troubles, Orange's decision to take up arms, the stunning success of the Sea Beggars and the capture of Den Briel, the meteoric rise of Holland as pivot of the Revolt, and the punishing warfare waged by Alba and his son Don Fadrique. In the version of the Revolt created by pamphleteers and early historians, Alba has the role of perfect villain: despotic, cold, and sinister in attitude and appearance, the central protagonist of the Black Legend of Spanish tyranny so skillfully promulgated in England and the Netherlands.[7] It was exactly these years, too, that witnessed the transformation of Orange from a court insider to redoubtable father figure of the Revolt, protector of liberty of conscience and political privileges, and avenger of Spanish tyranny.

In this chapter, I explore Alba's rule as a response to the depredations of iconoclasm, and argue that his punitive measures gave a new direction to the Revolt's politics by allowing the Beggars, now associated with religious violence, to present themselves as defenders of the old order, invoking the potent legacy of late-medieval civic constitutionalism. What is more, Alba's conviction that the reestablishment of Habsburg authority rested on his heightened command of public space prompted the opposition to castigate him as a usurper of royal prerogatives, and cast themselves as loyal vassals of the king. Armed with nothing more than basic instructions for his rule—to extirpate heresy and reestablish authority—Alba responded to iconoclasm and the erosion of royal power with a political strategy of exemplary punishment that combined rites of destruction, the management of public space, and the promotion of images of lordly authority. His justification for such action blended sixteenth-century metaphors about purging the social body of religious malignancy with classically inspired rituals of triumph and punishment gleaned from his mentor, Charles V. To achieve these ends, Alba concentrated all political authority in his person; established a punitive court to punish wrongdoers; reinforced the heresy placards; reasserted Catholic religious practice and liturgy; pursued the Beggars; arrested and executed the counts of Egmont and Hornes; billeted troops in troublesome cities; and

---

Antonio Ossoiro, *Vida y hazañas de don Fernando Alvarez de Toledo, Duque de Alba*, ed. José López de Toro (Madrid, 1945). Indispensable are Alba's letters, the bulk of which are in *Espistolario Alba*.

7. On the Black Legend, see Sverker Arnoldsson, *La Leyenda Negra: Estudios sobre sus origines* (Götenborg, 1960); K. W. Swart, "The Black Legend during the Eighty Years' War," in *Britian and the Netherlands: Some Political Mythologies*, ed. J. S. Bromley and E. H. Kossmann, vol. 5, Papers Delivered to the Fifth Anglo-Dutch Historical Conference (The Hague, 1975), 36–57, and Judith Pollmann, "Eine natürliche Feindschaft: Ursprung und Funktion der schwartzen Legende über Spanien in den Niederlanden, 1560–1581," in *Feindbilder: Die Darstellung des Gegners in der politischen Publizistik des Mittelalters und der Neuzeit*, ed. F. Bosbach (Cologne, 1992), 73–93. See also W. S. Maltby, *The Black Legend in England, 1558–1660* (Durham, 1971).

asserted his mastery over urban public space, most dramatically by building a military citadel in Antwerp, a city he considered the center of the troubles. Alba even countered iconoclasm by his own brand of image-making, having a statue of himself as victor over heresy installed in the new Antwerp citadel.

Although Alba's actions were not entirely new to Low Country rulers, rebels in the Netherlands reviled the duke as a tyrant unprecedented in their history, denouncing him as a new idolater who commissioned artwork for self-glorification while murdering innocents and brazenly trampling on political liberties. In doing so, they forgot the original caution exercised with him, such as William of Orange's letter of September 8, 1567, offering his services to Alba on his arrival.[8] Alba's heavy-handed military occupation spurred important realignments in the Revolt, and inspired a shift in the politics of the opposition to Philip II's policies. In the aftermath of radical iconoclasm, the Beggars' campaign had become irrevocably tainted with the stain of image-breaking and other violence. Never comfortable with the inversion antics and anticlericalism of the Beggars' vernacular style, great noblemen like Orange had actively shunned association with the movement. By the end of 1567, surviving members of the original Compromise began to speak of "fatherland" and "freedom" as their casus belli.[9] By 1572, when Orange launched his famous invasion of the Netherlands against Alba, the Antwerp chronicler Godevaert van Haecht observed that his men eschewed popular acclaim for themselves as Beggars and insisted they be referred to as defenders of the "fatherland."[10]

Rebels responded to Alba's governorship with a stream of patriotic lore vented in cheap print, engravings, and pamphlets that portrayed the Netherlands as an imagined *patria* of virtuous citizens hounded by a zealous despoiler of cities and their rights. This lore also cast Alba as an idolatrous tyrant and, more important, portrayed him as a usurper of proper royal authority. In no small measure Alba's punitive rule prompted such criticism. It was, however, also the result of his keen attention to the rituals of public punishment, and more generally, to the fact that he was the first governor general to rule with such a robust public profile on behalf of an absent king, something, as I have noted, that Margaret of Parma and other previous regents avoided. Alba's double sin—assuming royal attributes and presenting himself as an object of worship—was a serviceable trope, for it pleased both political rebels, whose opposition to the duke could be easily justified as an attack on villainous rule, and Calvinists, who could present Alba as a new Nebuchadnezzar. Alba's reign opened up a new chapter both in the Revolt and in its political culture, in which an unbending tyranny was contrasted with the historically guaranteed freedoms

---

8. In Kervyn de Lettenhove, ed., *Documents inédits relatifs à l'histoire du XVIe siècle* (Brussels, 1883), 1:45–46.

9. See the discussion of a late 1567 document in which original signatories to the Compromise invoke such patriotic language in Pollmann, "Eine natürliche Feindschaft," 73–74.

10. *Kroniek Van Haecht*, 2:199.

and rights of the urban sphere. Over the course of Alba's six-year rule, the Beggars transformed themselves into defenders of civic liberties, *patria*, and good kingship, adopting the party name of "the Patriots" by 1576, while Calvinists rallied against the idolatry of a tyrannical ruler who usurped the authority of the king.[11]

Exemplary Punishment

In an anonymous print created sometime during the wonder year, churchmen, Beggars, and iconoclasts are positioned alongside one another. In the foreground, the pope appears as the Whore of Babylon. He is seated upon the Seven-Headed Beast of the Apocalypse, receiving the urgent prayers of clergy and dwarfed by a winged devil saddled with liturgical objects, a depiction that draws on prototypes popularized in German woodcuts during the Reformation.[12] Despite this indebtedness, the print is uniquely Netherlandish in subject matter. The winged devil exclaims, "To pray or shit, it is all in vain; I have had my best chance," while men sweep up the detritus of broken images with vigorous, athletic strokes. Billowing pants, fashionable hats and capes, even the exposed buttocks of the lead sweeper point to the masculine vigor of the men engaged in *schoonmaakactie* (cleaning up). The text urges them "to sweep quickly and not become weary, for all this merchandise belongs to the devil." The background scene confirms the identity of the sweepers. It depicts the prior moment that has prompted the sweeping: similarly dressed men are using hammers and ropes to destroy images and statues, their Beggars' pouches visible. The print contrasts Catholic clergy and the pope to the Beggars, depicted not merely as noble opponents of Philip II's government, but as the actual iconoclasts. Such an equation between Beggars and iconoclasts was understandably more common in Catholic sources. One Catholic song from the wonder year asserts that Beggars and iconoclasts are one and the same: "They [the Beggars] say this is God's word that images must be destroyed and hurled from churches; but I say let them have their words, it is the devil's work."[13]

That in both the satirical print and the Catholic ballad the Beggars served as a conve-

---

11. The fullest treatment of this evolution is Alastair Duke, "From Beggars to Patriots: The Construction of Rebel Identities in the Revolt of the Netherlands, ca. 1566–1579" (forthcoming). For the classical and early modern strands behind the emergence of "patria" and "patriots" as political terms, see Robert von Friedeburg, "The Office of the Patriot: The Problem of Passions and Love of the Fatherland in Protestant Thought, Melanchton to Althusius, 1520s to 1620s," in *Nation, Ethnicity and Identity in Medieval and Early Modern Europe*, Studies in Medieval and Renaissance History, 3rd ser., vol. 3 (New York, 2006), 241–74.

12. Horst, *Opstand in zwart-wit*, 48. See also James Tanis and Daniel Horst, *Images of Discord: A Graphic Interpretation of the Opening Decades of the Eighty Years' War* (Grand Rapids, 1993), 38–39, with an English translation of the print's text. On print propaganda in the German Reformation, R. W. Scribner, *For the Sake of Simple Folk: Popular Propaganda in the German Reformation* (Cambridge, 1981).

13. NG, 1:284.

The Beggars and the Iconoclasts. Anonymous, ca. 1566. While the Beggars engage in iconoclasm and cleaning up, Catholic clergy make urgent appeals to the pope, depicted as the Whore of Babylon seated upon the Seven-Headed Beast of the Apocalypse. Courtesy of Rijksprentenkabinet, Rijksmuseum, Amsterdam.

nient shorthand for the troubles of 1566 suggests that in the aftermath of iconoclasm few propagandists found it in their interest to sort out the actual political and social categories that distinguished the grands seigneurs from the lesser Order of the Compromise and the Beggars, and both from the Calvinist consistories, ministers, lay preachers, and actual iconoclasts. The Beggars were so intimately allied with the first opposition to Philip II's governmental policies that in the period after the summer riots they stood for everything committed against either Church or king. In this formulation, if the Beggars were the iconoclasts, then the king was the Church, a point made clear in portraits of Philip II that appeared in print around 1568. In the earliest of such depictions, engraved by Hieronymus Wierix, a framed double portrait of Christ and Philip II is accompanied by the briefest of Latin exhortations: "Fear God and honor the King," along with an excerpt from 1 Peter 2:13–15: "For the sake of the Lord, accept the authority of every social institution: the king as the supreme authority, and the governors as commissioned by him to punish criminals and praise good citizenship. Such is God's will."

Double portrait of Philip II and Christ, ca. 1568. Print published by Hans Liefrinck after an engraving by Hieronymus Wierix. Courtesy of Koninklijke Bibliotheek van België.

This direct linkage of Church, Crown, and political authority is precisely what the Duke of Alba was sent to the Netherlands to achieve. In the eyes of Philip II and Alba, the Beggars were indistinguishable from the iconoclasts, even though there were Catholic noblemen in the Compromise, many of whom were aghast at the hedge preaching and the iconoclastic riots. Whatever religious belief may have animated the Beggars and the noblemen in their orbit—Orange's plea for liberty of conscience, for example—it was but a diversion covering a political rebellion against the king. In a letter dated June 30, 1566, to Cardinal Granvelle, the jurist Christoffel d'Assonleville expressed this sentiment directly. The Beggars, he asserted, used religion "as a mask" to vent antiroyalist policies, a point made frequently in court circles, including by Alba himself, and in the formal denunciation drawn up against William of Orange after Alba's arrival in Brussels.[14] The Beggars,

14. *Corr. Granvelle*, 1:341. See the royal mandate to Alba printed in Martin Fernández Navarrete, D. Miguel Salvá, D. Pedro Sainz de Barandá, eds., *Colección de documentos inéditos para la historia de España* (Madrid, 1844), 4:390. The accusation of the same against Orange is found in ibid., 4:432.

the various Protestant communities, the iconoclasts—they were at once unrepentant heretics and political rebels, guilty of profaning God and fomenting the dreadful lèse-majesté. While debate over how best to deal with the Netherlands had polarized the court in Castile, with the faction led by Alba preaching a hard line and the faction led by Ruy Gómez de Silva favoring moderate accommodation, the iconoclastic riots swung the argument toward the former. Punishment would be exacted, an army must be dispatched, and the king would make the arduous trip there to settle the matter.[15]

The patent Alba received on November 29, 1566 for his rule as captain general used the rhetoric of paternalism—the prince preferred clemency to the rigor of justice—and the reality of severe punishment. The Beggars were political rebels who had cynically manipulated religion, and the iconoclasts were their violent handmaidens, making both equally guilty of profaning king and God.[16] To restore royal order, the duke was granted full military powers. In essence, this established a de facto one-man rule in order to avoid the quagmire of Low Country consultative politics, with its endless negotiations with governmental councils, regional Estates, the States General, urban burgomasters, and aldermen. Alba thought his task would be temporary—a short, grim job that had to be concluded as prelude to the arrival of Philip II, and one that would test his proven skills as a soldier. At Philip's court, Alba had pushed for a military occupation of the Netherlands, but only as prologue to the king's arrival. He never anticipated his rule would stretch for six years, and that Philip, overtaken by domestic affairs and political challenges in the Mediterranean, would never make the trip to Brussels.[17] While Alba did rule with the military dispatch and brutality expected of him, it was ultimately his financial policies, particularly the Tenth Penny value-added tax that he struggled to impose, and his extralegal pursuit of heretics and rebels, that brought down his governorship. The Castilian soldier, in effect, was wrecked upon the shoals of Low Country legal and financial intricacies, the Achilles heel of many Burgundian and Habsburg princes. But before these financial per-

---

15. Lagomarsino, "Court Factions and the Formulation of Spanish Policy," 222–88; Maltby, Alba, 133–34; Kamen, Duke of Alba, 65–66.

16. A copy of the patent is in Navarrete, Colección de documentos inéditos, 4:388–96. For Alba's confirmation of receipt of the patent, see his April 27, 1567, letter to the king in ibid., 4:354–57. The phraseology of clemency in lieu of the reign of justice is a standard legal formulation in letters of remission issued by the dukes of Burgundy in the fifteenth century. The supposed "secret instructions" to Alba from the king that Maltby, Alba, cites is a short list of directives: punish heretics, enforce the placards, seize arms, arrest rebels, and build citadels in select cities. Despite Maltby's assertion of its authorship, there is no secondary evidence to prove the case. A copy of the abbreviated text appears in A. L. E. Verheyden, Le conseil des troubles: Listes de condamnés (1567–73) (Brussels, 1961), 50. Since it refers to Philip II in the past tense as "of high and glorious memory," it was probably drawn up after 1598.

17. Maltby, Alba, 135; Kamen, Philip II, 119–20; on the larger international framework Philip II had to evaluate the problem of the Netherlands against, see Geoffrey Parker, The Grand Strategy of Philip II (New Haven, 2000).

ils weighed him down, it was Alba's military occupation of cities that convinced many Netherlanders that the duke schemed to impose an unprecedented tyranny on them.

Martial Space

As steward of Philip II's court, Alba knew intricately the world of ceremony and had been instrumental in introducing Burgundian court protocols to Spain in 1548.[18] He had accompanied Philip during the great 1549 progress through the Netherlands to initiate the Castilian prince in the Burgundian cultural world of masquerades, jousts, and banquets and to introduce him as the heir to Charles V.[19] Great Joyous Entries were a centerpiece of the journey, including one into Brussels on April 1 in which Philip was reunited with his father after a six-year separation, an event that inspired a series of tableaux vivants concerning filial piety.[20] No such positive themes were struck when the soldier-governor Alba entered Brussels on August 22, 1567, after a four-month passage through Italy, the Alpine pass of Mount Cenis, Franche Comté, Lorraine, Luxembourg, and finally into Brabant with ten thousand Castilian and Neapolitan troops and their camp followers.[21] Several of the top nobility had earlier met Alba on August 3 when he reached Thionville, including Egmont, who, according to the chronicler Pontus Payen, failed to take a cue when Alba and his men observed darkly that here was a "traitor to God and king."[22] Not an eyewitness to the event, Payen probably indulged in literary embellishment, but even if it were true, it does not explain the chilly nonreception Alba received in Brussels. Miguel de Medivil, one of the duke's military receivers, wrote that Alba and his elite clique of "caballeros y gentiles hombres" entered the city at 3 p.m., "but without any welcoming delegation on the part of the city."[23]

That an official train with the king's commander at its head would be denied the basic salutations of an official welcome was an obvious rebuff on the part of civic authorities. If nothing else, it portended the conflict to come between Alba's roughshod justice and a citizenry obsessed with traditional rights and privileges. A student of court etiquette, Alba headed immediately to the Coudenberg Palace to announce his arrival to Margaret of Parma. In the confusing early months after iconoclasm, the regent had favored a military solution from Spain, but her victory over Calvinist militants in the Westkwartier, Tournai,

18. Maltby, *Alba*, 66–68; Kamen, *Duke of Alba*, 34.
19. Maltby, *Alba*, 66–68; Kamen, *Philip of Spain*, 36–44.
20. Meadow, "Ritual and Civic Identity," 38. The best source for the Brussels entry is Calvete de Estrella, *El felicissimo viaje*, 1:175–89.
21. Geoffrey Parker, *The Army of Flanders and the Spanish Road, 1567–69* (Cambridge, 1972; rev. ed., 1990).
22. Payen, *Mémoires*, 2:21. Maltby, *Alba*, 143, accepts the account, while Herman van Nuffel, *Lamoraal van Egmont in de geschiedenis, literatuur, beeldende kunst en legende* (Louvain, 1968), 45 doubts its veracity since Payen was not there and since it would have revealed Alba's hand to Egmont.
23. Navarrete, *Colección de documentos inéditos*, 4:397–98. See also Kamen, *Duke of Alba*, 81.

Valenciennes, and Antwerp with the help of such loyal grandees as Philip of St. Aldegonde, Baron of Noircarmes, and Maximilien Vilain, Lord of Rassenghein, had changed her mind. Alba knew this, but he also knew that no matter what her official position, this illegitimate sister of the king had the wrong birth and sex to match his status as soldier, knight of the Golden Fleece, and court insider. Once in her presence, according to de Medivil, Alba rushed to "kiss her hand," doffed his hat, and greeted her "with the courtesy and reverence as if he had arrived before a Queen." By contrast, the regent responded stiffly. Things went badly from the moment the duke first entered Margaret's courtyard, when her household archers skirmished with his bodyguards. A second meeting on August 26 between the two went no better: Alba presented his patent, claimed military authority, described his plan to billet his troops in Antwerp, Ghent, Brussels, and other cities—which she protested as too burdensome—and essentially marginalized her rule. On September 13 the regent tendered her resignation, transferring government and military power to Alba's hands.[24]

Even before the regent's departure, Alba had begun to billet his *tercios*—the infantry units of the Spanish army—and launched the notorious Council of Troubles. This special tribunal to punish rebels and heretics was seated in Brussels, and over the next two years was assisted by 170 regional investigators, most of them Netherlanders.[25] The soldiers and legal officers were complementary sides of a policy to purge the social body of wrongdoers. The policy aimed to restore the link between political authority, Catholic practice, and a disciplined public sphere that had been essential to the king's placards, but also to the ordinances issued in the first half of the sixteenth century by urban magistrates in places like Ghent and Antwerp. Despite his martial ethos, Alba's program had a strong cultural foundation, focusing on the regulation of public behavior, the full reassertion of Catholic worship, the completion of Granvelle's stalled reorganization of Netherlands bishoprics, the censorship of books and other printed media, and the regulation of schools and teachers.[26] The League and Beggar campaigns of 1563–66 had been waged in public and through anticlerical symbols of inversion, and the iconoclasts had violently assaulted religious spaces and objects. To expunge their deeds, Alba felt compelled to master public life anew, even if this required trampling on civic and regional rights.

24. Ibid., 4:398–404 for the August 22 and 26 meetings. A dramatic account is in Motley, *Rise of the Dutch Republic*, 2:114–17.

25. The best introduction to this tribunal is Hugo de Schepper and Guido Marnef, "Raad van Beroerten (1567–1576)," in *De centrale overheidsinstellingen van de Habsburgse Nederlanden (1482–1795)*, ed. E. Aerts et al. (Brussels, 1994), 1:469–77. Despite miscalculations, still important is Verheyden, *Conseil des troubles*, with its list of those summoned and its appendix of documents. Verheyden's figures, however, were determined to be too high because of double listings. For a correction, see M. Dierickx, "De lijst der veroordeelden door de Raad van Beroerten," *Revue Belge de Philologie et d'Histoire* 40 (1962): 415–22.

26. Maltby, *Alba*, 205–24 for ecclesiastical and financial reforms, and for Alba's own summary of his tasks, see Navarrete, *Colección de documentos inéditos*, 4:497–506, letter dated June 9, 1567.

Quartering troops in difficult cities was the first step in quelling disorder and transforming public space into policed space. When Alba entered Brussels, he did so at the head of his ten thousand Spanish and Neapolitan troops plus a small band of German infantry who were to replace the approximately same number of Walloon and German troops under the regent's command. On arrival, he began garrisoning these men near Brussels, in Ghent, Lier, Enghien, and Diest, among other places, even though the regent had complained that this unfairly singled out certain cities such as Brussels itself, whose population had not rebelled.[27] Many of Alba's soldiers thought poorly of the Netherlands, no surprise in a tense environment constantly humming with violence. From the start, the soldiers raised the ire of local residents, who resented their presence and suffered from their casual violence and insults. It was the troops' contemptuous behavior and their later mutinies that helped to widen discontent against Alba and his successors, including among Catholic nobles and townspeople who might otherwise have remained obedient. In the ethnographic imagination of certain Castilians, the Netherlanders were heretics given over to Bruegelian excesses of food and drink.[28] Alonso Vásquez, who served from 1577 until 1592 in the Low Countries and France, seemed to distill the opinions of many of his contemporaries in his 1616 *The Wars of Flanders and France*. He praised the Low Countries as a "very rich and powerful" land of cities and enterprising merchants. But after that he had little positive to say, be it the weather—nine months of winter and three months of "hellish" summer, using the wordplay in Spanish, "nueve meses de invierno y tres de infierno"—or the people and their disposition—"heretics and disobedient to their rightful lord and prince."[29] Echoing earlier observations located in sources as diverse as Lodovico Guicciardini's writing and Charles V's placards, he described Netherlanders as urbane and educated: gifted in the ability to speak many languages, unusually literate, and fond of books. These positive qualities notwithstanding, they were also rebels, prone to taking up arms against their natural lords. Their Dionysian impulses ran strong: from the time they were mere babes, Netherlanders were big drinkers; even as infants drinking from wooden cups shaped like a woman's breast. They were lovers of festivals and carni-

---

27. Parker, *Dutch Revolt*, 104. On the Army of Flanders, see Parker, *Army of Flanders*, a military, social and cultural analysis of this fighting force that drew on troops from several European states, the Netherlands included. On its size and composition, see appendix A, 271–72.

28. J. Brouwer, *Kronieken van Spaansche Soldaten uit het Begin van den Tachtigjarigen Oorlog* (Zutphen, orig., 1933; 2nd ed., 1980), a useful anthology of excerpts of the most important Spanish chronicles of the Dutch Revolt. See also E. Gossaert, *Les Espagnols en Flandre* (Brussels, 1914), and L. van der Essen, "Croissade contre les hérétiques ou guerre contre des rebelles?" *Revue d'Histoire ecclésiastique* 51 (1956): 42–78.

29. I have used the excerpt in Brouwer, *Kronieken van Spaansche Soldaten*, 86–126 of Alonso Vásquez, *Guerras de Flandes y Francia en tiempo de Alejandro Farnese* (Madrid, 1879). For a study of Spanish perceptions of the Netherlands in chronicles and imaginative literature for the sixteenth and seventeenth century, see Yolanda Rodríguez Pérez, *De Tachtigjarige Oorlog in Spaanse ogen: De Nederlanden in Spaanse historische en literaire teksten* (circa 1548–1673) (Nijmegen, 2003). On Vásquez, see ibid., 169–72.

vals—both the occasions of heavy drinking, since they used any celebration as an excuse to run to the tavern. Rude in social mores, they also gave an unusual space to women, who worked, ran businesses, and even freely read. Although impressively learned, the minds of Netherlanders were corrupted by heretical books and ideas, especially since censorship was weak.[30] Vásquez imagined a people savvy but disordered, excessively carnal in appetites and behaviors, incautious in maintaining fixed gender roles, and smart but politically troublesome at best. The well-ordered Castilian notion of Church and Crown, of work and household, seemed wholly absent in the Netherlands.

Billeting troops is never an easy task. But the palpable contempt of the soldiers for their hosts, which was heartily returned, can be discerned in Marcus van Vaernewijck's chronicle of the occupation of Ghent, the best description of the effects of Alba's military in its first year of occupation. Because Ghent already had a "Spanish citadel" built by Charles V in 1540, because Ghent was reasonably near Brussels, and because of its prominent role in image-breaking and Calvinist agitation, Alba found it an ideal site for stationing some of his men.[31] On August 30, nineteen companies of *tercios* made a dramatic entry into the city through the Keizerpoort, the same gate at which the statue of Charles V and the Virgin Mary had been destroyed in the iconoclastic riots.[32] They were accompanied on their way to the Friday market by all sorts of camp followers, including prostitutes on horseback and "barefooted ruffians." On September 1 the senior alderman was forced out of bed in the middle of the night to surrender the city's keys to the officers of the citadel, an act signaling that the Spanish expected full submission from Ghent's citizenry. The next day, the *tercios* held a giant muster in Saint Bavo's Cathedral, forcing clergy and canons into the crypt to hold mass, and carelessly breaking a stained-glass window. Van Vaernewijck, an Erasmian Catholic and foe of the Beggars, observed that the window-breaking incident prompted some citizens to mutter that the soldiers were nothing more than "kerckbrekers," church-breakers.[33] Such an utterance did not bode well for the occupation of Ghent. What is more, the soldiers aggressively ransacked houses for bedding and household provisions, forcing good Catholics to go without beds, and intensified their hectoring of the aldermen, provoking the ire of Protestant and Catholic Gentenars alike.[34]

Over the ensuing months of the Army of Flanders' presence in Ghent, hatreds grew sharper. This had to do with the presence of so many thousands of troops who suspected their hosts of being, as Van Vaernewijck reports, "sodomites, traitors to king, and Luther-

30. Brouwer, *Kronieken van Spaansche Soldaten*, 88–99.
31. On the Spanish citadel in Ghent, see Gachard, *Relation des troubles de Gand*, 101. For the selection of the seigneury of Saint Bavo's, see Boone, "Urban Space in Late Medieval Flanders," 638.
32. BT *Van Vaernewijck*, 3:1; Ghent's aldermen had nervously issued a civic ordinance calling on citizens to treat the "regiments from Naples" with calm. See SAG 93/28 DD, fols. 260v–261v.
33. BT *Van Vaernewijck*, 3:15.
34. Ibid., 3:21–26; SAG 93/28 DD, fols. 263v–264v, and fol. 268r–v.

ans"—a vivid conflation of sexual, political, and religious sins. The cost of providing for this garrison of some three thousand was steep: at first, food and goods, but by October 24, a one-time sum of 240,000 Flemish pounds, and by November, a month salary of 100 Flemish pounds per soldier.[35] Ghentenars' antipathy also had to do with a growing number of acts of violence: from petty thieving on the part of the soldiers to armed assaults, incidents that Alba himself took action to quell, even ordering the execution of some wrongdoers.[36] Much of the conflict was played out on religious terrain. On September 8, for example, at the house of a small-time furrier and cloth seller, several soldiers nearly rioted when they observed an ordinary painting of Jesus on the Cross with what appeared to be a stab mark through the leg. The men proclaimed the discovery of a heretic and iconoclast, summoning the bailiff and his men who hauled the members of the household to jail. During the inquest, the husband explained that he sold not only cloth and furs, but also old paintings in need of repair.[37] Tensions ratcheted up after two executions of Spanish soldiers for robbery that had included the Augustinians among the targets. The irony of stealing from a religious house provoked the acid observation by local Calvinists that the pope had sent "violators of churches, thieves, murderers, violent thugs, tyrants, rascals, and criminals" as protectors of religious order in Ghent.[38] Already by October 10 the nominally loyal aldermen had lodged a complaint to Brussels against the *tercios* in Ghent. The soldiers, grumbled the aldermen, routinely engaged in thievery, random pillaging and impious acts, even eating meat on Fridays. Indeed, under the guise of hearing mass, the soldiers had robbed a church; their assaults and murder of citizens had rendered ordinary life and work impossible.[39]

Alba responded to these protests with a few high-profile executions of guilty soldiers, but the situation only deteriorated. Ghent had become akin to a besieged city, nominally free to engage in its usual traffic of goods and people, but in reality imprisoned by the coercive supervision of the Army of Flanders. On October 7 a soldier violently struck the cheek of an assistant sexton at mass at Saint Jacob's for failing to provide cushions so that the Spanish could kneel while taking Communion. Even more scandalously, a group brought paid prostitutes to the upscale Lange Muidestraat and heckled several respectable housewives to kiss their behinds.[40] In response to yet another complaint against such behavior issued by the aldermen to Alba, a procession with the Host was ordered for Sunday October 19, in order to pray for better times and for "unity in the Catholic religion."[41] Van

---

35. Dambruyne, *Corporatieve middengroepen*, 467.
36. BT Van Vaernewijck, 3:97 for the quote; for the incidents of stealing and punishments meted out see, ibid., 3:42–44, 62–66, 143–50.
37. Ibid., 3:24–25.
38. Ibid., 3:102.
39. Ibid., 3:100.
40. Ibid., 3:104, 107.
41. SAG 93/28 DD, fols. 266v–267v.

Vaernewijck considered it one of the finest religious events he had seen in years. Mass was held in Saint Bavo's, the church aglow with thousands of burning candles. But the celebration failed to assuage the soldiers, who complained that the Ghentenars's religious expression was more show than substance—true enough in the sense that they had been required to attend, as was typical with such civic decrees.[42]

Not even the execution of four iconoclasts from the 1566 riots on December 11 could help bridge the implacable divide between contemptuous soldiers and weary Ghentenars. The crowd that gathered to watch was clearly agitated, and the soldiers responded by setting upon them, wounding several, and killing a few. Van Vaernewijck attended the troubled executions and was dumbfounded at the Spanish violence at an event intended to prove that Ghent did indeed punish those guilty of iconoclasm. Even Alba was embarrassed, and sent his son Fadrique to Ghent to punish the riotous soldiers, two of whom were subsequently executed and whose corpses were slowly and gruesomely quartered, though many Ghentenars opted not to attend.[43] After several more incidents of violence and insults, most notably the usurping by some soldiers of the forward place typically reserved for the aldermen in a procession with the Host on January 4, 1567, Van Vaernewijck himself could not conceal his disillusionment with the soldiers sent to protect the royal authority that he never ceased defending.[44] He reports that Ghentenars considered the soldiers false Christians, rogues, and rapists who assaulted local women; they were nothing more than animals who made him nostalgic for the last occupation of Ghent under Charles V in 1540. This unhappy event in Ghent's history, reasoned Van Vaernewijck, at least had prompted the arrival of German soldiers, reasonable men when compared to the Italian and Spanish troops who largely made up these particular *tercios*.[45] City aldermen nervously tried to keep the peace, passing ordinances forbidding the exchange of strong words or blows between local inhabitants and the soldiers, and urging Ghentenars to take complaints to them rather than trying to settle such matters themselves.[46]

Apart from the soldiers' casual brutality, their religious practice puzzled Van Vaernewijck. How dared they take a more forward place in a religious procession than the town fathers, on the one hand, while on the other, their men posted in the streets did not even raise their heads from their dice games when the train of clergy, Host, and pious observers marched by?[47] These were the same men who prevented the executioner from strangling four condemned Anabaptists before lighting the fire beneath them, and threw more wood on the burning pyre, who mocked the cries of pain as a defrocked priest was executed, whose penitential procession during Easter week involved self-flagellation, who knelt

---

42. Ibid., fol. 267v, and BT *Van Vaernewijck*, 3:112.
43. BT *Van Vaernewijck*, 3:143–57.
44. The decree for the procession is in SAG 93/28 DD, fols. 275r–276v.
45. BT *Van Vaernewijck*, 3:194–97.
46. For an example, dated May 23, 1567, see SAG 93/28 DD, fols. 277r–278v.
47. BT *Van Vaernewijck*, 3:195–96.

excessively and dramatically before the Host when a priest gave the last rites to a fellow soldier, but who took bedding away from poor families so that newborns went wanting.[48]

Van Vaernewijck's observations were strongly worded but not unprecedented; to take one example, they resemble many of the same points a chronicler in Utrecht made about the Army of Flanders' soldiers assigned to its Vredenburg fortress, a citadel Charles V ordered built in 1529.[49] Little wonder that when Alba ordered the redeployment of most of the Spanish *tercios* from Ghent on June 23, 1568, Van Vaernewijck reported a city elated, freed from what had felt like "Egyptian bondage." Surveying the damage, he saw not a city of workers and merchants, vibrant in culture, but a shattered locale that military occupation had turned more into a "slaughterhouse" than a bustling marketplace, with gallows everywhere and hatreds deeply set.[50]

Van Vaernewijck's account of the Army of Flanders' occupation of Ghent makes clear just how polarized were the perceptions of the citizenry and the soldiers. The troops considered the town the realm of heretics and rebels, with iconoclasts lurking in its houses, its economic and political elite disloyal schemers, and its citizenry in general prone to false displays of Catholic religious practice, such as showy processions. The city was under occupation, goods were theirs for the taking, and the citizens required vigilant policing lest they riot again. Ghentenars, by contrast, considered the troops violent thugs who had converted a city of trade and commerce into one big citadel of repression. The soldiers might suspect everyone of being a heretic and iconoclast, but they themselves cynically displayed false piety—robbing cloisters, violating churches, gambling when they ought to be praying—and intemperate moments of devotion, with excessive kneeling and curious flagellation. These perceptions, of course, were filtered through the lens of Van Vaernewijck, a humanist, merchant, and man of letters quick to see the soldiers as plebian ruffians whose particular forms of Catholic behavior were as irksome as the iconoclasts' radicalism. To Van Vaernewijck, both sets of actors were deficient in reason. By contrast, he admitted to a begrudging admiration for his foes the Calvinists. The execution of one of Ghent's richest iconoclasts on March 30, 1568, the merchant Lieven de Smedt, became an occasion for Van Vaernewijck to stake out an argument for clemency, based principally on the Calvinists' pious dedication to scripture.[51] Man of commerce and letters and foe of

---

48. Ibid., 4:310–12; ibid., 4:4–5, 31–32, 50–52, 133. Other observers were puzzled by Spanish religious practice, and particularly flagellation. See, for example, the comments by the Franciscan sister in Van Alfen, *Kroniek eener Kloosterzuster*, 24.

49. S. Muller, "Verhaal van het beleg van het kasteel Vredenburg te Utrecht in 1576 door eenen ooggetuige," *Bijdragen en Mededelingen van het Historisch Genootschap* 6 (1883): 147–209, esp. 170–72.

50. BT *Van Vaernewijck*, 4:130–33, 281.

51. Ibid., 3:306–7. On this cloth dealer, see Delmotte, "Het Calvinisme in de verschillende bevolkingslagen," 167, and his deposition and sentence in RvB, no. 1, fols. 117v, 119v, and 132v, and ibid., no. 72, fol. 312r.

the Calvinists and the Beggars, Van Vaernewijck in his chronicle of Ghent's military occupation captures a shift in political perception that soon reverberated throughout the Netherlands. In 1566 Van Vaernewijck had railed against the Calvinist open-air sermons and the abhorrent lawlessness, impiety, and destructive violence of iconoclasm. By 1568 his principal antagonists were not so much pious adherents of the Reformed faith as the Army of Flanders. The city, its liberties, and its public life were imperiled by Alba's brutal occupation, and the very men sent to punish the *beeldenstormers* were themselves guilty of religious impiety and disrespect for life and property. In the shift away from denunciations of the chaos of the wonder year to an angry, sorrowful description of Ghent under the thumb of the Army of Flanders, Van Vaernewijck captures how concern for urban rights and the liberties of its civic sphere came to the fore as a response to Alba's governorship.

Exemplary Punishment

The Council of Troubles, the duke's tribunal to punish iconoclasts and other wrongdoers, was Alba's most important achievement in the Netherlands—and his most enduring albatross. Along with the hated Tenth Penny tax, the Council became the signature of Alba's sinister reign, decried in print and song in the early *vaderlandse geschiedenis* (history of the fatherland) of the Dutch Golden Age as a tyrant's tool that had summoned thousands, confiscated its victims' goods in violation of customary law, and then executed them by sword, cord, or fire. Because the specter of the Inquisition had been one of the great preoccupations of the nobility's brief against Philip II in the early 1560s, the Council came to be seen as the realization and intensification of everything the Compromise had tried to oppose. Netherlanders were not wholly mistaken in this assumption. Although not an ecclesiastical body, and though it claimed no inquisitorial jurisdiction, the Council embodied Philip II's directive to Alba to enforce the placards through a policy that stopped short of creating a new Inquisition.[52] The Council served as the legal clearinghouse for all that the wrongdoing Netherlanders had inflicted on Church and king, and a mechanism to mete out punishment effectively. Its efficient operation and victims, mostly notably the high-profile executions of Lamoral, Count of Egmont, and Philip de Montmorency, Count of Hornes, convinced its critics that its purpose was to brazenly suspend legal privileges. Alba's strategy of exemplary punishment was intended as a prelude to the offer of a general pardon, eventually granted on July 16, 1570, but the strategy deepened the sense of his rule as brutal tyranny and created a pantheon of martyred heroes that gave the incipient Revolt new direction.

Alba incorporated the Council only five days after his arrival in Brussels, though many elite dissenters like Hoogstraten, Brederode, and Orange had wisely fled to Germany. The

---

52. Verheyden, *Conseil des troubles*, 508; Goosens, *Inquisitions modernes*, 2:108–112, 150.

mix of Netherlander and Spanish councilors included Charles de Berlaymont, the regent's trusted advisor who had derided the Compromise noblemen as beggars during the April 5, 1566 petition to moderate the heresy placards; Philip of St. Aldegonde, Baron of Noircarmes, who had put down the Calvinist insurrection around Valenciennes and Tournai in the fall of 1566; and Juan de Vargas, a close advisor to Alba from Spain. They deliberated over thousands of cases assembled by nearly two hundred regional investigators, who patiently identified suspects and recorded depositions. To a set of provinces like the Netherlands, whose political elites zealously cherished local privileges, the centralized Council was tyranny incarnate, riding roughshod over such prized rights as trial in one's local jurisdiction and protection against forfeiture of goods and property.[53]

The tribunal worked diligently, gathering exact information in even the most rural corners of the urbanized Low Countries. The Pays de l'Alleu, a territorial enclave between Flanders and Artois that was home to small communities such as Venthie, Lestrem, and Fleurbaix, had been a hotbed of radical Calvinism, iconoclasm, and armed insurrection in 1566. Arriving there in the first week that the Council was established, commissioners deposed thirty-eight witnesses in nine days, from pastors to farmers, merchants, and shopkeepers. The investigators sought precise information about the summer hedge sermons, about Calvinist consistories, about the spaces and places of iconoclasm, and, most importantly, about the participants.[54] This line of inquiry was applied in places large and small, in 's-Hertogenbosch, Valenciennes, Utrecht, and Amsterdam. The identity of Calvinists and iconoclasts and the acts they committed preoccupied the Council: attendance at a hedge sermon, an attack on a church, participation in a conventicle, or the taking up of arms were some of the most regularly cited transgressions. So flooded was the Council with reports and names that Alba decided by April 1568 to hear only those cases not covered already by the placards.[55] In the nine years of the Council's operation, 8,568 people were tried for heresy, treason, or both. Most were convicted in absentia, having fled prior to Alba's arrival, to England, the Rhineland, and other safe havens, so that 1,083 were actually executed and 20 banished. While the numbers are not as high as legend would have it, they are impressive, especially because most of the executions occurred in the first two years of the Council's term. Cities like Ypres, Antwerp, Tournai, Valenciennes,

---

53. These legal battles had their origins in Charles V's and Philip II's placards. See Alastair Duke, "Salvation by Coercion: the Controversy surrounding the 'Inquisition' in the Low Countries on the Eve of the Revolt," *Reformation and Revolt*: 152–74. A review of the Council is in de Schepper and Marnef, "Raad van Beroerten (1567–1576)"; see also Maltby, *Alba*, 154–56, and Verheyden, *Conseil des troubles*, especially the transcribed documents in the appendix.

54. *Troubles religieux*, 2:267–320, depositions taken by Charles de Bonnieres, Lord and Baron of d'Auchy, Pierre Couronnel, councilor to the Council of Artois, and the court's commissioners, transcribed from the RvB, vol. 9, fols. 1ff.

55. Maltby, *Alba*, 155.

Ghent, Amsterdam, Haarlem, Utrecht, and Groningen each had hundreds of accused, with Tournai leading with 1,083 convicted.[56]

In the political sphere, no punishment was more shocking than the executions of Egmont, grand seigneur and hero of the battle of Saint Quentin, and Hornes, member of the League, former attendant of Philip II's bodyguard, and scion of the Montmorency clan.[57] Their surprise seizure, their imprisonment and trial, and their execution in Brussels' great central square on June 5, 1568, consecrated the two as the Revolt's first political martyrs, celebrated in print, text, and song, much like the Protestant victims canonized by Van Haemstede and Crespin. The suddenness of their death sentences and their execution in Brussels' great square stunned all Netherlanders, even Catholic loyalists.[58] In Alba's own words, the punishment was "exemplary." In letters to Philip II and his eventual successor, Don Luis de Requesens, Alba spoke directly about the efficaciousness of high-profile executions. Punishing the lower classes was important within reason, but a few well-chosen elite victims would yield maximum public impact "because it is not the intention of His Majesty to have a blood bath."[59]

With their deaths, Egmont and Hornes became political heroes and victims of an unjust tyrant. They had been foes of the iconoclasts and considered themselves good vassals of the king. Neither man was Protestant nor even close to the Beggars, and as knights of the Order of the Golden Fleece, they had elite Burgundian credentials and the legal right to be tried by a court of their peers.[60] But they, along with other disobedient noblemen,

---

56. Verheyden, *Conseil de troubles*, with its master list, corrected by Dierickx's "De lijst der veroordeelden door de Raad van Beroerten."

57. Théodore Juste, *Le comte d'Egmont et le comte d'Hornes* (Brussels, 1862), based largely on printed correspondence and Council of State records in the Algemeen Rijksarchief Brussel. Egmont's interrogation before the Council of Troubles in RvB, vol. 156, with an imperfect French translation of the Spanish original in F. de Reiffenberg, ed., *Correspondance de Marguerite d'Autriche, duchesse de Parme, avec Philippe II* (Brussels, 1842), 297–349. Hornes's deposition exists only in the copy found in *Supplément à l'histoire des guerres civiles de Flandre sous Philippe II du père Famian Strada*, 2 vols. (Amsterdam, 1729), 1:103–210. A good evaluation of both sources is in Parker, *Dutch Revolt*, 287. Overviews of the two men include A. Schillings, "Philips de Montmorency, graaf van Hoorne," in *Tijdschrift voor Geschiedenis* 28 (1913): 321–27, P. B. de Troeyer, *Lamoraal van Egmont: Een critische studie over zijn rol in de jaren 1559–1564 in verband met het schuldvraagstuk* (Brussels, 1961), Simon Groenveld, *De graven Egmont en Horn: Slachtoffers van de politieke repressie in de Spaanse Nederlanden* (Brussels, 2003), and Aline Goosens, *Le comte Lamoral d'Egmont (1522–1568): Les aléas du pouvoir de la haute noblesse à l'aube de la révolte des Pays-Bas* (Mons, 2003).

58. On executions as spectacle, see Pieter Spierenburg, *The Spectacle of Suffering: Executions and the Evolution of Repression from a Preindustrial Metropolis to the European Experience* (Cambridge, 1984), and on executions of Protestants as public ritual in sixteenth-century France, see David Nicholls, "The Theater of Martyrdom in the French Reformation," *Past and Present* 121 (1988): 49–73.

59. Navarrete, *Colección de documentos inéditos*, 4:497–98, letter dated June 9, 1568, to Philip II, and *Epistolario Alba*, 3:675–76, letter of September 19, 1567, to Requesens.

60. Alba clearly was concerned with their status as knights of the Golden Fleece, and in his correspondence discussed the matter with Philip II: Maltby, *Alba*, 145. See, for example, Alba's careful references to

had earned Margaret of Parma's distrust well before Alba's arrival. Already on August 27, 1566, with the iconoclastic riots in full swing, the regent had angrily denounced Orange, Hoogstraten, Hornes, and Egmont as poor managers during the troubles, and, more damning, of being against "God and the king." Orange's plan, she wrote Philip II, was to become master of the state and divvy up spheres of influence among his fellow grandees.[61] No wonder that the Council of Troubles condemned all the signatories of the 1566 Compromise to death (or life-long banishment if they were tried in absentia) for the crime of lèse majesté.[62]

Although Hornes had not been a member of the Compromise, he had been part of the 1563 League and had made concessions to Calvinists in the aftermath of the iconoclastic riots. The case against Egmont was more tenuous. As a member of the Council of State and as governor of Flanders, he was no foe of royal power. Egmont was Catholic and royalist. Further, he was a military hero of the iconic battle of Saint Quentin that was celebrated in Philip II's Escorial, and also of the battle of Gravelines in 1558—a man, as one observer of the execution noted in a letter to Cardinal Granvelle, whom people said "twice saved the king's crown."[63] Egmont's membership in the League and his general protests in the 1560s had everything to do with protecting noble prerogatives and regional privileges and almost nothing to do with Reformed sentiment or antimonarchical commitments. While Egmont had arranged a religious accord in Flanders between Catholics and Protestants, he acted only at the regent's directive and had diligently punished the iconoclasts in Ghent, Ypres, and elsewhere. Despite his later canonization as victim of Alba's tyranny, he was an ambiguous icon to memorialists of the Dutch Revolt, some of whom even bitterly criticized him in a ballad found in *A New Beggars' Song Book*.[64] The preface to the song reads: "Here is presented a new song about the Count of Egmont and how through avarice he let himself be bribed into the Papist camp, being the cause of the two counts' beheading." Set to the melody of Psalm 16, the ballad recounts a tale of Egmont's duplicity, alleging that he betrayed Calvinists and iconoclasts, twenty-two of whom he had executed and thirty whipped.[65]

Egmont could surely have been reconciled with the Crown, and so too could Hornes, who had practical experience in Spain, but the policy of exemplary punishment as outlined by Alba required high-profile victims. Alba's action, therefore, was grounded less in po-

---

past chapter meetings of the Golden Fleece in which knights were tried for lèse majesté in *Epistolario Alba*, 2:12–16, dated January 19, 1568.

61. Quoted in Juste, *Le comte d'Egmont et le comte d'Hornes*, 151.
62. See order of October 9, 1567, in "Registre des procès-verbaux du Conseil de Troubles," excerpted in Verheyden, *Conseil des troubles*, 509.
63. *Corr. Granvelle*, 3:254, letter of Pierre Aguilon June 5, 1568.
64. On the ballads concerning Egmont, see the synopsis in Van Nuffel, *Lamoraal van Egmont*, 30–36.
65. GB, 1:67–68.

litical pragmatism than a sacrificial rite: the dramatic execution of two powerful noblemen, reconciled before death to Church and Crown, to serve as prologue for an eventual general pardon that he would grant. In his patent to Alba, the king had urged him to temper punishment with the offer of clemency; Alba readily agreed—such paternal succor being common to princely discourse—but no pardon could be issued until key noblemen were punished and enough property confiscated from them and others to make the offer of reconciliation feasible and affordable.[66]

Part of the shock of the arrest of Egmont and Hornes was that Alba dared to break the elite bonds of the Order of the Golden Fleece. He seized two fellow knights, neither of whom had overtly professed disloyalty to king or God, and then violated Golden Fleece privileges by forgoing a trial before their peers and transferring the men outside their jurisdiction, to Ghent in Flanders.[67] Alba was well aware of how transgressive his acts were, a point proven by the care with which he searched for historical precedence for his actions in letters to Philip II and others.[68] Alba considered the risk worth taking, since he was firmly convinced that the executions, if carefully scripted with victims reconciled before death, would serve as the perfect example of the price of political disobedience. But though the beheading of Egmont and Hornes was sensational, it also provoked two consequences that played into the hands of the incipient opposition. The two grands seigneurs became martyred heroes around whom dissenters could rally, and they were memorialized even more widely than the Protestant victims championed in songs and books. In early histories of the Dutch Revolt, the two men's deaths became a shorthand for Alba's tyranny, so much so that Egmont's memory was rekindled in the modern romantic imagination thanks to his apotheosis as an apostle of liberty by Goethe and Beethoven.[69] The circumstances of their deaths also had uncanny Christological chords: two vassals of the king sentenced to death by a tyrannical provincial governor, who considered their deaths as a gateway to a general pardon, their blood shed for the forgiveness of others.

Both Egmont and Hornes had been arrested in Brussels after having dined with Alba only days after his arrival in the Low Countries on September 9, 1567. They had been reviewing plans for citadels in Antwerp, Thionville, and Luxembourg as part of Alba's over-

---

66. Navarrete, *Colección de documentos inéditos*, 4:388–96. For Alba on the general pardon, see ibid., 4:503–5.

67. Juste, *Le comte d'Egmont et le comte d'Hornes*, 301.

68. *Epistolario Alba*, 1:674. In this September 14, 1567, letter to de Chantonnay, Alba turns the tables on his critics by arguing that the crimes of Egmont and Hornes were all the more odious because they were Golden Fleece knights. On January 19, 1568, Alba wrote Philip II that Maximilian of Austria in 1481 had tried five Golden Fleece knights for the crime of *lèse majesté* in 1481, ibid., 2:13.

69. For the cultural and historiographical fortunes of Egmont through the centuries, see Van Nuffel, *Lamoraal van Egmont*.

all plan to manage urban public space, collaborating in the very process to which they would fall victim.[70] Though Egmont protested that as a knight of the Golden Fleece he would only surrender his sword to his sovereign lord, he was quickly subdued by Alba's men, and then transferred with Hornes, in violation of the Privilege of Brabant, which proscribed transfer after arrest beyond legal boundaries of the province, to Gravensteen Castle in Ghent. There they spent the next nine months, Egmont hearing eighty-two charges against him by the Council of Troubles on January 11, 1568, and Hornes sixty-three.[71] On June 1, eighteen noblemen of the Compromise were beheaded at the Horse Market in Brussels. Two days later, Egmont and Hornes were transferred to Brussels via Dendermonde and held in separate sealed rooms in the crossbowmen's meeting house, the Broodhuis, directly across from the town hall. As they departed Ghent, Van Vaernewijck reported a dapper looking Egmont and an emboldened Hornes who tipped his hat to onlookers. An enormous crowd had gathered to pay their respects, many crying as the men were taken away. In characteristic fashion, the chronicler used the occasion to ponder the fate of things: Egmont, a man of near-royal status in Flanders, had become a mere impoverished prisoner, taken by force out of a city into which he had made many splendid entries.[72]

The Council pronounced death sentences on them for the crimes of *lèse majesté* on June 4, and both men prepared to die the next day. Their executions carried the heavy ceremonialism that Johan Huizinga found so much a part of "life's intensity" (*'s levens felheid*) in the late-medieval Burgundian Netherlands.[73] Befitting a grand seigneur, Egmont had a particularly theatrical exit. He received news of the death sentence at 11 p.m. the night before his execution. It was delivered by Maarten van Riethoven, the bishop of Ypres assigned as his confessor. According to the report penned by a bishop's associate, Egmont spent the next few hours in prayer, and in writing a letter to the king to profess his loyalty, ask for forgiveness, and plead for mercy for his wife and children.[74] The commanding officer and his captain retrieved him at 11 a.m. and began the procession to the scaffold, Egmont reciting the Fifty-first Psalm ("Have mercy upon me, O God"). Three thousand

---

70. Juste, *Le comte d'Egmont et le comte d'Hornes*, 299–301. A dramatic account is in Payen, *Mémoires*, 2:29–30.

71. Juste, *Le comte d'Egmont et le comte d'Hornes*, 323.

72. BT Van Vaernewijck, 4:102–4. Also of value are the accounts of the Brussels burgher Jan de Pottre, in de St. Genois, *Dagboek van Jan de Pottre*, 30, and Alonso Ulloa, *Gründliche Beschreibung des Niederländischen Kriegs* (1570), cited and excerpted in Van Nuffel, *Lamoraal van Egmont*, 19, and n. 20. See also the account of their execution provided by a jurist friend of the archbishop of Ypres, confessor to Egmont before his death, in *Historia Episcopatus Iprensis* (Bruges, 1851), 52–54.

73. Huizinga, *Autumn of the Middle Ages*, 1.

74. *Historia Episcopatus Iprensis*, 52–54; a Dutch translation of Egmont's letter is in Bor, *Oorsprongk*, 1:240. A summary account with all sources consulted is in Van Nuffel, *Lamoraal van Egmont*, 17–18. See also Morillon's account to Granvelle of his conversation with the bishop of Ypres in *Corr. Granvelle*, 3:274–77, letter dated June 13, 1568.

Spanish troops lined the great square, where stood the scaffold covered in black cloth and outfitted with two velvet cushions and a table with a silver crucifix. In good Burgundian style, Egmont was splendidly dressed. He had cut off the collars of his red damask robe over which he wore a gold-bordered black cape. He sported the gold firesteel collar of the Golden Fleece and a fanciful black silk hat with black and white feathers. On the scaffold, he asked if there was a pardon at hand. Since there was none, he prepared to die, taking off his robe, and, of greatest symbolic import, his Golden Fleece collar. After final prayers with the bishop, Egmont kissed the crucifix, removed his hat, covered his eyes with a cap, and spoke one of Christ's seven utterances on the cross—"Father, into thy hands I commend my spirit" (Luke 23:46)—before the discreetly hidden executioner struck his clean blow.[75] Hornes immediately followed, accompanied by his confessor Gislus Vroede, future suffragan of the archbishop of Mechelen. Unlike Egmont, Hornes addressed the crowd before the axe swung, though he curiously did not kiss the crucifix and apparently had refused confession earlier. It is this behavior that spurred the account expressed in song and early histories of the Dutch Revolt that Hornes died Protestant, though the testament he dictated was Catholic and though Alba reported to Philip that both men met their fate firmly within the fold of the Church.[76]

The heads of Egmont and Hornes were affixed to pikes and left upon the scaffold for two hours. This act, more than any other, infuriated Orange, who fumed about the executions in a letter dated June 18, 1568, decrying the "great mockery and dishonor" of such defamation.[77] The wording of his letter implied that Alba had violated cultural norms; Egmont and Hornes had been locked up prior to their execution in the Broodhuis, a spot Orange noted that was typically used to "hold celebrations and meetings." They were executed on the eve of Pentecost, "publicly upon the square." The secular and sacred associations Orange invoked were those of celebration, whether it be a guild festival or a religious day typically associated in the Netherlands with plants and flowers.[78] Both carried public connotations, involving splendid processions. In their place, the nefarious Duke of Alba served up a tragedy instead, with the insult of heads on pikes. Some early sources intimated that their heads were sent to Spain as proof of their deaths, though there is no contemporary corroboration of this suspiciously Herod-like act.[79] The bodies of Egmont and Hornes were carried to the church of Saint Gudule, the Brussels church at

---

75. The two eyewitness accounts are St. Genois, *Dagboek van Jan de Pottre*, 30, and Ulloa, *Gründliche Beschreibung des Niederländischen Kriegs*, 29–32. A full account of the Egmont's execution is in Juste, *Le comte d'Egmont et le comte d'Hornes*, 350–52.
76. Juste, *Le comte d'Egmont et le comte d'Hornes*, 349.
77. *Archives d'Orange-Nassau*, 3:246–47.
78. On Pentecost, see Celis, *Volkskundige kalender voor het Vlaamsche land*, 52–54.
79. Motley, *The Rise of the Dutch Republic*, 2:208, accepts the report. See also Gachard, *Notice sur le Conseil de Troubles*, 29, citing a letter by Council of State member Geronimo de Roda, and *Kroniek Van Haecht*, 2:27.

which Philip II had heard a young William of Orange proclaim him as the successor of Charles V in 1558. From there, Egmont's remains were taken to the cloister of Saint Clare, embalmed, and buried in Sottegem, while those of Hornes were transported to a church in Weert, his ancestral home. Eyewitnesses like Alonso Ulloa recount how mourners immediately contested Alba's rites of effacement. After the beheadings, the crowd dipped handkerchiefs into the blood as it spilled off the scaffold and pooled on the ground, and at Saint Clare, throngs of people arrived to touch Egmont's coffin, as if it contained the bones of a saint. In the meantime, Alba ordered the removal in Brussels of the escutcheons and other heraldic devices of the two men.[80]

The repercussions of the executions were electric, the exemplariness intended by Alba producing instead a ritual cynosure around which Orange and others in exile rallied. Alba had issued a sentence against Orange in March 1568 after he failed to answer an earlier summons to appear before the Council of Troubles issued on January 19. The edict confiscated Orange's Netherlands patrimony, condemned him as a traitor, and was accompanied by the abduction of his eldest son from Louvain to be held indefinitely in Spain. In response, the prince decided in favor of armed revolt. As part of a multipronged invasion plan, Orange readied himself to launch a military campaign into Brabant while his brother Louis of Nassau led forces into Friesland in late April. The northern military campaign went poorly. Orange's brother Adolf was killed at the battle of Heiligerlee on May 23, and on July 23 Louis' forces suffered a crushing defeat at the battle of Jemmingen. Orange's plans to invade through Brabant had to be delayed until early fall as he scrambled for support among skeptical German princes.[81]

However swiftly Alba moved to erase the presence of Egmont and Hornes, the two immediately became consecrated martyrs with tangible relics. Their legacy grew in the poplar media of balladry and print. Egmont was a figure who provoked some consternation in Calvinist circles. The Antwerp chronicler Godevaert van Haecht had considered him disloyal to the Beggars' cause, echoing the sentiment of the explicitly anti-Egmont ballad. But more common was Egmont's celebration as a heroic grandee betrayed, his loyalty to Philip as a soldier and vassal proof positive that the duke and king were tyrants.[82] Egmont had died a political and religious good death, professing loyalty to God and king. In this sense, the execution should have been a ritual catharsis. But so stylized was his expiation of misdeed that no such purging was possible, since it reminded contemporaries that Egmont was a dignified grandee whose punishment was disproportionate to his crime. In perhaps the best-known ballad about the executions, Egmont was lionized as "a

---

80. Juste, *Le comte d'Egmont et le comte d'Hornes*, 353.
81. Swart, "Wat bewoog Willem van Oranje?" and Parker, *Dutch Revolt*, 108–11.
82. Van Nuffel, *Lamoraal van Egmont*, esp. 26–27; *Kroniek Van Haecht*, 2:27.

lord of great power" who went to the scaffold "as a sheep goes to slaughter," the paschal language as obvious as it was potent. The song continues:

> Bravely he went to the city where he was to die and calmly he spoke: "You lords and citizens gathered here, there is no pardon. Hence I am a poor count and no nobleman."

The ballad details Egmont's last rites on the scaffold, and, before moving on to Hornes, concludes: "One could see his blood flow, noble, from the Order [of the Golden Fleece]."[83] Just as Orange's succinct comments about the execution of Egmont and Hornes juxtaposed festive and religious space and time against its violation by Alba, the ballad turned on contrasts. On the scaffold, Egmont considers himself a poor count, but the blood from his execution confirms his heraldic greatness. He portrays himself as "no noblemen," but he is reclaimed through his sacrifice as a heroic grandee.

As more songs were composed and chroniclers memorialized the executions as a central chapter of the narrative of the Dutch Revolt, Egmont and Hornes received equal attention in visual prints. The earliest, produced around 1568 by Frans Hogenberg, depicts the execution set above a German caption.[84] Hornes kneels before the executioner, next to the decapitated body of his fellow nobleman. The scene is frontally framed to highlight the public nature of the executions—a scaffold on the great square set beneath windows for observers to see—but isolates Hornes and the corpse of Egmont in a space of soldiers, lances, and other weapons. In doing so, Hogenberg presents the execution as an executive action; the crowd is static as soldiers seal off the scaffold on behalf of Alba.

The public deaths of Egmont and Hornes occasioned sparring over their memory between Alba and his subjects. Alba's removal of Egmont's insignia and banners from his residence in Brussels, as well as all other symbols, heraldic or otherwise, echoed the classical practice of defamation, in which any representation of an adversary is expunged or derisively portrayed.[85] Sympathizers of Egmont and Hornes counteracted by fashioning new political relics as tangible objects of worship: blood-soaked handkerchiefs and venerated corpses.

Alba's practice of exemplary punishment and ritual defamation was not limited to the execution of Egmont and Hornes. Before these, the duke had ordered the destruction of the Brussels residence of Floris van Pallant, the Count of Culemborg, a member of the Compromise who sought refuge with Orange in Germany. Alba had the residence razed

---

83. NG, 1:348–49, and GB 1:62 [de Bruin and Oosterman, *Repertorium* T0424].

84. Horst, *Opstand in zwart-wit*, 80–82, reproduced in a smaller size and with less text that same year by the workshop of Wolfgang Meyerpeck in Leipzig; see Kinds, *Kroniek van de opstand in de lage landen*, 53.

85. For the Roman practice, see Eric R. Varner, *Mutilation and Transformation: Damnatio Memoriae and Roman Imperial Portraits* (Leiden, 2004).

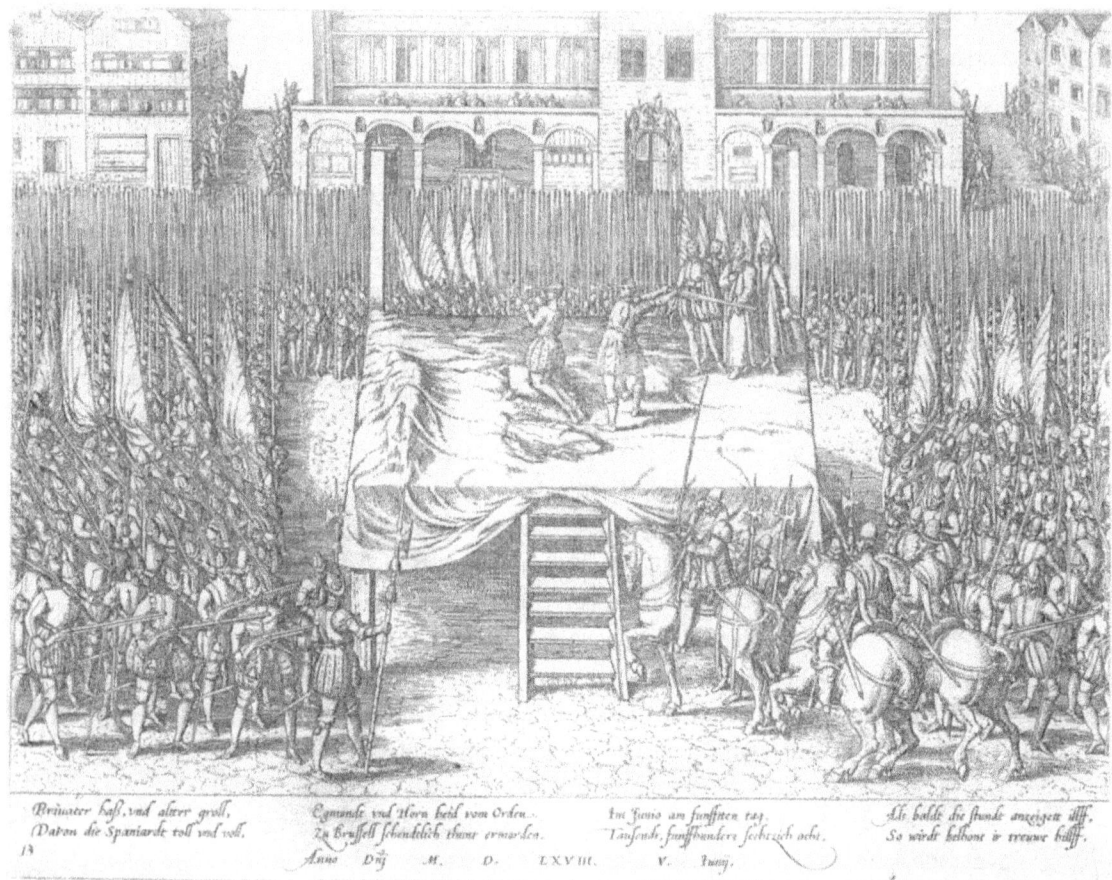

The execution of Egmont and Hornes. Frans Hogenberg, 1568. Courtesy of the private collection of Karel Kinds.

on May 28, 1568, and the earth strewn with salt as an act of purification—not unlike the ritual profanation and enwalling of the Augustinian cloister in Antwerp in 1523 that had produced the first two Protestant martyrs in northern Europe.[86] The Culemborg residence had hosted the notorious April 8, 1566, inaugural banquet of the Beggars. In its place, Alba erected a classically inspired column upon a pedestal designed by Jehan Guilgot of Brussels, which boasted inscriptions in Latin, Dutch, French, and Spanish marking the "cursed memory" (excrandam memoriam) of the conspiracy launched against Philip II on that very spot.[87] With the troublesome grandees executed and others in exile, with their public heraldry removed, and with the Beggars' house of inspiration razed, Alba moved

86. Scheerder, De Inquisitie in de Nederlanden, 38–39.
87. Tóth-Ubbens, Verloren Beelden, 54–55.

forward with his plan to build citadels to ensure foolproof control over the public realm. But as he asserted his mastery over public life, the opposition in exile seized on his unpopular occupation to shed their taint of radical iconoclasm and Beggars' transgressions and to position themselves as defenders of an old order—of civic rights, of noble prerogatives, of the proper relationship of subjects to lordship, of the integrity of the Order of the Golden Fleece and its knights' dignity and legal rights, all of which Alba clearly intended to undo.[88] Over time, the death of Egmont and Hornes became a master symbol of Spanish tyranny against the virtuous nobility and the civic realm. Indeed, the Peace of Münster, signed in 1648 between Philip IV and the United Provinces, took place on June 5 because, in the words of the Portuguese ambassador who witnessed the signing, it was "on that day and at that time eighty years ago that the counts of Egmont and Hornes had been executed by the Duke of Alba in Brussels; and the Estates wished their freedom to begin at the same day and time as those gentlemen had died in defense thereof."[89]

Fortress Antwerp

The plan Alba brought with him to the Netherlands for building military citadels in troublesome cities was a centerpiece of the Spanish design for supervising public life, which had been put into practice earlier in Italy with new military fortifications during the interminable wars between the French and Habsburg imperial forces.[90] In the Low Countries, these military complexes became the targets of the rebels' disdain, portrayed as sinister lairs for gaining a stranglehold on urban life. Alba's plan was hardly new; as early as Ghent's revolt against Charles the Bold in 1467 the Burgundian prince had considered placing a citadel in the city, a plan not realized until 1540 under Charles V. Utrecht also saw the building of the Vredenburg fortress in 1529, the year the town came under Habsburg rule.[91] After the iconoclastic riots, Margaret of Parma advocated even more citadels,

---

88. The fate of Egmont and Hornes elicited comment not merely in the Low Countries but elsewhere in Europe, including from Michel de Montaigne. See *The Complete Works of Montaigne*, trans. and ed., Donald M. Frame (Stanford, 1943), 192. See Anton van der Lem, "Echoes de la révolte: Montaigne et les Pays-Bas du XVIe siècle," in *Montaigne and the Low Countries (1580–1700)*, ed. Paul J. Smith and Karl A. E. Enenkel (Leiden, 2007), 47–62.

89. Francisco de Sousa Coutinho to the King of Portugal in E. Prestage, *Correspondência diplomática de Francisco de Sousa Coutinho durante a sua embaixada en Holanda, 1643–1650*, 3 vols. (Coimbra and Lisbon, 1920–55), 3:13.

90. For case studies, see Simon Pepper and Nicholas Adams, *Firearms and Fortifications: Military Architecture and Siege Warfare in Sixteenth-Century Siena* (Chicago, 1986), for Siena and for Florence, J. H. Hale, "The End of Florentine Liberty: The Fortezza da Basso," in *Florentine Studies*, ed. Nicolai Rubenstein (London, 1970), 501–32.

91. Boone, "Urban Space in Late Medieval Flanders," 638. On Vredenburg, see T. J. Hoekstra, *Vredenburg Castle at Utrecht* (Utrecht, 1982). On the introduction of Italian-style military citadels and fortifications into the Low Countries, see the architectural study by Charles van den Heuvel, *"Papiere Bolwercken": De introductie*

since it was plain to her that the reason Tournai was subdued more quickly than Valenciennes in 1566 was because it already had such a fortress.[92] The plan to build Valenciennes' citadel languished because of money problems, but citadels were either planned or underway elsewhere, especially in Antwerp, to which Alba paid obsessive attention. To Alba, the Antwerp citadel was the master urban symbol of his reign, the linchpin of his bigger plan to create lasting changes in the built environment.[93] But to his opponents, searching for a new political footing after the iconoclastic riots, his citadel stirred a civic consciousness, rallying opposition to him as a governor who sought to strip urban life of its liberties and to police its public space.

Alba's keen interest in Antwerp was understandable. It was not only the Low Countries' largest city, it had been as well the epicenter of the troubles, and was by cultural makeup a commercial entrepot whose lifeblood was a fluid exchange of peoples, ideas, and goods. While the city was not prone to regular social revolt, Antwerp's vigorous Protestantism during the wonder year and its fiercely independent magistrates made it problematic. Moreover, without a citadel, troops could only be quartered in private residences, a situation that had provoked headaches when Margaret of Parma did it in the spring of 1567.[94] Antwerp was also the city that had successfully rebuffed Granvelle's attempt to seat its bishop, preventing the ecclesiastical reorganization of the Netherlands that Alba was determined to finish. And of no small matter, Antwerp was part of William of Orange's sphere of influence, since he held its title of burgrave, and had spent from July 1566 to his exit in April 1567 exercising his superintendency there.[95] So associated with Antwerp was Orange by the end of the wonder year that his departure to Dillenburg on April 22, 1567, became the occasion of pious commemoration. The Antwerp chronicler Van Haecht notes that Orange invoked Psalm 130—"In the deepest need I call to thee, O Lord,"—as he rode out of the city.[96] There is a ballad commemorating the event that likens Orange's departure to the Diaspora of the ancient Israelites. Hundreds accompanied Orange with the exclamation "We will live or die with you!" in order to avoid the bloodthirsty regent and the

---

van de Italiaanse stede- en vestingbouw in de Nederlanden (1540–1609) en het gebruik van tekeningen (Alphen aan den Rijn, 1991).

92. Steen, A Chronicle of Conflict, 15–16.

93. On the failure of the citadel of Valenciennes, see Beuzart, La Répression à Valenciennes après les troubles religieux, 74. On the Antwerp citadel, see Hugo Soly, "De Bouw van de Antwerpse citadel (1567–1571): Sociaal-economische aspecten," Belgisch Tijdschrift voor militaire Geschiedenis 21 (1976): 549–78; H. Wauwermans, Les citadelles du sud et du nord d'Anvers (Brussels, 1880); Van den Heuvel, "Papiere Bolwercken", 105–11; Bor, Oorsprongk, 1:219.

94. E. Rooms, "De materiële toestand van het garnizoen te Antwerpen (1566–1577)," Belgisch Tijdschrift voor militaire Geschiedenis 20 (1974): 633–54.

95. Wells, "Antwerp and the Government of Philip II," 439–527.

96. Kroniek Van Haecht, 1:211–12.

reign of idolatry she would again usher in.⁹⁷ Because of this association between Orange and Antwerp, and because of its buzz of cultural and religious exchange, Alba was determined to clamp down on it.⁹⁸

Even before the iconoclastic riots, Cardinal Granvelle wrote about Antwerp to Gonçalo Perez, on January 23, 1565, "The presence of His Majesty and the construction of a citadel are what is needed to keep order in this city."⁹⁹ No surprise, then, that Margaret of Parma laid the groundwork for the citadel before Alba's arrival, exclaiming that "everything bad comes from this city."¹⁰⁰ In March 1567, she sent the Italian military architect Francesco de Marchi to Antwerp to scout out a good location and begin the design. Once Orange departed the city, Margaret took up residence there herself on April 28, backed by the firepower of some 3,200 Walloon troops. Her arrival in Antwerp was staged as a Burgundian, Catholic rechristening of the city—a countercoup to Orange's exit. She entered with a small band of trusted Golden Fleece advisors, Egmont included, much to the nervous acclaim of overly polite magistrates. The magnificent train of high dignitaries on horseback wound its way to the Onze-Lieve-Vrouwekerk, where the regent entered the church through the north portal, the door through which the iconoclasts had stormed the church. Rogier van Tassis, dean of the canons, greeted her and together they went to the high altar to celebrate mass and hear a Te Deum. Once her presence had graced the church, Margaret made her way to the Saint Michael's Abbey, the traditional residence of visiting royalty. With this ritual cleansing, the wonder year was over.¹⁰¹

Perhaps this ceremonial righting of the wrongs of 1566 left the regent too optimistic, for she reported to Philip II that Antwerp did not oppose the construction of a citadel. In fact, almost no one there wanted one. When Margaret left Antwerp on July 18 the city's Broad Council was still wholly against the project, and the regent herself bitterly remarked to the magistrates that they were foolish to think that the citadel was negotiable.¹⁰² Alba quickly assumed responsibility for the project on his arrival in Brussels, and appointed the Italian engineer Francesco Paciotto its designer and contractor. The Flemish engineer Jacques van Noyen had originally proposed the area near Saint Michael's Abbey inside the city as the citadel's location, clearly in the zone of royal space. For ease of construction, however, Paciotto changed the location to outside Antwerp's walls, to the south between the Kronenburgpoort and the Begijnenpoort, the site proposed by De Marchi after he

97. NG, 1:313–15 [de Bruin and Oosterman, *Repertorium* T2146].
98. *Epistolario Alba*, 2:33–34.
99. *Corr. Philippe II*, 1:338.
100. Ibid., 1:505, cited in Soly, "Bouw van de Antwerpse citadel," 550.
101. *Chronijck der stadt Antwerpen toegeschreven aan den notaris Geeraard Bertrijn*, 185–86, and *Kroniek Van Haecht*, 1:217.
102. *Corr. Philippe II*, 1:505, letter of February 1, 1567, while Orange was still there. Soly gives a summary of her efforts, "De Bouw van de Antwerpse citadel," 550–52.

scrapped his idea of putting the citadel alongside Antwerp's Nieuwe Stad on the city's north side.[103]

The walls to which the citadel would be adjoined were themselves fairly new, and a preview of the military fortifications the Spanish brought with them to Netherlands' cities.[104] Built between 1542 and 1562, the enceinte consisted of a polygonal wall with nine and a half bastions and five gates, cleanly ringed by a deep moat—a defensive structure that made it a public works showcase for the rest of Europe. The Spanish walls gave Antwerp a fortress look, appealing both to city fathers, who were willing to incur the enormous costs to advertise the city's impregnability, and to the Spanish Habsburg rulers committed to the supervision of urban space. Antwerp had been rarely attacked and was not a city with a history of internal unrest. This new fortification, therefore, was disproportionate to any actual threat. At its inception in 1542 it was more a preventive measure, as Charles V stepped up civic and religious ordinances to monitor urban life. Hieronymus Cock's 1557 bird's-eye view of the city portrays Antwerp as a dense, compact city: boats ply the waters of the Scheldt River on the opposite side and move freely back and forth as symbols of accessibility and commercial bustle, while a frontal view of its new moat and walls remind that viewer that ingress into the city was nevertheless stoutly demarcated (see chapter 4, Cock's bird's-eye view of Antwerp).

Once the new site for the citadel was determined, Alba followed its building very closely. Liège and Ghent had provided examples of the efficacy of a citadel for punishing recent offenses and insuring against future troubles. Two years after the sack of Liège in 1467 by Charles the Bold's forces, its governor Guy de Brimeu had seized the island in the river Meuse known as the Ile de la Cité, renamed it the Ile le Duc, and began constructing a citadel there.[105] Charles the Bold had apparently considered doing the same in Ghent after the riot of the Saint Lievens's pilgrims marred his inaugural entry in 1467, a plan not realized until after the 1539 revolt. Ghent's citadel was placed in the seigneury of Saint Bavo's, a strategic location on Ghent's eastern flank, but one that required the demolition of its venerable Benedictine abbey and church. The monks, made canons, were transferred to Saint John's, rechristened the Saint Bavo's Cathedral. Tearing down a privileged Benedictine complex was an audacious meddling with sacred property as punishment for a revolt whose driving motor was guild agitation.[106] There is no doubt

---

103. Soly, "De Bouw van de Antwerpse citadel," 553. On the problems of the Saint Michael's location, see Navarrete, *Colección de documentos inéditos*, 4:473, letter of Philip II to Alba, October 11, 1567; Van den Heuvel, "*Papiere Bolwercken*", 171–72, appendix 3, the report ordered by Pacciotto on the reasons for the final choice of location.

104. On Antwerp, see Lombaerde, "Antwerp in its Golden Age," 99–127, esp. 100–03. On fortifications in general, see James D. Tracy, ed., *City Walls: The Urban Enceinte in Global Perspective* (Cambridge, 2000).

105. Werner Paravacini, *Guy de Brimeu: Der Burgundische Staat und seine adlige Führungsschicht unter Karl dem Kühnen* (Bonn, 1975), 302–7; Boone, "Urban Space in Late Medieval Flanders," 638.

106. On the 1467 revolt and Saint Lieven worship, see Arnade, "Secular Charisma, Sacred Power";

that the citadel's construction was punitive in purpose, symbolized best by the fact that the walls and gates that the emperor had ordered demolished as part of his punishment of Ghent's rebellion were reused as building supplies for this new work.[107] While the presence of Ghent's citadel did not prevent the outburst of iconoclasm in the city in August 1566, it made it easier, as we have seen, to supervise the town when Alba and his troops arrived.

These successful precedents for urban citadels provided the justification for building one in Antwerp. It was to be a Renaissance showcase to match Antwerp's new enceinte, so acclaimed by military engineers and architects. Observers such as Welsh soldier and mercenary Roger Williams considered the lavish attention showered on Antwerp's citadel a poor decision, having more to do with Alba's obsession than anything practical, especially since work on the one in the strategic coastal city of Vlissingen in Zeeland was lagging.[108] On October 25, 1568, ground was broken for the Antwerp citadel, with several windmills taken down and small farmers displaced from their land.[109] Alba himself came to supervise, settling in at Saint Michael's Abbey, the usual in-town residence of court dignitaries. Fearing the demolition of space and property might elicit protests, Alba posted German troops at the Kronenburgpoort to police the construction. Finished in June 1571, the citadel was an enormous public works project that cost a stunning 801,900 guilders, five times more than the money spent on the city's new town hall in the first half of the 1560s. The evasions and protests from the political class that met Margaret of Parma when she started the effort were quickly silenced as Alba imposed his will on the cowering town fathers.[110]

Alba's micromanagement of the citadel's construction was one reason—irregular pay another—that Paciotto abruptly returned to Italy and was replaced with Bartolomeo Campi, much to Alba's disappointment.[111] When heavy rains damaged part of the curtain of a bastion in September 1569, Alba, though sick, gathered up enough strength to go to

---

Boone, "Urban Space in Late Medieval Flanders," 637–38. As Boone has observed, perhaps the singling out of Saint Bavo's was related to 1467 after all, since it was in its church that the relics of Saint Lieven were housed, whose translation had inspired the riot against Charles the Bold and whose veneration by artisans was unmatched.

107. Boone, "Urban Space in Late Medieval Flanders," 638; Arnade, *Realms of Ritual*, 205. On the changes to the seigneury of Saint Bavo's, see Christine Laleman, "Woord, beeld en materie: Het Sint-Baafsdorp in Gent," in *Qui valet ingenio: Liber amicorum Johan Decavele*, ed. Joris de Zutter, Leen Charles, and André Capiteyn (Ghent, 1996), 289–317.

108. D. W. Davies, ed., *The Actions of the Low Countries by Sir Roger Williams* (Ithaca, 1964), 33–34.

109. *Chronijck der stadt Antwerpen toegeschreven aan den notaris Geeraard Bertrijn*, 205–09; *Kroniek Van Haecht*, 1:237–39.

110. Soly, "De bouw van de Antwerpse citadel," 554–55. The Broad Council approved a subsidy of 400,000 guilders for construction as early as November 27, 1567, financed largely through taxes on property and other immovables and increased levies on foodstuff, beer, and wine.

111. *Epistolario Alba*, 2:17–20; Van den Heuvel, "Papiere Bolwercken", 155.

Antwerp and row through the moat to inspect it first hand.[112] No wonder that the finished product strongly bore his mark. The result was a pentagonal fort with five bastions, four of which were named after Alba: Duke, Ferdinand, Toledo, and Alba, with the fifth named after the design architect Paciotto. Placed on the southern edge of the city, the citadel had one of its 300-meter-long sides facing the Scheldt, another two toward the city, separated by the protective esplanade, and two more facing open space. A capacious moat surrounded the complex, with three gates connected by three stone bridges. The principal gate faced the city, between the Duke and Ferdinand bastions, and was decorated with Alba's heraldic devices. The other two gates faced the Scheldt and the open countryside. A "joincte," itself costing 142,000 guilders, linked the complex to the Keizerpoort, integrating it into the recently completed Spanish walls.[113] Inside the enormous complex was a small chapel, a large tree-lined plaza in the center, barracks to house soldiers, and toward the north bastion the "king's residence and house" for the citadel's governor. The chapel was dedicated to the apostles Philip and Jacob. It featured a stained-glass window decorated with a crucifix, the escutcheons of Philip II and Alba, and a depiction of the Resurrection. In 1570 the chapel was replaced by a larger church.[114] Before its completion, in 1568, the citadel already housed thirteen *tercios*, or between 1,560 and 2,080 soldiers.[115]

Conceived explicitly by Alba to "obviate and prevent troubles, uprisings, sedition and insolent behavior that may occur in Antwerp," the citadel thrilled the duke, who boasted to Philip II that it was "the strongest fortress in the world."[116] In a revised print of Cock's 1557 bird's-eye view of Antwerp, the citadel almost overwhelms the cityscape, its strong, clean symmetrical lines a contrast to the denseness of the urban tissue. Completed at enormous cost and with the untiring supervision of Alba himself, the citadel became a signature of the duke, the bastions bearing his name and titles, the chief gate his heraldry, and the chapel his escutcheon. So configured, the citadel was the perfect military complement to the public rechristening of Antwerp. On April 28, 1568, before its completion, all of Antwerp's weapons and other munitions were moved from the town hall—symbol of the city's merchant independence—to the citadel, a transfer of the heft of urban military power from the hands of the magistrates to Alba's. The next day, the first mass was sung at the citadel's chapel, consecrating the new fortress's authority. Separated by the protective esplanade, the citadel was physically linked to the city by the engineering mar-

---

112. Maltby, *Alba*, 152, as reported in the duke's letter of September 12, 1569, to Philip II in Navarrete, *Colección de documentos inéditos*, 38:182.

113. Soly, "De bouw van de Antwerpse citadel"; Piet Lombaerde, "Architecture and Urban Space," in *Urban Achievement*, 105.

114. F. Prims, "Het einde der kasteelkerk," *Antwerpiensia* 9 (1935): 256–74.

115. Soly, "De bouw van de Antwerpse citadel," 562.

116. Quote on citadel's purpose in ibid., 553; on Alba's boast that the citadel was "la mas fuerte plaça del mundo," see *Corr. Philippe II*, 2:16, letter of March 11, 1568.

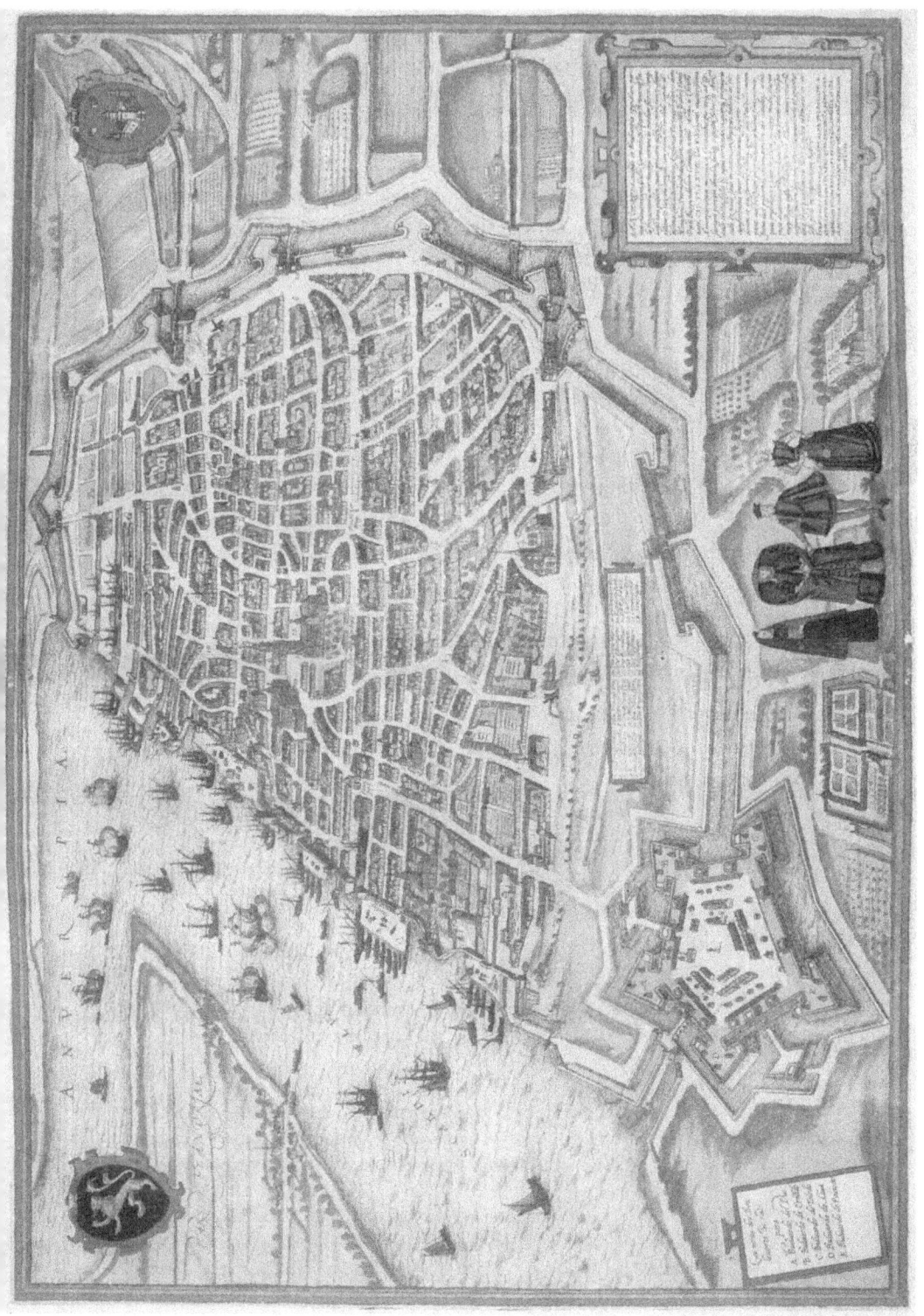

Bird's-eye view of Antwerp with its new citadel. Georg Bruan and Abraham Ortelius, *Civitatis Orbis Terrarum*, Cologne, 1572. Courtesy of Bijzondere Collecties, Universiteitsbibliotheek, Universiteit Leiden.

vel of the "joincte," denoting that its spatial demarcation notwithstanding, the citadel was inextricably part of the city. In 1567 Ludovico Guicciardini had waxed poetic about Antwerp's independence, so rich in privileges that it is "almost a free city, like a republic."[117] The citadel was an announcement than any such pretence of independence would now come up against Habsburg political and military supervision. The heady freedom Guicciardini gushed about—itself a fiction, since, as we have seen, social regulation of public behavior intensified during the sixteenth century—was henceforth subsumed to the Habsburg regulation of public life.

Image Worship: The Castilian Nebuchadnezzar

From the time of their introduction in the Low Countries, citadels had strong spatial and political valences, but none was associated more directly with a ruler than that of Antwerp. Bearing Alba's heraldic symbols, name, and titles, the Antwerp citadel was more than just a Habsburg fortress; it was a monument to the trusted right-hand man of Philip II, who had so swiftly subdued religious and political turmoil. This tight association between Alba and the citadel was enhanced substantially in May 1571 when Alba had a five-meter bronze statue of himself trampling on an allegorical two-headed, six-armed creature placed in the middle of its interior plaza. Among Renaissance princes, such triumphal artworks after classical fashion were common. Even so, Alba's monument elicited an unusual amount of criticism—and not limited to the Patriots. The statue became a rallying point for opposition against him, a symbol of the governor general's arrogance and idolatrous behavior. Well into the seventeenth century, decades after the statue had been removed, its fragments and memory were the stuff of condemnation and poetic contemplation. Alba's statue sparked controversy for two reasons: first, as a public testimonial to his authority, it smacked too much of pride and seemed audaciously regal; and, second, as a free-standing image, it was arrogantly idolatrous, turning the duke into a thing of worship.[118]

Alba was already vulnerable to such accusations. His general pardon offered on July 16, 1570 in Antwerp to Protestants willing to meet its precise terms earned the ire of, among others, chronicler Godevaert van Haecht, who thought the "very richly apportioned" stage

117. Guicciardini, Description de la cité d'Anvers, 76.
118. The following studies have assembled a wealth of primary and secondary sources on Alba's statue: L. Smolderen, La statue du duc d'Albe à Anvers par Jacques Jonghelinck (1571) (Brussels, 1972); L. Smolderen, Jacques Jonghelinck: Sculpteur, médailleur et graveur de sceaux (1530–1606) (Louvain-la-Neuve, 1996), 117–51; and Jochen Becker, "Hochmut kommt vor dem Fall: Zum Standbild Albas in der Zitadelle von Antwerpen, 1571–1574," Simiolus 5 (1971): 75–115, particularly on the literary theme of hubris that writers aimed at the statue after its removal. See also, Berwick y Alba, Discursos, 86–90, 129–30, for an anonymous document from the archives in Simancas that explains the symbolism of the statue: "Declaración de la estatua de metal del Duque de Alba y de otros que se ha puesto en el castillo de Amberes."

The five-foot bronze statue of himself that the Duke of Alba had commissioned to celebrate his triumph over heresy and rebellion, which was allegorized as a two-headed, six-armed creature. The statue elicited widespread criticism of Alba's vanity. Sculpted by Jacques Jonghelinck. Print by Philips Galle. Courtesy of Koninklijke Bibliotheek van België.

upon which Alba sat in the central marketplace was gilded poison, the rich red drapery of its covering "blood cloth."[119] The statue only confirmed what Van Haecht and others had earlier suspected: Alba had arrogated to himself the prerogatives of royal ceremonialism, trampling on the proper balance that Burgundian public life required between civic liberties and the king's ritual protocols.

Alba developed the idea for the statue in the flush of his early success as captain gen-

---

119. *Kroniek Van Haecht*, 2:129. Alba's own account of the pardon ceremony described its success, and the "gran contentamiento del pueblo," in *Epistolario Alba*, 2:388. See also Gustaaf Janssens, "'Superexcellat autem misercordia iudicium.' The Homily of François Richardot on the Occasion of the Solemn Pardon in the Netherlands (Antwerp, 16 July 1570)," in *Public Opinion and Changing Identities*, 107–23.

eral of the Netherlands. Only a year after his arrival, the Council of Troubles operated efficiently and Egmont, Hornes, and signatories of the Compromise were either dead—the unexpected death of Hendrik van Brederode in February 1568 in exile in Recklinghausen was a blow to the rebels—or in flight. Best of all, the anticipated multipronged invasion of the Low Countries by Orange and his associates in the spring and summer of 1568 fared poorly, despite the early victory of his brother Louis of Nassau at Heiligerlee in May, and despite the auspicious beginnings of the Sea Beggars, the rebels' ragtag navy, in the estuary of the Ems. Even before Orange's failed incursions into Brabant in October with thirty thousand troops, the rebels took a crushing blow in East Friesland's Jemmingen Peninsula on July 28 in a fierce battle between the forces of Alba and Nassau. Although Nassau luckily escaped, nearly seven thousand of his men died; the broad-brimmed hats of the Orangist troops choked the Ems River as they floated downstream and out to sea, according to witnesses in Emden.[120] Alba had delivered a rapid, stunning victory.

Alba's return to Brussels on December 22 occasioned celebrations, the military victor reentering the capital fresh from war in the provinces in good classical fashion. The reception was all the sweeter since Alba had been denied the protocols of a welcome delegation when he had first arrived with his enormous train of men in Brussels in August 1567. This time houses were bedecked, bells pealed, and cheers rang out. Delegations from the provinces, the city's magistrates, and clergy from Mechelen, Arras, and Cambrai came to greet him; a Te Deum was ordered, and other celebrations held, including a Burgundian tournament in the grand square and even a Castilian bullfight.[121] Alba's star shone brightly, so much so that Pope Pius V sent him a sword and hat usually reserved to reward the deeds of great Christian princes. His nuncio, Giovanni Battista Castagna—the future Pope Urban VII—compared Alba to Gideon, gushing "that God has reserved for him the greatest honor befitting the principal minister of the greatest monarch."[122] Alba clearly reveled in the *adventus* motifs of the victorious commander. Awash in adulation, he approved plans to erect an allegorical, free-standing monument of himself crushing his hydra-headed enemies. In theme, the statue was loosely based on the story of Hercules defeating the hydra Lerna. The Antwerp sculptor and court favorite Jacques Jonghelinck executed the sculpture, apparently at the urging of the Spanish theologian Benito Arias

---

120. For a full account, see Maltby, *Alba*, 167–71. For a wealth of primary sources, see L. P. Gachard, ed., "Correspondance du duc d'Albe sur l'invasion du comte Louis de Nassau en Frise, en 1568, et les batailles de Heyligerlée et de Gemmingen," *Bulletin de la Commission Royale d'Histoire* ser. 1, vol. 16 (1850): 221–384.

121. St. Genois, ed., *Dagboek van Jan de Pottre*, 32; Maltby, *Alba*, 179; Smolderen, *Statue du duc d'Albe*, 4.

122. Giovanni Battista Castagna's letter to Alba, June 25, 1568, in L. P. Gachard, ed., *Les bibliothèques de Madrid et de l'Escurial* (Brussels, 1875), 112. Not everyone, however, was so outwardly happy; a satirical handbill circulating in cities in the Low Country fumed that "The pope sends a golden sword to the Duke of Alba to enrage the Beggars, yes, so that the bloodthirsty tyrant can kill God-fearing men and women who serve the Lord with pure heart in order to hurt and sting [our] religion." See NG, 1:372.

Montano, who had been sent to the Low Countries in 1568 to assist in the publication of a polyglot Bible by the famed Plantin publishing house in Antwerp.[123]

Apart from the Hercules motif, it is not hard to locate a contemporary work that prefigured Jonghelinck's art piece: Leone Leoni's statue of Charles V defeating an allegorical Fury, with its free-standing depiction of the soldierly Charles crushing his adversary beneath his right foot. As Luc Smolderen has pointed out, however, the generalized abstraction of Leoni's work—an ur-hero over an ur-adversary—bears none of the attention to actual historical detail contained in the Antwerp statue.[124] Perhaps a more exact prototype is a miniature wooden statue executed around 1560 by an unknown artist of an armored Alba slaying a three-headed adversary, identified later as Pope Paul IV, Queen Elizabeth, and the Saxon elector Johann Friederich I.[125] In an important way, the Antwerp statue blends elements of both works while extending the genre. Because of its intricacy and thematic incorporation of actual historical events, the Antwerp statue is certainly more ambitious than its supposed prototypes. Jonghelinck's statue presents a narrative of the Revolt, defines its protagonists, and proclaims Alba as the resolution of the troubles. Thinking his governorship nearly done, Alba conceived the statue as the visual encapsulation of his temporary reign—a tribute to the memory of the turmoil and its successful conclusion.[126]

Employing a ritual motif used by Charles V in building Ghent's citadel, the statue was fashioned out of the very materials of the rebels' defeat: the bronze canons captured by Alba at Jemmingen.[127] The smelted canons made concrete the theme of defeat otherwise presented allegorically in the sculpture. It was not very hard to interpret the historical events that the statue presented through allegory. The sculpture portrayed Alba in military regalia, including his Golden Fleece collar, and facing east. Alba grasps a baton in his lowered left hand, symbol of his military command, but firmly extends his right hand toward Antwerp, a gesture that most early observers interpreted as conciliatory, though Orange fumed in 1572 that it symbolized instead the abolition of the Low Countries' cherished liberties and privileges.[128] At his feet is the two-headed, six-armed hydra, brandishing in its

---

123. For a comprehensive study, see Smolderen, *Jacques Jonghelinck*. The attribution was Maximilian Morillon's, one accepted by all early historians: see *Corr. Granvelle*, 5:138, letter of June 14, 1574. On Montano, see Bernard Rekers, *Benito Arias Montano, 1527–1598: Studie over een groep spiritualistische humanisten in Spanje en de Nederlanden op grond van hun briefwisseling* (Amsterdam–Groningen, 1961), and the summary overview in Smolderen, *Statue du duc d'Albe*, 7–8 and n. 14.

124. Smolderen, *Statue du duc d'Albe*, 68.

125. Tanis and Horst, *Images of Discord*, 33–34.

126. See the comments to this effect in Davies, *The Action of the Low Countries by Sir Roger Williams*, 35.

127. Smolderen, *Statue du duc d'Albe*, 9–10; on the capture of sixteen artillery pieces, including six bronze canons, see Gachard, "Correspondance du duc d'Albe sur l'invasion", 375.

128. Orange's important 1572 admonition to Estates and cities, dated June 16, is entitled: "Sendbrief in forme van Supplicatie aen de Coninklijke Majesteit van Spaengien," in Bor, *Oorsprongk*, 1:464–72.

various hands a broken hammer, an axe, a torch, a club, a purse, and a request contained in a booklet. The two-headed beast wears a Roman breastplate, and a pouch slung over his shoulder, along with Beggars' symbols—a miniature bowl and flask. Its legs are pockmarked with lesions, though this is not readily apparent in Galle's engraving, and its two faces grimace in defeat, while masks and shield lie at its feet. Two bas-relief sculptures grace the sides of the pedestal: one the left side is a good shepherd above whom a winged angel extends an olive branch with the Greek inscription "Dawn chases evil away;" on the right side is an altar upon which burns a sacrifice, accompanied by the inscription "For God our sacred father," in Latin. Directly beneath the sculpture is Montano's dedication to Alba as defender of religion and justice and extinguisher of rebellion and sedition.

For all its classical pretensions, the statue is a decidedly contemporary register of the troubles—a visual condemnation of Beggars and iconoclasts. To most early modern observers, the two-headed figure was an allegory of the nobility and the people.[129] Perhaps the strongest clue to the allegorical intentions of Montano, Alba, and Jonghelinck is discerned in an anonymous document housed in the royal archives in Simancas.[130] According to it, the hand with the booklet symbolizes the April 5, 1566 petition submitted by the Compromise to Margaret of Parma; the hand with the broken hammer, the destruction of churches; the hand with the ax, the destruction of images; the hand with the club, rebellion; the hand with the lighted torch, the fire put to churches; and the hand with the pouch, the three million guilders Calvinists tried to offer in 1566 to buy their religious freedom.[131] The two-headed figure depicts heresy: one head represents the people, the other, the nobility. The pouch and miniature flask are Beggars' insignia, while the two masks at the side of the figure represent duplicity. The figure thus portrays the troubles as a conjoined uprising of the people and the nobility, with three hands doing the plebian work of iconoclasm and religious violence and three hands doing the work of elite rebellion. Whatever their social differences and however distinct their acts of disloyalty, the people and the nobility are two heads of the same seditious body, trampled beneath Alba's feet. In the statue's ideology, the manual work of iconoclasm and the legal and financial maneuverings of the nobility were parallel sides of united sedition that the duke had decisively snuffed out.

Soon after its completion, the statue elicited criticism, eagerly from the Patriots, for whom it came to represent a renascent idolatry, but from others as well, including some in royal circles who interpreted it as testament to Alba's cultivation of vanity at the expense

---

129. On the various readings of the two-headed figure, see Smolderen, *Statue du duc d'Albe*, 31–32.

130. *Declaración de la estatua de metal del duque de Alba y de otros que se ha puesto en el Castillo de Amberes*, Archivo General de Simancas, Papeles de Estado. Legajo 549. fol. 153, in Berwick y de Alba, *Discursos*, 129–30.

131. On the three million guilder request, see J. Scheerder, "Eenige nieuwe bijzonderheden betreffende het 3.000.000 goudgulden rekwest, 1566," in *Mélanges d'histoire offerts à Léon van der Essen*, 2 vols. (Brussels, 1947), 1:559–66.

of his king.[132] Protestants and rebels in the Netherlands also had a similar reaction, including the Antwerp chronicler Van Haecht and Orange himself. In a pamphlet in 1573 that takes the form of a missive to Philip II, Orange reminded the king that Alba had diminished his authority by glorifying himself rather than king or God.[133] Alba's enemies at court in Castile used the statue to circulate rumors intended to discredit him. One recounted how the king himself had earlier refused the request of an Italian artist in Milan to place his arms and portraits on the city's gates because it smacked too much of vanity, and another that Alba was preparing a series of tapestries that included an image of himself about to crown Philip II.[134] As an intricate allegory of Alba's reign, the statue accomplished iconographically and politically what the duke had desired. But its commission and execution had the unintended consequence of casting Alba as a ritual poseur, as a usurper of the king's authority, as a new Castilian Nebuchadnezzar who curries idolatry and presents himself as an object of devotion. Like the brutal occupation of Ghent, the building of the Antwerp citadel had shown Alba to be a foe of the political checks and balances of the civic realm. To him, urban life in the wake of rebellion and iconoclasm required the militarization of its space. The free-standing statue was an even greater breach than the citadel, inasmuch as it usurped the public face of the king's authority and smacked of prideful excess. It encapsulated all that was wrong with Alba's governorship, and gave the rebels a new target after the weakening of the Beggars as a symbolic reference point.

The criticism against Alba accelerated after he proposed three new taxes to the States General in March 1569: the Tenth-, Twentieth-, and Hundredth-Penny taxes. As a one-time levy of 1 percent on all capital, the latter tax passed easily, but the Tenth-Penny tax and the Twentieth as permanent taxes to be implemented by royal collectors proved too much for the regional Estates, whose members prided themselves on their power to grant aid money and oversee its collection. There was immediate opposition, and Alba quickly sank into the quagmire of Low Country financial politics, pressing hard at first, then conceding on certain grounds, only to insist afterward on the taxes' collection.[135] The various Estates sent delegates to lodge protests in Spain; merchants and others went on a tax strike, and trade and commerce suffered.

As the discontent festered, the Sea Beggars stole the political limelight when, under William II de la Marck, Lord of Lumey, they successfully invaded the small seaport town of Den Briel in Holland on April 1, 1572, inaugurating the revolt of Holland and Zee-

132. The theme of hubris is explored in Becker, "Hochmut kommt vor dem Fall."
133. *Sendbrief* in Bor, *Oorsprongk*, 1:464–72. See also *Kroniek Van Haecht*, 2:150.
134. Smolderen, *Statue du duc d'Albe*, 43; the tapestry rumor is found, among other places, in an anonymous document reproduced in Berwick y de Alba, *Contribución al estudio de la persona del III Duque de Alba*, 34.
135. F. H. M. Grapperhaus, *Alva en de Tiende Penning* (Zutphen, 1982); J. Craeybeckx, "Alva's Tiende Penning een mythe?" in *Vaderlands Verleden in Veelvoud*, ed. G. A. M. Beekelaar et al. (The Hague, 1975), 182–208.

land.¹³⁶ One of their very first targets was the citadel then under construction in Vlissingen. The Welsh observer Roger Williams commented that had Vlissingen's citadel been completed before the less necessary one in Antwerp, this fresh round of revolts might have been prevented.¹³⁷

As the upheaval spread through Holland's and Zeeland's cities, rebels decried Alba's tyranny, proclaimed their allegiance to Orange, and triggered sporadic bouts of iconoclasm, despite Orange's disapproval.¹³⁸ By destroying a citadel and cleansing churches, the Sea Beggars and Orange's other sympathizers targeted two varieties of repression, one military and political, the other religious. Over the next year, fierce fighting engulfed the provinces, including several devastating sieges of cities both in the south and north. Alba was exhausted, unable to stem the new troubles, and found himself the subject of increasing ridicule; in a remonstrance published in June 1572, Orange used Spanish notions of ethnic and religious purity (*limpieza de sangre*) to denounce Alba as the son of unbelieving Jews and the commander of troops of "despicable disciples of African slaves." In early 1573, the duke received the news that Philip II planned to recall him.¹³⁹ On November 29, 1573, Don Luis de Requesens, former governor of Lombardy, assumed the governorship at a ceremony in Brussels, and the duke very quickly departed Brussels on December 16 for Madrid.¹⁴⁰ His exit occasioned stinging rebukes and hurrahs of self-congratulation from the rebels not seen since Granvelle's departure. Several ballads mockingly denounced the failed tyranny of the "old man" and "grey old one." "The old man was so angry," exclaimed one, "that instead of bowing down before him or paying the Tenth Penny people preferred instead to shout 'Vivent les Gueux!'"¹⁴¹

It is in the context of the Revolt's second wind and Alba's woes that the virulent campaign against his statue, his authority, and his reign must be understood. A fresh round of ballads, satires, and prints mocked the duke mercilessly as a tyrant, usurper of royal

---

136. For a political and social analysis of the Sea Beggars, see Johannes Cornelis Alexander de Meij, *De Watergeuzen en de Nederlanden, 1568–1572* (Amsterdam, 1972).

137. Davies, *The Action of the Low Countries by Sir Roger Williams*, 54–55. On Vlissingen's citadel, see Van den Heuvel, "Papiere Bolwercken", 126–29.

138. Maltby, *Alba*, 225–61, with a focus on military events; Israel, *Dutch Republic*, 168–78, for a succinct analysis, with attention to why Holland emerged as the new locus of the revolt. For bouts of iconoclasm in Holland and Orange's role in general, see "Copia de relacion de algunas cosas que el príncipe de Oranges ha hecho en Hollandia, y el estado en que aquella se halla al presente," in Simancas, Archivos de Estado, Papeles de Estado, liasse 555, published in *Corr. Taciturne*, 6:301–305.

139. Document 14 in *Texts Revolt*, 95, Orange's famous June 16, 1572, Vermaninghe (Remonstrance). The Jewish references were conflated with invocations of "Moorish" habits, both marking the Spanish as non-Christian; see Swart, "Black Legend," 46.

140. Maltby, *Alba*, 261.

141. See "Wie Wil hooren een nieu liet. . . . Van den ouden Man die duc dalve hiet," NG, 2:93–94 [de Bruin and Oosterman, *Repertorium* T7158]; cf. "Ick wil te landts uut rijden Sprack daer den Ouden Grijs," in ibid., 2:91–92.

authority, and idolater.[142] Two of the first salvos came in the form of popular prints: an engraving circa 1569 of the Duke of Alba upon a throne overseeing a landscape of political repression and religious persecution, an image reworked and reproduced repeatedly in the seventeenth century; and a satirical depiction of Alba's Antwerp statue. Both images spoof Alba's royal pretensions by depicting him seated upon a throne commanding a vast tableau of repression or making himself over into a worshipful image. This criticism was not lost on Orange, who in his 1573 complaint to Philip II used Alba's July 16, 1570, announcement of a general pardon as a case in point. He wrote: "Alba, following the example of the tyrant Herod, took your royal chair, which had never before been touched by any *stadholder*, and covered it with a golden cloth, on which he, in your absence, sat like an idol in the crowded square of Antwerp."[143]

In its ridicule of Alba's violent rule, the throne print reprises themes of political submission from the late-medieval era to bolster its contemporary criticism of the duke's monarchical pretensions. Seated upon a throne whose baldachin bears the tools of torture, Alba is presented as a royal pretender in league with Cardinal Granvelle, who bellows in his ear to persecute the evangelicals. To their left, a devil holds a papal tiara and royal crown as rewards for their good work. The background is a vista of torture and execution, including the beheading of Egmont and Hornes, whose blood forms a pool out of which a cardinal fishes. The inscription "the rod of God" is placed above Alba's head in Latin, French, and German, making the point, as Daniel Horst and James Tanis have observed, that many saw the duke's reign as punishment from God for the sins of society.[144] But perhaps the print's most compelling aspect is its foreground. On their knees before Alba are the Seventeen Provinces allegorized as young, chained maidens led by Brabant, who carries an open book entitled "God's Word." To their right are the men of the States General, immobile and silent. In the duke's hand is a copy of the privileges of some city or province, and at his feet, the ripped-up charters of liberties he is in the process of annulling. With its depiction of shackled provinces kneeling before the duke, and with the foreground action centered on the destruction of privileges, the print recalls earlier lordly punishments, the *amende honorable*, and the confiscation of privileges, most notably.

But if the throne-of-Alba print referenced these past indignities as it simultaneously

---

142. A good sampling of the print images can be found in Tanis and Horst, *Images of Discord*, esp. 25–34, but the genre—at least six surviving prints and twenty-two paintings from 1569 through 1650—is the subject of Andrew Sawyer's "The Tyranny of Alva: The Creation and Development of a Dutch Patriotic Image," *De Zeventiende Eeuw* 19 (2003), 2: 181–211. See also the analysis in Van Nierop's "Alba's Throne." Graphic images mocking Alba receive sustained attention in Horst's *Opstand in zwart-wit*, 63–108.

143. Sendbrief in Bor, *Oorsprongk*, 1:468; English quote in Tanis and Horst, *Images of Discord*, 30. For the pardon, see F. Prims, *Geschiedenis van Antwerpen*, 7:109.

144. Tanis and Horst, *Images of Discord*, 51, with an excellent analysis of the print and its adaptations. Sawyer, "Tyranny of Alba" makes a convincing case that the submission motif draws visually on Dirck Volkertsz. Coornhert's print, *The Submission of the Cities of Germany*, ca. 1555–56.

A "Throne of Alba" print. Anonymous, 1569. The first of a genre of prints that made fun of Alba as a pretender to royal authority and instigator of tyranny and discord. Courtesy of Rijksprentenkabinet, Rijksmusuem, Amsterdam.

castigated the duke's displacement of the king, the parody of Alba's Antwerp statue, produced sometime between 1571 and 1572, functioned as a spur to action. An armored William of Orange stands to the statue's right in front of a representation of the Tenth Penny tax—the hero eager to fight against "violence, taxation, injustice and tyranny." The statue, moreover, sits not in the citadel but in a vast field of war; Alba is ringed by an allegory of time proclaiming his final days as a tyrant and a winged devil wearing the papal tiara. In lieu of the two-headed, six-armed hydra, beneath his feet stands truth with her mouth gagged, justice with a broken scale, a widow, and an orphan, with the duke's foot upon the skull of one of his victims. Impoverished widows and parentless children had long been cited as the social by-product of the hated Inquisition; even before image-breaking struck Ghent in late August 1566, Van Vaernewijck voiced just such a critique of the ef-

A parody of Alba's Antwerp statue. Anonymous, ca. 1571–72. William of Orange comes to rescue the people of the Netherlands, as Truth is crushed beneath the tyrant's feet. Courtesy of Rijksprentenkabinet, Rijksmuseum, Amsterdam.

fects of inquisitorial practice on domestic life.[145] Inside the pedestal are the stored hearts the duke had wrested from his victims, now being reclaimed by emboldened Beggars.

With Alba's tyranny the pivot around which the rebels could fashion such an imaginary, it is not surprising that the duke's departure was equated with his downfall, nor that his statue's future was short-lived. In his 1573 letter to Philip II, Orange himself compared the duke to none other than Nebuchadnezzar, the Babylonian king who compelled others to worship falsely. But even worse than his predecessors, Alba ruled without consultation. He sought not only to usurp royal prerogatives but also to diminish Philip II's stature.[146] By making this analogy Orange tapped into a religio-political strain of criticism that harked back to Pieter Aertsen's painting of the refusal of three Jewish officials, Shadrach,

145. BT Van Vaernewijck, 1:70.
146. Sendbrief in Bor, Oorsprongk, 1:468.

Meshach, and Abednego, to worship the Babylonian king's great idol recounted in the Book of Daniel (see figure in chapter 3). It would not be long before the connection between such idolatry would be linked not just to a prideful governor but to royal power itself. In the anonymous 1576 treatise *Address and Opening to Make a Good, Blessed and General Peace in the Netherlands* the author sought to make a direct link between kingship and biblical idolatry, reasoning, "Therefore we read that God became very angry, when His people of Israel, unsatisfied with a legal government, wanted to have Kings, just like the pagans had, who would be worshipped by the community like idols, and whose will and resolution would be regarded as the supreme and irrefutable law."[147] Even before such a direct coupling between monarchical representation and biblical idolatry, Spanish authorities deemed it wise to have the Antwerp statue removed. Before Requesens arrived in Brussels in November 1573 to succeed Alba, the king's secretary, Gabriel de Zayas, in March had recommended such a move. In June 1574 Requesens ordered the commander of the citadel, Sancho d'Avila, to take down the statue; it was whisked away, stored, and later quietly smelted down, sometime between February 1576 and March 1577.[148]

After its demise, the statue lived on, inspiring both urban legends and poetic musings about what it had represented. One cultural legend recounts that the statue met its demise at the hands of Antwerp's own rioters, who set upon the citadel in August 1577 and violently tore down the bastion facing the city.[149] This invented account of the statue's fate catered to Calvinist sensibilities as yet another act of iconoclasm, a casting down of an image of authority that carried strong political and religious messages. The new Nebuchadnezzar had been defeated by image-smashing burghers after his humiliating departure from Brussels. An anonymous print celebrating the surprise deaths of Alba's two successors as governor general, Luis de Requesens and Don Juan, portrays Alba precisely as the humiliated Babylonian king of the Book of Daniel. Alba is shown groveling on the ground before an overflowing, blood-soaked pot holding the heads of Egmont and Hornes while a caption compares his fate to Nebuchadnezzar's, who spent seven years with a madness that made him act like a beast, eating wild grass. Behind the vanquished duke is the hated statue in Antwerp, the symbol of his idolatrous behavior and the reason for his precipi-

---

147. *Vertoog ende openinghe om een goede, salighe ende generale vrede te maken in dese Nederlanden*, trans. in Van Gelderen, *Dutch Revolt*, 104.

148. Smolderen, *Statue du duc d'Albe*, 50–54.

149. Widely popularized by the seventeenth-century chronicle of the Jesuit Famianus Strada, this fiction of retribution against the statue was amplified by later historians, and even celebrated in the modern romantic imagination, including an 1888 painting by Karl Verlat of heroic workers destroying the image of their oppressor, with women in the forefront and a muscular, sledgehammer-wielding Man of the People overseeing the destruction. See Smolderen, *Jacques Jonghelinck*, 142–43 for the sources, especially Strada. For this urban myth and a closer study of the sources of its origin, see too L. Smolderen, "La statue du duc d'Albe a-t-elle été mise en pièces par la population anversoise en 1577?" *Jaarboek van het Koninklijk Museum voor Schone Kunsten-Antwerpen* (1980): 113–36.

tous downfall.[150] Such Calvinist references to scripture were common in late sixteenth- and seventeenth-century Dutch literature. But the statue inspired other memorials too. A piece of Alba's statue, namely the thumb of his right hand, was preserved in the collection of the seventeenth-century humanist Pieter Cornelisz. Hooft, and reproduced in a 1719 tract published by J. van de Poll in Amsterdam.[151] Among literary circles, the thumb acquired the stature of a political relic, alluringly Catholic in appeal, and a source of poetic musing on the brevity of power and the problem of tyranny. Hooft himself composed a verse about its once awesome strength:

> The thumb, the true backhand. It, which in the past had itself been kissed by the whole Netherlands, although it oppressed them, is now wrung by the sailor who uses it as a dowel.[152]

The statue had achieved a status in its afterlife never fully realized during its short number of years as a public monument.

The celebrated treaty of 1576, the Pacification of Ghent, temporarily united the northern provinces of Holland and Zeeland and those that had remained loyal in a common effort to drive out Spanish forces; it established a provisional government under the aegis of the States General.[153] Among its articles was one directed against Alba's cultural campaign to master public life through memorials and representations such as the Antwerp statue, the column in Brussels, and the minting of medals celebrating his victories: "The pillars, trophies, inscriptions, and other representations (*andere teekenen*) erected by the Duke of Alba to the shame and disgrace of the aforementioned and all others shall be destroyed and demolished."[154] The treaty was penned in the same year that the hortatory *Address and Opening to Make a Good, Blessed and General Peace in the Netherlands* equated ceremonial representations of kingship with idolatry. While the States General was not yet willing to repudiate Philip II as sovereign, article twelve of the Pacification made it clear that Alba as captain general had attempted to buttress his reign through the orchestration of public images of authority. Alba had reigned so harshly as a response to the deterioration of Habsburg authority during the wonder year, having attempted to refurbish the religious

---

150. A description is in Tanis and Horst, *Images of Discord*, 30.

151. *Ter gedachtenisse van de duym des metalen gedenkbeelds, voorheen in bewaring bij P. C. Hooft, nu in eigendom van Buren* (Amsterdam, 1719), discussed in Becker, "Hochmut kommt vor dem Fall," 109–112.

152. "Op den dujm van 't metaelen beeldt des Hartoghen van Alva," reproduced in Becker, "Hochmut kommt vor dem Fall," 109. My thanks to Walter Simons who helped me with this tricky translation.

153. M. Baelde, "De Pacificatie van Gent in 1576," *Bijdragen en Mededelingen betreffende de Geschiedenis der Nederlanden* 91 (1976): 369–93. For the Pacification of Ghent, see A. S. de Blécourt and N. Japikse, eds., *Klein plakkaatboek van Nederland: Verzameling der ordonnantiën en plakkaten betreffende regeeringsvorm, kerk en rechtspraak (14e eeuw tot 1749)* (Groningen, 1919), 113–17.

154. De Blécourt and Japikse, *Klein plakkaatboek van Nederland*, 116.

The Death of Don Juan. Anonymous, 1578. Alba is satirized as a beastlike Nebuchadnezzar on the ground before a bloody pot with the heads of Egmont and Hornes with his infamous Antwerp statue in the background. Courtesy of Rijksprentenkabinet, Rijksmuseum, Amsterdam.

and political times, spaces, and objects so important to Burgundian-Habsburg authority, which the iconoclastic riots had fractured. He corrected what had been put asunder, rechristening public life through a cultural program of martial supervision, exemplary punishment, control of public space, and testaments to his authority as a means to facilitate his other goals, including the completion of the stalled ecclesiastical reorganization of the Netherlands, the punishment of wrongdoers, and military victory over rebels and their hastily assembled armies.

To Calvinists and political rebels, of course, this course of action was anything but corrective. Marnix, Lord of St. Aldegonde's 1570 *A Defense and True Declaration of the Things Lately Done in the Low Country* characterizes the duke as one who "made profane things holy, and holy things profane."[155] He billeted troops in cities like Ghent in the name of Church and king only to have irreverence and violence visited upon its townspeople. He issued warrants of arrest for thousands of pious men and women and put to death over a thousand,

155. Van Gelderen, *Dutch Revolt*, 61.

including the outwardly loyal Egmont and Hornes. He built citadels less for urban protection than for state coercion. Most notoriously, he erected a pillar in Brussels and a monument to himself in Antwerp that fostered a cult of political idolatry straight out of the Book of Daniel. Moreover, his very person was sinister. Tall, thin, with dark-black eyes and a forked, pointed grey beard was how contemporaries described him—the perfect protagonist of a Black Legend in the making, a governor whose likeness appears in Pieter Bruegel the Younger's *Massacre of the Innocents*, after his father's original, when it was safe to make explicit reference to this vanquished foe.[156] Alba's unbending Catholicism and political authoritarianism and especially his failed attempt to implement the Tenth Penny tax made him the perfect foil for royal arrogance and an adversary easy to satirize—an imperious ruler who ended his reign in the Netherlands as an "old grey man." More than anything else, Alba's policies allowed the Beggars in rebellion, hiding, or exile to make themselves anew into defenders of liberty and *patria*. As Alba made his exit, the fighting still burned hot in Holland, and William of Orange soon reentered the political stage, playing the good father and valiant leader of territories in revolt. Alba's defeat brought about Orange's apotheosis. As cities were pummeled by sieges and sacks, the core provinces temporarily united against Spanish depredations, but they remained stubbornly divided over the future direction of the Revolt.

156. See the physical description by Frédéric Badoaro in 1557 in L. P. Gachard, ed., *Relations des ambassadeurs vénitiens sur Charles-Quint et Philippe II* (Brussels, 1856), 72, and Maltby, *Alba*, 157. On the Massacre of the Innocents and its political context, see David Kunzle, "Spanish Herod, Dutch Innocents: Bruegel's *Massacre of the Innocents* in their Sixteenth-Century Political Contexts," Art History 24, no. 1 (February 2001): 51–82.

CHAPTER 6 SPANISH FURIES
SIEGES, SACKS, AND THE CITY DEFIANT

The Reformed political imagination that shaped chronicles, ballads, and broadsheets about the Dutch Revolt preferred clean opposites to the more messy reality of an uprising rife with factional politics and divergent religious commitments. In the emerging master narrative, voiced everywhere from the Beggars' ballads to the burgeoning pamphlet literature, the conniving Granvelle had squared off against the king's righteous vassals, particularly the trinity of Orange, Egmont, and Hornes. The success in exiling the cardinal, however, had opened the door to the political, religious, and representational crisis of iconoclasm. The paroxysms of violence in 1566 had brought the captain generalship of Alba, usurper of the king's authority, violent punisher of the people of the Netherlands, and idolater par excellence. Alba's unbending authoritarianism had provoked warfare and, with it, the righteous opposition led by William of Orange. He was no easy hero to Catholics, who suspected his Protestantism, or to militant Calvinists, who suspected his early ties to royal authority, his *politique* sensibilities, and his ambivalence about Reformed practice, but Orange nevertheless emerged as the trusted defender of the "fatherland"—the loyal vassal contesting a royal policy gone wrong, and the paternal symbol of oppositional sentiment.[1]

To Dutch propagandists, it was not long before Orange and Alba figured as symbolic opposites in an unambiguous fight between right and wrong, as in a 1572 anonymous print contrasting the two.[2] It depicts a militant Alba leading a shackled, naked personification of the "Nation of the Netherlands," with "the Poor Common Man" reduced to beggary at the duke's feet—yet another evocation of the symbol the Beggars had so successfully wielded. The text deplores the miserable state to which Alba has reduced the Netherlands. The bound woman and the beggar stand for enslavement and economic woes, and are set against a background in which soldiers of the Army of Flanders pillage

---

1. On Orange as symbol and figure from the sixteenth century onward, see Haitsma Mulier and Janssen, *Willem van Oranje in de historie*.
2. On Alba and Orange in the pamphlet literature as contrasting figures, see P. A. M. Geurts, *De Nederlandse opstand in de pamfletten, 1566–1584* (Utrecht, 1983), 178–80, 183–86.

William of Orange as military hero and sage leader contrasted with the tyrant Alba, who has a shackled Netherlands at his side. Anonymous, 1572. Courtesy of Stichting Atlas van Stolk, Rotterdam.

and attack. Opposite them stands a martial Orange, ready to restore the dignity and economic vitality of the beleaguered Low Countries. He is surrounded by symbols of commercial vitality and political and religious accord, including Honor, Prudent Counsel, and Wealth. The print freely mixes these religious, political, and commercial motifs to brighten the contrast between the rapacious Alba, shears in hand to rob the Netherlands, and the dapper Orange, with his sword and a laurel of honor above his head. The print must have proved popular, since it was reproduced some four years later, around 1576, as an anonymous engraving attributed to Theodore de Bry. De Bry's version is mostly faithful to the original, except that the background now depicts the sack of Antwerp at the hands of Spanish forces in 1576. Alba's citadel, rioting soldiers, and a burning town hall all plainly reference the depredations of the reviled attack that took place on November 4.[3]

De Bry's change of setting is understandable in light of the intense warfare Spanish and Netherlander forces waged regularly on urban terrain. The 1572 revolt had been triggered by Alba's disregard for political consultation and by his hated fiscal policies, but the

   3. Tanis and Horst, *Images of Discord*, 76–78, and Horst, *Opstand in zwart-wit*, 138–39.

A 1577 reworking of the 1572 print of Orange and Alba, with the notorious sack of Antwerp in 1576 as its background. Anonymous (attributed to Theodore de Bry). Courtesy of Museum Boijmans-van-Beuningen, Rotterdam.

conflict soon broadened because of the conduct of the Spanish-led Army of Flanders and its soldiers' propensity for staging violent mutinies.[4] In fact, it was the sack of Antwerp on November 4, 1576, that gave added weight to the States General's decision to issue the Pacification of Ghent, in which the formerly differing provinces agreed to work together with Holland and Zeeland to expel the occupying army.[5] Although they postponed—with dire consequences—a religious solution for the Netherlands, delegates reached immediate consensus on the need to rid the provinces of the hated soldiers. That conservative Walloon royalists could join Calvinists opposed to Philip II had much to do with cities across the various provinces having been devastated by swift mutinies and prolonged sieges from the Army of Flanders.

The urban violence also spurred writers and artists to memorialize these events in prose and print, producing the potent image of the soldiers and Spanish administrators as vio-

---

4. Parker, Dutch Revolt, 171–72, and Parker, Army of Flanders, 185–207 on mutinies.
5. M. Baelde, "De Pacificatie van Gent in 1576," Bijdragen en Mededelingen betreffende de Geschiedenis der Nederlanden 91 (1976): 369–93; Koenigsberger, Monarchies, States Generals and Parliaments, 272–73.

lent ruffians, breaking, killing, and robbing with the same intensity and some of the same symbolic goals as the *beeldenstormers* of 1566. If the targets of Calvinist iconoclasts in 1566 were Catholic religious objects and spaces of importance to Church and state, the soldiers of the Army of Flanders went after items dear to the urban burgher culture of the Low Countries: property, money, and other symbols of commercial vitality and political rights. The depredations stirred deep anger and raised the status of William of Orange, elevating the once Burgundian insider who had steered clear of the Beggars and failed to embrace the Calvinist insurgency in 1566 to the great defender of bedrock privileges and protector of domestic order. They also stoked radical sentiments not only in Holland and Zeeland, the cornerstone of the 1572 uprisings, but in Flanders and Brabant as well, where many cities opted for Calvinist regimes in 1577 and 1578. Most notable of these was Ghent. Here, a revolutionary government blended tried-and-true guild radicalism with a pugnacious Calvinism and invested in a new fortification system to foster a public image of a defiant city, ready to rebuff any violence from the Habsburg army.

The fight for ancient privileges and freedoms, the campaign against an occupying army, and the language of paternal succor became concentrated in the figure of Orange, who labored tirelessly to hold together Zeeland, Holland, Brabant, and Flanders, the core provinces of the Netherlands. The events of 1572–76 consolidated the Revolt, temporarily uniting divergent provinces. More lasting were the cultural forces that the urban violence unleashed, none more central than a revitalization of the late-medieval concern for the *ghemeente*, or civic community. This civic ethos was enriched by early strands of civic republicanism modeled after classical, Ciceronian precepts of virtue that had begun to emerge in the writings of Netherlanders such as the Ghent humanist Nicolaus Biesius and the Bruges lawyer Frans Goethals by the middle of the sixteenth century. The vernacular praise of a virtuous citizenry threatened by the tyranny of a prince's army offered a popular equivalent to such humanist sentiments, bolstering the already solid groundwork for protorepublicanism to seize the urban political landscape.[6] Still, scholars as diverse as Ernst Kossmann and Herbert Rowen have questioned how a revolt that gave birth to the seventeenth-century United Provinces was itself without great treatises on republicanism, how its political practice was without robust theoretical moorings.[7] The sieges and sacks of Low Country cities and the new party affiliation of the Patriots that arose are reminders that civic republicanism developed less through the small harvest of learned works from men like Goethals than through the grit of popular politics. The experience of urban vio-

---

6. Tilmans, "Republican Citizenship and Civic Humanism in the Burgundian-Habsburg Netherlands," in *Republicanism*, 1:107–25.

7. For a historiographical discussion, see Velema, "'That a Republic is Better than a Monarchy'"; Ernst Kossmann, *Politieke theorie in het zeventiende-eeuwse Nederland* (Amsterdam, 1960), and Herbert Rowen, "The Dutch Republic and the Idea of Freedom," in *Republicanism, Liberty and Commercial Society, 1649–1776*, ed. David Wootten (Stanford, 1994), 310–40.

lence and resistance reinvigorated a deeply felt ethos of the city as the wellspring of political identity. In the violence of pillage and the heroics of resistance, civic rights and privileges became more than rhetorical devices and abstractions; they became the very real sinews of a fight to define the constitutive elements of political life.[8]

Beggars as Iconoclasts: The Revolt Anew

After the Calvinist insurrection of 1566–67 and Orange's military campaign of 1568 fizzled, the Reformed communities faced the choice of life "under the cross" in the Low Countries or a forced exile that Calvinists interpreted as akin to the Diaspora of the Israelites. Orange's own departure from Antwerp on April 22, 1567, occasioned a refrain that struck this exilic chord.[9] In contrast, the seizure of Den Briel on April 1, 1572, by Orange's Sea Beggars—the spark of the revolt of Holland—ushered in the end of the Babylonian captivity and the triumphal return of the insurgents. The Beggars were back, Baal's temple overturned, and the Duke of Alba blindsided.[10] While the attack on Den Briel inaugurated new city regimes favoring Orange's cause in Holland, its protagonists were hardly honorable foot soldiers of the impugned fatherland. They were a volatile mix of petty Calvinist noblemen joined with freebooters who had been cruising the waters off Zeeland, Holland, and Friesland since 1568 with a fleet of some twenty ships and around 1,200 men, 90 percent of whom were seamen, laborers, and craftsmen. Orange himself first tapped their potential in February 1569 when he offered them letters of commission as part of his attempt to curry allies after his failed military campaign of 1568. By fall 1571, the Liège nobleman William II de la Marck emerged as the fleet's senior admiral, and this group of mostly privateers soon gained political credibility. De la Marck was an outspoken opponent of royalist policy and a signatory to the Compromise in 1566, and his right-hand man, the minor nobleman Willem Blois van Treslong, was an even more aggressive political rebel.[11]

The Sea Beggars' privateering streak and Protestant ethos proved an electric mix that prompted attacks on ecclesiastical property as well as commercial products. Their earli-

---

8. On the political importance of privileges, see Catherine Secretan, *Les privilèges, berceau de la liberté: La révolte des Pays-Bas, aux sources de la pensée moderne (1566–1619)* (Paris, 1990).

9. GB, 1, 45 [de Bruin and Oosterman, *Repertorium* T2146].

10. Ibid., 2, 3–9 for the Den Briel ballads. On the internal dynamics of the revolt of Holland, see J. J. Woltjer, *Tussen vrijheidsstrijd en burgeroorlog*, 9–63; K. W. Swart, *William of Orange*, 29–75; and Parker, *Dutch Revolt*, 130–68. For the religious terrain, see A. C. Duke and R. L. Jones, "Toward a Reformed Polity in Holland, 1572–78," in *Reformation and Revolt*, 199–226. For a microhistory of violence in Holland's North Quarter during these critical years, see Van Nierop, *Het Verraad van het Noorderkwartier*. On the capture of Den Briel, historians have relied on the narrative summary of Bor, *Oorsprongk*, 1:366–77.

11. De Meij, *Watergeuzen en de Nederlanden*, esp. appendices 2 and 3, 313–28 for the social composition of the Sea Beggars.

est recorded forays in Groningen and Friesland in August 1569 against Rottum and Dokkum involved the confiscation of religious goods and the plundering of a nunnery. These attacks were followed by a dozen others against religious interests.[12] Still, the Sea Beggars were not a well-known force until their raid against Den Briel on April 1, 1572. However minor a town, Den Briel was the spark that lit the tinderbox in Zeeland and the much more thickly populated Holland against Alba and the king. It was part of a much bigger, multipronged invasion of the Netherlands mapped out by Orange and his associates, whose success depended on gaining English and French support.[13] Located in southern Holland, Den Briel was easy prey: its small garrison of Spanish soldiers had left for the winter, never to return, thus it was an unprotected coastal town, ideal for a base of operations. Den Briel, which had a medieval curtain wall, was Treslong's hometown. As a veteran of the battle of Jemmingen, and someone who had lost a brother to Alba's Council of Troubles, this pugnacious nobleman harbored anything but peaceful intentions. Treslong, de la Marck, and their men took the city easily, employing rites of inversion and iconoclasm akin to the religious violence of 1566 but more fatal. The small city's churches were plundered and its ecclesiastical goods and vestments appropriated by Treslong and his men, who, according to the early historian of the Dutch Revolt Pieter Bor, took to wearing priestly vestments and drinking out of chalices aboard their ships, donning this garb in much the same way the original Beggars had put on mendicant outfits. The Beggars also seized nine monks, condemned them to death, and then taunted them on their sorrowful march to the gallows.[14]

Holland was no stranger to iconoclasm, but what the Sea Beggars brought was a more virulent strain, accompanied by the murder of members of Catholic religious orders. As the devout Catholic Wouter Jacobz., prior of Stein in Gouda, lamented in his account of events in Holland (written from his refuge in loyalist Amsterdam), the majority of the population did nothing to rebuff this violence:

> As long as people have been assured about their external freedom and their own welfare, they care not whether God's temples are despoiled, the holy statues broken, whether God's servants, the priests, religious and upright Catholics, are mocked, driven forth, plundered, and miserably murdered, nor finally also whether the worship of God and the most holy sacraments are hindered, blasphemed, and scandalously abused, being trodden underfoot and brought to nought as they please.[15]

12. Ibid., appendix 1, 310–12.
13. Holland's political institutions and fiscal policies in the late-medieval and early Habsburg period that explain its preparedness to inaugurate the revolt in 1572 has been explored in James Tracy, *Holland Under Habsburg Rule, 1505–66* (Berkeley, 1990). See also J. W. Koopmans, *De Staten van Holland en de opstand* (The Hague, 1990).
14. Bor, *Oorsprongk*, 1:366, 370.
15. *Dagboek Jacobsz.*, 1:3.

In 1566 Holland had experienced outbursts of iconoclasm that ran the gamut from genuine riots in cities such as Amsterdam, Delft, and Leiden to the orderly removal of images, whether by noble or magisterial fiat.[16] Anticlericalism had run high for years, and the county's greatest nobleman, Hendrik van Brederode, had been the undisputed leader of the Beggars before his untimely death in 1568.[17] But the murder of clergy had not been an element of the county's *wonderjaar*, and had scarcely figured in the south, except during a short-lived circuit of plunder in the troubled Westkwartier by a ragtag band of exiles dubbed the Wood Beggars.[18] The violence by the Wood Beggars was rapid, specific, and intense—including the torture and castration of priests—and ended with a second bout in September 1568 that resulted in their capture and swift execution.[19]

Whether committed by Wood Beggars or Sea Beggars, the new attacks added more overt forms of violence against clergy to the now familiar rites of inversion. In the twenty-four years between 1567 and 1591, an estimated forty-nine Catholic clerics died at the hands of the rebels, with most killed in Holland in 1572.[20] Wouter Jacobsz. recounts how the Beggars threatened to murder all clergy as they entered towns and cities, how priests were afraid to appear in public, and how nuns in Gouda had been harassed and even raped, taunted as mere "whores of the sacrament."[21] Despite the more intense violence, the tumult spread rapidly, anchored in Holland, a county that had a long tradition of urban particularism and robust Estates much like Brabant and Flanders.[22] While Calvinists

16. Duke and Kolff, "Time of Troubles"; Van Nierop, *Beeldenstorm en burgerlijk verzet in Amsterdam*; J. Smit, "Hagepreken en beeldenstorm te Delft," *Bijdragen en Mededelingen betreffende de Geschiedenis der Nederlanden* 45 (1924): 206–50.

17. H. de la Fontaine Verwey, "Le rôle d'Henri de Brederode et la situation juridique de Vianen pendant l'insurrection des Pays-Bas," *Revue du Nord* 40 (1958): 297–303; Duke and Kolff, "Time of Troubles," 317.

18. Backhouse, *Beeldenstorm en Bosguezen*, 135–36. Like many of his contemporaries, the cosmopolitan Marcus van Vaernewijck in Ghent recoiled at the deeds of the Wood Beggars, and recounted how priests were castrated before being murdered in slow, taunting fashion—a form of torture confirmed in legal documents; see BT *Van Vaernewijck*, 3:200–202.

19. Backhouse, *Beeldenstorm en Bosgeuzen*, the most in-depth study, summarized in his "Guerilla War and Banditry in the Sixteenth Century: The Wood Beggars in the Westkwartier of Flanders, 1567–68," *Archiv für Reformationsgeschichte* 74 (1983): 232–56. Many of the compelling details about the Wood Beggars are found in the deposition of their leader, Jan Camerlynck after his capture. For a transcription, see Backhouse, "Dokumenten betreffende de godsdiensttroebelen in het Westkwartier."

20. Gregory, *Salvation at Stake*, 274. The most celebrated was the execution of nineteen monks from Gorcum in Den Briel July 9, whose hanging and dismemberment inspired a vigorous Catholic martyrology. There were further attacks that same summer against clergy in Enkhuizen and Roermond. On the Gorcum martyrs, see E. H. J. Reusens, *Iconographie des bienheureux martyrs de Gorcum* (Louvain, 1867), and G. van der Elsen, "Iets over de geschiedenis van de HH. Martelaren van Gorcum," *De Katholiek* 88 (1885): 58–63.

21. *Dagboek Jacobsz.*, 1:21–50, and 48 for the quote.

22. Tracy, *Holland Under Habsburg Rule*; Van Nierop, "Troon van Alva," 219–22; Israel, *Dutch Republic*, who stresses Holland's internal differences, 170, with the accent on a less divided nobility and a stronger Protestant base. Cf. Geyl, *Revolt of the Netherlands*, 119–44.

were in the minority, anti-Spanish sentiment ran high, as did resentment of the oligarchic, conservative magistrates of the major towns. Still, most towns in Holland went over to Orange under pressure of the Sea Beggars rather than by spontaneous uprisings in favor of rebellion, which happened only in the cities of Enkhuizen and Vlissingen.[23] Orange was quick to respond to the urban conquests sweeping both Holland and Zeeland, and began to exercise his erstwhile authority as their stadholder and as Utrecht's, even though legally he had forfeited these appointments on his exile and had been replaced by Maximilien de Henin, Count of Bossu. On April 14, 1572, only two weeks after the seizure of Den Briel, Orange issued a stirring protest to his fellow Netherlanders against the "present slavery of cruel, foreign, and bloodthirsty oppressors." It was replete with the increasingly familiar evocation of ancient "rights and liberties," of the need to defend the "fatherland" against "Spaniards, bishops, and inquisitors" intent on imperiling townsmen and "your wives and daughters." The rhetoric was sharp and smart, and noticeably directed to the artisans and craftsmen invested in the domestic and property order of Low Country cities. These heads of the small republics of so many households were portrayed as pitted against a rapacious external and clerical enemy in whom the threats of sexual and physical violence merged. In Orange's words, it was a fight for "liberty of conscience, fatherland, life, wife, child, privileges, rights, and goods."[24] His was a declaration of the Revolt whose new watchword would be the imperiled urban realm—the *ghemeente* so commonly invoked in the late-medieval discourse of civic political life.[25]

Despite their Catholic majority, Zeeland and Holland became the new center of gravity for Orange and the Revolt, while the external pressure of the Sea Beggars and Bossu's pursuit of them provoked internal realignments of power in the various cities. Vlissingen—

---

23. Henk van Nierop, "Confessional Cleansing: Why Amsterdam did not Join the Revolt (1572–1578)," in *Power and the City in the Netherlandic World*, ed. Wayne Te Brake and Wim Klooster (Leiden, 2006), 85–102; a case study of an internal urban realignment that brought the Beggars to power is C. C. Hibbens, *Gouda in Revolt: Particularism and Pacificism in the Revolt of the Netherlands, 1572–1588* (Utrecht, 1983), important because Gouda had gone over early to Orange in 1572, though it had not been a source of trouble in 1566.

24. *Corr. Taciturne*, 6:297–301. It was in Hendrik Geldorp's 1571 *Belgicae liberandae ab Hispanis Hypodeixis, ad P. P. D. Gulielmum Nassavium, principem Aurantium* that Orange was first referred to as "father of the fatherland"; for an excerpt and translation, see *Texts Revolt*, 92. On the elevation of Orange as leader of the Revolt, see also H. Cellarius, "Die Propagandatätigkeit Wilhelms von Oranien in Dillenburg 1568 im Dienste des niederländischen Aufstandes," *Nassauische Annalen* 78 (1968): 119–48; R. van Roosbroeck, "Over een anoniem manifest, 1571," *Bijdragen tot de Geschiedenis* 17 (1926): 72–78; and G. Schmidt, "Des Prinzen Vaterland? Wilhelm I. von Oranien zwischen Reich, Deutscher Nation und den Niederlanden," in *Deutschland und Europa in der Neuzeit. Festschrift für Karl Otmar Freiherr von Aretin zum 65 Geburtstag*, ed. R. Melville et al. (Wiesbaden, 1988), 223–39.

25. On this civic sensibility, see Marc Boone, "'Cette frivole, dampnable et desraisonnable bourgeoisie.' De vele gezichten van het laatmiddeleeuwse burgerbegrip in de Zuidelijke Nederlanden," in *Burger: Een geschiedenis van het begrip 'burger' in de Nederlanden van de Middeleeuwen tot de 21ste eeuw*, ed. Joost Kloek and Karin Tilmans (Amsterdam, 2002), 33–53.

its unfinished citadel a symbol of Alba's supervision of urban space—became the second city to rebel, on April 6. When the more important Enkhuizen took up the Beggars' cause in early June, the tide turned. By the time Bossu summoned the Estates of Holland together in The Hague in July, of the six cities that traditionally dominated the representative body, only Amsterdam and Delft remained in the loyalist camp. In a counter gesture, the other rebel cities gathered on July 19 in Dordrecht and proclaimed their allegiance to Orange as their true *stadholder*, a critical first step in their eventual abrogation of royal authority.[26] At the same time, Orange's brother Louis of Nassau had opened a southern front in the rebellion. Bolstered by French Huguenot support, he seized Mons in Hainault, while the Count van den Berg entered the central Netherlands via Germany, capturing Zutphen on June 10. By late summer, the provinces were engulfed in warfare. But the expectation of further help from the French Huguenots collapsed with the August 24 Saint Bartholomew's Day Massacre and the death of Coligny.[27] Despite this great blow, Orange's campaign did not falter as it had done in 1568, and the urban-rich terrain of the southern and northern Low Countries became the site of prolonged sieges, terrifying sacks, and chilling violence.

The City Despoiled

After five years of incessant fighting, the beginning of 1577 saw the possibility of a reprieve. The new Habsburg governor general, Don Juan of Austria, agreed to the Pacification of Ghent and the departure of the Army of Flanders from the Low Countries if the States General recognized his authority and confirmed the public observation of Catholicism. This deal, struck on January 27, raised hopes, but then disintegrated. Neither Orange nor the Estates of Holland and Zeeland supported the accord, suspecting that the Pacification guaranteed neither their rights and privileges nor the free expression of Calvinism.[28] Frustrated, Don Juan recalled the troops and reignited conflict. Thus was in-

---

26. R. C. Bakhuizen van den Brink, "Eerste vergadering der Staten van Holland (19 Juli 1572), in his *Van Hollandsche Potaard: Studiën en fragmenten* (Brussels, 1943), 201–28; Koenigsberger, *Monarchies, States Generals and Parliaments*, 246–47; for Marnix's instructions, see R. C. Bakhuizen van den Brink, *Cartons voor de geschiedenis van den Nederlandschen vrijheidsoorlog* 2 vols. (The Hague, 1891–1898), 1:190–94; J. C. Boogman, "De overgang van Gouda, Dordrecht, Leiden en Delft in de zomer van het jaar 1572," *Tijdschrift voor Geschiedenis* 57 (1942): 81–109. For the role Holland's fiscal policies played in securing the borders of its province and ensuring its political and economic separateness, see James Tracy, *The Founding of the Dutch Republic: War, Finance, and Politics in Holland, 1572–1588* (New York, 2008).

27. On the military history, see Parker, *Dutch Revolt*, 131–42. For the intense preparations for warfare, correspondence with actual and potential supporters, and exchanges among the Nassau brothers, see volumes 3 and 4 of *Archives d'Orange-Nassau* that cover the years 1567–74.

28. The transcript of a meeting between Orange, his deputies from Holland and Zeeland, and Don Juan's negotiators at Geertruidenberg in May 1577 to discuss their differences over the Pacification and its

augurated a confusing period of claims and counterclaims of authority by Orange, by the States General, by its own new hand-picked governor general, Archduke Matthias (nephew of Philip II), and by Don Juan, who had never relinquished power. As complicated as the political landscape became, one core sentiment prevailed: the Netherlanders' virulent hatred of the Army of Flanders. This was true even among certain conservatives like the Duke of Aarschot, who was worn out by the soldiers' depredations, sacks, and mutinies.[29] Even that central organ of Habsburg authority, the Council of State, had been forced by popular outcry on July 27, 1576, to declare all mutineers rebels—an edict broadened by the States General on September 22 to include *all* Army of Flanders soldiers.[30]

When the second phase of the Dutch Revolt began in 1572, anger had been directed against Alba as the source of all misdeeds, just as it had been directed against Granvelle during the first troubles in the 1560s. By the mid-1570s, Netherlanders saw the Army of Flanders as the greatest troublemaker. This vast assemblage of fighting men, their providers, and their camp followers was a heterogeneous mix of infantry and cavalry, of the top *maestros del campo* (commanders), pike men, harquebusiers, and common foot soldiers, of men drawn from as faraway as Naples and as close as the Netherlands itself, an ethnic mosaic of Spaniards, Italians, Burgundians, Netherlanders, and Germans. In fact, at the peak of fighting in 1576, the infantry of the Army of Flanders consisted of 21,226 Germans, 22,616 Netherlanders, and only 6,125 Spaniards.[31] To the rebel propagandists, however, the Army of Flanders was Spanish *tout court*—true only insofar as they were Philip II's forces and were commanded mostly by Spanish senior officers.

None of these details mattered to the author of "a new ballad" composed in 1577. In a series of cleverly rhymed stanzas, the balladeer catalogued the misdeeds of the "Spanish soldiers" since their arrival in 1567, opening with a lachrymose paean to the ruin of the Netherlands' riches which, as we have seen, had become a central concern of print and visual propaganda:

> O Netherlands, Netherlands! Noble place,
> Your magnificent crown above all other lands,

---

implementation has survived. See "Vraye narration de costé et d'aultre entre les députez de Don Jehan et monseigneur le prince et députez de Hollande et Zeelande," in *Representative Government in Western Europe in the Sixteenth Century*, ed. G. Griffiths (Oxford, 1968), 452–62.

29. On the mutinies, see Parker, *Army of Flanders*, 185–206, and his "Mutiny and Discontent in the Spanish Army of Flanders, 1572–1607," in *Spain and the Netherlands, 1559–1659: Ten Studies*, ed. Geoffery Parker (London, 1979), 106–21, both of which explore such mutinies within the broader tradition of early modern forms of popular protest.

30. P. Génard. ed., *La furie espagnole: Documents pour servir à l'histoire du sac d'Anvers en 1576*, in *Annales de l'Académie d'archéologie de Belgique* 32, 3rd ser., vol. 2 (1876): 159–62, for the text of the September 22 decree and for the general context.

31. Figures from Parker, *Army of Flanders*, appendix A, 271.

A lovely, bejeweled spot, you were considered;
Nowhere else had such riches and treasure,
Where many acquired money,
So that all powerful merchants eagerly sought you.
They came to the Netherlands to seek prosperity,
Because you had such abundant profit;
But with bloody tears I must report,
That you so highly esteemed have now fallen;
In you so many had grown prosperous,
Living in peace and rest.
Now one sees everyone ultimately consigned to sighing and trembling with fear,
Because those who came to this land as friends want to ruin it.[32]

The balladeer recounts how the soldiers began their "tyrannical labor" by imprisoning noblemen and hounding ordinary citizens, so that their "friendship" was nothing more than a pure desire to pillage. "Wolves in sheepskin," the soldiers ravaged cities, stole goods, held citizens for ransom, raped women and girls without discrimination, even plundered religious houses, not unlike the iconoclasts. The balladeer builds narrative momentum as he reviews the cities desecrated: first Mechelen in 1572, but then, among others, Zutphen, Naarden, Haarlem, Aalst, and in 1576 Antwerp, the apex of mutinous violence. The ballad ends with a patriotic call to oust the "bits of bacon"—a slur on the Spanish as swine—from the Netherlands and place trust in Orange.[33]

With its catalogue of cities that fell victim to sieges, sacks, or mutinies, the "new ballad" makes clear that as peace faltered and fighting raged on, writers in the mid- to late 1570s were shaping a new chapter in the emerging storyline of the Dutch Revolt. Cities besieged by the Army of Flanders between 1572 and 1577 became the stuff of legend, hallowed sites of unspeakable violence and heroic suffering, their resistance made famous by the Revolt's earliest historians, Emanuel van Meteren and Pieter Bor, and by the local

---

32. Opening stanza of "Een nieu balade," part of a sixteenth-century bundle of poems, refrains, and ballads, the majority concerning Orange and Ghent in the late 1570s, now at the University of Ghent Library, Handschriftenzaal, MS. no. 583, published by Ph. Blommaert, *Politieke Balladen, Refereinen, Liederen en Spotgedichten, der XVI eeuw* (Ghent, 1847), 1–11.

33. On the meaning of *spekken*, see Swart, "The Black Legend during the Eighty Years' War," 49. Swart understood "spekken" to refer originally to the Beggars, but according to Meijer Drees, *Andere landen, andere mensen: De beeldvorming van Holland versus Spanje en Engeland omstreeks 1650* (The Hague, 1997), 96, the term referred more generally to lean, hungry people, and was applied originally to the Spanish soldiers, who ravaged the land. In all likelihood, the slang term carried meaning because of its punning quality: it described someone who was ravenous and also referenced swine or pigs. The slur "spek" was closely allied with the Netherlanders' appropriation of the Spanish "Marrano," a term originally applied to Christianized Jews in Iberia but which Netherlanders used generally to describe their Spanish enemies.

chroniclers and balladeers who preceded them.[34] In contrast to critiques of corrupt councilors or the specter of the Inquisition that had so preoccupied pamphleteers in the 1560s, by 1572 the threat that Spanish officials posed to long-cherished political rights and privileges became a more central concern of their writing.[35] Cities were the great repositories and beneficiaries of these much-touted rights and privileges, making their sieges and sacks not merely morally odious but sources of enormous legal and political worry. Urban sacks also ravaged a city's economic welfare as well as its charters of liberties, and much of the popular denunciations of them focused in straightforward, urgent fashion on these problems. But not all the protest against such violence was couched in the language of legal charter and economic privilege. Contemporaries such as the graphic artist Frans Hogenberg or chroniclers such as Bor and Van Meteren seized on the imaginary of the household imperiled—women raped, men murdered, children orphaned, goods pilfered—as the signature of the Army of Flanders.

This domestic rendering of an urban sack or siege tapped into established artistic genres, gender hierarchies, and literary motifs. Fundamental was Roman imperial violence against cities and its prose accounts by Tacitus and Livy, especially their use of the Latin *diripio*, a term that simultaneously invoked the physical violence of the sack and sexual violence of rape that usually accompanied it.[36] Concern about the rapacity of an occupying Spanish force was nothing new in the Low Countries, since there had been complaints in the early 1560s before the Revolt broke out about the conduct of the three thousand Spanish troops stationed in the Low Countries by Philip II when he departed for Castile in 1559. In 1560 Granvelle himself told Philip II's secretary that popular sentiment was building against the Spanish soldiers, and that they were perceived as a threat to privileges and freedoms.[37] The garrisons became such a political headache that Philip II had the men reassigned to the Mediterranean in January 1561—a political victory that was not lost on the Netherlanders facing the enormous Army of Flanders in the 1570s. What is more, outcries about the violence done by an army against urban domestic life was hardly specific to the Spanish during the Dutch Revolt. Such concern was voiced regularly elsewhere, including

---

34. Van Meteren published the earliest pieces of his work in Dutch in 1599; for Bor, the date was 1595. These works were greatly elaborated and brought out in handsome folio editions in the seventeenth century. On these two, as well as Everhard van Reyd, as the first historians of the Dutch Revolt, see A. E. M. Janssen, "A 'Trias Historica' on the Revolt of the Netherlands."

35. On the pamphleteers' focus on rights and privileges, see Geurts, *Nederlandse Opstand in de pamfletten*, 149–51; and especially, Van Gelderen, *Political Thought*, 115–32, and Martin Van Gelderen, "Conceptions of Liberty during the Dutch Revolt (1555–1590)," *Parliaments, Estates and Representation* 9 (1989): 137–53.

36. Adam Ziolkowski, "*Urbs direpta*, or how the Romans Sacked Cities," in *War and Society in the Roman World*, ed. John Rich and Graham Shipley (London 1993), 69–91.

37. *Corr. Philippe II*, 1:90. Cf. Strada, *Thien eerste boecken der Nederlandsche Oorlogen*, 1:132. See also E. van Autenboer, "De houding der Nederlanders en bijzonder der Mechelaars tegenover de Spaansche troepen in 1560," *Mechelse Bijdragen* 3 (1943): 87–98.

the fifteenth-century Burgundian period in the Low Countries, when cities fell victim to ducal reprisals. During Charles the Bold's campaign against Liège in 1468, the chronicler and canon of Saint Martin's, Theodoricus Pauli (Thierry Pauwels), recounted the cruel slaughter of men, women, and children and the random mutilation of their corpses in the same emotional pitch as rebels later sounded when describing Alba's assaults.[38]

Outcry against the Army of Flanders invoked older traditions, such as the biblical story of the Massacre of Innocents (Mathew 2:16–18), studied by the art historian David Kunzle, as well as classical lore such as the rape of Cassandra in the Trojan war as metaphor for military conquest, and the rape of Lucretia as foundational tale of the Roman Republic. The tropes about domestic disorder and rape that memorialists in the Netherlands invoked in decrying urban pillage were not so much novel as put to rhetorical work at a defining moment in the Revolt when such exhortations were pertinent.[39] The now problematic trademarks of the Beggars and the iconoclasts could be set aside in favor of the most enduring political symbol in the Netherlands: the civic patriot fighting on behalf of the commune against princely transgressions. Not only did this draw on urban valor and civic virtue, the richest sources of political identity in Dutch political culture, but it gained weight by its reference to family and household—a master image in the Protestant social ethic and in the guild governments of the late-medieval cities.[40] This formulation worked so well because it not only replicated the conceptual vocabulary of a centuries-deep tradition of urban dissent; it also played to the cultural conceits and legal realities of the guild masters and small craftsmen who bulked large in the political and economic life of the cities.[41] Their fight against tyranny was rendered direct, personal, and visceral by the use of domestic analogies and metaphors: these heads of households, masters of home and *ateliers*, took up the fight to protect children, women, property, and family against a king who had forfeited his paternal duties. The exhortations of the Patriots on behalf of the im-

---

38. Theodoricus Pauli, *De Cladibus Leodiensium*, in *Documents relatifs aux Troubles du Pays de Liège*, 224.

39. Diane Wolfthal, *Images of Rape: The "Heroic" Tradition and Its Alternatives* (Cambridge, 1999), 60–62; David Kunzle, *The Soldier in Netherlandish Art, 1550–1670* (Leiden, 2002). On rape and nationhood in the Dutch Republic, see Amanda Cathryn Pipkin, "Every Woman's Fear: Stories of Rape and Dutch Identity in the Golden Age," (PhD diss., Rutgers University, 2007), esp. 1–52. On the republican leanings of Low Country civic life, especially the influence of civic humanism and the valorization of the free citizen, see Karin Tilmans, "Republican Citizenship and Civic Humanism in the Burgundian-Habsburg Netherlands (1477–1566)," in *Republicanism*, 2:107–26.

40. On the household moralism and gender valences of the Reformation, see Lyndal Roper, *The Holy Household: Women and Morals in Reformation Augsburg* (Oxford, 1989); and Merry Weisner, "Family, Household and Community," in *Handbook of European History in the Later Middle Ages, Renaissance and Reformation, 1400–1600*, ed. Thomas A. Brady Jr., Heiko A. Oberman, and James Tracy (Leiden, 1994), 51–78.

41. Boone and Prak, "Rulers, Patricians and Burghers." On the tradition of urban revolt, and on late medieval guild culture and protest, see Marc Boone, "'Armes, coursses, assemblees et commocions': Les gens de métiers et l'usage de la violence dans la société urbaine flamande à la fin du moyen âge," *Revue du Nord* 87 (2005): 7–33.

periled city undoubtedly drew additional inspiration from such tributes to civic republicanism as the 1566 *De foelice et infoelici republica* of Frans Goethals that praised Bruges as a "republic of artisans" rich in constitutional liberties. But the Patriots did so with tales of very real urban desecrations, giving popular voice to the still relatively minor genre of Low Country civic humanism.[42]

What is more, memorializations of the sexual and domestic transgressions of the urban sacks were particularly well timed for the Patriots. These protests emerged just as the king was being discredited—the Estates of Holland were actively considering Philip II's repudiation by October 1575—and as some in Reformed political circles were touting William of Orange as a new *pater familias* to fill the vacuum left by the removal of the paternal sovereign.[43] The city besieged became symbol of a world gone awry, of a political order overturned as the result of so many domestic assaults; William of Orange the new father of the fatherland was touted as one who could restore cherished rights and privileges and secure peace. The prince's struggle for fraternal rights had a bedrock legitimacy because it was rooted not merely in abstract principles or local interests, but in something more viscerally fundamental: the prince's own family. Orange fought as part of a cohort of brothers: the senior of five brothers allied in a common cause, three of whom would meet their end on the battlefield, while William himself would succumb to an assassin's bullet in 1584.[44] The brothers' union of purpose and sacrifice resonated with the fraternal-soaked imagery long associated with metaphors of classical republicanism, while it eerily resonated for Calvinists—as the Leiden rhetorician Jan Fruytiers pointed out in 1574—with the five Jewish Maccabee brothers of the second century BCE and their fight against tyranny and idolatry.[45]

Sieges and sacks were so common to sixteenth-century warfare that there existed among military theorists protocols for plundering a city, typically allowed when townspeople defied an order to surrender.[46] The cities of the Low Countries had experienced their share, as in the example of Liège in 1468, when Charles the Bold gave his forces free

42. Tilmans, "Republican Citizenship and Civic Humanism," esp. 122–23, and Franciscus Goethalsius, *De Foelici et Infoelici Republica, ad Senatum Brugensem* (Louvain, 1566), fol. 46r.

43. On October 13, 1575, the Estates discussed the possibility of the abjuration of Philip II. See Koenigsberger, *Monarchies, States Generals and Parliament*, 258, and in general on the Estates of Holland in this crucial period, J. W. Koopmans, *De Staten van Holland en de Opstand: De ontwikkeling van hun functies en organisatie in de periode 1544–1588* (The Hague, 1990).

44. *Archives d'Orange-Nassau*, 4:xliv–xlv.

45. Jan Fruytiers, *Corte beschryvinghe vande strenghe Belegheringhe ende wonderbaerlicke Verlossinghe der Stadt Leyden in Hollandt*, first published in Delft in 1574, reproduced in facsimile in Robert Fruin, et al., eds., *De oude verhalen van het beleg en ontzet van Leiden* (The Hague, 1874), 19–20. My thanks to Anton van der Lem for this reference to the Maccabees in the account by Fruytiers.

46. Best known is the 1527 sack of Rome, for which see André Chatel, *The Sack of Rome, 1527*, trans. B. Archer (Princeton, 1983), and Kenneth Gouwens, *Remembering the Renaissance: Humanist Narratives of the Sack of Rome* (Leiden, 1998).

reign to loot, although he ordered the relics of Saint Lambert guarded. Already by 1440, defiant cities that rebelled against their Burgundian overlord risked being labeled guilty of the crime of *lèse-majesté* and incurring the fullest punishment: a razing or a sack.[47] Furthermore, in the wars of the Dutch Revolt, trouble among poorly treated and often unpaid soldiers was not limited to the Army of Flanders. Orange grumbled about his own soldiers. In a September 13, 1573 letter to his brothers Louis and Jan, he complained that a sense of obedience among his troops was sorely wanting, especially among the French and English, because of modest wages and delinquent pay. Nor were Orange's men without their own acts of revenge. In August 1573, Leiden's magistrates complained to Orange on two occasions that his garrison troops were guilty of rape, of meddling with public meetings, and of threatening sacks to such a degree that they feared a popular uprising against these men.[48]

The sacks engaged in by the Army of Flanders, however, were particularly galling to Netherlanders because they occurred not only against rebellious cities such as Haarlem, but also against those that had offered an olive branch or had stayed, if warily, in the royalist camp.[49] Their counterpart was sieges, prolonged square-offs of militia and garrisons against companies of the army that could stretch out for months, as happened in Haarlem, Alkmaar, and Leiden in 1573 and 1574. These cities' half-wasted and defiant citizenry became in the hands of pamphleteers and chroniclers paragons of urban defiance, of a domestic order brave and united in opposition to Spanish victory. Dolorous reports of cities punished mercilessly were therefore balanced by triumphalist accounts of urban victory, most famously in the songs of the Beggars.[50] Alba's plunder of Mechelen that began on October 2, 1572, was the first great sack decried by the Patriots. Because it was particularly audacious—the city had tried to appease Alba and welcome him—and purposely exemplary, the sack gained the attention of pamphleteers and chroniclers, whose accounts made it the epitome of soldierly violence.[51]

---

47. Boone, "Urban Space in Late Medieval Flanders," 645. See, more generally, the collection of essays on urban desecrations and reconstructions from the medieval to the modern era in *Destruction et Reconstruction de villes, du Moyen Age à nos jours / Verwoesting end Wederopbouw van steden, van middeleeuwen tot heden*, Gemeentekrediet, Brussels, n. 100 (Brussels, 1999), with an introduction by Martin Körner, 7–20.

48. Swart, *William of Orange*, 54–55. Seizing Geertruidenberg in Brabant in 1573 without losses on their side, Orange's men "did not touch the goods or property" of the town yet "cut the throats" of the garrison of about one hundred and sixty men. See *Archives d'Orange-Nassau*, 4:196–97.

49. Jean-Léon Charles, "Le sac des villes dans les Pays-Bas au XVIe siècle: Étude critique des règles de guerre," *Revue Internationale d'Histoire Militaire*, 24 (1965): 288–310. The Spanish soldier and diplomat, Bernardino de Mendoza, justified the 1572 sack of Naarden according to these protocols. See Bernardino de Mendoza, *Commentaires*, 2 vols. (Brussels, 1860–63), 2:33–34. For a review of the sacks under Alba, see also L. van der Essen, *Kritisch onderzoek betreffende de oorlogvoering van het Spaanse Leger in de Nederlanden in de XVI eeuw, nl. de bestraffing van opstandige steden* (Brussels, 1950).

50. These are collected in GB, and NG, vol. 2, excerpted from the *Geuzenliedboeken* and additional sources.

51. On the sack of Mechelen, see Guido Marnef, *Het Calvinistisch Bewind te Mechelen, 1580–85* (Kortrijk-

Mechelen was the seat of Granvelle's archbishopric and the city in whose Renaissance palace Charles V was raised and young William of Orange had served as a page. But the once loyal city had opened its gates to Orange's lieutenant Bernard van Merode on August 29, 1572 over the objections of the city's sheriff. Orange himself arrived on September 18 and garrisoned the city with three hundred infantry and five hundred cavalry under the command of Van Merode, before his departure five days later.[52] Alba's men marched on the city later that month. Well aware their forces were not sufficient, Van Merode and his men retreated on October 1; so too, if Morillon's account to Granvelle is accurate, did thousands of the city's citizens.[53] When Alba appeared before the city gates on October 2 a nervous delegation of ecclesiastics and citizens processed before him intoning penitential psalms. Alba ignored these entreaties and decided to allow his men "to refresh themselves a little," probably to ease their frustration over back pay owed and because they had not been allowed to loot Mons.[54] Before the incense swinging and psalms were finished, Alba's troops were scrambling over the city's walls.

The plunder was spectacular. An eyewitness to events, Jean Richardot, still spoke of it dramatically four years after the event: "One could say a lot more about it if the horror of it did not make one's hair stand on end—not at recounting it, but just at remembering it!"[55] Alba himself boasted to Philip II that the sack was so thorough that "not a nail was left in the wall."[56] For three days, Alba's men ransacked, pillaged, stole, ransomed, and assaulted. That clergy and Catholic religious objects were among the people and items the soldiers assaulted clearly infuriated eyewitnesses like the contemporary author of an anonymous, dramatic account, himself a foe of the Patriots, who reported that the rioting

---

Heule, 1987), 79–85; Henri Installé, "Verwoesting en wederopbouw te Mechelen in de zestiende eeuw," in *Verwoesting en wederopbouw van steden*, 155–184, esp. 161; E. van Autenboer, "Mechelen in de 16de eeuw: Schade wordt toegebracht en hersteld," in *Koninklijke Kring voor Oudheidkunde, Letteren en Kunst van Mechelen* 89 (1985): 197–242; and Craig Harline and Eddy Put, *A Bishop's Tale: Mathias Hovius among his Flock in Seventeenth-Century Flanders* (New Haven, 2000), 14–15. For sixteenth-century accounts, see *Mechelen met verraedt ingenomen 12 Augusti 1572*, Bibliothèque Royale de Belgique, MS. 6203, fols. 21r–30v, an overview of the sack by an anti-Orange partisan nevertheless horrified by the destruction; *Waerachtige beschryvinge van de destructie geschiet binnen de stadt Mechelen gedaan by den Spaingaerden in den jaer 1572*, Bibliothèque Royale de Belgique, MS. 17219–20, 2r–19v, written anonymously in Antwerp in 1581; and an eyewitness to the violence of the Army of Flanders, "Discours du pillage de Malines fait le 2e Octobre, 1572," in *Mengelingen van Historisch-Vaderlandschen Inhoud*, ed. J. F. Willems (Antwerp, 1827–30), 391–422. For military events, see Maltby, *Alba*, 225–61; Parker, *Dutch Revolt*, 139–40.

52. On Orange and Mechelen, see Marie-Ange Delen, *Hof en hofcultuur rondom Willem van Oranje (1533–1584)* (Amsterdam, 2000); on events, Marnef, *Calvinistisch Bewind te Mechelen*, 79–82.

53. *Corr. Granvelle*, 4:454, letter of October 17, 1572.

54. Quote in Parker, *Dutch Revolt*, 141.

55. This quote is well known, from L. P. Gachard, ed., *Rapport sur les différents séries de documents concernant l'histoire de la Belgique qui sont conservées dans les archives à Lille* (Brussels, 1841), 234. It is cited in Parker, *Dutch Revolt*, 141, whose translation I use, and in Motley, *Rise of the Dutch Republic*, 2:410.

56. *Corr. Philippe II*, 2:263.

soldiers "first killed several men and women, forcing open the doors of houses, and sacking randomly everyone and everything they encountered, be it the goods and persons of the officers of the Grand Council [the Burgundian Parliament], the clergy, the nobility, women and girls, widows and good Catholics, rich and poor alike."[57] The soldiers stole or destroyed reliquaries, altar clothes, precious jewels, priestly vestments, and the damask, velvet, and other luxurious outfits in which the city's statues of the Virgin Mary were dressed for feast days; the author even described how soldiers threw the holy wafers on the ground as they took chalices.[58] Mechelen's future bishop, Mathias Hovius, was with his parishioners when soldiers burst into his parish church, ransacked its holy objects, and even put a knife to the chest of the young priest as he heard confession from a woman, obliging him to hand over some coins.[59] But the soldiers exercised some discernment, leaving untouched the reliquary of Saint Rombout that housed the relics of the city's beloved saint, honored in an annual Eastertime procession.[60] No such caution, by contrast, was exercised in their violence against people and their goods. The eyewitness claimed scores were assaulted and killed, and women raped.[61] An anonymous memorialist of the sack, writing in 1581, lamented that the looting soldiers "spared neither friend nor foe, widow or orphan, young or old, poor or rich" and even tortured some men, hanging them by their testicles and castrating several.[62] Lest one suspect propagandistic exaggeration on the part of this Patriot, the eyewitness in Mechelen confirmed the same. He also described how women were hung by their breasts, how married women and young girls were raped and how a pregnant woman was stabbed in the stomach, this violent assault inducing labor and resulting in a premature infant who died almost immediately.[63] Loot was carted off to other cities. A year later, magistrates were still beseeching the help of other cities in recovering "the ciboria, chalices, and other goods" the sackers had taken away and sold.[64]

On October 4, Alba published a defense of the sack as just deserts for Mechelen's earlier acclaim for Orange.[65] The duke failed to erase the sting, especially since the sack vio-

57. "Discours du Pillage de Malines," 404.
58. Ibid., 407.
59. Ibid., 410, and Harline and Put, A Bishop's Tale, 14–15.
60. "Discours du Pillage de Malines," 409. On Saint Rombout, see E. van Autenboer, Volksfeesten en Rederijkers te Mechelen (1400–1600) (Ghent, 1962), 30–31.
61. "Discours du Pillage de Malines," 415.
62. Waerachtige beschryvinge, 9r–10v.
63. "Discours du Pillage de Malines," 414.
64. Van Autenboer, "Mechelen in de 16de eeuw," 202. The emphasis on both rape and the destruction of church property echoes polemical commemorations of the sack of Rome in 1527: André Chastel, The Sack of Rome, 1527, trans. Beth Archer (Princeton, 1983), 36.
65. Verklaringe der rechtveerdige saken van de plonderinge geschied in de stad Mechelen in Bor, Oorsprongk, 1: 409–10.

lated written codes of conduct, because Mechelen had not resisted Alba. Commentators ranging from contemporaries of the sack to nineteenth-century historians like Motley emphasized the ironic point that in their looting, breaking, stealing, and other acts of aggression, particularly against religious objects, Alba's soldiers resembled none other than the iconoclasts of 1566.[66] This criticism was not entirely new, and it resonates with the charges Catholic writers leveled against Charles V's imperial troops who sacked Rome in 1527, though in this famous case it was the Germans who were blamed the most because they were deemed Lutherans.[67] In the Netherlands, the Catholic Marcus van Vaernewijck had reported that Ghentenars condemned soldiers in the city as "church breakers" in 1567.[68] During the 1573 siege of Haarlem, the Catholic prior Wouter Jacobsz. blamed the Spanish failure of a quick victory on their sinful behavior, including the plundering of churches, altars, and statues:

> It was reported widely that the leaders of the army gambled daily and led lewd lives. The soldiers went continually from one village to another, plundering not only the houses of the inhabitants and the belongings of the church, but also smashing the holy altars, and destroying the statues; indeed they did not scruple to treat the holy sacraments irreverently. Their way of life was such that it was greatly to be feared that the same had been an important reason for this wretched defeat. Keeping the law of the holy church and her ordinances meant absolutely nothing to them.[69]

The fate of Mechelen gained added attention when the industrious Hogenberg issued a print. As the accompanying German text makes clear, the emphasis is on plunder, with goods carted off in large bundles and baskets and, in the lower left, a chest forced open. Hogenberg did not, however, portray any of the religious objects attacked or stolen, but zeroed in on the physical violence against persons, placing two destitute, naked women and their children in the print's foreground. Unlike other contemporary graphic prints, including the 1572 portrait of Orange and Alba, Hogenberg's two women and children in Mechelen are not simply allegorical representations of lofty abstractions, such as The Netherlands or Everyman. They serve as poignant instances of the very real violence done against specific persons and groups, especially the family. The city as a community of so many independent households had been rent asunder, the men slain, their artisanal and merchant wealth plundered, their wives raped, and their children left destitute.

When the historian Pieter Bor, whose first volumes on the great panorama of the trou-

66. Motley, *Rise of the Dutch Republic*, 2:409–10.
67. See, for example, Balthasar Castiglione's letter, written in his capacity as papal nuncio, to Alfonso de Valdés, apologist for the sack, in John Longhurst, ed., *Alfonso de Valdés and the Sack of Rome: Dialogue of Lactancio and an Archdeacon* (Albuquerque, 1952), 103–8.
68. BT Van Vaernewijck, 3:16.
69. *Dagboek Jacobsz.*, 1:166.

The plundering of Mechelen in 1572 with destitute women and children in the foreground. Frans Hogenberg. Courtesy of the private collection of Karel Kinds.

bles were published at the end of the sixteenth century, briefly described the sack of Mechelen, rape was his leitmotif of this "fury." Girls and women were sexually assaulted, often in front of their parents or husbands.[70] Similarly, years before Bor wrote his account and even before the Mechelen sack itself, Marnix, Lord of St. Aldegonde had railed in his 1570 *A Defense and True Declaration of the Things Lately Done in the Low Country* against troops of the Army of Flanders who "might violently abuse the riches, wives, children and lives of the citizens, according to their evil lust." He spoke of the soldiers' "fury," their pillage of men's coffers, rape of their wives, and murder of their children.[71] The sexual appetites of

70. Bor, *Oorsprongk*, 1:409.
71. *A Defence and True Declaration of the Things Lately Done in the Low Country whereby may easily be seen to whom all the Beginning and Cause of the Late Troubles and Calamities is to be Imputed*, the 1571 English translation of the 1570 Latin text in Van Gelderen, *Dutch Revolt*, 59–60.

the Spanish soldiers factored too into Orange's 1572 remonstrance: "Your wives have been subjected to the disgraceful embracements of the circumcised Moors . . . and your daughters have been given love potions with the result that they have lost all their senses and made the most shameful love with these unchaste rogues."[72]

In his conflation of the sexual and political dangers that the Spanish represented, Orange made explicit the allure of the soldier. The sack of Mechelen gave this motif a darker, violent hue with its story of plunder and forced sexual violence, of a domestic order violated. The urban, propertied man—craftsman or merchant—was the targeted reader of such accounts, the subject whose dependents—adult women and children—and goods had been so viciously assaulted. In his *Defense and True Declaration*, Marnix played on familial emotions, accusing Alba of dissolving Reformed marriages, rendering their offspring illegitimate, forcing new marriages that were in fact bigamous and adulterous, and even compelling widows against their will to marry his "cut-throat" soldiers.[73] Between the soldiers' violence and Alba's legal, financial, and religious policies, the domestic order had been torn apart, a potent analogy to the ungluing of the political order. The legal principles that protected the urban subject and his wealth were the municipal privileges of the Low Countries, ensuring that the trio of household, marketplace, and town hall ran smoothly. In Mechelen in 1572, these rights fell victim to Alba and his men. As part of the punishment, the duke had the city's privileges confiscated, its magistrates dismissed, and its guilds—including its military guilds of archers and crossbowmen, the *schuttersgilden*—abolished. In tandem with the assaults on persons, households, and livelihoods, Alba had overturned Mechelen's political order, restored only by his successor Requesens in 1574 as part of a general pardon.[74]

As important as the classical tropes and the domestic analogy were in the accounts of Mechelen's sack, these tales of murder, rape, and pillage also owed much to reports of Spanish depredation in the Americas, especially the *Brevíssima Relación de la Destrucción de las Indias* by Bartholomé de Las Casas, which was translated into Dutch in 1578 with the revised title *The Mirror of Spanish Tyranny* (*Spiegel der Spaensche tyrannye*). It was in subsequent Dutch editions of Las Casas—an astonishing twenty-five before 1648—that illustrations were first included. As popular as the text became and as much as it made Spanish actions in the Americas the yardstick against which Habsburg deeds in the Netherlands could be compared, *Brevíssima Relación de la Destrucción de las Indias* had been scarcely read up until the time that rebels discovered it. However, it had vibrant antecedents, including Girolamo Benzoni's *Historia del mondo nuovo* (1565), translated into many different languages, Dutch included, which popularized tales of tyranny in the

72. Quoted in Swart, "Black Legend," 50.
73. *Defence and True Declaration* is in Van Gelderen, *Dutch Revolt*, 61.
74. E. van Autenboer, "Het Algemeen Pardon van 1574 en Mechelen," *Mechelse Bijdragen. Mechelse Kring voor Oudheidkunde, Geschiedenis en Folklore*, 11 (1949): 59–75.

Americas that had been confined previously to French Calvinist circles.[75] Well before Las Casas, Dutch rebels were already referencing Spanish atrocities in the Americas. Marnix's 1570 *Defense and True Declaration*, for example, included a jeremiad to Netherlanders to pay heed to events in the "Indies," where the Spanish practiced unparalleled butchery.[76] The sack of Mechelen offered the first instance of urban butchery on local soil by the Army of Flanders. It also allowed those such as Hogenberg to offer their graphic depictions as visual narratives of rape and murder, proving the contention by Marnix and others that Spanish deeds in the faraway Americas could be replicated with the same ferocity locally.[77]

As more sacks followed on the heels of Mechelen, reports of the savagery of the Spanish soldiers took on darker hues. This was particularly true of the retributions against the small city of Zutphen in Gelderland on November 14 and Naarden in Holland on December 2. Emboldened by the victories of the Army of Flanders in Brabant, Alba had headed for Holland. Orange had fled there, deciding gloomily, as he wrote to his brother Jan, to make it his "tomb."[78] Before crossing into Holland, Alba's men pursued Orange's army in Gelderland, and on November 14 set upon the modest town of Zutphen. With a population of 7,500, the city was large enough to offer Alba a northern reprise of Mechelen's sack, to shock other rebellious cities into submission. In this goal the duke succeeded; so thorough was the plundering that other rebel pockets in Gelderland and Overijssel surrendered, with the effect felt in other provinces, most noticeably Friesland. With the northeast retaken, Alba finally turned to Zeeland and Holland. Once again, an exemplary sack served as the opening salvo to Alba's new campaign. This time the victim was Naarden in Holland's east, sacked even though its magistrates had made last-minute preparations to surrender to the Army of Flanders.[79] The sacks of Zutphen and Naarden were unalloyed in their violence, but their effects were fundamentally different. Zutphen provoked the surrender of the northeast while Naarden only stiffened Orangist opposition in the rebellious cities of Zeeland and Holland.[80] Both, however, became watchwords for Spanish butchery by rebel propagandists and early historians. The canonization of Zut-

---

75. Such analogies eventually culminated in the 1620 *Mirror of the Spanish Tyranny in the Netherlands*, a compendium of Spanish atrocities in the Netherlands whose title paralleled the Dutch translation of Las Casas's work, and whose popularity inspired twenty editions before the close of the seventeenth century, and even a primer version for school children. On the evolution of Dutch representations of the Americas, and on the use of the "Indies" as a parallel case of Spanish tyranny evoked during Alba's reign and thereafter, see Benjamin Schmidt, *Innocence Abroad: The Dutch Imagination and the New World, 1570–1670* (Cambridge, 2001), esp., 46–54, 73–88, and 95–99.

76. Van Gelderen, *Dutch Revolt*, 4, 59, from his edition of the pamphlet.

77. *De Spiegel der Spaensche Tyrannye geschiet in Nederlandt* (Amsterdam, 1620).

78. Letter of October 18, 1572, to Jan, *Archives d'Orange-Nassau*, 4:4.

79. For the two sacks and Alba's military campaign, see Maltby, *Alba*, 240–45.

80. On military events and the effects of the two sacks, see Maltby, *Alba*, 241–45, who downplays Bor's account of Naarden for its fictive stylization.

phen and Naarden as sites of Spanish desecration owes much to Hogenberg's depiction of their fate and to Alba's own harsh condemnation of the two cities—he ordered his son Fadrique to kill all of Zutphen's men and boasted to Philip II that "not a man born escaped" in Naarden. This process continued with the late sixteenth- and early seventeenth-century canonizers of the Dutch Revolt, particularly Van Meteren and Bor, and their gripping tales of rape, plunder, and grisly executions.[81]

Zutphen's sack reprised the Army of Flanders's punishment of Mechelen on a smaller yet more fierce scale. Alba's son Don Fadrique easily entered the city—the Spanish officer Bernardino de Mendoza had described Zutphen as poorly fortified—ordered the garrison killed, and then let his men indiscriminately murder and plunder. Contemporary reports about this massacre are meager, though Count Nieuwenaar wrote to Orange's brother Louis that the city had experienced a great "wail of agony" (*jammergeschrey*) at Fadrique's hands.[82] Because Zutphen's sack provoked the capitulation of the northeast, accounts about it are colored by a funereal tone. Naarden's sack and razing, by contrast, elicited wider commemoration, no doubt because it failed to dampen Holland's opposition and instead served as the agonizing prologue to the epic sieges of Haarlem, Alkmaar, and Leiden. Neither Frans Hogenberg nor Pieter Bor was an eyewitness to the sack, but both were contemporaries, born in 1538 and 1559 respectively, and each gave considerable weight to Naarden's fate. Hogenberg's illustration of Naarden's sack is even more violent than his print of Mechelen's, with depictions of murder, executions, and a raging fire and mass slaughter in the marketplace as his graphic centerpiece. Bor's written account similarly gives narrative emphasis to sexual violence and murder: the victims are raped and disemboweled.[83] In Bor's vivid description, based on the dramatic eyewitness account of Lambertus Hortensius, rector of Naarden's Latin school, Spanish trickery made this sack all the more appalling; after a delegation had offered to surrender, around five hundred townsmen were ordered to gather in the town's parish church, where they were ambushed and killed, even as their wives were preparing food to greet the Spanish forces. More plunder and murder followed this surprise massacre, as Bor highlights with stories of girls and pregnant women raped, fetuses cut out of wombs in ways that nodded to Las Casas' account of atrocities in the Americas.[84]

The Black Legendesque veneer to Bor's account is only heightened by his description

---

81. Alba on Zutphen is in *Corr. Philippe II*, 2:180, and on Naarden in Berwick y de Alba, *Epistolario Alba*, 3:261: "Degollaron burgueses y soldados sin escarpse hombre nacido."

82. *Archives d'Orange-Nassau*, 4:29, letter of November 29, 1572; Mendoza, *Commentaires*, 2:29–31; cf. Bor, *Oorsprongk*, 1:415. Lambertus Hortensius, *Over de opkomst en ondergang van Naarden*, ed. P. Peerlkamp (Utrecht, 1866).

83. Bor, *Oorsprongk*, 1:417–20.

84. Ibid. Spanish accounts differ, and Alba himself wrote to Philip II that townsmen never offered surrender. See Maltby, *Alba*, 244, and Alba's December 19, 1572, letter to Philip II *Espistolario Alba*, 3:261–62.

The sack of Naarden (Naerden) in 1572. Soldiers plunder, execute civilians, and set fire to the city. Frans Hogenberg. Courtesy of the private collection of Karel Kinds.

of the fate of the Latin rector Hortensius's illegitimate son, murdered with his heart torn out before his father's eyes. Although Hortensius's own account confirms this tragedy, it makes no mention of this gruesome form of murder. Bor was not alone in the use of this vivid analogy. Made sometime in the 1570s, a print entitled *Lament over the Desolation of the Netherlands* and attributed to Hans Collaert van Oude after an original by Ambrosius Francken featured Belgica personified as a young woman assaulted and raped by four soldiers who remove her heart. That the print's concern is the depredations by troops of the Army of Flanders is suggested not only by the depiction of four of its soldiers but also by the smoldering ruins of a building in the center background and the plunder of a village and a city to its left and right. The allegorical figures of Ambition and Greed flank the rape and murder scene; Greed's hand plunders a chest of coins, while her avarice is symbol-

Lament over the Desolation of the Netherlands ("Belgica" in Latin). Hans Collaert van Oude after Ambrosius Francken, ca. 1577. The Netherlands is personified as Belgica, a young woman murdered by four soldiers who remove her heart and steal her money. Courtesy of Stichting Atlas van Stolk, Rotterdam.

ized by a bulging money bag and keys hanging from her belt. The print's caption laments Belgica's loss of wealth and beauty at the hands of foreigners who rob her; the violent rape is symbolized by the excised heart, while the plunder of goods is symbolized by the looted chest.[85] By the mid-seventeenth century, historians such as P. C. Hooft would embellish Bor's version to accuse the Spanish of practicing cannibalism on the corpses at Naarden, valorizing this particular sack as the apex of Spanish savage tyranny.[86]

85. Tanis and Horst, *Images of Disord*, 105–6.
86. P. C. Hooft, *Neederlandsche histoorien sedert de ooverdraght der heerschappye van Kaiser Karel den Vyfden op Kooning Philips zynen zoon* (Amsterdam, 1642), 279. During the siege of Leiden, the chronicler Jan Fruytiers imputed the same behavior to a Zeeland Sea Beggar who murdered a Spanish soldier on a dike outside the besieged city, removed his heart, and sank his teeth into it. The excised heart was said to have been on display afterward in Delft. See Fruytiers, *Corte beschryvinghe*, 14. Ritual dismemberment was commonly practiced on the late-medieval battlefield, and there were tales of cannibalism. See Valentin Groebner, *Defaced: The Visual Culture of Violence in the Late Middle Ages*, trans. Pamela Selwyn (New York, 2004), 226–29, and the tales of ritual cannibalism in the punishment meted out to Pazzi conspirators against the Medici brothers, Lauro Martines, *April Blood: Florence and the Plot against the Medici* (Oxford, 2003), 145–49.

The City Defiant

As Burgundian metropolis, archbishopric, and royal residence, Mechelen was very different from modest Zutphen and Naarden. Yet no matter how distinct, all three cities stood equal in the rebels' minds by 1573 as concrete proof of Spanish tyranny. Murder, theft, and rape were compounded by the ransacking and burning of churches and town halls. But while many were cowered into submission, the Patriots marveled at how the Revolt continued to build momentum in the very cities so maltreated by the Army of Flanders. Their literature soon extolled heroic townspeople who repaired the frayed political order, fought back against their attackers, and summoned the highest *burgerlijcke* values of stoicism, courage, and can-do pugnacity. Letters and chronicles told of men who soldiered bravely, aided by children and women who exercised martial prowess and manly skills. The sieges of Haarlem, Alkmaar, and Leiden in Holland functioned in such narratives as inspiring counterweights to the pernicious sacks. Energetic urban militia and local garrisons led the resistance against better-outfitted units of the Army of Flanders, assisted by women and children who rained stones, pitch, lime, and hot oil on the heads of the foreign soldiers from the city's ramparts. The propaganda that Netherlands Patriots harvested from these military trials was metaphorically rich, and was used as a yardstick for assessing Philip II's kingship. The urban fraternal and domestic order had held its own against a mighty king whose policies could no longer be blamed on bad councilors, but rather on his own abuses. As Johan Junius de Jonghe, governor of Veere in Zeeland, gravely concluded in 1574, a prince "without his people is no prince at all."[87]

The first great siege was Alba's effort to capture Haarlem and thereby cut Holland in half.[88] It dragged on from December 1573 to the next summer, when Haarlemers finally surrendered on July 12 upon promise that the city would be sparred a sack. It was a stipulation Don Fadrique was unable to honor, when his soldiers mutinied, angered over pay owed and the miserable conditions they endured during the long, cold months of the campaign. Despite the failure to keep Haarlem in the rebel camp, and despite Orange's inability to relieve the city, the Patriots touted the city's defiance as a Herculean accomplishment. One commemorative ballad intoned:

---

87. *Sekere brieven waer inne den aenghevanghen vredehandel deses Jaers LXXIIII vervaetet is* (Delft, 1574), a collection of documents laying out Holland's and Zeeland's political position after peace negotiations with Requesens had failed at Breda, with Junius's *Discourse* included. For an analysis and the quote, see Van Gelderen, *Political Thought*, 130.

88. J. W. Wijn, *Het beleg van Haarlem* (Amsterdam, 1942); Piet Huurdeman, *Het beleg van Haarlem* (Alkmaar, 1980); and C. C. van der Valkenburg, ed., *Men sagh Haerlem bestormen* (Haarlem, 1973); Maltby, *Alba*, 243–61 for overviews. Contemporary accounts include P. Sterlinckx, *Een corte waerachtige beschrijvinghe van alle geschiedenissen, aenslaghen, stormen, schermutsingen, ende schieten voor de vroome stadt Haarlem in Hollandt geschiedt . . . van 3 Dec. 1572 tot den 12 Sept. 1573* (Delft 1573), and Mendoza, *Commentaires*, 2:35–125, as well as the Beggars' songs and other ballads collected in NG, 2:43–48.

God in Heaven look below in the earthly valley at all your children,
For the Duke of Alba pursues great and ordinary Christians with determined cruelty.
Outside of Haarlem, he comes to war,
He sends three trusted companies and demands to know if Haarlem, that valiant city,
  will surrender to the king's side or face the penalty of sword and fire.
"We will win by our storm and spare no one. Will you not accept our mercy?" [asks a
  Spaniard]
A worthy burgher replies, "We know what your mercy was worth to the poor burghers
  of Naarden, who were all grievously murdered. Men, women, children: you cut
  them all down.
The citizens of Zutphen had opened their gates to accept your mercy,
But were all slain and captured."
"We will not give up the city," spoke the senior commander.
"We want to keep the town for the king and put ourselves in God's hand."[89]

The "senior commander" was Haarlem's military governor, Wigbolt Ripperda. On the eve of the arrival of Don Fadrique's troops, with the help of the city's militia, he had purged wavering magistrates. Further, he had denounced the town's pensionary as a collaborator; he was executed at Delft at Orange's command.[90] It was a lopsided stand-off: Haarlem, a city of around 11,500, with a modest garrison, could hardly withstand Don Fadrique's resources in arms and men. Though the city boasted a strong curtain fortification, it had only one new bastion.[91] But withstand it did, partly owing to the cold, bitter weather and partly owing to its people's own resourcefulness, including building new defensive structures inside the city and mounting surprise raids against the dug-in Spanish forces. As they kept the soldiers at bay, the Haarlemers taunted them by taking religious statues from the cleansed churches and placing them on the ramparts to be shot, and by dressing up in ecclesiastical vestments and parading on the city wall.[92] But the city could not hold out forever, and finally, half-starved, exhausted, and without relief from Orange's men, the town capitulated on July 12. Despite promises of mercy, Alba had the garrison of some two thousand executed, sparing only several hundred German and English soldiers. He also rounded up and arrested citizens and imposed a hefty war indemnity, although he failed to prevent an unexpected mutiny of his unpaid and weary forces outside the city after the siege was over.[93]

89. NG, 2:43–44, and GB, 1:139 [de Bruin and Oosterman, Repertorium T5319]
90. Wijn, Beleg van Haarlem, 37–62, on this and other critical events in December.
91. The English soldier Walter Morgan noted that Haarlem was easy prey "because the toune was all-toogether unfortyfyed." See Walter Morgan, The Expedition in Holland, 1572–1574, ed. D. Caldecott-Baird (London, 1976), 114.
92. Mendoza, Commentaires, 2:92.
93. For a military narrative, see Maltby, Alba, 243–61; on the mutiny, Parker, Army of Flanders, 198; on the

If Haarlemers were victims of Alba's harsh peace—even Granvelle denounced his tactics as unduly bloody and counterproductive—they had displayed considerable valor during the siege months.[94] Writers and memorialists in the Patriot camp praised Haarlemers' courage, citing the martial boldness displayed by devoted wives and children as well as husbands and fathers, as if the siege was an endurance test that expunged the stain of victimhood left by the sacks of Mechelen, Zutphen, and Naarden. As the commemorative ballad about Haarlem makes clear, it was these poor towns' fates at Alba's hands that fired the city's resolution to fight. Perhaps it was also reports of raped women and orphaned children that prompted chroniclers of the Haarlem campaign to emphasize the reverse: women and children at the ramparts fighting back with whatever means was at their disposal. They dumped hot coals and oil on their enemies, and when the food ran out, they survived stoically on the meat of horses, cats, dogs, even mice. Protagonists rather than victims, women and the young were important in preventing a quick takeover of the city by the Army of Flanders.[95]

It is within this topos of siege heroism that the legend of the "manly woman," *Kenau Simonsdochter Hasselaer* must be understood. Chroniclers mined popular legends of Amazon warriors in recounting the tale of the wife of a shipbuilder turned battle commander who took up arms against Don Fadrique's men to protect home, hearth, and urbs.[96] About her actual activity during the siege little is noted in the historical record, though she is mentioned in a contemporary chronicle authored by Johannes Arcerius Frisius.[97] But that did not prevent Hasselaer's rapid elevation as heroine, already the subject in 1573 of a now lost German woodcut, but mentioned continuously thereafter, including in an early but undated German print, where she is portrayed as the biblical Judith, brandishing the head of one Don Pero (for whom there is no historical record) in lieu of Holofernes. Hasselaer stands in front of Haarlem, the don's head firmly in her right hand, the freshly slain corpse

---

final month of July, Wijn, *Beleg van Haarlem*, 180–204. Even Spanish detractors like the chronicler Pedro Cornejo commented on the Haarlemers' fortitude to endure hunger as if they were enjoying a banquet; Rodríguez Pérez, *Tachtigjarige Oorlog*, 64.

94. Granvelle to Don Juan, August 28, 1573, quoted in Parker, *Dutch Revolt*, 160.

95. NG, 2:44 [de Bruin and Oosterman, Repertorium T5319]; Bor, *Oorsprongk*, 1:423.

96. The theme of urban heroines during sieges was not specific to the Dutch Revolt. In fifteenth-century France, Jeanne Laisné of Beauvais was celebrated for seizing a Burgundian flag and rallying townspeople when Charles the Bold besieged the town in 1472. See C. Beaune, *The Birth of an Ideology: Myths and Symbols of Nation in Late-Medieval France*, trans. S. R. Huston (Berkeley, 1991), 145.

97. He coined the expression "een seer manlycke vrou" in his 1573 *Historie ende een waerachtig verhael van al die dingen die geschiet sijn, van dach tot dach, in die lofweerdichste ende vermaerdste stadt van Hollandt, Haerlem ghenoemt, in dien tijt als die van den Hertoge van Alba belegert was*. For a discussion, see G. H. Kurtz, Kenau Symonsdochter van Haerlem (Assen, 1956), 55; G. H. Kurtz, "Kenau," in Van der Valkenburg, *Men sagh Haerlem bestormen*, 65–75; and most recently, Els Kloek, *Kenau: De heldhaftige zakenvrouw uit Haarlem (1526–1588)* (Hilversum, 2001), with an emphasis on the actual historical person.

SIEGES, SACKS, AND THE CITY DEFIANT 239

An undated German print celebrates the legendary Kenau Simonsdochter Hasselaer, manly heroine of the siege of Haarlem, depicted as the biblical Judith and holding the head of the fictional Don Pero. Courtesy of Rijksprentenkabinet, Rijksmuseum, Amsterdam.

crumpled bloodily at her feet. She is stern in bearing, and armed with lance, pistol, and sword. A German text boasts about the women who fight the "Spanish Moors" for the protection of the fatherland. The indignity of Hogenberg's destitute, naked, and violated women of Mechelen has been exorcised by this housewife as soldier-Amazon, symbol of the city defiant and the domestic order supercharged. The image of the Dutch Amazon not only fired the rebels' imagination; it also played to gender imaginaries that the Spanish themselves had invoked, including the soldier Alonso Vásquez, who wrote that Dutch women have an "energetic, manly nature" and show great courage during warfare.[98]

Hasselaer's fortunes would only rise in the young Dutch Republic, where she functioned as one of several emerging patriotic legends.[99] Exceptional as she was, Hasselaer was not sui generis, but stood for a vision of the city as a collectivity of households united to repel the Spanish tyrants. This communal theme intensified with the sieges of Alkmaar and Leiden, famous because both ended with the retreat of Spanish forces. Alkmaar's was

98. Brouwer, *Kronieken van Spaansche Soldaten*, 93–94.
99. Schama, *Embarrassment of Riches*, 88–89; Kurtz, "Kenau," 65–75; Kloek, *Kenau*.

short, running from August 31 to October 8, 1573, but it was nonetheless intense.[100] Leiden's was truly epic, involving two separate phases, the first from October 31, 1573 to March 21, 1574, and the second from May 1574 until the city's relief on October 3, 1574.[101] Part of the thrill of Alkmaar's victory had to do with just how determined Alba had been to take it; he even wrote to Philip II that he was determined "not to leave a creature alive and put them all to the knife" because they have not profited by the example of Haarlem.[102] Don Fadrique's men surrounded this North Quarter city, but with Orange's permission, Diederik Sonoy, his commander in north Holland, opened key dikes and sluices, forcing Fadrique to raise the siege. That the townspeople were prepared to drown rather than surrender became the stuff of legend. So too did the heroics displayed by its women and children, determined to avoid the fate of their compatriots elsewhere. One of the stirring ballads about Alkmaar evokes both themes in its opening stanzas. The refrain laments this period of "war, want, floods, plague, and tyranny," denounces Alba as Nero and Pharaoh combined, and bemoans the taking of Mons, Mechelen, Zutphen, and Naarden, because "women and children" were assaulted in such a way "that no Turk would so perpetuate."[103] These dependents, as well as their pious menfolk, suffered great want. Hungry, they were reduced to eating cat, dog, and horseflesh, but gleefully rushed to the city's walls to rain down on the soldiers' heads whatever their dwindling cupboards had left, including boiling water and oil, pitch, lime, as well as the contents of their chamber pots.[104]

The theme of civic solidarity, starvation, and Exodus-like deliverance through the flood waters reached a crescendo with the second siege of Leiden. Alba's successor Requesens had been forced to raise the first siege in March 1574 in order to counter an invasion by Louis of Nassau from Germany into the eastern Netherlands. After the decisive victory by

100. On Alkmaar, see Ev. Wasdorp, *Het beleg der stede Alkmaar in 1573 naar aanteekeningen van ooggetuigen geschetst* (Arnhem, 1862); J. J. de Gelder, *Brieven en andere bescheiden rakende het beleg van Alkmaar in 1573 naar de oorpronkelijke stukken* (Alkmaar, 1865); and Nanning van Foreest, *Een cort verhael van de strenghe belegheringe ende aftreck der Spangiaerden vande stadt Alcmaer gheleghen in Holland* (Delft, 1573), a Dutch translation of the Latin original, for which see the reprint and the introduction by Henk van Nierop, "Alkmaar in de Opstand," in Nanning van Foreest, *Kort verhaal van het beleg van Alkmaar: Een ooggetuigenverslag*, ed. M. Joustra (Alkmaar, 2000), 7–18.

101. For reprints of early accounts of Leiden's siege, see Fruin, *Oude verhalen*, including Fruytiers's *Corte beschryvinghe*. For analyses, see R. H. Bremmer, "Het Beleg en ontzet van Leiden," *Nederlands archief voor Kerkgeschiedenis* 47 (1965–6): 166–94, and Raymond Fagel, *Leids beleg en ontzet door Spaanse ogen* (Utrecht, 1997). The sieges of both Alkmaar and Leiden produced numerous commemorative ballads, the principal ones of which appeared in the published *Geuzenliedboek* and the others in sixteenth- and seventeenth-century chronicles: NG, 2:49–66 for Alkmaar, and 2:131–42 for Leiden. Leiden's siege also was the subject of the 1606 play by the rhetorician Jacob Duym, *Benoude belegheringe der stad Leyden* (Leiden, 1606).

102. Letter of August 30, 1573, in *Epistolario Alba*, 3:491–96.

103. NG, 2:48–49, and GN, 1:149 [de Bruin and Oosterman, *Repertorium* T4614]; Nanning van Foreest, *Cort verhael*.

104. Nanning van Foreest, *Cort verhael*.

the Army of Flanders at Mook on April 14, in which Orange's brothers Louis and Hendrik perished, the Leiden siege resumed under the command of Francisco de Valdez.[105] The upcoming fight did not seem to bode well for Leiden, a town of fourteen thousand with only its civic militia of *schutters* as the backbone of its resistance, though balladeers made much of these "strong, courageous, and valiant burghers without even a garrison in the town."[106] Orange had set up camp at Delft with fifteen thousand troops. With the sting of his failure to relieve Haarlem strong, he was determined to come to Leiden's aid, encouraging their resistance through messages sent via carrier pigeon.[107] Dutch narratives of the siege take on exaggerated, epic dimensions in which the suffering of the citizens is miraculously relieved by Leiden's deliverance at the hands of floodwaters. On October 3, 1574, Admiral Boisot and his flotilla of Zeeland Sea Beggars reached Leiden's walls after rain and wind finally raised the water levels a month after the dikes along the Maas had been broken in an attempt to open a route to the besieged city. Orange had been laid low by a terrible illness in August, which left him bedridden for weeks in Rotterdam, his suffering surpassed only by the parallel misery of hunger and illness inside Leiden's walls.[108] On July 1, its citizens had already heartened the prince by their stirring declaration that they would rather die of hunger than become slaves of the Spanish.[109] Indeed, the rhetoric of correspondents, chroniclers, and later balladeers employed such pregnant terms as "liberty," "privileges," and "fatherland" to a degree not seen in other sieges.[110]

Hunger was Leiden's means of heroic suffering, and the first great chronicler of the siege, the rhetorician, writer, and eyewitness Jan Fruytiers, on whose work Pieter Bor and subsequent Dutch historians based their own accounts, made it their badge of defiance. Food supplies dwindled fast, severe rationing was imposed, and some women, children, and the non-able-bodied were sent packing to other cities.[111] Balladeers and other Dutch chroniclers were rapturous about Leideners' heroism. Jan Fruytiers singled out the stoicism of townswomen, less for the martial valor of their equivalents in Haarlem and Alkmaar than for their willingness to endure hunger. They had earned their husbands' admiration, Fruytiers insisted, "because there were many who would rather die of hunger

---

105. On Orange's despair at the loss of his brothers, see his April 22, 1574, letter in *Archives d'Orange-Nassau*, 3:378–81.

106. NG, 2:136 [de Bruin and Oosterman, *Repertorium* T6654].

107. Bremmer, "Het Beleg en ontzet van Leiden"; Fagel, *Leids beleg en ontzet door Spaanse ogen*. As Fagel makes clear, military events are closely recounted in Mendoza's superb *Commentaires*, 2:252–85.

108. On Orange's illness, see the correspondence in Groen van Prinsterer, *Archives d'Orange-Nassau*, 5:38–40, 50–53.

109. Bor, *Oorsprongk*, 1:505: "geresolveert zijnde den uittersten hongersnood liever te lijden dan haerder vyanden slaven te werden."

110. This is especially true in the ballads and refrains; see NG, 2:131–44.

111. Mendoza, *Commentaires*, 2:263; Bor, *Oorsprongk*, 1:553; see also Fagel, *Leids beleg en ontzet door Spaanse ogen*, 21.

in their houses than to put themselves in the hands of tyranny. We all too well remember the examples of Naarden, Zutphen, Mechelen, and Haarlem."[112] Instead, Leideners subsisted on a ration of malt cake, water, and the meat of horses, dogs, cats, mice, and rats. In the high point of Fruytiers's narrative, the Leideners proclaim their starvation as their duty for the fatherland, intoning from the city ramparts:

> You call us rat eaters and dog eaters, and it is true that we lack provisions. If you hear dogs bark and horses bray, then know that we are holding out. And even when we are on the verge of perishing, be sure that we will each devour our left arm, retaining our right to defend against your tyranny and prevent your bloodthirsty men from scaling our walls.[113]

Fictive or not, the proclamation expunged the blemish of all previous sacks by its romantic liberty-or-death fist-shaking, repeated in variation in other accounts, including a Beggars' song in which the citizens exclaim: "See, so long as we have hands, one to eat and the other to fight, we will not perish." The song concludes with an exhortation for Orange to "fight for your fatherland."[114] In 1606 the rhetorician Jacob Duym, using these literary prototypes, based a play on the siege of Lieden, replete with clichéd bathos. The drama featured villainous Spanish soldiers, grave city magistrates, resolute burghers who prefer death to a life of slavery under a tyrant, and brave housewives, who suffered near starvation on behalf of city and *patria* as their children cried out, "Oh mother, give us bread!"[115] Perhaps the most startling feature of Leiden's heroism to emerge in the seventeenth century was the story of Burgomaster Van der Werf, embellished from an incident inserted in the 1577 second edition of Fruytiers's account of Leiden's siege. During the critical fourth month of the siege, when supplies dwindled, hunger was everywhere, and citizens and magistrates desperate over how to proceed, Van der Werf offered to kill himself and bequeath his body as food, a Christ-like sacrifice that literally made the body of the citizen the means of Leiden's communal salvation.[116]

The fame of Leiden's siege and the deeply felt emotional tone of its commemoration

---

112. Fruytiers, *Corte beschryvinghe*, in Fruin, *Oude verhalen*, 20.
113. Ibid. This topos of starvation before subjugation figured in other accounts, including the 1575 *Discours du siège que les Espaignolz ont tenu devant la ville de Leyden en Hollande*, 21, attributed by Robert Fruin and his fellow editors to Guillaume de Maulde, whose name accompanied one of the three extant copies of this treatise: Fruin, *Oude verhalen*, 28–29.
114. NG, 2:137–39, and GB, 1:18 [de Bruin and Oosterman, *Repertorium* T7522].
115. Duym, *Benoude belegheringe der stad Leyden*, esp. Ciii–Fiv.
116. Van der Werf's offer first appeared in the 1577 reworking of Fruytiers's 1574 text, for which see Fruin, *Oude verhalen*, 36–7. Its reworking in later periods, the seventeenth century most importantly, is traced in Marijke Meijer Drees, "Burgemeester Van der Werf als vaderlandse toneelheld: een politieke autoriteit in belegeringsdrama's," *De zeventiende eeuw* 8 (1992): 167–76.

had everything to do with the miracle-like storm and rising waters that delivered Leiden's citizens from starvation, and with the fact that lifting Leiden's siege forced the Spanish concession of most of Holland, save Haarlem and Amsterdam. Brave citizen militias, stoically suffering and strong wives, rampart-scampering and stone-throwing children had together endured cold, hunger, and death, and willingly risked self-inundation by cutting the very dikes that kept the sea out, all to repulse the Goliath-sized Army of Flanders. The city had been redeemed, exultantly savoring the liberties and privileges defended by its townspeople. Yet despite the civic triumphalism of the Dutch rebels, the Army of Flanders persisted, even if its companies had taken a beating. Frustrated by a bogged-down war, maltreated by their officers, its rank-and-file soldiers increasingly mutinied, terrorizing the cities they seized. These spontaneous revolts of soldiers only widened the gulf between Habsburg authorities and Low Country townspeople and nobles, who had no real chance at reconciliation and peace, and set the stage for the infamous sack of Antwerp on November 4, 1576.

The Spanish Fury in Antwerp

The city besieged, the city destroyed, the city defended, and the city reclaimed: these urban trials and triumphs were the yin and yang of the Dutch Revolt in the critical two years of 1572–74. The sack and the siege offered patriotic fodder and an ethos of civic heroism for the rebels to spin tales of brave urban men and women enacting the highest values of citizenship. Yet despite the successes of Alkmaar and Leiden, neither victory stopped the Army of Flanders's depredations. It was events in Brabant, notably the mutiny of soldiers in Antwerp in 1574, the mutiny in Aalst in 1576, and above all the sack of Antwerp in 1576, that moved the States General to rid the Low Countries of these men. Apart from the political role Antwerp's sack in 1576 played in the intensification of the Revolt, it did symbolic work as the greatest example of Spanish villainy against the civic realm, offering to the Patriots an instance of urban martyrdom as powerful as the deaths of Egmont and Hornes in 1568.

As Geoffrey Parker has explored, the mutinies of the Army of Flanders were frightening events, the social consequence of amassing thousands of poor work-a-day soldiers like the *picas secas* (pike men) and the harquebusiers in units that endured trying conditions, arrogant officers, and great disparity in pay.[117] Alba's successor, Requesens, had despaired after the mutiny in Antwerp in 1574 that "it was not the Prince of Orange who had lost the Low Countries, but the soldiers born in Valladolid and Toledo," with their ru-

---

117. Parker, *Army of Flanders*, 185–206, and his "Mutiny and Discontent in the Spanish Army of Flanders," with important prosopographical information. See, too, Van der Essen, *Kritische studie over de oorlogsvoering van het Spaanse leger* for the Alba period and the identically titled vol. 2, for the period of Requesens (1573–76) (Brussels, 1952).

inous attack on this commercial metropolis.[118] The mutinies were devastating to Low Country cities because of their frequency; between 1572 and 1607 there were more than forty-five, including a main cycle in 1573–76 at the height of the fighting between the Army of Flanders and the Patriots. Mutineers typically elected leaders, an *electo* for Spanish troops or an *ambosat* for the Germans. Once organized, they drew up grievances that typically centered on the demand for back pay, but included appeals for better camp conditions—from medical services to the freedom to change units. Given the tough fighting the soldiers endured, such requests were not surprising. Nor were the financial demands; even the Spartan Duke of Alba expressed astonishment on the eve of the siege of Haarlem that his men "can bear" the wet, cold conditions with twenty months' pay owed to them. When Haarlem surrendered in July 1573, the soldiers got only four months' pay, and bitterly responded with a mutiny.[119] As in other social revolts in early modern Europe, soldiers who mutinied risked incurring severe punishment, but often gained temporary respect from their superiors; Alba himself referred to the Haarlem mutineers as "magníficos señores hijos," not unlike the other polite salutations senior officers used in their negotiations with Army of Flanders mutineers whom they more usually described as lackeys, vagabonds, and pay-grabbers.[120]

Just as it is too easy to see the iconoclasts of 1566 as people programmed by their Calvinist ministers, so it is too simple to interpret the mutinies in the Army of Flanders as merely about money, though it was a powerful motive. Parker has explored the broader social domain of these mutinies, including the soldiers' demands for better religious services, for improved medical help, and for fairer judicial treatment, and has demonstrated the compelling ways in which mutineers formed protest committees and had grievances printed as fly sheets.[121]

The mutinies achieved more still. In both the behavior displayed and the institutions targeted, mutinies imperiled symbols of urban political order dear to the Patriots, and spawned legends similar to those of the sacks of Mechelen, Zutphen, and Naarden. The two attacks on Antwerp in the 1570s are cases in point. The April–May mutiny of 1574 for back pay was prologue to the more spectacular sack of November 1576, which became one of the most remembered events of the Dutch Revolt, rousing the kind of visceral anger among the provinces that the *beeldenstorm* had among Catholic loyalists. The strong reaction to the sack owed much to the rioters targeting the city's built environment, especially

118. Quote in Parker, *Army of Flanders*, 185, Hernando Delgadillo to Juan de Albornez, July 9, 1574.
119. Parker, *Army of Flanders*, 198; Maltby, *Alba*, 258.
120. Quote in letter of Alba to Philip II, August 30, 1573, in *Epistolario Alba*, 3:471–74; Parker, *Army of Flanders*, 200.
121. "Mutiny and Discontent." The fly sheets for the 1574 Antwerp mutiny have survived: Archivo General de Simancas, E 558/41, 42, 44, 45, 48, 50, and Instituto de Valencia de Don Juan, 67/311–12 and 315–17.

the town hall, that great architectural symbol of the city's political pride and its environs. The assault on Antwerp was intense, violent, and spatially dispersed, but had a focal point in the town hall just as the iconoclasts had theirs in the Onze-Lieve-Vrouwekerk. The great damage done to this political landmark was accompanied by harrowing tales of the social and domestic order overturned, culminating in the incident recounted by Pieter Bor and other historians of the violent disruption of a wedding party, the murder of the groom, and the kidnapping and rape of the bride. The burnt-out town hall and the family violated became public and private counterparts of a narrative of a city despoiled—the civic sphere destroyed, the household violently assaulted. Antwerp desecrated became shorthand for all of the urban violence committed by the Army of Flanders since Alba's arrival in 1567.

Because it was so spectacular, Antwerp's "Spanish fury" of November 4, 1576 eclipsed the mutiny of two years before, which had been mostly bloodless.[122] The 1574 upheaval's pain was principally financial, since the violence required local creditors to front money to pay off the rioting soldiers. The uprising did, however, involve a dramatic takeover of Antwerp's public space from mid-April to late May, and occasioned rites of inversion worthy of an early modern social upheaval—a sore reminder that with the citadel hugging its outskirts, Antwerp was a city supervised. To settle the upheaval, officials were forced to pay all 4,562 soldiers half of their original demand, while turning a blind eye to whatever looting or stealing they had done to make up the difference. Antwerp's bankers underwrote loans for the enormous sum of one million florins, while the victorious soldiers celebrated, according to the chronicler Van Meteren, by dressing in gold finery and parading about as "if they were great masters and lords." Governor General Requesens pardoned them, an event celebrated in the Onze-Lieve-Vrouwekerk, after which the men gathered on the Meir Bridge, gaming, drumming, drinking, and celebrating their carnivalesque, temporary mastery over Antwerp.[123]

The ritual inversion and financial strain of the 1574 mutiny in Antwerp, considered alongside the several years of continual fighting, periodic sacks, and famous sieges, helped to coalesce anger among the Low Country populace and their representative institutions. The matter came to a head in the fall of 1576, when yet again underpaid and over utilized rank-and-file soldiers mutinied, this time on July 25, only sixteen miles outside of

122. See the memoirs of Frédéric Perrenot de Champagney, in "Par quel moyen les Espaignols amutinez entrèrent en Anvers le XXVI d'Avril 1574," in A. L. P. Roubaulx de Soumoy, ed., *Mémoires de Frédéric Perrenot Sieur de Champagney, 1573–1580* (Brussels, 1860), 33–67, and Mendoza, *Commentaires*, 2:231–38. Subsequent accounts are based largely on Van Meteren (a native of Antwerp), *Historie der Nederlandscher ende haerder Na-buren oorlogen*, fols. 100r–101v, and Bor, *Oorsprongk*, 1:493–94. An analysis of the mutineers' fly sheets is in Parker, "Mutiny and Discontent," 108–10. A factual summary is in Mertens and Topfs, *Geschiedenis van Antwerpen*, 5:8–16. The mutiny was also the topic of Beggars' ballads: NG, 2:120–23, and GB, 1:212 and 214 [de Bruin and Oosterman, *Repertorium* T7139 and T4478].

123. Van Meteren, *Historie*, 101v.

Brussels in Aalst, a small town that had done nothing to prompt the soldiers' wrath.[124] The sack was not only characteristically brutal; it also occurred at a remarkably tense political moment. Efforts to achieve peace the previous year had failed since Orange had not budged from the three essential conditions he had laid out to his brothers in 1573: "liberty of conscience," that is, the free exercise of Protestantism; the restoration of traditional rights and privileges; and the departure of the Army of Flanders.[125] New offensives by Requesens, including the siege of Zierikzee, had not turned the tables in favor of the Spanish, but had merely cost more money.

On September 1, 1575, Philip II suspended interest payments and declared bankruptcy, thereby impoverishing the Army of Flanders. To make matters worse, Requesens unexpectedly died on March 5, 1576, prompting the Council of State in Brussels to assume his political authority in the absence of an appointed successor. The Council's most senior members, Viglius and Berlaymont, were both aging and no longer effective. The council was divided into two camps: that of Gerónimo de Roda, Alba's original appointee to the Council of Troubles, and that of the Duke of Aarschot from the powerful Croy family, a nobleman who had decided that the Army of Flanders must go as a condition to secure peace.[126] Anti-Spanish sentiment snowballed in Brabant and Flanders, where Calvinist sentiment was still strong and conservative noblemen and town magistrates increasingly fretted over the erosion of their traditional spheres of influence. A ballad of the time captured the mood when it imputed to the "Spanish" soldiers pure bloodthirstiness:

> All the Spanish shout loud and clear:
> Pay us or face death. Or we will bring the cities under our feet,
> And wash our hands in burghers' blood.[127]

Orange had intercepted a letter by an officer of the Army of Flanders who wrote nervously that Brussels was on edge and that the Spanish were being attacked in public, including the murder of servants of Berlaymont and Roda.[128] On July 26, the day after the attack on Aalst, the Council of State felt so boxed in that it published a decree declaring the mutineers from the Army of Flanders to be rebels against God and king, though tellingly the edict was neither registered nor published in Antwerp, for fear it might provoke d'Avila and his men in the citadel.[129] The next day, the Council reluctantly allowed

---

124. Mendoza, *Commentaires*, 2:381–82.
125. Letter of February 5, 1573, in *Archives d'Orange-Nassau*, 4:50.
126. For political events, see Parker, *Dutch Revolt*, 166–71. On the Breda peace initiative of 1575, Koenigsberger, *Monarchies, States Generals and Parliaments*, 258–59.
127. NG, 2:167, and GB, 1:261 [de Bruin and Oosterman, *Repertorium* T7033].
128. *Archives d'Orange-Nassau*, 4:386–89. See also Mendoza, *Commentaires*, 2:384–85 on murder of one of Roda's servants.
129. Transcribed in Génard, *Furie espagnole*, 12–13.

the Estates of Brabant to raise troops to protect the province from soldiers outraged to have been branded as outlaws. But when the Council refused to allow the Estates of Hainault and Brabant to consult together for their common defense, its delegates interpreted this as a violation of a right guaranteed by the 1549 Pragmatic Sanction. On September 4, with the new governor general Don Juan not yet in the Netherlands, troops from the Estates of Brabant raided the Council of State meeting, arrested its officeholders, and paved the way for the Estates of Hainault and Brabant to plan for an independent meeting of the States General. An anonymous pamphlet that appeared immediately to justify the mysterious takeover of the Council of State recycled the accusations about Spanish depredations recounted in narratives about sieges and sacks: the Spanish had come to pillage and rob the Low Countries' riches, since Alba had given them "liberty and license to live at their pleasure through pillage, ransoming, attacks, murder, and the rape of women and girls."[130]

Political developments accelerated as tensions built. The regional Estates were busy laying the groundwork to meet; on September 8, Brabant and Hainault invited all provinces except Holland and Zeeland to send delegates. The Council of State was effectively paralyzed after its members were temporarily arrested; of its key figures, Roda had managed to escape to Antwerp's citadel, where he set up a one-man royalist counter-effort. The Estates of Brabant began negotiations with their increasingly independent peers in Holland and Zeeland. Its delegates also republished the Council of State's original ban against Army of Flanders mutineers on September 22 but broadened it to include all its soldiers, whether openly disobedient or not.[131] Talks among the Estates at Ghent led to a decision to seek peace only after the Spanish troops were expelled. The restless and angry units of the Army of Flanders responded by banding together, ready to strike sometime, somewhere.

With Roda installed in its citadel, powerful Antwerp was vulnerable. Rich in goods, money, and households, Antwerp beckoned like an urban smorgasbord to weary, maltreated, and violent soldiers.[132] As the States General deliberated in Ghent, units of the

---

130. "Justification du saisissement et sequestration d'aucuns Seigneurs du Conseil d'Estat et aultres au Pays-Bas," in Génard, Furie espagnole, 106–7.

131. "Placcaet opte rebellie vanden Spaignaerden met heuren aenhangeren ende resistencie tegen de selve ende des dyen aencleeft," in Génard, Furie espagnole, 159–62.

132. On the Spanish Fury of Antwerp, see the enormous collection of archival and print documents assembled in Génard, Furie espagnole in addition to his "Les poursuites contre les fauteurs de la Furie espagnole ou du sac d'Anvers de 1576," Annales de l'Académie d'Archéologie de Belgique 35 (Antwerp, 1879): 25–170, which contains a transcript of the inquest into paymaster Francisco de Lixalde's role in the looting of his neighborhood in Antwerp from Stadsarchief Antwerpen, Certificatieboek 38/164–74, Dec. 4–5, 1577. Contemporary narrative accounts include Mendoza, Commentaires, 2:381–430; Roubaulx de Soumoy, Mémoires de Frédéric Perrenot, 72–152; George Gascoigne, The Spoyle of Antwerpe, Faithfully Reported by a True Englishman, who was Present at the Same, November 1576, in An English Garner: Tudor Tracts, ed. A. F. Pollard (New York, 1903),

Army of Flanders and their commanders, some mutinous, others not, began to plan an attack on Antwerp, whose citadel was now the nerve center of coordination. Having experienced one full-scale mutiny in 1574, Antwerp's governor, the moderate Frédéric Perrenot, Lord of Champagney, brother of the pilloried Granvelle, sensed another in the offing, and was deeply suspicious of d'Avila, the citadel's commander. To bolster his strength, Champagney dismissed a garrison of German soldiers whom he did not trust and replaced them with eight new companies under the command of Otto Oberstein. But d'Avila also raised his number of men, bringing in additional units. September and October saw tense back-and-forth negotiations and continual troop buildup. As it became clearer that an attack was imminent, the States sent five thousand Walloon infantry under the command of the Marquis of Havré, Aarschot's brother, and of Philip, Count of Egmont and son of the executed hero; Orange ordered fourteen companies of his men readied to aid the town, though they were upstream from the Spanish fortress.[133]

In wet weather and a dense fog, soldiers and townspeople together began to erect a rampart and ditch to seal off the citadel from Antwerp, working furiously as men from the citadel took random shots at them through the blinding mist. The States troops were hardly model defenders; some threatened local Spanish residences with looting, and desisted only on promises of beer and other provisions.[134] The next day, November 4, was a Sunday, and work was halted on the defensive ramparts. This was a mistake, since mutinous units from outlying areas had been continuously streaming into the citadel. Included among the new arrivals were two thousand of the hardened Aalst mutineers under their *electo*, Juan de Navarase. They reached Antwerp's citadel early in the morning on November 4 and refused rest, saying, according to the eye-witness Bernardino de Mendoza, "they would dine in Paradise or eat in Antwerp."[135] With men from Lier, Maastricht, and other areas also in the citadel, the number of troops swelled to around four thousand infantry and eight hundred cavalry, less than the nine thousand infantry and twelve hundred cavalry Champagney had inside Antwerp, but far more united and determined.[136]

The mutineers struck early Sunday morning, pouring out of the citadel and across the esplanade, easily breaching Champagney's unfinished fortifications. The Aalst *electo* Navarese held aloft a flag with the Virgin on one side and Christ crucified on the other and

---

6:419–49; Hessels, *Abrahami Ortelii . . . Epistulae*, 1:145–54, the Nov. 14, 1576, letter (no. 64) Gerard Janssen to Jacob Cool, Antwerp. An analysis of its prelude is in Etienne Rooms, "Een nieuwe visie op de gebeurtenissen die geleid hebben tot de Spaanse Furie te Antwerpen op 4 November 1576," *Bijdragen tot de Geschiedenis* 54 (1971): 31–54. A concise overview of events is in Jervis Wegg, *The Decline of Antwerp under Philip of Spain* (London, 1924), 189–206, based on printed accounts, especially Champagney's; and Mertens and Topfs, *Geschiedenis van Antwerpen*, 5:35–52.

133. Roubaulx de Soumoy, *Mémoires de Frédéric Perrenot*, 120–23, and Rooms, "Een nieuwe visie,"
134. Génard, *Furie espagnole*, 449–51, including payments to brewers.
135. Mendoza, *Commentaires*, 2:425.
136. These numbers calculated by Rooms, "Een nieuwe visie," 51.

was cut down as his men clashed with the small units of Walloons and Germans willing to fight. But otherwise, Antwerp was completely swarmed, with the garrison and States troops mostly taking flight. The city was ransacked, with sustained resistance mounted only at key public spaces: the town hall and the market square, the bourse, and the Meir Bridge. The English merchant George Gascoigne, holed up at his nation's trading house, penned a memorable account of the slaughter. He recounted the wild dash through Antwerp's streets by various Spanish units, all with "their lackeys and pages followed with firebrands and wild fire, setting the houses on fire in every place their masters had entered" so that whole neighborhoods went up in smoke.[137] When Gascoigne ventured out of his residence into the streets, he saw maddening chaos and heard sharp exchanges at the bourse; one despondent citizen declaring: "Alas, sire, there is no order; and behold the ruin of this town!"[138]

As Antwerp succumbed to fire and plunder, Champagney and Havré escaped to Orange's fleet, while Oberstein drowned, Egmont was taken captive, and Gascoigne and his compatriots, like so many other trading companies, fended off attackers by promises of cash, silver dishware, and other goods. The Antwerpener Gerard Janssen penned a dramatic account of German soldiers from the Army of Flanders storming his house, where he hid, terrified, in his cellar. As the soldiers raided his pantry for beer and food, he evaded their detection until they returned to look for jewels and other goods. Once discovered, he was forced to hand over cash and bonds, then ransom himself with his household belongings.[139] The Englishman Gascoigne was thunderstruck by the rapacity of the rioters and their arc of destruction:

> They neither spared age nor sex, time nor place, person nor country, profession nor religion, young nor old, rich nor poor, strong nor feeble; but, without any mercy did tyrannously triumph, when there was neither man nor means to resist them. For age and sex, young and old: they slew great numbers of young children, but many more women more than four score years of age. For time and place: their fury was as great ten days after the victory as at the time of their entry; and as great respect they had to the Church and Churchyard, for all their hypocritical boasting of the Catholic religion, as the butcher had to his shambles or slaughter house. For person and country: they spared neither friend nor foe, Portuguese nor Turk. For profession and religion: the Jesuits must give their ready coin; and all other religious houses, both coin and plate: with all short ends that were good and portable. The rich was spoiled because he had, and the poor were hanged because they had nothing. Neither strength could prevail to make resistance, nor weakness move pity for to refrain their horrible cruelty.[140]

137. Gascoigne, *The Spoyle of Antwerpe*, 438.
138. Ibid., 440.
139. Hessels, *Abrahami Ortelii*, 1:150–52.
140. Gascoigne, *The Spoyle of Antwerpe*, 444.

While precise numbers are not available, the city suffered enormously, with about eight thousand residents perishing.[141] Notes used to prepare a now lost report on the sack by Antwerp's magistrates tallied the loss of some 1,400 houses and buildings.[142] In a bitter letter to the States General, Antwerp's magistrates described the sack as the fall of the world's greatest civic emporium at the hands of murderous thugs:

> It is well known that not long ago the city of Antwerp was the single and true asylum and place of all the nations of the universe, abundant in all sorts of goods and riches, the deviser and nourisher of all industry and craft, nourishers of the true Roman Catholic religion, instigator of all knowledge and virtue, and for all its preeminence still loyal and obeisant to its prince and lord sovereign. But in this moment, it has fallen from its high perch of honor and prosperity to the bottom and abyss of all misery and calamity, becoming a cave of brigands, thieves, murderers, rapists, villains, enemies of God and their lord and master of the fatherland and of all good citizens, inhabitants, and visitors of this city of Antwerp.[143]

The sack of Antwerp was the apex of several years of terrifying sacks and sieges, the sorrowful terminus to a cycle of urban violence that had begun with Alba's attack on Mechelen in 1572. It became to the Patriots and their heirs the pinnacle of Spanish tyranny and a brief on behalf of urban liberty. A Beggars' ballad stirringly opens:

> Netherlanders wake up! Wake up! It is not the time to fall in disgrace. See how the faithful prince will fight the Spanish brood before they make you mourn for your life and goods. Take merry Antwerp as your example. It was Europe's temple of triumphant trade. Of fine commerce there was nowhere else like it. What else can you declare? It was the world's crown. Its richness was evident in its many churches and buildings built there. Need I mention the town hall and the two bourses, or the Pand [public art market] and also the Easterling House [Hanseatic House]? But how we have seen you slip, O majestic city. Your trade plummeted, your houses stand desolate. This villainy was done by the father of tyranny, the Duke of Alba, a Spanish traitor, thirsty for Christians' blood. He has stolen the crown off your head and built a murderer's nest [the citadel], which has now robbed you.[144]

Apart from the verbal flogging that popular balladeers still reserved for Alba, what stands out in these stanzas is the emphasis on the citadel as the seat of all troubles and the role

---

141. A precise calculation of those killed is impossible. Génard attempted to trace names of all the victims recorded in city records, though he only located several hundred. The figures come from contemporary chroniclers. For a discussion, see Génard, *Furie espagnole*, 553–82.

142. "Actes exécrables commis par les Espaignolz," in Génard, *Furie espagnole*, 447–48.

143. Génard, *Furie espagnole*, 633.

144. NG, 2:175–76, and GB, 1:273 [de Bruin and Oosterman, *Repertorium* T6809].

the stock exchanges and the town hall play as symbols of Antwerp's greatness. The ballad lauds Antwerp as a commercial gem, a plural center of exchange stunted by the citadel soldiers who stood watch over the city like punishing sentinels.

The town hall was a precise target of the mutineers' wrath. Situated on the west side of Antwerp's Grote Markt (market square), it was relatively new, having been constructed between 1561 and 1565. Designed by the architect and sculptor Cornelis Floris II de Vriendt, it was modeled on Italian palace architecture, and divided by a high central projection and façade embellished with carved reliefs in the arch spandrels and free-standing sculptures.[145] As Holm Bevers has explored, the town hall featured classical arches and the division of its floor plan into rhythmic bays, making it akin to the triumphal arches used so frequently in sixteenth-century entries. The building was studded with dramaturgical flourishes and had been intended to be incorporated into an entry ceremony for Philip II that never occurred. The positioning of the building on the west side of the Grote Markt made it maximally viewable from Antwerp's processional routes. Equally important was its sculptural program, with allegorical figures, heraldic emblems, and two obelisks in the central façade. Prudentia, Justitia, and Ratio reminded the magistrates of their political virtues; the obelisks were classical embellishments whose pedestals bore the classical band S.P.Q.A. (Senatus Populusque Antverpiensis). But even more prominent was the figure of Silvius Brabo, the mythic Roman slayer of the giant Druon Antigoon who had prevented settlement on the Scheldt by his demand of a half of a traveler's goods, on pain of losing his or her right hand. The focus on Brabo was a departure from earlier cultural traditions, which had more commonly alluded to the giant Antigoon as symbol of civic identity, as in the 1549 entry of Charles V and Philip II when Antigoon was featured in a tableau vivant.[146] The statue of Silvius Brabo was placed in the central façade in late spring 1566, at the height of tensions over the city's privileges with Margaret of Parma and her administration. At the time, Brabo was touted not merely as the slayer of the giant Antigoon but also as the first Duke of Brabant. His person, therefore, was associated with civic constitutional and provincial rights—the perfect symbol not only of the civic order but for the privileges that the town hall served.[147]

If the soldiers had been motivated purely by a desire for goods and specie, they would have ignored the great Renaissance-style *stadhuis* in the city's center, and would not have set fire to the archives of privileges and other documents it housed.[148] But they did both and made the attack on the town hall the centerpiece of the fighting. The English witness

---

145. A formal description and analysis is in Holm Bevers, *Das Rathaus von Antwerpen (1561–1565)* (Hildesheim, 1985), and his summary in Van der Stock, *Antwerp*, 243.

146. Meadow, "Ritual and Civic Identity," 56–57.

147. On the allegorical program, Bevers, *Rathaus von Antwerpen*, 41–81.

148. On the attack and damage to the town hall, see the documents in Génard, *Furie espagnole*, 523–24, 632.

Gascoigne recounts how the mutineers zeroed in on the town hall, and describes its attack in the same breath as the rape of Antwerp's women—underscoring that the town hall and the family were inseparable strands of public life: "But I may not pass over with silence the willful burning and destroying of the stately Town House, and all the muniments and records of the city: neither can I refrain to tell their shameful rapes and outrageous forces presented unto sundry honest dames and virgins."

In a letter about the sack to the States General, Antwerp's magistrates were even more distraught about the damage to the town hall:

> Not even that temple and holy office of justice, the very magnificent town hall of the aldermen, escaped the flames, an edifice so sumptuous that it numbers among the miracles of the world, a ruin compounded by the loss of its charters, muniments, books, registers, seals, legal cases, and countless other documents concerning kings, potentates, princes, republics, and nations of the world; even the estates and instructions of poor orphans and other private persons are now reduced to ash and cinders.[149]

Although the town hall was badly gutted by fire set by rioting soldiers, with the help of an unnamed soldier significant portions of its archives were hauled out, though the remainder perished.[150] Antwerp's militia had tried to defend the cherished building, fighting to hold it from the mutineers until fire forced them to jump out of its windows as the flames were spreading to the surrounding upscale neighborhoods, resulting in more than six hundred houses destroyed.[151] Although it was eventually restored, the town hall sustained extensive damage, enough to make it the lasting emblem of the Spanish Fury in Antwerp.[152]

The town hall and the citadel had been Antwerp's two great public works in the 1560s, and the two functioned as opposites to many Antwerpeners: the town hall, the seat of government and monument to urban independence; the citadel, the hated "murderers' nest" that stood as a sore testament to Antwerp's submission to Spanish authorities. That it was mutinous forces from the citadel who rained destruction on the town hall made the sting of its loss all the worse. The town hall was Antwerp's public encapsulation of former pensionary of Antwerp Jacob Wesenbeke's holy troika of liberty, freedoms, and privileges—the bedrock of the rebels' political platform. Its attack was a vivid realization of the complaints popularized by Wesenbeke and his successors in the pamphlet literature

---

149. Ibid., 635–36; Gascoigne, The Spoyles of Antwerpe, 438.

150. Génard, Furie espagnole, 523, with excerpts from records concerning payments to those who helped rescue documents from the flames.

151. Mendoza, Commentaires, 2:427–28; see also Bor, Oorsprongk, 1:731; Van Meteren, Historie, 121v; Génard, Furie espagnole, 463–70.

152. Guicciardini, Description de la cité d'Anvers, 76.

SIEGES, SACKS, AND THE CITY DEFIANT 253

Antwerp's town hall, the proud symbol of its civic rights, set afire during the Spanish Fury of November 4, 1576. Frans Hogenberg. Courtesy of the private collection of Karel Kinds.

on Spanish hatred of legal privileges.[153] These rights were hallowed parchments, and the "temple" of justice their repository. In visual depictions of the sack of Antwerp, the burning town hall exemplifies the general horror, most literally in Frans Hogenberg's print, and allegorically in the engraving by Antonie van Leest, in which two soldiers remove a personified Belgica's heart before a town hall engulfed in flames. The text that accompanies Van Leest's illustration is a plaintive wail about the loss of "my beautiful privileges."[154] To assault the town hall was to violate that which made Antwerp free.

153. Van Gelderen, Political Thought, 115–19; Geurts, Nederlandse Opstand, 149–51.
154. The engraving and text were inserted into Jan Baptist Houwaert's 1577 allegory of Spanish tyranny, *Milenus clachte, waer inne de groote tyrannie der Romeynen verhaelt /ende den handel van desen tegenwoordighen tyt claerlijck ontdect wordt . . . toeghescreven den doorluchtigen Prince van Orangien*, in its third section, Antijcke Tafereelen (Antwerp, 1577). See also Bevers, *Rathaus von Antwerpen*, 48.

Belgica's heart is removed by a soldier while Antwerp's town hall is in flames behind her. Antonie van Leest. Courtesy of Stichting Atlas van Stolk, Rotterdam.

Hogenberg's frontal view of the town hall in flames captured the horror of the Spanish Fury in the public sphere. His other popular image of the 1576 violence blends a public glimpse of the bloodshed with interior, domestic viewpoints of the attack through the use of cutaway images of buildings. As soldiers stab and shoot citizens on the streets, they torture the naked limbs of terrified citizens attempting to hide inside houses and storefronts. That not even the private home was safe is reinforced by archival records that point to the robbery, manhandling, and murder of residents, best exemplified in the case of relatives of Francisco de Lixalde, paymaster of the Army of Flanders, who robbed, roughed up, and humiliated more than fifteen neighbors in Beddestraat.[155]

Memorialists of the sacks of Mechelen, Zutphen, and Naarden played up tales of domestic robbery and rape to serve as powerful, gendered metaphors of the city despoiled.

155. Stadsarchief Certificatieboek 38/164–74, printed in Génard, *Les poursuites contre les fauteurs de la Furie espagnole*, 6–21.

The rape and torture of Antwerp's civilians in both private and public space during the Spanish Fury. Frans Hogenberg. Courtesy of the private collection of Karel Kinds.

As printmaker of the sacks of Mechelen and Naarden, Hogenberg not surprisingly accented this gendered theme in his Spanish Fury series. But it was the historians Pieter Bor and P. C. Hooft who sharpened the domestic motif by giving story to a single incident of Antwerp's sack: the violent breaking up of a family's wedding celebration. Neither Bor, still a young man, nor Hooft, who was not born until 1581, witnessed Antwerp's sack, though each was well informed, especially Hooft, whose wife's grandmother lived through it and passed on harrowing tales of family members robbed and tortured.[156] Nor does the story leave traces in the archival documents that have survived. But to later Protes-

---

156. Génard, *Furie espagnole*; Bor, *Oorsprongk*, 1:731–32; Hooft, *Neederlandsche histoorien*, 463–65. Although a native son of Antwerp, Van Meteren did not mention the incident in his brief consideration of Antwerp's fate; see Van Meteren, *Historie*, 120r–121r.

tant imbibers of the Black Legend such as Motley, the accounts of Bor and Hooft of a family wedding celebration overturned, whether real, embellished, or fictive, came to embody Spanish tyranny.[157]

The story of the disrupted wedding was operatic tragedy. As two well-to-do families celebrated the nuptials, Spanish soldiers rushed in, robbed the household and killed the groom. A horrified patriarch, mad with grief, struggled helplessly to defend his daughter, the bride, but was cut down in front of her. The beautiful bride was brought to the citadel, where she tried to hang herself with her necklace. Instead, she was stripped of her valuables and clothes, whipped, and sent naked back into the city, where a soldier killed her. The widely read, handsome folio edition of Bor's chronicle published between 1679 and 1684 contains a dramatic illustration of the event by Jan Luyken. The handsome groom lies dead at his bride's feet, and the unlucky young woman is being torn from the hands of her father while her mother faints. As soldiers pillage the house, the streets are filled with horrific violence, and a church is ablaze. The family is undone: its sanctified home plundered, its familial bonds violently severed, and its very celebration of reproduction becomes instead its blood-soaked termination. Nothing is inviolate, not even a church, which only the iconoclasts had previously dared to attack.[158]

The accounts of the disrupted wedding reference the interdependent realms of urban desecration: the family as the foundation of the urban order, its public life in the streets and squares, and its religious domain. The violated, naked bride encapsulates the horror of the Fury in one agonized body, and functions more generally as an allegory of Belgica plundered. Her fate is a sorrowful fulfillment of Orange's warning in 1572 that the Spanish came to overturn the civic order by threatening property, goods, women, and children.[159] Years before the Spanish Fury in August 1569, the magistrates of Antwerp had celebrated the wedding of Sancho d'Avila, commander of Alba's citadel, to a Bruges Spanish nobleman's daughter with a procession, tournament, and fireworks.[160] What d'Avila had given them in return was a wedding cut short, a family murdered, and a city with its public domain and private residences plundered and torched. The town hall ablaze, many of its privileges lost, and the family murdered: these were the arresting images by which Dutch writers and artists captured the "tyranny" of the Army of Flanders on behalf of the Revolt.

---

157. Motley, *Rise of the Dutch Republic*, 3, 114–15, after Bor. The theme of a wedding disrupted may have been borrowed from commemorations of the 1572 Saint Bartholomew's Day massacre in Paris and its theme of a royal wedding gone astray, though there is no direct allusion to it. For its violence, see, in particular, Diefendorf, *Beneath the Cross*, and Denis Crouzet, *La nuit de la Saint-Barthélemy: Un rêve perdu de la Renaissance* (Paris, 1994).

158. Génard, *Furie espagnole*, 535–46.

159. *Corr. Taciturne*, 6:297–301.

160. *Antwerpsh Chronykje*, 208.

A wedding celebration is violently broken up by soldiers of the Army of Flanders. The incident became the symbol of the 1576 sack of Antwerp. Illustration by Jan Luyken in Pieter Bor's *Oorsprongk, begin en vervolgh der Nederlandsche oorlogen, beroerten, en borgerlyke oneenigheden* (1679–84). Courtesy of Bijzondere Collecties, Universiteitsbibliotheek, Universiteit Leiden.

The effect of the Spanish Fury in Antwerp was sensational. Antwerp's magistrates had angrily reported the outrage in a letter to the States General in session in Ghent. A Jesuit in Antwerp said the sack was akin to Judgment Day.[161] The destruction—and the damage done to Antwerp's all-important banking houses and credit markets—added momentum to the accord the Estates were finalizing in Ghent. On November 8, the States General issued the Pacification of Ghent, which called for the immediate expulsion of the Army of Flanders as a precondition for negotiations with the king and a religious settlement. Its preamble pinned the blame for the decade of incessant warfare on the rapacity of the Spanish, particularly the soldiers. Although lacking the imprimatur of Holland and Zeeland, the Pacification of Ghent held out the promise of peace even as it sidestepped how the status quo ante bellum was to be achieved. On January 9, 1577, the provinces proclaimed their

---

161. Génard, *Furie espagnole*, 545, 635–36.

support for the Pacification in the Union of Brussels, and on February 12, the new governor general, Don Juan, warily agreed to its terms.[162]

The Army of Flanders had no defenders. They were criticized at the outset by the humanist Catholic chronicler Marcus van Vaernewijck, by the fiercely anti-Beggar prior of Stein, Wouter Jacobsz., and even by the loyalist, the Duke of Aarschot. No less than Governor General Requesens had despaired of their ruinous mutinies and behavior. Beggar pamphleteers and balladeers described the soldiers as a murderous hoard. Orange's 1573 missive accused Alba and his soldiers of "plundering, robbing and ravaging, evicting and desolating . . . the subjects of your Majesty, noble as well as common, poor and rich, young and old, widows and orphans, men, women and young maidens."[163] A French-speaking balladeer summarized the feelings of most Netherlanders in his bitter farewell to the soldiers of the Army of Flanders:

> Adieu, captains of all evil. Adieu, principal enemies of the Low
>   Countries and all virtues.
> Adieu, plunderers, murderers, and wretches, killers, and tyrants.
> Your villainous deeds are shameful.
> Adieu, rapists of fair virgins. Adieu, conspirators of iniquitous deeds.
> Cover your face on account of your enormous deeds.
> Adieu, spoilers of sacred places.
> Adieu, thieves of goods of owners who never forfeited them.[164]

Just like the iconoclasts in 1566, the soldiers of the Army of Flanders could be easily dismissed as "canaille"—and worse.[165] This anonymous balladeer went so far as to accuse the soldiers and their paymasters of "libertinism and atheism," of being men of "Jewish race" and "perturbers of the Republic."[166] But Orange, his allied pamphleteers, and early Dutch historians went further in denouncing the Army of Flanders's perfidy by reference to the propertied, domestic order the soldiers had shattered in cities. Desolate children and sexually assaulted women became potent symbols of a king and his officials who had broken their inaugural oaths to uphold their subjects' rights. Antwerp's fire-damaged town hall, its ravaged archives, and the violent overturning of a private wedding ceremony stood as proof of a fatherland whose household and livelihoods were in peril by an unchecked tyranny. The iconoclasts had rent asunder the sacred places and objects of

162. Baelde and Van Peteghem, "Pacificatie van Gent"; Koenigsberger, *Monarchies, States Generals and Parliaments*, 270–72.
163. *Sendbrief* in Bor, *Oorsprongk*, 1:464–72. I have used the English excerpt in Schmidt, *Innocence Abroad*, 82.
164. NG, 2:202.
165. Parker, "Mutiny and Discontent," 113.
166. NG, 2:203.

Catholic religious worship and Burgundian political authority and, by doing so, wounded the appeal of the Beggars' movement. Alba and his men had wreaked equal havoc on the political and urban landscape and, by doing so, compromised the king and stirred civic outrage. By late 1576, Holland and Zeeland were prepared to renounce the sovereignty of Philip II as the other provinces struggled with religious sectarianism and the problem of princely injustice. As the Good Shepherd Philip II watched his image tarnish, William of Orange assumed the position of the valiant defender of family, household, and fatherland. The Revolt was now vigorously advanced in the language of civic order and virtuous citizenship—with its privileges and its domestic foundations—born not of political theory but in the violence of warfare.

CHAPTER 7 FATHER OF THE FATHERLAND
WILLIAM OF ORANGE AS CIVIC PATRIOT

Around 1580, shortly before the States General in Antwerp issued their Act of Abjuration of Philip II's sovereignty over the rebellious provinces, Theodore de Bry made an engraving that juxtaposed William of Orange with Philip II and Pope Gregory XIII. The print's theme is the desire for peace in a world troubled by mankind's follies and by the ugly grip of the devil, depicted as a clawed beast with drooping breasts. This horrid she-devil entices idolaters as she hovers over a globe that holds biblical scenes of the Fall and the Apocalypse. On the right, Philip II and Gregory XIII pray to Christ for peace, yet they are positioned by De Bry to face the sinful world and the devil. In posture and gesture, both leaders mimic the biblical kings inside the globe who worship the Seven-Headed Beast of the Apocalypse. Philip II and Gregory XIII, praying, are accompanied by a group that includes an unnamed bishop. But the most notable figure in the company is Philips Willem, Orange's captive son, who had been forcibly taken by Habsburg authorities to Castile when his father fled to Dillenburg in 1567. In the text next to him, Philips Willem pleads to return to the Netherlands. It is not clear in the print whether Orange hears his son's pleas or anything else in this landscape of worldly troubles, since he kneels with his back to the globe. Ever the pious warrior, the prince in military dress prays before Christ, asking for his people's deliverance from sin and the restoration of peace.

By contrasting Orange with pope and king rather than the usual Alba, De Bry tells us a great deal about how elevated the prince's political stock had become among the Dutch rebels by 1580. Miniature illustrations above both Philip II's retinue and William of Orange provide one axis of the contrast. Over the royal party is a depiction of Daniel's release from the lion's den, perhaps a reference, as James Tanis and Daniel Horst have suggested, to Philips Willem's status as captive among foes.[1] The illustration placed above William of Orange repeats the filial theme in a jarringly different manner. A man kneels in prayer before a statue of a "strange god," while being stabbed in the back by a younger man. In

---

1. Tanis and Horst, *Images of Discord*, 90–91.

WILLIAM OF ORANGE AS CIVIC PATRIOT 261

William of Orange, on the left, kneels before Christ, while Philip II, Pope Gregory XIII, and others, including Orange's kidnapped son Philips Willem, pray in front of a she-beast reigning over a sinful world. Theodore de Bry, ca. 1577–80. Courtesy of Simon van Gijn-museum aan huis, Dordrecht.

the center right foreground of the murder scene is a pillar upon which an open tablet features the first commandment proscribing the worship of other gods. It is a probable depiction of the biblical story of the Assyrian king Sennacherib (ca. 705–681 BCE), son of the famed Saragon. As he strove to maintain the military empire of his father, Sennacherib skirmished with nearby kingdoms and invaded Judah, besieging Jerusalem. While he routed his enemies, captured Babylon, and built a splendid palace for himself at Nineveh, Sennacherib died at the hands of his jealous sons while he was in prayer before the god Nisroch (2 Kings 19:37, and Isaiah 39). In his appropriation of this biblical tale, De Bry has sharpened its emphasis on idolatry and linked it to filial betrayal: the king is stabbed in the back by his son at precisely the moment he offers prayers to Nisroch. Portrayed as the polar opposite of such woe is Orange, the model Christian soldier. But the prince is a hero himself beset with filial woes, his eldest son held in the enemy camp. Sennacherib stands for wicked kingship, and, by easy analogy, Philip II: Sennacherib was a grasping ruler whose imperial army ransacked cities—certainly a reference to the siege motif still fresh on Netherlanders' minds—and whose idolatrous appetites resulted in his death at the hands of his unfaithful sons. To De Bry, William of Orange and his son Philips Willem are archetypes of the nation as family, devout but tragically separated by a punishing king. The king is cut from the same moral fabric as the Assyrian Sennacherib, besieger of godly cities, idolater par excellence, and father of a family itself succumbing to self-destruction.

De Bry's print indicates that the Reformed political imagination in the Netherlands on the eve of the abjuration of Philip II still trafficked in a binary symbolism that posited pious rebels against a sinful opposition guilty of the twin vices of tyranny and idolatry. New, however, are the explicit contrast between Orange and the king, and the secondary echo of Philip II-Sennacherib as desecrator of sacred cities. No doubt both themes come out of the experience of the violence against cities in the 1570s and the triumphant mood savored by the Patriots in the aftermath of the Pacification of Ghent and the expulsion of the hated Army of Flanders. While even the most dedicated rebels were not yet ready to pillory Philip II in public, the king began to recede from their political rhetoric, and his demotion increasingly profited William of Orange, simultaneously touted as leader of the Revolt and assigned paternal imagery previously the provenance of Burgundian and Habsburg royalty. A coterie of writers and artists hailed Orange as *pater familias* of a land whose king had failed in his political obligations, transferring to him the paternal hallmarks of royalty to match the fraternal associations the civic traumas of the 1570s helped nourish.

Since the failure of his military campaign against Alba in 1568, Orange had linked his cause to the Revolt, becoming its most visible spokesperson. In the second half of the 1570s, the prince served as an invaluable symbol to the Patriots, the princely embodiment of an inchoate civic republicanism that interpreted lordly sovereignty as the guarantor of civic and provincial interests. As the king assumed the hue of tyranny once reserved for Alba, Orange gained new associations, none more potent than *pater patriae*, or father of the fatherland, a designation previously ascribed in the Burgundian Netherlands only to Valois and Habsburg princes.[2] Not ready to repudiate monarchy, the Patriots nevertheless were eager to transfer some of its symbolic heft to Orange, while maintaining the civic, fraternal imagery that had become a standard part of his profile. What is more, the bur-

2. On the conceptual history of *patria*, fatherland, and related patriotic semantics in the Low Countries, see Karin Tilmans, "De ontwikkeling van een vaderland-begrip," and E. O. G. Haitsma Mulier, "Het begrip 'Vaderland' in de Nederlandse geschiedschrijving van de late zestiende tot de eerste helft van de achttiende," in *Vaderland: een geschiedenis van de vijftiende eeuw tot 1940*, ed. N. C. F. van Sas (Amsterdam, 1999), 163–80. By comparison, references to *patria* emerged in the territories of the empire in the late fifteenth century for the areas of the *regnum teutonicum*. Yet the term "patriots" as a political badge took hold in the early seventeenth century, and across northern Europe, making the Dutch Revolt a key conduit of this semantic shift. For a series of case studies, see Robert von Friedenberg, ed., *Patria und Patrioten vor dem Patriotismus* (Wiesbaden, 2005).

nishing of Orange's image occurred in tandem with the new swell of civic boosterism. In the wake of the expulsion of the Army of Flanders, the cities of the Low Countries asserted their age-old rights and privileges, and made ridding themselves of the hated citadels essential to this urban refurbishment. Orange became a key reference point, fraternal defender of this civic order but also wise father to the imagined *patria* at large. By 1577 he had even mastered the greatest Burgundian princely ritual, the entry ceremony, resuscitating the fifteenth-century civic idioms that the Habsburg rulers had downgraded, while borrowing some of the sacred imagery with which they had inflated it. By 1581 invocations of Philip II had become so muted that the Patriots could comfortably renounce his sovereignty while transferring much of the princely sheen to Orange and to the States General's hand-picked successor to the king, the Duke of Anjou. Orange became the perfect cultural and political barometer for a political sensibility in which monarchy and civic and provincial authority were in tension, their alignment not disputed but never precisely fixed. He was princely and paternal, yet no usurper of Philip II's titles; he was lordly in stature, but a fraternal defender of the civic order who fought in league with his brothers to redeem a fatherland imperiled by tyranny. His hereditary nobility recalled his Burgundian eliteness, while his fraternal, republican symbols solidified his ties to the urban sphere and its political aspirations.

The City Renewed:
Casting Down the "Murderers' Nest"

The apparent unity welding the core provinces of Brabant, Flanders, Zeeland, and Holland by the sealing of the Pacification of Ghent on November 8, 1576 soon dissipated. Although the hated Army of Flanders began to retreat in April 1577, the attempt by the southern Catholic conservatives and Orange, Holland and Zeeland to iron out differences over religious policies and political allegiances collapsed at talks held at Geertruidenberg May 13–27, 1577.[3] Meanwhile, Don Juan's failed effort to reassemble a force from the Army of Flanders to quell the armies of the States General in July of that year finished his credibility. The States General grew divided between those in Orange's orbit and those in the camp of the Catholic Philippe de Croy, Duke of Aarschot, who sought an accommodation with Philip II, albeit one that would preserve the traditional power of the nobility. Aarschot, a determined foe of the Beggars in 1566, scored a major victory when he maneuvered the selection of the young Austrian Archduke Matthias in the States General as governor general on December 7, 1577, thereby nullifying Don Juan's power while retaining the framework of Habsburg sovereignty. Now fully discredited, Don Juan con-

---

3. "Vraye narration de costé et d'aultre entre les députez de Don Jehan et monseigneur le prince et députez de Hollande et Zeelande," in Griffiths, *Representative Government*, 452–62.

signed himself to fighting the States' troops until his death from the plague on October 1, 1578. Always the deft politician, Orange managed, despite Aarschot's opposition, to win appointment in the States General as Matthias's lieutenant general and, more remarkably, as *ruwaart* of Brabant, a position akin to *stadholder*. Orange's fortunes were clearly on the rise in the south. Yet he faced the Herculean task of managing radical Calvinist impulses resurfacing in Flemish and Brabantine cities, Ghent and Antwerp especially, while countering the royalist leanings of Aarschot.[4]

Despite the States General's feeble attempts to exercise authority over the north—this campaign included appointing the conservative Catholic noble Georges de Lalaing, Count of Rennenberg, as *stadholder* of Friesland and Groningen—the separate development of the Revolt in Holland and Zeeland only intensified. The Alteratie (change of civic rule) in Amsterdam in May 1578 enhanced this development. Despite Amsterdam's history as a royalist stronghold from which Alba and his son Fadrique had run their campaign against the rebels of 1572–73, and even though at least half of its inhabitants remained Catholic, Amsterdam fell under the control of a Calvinist regency. Since June 1575 Holland and Zeeland had been joined in a defense pact that laid the groundwork for a separate state abiding by the Reformed religion. Strengthened by Amsterdam's Calvinist turn, these tendencies finally resulted in the January 1579 Union of Utrecht. The agreement made no mention of the Spanish king and allowed its signatories to implement their own religious policy provided that freedom of conscience was secured. It permitted Holland and Zeeland to maintain a monopoly for the Dutch Reformed Church, and to secure a measure of political independence from the States General. In the southern territories, Calvinist radicals gained power in key cities in Flanders and Brabant. Meanwhile, Aarschot's royalists, horrified by these events, banded together into a formidable bloc to seek reconciliation with the king. Dogged by divisions, Orange had to tread in difficult waters even as his fortunes soared with his triumphant restoration of power—and physical return—to his power base in Brabant.[5]

In the immediate aftermath of the Pacification of Ghent, these crosscurrents of religious and political troubles made peace seem parlous. But elation at the banishment of the hated Army of Flanders, desecrator of the civic order, overrode any pessimistic foreboding. In the wake of the Pacification's promulgation, Low Country' cities with the despised Spanish citadels moved swiftly to alter or dismantle them, a public expunging of

---

4. On Orange's political dilemmas, see Johan Decavele, "Willem van Oranje de 'Vader' van een verscheurd 'Vaderland' (1577–1584)," *Handelingen der Maatschappij voor Geschiedenis en Oudheidkunde te Gent* 38 (1984): 69–86, and Swart, *William of Orange*, 103–85; in general of this period, G. Malengreau, *L'Esprit particulariste et la Révolution des Pays-Bas au XVIe siècle, 1578–1584* (Louvain, 1936).

5. On the Walloon conservatives, see H. de Schepper, "De mentale rekonversie van de Zuidnederlandse adel na de Pacificatie van Gent," *Tijdschrift voor Geschiedenis* 89 (1976): 422–23; on the conditions set by the States General for the reception of Archduke Matthias as governor general, see the original text in Griffiths, *Representative Government*, 463–68; on Holland and Zeeland, see J. C. Boogman, "The Union of Utrecht: Its Genesis and Consequences," *Bijdragen en Mededelingen betreffende de Geschiedenis der Nederlanden* 94 (1979): 377–407.

the hated "murderers' nest" that had symbolized the supervision of urban public life by Habsburg authorities.[6] Rid of these citadels and their men, cities would be free of a burden they had borne since Alba, a critical step toward fulfillment of the patriotic zeal for a rejuvenated civic freedom. As one petition in October 1577 to the States General to dismantle the citadels of Antwerp and Ghent put it, "We are a people descended from free ancestors."[7] In Antwerp and Utrecht, the eagerness to get rid of their citadels spawned public legends of heroic shovel- and pick-wielding citizens, bolstering an elated spirit of urban populism. As the Estates of Friesland wrote in 1577 about their effort to take down Alba's citadel in Groningen, "We are destroyers of citadels but builders of free cities."[8]

Not long after the Pacification of Ghent, cities with citadels such as Antwerp, Ghent, Groningen, Utrecht, Valenciennes, Béthune, and Lille began to petition the States General for their partial dismantlement or demolition.[9] Utrecht's action against its Vredenburg Citadel set the tone for events elsewhere. Constructed in 1529 by Charles V as a redoubt against the hostile Duke of Guelders and as an affirmation of his lordly authority, Vredenburg at the start of Alba's regime in 1567 had a garrison of the Army of Flanders assigned to it. More troops arrived in 1571, and on February 12, 1572, Alba stigmatized Utrecht by ordering its archives, the repository of its privileges, transferred under guard to Vredenburg.[10] After the Pacification of Ghent, opposition to Vredenburg mounted. Exacerbating the controversy over its future were internal divisions over who was the rightful candidate to succeed as Utrecht's *stadholder*. On the one hand, there was Gilles de Berlaymont, Baron of Hierges, put into office by the king but temporarily in alliance with the States General. On the other hand, there was William of Orange, supported by master artisans and other craftsmen and a claimant to the title since 1572. This was no minor matter in Utrecht, the seat of the northern Netherlands' most important bishopric. In 1566 the city had been shaken by iconoclasm—225 Utrechters were summoned before the Council of Troubles under Alba—but it returned to Spanish control firmly in 1567, and in 1572 it had served as a strategic base for Army of Flanders' military expeditions against Holland's Beggars.[11]

---

6. Bor, *Oorsprongk*, 1:802, referring to the dismantling of Utrecht's Vredenburg Citadel. Orange too had insisted on the partial demolition of the citadels as a condition of peace with Don Juan. See *Archives d'Orange-Nassau*, 4:559–61.

7. J. M. B. C. Kervyn de Lettenhove, *Les Huguenots et les Gueux*, 6 vols. (Bruges, 1883–85), 4:471.

8. J. Grooten, "Het kasteel van Coevorden in de zestiende eeuw," *Nieuwe Drentse Volksalmanak*, 102 (1985): 1–20. I thank Charles van den Heuvel for this reference.

9. André Despretz, "Stadsversterkingen en burgerwacht tijdens de instauratiejaren der Gentse Calvinistische Republiek (1577–1579)," *Handelingen der Maatschappij voor Geschiedenis en Oudheidkunde te Gent*, 20 (1966): 3–18.

10. J. E. A. L. Struick, *Utrecht door de eeuwen heen* (Utrecht and Antwerp, 1968), 158.

11. A. van Hulzen, *Utrecht in 1566 en 1567* (Groningen, 1932); Jan van Vliet, *Ketters rond de Dom* (Utrecht, 1987); and Benjamin J. Kaplan, *Calvinists and Libertines: Confession and Community in Utrecht, 1578–1620* (Oxford, 1995), 20–21, and 135–36 on Orange gaining the stadholdership.

Even before the Estates of Utrecht confirmed its support of Orange in October 1577, there was popular outcry for Vredenburg's physical dismantlement, after a winter of turmoil between citadel soldiers and townspeople. An anonymous chronicler from Utrecht captured much of the tension during this period.[12] Since their arrival, the soldiers of the Army of Flanders in Vredenburg had behaved scandalously, pilfering goods from citizens, harassing married women, widows, and orphans and fancying themselves "kings, dukes, and counts" in an inversion imaginary fed by their arrogance.[13] But matters intensified after the sack of Antwerp and the signing of the Pacification of Ghent, as angry, restless soldiers realized their days in Vredenburg were numbered. On December 21 and 22, fighting broke out in the city between them and men from Utrecht's local militia. In the mêlée, cannon shot and fire destroyed houses around Vredenburg. The chronicler was aghast: citizens wondered, he mused, whether the trial of enduring these armed rascals was punishment from God for their transgressions.[14] After persistent demands for the garrison troops to leave, Francesco Fernando d'Avila agreed to remove his contingent from Vredenburg on February 11, 1577. Despite this victory, popular demands to dismantle the citadel mounted while the Estates of Utrecht equivocated about the wisdom of such an action. On May 2 a throng of artisans marched on the citadel to force a decision—craftsmen formed the backbone of Orange's support in the city—well in advance of the official decree to dismantle it granted by the States General on August 18.[15]

By the seventeenth century, the popular agitation against the Vredenburg citadel had spawned the legend of Catrijn van Leemput, heroic citizen-warrior in the tradition of her Haarlem counterpart Kenau Simonsdochter Hasselaer. Much like Hasselaer, Van Leemput was a real historical person alchemized into political mythology. As the tale has it, Van Leemput successfully resisted an assault by two soldiers by wielding a knife hidden in her clothes. Later, she led a citizen army—picks, shovels, and hammers aloft—in the assault on the hated citadel.[16] Van Leemput is the vindication of rape victims of the civic sacks, fending off a personal attack to lead a group effort against the fortress of their oppression. More than just its physical eradication, Vredenburg Citadel's dismantlement represented the enactment of a different kind of destruction executed by the very same means—work tools and craftsmen's hands—that *beeldenstormers* had employed a decade earlier.

The theme of the city renewed after the expulsion of the Army of Flanders gained even wider currency with the efforts to take down parts of the citadels of Ghent and Antwerp. These too came under attack in the summer of 1577, with permission likewise granted by

---

12. Muller, "Verhaal van het beleg van het kasteel Vredenburg," 147–209, esp. 170–72.
13. Ibid., 168–70.
14. Ibid., 173, 195–203.
15. T. J. Hoekstra, *Vredenburg Castle at Utrecht* (Utrecht, 1982).
16. Her exploits were celebrated in Johan van Beverwijck, *Van den Uutnementheyt des Vrouwelicken Geslachts* (Dordrecht, 1643). See also J. G. Riphaagen, "Trijn van Leemput (–1607), heldin van de Vredenburg," in *Utrechtse Biografieën: Levensbeschrijvingen van bekende en onbekende Utrechters* (Utrecht, n.d.), 1:97–101.

the States General. Well before the States General broke with Don Juan, all three members of Ghent's Broad Council had asked permission on January 7, 1577, to take action against the citadel, home to around three thousand soldiers until their expulsion on November 13, 1576, days after the Pacification. As in Utrecht, the sting of Antwerp's Spanish Fury was still fresh in Ghent, and its citizens doubtless were emboldened because Orange had marched against the Army of Flanders garrisoned in the citadel before the Pacification was signed. But Ghentenars' antipathy to the citadel went deeper. Supported by taxes that fell most heavily on craftsmen and artisans, the citadel with its soldiers was resented because it symbolized "the public suppression of rights, charters, and privileges."[17] Built in 1540, it was a stinging reminder of the humiliation of Charles V's victory over the city after its revolt. On August 21, 1577, the States granted Ghent's request, and work to dismantle part of the citadel started on September 30.

Heightening the significance of the partial destruction of the Ghent citadel was its direct linkage to a larger public works project: the construction of new city walls. This fortification project was begun on October 12, 1577, but not finished until 1581, though most of the work was done in the first year. The two civic projects were intimately linked. Ghent's citadel was not so much dismantled as redesigned, its two western bastions facing the city torn down, so that the remainder could be fluently integrated into the new enceinte.[18] The conjoining of the two projects could not have had a clearer message: a city freed from its Spanish yoke is a city strong and fortified, the new triangular bastioned walls and deep moats projecting an urban order not merely restored, but strengthened. Just such a sentiment appears in a poem praising Jan van Hembyze, the radical leader of Ghent's Calvinist turn. On the occasion of Van Hembyze's forced departure from Ghent in August, 1579, the poet lauds him as a leader who transformed Ghent from a city "naked" to one strong and fortified, a city of new bastions.[19] Ghent had even exacted a labor corvée to support the fortifications' project: a rotational system imposed on neighborhoods that guaranteed at least 450 citizen-hands at work at any given time, though this gave way within a half year to the right to pay a tax instead as support. If the spirit of citizenship was evoked to support the efforts, so too was interurban fraternity: Antwerp and Ghent pledged workers to one another to help in their efforts to transform their citadels.[20] When William of Orange entered Ghent on December 29, 1577, 170 Antwerpeners accompanied him, and, according to a local chronicler, they set about helping to dismantle the citadel the very next day.[21]

17. For the January 26, 1577, request, see SAG, 120, no. 2, 86, and for the quote, see SAG, reeks 107, no. 3, fol. 145r, cited in Dambruyne, *Corporatieve middengroepen*, 646, n. 184.
18. Despretz, "Stadsversterkingen en burgerwacht."
19. Decavele, *Eind van een rebelse droom*, 96.
20. Ibid., 96; Despretz, "Stadsversterkingen en burgerwacht."
21. P. C. van der Meersch, ed., *Memorieboek der stad Ghendt, van 't jaer 1301 tot 1793*, 3 vols. (Ghent, 1854), 3:34.

Antwerp's actions against its vilified citadel received even greater public airing than Utrecht's or Ghent's, understandably so since its citadel had been the launching site of the Spanish Fury against the city. Nor did anyone forget that the Antwerp citadel was the Duke of Alba's favorite public works project, its bastions mostly named after himself. Antwerp's undertaking spawned a vibrant tale about tool-wielding citizens who bravely marched on the citadel, an account that must have influenced the seventeenth-century legend of Van Leemput in Utrecht. The attack on Antwerp's citadel functioned as a jubilant cleansing ritual before the fortress's redesign as civic property and eventual home to William of Orange and his court when he returned to Brabant in January 1578.[22] A ballad commemorating the end of Alba's citadel features the plaint of "Madonna Citadel,"

> Oh, how I have been oppressed and am bereft of comfort because I am little loved in this land. What dejects me the most, ah woe, is that I must die when I am so young.[23]

The citadel laments her lack of friends and the fact that her Spanish guardians have become outlaws. Everyone hates her, especially women, "who had lost their husbands and now are widows . . . they have vigorously sworn that I must die!" Indeed, "everyone has reason to hate me" the citadel laments, because "my robbers' nest is full of the goods and blood of orphans."[24] As the ballad makes clear, Antwerp's citadel was inextricably associated with the city's sack by the Army of Flanders. Its gendering in a mock virginal Catholic cloak as "Madonna Castilla" is played off against invocations of the Spanish Fury as murderous rape that left vulnerable young widows and destitute orphans in its wake. The ballad partakes of the same domestic metaphors that gave narrative verve to the official commemorations of sacks and sieges. Little wonder then that commemorations of the partial dismantlement of the citadel would tap into these same stock currents and feature the storyline of a heroic throng of citizens attacking the symbol of their misery, the citadel that nearly ruined family and city.

In actuality, Antwerp's citadel had briefly fallen into sympathetic hands when on February 12, 1577, the lieutenant of the despised Gerónimo de Roda handed its supervision over to the Duke of Aarschot's men. The Army of Flanders garrison gave way to the States General's soldiers, who were mostly Walloons —but not for long, because Don Juan decided to substitute German mercenaries under the authority of the loyal Louis de Blois, Lord of Treslong. After Don Juan's failed attempt to take the city on August 1, however, the new governor of Antwerp, Jan van Redeghem, Lord of Liedekercke, took firm control

---

22. On Orange's residency in Antwerp's citadel, see Delen, *Hof en hofcultuur rondom Willem van Oranje*, 96–111; and Prims, "De huisraad van Oranje te Antwerpen," and Prims, "Met Oranje op den Kasteelplaats," *Antwerpiensia* 7 (1933–34): 128–42.

23. *Bekentenisse ende verscheydinghe van Madonna Castillia tot Antwerpen* (1577).

24. Ibid.

of the citadel and expelled the now fully discredited garrison. Buoyed by success, Antwerp's magistrates officially submitted a request on August 19 to demolish some of the citadel's bastions, and work began days later when permission was granted.[25]

As with Ghent, authorities preserved much of Antwerp's citadel for integration into the city's walls. The dismantlement of the Ferdinand bastion and several curtains that faced the city took on the air of civic celebration, inaugurated by a march on the hated "murderers' nest" by jubilant citizens brandishing household and work tools. The elation of saving Antwerp from yet another sack, this time at the hands of the treacherous Don Juan, inspired popular art. A series of seven prints by Hieronymus Wierix in 1578 after a design by Maarten de Vos culminates in a depiction of the march on the citadel, with a throng of men, women, and youth holding high pickaxes and shovels as they head toward the "Duke of Alba's temple." Lest the message be obscure, the print features an allegory on the upper right of Liberty removing the chains from her shackled feet with a key. Freedom is regained, and, in the words of the text underneath, commerce can once again flourish. This same theme echoes in one of two allegorical prints produced by Jacques de Gheyn I in 1577. It features a bird's-eye frontal view of Antwerpeners engaged in the actual physical work of destruction. Allegorical figures frame the action: on the left are Peace and Justice, heralded by the Latin text as better bastions for the city than the citadel, and on the right are Truth and Love, who restore the Maiden of Antwerp's vigor.[26] The text, in Latin, French, and Dutch, emphasizes the civic unity behind the enterprise. Von Redeghem, the new governor of Antwerp, and Pontus de Noyelles, the Lord of Bourse—both instrumental in ridding Antwerp of the German garrison—cast the first stones against the citadel, followed immediately by "noble, rich, and great and ordinary" folk who together set to work.[27] If Wierix's print features a popular rally of citizens armed with everyday tools, De Gheyn's zeros in on the collective action against the bastions facing the city, presented as an act of civic iconoclasm against a public landmark whose emotional charge was no less incandescent than was the church of Onze-Lieve-Vrouw to the Calvinists in 1566. Both structures were assaulted, but only partially, and both at the hands of well-organized bands armed with nothing more than their everyday tools.

After the return of William of Orange to Brabant in January 1578, Alba's citadel was assigned a new civic purpose, as home to the court of William of Orange, his third wife Char-

25. Prims, *Geschiedenis van Antwerpen*, 8:137–39; C. van den Heuvel, "The Use of the Map in Town Planning-Historical Research: The Partial Demolition and Insertion of the Citadel of Antwerp, in *Taking Sides/ En marges des rives. Antwerp's 19th-Century Belt: Elements for a Culture of the City/La ceinture du XIXe siècle à Anvers: Éléments pour une culture de la ville* (Antwerp, 1993), 169–171; Lombaerde, "Herrschaftsarchitektur."

26. Formal analysis is in Horst, *Opstand in zwart-wit*, 224–34.

27. The taking down of the citadel inspired a genre; there are at least seven known paintings of its dismantlement at the hands of jubilant citizens; see the catalogue of the Hans Vredeman de Vries exhibition in Antwerp in 2002, Heiner Borggrefe et al. eds., *Tussen stadspaleizen en luchtkastelen. Hans Vredeman de Vries en de Renaissance* (Ghent, 2002), no. 133, 291–95.

Antwerp's ordinary citizens with their work tools celebrate as they march to dismantle Alba's hated fortress. One of seven prints issued by Hieronymus Wierix after a design by Maarten de Vos, 1578. Courtesy of Rijksprentenkabinet, Rijksmusuem, Amsterdam.

The partial dismantling of Antwerp's citadel, with the allegorical figures of Peace and Justice to the left, and Truth and Love to the right. Jacques de Gheyn I, 1577. Courtesy of Rijksprentenkabinet, Rijksmuseum, Amsterdam.

lotte de Bourbon, the children from their marriage, three older children from the prince's first two marriages, a natural son, and his fairly large court of some 180 persons.[28] During his occupancy until 1583, Orange had the former governor's house reconstructed into a Renaissance-style palazzo to befit his princely status, just as in Vlissingen in 1582 he had a residence built from materials appropriated from Alba's unfinished citadel there. While in Antwerp, Orange and his wife had four more children. All daughters, they were named

28. Delen, *Hof en hofcultuur rondom Willem van Oranje*, 104, whose analysis is based on a surviving court list and ordinances for the Antwerp period of residency; Swart, *William of Orange*, 144–45. On the refurbishing of the governor's house in the citadel for Orange and on Vlissingen, see Lombaerde, "Herrschaftsarchitektur," 325, 329–30.

Catharina Belgica, Charlotte Flandrina, Charlotte Brabantina, and Emilia Antwerpiana respectively, each striking a patriotic chord associated with the triumphant return of Orange to the south. Antwerp's citadel had represented the destruction of the family—in the legend of the wedding party cut down during the Spanish Fury and in the Madonna Castillia ballad that wept for the orphans and widows the citadel created, to take two examples. But it now housed the Revolt's father figure and nurtured his court and family whose newborn girls bore names tied to the heroic city, its province Brabant, and its ally Flanders. The city unshackled of its chains by ordinary citizens was a city renewed through the restoration of household and family, best illustrated by Father William and his specially named new children.

FATHER, FAMILY, AND BROTHERS

When Orange moved his family and court to Antwerp's rededicated citadel, he was riding a spike in popularity, having returned triumphantly from Holland to Brabant a decade after he hastily fled to Dillenburg to escape Alba's judgment. It was between this period of enforced exile and his homecoming to Brabant that he became increasingly considered head of the Revolt, a status all but guaranteed when he regained the stadholdership of the rebellious provinces of Zeeland and Holland in 1572. Still, Orange was never a universally acclaimed leader, an impossible position in a conflict intractably fragmented along political and religious fault lines. What is more, there were considerable problems in conceptualizing the Netherlands as a unified *patria* to which Orange could appeal, even though émigrés in the 1550s and 1560s began increasingly to talk of "our fatherland, the whole Netherlands," in the words of the Calvinist Marten Micron in London.[29] *Patria* and its vernacular equivalents—community, land, general lands, even fatherland—were plastic terms whose meanings varied from the spiritual realm to the local turf. Although they had been invoked in Dutch sources prior to the Revolt, they had mostly functioned as provincial or urban designations.[30] Orange's challenge was to hold in balance two impulses that nourished his stature but tacked in opposite directions: the fraternal rhetoric of civic brotherhood and urban liberty that the Patriots cultivated, full of prideful localism, and the royal paternalism that cast him as father of a united fatherland, with its appeal to the common political good.

A further, equally paralyzing challenge to Orange's universal appeal was the vexing problem of religious allegiance. Since Orange's impassioned defense of freedom of conscience in the Council of State in 1564, he had pursued a policy of religious coexistence among Protestants and Catholics. He did so for the same pragmatic reasons that had mo-

---

29. Duke, "The Elusive Netherlands," 37, quote from M. Micron, *De christlicke ordinancien der Nederlantscher ghemeinten te London (1554)*, ed. W. F. Dankbaar (The Hague, 1956), 35–37. See also S. Groenveld, "'Natie' en 'patria,'" republished in Van Sas, *Vaderland*, 55–82.

30. Tilmans, "De ontwikkeling van een vaderland-begrip," esp. 14–23.

tivated the more resolutely Catholic Egmont to argue that same year that the draconian measures to enforce religious unity in the Netherlands were impractical because the Low Countries were a compact set of territories abutting Protestant lands.[31] But the goal of religious accommodation proved elusive in the calcified atmosphere of Catholic and Calvinist fighting, and there was no lack of criticism of Orange himself as a man in-between, a composite of different beliefs, even after his profession of Calvinism in 1573. In a 1580 dig at Orange, an anonymous author portrayed him as craftily silken in personality, and Janus-like in faith: "He comports himself so dexterously that not even the most astute can know [his religion]: the Catholics see him as Catholic, the Lutherans, as Lutheran." In point of fact, the observer charged, he was a bit of both, manipulating religion as "a political invention," a horror that inevitably leads to atheism.[32]

The polemic did have an element of truth. Although Orange took up the cudgel against Philip II's policies early as a member of the Council of State and knight of the Golden Fleece, he was no youthful revolutionary. Rather, he showed himself more willing to play the dissenting statesman who sought compromise, than the charismatic Beggar, a role cherished by Hendrik van Brederode until his untimely death in 1568.[33] Orange's decision to embrace rebellion came after Brederode's death robbed the opposition of a leader and, more decisively, after his own condemnation by Alba's Council—he was summoned to appear before the tribunal on January 19, 1568—and after the arrest of his close colleagues earlier that fall. The die was cast for the incipient Revolt when the prince crossed the Maas River on October 5, 1568, having defended his position as a loyal vassal of a misguided king in his *Justification of the Prince of Orange* issued months earlier, in April.[34] In a clever sequence of arguments, Orange denounced the heresy placards, pinned the blame for the troubles on Cardinal Granvelle "and his creatures," presented himself as a loyal servant unjustly robbed of his goods and rights, and, in line with the writings of his associate Jacob van Wesembeke, linked his position to the fight to preserve the inviolable rights and privileges upon which the cardinal and his followers had so carelessly trampled.[35]

Orange's *Justification* bore his imprint, but it was probably written in collaboration with

---

31. Rachfahl, *Wilhelm von Oranien*, 2:474–75.

32. Bibliothèque d'Arras, MS. 249, *Commencement de l'Histoire des troubles des Pays-Bas, advenuz soubz le gouvernement de Madame la Duchesse de Parme*, cited in *Correspondance Taciturne*, 2:iii–v.

33. Rachfahl, *Wilhelm von Oranien*, a political consideration of Orange's career to 1568; see also Duke, "From 'Loyal Servant' to 'Irreconcilable Opponent' of Spain," in Swart, *William of Orange*, 17–18, especially the point that although cautious, Orange pushed more vigorously than his peers for a resolution to the religious debates.

34. *La Justification du Prince d'Orange contre les faulx blasmes, que ses Calumniateurs taschent à luy imposer à tort*, in *Apologie de Guillaume de Nassau, Prince d'Orange*, ed. A. Lacroix (Brussels and Leipzig, 1858), 157–205, and 207–12 for the January 19, 1568, condemnation of Orange.

35. On the influence of Wesenbeke on the tone of the *Justification*, see Van Gelderen, *Political Thought*, 120.

Wesembeke and the Huguenot Hubert Languet, part of his tight circle of exiled writers and associates.[36] It marked Orange's first public efforts to craft his profile as an impugned grandee forced to take up arms—the first move to present himself as an inspirational, self-sacrificing leader of the incipient rebellion.[37] However ideologically astute, this effort also carefully rode the prevailing political winds. As the Revolt matured, especially after the quick pace of events in Holland and Zeeland in 1572, Orange's self-presentation shifted from that of faithful vassal bravely opposing wrongful state policy for the honor of his lord to independent political leader fighting an unjust king. Orange now became the wise prince and pious warrior, one whose paternal gifts were complemented by the civic commitments of his fellow citizens and the fraternal bonds of the Nassau family. Orange's return to Brabant in 1577 saw an intensification of such rhetoric, distilled in different versions in a cluster of entry ceremonies staged that year on his behalf in Brussels and Ghent, and later in Amsterdam in 1580. In these ceremonies, Orange co-opted the premier Burgundian public ritual both to vaunt his authority and to restore the full civic dimension of its rites.[38] These were bravura performances that officialized Orange's charismatic authority and helped to fortify him against the political troubles that beset him in the final years of his life when he pursued his ill-fated French policy.

Such heady acclaim for the prince was the result of a decade of concerted efforts to link his profile to the Revolt. It was in 1568 that Orange began to tap a small, vibrant group of literary figures and writers who resided either with him in Dillenburg or the Calvinist stronghold of Emden. Men like the Antwerp pensionary Jacob van Wesenbeke and the lawyers Gilles le Clercq and François Baudouin busied themselves presenting Orange as a wise, valiant hero, cobbling together a stock of easily understandable associations for the prince.[39] From the outset, printed pamphlets like the *Justification* were essential to this effort, but the Orangists quickly seized on other media to make their case, particularly artwork and popular balladry.[40] No surprise, then, that the military campaign inaugurated

36. Ibid.; Cellarius, "Die Propagandatätigkeit Wilhelms von Oranien."

37. On Orange's "think-tank" and its development after 1568, see René van Stipriaan, "Words at War: The Early Years of William of Orange's Propaganda," *Journal of Early Modern History* 11, no.4–5 (2007): 331–49.

38. Official booklets were prepared by rhetoricians and publishers to memorialize these entries: Jan Baptist Houwaert, *Declaratie van de triumphante Incompst vanden Doorluchtigen . . . Prince van Orangien binnen die princelijcke Stadt van Brussele* (Antwerp, 1579); Lucas d'Heere, *Beschrijvinghe van het ghene dat vertoocht wierdt ter Incomste van d'Excellentie des Princen van Oraengien binnen der stede van Ghendt den XXIX Decembris 1577* (Ghent, 1578); Gillis vanden Rade, *Incomste vanden doorluchtighen Vorst ende Heere mijn Heere den Prince van Orangien binnen der Vermaerde Coopstad van Amsterdam den XVII Martii 1580* (Antwerp, 1580).

39. Van Stipriaan, "Words at War," is particularly insightful for the launching of this enterprise and the social networks Orange managed.

40. On the genre of the pamphlet in the Dutch Revolt, see Duke, "Posters, Pamphlets, and Prints," and, for the early Republic, Craig Harline, *Pamphlets, Printing and Political Culture in the Early Dutch Republic* (The Hague, 1987).

by Orange in 1568 gave occasion both to the first song heralding the prince's actions and to the first visual representations of Orange as righteous leader. By far the most famed of these early cultural efforts was the "Wilhelmus," the composition in the Beggars' ballad repertoire that in an updated version in 1932 became the national anthem of the Netherlands.[41] It appeared in the 1577–78 first edition of the *Beggars' Songbook*, but its author and exact date of composition have proven elusive—Orange's tireless secretary Philips van Marnix, Lord of St. Aldegonde is often mentioned, and also the Antwerp rhetorician Willem van Haecht and the Leiden rhetorician Jan Fruytiers.[42] Most experts are convinced the "Wilhelmus" was written sometime between 1568 and 1572, because its first documented use was during the 1573 siege of Haarlem, when a member of the civic garrison sang it defiantly atop the city's walls. The song mentions Orange's taking up arms in 1568 and the death of his brother Adolph at Heiligerlee in Ommelanden on May 23 that same year. The Antwerp chronicler Godevart van Haecht wrote that Patriots sang it aboard the Sea Beggars' ships, an assertion confirmed by a sentence imposed in Amsterdam on one Pieter Heyndricks on December 31, 1574, accused of singing a stanza or two of the song as he left a church. Heyndricks testified that he had never seen the ballad in print but had learned it on shipboard.[43]

The "Wilhelmus" is an acrostic ballad of fifteen stanzas in which the first letter of every line combines to spell Willem van Nassou. Its formal composition bears striking resemblance to the poetic meter of the rhetoricians. Its melody, first written down in 1574, is based on a French Catholic composition about the failed siege of Chartres by Huguenots in March 1568. The "Wilhelmus" apparently circulated quickly; not only was it sung as early as 1573, but it proved enduringly popular in the seventeenth century. Moreover, the melody was adapted to new works, including at least thirty Catholic, twenty-four Anabaptist, twenty-two Beggars, five Calvinist, and seven secular compositions.[44] The song's verses break no imaginative ground, though they cleverly meld patriotic lore and Calvinist sentiment to present Orange as a faithful vassal to Philip II—"I have always honored the king of Spain"—and as a soldier "true to the fatherland." Orange pledges that "my shield and faith art Thou, O God, my Lord," as he battles Spanish tyranny, casting himself as David seeking shelter from Saul's misrule, but promising a return to avenge the

---

41. De Bruin, "Het Wilhelmus tijdens de Republiek"; Bostoen, *Wilhelmus en de anderen*; J. de Gier, ed., *Het Wilhelmus in artikelen: Een bundel herdrukte studies over het Wilhelmus* (Utrecht, 1985); A. Maljaars and S. J. Lenselink, *Het Wilhelmus: Een bibliografie* (The Hague, 1993).

42. Van Stipriaan, "Words at War," on Fruytiers, based on stylistic argument about the interchangeable use of the pronouns "du" and "ghy" in the ballad. Van Stipriaan also assesses the historiography of the song's authorship and date of composition, and offers a valuable summary of the debates over dating and the original language of composition between two leading scholars of the ballad, Ad den Besten and Abraham Maljaars.

43. De Bruin, "Wilhelmus tijdens de Republiek," 20, from the Amsterdam *Confessieboeken*.

44. Grijp, "van geuzenlied tot Gedenck-clanck."

impoverishment of his "noble Netherlands." Orange is portrayed as a reluctant opponent of royal policy: though he has never impugned the king, his obedience to the greater majesty of God justifies his political actions.[45]

The "Wilhelmus" is a predictable homily about Orange's self-sacrifice—exiled, without property, and having already lost his brother Adolph in battle—and a paean to his larger-than-life status, the prince cast as the Israelite David in the service of God and *patria*. Hebrew analogies to contemporary struggles, as we have seen, were common in Calvinist writings, and the depiction of Orange as the righteous soldier of homeland and God in the "Wilhelmus" is found as well in early portraits. In 1569 Mathis Zyndt produced the first significant print that depicted Orange as a military leader. Based on a slightly earlier German print by Balthasar Jenichen that had contrasted Orange and Philip II, Zyndt showcases Orange as Joshua, the prince placed on the right foreground of a scene that shows him crossing the Maas to take up arms in 1568. Orange is studded with allegorical attributes, including the symbol of Prudence atop his head piece.[46] The German text is equally pertinent, an impassioned plea for the protection of the "Vatterland," with its suffering "rich and poor, widows, wives, and young children." David and Joshua: thus early in his armed struggle Orange is compared to the greatest Hebrew political figures. David served as a perfect analogy of the courtier turned heroic leader, whose Saul easily stood for Philip II. The same holds for Joshua, warrior for the Promised Land; Zyndt's print evokes a parallel between Orange's crossing of the Maas on October 5, 1568, to invade Brabant with Joshua leading his tribes into Canaan across the Jordan (Joshua 3:1–17).

These were exalted analogies for a series of efforts that floundered, as Orange's forces repeatedly suffered defeat at Alba's hands. The writings and artwork were pitched not only to rouse popular support during Alba's occupation of the Netherlands, but also as part of a campaign to elicit the help of German evangelical princes whose assistance Orange desperately needed.[47] While Orange's self-presentation prior to 1572 was careful to tout his dissent as being taken up reluctantly against a king he had faithfully served, all the essential elements of his later public image were laid down. Biblical analogies dominated the rhetoric, with the references to David and Joshua proving effective because so well known. Just as compelling were the more subtle appeals to fatherland and family, particularly the acknowledgement of Orange's fraternal self-sacrifice for the sake of the struggle, best illustrated by the references in the "Wilhelmus" to the death of his brother Adolph. In the years that followed, familial imagery accompanied Orangist rhetoric, cropping up alongside the tried-and-true analogies to great Hebrew figures. With the securing of the rebellion in Holland and Zeeland in 1572, the Patriots increasingly appealed to

45. The text is published in the 1577–78 *Geuzenliedboek*, fols. 29r–31r, with a transcription in De Bruin, "Wilhelmus," 39–41 [de Bruin and Oosterman, *Repertorium* T7365].
46. Horst, *Opstand in zwart-wit*, 109–11.
47. Duke, "From 'Loyal Servant' to 'Irreconcilable Opponent' of Spain," in Swart, *William of Orange*, 22.

One of the first prints of William of Orange as a military hero, issued a year after his 1568 campaign against Alba. The prince is allegorized as Joshua, and the accompanying text makes mention of the fight for the "fatherland." Mathis Zyndt, 1569. Courtesy of Rijksprentenkabinet, Rijksmuseum, Amsterdam.

fatherland, the common good, and what Martin van Gelderen has called the "inseparable trinity" of the Revolt: liberty, charters of privileges, and rule by representative Estates.[48] A public accustomed to a lordly tradition of paternalism and a civic one of privileges responded more readily to the fatherly image and the vocabulary of rights than to the more resolutely Calvinist invocation of Hebrew heroes. But such a broadening of associations for Orange was not simply political calculation. His self-presentation as servant to the fatherland apparently colored his own sense of self, to judge from the rare glimpses we have of it. Even in private matters like his marriage to Anne of Saxony, later annulled because of her affair with the father of the artist Rubens, Orange characterized himself as a stoic

---

48. Van Gelderen, *Political Thought*, 119, popularized by Jacob van Wesembeke. See also his concise "Conceptions of Liberty during the Dutch Revolt (1555–1590)," in *Parliaments, Estates and Representation* 9 (1989): 137–53.

Patriot, imploring his distracted wife to be faithful because he had committed his whole person to "the glory of God and the liberty of his fatherland."[49]

In the print marketplace, Orange's image as righteous prince was sharpened by contrasting him with the Duke of Alba as his sinister antithesis. Such was the case in the 1572 anonymous print we saw in chapter 6 that featured the two opponents, or in a Beggars' song, with its stirring first stanza:

> Quick seventeen Provinces!
> Come to your feet now.
> Come in good cheer to meet the prince.
> Take your position with his banners.
> Everyone as a loyal man.
> Help to dislodge the tyrant, the Duke of Alba.
> Believe this loyally,
> He [the prince] comes not to ruin you.
> But to restore your deprived assets and goods,
> In favor of the King of Spain.
> Assist open-heartedly the Prince of Orange as his lieutenant.
> His drums and his trumpets bring you no danger.
> They are only to resist the bloodthirsty Duke of Alba.[50]

While Orange's administration of Holland and Zeeland as *stadholder* was not without headaches—as Koenraad Swart has pointed out, he wrestled with their respective Estates, heard complaints about his own poorly behaved soldiers, and had to push as hard as any government official to secure financial support for the rebellion—he was presented in the political pamphlets as the model of selflessness.[51] In a printed admonition by the Estates of Holland and Zeeland in 1574 to the States General in Brussels concerning the governorship of Alba's successor, Requesens, the prince is compared to a pelican, the Christlike analogy of one who sheds his blood for his own children, in a text replete with references to the "beloved fatherland" and the "common fatherland."[52] At the pamphlet's end, Orange's nobility is proved by what he has sacrificed for the struggle: land and possessions, of course, but also his brothers, who have perished "for the dear fatherland."[53]

---

49. *Archives d'Orange-Nassau*, 3:327, letter of November 11, 1569. For a lively overview of Orange's troubled marriage, see Simon Schama, *Rembrandt's Eyes* (New York, 1999), 59–71, and R. C. Bakhuizen van den Brink, *Het huwelijk van Willem van Oranje met Anna van Saxen* (Amsterdam, 1853).

50. NG, 2:20–21 [de Bruin and Oosterman, *Repertorium* T6104].

51. Swart, *William of Orange*, 47–61.

52. *Vriendelicke Vermaninghe aen de Staten van Brabandt etc. op de Supplicatie by hem aen Don Loys de Requesens . . . onlangs overghegheven om voorts S. Maj. In Spangien verhandtreyct te worden* (Delft, 1574), A1–r.

53. Ibid., Bii–v. This section of the pamphlet is in *Texts Revolt*, 117.

The "Wilhelmus" likewise invokes this fraternal dimension of Orange's struggle by referring to the death of Adolph of Nassau in 1568, a tendency deepened by early historians of the Revolt like Emanuel van Meteren, who praised Orange as one of a valiant band of brothers who had sacrificed everything for the struggle.[54] The 1574 admonition by the Estates of Holland and Zeeland carries extra emotional weight because in April of that year two of Orange's other brothers, Louis and Hendrik, had died at the battle of Mook; the prince anguished over the loss in correspondence to his only surviving brother Jan.[55] But these were not the only family losses that gave meaningful texture to the output of Orange's propagandists. In what would eventually become standard fare, the 1568 Justification bewails not only the confiscation of the Prince's considerable assets, but also the seizing of his oldest son, Philips Willem, then a student at Louvain, and his forced residency in Spain. They were never reunited.[56]

In one breath pamphleteers and chroniclers lamented the city imperiled by the Army of Flanders as a family rent asunder and hailed Orange as "father of the fatherland." A 1571 text by the Dutch schoolmaster Hendrik Geldorp apparently first used the term, and its popularity grew steadily. This Roman title was hardly new, but it had been previously the provenance of Burgundian and Habsburg princes, a heritage still evoked during the Revolt. When ambassadors from the Estates General were negotiating the offer of lordship over the Netherlands with the Duke of Anjou in September 1580, they recalled Philip the Good's historical role in protecting local privileges in the fifteenth century, hailing him as "father of the fatherland."[57] Orange's assumption of the title was remarkable not merely because the Burgundian association of *pater patriae* had not been forgotten, but more obviously because this term had never been applied in the Low Countries to anyone other than sovereign princes. Apart from its usefulness in figuratively bestowing Roman and royal attributes on Orange, the paternal terminology also emphasized a resonance between Orange's own family's sacrifices and the larger political family of the citizenry.[58] Beginning with the "Wilhelmus," Orangist literature never ceased to mention either the kidnapping of his oldest son or the sacrifice of his three brothers. In some instances, Orange's own tribulations were juxtaposed with the heroic suffering of the Dutch people to illustrate that common travail. Bor's description of the epic siege of Leiden in 1574 intersperses the misery endured by the starving citizens of the besieged city and Orange's terrible illness that August in Rotterdam: the citizens near starvation, the prince so fever-ridden he could not

54. For a discussion, see A. E. M. Janssen, "Prins Willem van Oranje in het oordeel van tijdgenoten," in *Willem van Oranje in de historie*, 21.
55. *Archives d'Orange-Nassau*, 4:378–81, letter of April 24, and letters of January 1575, 382–98.
56. *La Justification du Prince d'Orange*, in *Apologie de Guillaume de Nassau*, 204–5.
57. Griffiths, *Representative Government*, 491.
58. *Texts Revolt*, 92, an encomium penned in 1571 but not printed until 1574 in Latin as *Belgicae liberandae ab Hispanis Hypodeixis, ad P.P.D. Gulielmum Nassavium, principem Aurantium*.

rise from bed until a delegation from Leiden visited him at month's end. Inspired by the visit, Orange quickly recovered and—in a parallel narrative of recovery and redemption—Leiden was relieved by the controversial opening of key dikes.[59] Orange's family and his personal suffering could serve as a potent metaphor of the *patria*, with the prince both the fraternal hero and the first among brothers fighting on behalf of liberty.

Enter the Prince

Since his forced departure from Brabant in 1567, Orange had retained considerable support there, despite Walloon conservatives' efforts to sideline him. There is strong evidence that Orange played a hand in orchestrating the Brussels coup against the Council of State on September 4, 1576; once Don Juan's reputation was fatally tarnished by his attempt to recall the Army of Flanders in August 1577, Orange's stock rose.[60] That summer as the soldiers were being dislodged, Orange's visits to cities in Holland and Utrecht drew cheers. In his youth, Orange had been steeped in the ritual politics and cultural élan of the Burgundian theater state; throughout his life—sometimes to the disapproval of his Calvinist preachers—he retained a taste for banquets, jousts, and other noble sport.[61] What is more, he knew from experience that the Joyous Entry was the supreme Burgundian political ritual, one that carried great constitutional weight; its Dutch designation, Blijde Inkomst, was synonymous with the fourteenth-century Brabant document fetishized by the Patriots as the bedrock of their liberty.[62] At the peak of his popularity, Orange publicized his virtues through a small cluster of carefully planned entry ceremonies. Orange's trio of entries, in Brussels and Ghent in 1577 and Amsterdam in 1580, were critical moments in crafting his ritual profile, because they staged before the public eye the fraternal and paternal imagery previously circulated through the medium of print—in song, pamphlet, and graphic illustrations. This trio of entries positioned Orange as triumphal leader before an adoring crowd, but they also occasioned commemorative booklets, ensuring their recorded memory. Moreover, they were politically unique, having neither a constitutional dimension nor an inaugural purpose. Dressed up with all the triumphal symbols of a Blijde Inkomst, the entries were without contractual obligations, allowing their planners the freedom to praise Orange with exalted metaphors of princely heroism while portraying him as an inveterate defender of civic freedom. Orange was bathed in glory, but so too was the city, with neither forced to make concessions or acknowledge the political restraint required in a standard Joyous Entry.

59. *Archives d'Orange-Nassau*, 5:38–40, 50–53; Bor, *Oorsprongk*, 1:551; Swart, *William of Orange*, 78–79.
60. Swart, *William of Orange*, 105–8, 122–23.
61. For his ritual appetites and court culture, see Delen, *Hof en hofcultuur rondom Willem van Oranje*, 215–39.
62. Geurts, "Het beroep op de blijde inkomste."

The rehearsal for the entries in Brussels and Ghent was Orange's tour of the North Quarter of Holland and Utrecht in the summer of 1577. He was in Alkmaar from June 26 to July 20, Hoorn for the next five days, Enkhuizen from July 25 to July 29, and Medemblik until August 1, after which he went to Haarlem, escorted from city to city by civic guardsmen on horseback. According to the chronicler Bor, though none of the cities Orange visited in north Holland treated him to the standard princely fare of classical arches, he was greeted with cheers of "Father William" by the "common people," who viewed him as nearly godlike, the redeemer of their misery and liberator from "Spanish slavery."[63] On August 18 he entered Utrecht, flush with excitement over ridding the Vredenburg Castle of the hated garrison and eager to secure the stadholdership of the city and its environs. There he was greeted, predictably now, as a second David, though the entry was marred by a nine-year-old girl falling to her death from a balcony as she greeted him. Bor recounts how Orange stopped to view the corpse, to insure that the crowd did not trample on it, and to console the grieving parents—proof positive of his paternal compassion.[64]

But it was the highly managed entries into Brussels and Ghent soon thereafter that inspired the rhetoricians, guardians of the civic esprit, to hail Orange as the Revolt's salvation figure. From the time of the first stirrings of public outrage against the mutinous soldiers of the Army of Flanders in fall 1576, Orange had become a popular figure among Brussels' artisans, craftspeople, and other middling sorts.[65] His stock rose even higher after an internal political realignment in Brussels at the end of August 1577 turned municipal authority over to the Committee of Eighteen, comprising two delegates from each of the nine "nations" of guilds that normally had a hand in the selection of the aldermen. Consolidating power, the new committee had great sway over both the Council of State and the Estates of Brabant. It was the first rumble in a series of political reverberations in Brabant and Flanders that peaked with the establishment of a radical Calvinist regime in the city of Ghent.[66] Orange carefully maneuvered among these populist currents, especially after the States General invited him formally on September 6, 1577, to Brussels to advise them on a course of action in the aftermath of Don Juan's treachery.

Brussels that fall was a nest of political intrigue, with factions at the civic and state level jockeying for influence and promoting different leaders. None of this discord, however, hampered Orange's triumphal reception in Brussels on September 23, 1577, which was commemorated in an illustrated booklet prepared by the poet Jan Baptist Houwaert.[67] As

63. Bor, *Oorsprongk*, 1:830–31; see also A. E. M. Janssen, "Prins Willem van Oranje in het oordeel van tijdgenoten," in *Willem van Oranje in historie*, 22.
64. Bor, *Oorsprongk*, 1:831–32.
65. For example, see *Justification du saisissement et sequestration d'aucuns Seigneurs du Conseil d'Estat et aultres au Pays-Bas*, in *Furie espagnole*, 109.
66. A. Henne and A. Wauters, *Histoire de la ville de Bruxelles* (Brussels, 1845), 1:462.
67. Houwaert, *Declaratie van de triumphante Incompst*.

previously, noted, printed accounts of Burgundian and Habsburg entry ceremonies had been common in the Low Countries since Charles V's entry into Bruges in 1515, so that the genre was well established by the time Houwaert prepared his text. Apart from the observations of the English statesman Davison, or the perfunctory mention of the entry in Jan de Pottre's city chronicle, Houwaert's text is our only solid description of the formalities prepared by Brussels' chambers of rhetoric and its citizens.[68] The account is no simple transcript, but rather a spirited praise of Orange's virtues. True, the text is a careful redaction of the tableaux vivants and rhetorician performances offered to Orange, but it also was a polemic, with a preface denouncing Don Juan's treachery.[69] At the time of the entry, Houwaert was well established, both as a poet and in his position as master of accounts for Brabant. He was an enthusiast for Orange and had been arrested by Alba under suspicion of Protestantism but freed a year later after professing Catholicism. In 1578 Houwaert had penned *The Complaint of Milenus*, a treatise of classical *exempla* on lordly tyranny modeled after a prototype by the Spanish writer Antonio de Guevara; just months after his text for Orange's entry, he wrote yet another commemorative booklet, this one for Matthias of Austria's entry into Brussels on January 18, 1578, and he wrote a poem in praise of Orange's chosen favorite, the Duke of Anjou in 1582. He died in 1599 apparently reconciled to Spanish Habsburg lordship.[70]

Houwaert's booklet for the prince recounts Orange's progress from Antwerp to Ghent. It dutifully summarizes the tableaux vivants prepared by Brussels' three chambers of rhetoric and describes the bedecking of the city with coats of arms and sumptuous cloth, the fire illuminations, and the throaty acclaim by throngs of excited townspeople. It also reproduces the texts of the plays performed in Orange's honor by rhetoricians. In this sense, the entry text is utterly predictable, faithful to the expectations of its genre to laud lord and city. These pieties notwithstanding, Houwaert probably did capture the enthusiasm for Orange in Brussels at a time when the city was in thrall to its newly installed Committee of Eighteen. Even the English observer Davison, who both accompanied Orange on his entry and had private meetings with him, was struck by the clamor he witnessed, an impression he conveyed in letters to the queen's minister of state, Francis Walsingham, a leader of the anti-Spanish faction at the English court. At Antwerp, Davison wrote that "his Excellency arrived in this town yesternight, where he was received with that incredible joy and to that unspeakable comfort of all good Patriots, as if an angel had been sent from heaven to their safeguard." In Brussels he noted that Orange was wildly hailed "ut pater patriae," and he elaborated in a separate letter that "with such singular demonstra-

---

68. St. Genois, *Dagboek van Jan de Pottre*, 76; *Calendar of State Papers, Foreign series, 1577–78* (London, 1901), 170–72, 199–200, and 206; M. Soenens, "Fêtes et cérémonies publiques à Bruxelles aux Temps Modernes," *Bijdragen tot de Geschiedenis* 68 (1988): 47–108, esp. 47–55.

69. Houwaert, *Declaratie van de triumphante Incompst*, 7.

70. G. J. van Bork and P. J. Verkruijsse, *De Nederlandse en Vlaamse auteurs* (Weesp, 1985), 287.

tions of joy was he welcomed of every man, as if he had been an angel come down from heaven they would not have done no more."[71]

The éclat of the Brussels entry drew its charge from the conjunction of the new municipal government in the city, the poetic skills of Houwaert, and the cultural commitments of Brussels' three venerable chambers of rhetoric, the Book, the Cornflower, and the Garland of Mary (formed in 1507 by the merging of two fifteenth-century chambers, the Violet and the Lily). For a few decades, these chambers had exhibited strong Protestant leanings; in 1559, as we have seen, the Garland of Mary mounted a farce in Brussels' central marketplace entitled *Barefoot Brothers* that was a stinging jab at the Franciscans, earning them both a first prize in the competition and legal investigation into their religious commitments. Brussels' chambers also traditionally exercised regional leadership in organizing competitive matches among southern Low Country rhetoricians.[72]

A big entry ceremony was a rare event in any city, for which rhetoricians might wait for more than a decade. However, Orange's visit on September 23, 1577, ironically was sandwiched tightly between two others. Five months before the prince entered Brussels, there had been a reception to welcome Don Juan, a ceremony that involved an overly optimistic pageant car that featured an allegory with Peace trampling on a pile of discarded arms. Four months after Orange's celebration on January 18, 1578, there was a full-blown entry for Archduke Matthias with a commemorative booklet authored by Houwaert.[73] Because it did not carry the legal dimension of the other two entries—in both Don Juan's and Matthias' cases, the welcome ritual was for a new governor general—Orange's Joyous Entry was the least formulaic. The classic Blijde Inkomst was a constitutional rite dressed up in ceremonial finery; no matter how elaborate the praise, the entry always contained the admonition from town dignitaries to the sovereign to uphold rights guaranteed to them in urban charters of privilege. When Orange was welcomed in Brussels, he came with no formal legal obligation to either Brussels or Brabant—he had not yet been offered the position of governor of the province—but as an invited guest and advisor to the States General. As such, his entry did not require the constitutional formula of the traditional Joyous Entry, and its planners were thus freer to spend their energies in acclaiming him. Fully absent were triumphal arches done up in classical style, common fare for sixteenth-century princes like Philip II and Charles V when they entered Brussels in 1549, or for Archduke Matthias in 1578 just months after Orange's welcome. At the same time, there were no warnings about the limits on the exercise of sovereignty, no lecture, as Archduke Matthias was to receive, on his duty to protect and maintain the rights, liberties, and privileges of

71. *Calendar of State Papers, Foreign*, 170, 205–6.
72. Van Bruaene, "Minnelijke rederijkers, schandelijke spelen."
73. Soenens, "Fêtes et cérémonies publiques à Bruxelles," 53–55. J. B. Houwaert, *Sommare beschrijvinghe vande triumphelijcke Incomst vanden Doorluchtigen ende hooggheboren Aerts-Hertoge Matthias binnen die Princelijcke Stadt van Brussele* (Antwerp, 1579).

his provinces. Orange was hailed as the patriotic defender of a newly rejuvenated city, free from the Spanish tyranny, with all the positive acclaim of an entry ceremony and none of its admonitions.

Although Orange's entry diverged from the protocols of the sixteenth-century Joyous Entry, it drew inspiration from it. Apart from its different legal quality, it is the absence of the triumphal arch and the classical, imperial motifs—a feature of Habsburg entries since Charles V's into Bruges in 1515—that makes it distinct.[74] Instead, Orange was treated to the still popular tableaux vivants that were prepared by rhetoricians and other theater companies. Classical themes were popular, most notably a staging of the story of Perseus and Andromeda. But the most powerful models deployed were either allegorical, a common feature of urban *ommegangen*, or biblical, the pairing of Orange with Hebrew heroes. So conceived, Orange's entry drew from older ceremonial forms that stretched back to early fifteenth-century urban pageantry while hailing him as restorer of civic freedom. In the entry's final tableau vivant, four young women, allegorized as Love, Reason, Peace, and Justice, were rescued from imprisonment by a classical soldier-hero brandishing a weapon in one hand and in the other a book of privileges. Orange thus appears as the source of political renewal and rational rule who brings to Brussels not merely arms but an enormous package of legal freedoms.[75] In the woodcut illustration of the tableau, the hero stands to the front right; while he carries a lance in his right hand, it is held low, and the emphasis is placed on the hefty book of privileges he holds under his left arm. The hero is thus presented not in a pose of athletic prowess or military vigor, but as a book-bearing guarantor of privileges.

In perhaps the most striking departure from Burgundian and Habsburg entries, Orange came to Brussels by boat at the head of a substantial group of guild officials and town officials from Brabant's other great city, Antwerp. The delegation floated down a canal on a barge, the sluices and locks along the way festooned with candles and torches and crowded with people applauding the flotilla. There were periodic stops to view pageantry staged on the banks, such as Brussels' shooting companies, who discharged their bows and firearms in honor of the prince at the Sas lock as they neared the city. In Orange's company, the English agent Davison observed two hundred Antwerpeners marching along the banks with men from Brussels, accompanying the barge as it wended its way to the latter city. While water tournaments and other aquatic ceremonies were not unknown in princely entries, no great inaugural entry had ever proceeded by water. Chivalric protocols called for the lord to enter the city on horseback, the regal train met by an official welcoming party outside a standard city gate, in Brussels' case the Leuvenpoort.[76] Not so with

74. Sydney Anglo, ed., *La tryumphante Entrée de Charles Prince des Espagnes en Bruges 1515* (Amsterdam, n.d.).
75. Houwaert, *Declaratie van de triumphante Incompst*, 15; *Calendar of State Papers, Foreign*, 199–200.
76. Soenens, "Fêtes et cérémonies publiques à Bruxelles," 50.

An illustration of a tableau vivant during Orange's 1577 triumphal entry into Brussels that depicts the prince as a classical soldier-hero, weapon in one hand and a book of privileges in the other. Jean Baptist Houwaert, 1577. Courtesy of Bijzondere Collecties, Universiteitsbibliotheek, Universiteit Leiden.

Orange's entry, where interurban alliances—the bonds between Antwerp and Brussels—were celebrated, where urban might was displayed by the militia, and where the prince, at the head of a water flotilla, celebrated the maritime nature of the Revolt, manifest in the triumph of the Sea Beggars in 1572 and the manipulation of dikes and regional waterways that turned back Alba and Requesens. Orange might be a prince, but he was a prince of cities, one proud to use a barge as a ceremonial vessel and to forgo the Burgundian glamour of the handsomely bedecked horse. He entered Brussels on a merchant waterway that connected Brabant's two great cities and was not accompanied by a court retinue but by urban officials and guildsmen from both cities.

For all the civic fanfare, Orange was still the ritual center, and the progress from Antwerp to his residence in Brussels, which he had not seen in a decade, consecrated him as a salvic figure moving in space like a sacred object in a religious *ommegang*. This was especially true once Orange entered Brussels. Inside the city, the prince finally exchanged boat for horse and met Aarschot and his son, the Prince de Chimay, and dignitaries of the States General at the town hall. He took in the lavishly bedecked buildings, facades festooned with luxury cloth, and balconies so choked with spectators that Houwaert worried they might collapse. His arrival inaugurated three days of festivities—a blur of banquets and music, a menu of rhetoricians' plays, the tolling of church bells, and a city so beautified with candlelit paper lanterns that it shimmered like a sea of floating lights.[77] After meeting Aarschot and members of the States, Orange was treated to a tableau welcoming him as prince of peace, and like the two next stagings, it featured allegorical figures such as Justice and Prudence.[78] In this section of the booklet, Houwaert's prose soars, portraying Orange's arrival as a once-in-a-lifetime sensation, the crowd doffing hats, falling on their knees, shedding tears of joy, and acclaiming the prince as a political savior.

Sacred analogies cropped up in Orange's welcome even before he reached Brussels that September 23, particularly in the tableaux vivants the three Brussels chambers of rhetoric mounted on barges outside the city, near the sluice of Vilvoorde. The Garland of Mary, the Book, and the Cornflower embraced the theme of the prince as Old Testament hero. The connection to the earlier Orangist literature, balladry, and artwork was unambiguous; on one fancifully outfitted barge musicians played the "Wilhelmus" for the prince, with trees set in the boat bearing the arms of the Seventeen Provinces, Orange, and even the king in their branches. The first two tableaux, presented by the Garland of Mary and the Book respectively, offered comparisons of Orange to David defeating Goliath and to Moses: the Garland of Mary featured a text that praised the fatherland, and the Book extolled a prince of wisdom who prudently governs his land. The representations were lavishly done, but

---

77. Houwaert, *Declaratie van de triumphante Incompst*, 43–58.
78. Ibid., 44.

broke no new conceptual ground: the rhetoricians reprised now-familiar themes of Orange as slayer of the Philistine giant and as liberator of his enslaved people.[79]

The Cornflower's tableau was the most conceptually complex. It featured the figure of Joseph richly dressed in golden robes rescuing his brothers and father from the ravages of the drought, while he simultaneously tramples the figure of Discord under his feet. An orator nearby compares Orange to Joseph, and appeals to him as "Father" who has arrived to protect Brussels with his righteous virtue.[80] As a wise administrator, Joseph is an apt comparison to Orange, but he is also the most nuanced of the three biblical heroes featured. The Genesis story is of a family torn asunder by brotherly jealously. Joseph, his father's favorite, is sold into bondage by his scheming brothers, but he magnanimously redeems them years later when he is administrator of drought relief and skilled vizier at the pharaoh's court, having obtained his high position after overcoming a series of remarkable tribulations. The Joseph story is as much a narrative of familial strife and reconciliation as it is a morality tale of a sagacious administrator. The Cornflower's tableau focuses not so much on the earlier betrayal as on the happy outcome, with the family rescued by the sage brother. In the context of 1577, Joseph was indeed similar to Orange: a one-time favorite, he suffered forced exile in a family torn apart; after brute tests of his will, he rises to prominence outside his homeland and saves his father and brothers. The Arras chronicler Pontus Payen had already in 1567 likened the turmoil of 1566 to a civil war, a war that tore at the family, "father against son, brother against brother."[81] In the Cornflower's tableau, the fraternal strife in Joseph's family stands not for Orange's brothers, always depicted in happy unison, but for the *patria* as family, for the strife among the provinces only recently overcome with the Pacification of Ghent. Orange the model hero was Orange the unifier of a once divided land.

Orange's entry into Brussels on September 23, 1577, was a high point for him, the culmination of almost a decade of pamphlets, ballads, and prints that lionized him as the noble servant of a misguided king, and then as father of the fatherland. The political ideals espoused were not the reality, of course, as Brabant in the fall of 1577 and the Netherlands in general, were anything but unified, convulsed by a political three-ring circus with Don Juan, still titular head of the government, holed up at Namur, Orange reestablished in the south and soon selected as governor of Brabant, and the young Archduke Matthias the States General's choice as the new governor general. In this triangle of competing interests, who was the rightful leader? To the entry's planners, the answer was Orange, anointed in a ceremony that had for almost two centuries been the public vehicle to promote Burgundian and Habsburg authority. In the aftermath of the iconoclastic riots of

79. Ibid., 25–30.
80. Ibid., 33.
81. Henne, *Mémoires de Pontus Payen*, 2.

1566, Alba had vigorously promoted his public leadership and restored royal authority, only to be traduced by Reformed critics as an idolatrous tyrant. A decade later, political circumstances finally allowed Orange's apotheosis, turning this nominal Calvinist into an object of veneration. The idealization of Orange as a political image even seduced idol-fearing Calvinists like the Ghent artist Lucas d'Heere, who mused about enshrining Orange's virtues "after the old way" in a marble statue that he contemplated. After all, the prince had earned more praise than "ever an emperor had or any such tyrant." D'Heere imagined depicting Orange in a triumphant pose with throngs of people and even animals (sheep and wolf lying together) flocking to him and with a pedestal beneath that read "The father of our lands who merits the approval of everyone."[82]

The Brussels entry ceremony might have been the grandest for Orange in 1577, but it was not the only one that year. In Ghent, d'Heere worked with the city's chambers of rhetoric to design a Blijde Inkomst for the prince on December 29, 1577, providing a Flemish counterpart to Brussels' welcome. Like Houwaert, d'Heere produced a commemorative booklet of the entry, but more compact, without illustrations, and with a less fulsome tone. By 1577 d'Heere was a seasoned artist. His parents were both artists and he started his career as a painter. He contributed artwork to the 1559 chapter meeting of the knights of the Golden Fleece in Ghent's Saint Bavo's Cathedral, apprenticed a year in the service of Catherine de Medici in France, and returned to Ghent in 1560 to establish himself as a poet and as a member of the rhetoric chamber of Jesus with the Balsam Flower. He also openly professed Calvinism and published a Dutch translation of the French-language psalm book of Clément Marot and Théodore de Bèze. In 1567 d'Heere fled to England to avoid Alba's Council of Troubles, became active in the Dutch Reformed Church in London, and made contacts at the English court, spending time in Walsingham's circle where he apparently caught Orange's attention. He returned to Ghent a decade later when the Pacification of Ghent was promulgated.[83]

D'Heere's own personal odyssey and his pronounced Calvinism help to explain the harder edge to Ghent's entry ceremony for Orange, but so do circumstances in the city and in Flanders and Brabant in general. Much had happened in the few months since Orange had his grand reception in Brussels. The general political landscape had developed large fault lines, and Ghent underwent a major political realignment on November 1, when a Committee of Eighteen based on the model of Brussels seized power and set the city down a radical path of uncompromising Calvinism that included an effort to restore the political order of guild rule. Ghent became a turbulent Calvinist regime, more unbending than the Calvinist rule concurrently established in Antwerp or Brussels. The Committee of

---

82. D'Heere, Beschrijvinghe, 30.
83. On d'Heere, see Werner Waterschoot, "Leven en betekenis van Lucas d'Heere," in Verhandelingen en Mededelingen van de Koninklijke Vlaamse Academie voor Taal-en Letterkunde (1974), 16–126; and W. Waterschoot, "Lucas d'Heere in Gent," Jaarboek De Fonteine 31 (1980–81): 131–44.

Eighteen's rule eroded whatever stability Orange had counted on in the south, and held on defiantly, even after several internal upheavals, until its fall in 1584.[84]

The first rumblings of political trouble in Ghent came while Orange was in Antwerp in October 1577. Ghent was a city still smarting from the loss of its privileges in 1540, from the aftermath of 1566, and from the irrepressible history of guild agitation that stretched back to the late Middle Ages. D'Heere's return from exile in 1577 was part of a newfound optimism among Calvinists about Ghent's religious future. More generally, all Ghentenars saw an opportunity after the Pacification of Ghent for a political renewal, a return to an urban regime of rule by its Three Members, a restoration of its guild structure of fifty-four corporations that Charles V had reshuffled, a return of its guild and city charters, and a refurbished preeminence over its old hinterland, the Quarter, and Flanders in general. Hand in hand with Ghent's action against its citadel went a major effort to rebuild its fortifications, to present the city anew as strong and independent. But such an overhauling of the city's public image—in effect, an effort to reclaim its late-medieval glory—was not complete without the return of its legal privileges, and along with them, the power-sharing between the city's guilds and urban patricians that had been the basis of its city government in the halcyon days of the fifteenth century.

Ghent's effort to reclaim its privileges began in the city's Great Council, more than half of whose members were guild masters, on October 18. Council members directed the city's aldermen to seek the return of privileges, citing article ten of the Pacification of Ghent as legal justification.[85] Orange, who both in Holland and Brabant had consistently favored widening the political influence of the urban middling sort, threw his support behind Ghent's request. The States General was poised to agree, but encountered problems with Orange's rival, Aarschot, who just weeks before on September 20, had been named governor of Flanders.[86] When Aarschot came to Ghent at the head of an impressive roster of Flemish nobles and church officials on October 23 for a meeting of the Estates of Flanders, he publicly confirmed his opposition to restoring Ghent's privileges, even provocatively stating that "those calling for the privileges [to be restored] deserve hang-

---

84. Decavele, *Eind van een rebelse droom*, the best general overview of Ghent's Calvinist period. See also J. E. Neve de Mevergnies, *Gand en république: La domination Calviniste à Gand (1577–84)* (Ghent, 1940), and the richly documented A. Despretz, "De instauratie der Gentse Calvinistische Republiek (1577–1579)," *Handelingen van de Maatschappij voor Geschiedenis en Oudheidkunde te Gent* 17 (1963): 119–229, with a review of printed sources. On the Calvinist resurgence in the south, see G. Marnef, "Brabants Calvinisme in opmars: De weg naar de Calvinistische Republieken te Antwerpen, Brussel en Mechelen, 1577–1580," *Bijdragen tot de Geschiedenis* 70 (1987): 7–21, and Decavele, "De mislukking van Oranjes 'democratische' politiek in Vlaanderen."

85. SAG, 94bis, no. 27: *Registre sur la restitution des privileges en 1577, arrestation du duc d'Aerschot, 1577–1580* for a bundle of documents on this matter, including both the requests of the Great Council and the aldermen.

86. *Corr. Taciturne*, 4:lx–lxxxvi. On Orange's favoring of widening political rights among the urban propertied classes, see Swart, *William of Orange*, 119.

ing." Two emerging leaders in Ghent orchestrated a response: François van de Kethulle, Lord of Ryhove, and the more pugnacious alderman Jan van Hembyze, a patrician previously active in city government who had become radicalized, in part owing to the death of his son who had fought with the Sea Beggars. Late in the night of October 28, after a rambunctious public rally, these men had Aarschot and his son, the Prince of Chimay, and several high dignitaries and legal officers seized and imprisoned, including the bishops of Bruges and Ypres—fifteen high-ranking men in all.[87]

On November 1, Ghent's plotters formed the Committee of Eighteen, exuberantly declared the privileges restored, and started the city down the path toward a Calvinist regime. While Orange managed to secure Aarschot's release on November 10, the others remained prisoners, many of them until 1584. Orange openly sided with Ghent in the teeth of immediate, sharp criticism of the coup, and there is evidence that he earlier had tacitly approved of the plan for Calvinists to seize power in the city. His Ghent alliance was strategic, a way to strengthen his hand in Flanders. But it proved ultimately too costly, as the city swerved sharply within a year into radicalism, persecuting Catholics and reigniting iconoclasm, much to the prince's despair.[88]

Orange visited Ghent on December 29, 1577, by invitation of the Estates of Flanders and the city's new Committee of Eighteen, the former wanting the prince's help in dealing with the recent turmoil in Ghent, and the latter wanting his approval in the selection of two new banks of aldermen. Lucas d'Heere prepared the official welcome, assisted by his brother, the architect Jan d'Heere, and Jan Schoorman, the sculptor. Like their peers in Brussels, d'Heere and his associates promoted the theme of William of Orange as hero-redeemer of the fatherland. There were other essential similarities between the two ceremonies, even though they featured completely different tableaux. Ghent also invoked the theme of urban solidarity between itself and Antwerp; the prince arrived at the Dampoort with an escort of 170 soldiers from Antwerp, pledged to help dismantle the citadel and construct the fortifications.[89] Ghent boasted its martial power as well. The aldermen dis-

---

87. For a political narrative of events, see Despretz, "Instauratie der Gentse Calvinistische Republiek," 128; P. Rogghé, "De Orangistische Putsch van 28 Oktober 1577 te Gent," *Appeltjes van het Meetjesland* 18 (1967): 143–79, and chroniclers and documents, esp. SAG 94bis, no. 27, *Registre sur la restitution des privileges en 1577*; Van der Meersch, *Memorieboek der stad Ghent* 3:33, and P. B. de Jonghe, *Gendsche Geschiedenis ofte Kronijke van de beroerten en ketterije binnen en omtrent de stad van Gend sedert het jaer 1566 tot het jaer 1585*, 2 vols. (Ghent, 1781), 1, 310.

88. For an analysis, see Decavele, "De mislukking van Oranjes' 'democratische' politiek."

89. The best description of the entry is d'Heere's official booklet: d'Heere, *Beschrijvinghe*; see also Van der Meersch, *Memorieboek der stad Ghendt* 3:36–37, and the protocols Ghent's aldermen drew up in SAG, 94bis, no. 27, document 15: *Concept ghepreparaeert omme inne te haelen [de] Ex[cellen]tie van mijnen [heeren] de prince van Oraingien*. On the commitment of Orange's soldiers to help Ghent, see Despretz, "Stadsversterkingen en burgerwacht," 5. A succinct overview of the entry is provided by Werner Waterschoot, "Vorstelijke Intochten," in *Het eind van een rebelse droom*, 116–19.

patched two companies of its militia to greet the prince the day before, in nearby Temse, with another sent the next morning, Sunday, December 29, to prepare his escort for a late-afternoon, sunset entry. Six hundred additional militiamen formed part of the welcome delegation that rode outside Ghent's city walls to greet Orange's retinue.[90] Antwerp had also recently undergone a political realignment, with its own Council of Eighteen assuming power in the city, and the solidarity struck between it and Ghent could not have been better displayed then in the commingling of their soldiers as they escorted Orange into Ghent.[91] If the two cities projected interurban solidarity, their prince struck a fraternal chord by bringing his only surviving brother, Jan—who had been recently appointed stadholder of Gelderland—with him as he entered Ghent.[92] Jan was a newly converted Calvinist, so strict in his Reformed faith that it later led to estrangement between the two brothers when William formed an alliance with the French Duke of Anjou. Perhaps Jan's conversion was one reason why the prince brought him to newly radicalized Ghent; he was useful both as a symbol of brotherly accord and of the commitments of Orange to the Reformed religion.

Urban and fraternal camaraderie, essential ingredients of the Revolt's political language, were framing devices for Orange's entry into Ghent. Despite these contemporary references, the Ghent entry stuck to traditional ceremonial forms, making use of a fairly standard parade route through Ghent from the Dampoort to the center. Orange entered Ghent on a Sunday. It was not just any Sunday, but the Sunday after Christmas, following the three Advent Sundays, part of a religious time that fifteenth-century Burgundian princes wove into some of their most famous entries, such as Philip the Good's December 11, 1440, visit to Bruges.[93] Although the timing was probably coincidental, the winter setting evoked the liturgical glow of light the Burgundians had favored, bathing Orange in a candle-lit entry at sunset. Ghent's fifty-four guilds sent representatives to accompany the prince, each carrying a torch. The visual effect was to envelop Orange and his retinue in intense light as a cold, late-December darkness set in. But the political dimension was just as consequential: a public insistence that the guild structure that Charles V had abolished in 1540 was renewed and active in public life.[94]

The entry's theme of Ghent as a city renewed paralleled a broader message of the prince as defender of the fatherland and vanquisher of Spanish tyranny, illustrated in the three tableaux vivants prepared by Ghent's chambers of rhetoric. Ghent's entry did not include

90. SAG, 94bis, no. 27, document 15.
91. Marnef, "Brabants Calvinisme in opmars."
92. William's political relationship with his brother can be gleaned from their letters, J. H. Kluiver, ed., *De correspondentie tussen Willem van Oranje en Jan van Nassau, 1578–1584* (Amsterdam, 1984).
93. Kipling, *Enter the King*.
94. D'Heere, *Beschrijvinghe*, 18; for the use of a standard parade route, see also Waterschoot, "Vorstelijke intochten," 116.

the ever-favorite triumphal arch, probably for the same reason that Brussels had not: this was not a constitutional event à l'antique. The chambers of rhetoric plumbed instead the allegorical and biblical language of the urban tableaux vivants, so much a part of the civic fabric since the late Middle Ages. But Ghent was a city at a more radical moment than Brussels, just as d'Heere was an artist of explicitly pronounced Calvinism, a refugee retuned home after a decade abroad. It was also the city where the Pacification of Ghent was negotiated and in which Orange had strategically rid its citadel of the Army of Flanders, before official action to dismantle it had been taken. All of these factors explain why Ghent's entry, so similar in many ways to Brussels', worked more barbed political references into its staged allegories and biblical reenactments.

The first tableau vivant was by Jesus with the Balsam Flower, and held in front of Saint Jacob's Church. It staged Orange as Judas Maccabeus, the Israelite military hero who had defeated a much larger Syrian army, recaptured Jerusalem, and rededicated the Temple after one of its altars had been defiled by the Greek religious rites conducted on it by order of the Syrian king. Orange-Maccabeus stood positioned on the stage's right-hand side, in front of personifications of the Estates of Flanders, a soldier, Obedient Labor, and a boatman, Sturdy Heart, all four tableaux complemented by a torch-bearing Love of the Fatherland figure. Behind them were the privileges of Ghent they labored to protect, and above them, the hand of God extending from a cloud and offering grace. The stage's left side presented these heroes' enemies: three Spanish soldiers, Violence, Death, and Robbery; a horrid Janus-faced Treason; and, "dressed like a Spanish priest," a female personification of the Inquisition, poised to attack Maccabeus and his party. They were flanked at the front of the stage by the personifications of Rhetoric and History, the former welcoming the prince, the latter praising Orange-Maccabeus as a "true father" and commending the Estates for ridding Flanders of the Spanish tyranny.[95]

The analogy between Orange and Judas Maccabeus sharpened the theme of Spanish oppression. The first book of the Maccabees spoke powerfully to Ghent's Calvinists. One the one hand, Judas Maccabeus, as the underdog turned military victor fighting with four brothers, was an easy stand-in for Orange, and the story of the cleansing of the Temple after its tainting by idol-worshiping Greek Syrians held great appeal. After all, Ghent's Calvinists were heirs of the stinging 1566 iconoclastic riots. They would also become instigators of a new wave of iconoclasm that gripped Ghent not long after the entry, between July and September 1578, with yet another bout occurring in March 1579.[96] That the tableau was staged in front of Saint Jacob's, the parish church and neighborhood that had housed Ghent's thickest Calvinist population in 1566, only enhanced the idolatry subtext embedded in the choice of Judas Maccabeus as a prototype for Orange.[97]

95. D'Heere, *Beschrijvinghe*, 18–20.
96. Despretz, "Instauratie der Gentse Calvinistische Republiek," 170–77, 179–83.
97. Delmotte, "Calvinisme in de verschillende bevolkingslagen te Gent."

If the Army of Flanders was cast as the enemy in this first tableau, the staging in front of Ghent's town hall by its four other chambers of rhetoric vilified Alba. His vanquisher was none other than the Pacification of Ghent, personified by the Maiden of Ghent bedecked in Orange's colors of orange, white, and blue, and sporting a miniature paper replica of the city on her head. In a concession to the Pacification's implicit search for a religious accord, the Maiden was flanked by figures representing Protestantism and Catholicism, while she busily smelted seventeen links to affix on a golden chain, each link decorated with the arms of one of the provinces. Underneath the anvil (dubbed Strength) was Alba, tearing his trampled-on clothes and eating his bloody heart, a parody no doubt of his infamous Antwerp statue that had him crushing his enemies, iconoclasts included, beneath his booted feet.[98] The whole staging was accompanied by differently positioned maidens embodying virtues: Faith, Truth, Constancy, Discretion, and Agreement. On each corner of the tableau there were personifications of Rhetoric, and in its front middle, the classical figure of Mercury.

The stage in front of the town hall also featured a major tableau. Its centerpiece was yet another representation of Orange as military leader, fully armored and touted as "Protector of the Netherlands," a contemporary counterpart to his earlier Maccabee analogy. Flanked by Wisdom and Strength, the Protector brandished a sword in his left hand bearing the inscription, "For Faith and the Fatherland," and a heart dubbed "Helpful Loyalty" in his right hand. Unity and Accord, both depicted as young girls, stood in front of him and two other "nymphs" also paid him homage: Good, Willing Charity and Good Favor. At the hero's feet were his vanquished foes: Death, Plunder, and Rape, a pointed reference to the deeds of the Army of Flanders. Above the tableau were the coats of arms of Orange and Philip II joined with a legend reading: "My sincere desire is to honor the king," a nod to the second stanza of the "Wilhelmus," and an indication that at this point, no one was publicly ready to attack Philip II. When the prince passed before this staging, he was greeted in song, but not by the "Wilhelmus" performed in his Brussels entry, but by a verse lauding him as "Noble and pure Prince of Orange" whom his subjects welcome "with happiness flowing from love, as a courageous, proud lion."[99]

The final tableau of Ghent's entry was placed in front of the court of Wakken, Orange's place of residence during his stay. There were columns and an obelisk, festooned with the arms of the Estates of Flanders, and, in the middle, the Maiden of Ghent with the Lion of Flanders, depicted in her trellised garden, the popular *hortus conclusus* symbolism that Ghent, Ypres, and other cities had invoked since the late Middle Ages.[100] Allegorical

98. D'Heere, Beschrijvinghe, 21.

99. Ibid., 25.

100. For Ghent, the representation is first featured in the late fourteenth century and is the subject of a poem by Boudewijn vander Luere; see J. Reynaert, "Boudewijn vander Luere en zijn 'Maeght van Ghend,'" *Jaarboek van De Fonteine* 31 (1980–81): 109–30.

figures representing Love, Trust, Constancy, and Bravery flanked the Ghent Maiden as she offered her gold heart of sincerity to Orange. Once again, Orange was greeted with a verse, this time explicitly as "Good princely lord of the Netherlands, right father." The stage was ringed with fifty-four maidens, dressed in Orange's colors, who waved the guild banners of the city, the symbols of Ghent's artisanal might and a fitting denouement to the entry that celebrated the restoration of these corporations and their charters of privileges.[101] That evening, the town fathers held a lavish banquet, the high point of which was the toast offered by the figure "Community" to Orange as a "Prince of Peace" who sacrificed "his person and his possessions for the Fatherland" to defeat "Spanish Violence."[102]

The Ghent entry was freighted with an even heavier dose of urban boosterism than that of Brussels. It was an unabashed celebration of the city's privileges and guild might, with militia, artisanal, and legal invocations of power woven into the tableaux. The entry also more explicitly denounced the Army of Flanders and Alba. It featured a parody of the former governor general as crushed and defeated, rhapsodized about the Pacification of Ghent, and unequivocally touted Orange as a father figure. Its political and religious symbolism, however, was not wholly one-sided. Because at least half of Ghent's population remained solidly Catholic, the tableaux both advanced Reformed commitments, particularly in the figure of Judas Maccabeus as cleanser of ancient idolatry, and acknowledged Orange's hope for religious peace, particularly in the representation of the figures of Catholicism and Protestantism together.[103] In formal structure, the entry played up Ghent's civic rights and military prowess, and the fraternal bonds between Orange and his only surviving brother. Yet all references to Spanish tyranny notwithstanding, d'Heere and the rhetoricians chose to put the coats of arms of Orange and Philip II next to each other, and in doing so, to underline the prince's ultimate fidelity to his sovereign. Apart from this passing reference to royal heraldry, attention to Philip II was all but absent in the entry, the focus squarely on Orange as warrior-hero and redeemer of the urban order. The entry's anti-Spanish resentment was vented against Alba, with Philip II left wholly untouched. As in the Brussels entry, Orange was heralded as the savior of city and fatherland, but not as a replacement of the king.

However, the cheerful evocations of civic solidarity, paternal acclaim for William of Orange, and common destiny among the Netherlands provinces in the Joyous Entries into Brussels and Ghent of September and December 1577 proved short-lived. Fierce political differences emerged over the next two years among key noblemen and the provinces. Ghent plunged into internal turmoil and Calvinist rigidity, and the relationship between

---

101. D'Heere, *Beschrijvinghe*, 26–27.
102. Ibid., 28–29.
103. On the estimate of Ghent's percentage of Catholics and Calvinists, see Dambruyne, *Coporatieve middengroepen*, 655.

Van Hembyze and Orange soured, even though the prince managed some temporary successes in the city, including a short-lived declaration of religious peace. Holland, Zeeland, Utrecht, Friesland, Gelderland, and Ommelanden formed the Union of Utrecht on January 22, 1579. This initially chagrined the States General and Orange, as it vitiated the Pacification of Ghent's spirit of religious accord. Moreover, it consolidated the separateness of these territories, especially Holland, from the States General in Antwerp. Even before this northern Union was signed, the threat posed by the Calvinist regimes of Brussels, Antwerp, and especially Ghent, had prompted the Estates of Hainault, Arras and Douai to form their own Union of Arras. On May 17 these Walloon provinces proclaimed the maintenance of Catholicism and held out the possibility of reconciliation with Philip II, a development achieved by the new governor general, the Prince of Parma, son of the former regent, Margaret of Parma.[104] As the Netherlands hardened into rival blocs, Orange increasingly despaired. By fall 1579 the prince stopped using the valedictory formulas of "your compatriot" and "the common cause of our fatherland" in his correspondence with the States General.[105]

However hobbled, the Revolt continued, with Orange directing events from the refurbished citadel in Antwerp. The Calvinist cause in Holland had received a big boost on May 26, 1578, when a coup in Amsterdam purged the town council (*vroedshap*) of its tight-knit, conservative Catholic oligarchy, deporting thirty and replacing them for the most part with Reformed merchants who had returned from a decade-long exile.[106] With this "Alteratie"—accompanied by riotous bouts of iconoclasm—Amsterdam was finally within the Calvinist fold. In early 1580, Orange visited the city as part of a trip to Holland to push for reforms to the Council of State and other governmental offices to counteract the centrifugal pull from the regional Estates that had increasingly frustrated him.[107] His entry into Amsterdam on March 17, 1580, was memorialized in an succinct account published by Gillis vanden Rade in Antwerp, apparently aimed at readers in Brabant and Flanders eager to hear that Holland was pursuing common cause with their Patriots. The booklet, although published in Amsterdam, was distributed in Antwerp, by a privilege granted by

---

104. For general developments, see Parker, *Dutch Revolt*, 193–95; Swart, *William of Orange*, 157–60, 171, and, J. C. Boogman, "The Union of Utrecht: Its Genesis and Consequences," *Bijdragen en Mededelingen betreffende de Geschiedenis der Nederlanden* 94 (1979): 277–407.

105. Swart, *William of Orange*, 171. The last documented use of such phrases, according to Swart, was in a September 25, 1579, letter from Orange to the States General. See ibid., 171, n. 71, citing *Corr. Taciturne*, 4:185. Orange apparently replaced them with "vostre très-affectioné amy à vous faire service" and "vostre très-affectioné serviteur et amy": *Corr. Taciturne*, 4:253 and 5:68.

106. Amsterdam's former loyalty to the king had long piqued the Beggars, one of whose ballads in 1573, "Amsterdam Warned," fulminated: O daughter of Sodom awaken / You going with the Spanish tyrant / Your head stuck out over all Holland's cities / To lord your will triumphantly / You have brought all of Holland into discord. See NG, 2:88.

107. Swart, *William of Orange*, 204–5.

the city's secretary, J. van Asseliers.[108] It was the first significant princely entry into Holland since 1549, when Charles V made a circuit with Philip II through Dordrecht, Rotterdam, Delft, The Hague, Leiden, Haarlem, and Amsterdam, and other cities.[109] That fact alone is proof that however modest in form, the entry carried enormous symbolic weight, consecrating Orange as the heir to a ritual form not used for a prince since Charles V himself. Two days before the entry in Amsterdam, Philip II's government issued the *Edict of Proscription* to denounce Orange as the "sole head, author, and abettor of the Revolt" and offered financial rewards for his assassination. The king's actions gave the ceremony a sense of urgency and an air of heroic defiance. The entry also transpired months before several important political and personal developments for the Revolt and Orange. On September 19, 1580, the States General in Antwerp signed a treaty with the Duke of Anjou promising him lordship over the Netherlands. That fall, Orange prepared his famous *Apology* to repudiate the charges leveled against him and to publicly denounce Philip II.[110] Two and a half years after the Brussels and Ghent entries, the optimism stirred by the Pacification of Ghent had dissipated, and so too the sense that a unified fatherland could prevail. Moreover, Holland's Estates had grave reservations about Orange's promotion of the Duke of Anjou, a concern that ultimately prompted it, Zeeland, and Utrecht to declare their independence from Anjou's authority in February 1582.[111]

Notwithstanding worries over the fraying of a common vocabulary of patriotic opposition, Amsterdam greeted Orange with much the same gusto that Brussels and Ghent had done in 1577. Town fathers, citizens, rhetoricians, and shooting guilds were on display along with a rousing maritime entry that emphasized both the seafaring vitality of this city on the IJ and the Sea Beggars' character that had colored the Revolt of 1572 in Holland. The entry was also an obvious attempt to reassure Patriots elsewhere that the Revolt still had a common base. A flotilla of three galleys done up in Orange's colors and studded

---

108. Vanden Rade, *Incomste vanden doorluchtighen Vorst ende Heere*; J. C. Breen, "Het eerste bezoek van prins Willem I aan Amsterdam na de Alteratie van 1578, "*Jaarboek van het Genootschap Amstelodamum* 21 (1924): 63–81, and E. W. Moes, "De blijde inkomst van Prins Willem van Oranje binnen Amsterdam in 1580," *Amsterdamsch Jaarboekje voor 1897* (Amsterdam, 1897): 1–8 for a few additional items gleaned from the archives. See also Delen, *Hof en hofcultuur rondom Willem van Oranje*, 280–81, 284–85. For the intended audience, see D. P. Snoep, *Praal en propaganda: Triumfalia in de Noordelijke Nederlanden in de 16de en 17de eeuw* (Alphen aan den Rijn, 1975), 24.

109. Vanden Rade, *Incomste vanden doorluchtighen Vorst ende Heere*, 18.

110. For the Edict of Proscription, see Lacroix, *Apologie de Guillaume de Nassau*, 5–24, with the text of the Apology as well. For the negotiations and the September 19, 1580 treaty with the Duke of Anjou, see "Rapport fait au prince d'Orange et aux Etats Généraux par les ambassadeurs qu'ils avaient envoyés au duc d'Anjou, 12–17 September 1580," in *Corr. Taciturne*, 4:421–71, and Mack P. Holt, *The Duke of Anjou and the Politique Struggle during the Wars of Religion* (Cambridge, 1986), 134–38.

111. "Déclaration du duc d'Anjou concernant l'indépendance des provinces de Hollande, Zeelande et Utrecht," in *Documents concernant les relations entre le duc d'Anjou et les Pays-Bas* 5 vols., ed. P. L. Muller and A. Diegerick (Utrecht, 1899), 3:287–89, dated Feb. 22, 1582.

with imitation canons, six cloth-draped sailboats, three tree-lined boats, and a few small rowboats fetched Orange at Muiden and brought him into Amsterdam's harbor on the morning of March 17. The thunder of the booming guns that greeted him was so heavy that it shattered the glass of a nearby merchant's shop.[112] The city's waterways had been cleared of its usually active ships. Citizens stood in front of their houses to cheer the prince, though they were ordered to do so on threat of being fined. As with Brussels and Ghent, there were no triumphal arches, but instead some modest tableaux vivants mounted by the city's rhetoricians and some of its trade associations. One such was the staging of Neptune with a whale upon his back. Another was a beautiful maiden at the Damrak, sponsored by the Baltic shippers, who erected columns bearing their cities' arms on each corner of the tableau. The symbolism was economical and direct: Amsterdam was a proud maritime city of merchants, alternately represented by the classical god of the sea and by the ever-popular civic maiden. A little farther on, at the Papenbrug, the seafaring theme was enhanced by a water tournament in which men seated two apiece in rowboats tried to knock the lances out of their opponents' hands. As Vanden Rade notes, at least ten or twelve ended up in the frigid water. Following the sport was a formal welcome by four of Amsterdam's burgomasters in front of the gothic *stadhuis*. There, Amsterdam's *schutters*, who had earlier greeted the flotilla from the street bridges and had then marched to the city center, hailed Orange. The day ended when the prince retreated to his guest house in the Warmoesstraat adjacent to the Papenbrug. But festivities began anew the next night; townspeople lit candles and torches and hung paper lanterns everywhere, including the spire of the Oudekerk (the Old Church), which flickered with 150 or more lights.

The climax of the entry ceremony came Saturday night. The event was kicked off with volley after volley of flaming arrows shot by archers into the spring air. Under the supervision of the artillery master, Gerrit Henrickszoon, two miniature houses were set up on the Papenbrug: one, a wooden replica of the prince's residence at Breda, and the other, a model of Alba's former house in Antwerp's citadel—the choice of Alba and his Antwerp project a reminder of just how essential he had become to the civic memory of the Revolt, some seven years after his departure. Placed apart from one another, the houses were rigged to fire burning arrows at each other, with Alba's reduced to a smoldering ruin an hour after the volley started. At the Vismarkt (Fish market), the rhetorician chamber "In Love Blooming" erected a fire display in the shape of a crown spiked with oranges. Lit by a fuse, it produced a magnificent light show, a rousing end to an enthusiastic entry dedicated, among other things, to "the manly fight for freedom."[113] As an accompaniment, the rhetoricians had hung banners with verses in the name of Orange and Alba. Orange's

---

112. Vanden Rade, *Incomste vanden doorluchtighen Vorst ende Heere*, and Moes, "Blijde inkomst van Prins Willem van Oranje."

113. Ibid., and with some minor details also in Delen, *Hof en hofcultuur rondom Willem van Oranje*, 280–81, and 284–85.

paean was a biblically laced evocation of unity of the righteous against "the Whore of Babylon." More polemically, Alba was dismissed as an idol-maker who erected an image of himself as a god in Antwerp and who unleashed "Spanish bloodhounds" that left poor orphans and widows everywhere. Thus the short verse managed to sum up the cultural and social denunciation of Alba leveled against him during his governorship; he was both guilty of the worst kind of idolatry and of turning the city into a domestic ruin.

Compared to the entry ceremonies of Brussels and Ghent, Amsterdam's was more modestly conceived. The ritual tradition of the Joyous Entry was more deeply cultivated in the south, where the Burgundian dukes had a heavier ceremonial imprint. Yet despite its compactness, Amsterdam's celebration delivered much of the same punch as its Brabantine and Flemish counterparts, using aquatic themes to a much greater effect than in Brussels, and like d'Heere's program for Ghent, issuing tart political jabs. Amsterdam's 1580 entry ceremony is proof that no matter how much the Revolt had evolved since 1566, propagandists were drawing on the basic stock of motifs that Orangists had launched in 1568. These entries brought a fitting closure to the urban violence and warfare of the earlier 1570s; they were simultaneously ceremonial acclaim of a renewed civic sphere and a dramatic apotheosis of Orange's leadership and guardianship of urban and provincial rights. Orange's trio of entries between 1577 and 1580 thus seized the master ritual of Burgundian lordship and mined its political potential, exalting the prince and the city in tandem in a way an ordinary *Blijde Inkomst* could not, because its contractual elements stipulated the limits of each party's authority. Orange reaped the benefits of an imagined fatherland that cast him as the paternal leader and fraternal comrade, welcomed with similar rhetoric in the three cornerstone provinces of the Revolt: Brabant, Flanders, and Holland. In each entry, Alba served as Orange's convenient foil, while the Spanish king was plainly ignored, his ritual presence erased save for a few heraldic references. By 1581 Orange's profile had become so exalted that when Philip II was repudiated, the prince was an easy substitute for the king's lost virtues.

The Bad King

Since the "Wilhelmus" ballad, Orange had been cast in the role of defender of the fatherland in revolt, through the orchestration of a simple, compelling repertoire of fraternal and paternal symbols. But if Orange had evolved in his role as the righteous father, Philip II was still the king misled by evil councilors and poor governor generals, but was not himself the target of caricature. This depiction of Philip, however, changed dramatically after the famous Edict of Proscription issued against Orange on March 15, 1580, just two days before the Amsterdam entry. Issued by Philip II at the behest of Cardinal Granvelle, the edict declared Orange an outlaw and called for his assassination It hyperbolically accused him of masterminding the whole Revolt, from the wonder year to the current troubles—a crime all the worse since he was no more than a "foreigner and outsider," a German import.[114] The tone of the Proscription was exuberantly ad hominem, painting Orange as the sinister puppet master of the troubles; it even dipped into his private life to condemn his third marriage to Charlotte de Bourbon, an apostate nun.[115] Orange was the "head, author, and instigator" of the troubles, and a reward of 25,000 crowns and a title of nobility was offered to anyone who successfully eliminated him.[116]

Orange's response to the edict was his famous Apology, prepared by his court preacher, Loyseleur de Villiers, with the prince's apparent help, and read before the States General in December 1580. While it was formally addressed to delegates of the States, the text was intended for broad circulation, and was translated from the original French into Dutch, Latin, English, German, and perhaps Low German.[117] Much ink has been spilled over this text, since it offers an almost complete political biography of Orange at key moments of the Revolt and a summa of the ideas presented in the pamphlets written by the Patriots. In one sense, the Apology covers familiar ground. It stitches together well-rehearsed criticisms of Spanish tyranny, warns vigorously of the need to protect liberties and privileges lest the Netherlands succumb to the wretchedness imposed on the poor Indians of the Americas, and rails against Alba, the Inquisition, and the assault on liberty, making it a classic in the literature of the Black Legend. Different, however, is its tone and pacing. Historians from Swart to Van Deursen have been keen to point out its disjointedness and prolix quality and puzzled over its fierce character assassination of Philip II, whom Orange accuses of incest, adultery, and the murder of family members.[118] For a man famed for his caution and astuteness, Orange presents a rash and angry self-defense, not just in the Apology's language but also its fractured narrative structure, which differs starkly from the logical eloquence of his 1568 Justification.

Orange's Apology neither spares punches nor carefully parses words. After an opening defense of his family's historic link to the Low Countries to refute the accusation that he was an outsider, he defends the appropriateness of his third marriage with a sharp coun-

114. Ban ende Edicte by forme van Proscriptie uutghegaen ende ghedecreteert by onsen Allerghenadichsten Heere de Coninck, teghens Willelm van Nassau, Prince van Oragnien, als hooft, beroerder ende bederver van tgheel Christenrijck, ende namentlijck van dese Nederlanden, in De Moord van 1584: Oorspronkelijke verhalen en gelijktijdige berichten van den moord ghepleegd op prins Willem van Oranje, ed. J. G. Frederiks, (The Hague, 1884), 1–25.

115. Ban ende Edicte by forme van Proscriptie, in Frederiks, Moord van 1584, 8.

116. Ibid., 20–25.

117. For the circumstances of its writing, see Swart, William of Orange, 188–89, and Duke, "William of Orange's Apology," 4–5. The original French text is reproduced in Lacroix, Apologie de Guillaume de Nassau. All citations are to the English translation by Duke, "William of Orange's Apology," annotated and with an intro., in "William of Orange's Apology," Dutch Crossing 22, no. 1 (Summer, 1998): 3–96. On Villiers, see C. Boer, Hofpredikers van Prins Willem van Oranje: Jean Taffin en Pierre Loyseleur de Villiers (The Hague, 1952).

118. Duke, "William of Orange's Apology," 5 for a discussion of historians' reactions; see also Swart, William of Orange, 189–91, and Van Deursen and De Schepper, Willem van Oranje, 145.

terjab: Philip II was guilty of incest, having married his cousin Anne of Austria in 1570. As royal marriages among first cousins were not that extraordinary, Orange adds a startling charge: Philip II had slain his former wife, Elizabeth of Valois, in 1568—a wife to whom he had been unfaithful in the more usual sense—to enable this new marriage. What is more, the king had murdered his psychologically troubled son, Don Carlos. Orange explains this vicious behavior by pointing out that Philip II was descended from a bastard, Henry of Castile.[119] The shift in the presentation of the Habsburg ruler in Orangist literature was as dramatic as it was rapid. Philip II had abruptly morphed from a monarch duped by wicked advisors into "an incestuous king, who slew his son and murdered his wife."[120]

Such a sudden and sharp attack on the king provoked the ire of Castilians, and particularly that of Pedro Cornejo, a chronicler best known for his 1581 *History of the Civil Wars and Rebellion of Flanders*.[121] In his "Antiapology," Cornejo rails against Orange's "veritable demonic treatise," a blasphemous tissue of lies aimed at the gullible and "blind people of Flanders."[122] Orange's treatise promoted the heresy of "liberty and diversity of faith," bemoaned Cornejo, a sure recipe for anti-Catholic tyranny. Orange was a sinister man who railed against the king every time he opened his mouth, despite having received Philip II's generous patronage.[123] Cornejo was shocked by Orange's impugning the king's character, judgment, and rule.

But the intemperate attack on Philip II that infuriated Cornejo and puzzled an earlier generation of historians did have an obvious political logic: it paved the way for the legal abjuration of Philip II. At precisely the moment of the Apology's preparation, the States General had struck an agreement with the mercurial Duke of Anjou, a Catholic Valois prince, to assume lordship of the Netherlands. It was hardly an ideal arrangement. The negotiations that led to the deal between Anjou and the States General held at Plessis-lès-Tours in August and September 1580 were difficult, with the Netherlanders refusing to grant Anjou the title of "sovereign" by cunningly insisting that no such word existed in

---

119. Duke, "William of Orange's Apology," 28–29. For the actual facts of this marriage and Don Carlos's death, see Parker, *Philip II*, 92–93.

120. Duke, "William of Orange's Apology," 28.

121. Cornejo, *Historia de las civiles guerras y rebelión de Flandes* (Prague, 1581), evaluated by Rodríguez Pérez, *Tachtigjarige Oorlog*, 51–52.

122. *Antiapologia o contra defensa en dos partes dividada la primera en respuesta de una carta del principe de Orange*, A2r–A3v. The text is now available in a critical edition. See Anton van der Lem and Bahar Turkoglu, "L'Anti-Apologie, 1581, de Pedro Cornejo," *"Lias": Sources and Documents Relating to the Early Modern History of Ideas*, vol. 31, no. 2 (2004): 185–237. For examples of Cornejo's rhetoric in this work, see Rodríguez Pérez, *Tachtigjarige Oorlog*, 63–65, and a more sustained treatment in Yolanda Rodríguez Pérez, "The Pelican and its Ungrateful Children: The Construction and Evolution of the Image of Dutch Rebelliousness in Golden Age Spain, " *Journal of Early Modern History* 11, no. 4–5 (2007): 285–302.

123. *Antiapologia*, E3v, H2v.

Dutch. Instead, the States proffered Anjou the designation "prince and lord." What is more, they insisted on affirming a clause in the famous Joyous Entry text of Brabant that allowed for his removal from office if necessary—this before Anjou had even assumed formal lordship![124]

Orange harbored genuine hope for the arrangement with the Duke of Anjou, despite the States General's lack of enthusiasm. In January 1580, he had argued before the States General that the Netherlands did not have the means to govern itself, that reconciliation with Philip II was out of the question, that a foreign lord was necessary, and that Anjou best fitted the bill because he would solidify a powerful French alliance.[125] Others agreed, but on far less positive grounds. In *Emmanuel-Erneste: Dialogue of Two Persons on the State of the Netherlands*, Gerard Prouninck, a town official from 's-Hertogenbosch, used the succession debates to consider whether the Netherlands should be a free republic or under the administration of a new prince. Prouninck concluded that unlike the virtuous and disciplined Swiss, the Dutch were corrupt, self-interested, and divisive, and hence needed the kind of lordship Anjou would provide.[126]

However weak his endorsements, Anjou had been selected as the new lord, and Philip II now could be freely discredited, even if it would take another year to put into concrete effect. In large measure, Villiers and Orange were preparing the conceptual groundwork for this abjuration in their frontal assault on Philip II's character in the Apology. What others have seen as an embarrassing quality in this canonical text—that is, the slander against Philip—is less gratuitous than it might appear if these harsh words are compared to the rhetorical profile of Orange, set in motion in 1568, as righteous leader and father of the nation as family. If the prince was the good father who worked in conjunction with his self-sacrificing league of brothers, Philip II was the necessary opposite: the bad father, guilty of public governance gone awry and a private life in turmoil, a king who had failed his political subjects and murdered his own son and wife. In this sense, the contrast of Orange as the good father and Philip II as the wicked one is a potent anticipation of the gendered language of later republicanism, of what Lynn Hunt has dubbed the "family romance" of the French Revolution. In 1789 the fraternal language and rituals of Jacobin republicanism depended on depicting Louis XVI and Marie Antoinette as bad father and mother figures and, in general, on the deployment of domestic metaphors in the revolu-

---

124. "Rapport fait au prince d'Orange et aux Etats Généraux par les ambassadeurs qu'ils avaient envoyés au duc d'Anjou, 12–17, September 1580," in *Corr. Taciturne*, 4:421–72. On Orange's title in 1572, see Koenigsberger, *Monarchies, States Generals and Parliaments*, 257.

125. Van Gelderen, *Political Thought*, 170.

126. Gerard Prouninck van Deventer, *Emmanuel-Erneste: Dialogue de deux personages sur l'Estat du Pais Bas* (Antwerp, 1580), summary in Van Gelderen, *Political Thought*, 170–73, and Geurts, *Nederlandse Opstand*, 111–12.

tionary politics of the nascent republic.[127] On the eve of the repudiation of Philip II by the States General in 1581, Orange chose to play the role of the heroic father fighting against Philip II's murderous reign on behalf of a rejuvenated civic landscape. The loss of Orange's brothers proved the Nassau men's fraternal sacrifice to a revolt inching its way toward republican imagery; Orange's leadership on behalf of "yourselves, your wives and your children" proved the usefulness of conceptualizing the rebels as a civic family headed by a good father; and finally, the kidnapping of Orange's oldest son, Philips Willem, mentioned no less than seven times in the Apology, showed what the good father of a nation of families had endured in the painful sundering from his eldest son. While Philip II had viciously murdered his own son and heir, Orange, by contrast, had suffered a cruel separation from his. As he poignantly exclaimed in his Apology, "For am I not, my Lords, so inhuman as not to feel the affections of a father, nor yet so resigned that the sorrow for the long absence of my son does not often come to mind?"[128]

In the use of familial imagery as a political device, Orange's 1580 Apology dovetails nicely with the print by Theodore de Bry, discussed above, and produced around this time. In De Bry's visual imaginary, Orange is the pious warrior whose oldest son begs for his return to his father, while Philip II is the idolater-king analogous to Sennacherib, whose own family self-implodes. In the Apology, Orange deploys almost identical familial metaphors. He casts himself as the righteous father who has endured the loss of his brothers and the kidnapping of his son, sacrificing his family for the nation as family. Philip II had legislated a reign of idolatry—Orange points out that a man could be sentenced to die for merely looking askance at a statue—and forfeited the paternal concern by which a good lord should rule.[129] The king had shown himself no better than the bloodthirsty and equally idolatrous Alba—perhaps worse, because he was guilty of killing wife and son. The idolater father-king had proved so bad a tyrant that it took the nation as family, and Orange as the selfless new father, to repudiate his power. The subjects of the new political order in the Netherlands were not so much the "good children" typically invoked by Burgundian and Habsburg lords when deploying paternal rhetoric, but the fathers and brothers forced to fight for all the "widows and orphans" that Alba and Philip had left in their wake.[130]

Orange might be the good father, but whatever lord he chose to rule the Netherlands would rule a land of fraternal citizenry, a nation of many civic households protected by liberties, privileges, and freedoms, and unshackled from the tyranny of an idolatrous and murderous misrule. Philip II, in the words of the States General's July 28, 1581, Act of Ab-

---

127. Lynn Hunt, *The Family Romance of the French Revolution* (Berkeley, 1992).
128. Duke, "William of Orange's Apology," 43.
129. Ibid., 38.
130. On the rhetoric of just lordship and public good in the Burgundian Netherlands, see A. J. Vanderjagt, *"Qui sa vertu anoblist.": The Concepts of "noblesse" and "chose publicque" in Burgundian Political Thought* (Groningen, 1981).

juration, had failed to "love and support them [his subjects] as a father his children or a shepherd his flock."[131] The paternal terminology was forfeited to Orange. True, the prince would bequeath his political capital to the new Lord Anjou, welcomed into Antwerp on February 19, 1582, as "father" to the *patria*. But Anjou's charge was not to govern the Low Countries vertically as a prince holding a mandate over his dependents, but rather to defend the bitterly fought and scrupulously cherished rights and privileges of his citizen subjects.[132] Moreover, his reign was not only controversial but ritually and rhetorically problematic, given the heights to which the Patriots had raised Orange's stature. This was not yet a republic of free men, and the Netherlands were rent with divisions over the direction of the Revolt. Still, the Patriots had embraced the language of fraternal rights and the cultural posture of civic republicanism, and in the process they elevated the once-reluctant friend of the Beggars to leader of the Revolt, as father of the fatherland. Orange was no monarch, nor was he even the lord chosen to replace Philip II. But he was the unparalleled ritual successor to the Burgundian and Habsburg princes, making the representation of any replacement to Philip II inherently troubled, given that the tension between dynastic lordship and civic and provincial rights that harkened back to Charles the Bold was still unresolved, with Orange the only prince seemingly able to bridge the divide.

131. Mout, *Plakkaat van Verlatinge*, 71.
132. H. M. C. Purkis, ed., *La magnifique Entrée de François d'Anjou en sa ville d'Anvers* (Amsterdam and New York, 1973), 16, a facsimile edition of the original 1582 text published by Plantin in Antwerp.

CHAPTER 8   ABJURATION AND
ASSASSINATION
THE DILEMMA OF AUTHORITY

What did Netherlanders think of the Spanish author[
Orange's Apology? Their attitudes ran the gamut,
had already reconciled with Philip II to Orange's pa
inspiration from the prince's spirited self-defense to sharpen their polen
camp was the anonymous engraver of the print, issued around 1580–81, e
ing in My Garden, Spanish Pigs.¹ To compare the enemy to swine was bolc
nothing new, since the Army of Flanders had been routinely heckled as "s
bit of bacon, slang probably derived from the Spanish term "Marrano"
Jews.² Nor was animal imagery foreign to the libels that Catholics and (
ists and Orangists vigorously hurled at one another. A Catholic refrain co
in 1579 characterized the Beggars as filthy, blood-sucking lice who "st
rape."³ The Spanish pigs print, however, made the theme particularly e
ing late-medieval images of urban pride with newer ones of civic liberty–
the Patriots' political sensibility. Its central feature is a fierce, virile Lion
stands enclosed in a circular garden in front of a gate bearing Orange's cc
its trellised garden, the print evokes the popular late-medieval hortus con
Low Country cities regularly employed as a setting for either the Virgin
Tuindag veneration in Ypres, or for the city represented as a young maid

The lion in Holland's garden is rimmed with the flags of the province'
supported the Revolt. It proudly displays a liberty hat atop a tall pole—a
bol that had previously appeared on a few commemorative medals struc
revolt in 1572, and whose popularity was unmatched in the political icc

1. Text and summary in Horst, Opstand in zwart-wit, 287–90.
2. Swart, "The Black Legend during the Eighty Years' War," 84. As early as 15(
Antwerp against Granvelle accused him of wanting to make Brabanters "esclaves aux pc
for which see J. M. B. C. Kervyn de Lettenhove, Relations politiques des Pays-Bas et de l'An
Philippe II, 11 vols. (Brussels, 1882–1900), 2:675.
3. Blommaert, Politieke balladen, 107–11.

THE DILEMMA OF AUTHORITY   305

C Essez Poureeaux de rompre ma Haye,
Retire ta hûte, & ton Groin-verrat,
Où tu recepuras mortelle playe
De ma Massüe, ou par mon Geux Soldats
Mon Excellent Protecteur Orangeat,
Te fera l'assaut, par Mer, & par Terre:
Prens tes Truyes-ladres pout ton debat,
Et fuy-ten Gonjects, fay ailleurs la guerre.

Stop Rooting in my Garden, Spanish Pigs. Anonymous print, ca. 1580, around the time of the Abjuration of Philip II. It contrasts a liberty-loving lion defending a circular garden with the flags of Holland's cities. The Spanish enemy, portrayed as dirty, copulating swine, root in the mud beyond the walls. Courtesy of Rijksprentenkabinet, Rijksmuseum, Amsterdam.

seventeenth-century United Provinces.[4] So configured, the garden is a visual stand-in for the urban sphere, a privileged realm and enclosed space of a fiercely defended liberty. A distant city across a bay behind the garden—a calm presence in a sphere of otherwise

   4. Horst, *Opstand in zwart-wit*, 288. Such imagery was not unique to the Netherlands; by the early sixteenth century the kingdom of France was depicted as a garden with a lion, for which see R. W. Scheller, "Representatie en realisme: De vormgeving van het laat-middeleeuwse identifiteitsbesef," in *Openbaring en bedrog: De afbeelding als historische bron in de Lage Landen*, ed. B. Kempers (Amsterdam, 1995), 50–51. For the iconography of the republic, see also Andrew Sawyer, "Medium and Message: Political Prints in the Dutch Republic, 1568–1632," in *Public Opinion and Changing Identities*, 163–88.

frenzied action—beckons like an urban idyll. The lion's aggressive pose is in response to the chaos outside the enclosure: a shoreline swarming with swine that root for food and freely copulate with one another. One sow in the front, breasts heavy, drags her young behind her, a cross hanging off her neck. A pig in the right center of the picture scrambles up the hill with the banner of Alba's arms tucked under its leg. The pigs, visually coded as Catholic and Spanish, encapsulate pure animal instinct: feeding, mating, and reproducing. On the left, the waters of the bay roil as three ships of the Sea Beggars from Zeeland approach shore. The first bears the names of Vlissingen, Middelburg and Veere, and boasts Orange's arms and another liberty hat on its mast. The lion of Zeeland straddles the first two ships in a defiant roar, while geese, a popular symbol of the Beggars, are atop the decks. Pigs dangle from the spars of the second ship, while a desperate few spring into the water and attempt to join those swarming on shore. A text below the image in French and Dutch rails against the Spanish pigs and threatens to crush their heads and break their necks.

The Spanish pigs print is raw in its invective, casting the enemy as grunting swine and lauding the Patriots as liberty-loving defenders of the urban order, fortified by durable symbols of local might. Its visceral quality speaks volumes about how much political attitudes and cultural perceptions had hardened since the constitutional crisis of Habsburg authority and the trauma of the wonder year. It also says much about a deepening polarization of political and religious life in the Netherlands by the time of Orange's Apology. Holland and Zeeland had inched more and more toward independence after 1575, the year their Estates had considered repudiating Philip II's authority; Brabant and Flanders had urban Calvinist regimes that worried or alienated moderate Protestants and Catholics; and six southern provinces, Hainault, Artois, Walloon Flanders, Namur, Luxembourg, and Limburg, were already reconciled with the king. The father of the fatherland himself was trapped in these political cross currents, disliked by radical Calvinists who had no taste for his search for a religious peace and also by Catholic Netherlanders and royalists, who equally mistrusted him and taunted him in verse, as in a 1578 ballad about the Beggars in hell. In the verse, Orange and his wife, the apostate nun, are ridiculed as party to a sorry parade of "rogues, murderers, and iconoclasts, church violators who produced many scandalous children, apostates, ministers with their false doctrines, violators of peasants, pirates, and tramps, devourers of priests (Paep-eters), desecrators of the sacrament, and rapists."[5] With such diversity of political and religious commitments, a united front of opposition to Spanish authority among those provinces still in revolt seemed like an ideal that had slipped away. A prideful civic ethos had been revived, the rights of the States General enshrined, Philip II pilloried, and Orange hailed as the princely redeemer. But internal divisions remained fierce, religious accommodations had been

5. Blommaert, Politieke balladen, 41–43.

hardly addressed, and the knotty question of the future sovereign lordship was glaringly unresolved.

Abjuration and Oath Taking

In this delicate political landscape, the political elites—delegates of the States General especially—had to operate with more tact than anonymous polemicists and balladeers. Perhaps it is no surprise, then, that the defining text of the Revolt, the Abjuration of Philip II, occasioned no public ceremonies, no ritual cheering, and no commemorative medals. There was no public recognition of the Abjuration at all, apart from its official release of officeholders from their former oaths of loyalty to Philip II and their swearing of a new oath to the United Provinces and the regional Estate of the territory in which they held their position.[6] Yet no matter how cautious the States General had been about publicizing their move, there were unanticipated reactions to the Abjuration, including, for example, the public destruction of Philip II's coat of arms in Calvinist Mechelen and Bruges.[7] On August 27, Mechelen registered the Abjuration and immediately took down and destroyed the king's arms from the windows of the central town hall and elsewhere. Bruges did the same on September 2, but they proclaimed Philip II an enemy of the state, something the various Estates had opted against doing as they debated the final details of the Abjuration earlier in June. Most municipalities, however, removed the king's insignia without fanfare, as part of the requirement to purge all official documents and public buildings of the king's heraldry. In a sense, this official erasure of the king had been prepared years in advance by the Patriots as they slowly phased out his ritual invocations and representations in public life. However stridently the Abjuration blasted Philip II as a tyrant, the States General strove to make the transition to a new prince seamless, even muted. The public acts required to change political loyalties, however, proved such efforts impossible.[8]

Issued by the States General on July 26, 1581, after the decision had been made to offer lordship over the Low Countries to the Duke of Anjou, the Plakkaat van Verlatinghe (Edict of Abjuration) didactically reiterated political and legal arguments of Orange and others, but it broke no new conceptual ground. The Abjuration's core argument was succinctly formulated in a companion pamphlet, Political Education, issued a year later, that put forth that

---

6. A critical edition of the text is in Mout, Plakkaat van Verlatinghe. I quote from the English translation in Texts Revolt, 216–28. On the impact of late-medieval urban constitutionalism on the Abjuration, see Wim Blockmans, "Du contrat féodal à la souveraineté du peuple. Les précédents de la déchéance de Philippe II dans les Pays-Bas (1581)," in Assemblee di Stati e istituzioni rappresentative nelle storia del pensiero politico moderno (secoli XV–XX): Atti del convegno internazionale Perugia 16–18 settembre 1982 (Rimini, 1983), 135–50.

7. Marnef, Calvinistisch Bewind, 172–75, 179–80, and E. Varenbergh, ed., Guillaume Weydts, Chronique Flamande 1571–1584 (Brussels, 1869), 39–40.

8. Marnef, Calvinistisch Bewind, 180.

Philip II had become a "murderer" rather than a "father," a "butcher" rather than a "shepherd," and a "tyrant" rather than a "prince," and because of it his subjects "were no longer bound to obey him."[9] The Abjuration railed against the king's violation of the Netherlands' "ancient freedom" and presented a résumé of his tyranny since the wonder year of 1566, trotting out the now-familiar accusations that he subverted regional and urban rights and turned citizens into slaves. It found Philip in violation of the oaths that he swore to uphold legal privileges, declaring his sovereignty forfeit by reason of his constitutional transgressions. In rhetoric and argument, the Abjuration is a didactic examination of lordly duties and Philip II's violation of them. While regional Estates had eagerly approved Philip's removal in meetings prior to the Abjuration's publication, almost all cautioned against a public declaration of the king as an enemy of state, for the practical reason that it would interrupt economic relations with Castile and Portugal.[10] The States General desired to downplay the radicalism of their actions, and justified the "leaving" of Philip as sovereign by reference to what law and political custom required. In this regard, the Abjuration is not wholly disingenuous, since its language does hark back to earlier repudiations of lordship in the Low Countries. It carried echoes of the long-ago words of the twelfth-century Ghentenars when they declared against their ruler, Count William Clito, on February 16, 1128:

> Instead of treating us honorably, you have oppressed us. You have broken your promises and oaths by persecuting us unjustly and perversely. As a lawless and faithless count, you have only one thing to do, and that is to get out and leave your subjects free to elect a successor.[11]

Indeed, the Abjuration is less the defense of a radical political action than a matter-of-fact declaration of legal principle. While a retrospective of Philip II's tyranny is sketched, and the now common reference to "the privileges, traditional customs, and liberties of the fatherland, the life and honor of our wives, children, and descendents" is vividly evoked, the text does not obsessively justify its severing of sovereignty. It dwells instead on the practical implications of such a move, particularly the need to release office holders from oaths sworn to the king and the necessity to expunge the "name, titles, and arms" of Philip II from the public arena and the legal instruments of governance.

9. *Een Trouwe Waerschouwinghe aen de goede mannen van Antwerpen* (Antwerp, 1581).

10. Japikse, *Resolutiën der Staten-Generaal*, 3:280–86, discussed also by Mout, *Plakkaat van Verlatinghe*, 55–57. Only the Estates of Friesland and Ommelanden recommended declaring the king an enemy. For an analysis of the preparation of the Abjuration text, see J. P. A. Coopmans, "De herkomst van het Plakkaat van Verlatinghe," in *Justicie en Gerechticheyt*, ed. G. van Dievoet and G. Macours (Antwerp, 1983), 35–52.

11. Original Latin text in J. Rider, ed., *Galbertus Notarius Brugensis: De multro, traditione, et occisione gloriosi Karoli comitis Flandriarum* (Turnhout, 1994), 142. For an analysis of this, see Jan Dumolyn and Jelle Haemers, "Patterns of Urban Revolt in Medieval Flanders," *Journal of Medieval History* 31, no. 4 (2005): 369–95.

The Abjuration confirmed a *fait accompli*, but it required the public eradication of the king's authority in a political culture that, as we have seen, was thoroughly saturated with ceremonial evocations of Burgundian and Habsburg power and beset with worries from officeholders, even some Protestants among them, about the consequences of repudiating a sovereign.[12] Oaths were legal utterances, public testaments of one's commitment to a principle or duty; as such they were especially crucial to the Abjuration, because of the core charge that Philip II had failed to uphold the regional privileges to which he swore during the 1549 Joyous Entries. Fear of the oath as irrevocable is undoubtedly why protests from municipal officials against abjuring the king were common. In Bruges, for instance, one Jan Spestael chose to leave the city rather than publicly renounce Philip II, a protest that widened shortly thereafter, in early October 1581, among Catholic officeholders and guild deans.[13]

The anonymous writer of the text issued in Mechelen a year later in support of the Abjuration, *Political Education*, tackled the matter of the oath head on, no doubt aware that it had become a fractious political issue.[14] The author argued that the public disavowal of the king flowed from Philip II's failure to uphold his inaugural promises, a double infraction because kings are bound in word to God and to their subjects. The Abjuration's requirement that public officials swear allegiance to the "United Provinces" and their respective Estates because Anjou had not yet officially assumed his lordship functioned as a virtuous counterweight to Philip II's vitiation of his contractual obligations. It was the public marker of concord and good citizenship, a rite of communal witnessing. By contrast, Philip II had betrayed his subjects. He had severed his contract with them and, even more damning, insulted God with his princely violations and self-aggrandizement. To buttress this latter point, *Political Education*'s author alluded to the Book of Daniel's account of the attempt to execute the three Jewish officials, Shadrach, Meshach, and Abednego, for refusing to worship Nebuchadnezzar's golden idol—a scene painted by Antwerpener Pieter Aertsen in 1552 (see chapter 3).[15] Once again, and with a final flour-

---

12. Parker, *Dutch Revolt*, 200, who cites Anabaptists, who by principle refused oaths; Catholics, who were against abjuration altogether; and a Lutheran minister in Woerden, Holland, expelled by its Estates for preaching against the Abjuration. On June 6 1581, the States General had solicited responses from each provincial delegation about the abjuration of the king, the removal of his insignia from official documents and public buildings, and the use of the States General's seal in their place. See Japikse, *Resolutiën der Staten-Generaal*, 3:277, and the responses, ibid., 3:279–86. Much of this material is also summarized in L. P. Gachard, "La décheance de Philippe II," in L. P. Gachard, *Études et notices historiques concernant l'histoire des Pays-Bas*, 3 vols. (Brussels, 1890), 1:376–96; and Mout, *Plakkaat van Verlatinghe*, 55–57.

13. Varenbergh, *Guillaume Weydts, Chronique Flamande*, 40–42.

14. For the text of the oath, see Bor, *Oorsprongk*, 2:280. For its requirement by the States General, see Japikse, *Resolutiën der Staten-Generaal*, 3:295.

15. *Politicq Onderwijs* was published in Mechelen in 1582. It is translated in Van Gelderen, *Dutch Revolt*, 165–226, the Book of Daniel reference is on 208.

ish, Philip II is blasted as the idolater tyrant, guilty of the legal violation of his political commitments and of impugning God with his reign of false images.

By swearing new oaths, the king's former subjects were doing more than transferring sovereignty to a new prince. They were forming fraternal bonds of community and concord among themselves. This new oath promised a different political landscape and a new lord to revive a Burgundian golden era. But was there agreement among noblemen, delegates to the States General, urban magistrates in the provinces still in revolt, and political theorists that a prince was necessary to govern the Netherlands in the wake of the repudiation of the Spanish king? While few were willing to forgo a titular lord, the precise contours of princely authority were hardly clear. After all, the rhetoric of urban freedom that coursed through the Revolt, especially after 1572, increasingly harnessed metaphors of civic republicanism and showered Orange with paternal imagery that had once belonged exclusively to Burgundian and Habsburg lords. The Patriots repeatedly evoked freedom as a legal motif when they railed against lordly tyranny, borrowing generously from sixteenth-century resistance theory worked out in Huguenot France and elsewhere, and their own late-medieval constitutional traditions.[16] The new oaths the States General stipulated were not to Anjou, but to the regional Estates, a statement that real political authority lay with their own representative bodies.

Unresolved was the tension between the civic, the provincial, and the princely that had been a perennial dilemma in the Burgundian Netherlands. Men like Orange, steeped in the late-medieval Burgundian tradition of princely rule, understood the fight for urban and provincial rights as being easily, if imprecisely, compatible with the rule of a just lord. In the Apology and in other polemics, Orange typically presented Philip II as a unique tyrant, the errant son of the dignified Charles V and his Burgundian predecessors, who were fair rulers. Despite the urban populism in support of the prince, Orange never rejected princely rule per se, opting instead for his own adaptation of sixteenth-century resistance theory against an unjust lord.[17] Orange comported himself with Burgundian panache, ran a large, princely household, and had a marked taste for courtly life and the trappings of late-medieval chivalric culture, especially tournaments.[18] Those who wanted to explore what was dubbed the "Swiss" model—that is, a post-monarchical state as an urban confederacy—were in a small minority. They were represented best by the author of the 1578 *The True Patriot to the Good Patriots*, probably written by the Reformed minister Petrus Beutterich in support of Ghent's Calvinist regime. But even Beutterich did

---

16. Mout, *Plakkaat van Verlatinghe*, esp. 47–53, but also A. C. J. de Vrankijker, *De motiveering van onzen Opstand: De theorieën van het verzet der Nederlandsche opstandelingen tegen Spanje in de jaren 1564–1581* (Nijmegen and Utrecht, 1932), and, most important, the general conclusions in Van Gelderen, *Political Thought*, 260–87.

17. See, for one example, Duke, "William of Orange's Apology," 15.

18. Fully explored in Delen, *Hof en hofcultuur rondom Willem van Oranje*.

not embrace outright civic republicanism, but only sought to reject Anjou as Philip II's successor.[19]

Such sensibilities go far in explaining why the royal Anjou, with his Valois Burgundian ancestry, his direct access to his brother, the French king, and his watered-down sovereignty seemed the perfect prince to replace Philip II, even if Holland and Zeeland failed to submit to his authority, offering the title of count of their two provinces to Orange himself.[20] Anjou could revive Burgundian lordship, and with it the sheen of princely glory. Yet his authority would be circumscribed, subordinated to the popular sovereignty of urban magistrates and the States General. What better way to achieve this than a Joyous Entry that made the oath itself—that which bound prince to people and people to prince—the central ritual act of political renewal after it had been so tarnished by Philip II and his perfidy. The new prince's inauguration and public vows, however, had to straddle two important impulses in tension with one another: a romantic evocation of Burgundian lordship from an idealized past, and a supercharged civic ethos of urban rights and provincial authority.

The Image of Lordship

The abjuration of Philip II was a political watershed, even if cautiously announced. But despite accusations that the king had been an idolatrous tyrant, it neither inspired new forms of political representation in the public realm nor new political rituals. Instead, there was a noticeable effort to resuscitate tried-and-true Burgundian ceremony that best promoted a balance of urban rights and just lordship—the Joyous Entry as a constitutional rite that Philip the Good, Charles the Bold, and their successors had inflated with classical, sacred, and imperial trappings. After two centuries of Valois and Habsburg Burgundian rule, the rituals that had sealed authority since the rise of the Burgundian Netherlands as a late-medieval state proved of enduring importance in a post-iconoclastic era. But the Catholic imagery that the dukes of Burgundy so enthusiastically embraced was clearly unacceptable to Calvinist Netherlanders. Princely ritual after the Abjuration therefore adapted more ecumenical references to standard Hebraic heroes, to venerable civic symbols, and to classical allegories—a stylistic mix adumbrated by Orange's civic entries of the late 1570s. Still, not all critics were satisfied. There were strict Calvinists like Orange's brother Jan who fretted that the lordship of a prince like Anjou facilitated the return of the reign of an idolatrous prince, even if his public rule was expunged of Catholic

---

19. *Le Vray Patriot aux Bons Patriots* (1578), esp. C2v on the Swiss cantons. Portions of this text are translated in *Texts Revolt*, 159–62. A fine analysis of this debate is in Van Gelderen, *Political Thought*, 187–91, and, more generally, in Van Gelderen, "Conceptions of Liberty during the Dutch Revolt."

20. On Holland's and Zeeland's opposition to Orange's Anjou policy, see "Déclaration du duc d'Anjou," in *Documents concernant les relations entre le duc d'Anjou et les Pays-Bas*, 3:663–66.

props.²¹ But did the visual promotion of the sovereign's authority indeed contradict the Calvinist opposition to religious images and idolatrous rulers like Nebuchadnezzar, to which texts such as *Political Education* referred? Did it undermine the Orangists' disdain for Alba and his infamous Antwerp statue by making them guilty of the same visual worship of lordship? Calvinists like Jan of Nassau certainly thought so, and so too did certain Catholic opponents, including Maarten Donc, whose 1597 *A Short Distinction between Godly and Idolatrous Images* denounced Reformed theorists for their shrill proscription of all forms of religious image worship while they freely embraced "the likenesses of emperors and kings" depicted and honored in statues, prints, paintings, and other media.²² Yet such debates over the finer points of the theological consequences of political representation were largely academic. In the public arena, representations of lordship clearly flourished, calibrated to urgent political circumstances under which they were enacted. In the wake of Philip II's repudiation, the first, crucial test of sovereign lordship was the Duke of Anjou's reception in the Low Countries.

Of the three entries Anjou made to secure his authority in Brabant and Flanders, the Antwerp reception on February 19, 1582 was the most significant. It at once played to a nostalgia for Burgundian ritual and affirmed a civic constitutionalism by which the prince was bound in his oath-taking—exactly the point upon which Philip II had been repudiated, for failing to honor these oaths. The event merited not only a spectacular display of urban ceremony the likes of which Antwerp had not experienced since Philip II's entry into the city in 1549, but also a handsome folio about it, published by Christopher Plantin.²³ The commemorative book was the most elaborate entry *livret* to date, with twenty-one

---

21. On the Nassau brothers' disagreements over Anjou, see Swart, *William of Orange*, 250–51, and the letters exchanged on the matter in *Archives d'Orange-Nassau*, 8:303–5, and 344–46 especially.

22. Maarten Donc, *Een Cort onderscheyt tussen Godlijcke en Afgodissche Beelden* (1597), Biv r–v. Dort's work was part of a spate of positive endorsements of the role and function of images in religious life published in the era of the Revolt. Others who leveled the same criticism about secular image worship against Calvinists included Johannes Molanus, rector of the University of Louvain, in his 1570 *De Picturis et Imaginibus*, and Johannes a Porta, *D'net der Beeltstormers* (Antwerp, 1591). For a treatment of these three texts, see Freedberg, *Iconoclasm and Painting*, esp. 69–79.

23. See Purkis, *Magnifique Entrée de François d'Anjou*, for a facsimile edition. See also J. Diegerick, "Notice sur l'entrée solennelle du Duc d'Anjou dans la ville d'Anvers, le 19 février 1582," *Annales de l'Académie d'Archéologie* 11 (1854): 405–22, and A. Gielens, "De Kosten van de Blijde Intrede van den Hertog van Anjou (1582)," *Jaarboek Antwerpen's Oudheidkundige Kring* 16 (1940): 53–78. For both the entry and Plantin's text editions, see Emily Peters, "'Den gheheelen loop des weerelts' (The Whole Course of the World): Printed Processions and the Theater of Identity in Antwerp during the Dutch Revolt," (PhD diss., University of California, Santa Barbara, 2005), chap. 5. For Anjou's Antwerp entry contrasted to his July 27 and August 29 entries in Bruges and Ghent, see Anne-Laure van Bruaene, "Spectacle and Spin for a Spurned Prince: Civic Strategies in the Entries of the Duke of Anjou in Antwerp, Bruges, and Ghent (1582)," *Journal of Early Modern History*, 11, no. 4–5 (2007): 263–84, with attention to the difficulties encountered especially in Bruges and Ghent, where anti-Anjou sentiment was robust.

etchings and engravings, more expensive than woodcuts, and several deluxe copies with hand-colored illustrations. Shortly after his book's publication, Plantin produced a less pricey quarto version in both French and Dutch, with no illustrations.

That so much effort was expended to celebrate what turned out to be a disastrous, short reign is not surprising. Anjou's assumption of the dukeship of Brabant in Antwerp was the first political act of the investiture of sovereignty following the Abjuration. At that time, Antwerp was both the seat of the States General—it moved to Middelburg in August 1583, then to Delft and then The Hague—and the residence of Orange. It was also the commercial gem of Brabant, the province whose constitutional document, the 1356 Blijde Inkomst, with its famous clause of resistance that allowed subjects to renounce a lord who failed to uphold the duchy's privileges, had been elevated by Orangists as the master text of freedom that permitted their legal renunciation of the Spanish king.[24] In many ways, Antwerp in 1582 was the pulse center of the Revolt; it was ruled by a Calvinist government that had come to power in 1577 during the political turn that had installed like-minded regimes to Ghent and Brussels.[25] While Antwerp's magistracy did not assume the radical tone of Ghent's Calvinist regime, the city did experience a second bout of iconoclasm in May and June 1581. It passed off, however, without great turmoil, since many guilds and other corporate groups volunteered to remove their altars from chapels and churches.[26] After July 1, Catholics could no longer worship in public, though they were given two chapels where a mere six priests were allowed to conduct baptisms and marriages. On August 23, 1581, only a few days past the anniversary of the original *beeldenstorm* of 1566, Calvinists assumed official control of the Onze-Lieve-Vrouwekerk again. They had matters other than religion on their minds. Much like their counterparts in Ghent, these new Calvinist magistrates showed themselves to be shrewd managers of civic consciousness. Two acts that followed in the wake of Philip II's abjuration exhibit their determination to bolster Antwerp's civic pride and raise its political stature. On November 29, 1581, after two years of renovation, the city celebrated the restoration of the town hall, and the magistrates promptly began to conduct business there. Given that the damage to this monument to civic power had become for the Patriots a hallmark of Philip II's contempt for Antwerp's privileges, the town hall's repair carried momentous political weight. Not long thereafter, in November 1582, a new redaction of Antwerp's privileges and rights was also finished, a project authorized in July 1578.[27] A newly refurbished town hall and a new codification of the city's great privileges spoke to Antwerpeners of the rejuvenation of their political culture after the trauma of the sack of the city in 1576. It was a simple equa-

24. See, in particular, Geurts, *Nederlandse Opstand*, 149–51.
25. A factual account is offered in Prims, *Geschiedenis van Antwerpen*, 19:139–79.
26. Ibid., 186–87.
27. Floris Prims, *De groote cultuurstrijd. II. De christelijke republiek, 1581–1585* (Antwerp, 1943).

tion: the Army of Flanders had burned the town hall and damaged its charters of liberties; the Calvinist magistrates had revenged these insults by restoring both and reclaiming their pride of place in the civic landscape.

It was into this civic environment of Calvinist ascendancy and political renewal that Anjou entered on February 19, 1582. Plantin's edition of the prince's reception as Duke of Brabant is lavishly produced and expensively illustrated. Its French text, however, written by Orange's court chaplain Pierre Loyseleur de Villiers, suggests neither the enthusiasm of Houwaert's account of Orange's welcome in Brussels and the anonymous one of his reception in Amsterdam, nor the more polemical quality of d'Heere's description of Orange's visit to Ghent. While the book is both more elaborate and better produced than these other three texts, its tone is more legalistic and measured, an echo, otherwise muted in this handsome folio volume, of the ambivalence Antwerpeners felt about receiving a French Catholic prince into what was now officially a Calvinist city, although at least half of the population was Catholic.

Anjou was treated to an impeccably organized series of tableaux vivants and handsomely outfitted retinues of militia companies, city magistrates, delegates of the States General, and other queues of officialdom, all orchestrated by a committee headed by the artist Hans Vredeman de Vries.[28] Concord and harmony were the entry's guiding themes, and pageant organizers reached deep into Antwerp's traditional *ommegangen* and ceremonial protocols to acclaim the newly inaugurated Duke of Brabant and to champion the city, its economic vitality, and its cultural authority. Before entering the city via the Keizerpoort, Anjou was invested as duke by the Estates of Brabant outside the city's walls upon a magnificent dais with the full sweep of the city visible behind his gold-covered throne. It was a display of Antwerp's physical immensity, the magnificence of its fortifications, and the control local officials had gained over the once-despised citadel. Praised by the Estates of Brabant's councilor of law, André Hessels, as the embodiment of the illustrious house of Burgundy, Anjou had the articles of the Brabantine text of the Blijde Inkomst read aloud to him and heard an oration on the necessity of upholding its "liberties, rights, and privileges." Anjou was then presented with the keys to the city, which he promptly returned.[29]

As Anjou entered Antwerp, he was greeted with the first tableau, a chariot wagon featuring the Maiden of Antwerp flanked by Justice, Religion, and Concord. He was then escorted under a canopy along the route to view a full array of spectacles and tableaux vivants. Last of all was the Cave of Discord wagon that had featured prominently in the 1566 Assumption Day procession.[30] It reappeared more prominently three days later, when Anjou paraded from the traditional royal residence of Saint Michael's Abbey to the

---

28. On his role, see Van Brauene, "Spectacle and Spin for a Spurned Prince."
29. Purkis, *Magnifique Entrée de François d'Anjou*, 18–26.
30. Prims, "De Antwerpsche Ommeganck," 15.

central market to swear his oath of lordship in front of a crowd of citizens beneath the central bay of the restored town hall. In the Assumption Day procession of 1566, the Cave of Discord threatened a world teetering on disarray; now it was depicted as chastised and weakened, its three furies of Discord, Violence, and Tyranny forced into retreat by the rays of Apollo, a stand-in for Anjou, and by the ascendance of Concord.[31]

Anjou's oath-taking that day was the apex of the three days of his entry—the central ritual event of fidelity and community witnessing that the Abjuration itself had made of critical importance for officeholders. The plate Plantin prepared to illustrate the princely oath is more a hymn to Antwerp's civic might than it is to Anjou's investiture, an artistic maneuver that speaks volumes about the ritual placement of the prince in the new political scheme. The restored town hall looms imposingly, and Anjou himself, seated directly in front of it, peers across a semicircle of open space where soldiers are retrieving tossed coins, to look directly at a wagon cart featuring the Maiden of Antwerp. Enormous crowds of officials, onlookers, and militia companies ring the market square; on the right, fire displays brighten the winter cold and offer an atmosphere of good cheer. The illustration is a forthright celebration of the town hall, urban public space, and Antwerp's citizenry. In the buzz of activity, Anjou appears noticeably dwarfed—the center of attention, the object of praise, but also an adjunct to Antwerp's privileges and rights, whose provisions he is instructed to respect. Seated almost as a passive recipient of this inaugural celebration, he is a far cry from the image of Orange presented in the Brussels 1577 welcome, in which the final tableau featured the prince as a classical soldier-hero brandishing a lance in one hand and a book of privileges in the other.[32] Anjou, by contrast, might be the salve of Concord and the muse of Apollo—the house of Burgundy resurrected—but he was also the dutiful oath taker and guardian of privileges rather than their master, the object of praise but also the witness to a series of tableaux that celebrated the icons and symbols of Antwerp's civic consciousness. In the aftermath of Philip II's abjuration, the great Burgundian Joyous Entry could still proclaim a prince as ruler, but the images deployed were aggressively civic. Anjou was a prince, but a dependent one, and his oath was subsumed within a full civic context.

Anjou's reception, however politely circumspect, proved too optimistic, as the Cave of Discord was not yet so easily vanquished and the virtue of Concord—the entry's symbolic leitmotif—proved frustratingly temporary. His reign unraveled more quickly than even his critics might have predicted. First, Anjou began to press for the public allowance of Catholic practice again in Antwerp, a goal Orange himself had worked to accomplish, but one that piqued tempers in the city when it came from a foreign Catholic prince. When Anjou had Catholic mass celebrated in Saint Michael's the Sunday after his Joyous Entry,

31. Purkis, *Magnifique Entrée de François d'Anjou*, 38.
32. Houwaert, *Declaratie van de triumphante Incompst*, 15.

a near-riot ensued, forcing the magistrates to concede that Catholics could henceforth have mass celebrated there.³³ But what tipped the balance against Anjou in Antwerp was an assassination attempt against Orange the following month, on March 18. Orange nearly died from a bullet wound to his jaw; his several-month recuperation was interpreted as yet another trial on behalf of the fatherland. While the plot against the prince was hatched by a fiercely loyalist Spanish merchant and executed by his hapless servant, Jean Jaureguy, Antwerpeners suspected Anjou's involvement—the assassin was supposedly dressed in French clothes—and an angry crowd had to be kept from storming Saint Michael's Abbey, where Anjou resided. Plantin published a heroic account of the attempt on Orange's life and bundled it for sale with the cheaper quarto copies of the account of Anjou's entry.³⁴

Rumors of Anjou's involvement in the attack against Orange were not grounded in reality, since Orange and Anjou worked agreeably together. Anjou, however, grew quickly exasperated at being boxed in by an obstreperous States General. As the famed political theorist Jean Bodin trenchantly observed in 1583, the root cause of the tension between Anjou and the States was conflicting interpretations of sovereignty: Anjou wanted more centralized authority than the States were ready to concede.³⁵ As we have seen, the splendor of Anjou's own triumphal entry into Antwerp hinged on the twin themes of concord and Burgundian lordship, and both were embedded in a storyline of civic renewal. Anjou was hailed as a new lord, but one indebted to urban power and without the ritual charisma of Orange, the real heir to Burgundian splendor.

Anjou had been summoned as Philip's successor when the south had been facing its fiercest opponent: Alexander Farnese, the Duke of Parma and son of the former regent, Margaret of Parma. Farnese had succeeded Don Juan as governor general in 1578; concluded the Treaty of Arras on May 17, 1579, which reconciled the Walloon provinces with the king; and waged brilliant campaigns against the rebellious provinces.³⁶ Anjou was in a difficult situation, as the funding that the States had originally promised him failed to materialize, despite repeated requests and Orange's support. He fumed as he tried to manage the poorly organized States' troops whose salaries he could not pay on time. In fall 1582, Anjou secured 10,000 new soldiers from France, a seeming boon to the States' military campaign, and billeted them in Antwerp. But instead of using them in the service of the Revolt, Anjou directed them in an attempted coup against Antwerp on January 17,

33. Prims, *Geschiedenis van Antwerpen*, 19:179; Holt, *The Duke of Anjou and the Politique Struggle*, 170.

34. *Bref recueil de l'assassinat commis en la personne du . . . Prince . . . d'Orange . . . par Jean Jauregui* (Antwerp, 1581), and on the bundling of the two text, see Peters, "Den gheheelen loop des weerelt," 302, and Jardine, *Awful End of Prince William the Silent*, 63–67.

35. Griffiths, *Representative Government*, 505.

36. For military details and other elements, see Léon van der Essen, *Alexandre Farnèse, Prince de Parme Gouveneur Général des Pays Bas*, 5 vols. (Brussels, 1935–37), especially important since the work relies on the Farnesian archives, the Carte Farnesiane in Naples, that was mostly destroyed in 1943.

Anjou swears his oath as the newly inaugurated duke of Brabant before Antwerp's town hall. Plate twenty-one in La joyeuse et magnifique entrée de Monseigneur Françoys, . . . Duc de Brabant, d'Anjou, . . . en sa tres-renommée ville d'Anvers. Antwerp: Christopher Plantin, 1582. Courtesy of the Universiteitsbibliotheek Gent.

1583. Orange was dumbstruck by the actions of this controversial ally upon whose promotion he had expended so much political capital. Antwerp's magistrates, by contrast, had been more astute; tipped off in advance, they had secured the city with militia companies and closed the city gates. When Anjou's men rushed the city, reportedly shouting "Kill, kill, kill! Long live the mass!" they were repelled, and in the fight that ensued more than a thousand Frenchmen perished, including some lesser noblemen.[37]

37. The fullest account of the "French Fury" is the official report of the magistrates in Calendar of State Papers, Foreign, 1533–84, 18:24–31.

In the wake of this fiasco, Anjou's reign was all but finished, and Orange's reputation seriously eroded. The prince doggedly implored the States General to mend fences with the treacherous Anjou, since the French alliance still offered the rebels their best practical chance to retard Parma. He wearily reminded his peers that the Low Countries had suffered repeated assaults by Burgundian predecessors, but had never repudiated them.[38] While the States reluctantly conceded to Orange's plea in March, 1583, and while Anjou's forces, particularly the Swiss mercenaries, stayed and fought, Anjou himself returned to France in late June. He died of tuberculosis a year later, thirteen days after one last attempt by a deeply divided States General, now located in Holland, to reconcile with him.[39]

Martyrdom

Anjou's failed attempt to seize Antwerp doomed his rule in the Netherlands, even if he more or less held onto the title of lord until his death. With its inflated civic symbols and its presentation of Anjou as guarantor of liberties, the Antwerp entry of 1582 reveals not just mixed feeling among Netherlanders about this French Catholic prince, but more generally an unresolved ambivalence about lordship after the Abjuration of Philip II. While almost everyone was at pains to affirm the necessity of a sovereign lord in the Netherlands, after a decade and a half's campaign to present Orange as paternal defender of the *patria*, there was little room for another prince to gain ritual traction. Burgundian ceremonial forms had been effectively rekindled for Anjou, but they had to be emptied of their association with Catholic liturgy and devotional practices—precisely the elements that Philip the Good, Charles the Bold, and Charles V had cherished. Meanwhile, Holland and Zeeland had opted to offer their governorship to Orange instead of Anjou, and while these two vitally important provinces never ultimately blocked Anjou's selection by the States General, they did not advocate it. Never the ceremonial heartland of the Burgundian dukes, Holland and Zeeland were ready to accept Orange as a governing prince instead of as a *stadholder*, and to embrace the republican-tinged rhetoric of the nation as civic family. Flanders and Brabant, by contrast, strove to retain the Burgundian heritage of lordship and its ritual trappings, but to leaven both with a heavier dose of civic boosterism than the Valois dukes of Burgundy and their successors had allowed. Anjou's coup against Antwerp rendered such efforts futile. Orange had inherited too much of the ritual charisma of the Burgundian heritage, and the Abjuration had stipulated that officeholders forsake the king and swear fidelity not to Anjou, but to their regional Estates. There was little room for strong princely authority at this critical juncture in the Burgundian Netherlands, even if there was no outcry or principled opposition to monarchy itself.

38. Muller and Diegerick, *Documents concernant les relations entre le duc d'Anjou et les Pays-Bas* 4:335–41; Bor, *Oorsprongk*, 2:343, estimates the number of Anjou's men killed between 1,400 and 1,500.

39. Muller and Diegerick, *Documents concernant les relations entre le duc d'Anjou et les Pays-Bas*, 5:769–71.

Any search for a new public language of sovereign lordship was made moot by a much more pressing matter: defending the territories still in revolt against Parma. That too proved impossible, and the sparring over Anjou's future and Holland and Zeeland's increasing separatism prevented a coordinated effort to retard the Army of Flanders as it swept through Flanders and Brabant. Even though Anjou had assigned his Swiss mercenaries to the States General's forces when he fled, Parma made striking advances in spring of 1583. To make matters worse, Orange's popularity in the south faltered after Anjou's treachery. Dismayed by the intense criticism leveled at him following the failed attack on Antwerp, Orange decided to leave the south for Delft, in Holland, in July 1583. As Parma's campaign to gain back Brabant and Flanders quickened, the States General itself moved north, setting up in August first in Middelburg and then in Delft, where Orange had taken up residence in the Prinsenhof in January 1584. He was finally ready to accept the countship of Holland. Instead, on July 10, 1584, at the age of fifty-one, Orange fell victim to an assassin's bullet. Hailing from Franche-Comté and inspired by the Edict of Proscription against Orange, the fanatically Catholic Balthasar Gérard had remarkably managed to pose in Orange's court as a Huguenot exile eager to assist the Patriots' cause. Allowed access to the Prinsenhof, he shot the prince from behind a pillar as Orange left his midday meal. According to accounts by the States General and the Estates of Holland, as he died Orange muttered, "My God, have pity on me and these poor people."[40]

Orange had never achieved universal acclaim among those opposed to Philip II during the Dutch Revolt, but by dint of status, charisma, and leadership, he nevertheless had become the symbolic repository of many of the Revolt's goals. His increasing glorification, captured in his great triumphal entries of the late 1570s, sat uneasily beside the reality of the polarized perceptions about him. In his final years, Orange lost the support of the coalition of Catholics and Protestants he had labored to stitch together. His vision of a unified state secured through a religious peace was unrealized due to a rebellion now almost completely in the hands of urban Calvinists, with most of the Netherlands nobility, and almost all Catholics, reconciled with the Spanish king. He had pinned his hopes on Anjou and a Burgundian-tinged revival of a state compatible with a robust States General and a privileging of provincial and municipal rights. But his admirers clearly preferred that Orange himself publicly represent the state, whose political order he fought to establish, and their fraternal and paternal rhetoric in his honor contradicted Orange's own

---

40. The earliest accounts of Orange's assassination are in J. J. Frederiks, ed., *Oorspronkelijke verhalen en gelijktijdige berichten van den moord gepleegd op Willem van Oranje* (The Hague, 1884), R. Fruin, "De oude verhalen van den moord op prins Willem I," in R. Fruin, *Verspreide Geschriften*, 10 vols. (The Hague, 1900–05), 3:65–117, and L. J. van der Klooster, "Drie gelijktijdige berichten over de moord op prins Willem van Oranje," *Jaaarboek Vereniging Oranje-Nassau Museum* (1984): 37–83. See also Bor, *Oorsprongk*, 1:427–36. A factual summary is in Swart, *William of Orange*, 252–55; see Lisa Jardine, *Awful End of Prince William the Silent* on Orange's death as a protomodern political assassination.

model of the Netherlands ruled by a compact between a French lord and parliamentary bodies. In the end, his assassination resuscitated his damaged reputation and predictably raised his symbolic stock. His somber state funeral in Delft was his apotheosis, a political martyrdom for a fledging commonwealth in need of consecration and a key moment in a foundation narrative whose past heroes included the martyred Egmont and Hornes.

The details of Orange's assassination were the subject of an official account authorized by the Estates of Holland and written by Pierre Loyseleur de Villiers, the principal author of the Apology.[41] A recounting of Orange's death appealed to resolute Calvinists and humanist-influenced urban literati. Both groups had a taste for martyrdom and for the defense of faith or civic virtue in the face of inquisitors and tyrants. Orange's Apology had ended with a sacrificial *cri de coeur* that he would "purchase your freedom, if necessary, with my blood."[42] His assassination eerily fulfilled this vow, and Delft honored Orange's death with a dignified state funeral. They also promptly executed his assassin, the young Huguenot imposter Gérard, on July 14 with gruesome dismemberment—according to the death sentence and to eyewitness accounts, his heart was flung in his face.[43] There could be no less painful a punishment for the surrogate of the Spanish king who, in the words of one doleful ballad about Orange's death, killed "my father, next to God in worth."[44]

Orange's funeral outshone Gérard's brutal ending. As with the inauguration of Anjou, though in a more modest fashion, Burgundian motifs resurfaced. For all the vocabulary of civic rights and republican self-sacrifice that swirled around Orange, the Estates of Holland opted for a public burial on August 3 that had regal inflections. The Burgundian element is strongly echoed in the funeral cortege's layout, but even more so in its commemorative booklet, whose design borrows heavily from Charles V's 1558 royal funeral in Brussels memorialized by Johannes and Lucas van Deutecum in an edition printed by Christopher Plantin in Antwerp.[45] The artist Hendrik Goltzius commemorated Orange's funeral in a twelve-sheet series of engravings whose layout faithfully mirrored the Deutecum brothers' depiction of the rank and order of Charles V's.[46] Orange's Burgundian heritage was strong, and the link to Charles V personal, as shown by his prominent

---

41. *Verhael vande Moort ghedaen aenden Persoone des Doorluchtigen Hoochgheboorn Fursten ende Heeren Heern Wilhelms byder gratien Godts, Prince van Oraengien*, in Frederiks, *Oorspronkelijke verhalen*, 57–82.

42. Duke, "William of Orange's Apology," 84.

43. *Historie Balthazars Gerardt, alias Serach, die den Tyran van T'Nederlandt den Prince van Orangie doorschoten heeft: Ende is daerom deur grouwelijcke ende vele tormenten binnen de Stadt van Delft openbaerlijck Gedoodt*, in Frederiks, *Oorspronkelijke verhalen*, 85–99. According to Frederiks, a letter by Cornelis Aerssen to authorities in Brussels confirmed this manner of execution, see *Oorspronkelijke verhalen*, 135–36, but see also the official decree of punishment against Gérard, 42–45.

44. NG, 2:284–89 for the ballads about Orange's death, and for the quote, 287.

45. Johannes and Lucas van Deutecum, *La magnifique et sumptuese pompe funèbre*; Bor, *Oorsprongk*, 1:435, and the analysis in Delen, *Hof en hofcultuur rondom Willem van Oranje*, 311–13.

46. Henricus Goltzius, *Ordo apparatusque funebris Guilielmi illust. Pr. Auriacae comitis Nassaviae* (n.d.), whose prints are reproduced in Walter L. Strauss, *Hendrik Goltzius, 1558–1617: The Complete Engravings and Woodcuts* (New York, 1977), 322–35.

role in the emperor's abdication and funeral.[47] That the account of Orange's funeral procession imitated Charles V's tells us something about the usefulness of graphic prototypes in the print marketplace, but it was also an assertion that Orange himself had achieved an equal level of political stature and fame as a figure of unmatched importance to Holland and the Revolt. A formation of *schutters*, exemplars of the civic esprit, led the procession of two hundred mourners to Delft's Nieuwe Kerk, though Golztius's illustration depicts trumpeters in their place because he wanted to evoke the Deutecum brothers' text commemorating Charles V's funeral.

Not every element of Orange's funeral mirrored the cortege of Charles V. Absent were the Golden Fleece insignia, the great train of Burgundian noblemen, and the imperial regalia and allegories, such as the Ship of State, of the Brussels funeral of 1558. Goltzius makes no attempt to replicate these royal symbols. Orange's casket was carried amid a retinue of noblemen and delegates from the Council of State and the States General, mostly from Holland. Present too was his son Maurits, whose political fortunes were already on the rise, Maurits's half-brother Justinus, and Orange's nephew Willem-Lodewijk. Revealingly absent was his surviving brother Jan, whose anger over Anjou had unraveled what was left of the once much ballyhooed band of brothers who stood for fraternal bonds in the early days of the Revolt. Held aloft were heraldic devices of Orange and the House of Nassau: a helmet, coats of arms, a livery, and the sword of state. In a nutshell, the funeral's processional order so faithfully duplicated that of Charles that substitutions of men or insignia were made only when absolutely required, with one thing switched for its near equivalent to preserve a parallel structure: the men from the States General, for example, occupied the spot that in Charles V's funeral was assigned to the knights of the Golden Fleece. Orange's two great political débuts as a young statesmen had been at signature political rituals in Brussels: the Abdication and the funeral of Charles V. Despite the enormous changes in the political landscape of the Netherlands and in his own eventful career since those two events, Orange exited public life still awash in the glow of Burgundian ceremonialism, albeit now colored by symbols of his own household and the power of Holland, its noblemen, and its own Estates.

Orange's funeral ushered in a new chapter in the political culture of the Netherlands in the era after the Abjuration of Philip II. It captured both the persistence of Burgundian ceremonial forms and the vitality of the House of Nassau as the real locus of princely charisma. It also underscored the widening power of Holland, its cities, and its Estates. In this civic realm, Orange achieved his ultimate apotheosis as cult object to be worshipped, according to his grave's epitaph, as a "lover of God's word and hater of tyranny."[48] Such adulation was at root political, but it carried obvious religious overtones. Maximillian Morillon, Granvelle's longtime informant about Low Country affairs since

---

47. Schrader, "Greater Than Ever He Was."
48. Bor, *Oorsprongk*, 2:436.

Two of twelve engravings of William of Orange's funeral cortege in 1585, with the heraldry of the prince and the House of Nassau. Hendrik Goltzius, 1585. Courtesy of Rijksprentenkabinet, Rijksmuseum, Amsterdam.

the cardinal's forced departure in 1564, wrote disparagingly that Orange's mourners had encased his heart in a golden reliquary, turning it, of all things, into a relic, a thing of religious veneration.[49] In a whitewashed church cleansed by iconoclasm, the once-reluctant rebel was laid to rest in a modest tomb that an English observer in 1592 noted was poorly maintained, indicative of the parlous nature of Holland's new political circumstances.[50] In 1623 it was replaced with a baroque marble and bronze mausoleum in honor of the "father of the fatherland," a triumphal veneration for his family of civic patriots.[51] In death,

49. *Corr. Granvelle*, 11:81, letter of August 11, 1584.
50. Swart, *William of Orange*, 255.
51. E. I. Jimkes-Verkade, "De ikonologie van het grafmonument van Willem I, prins van Oranje," in *De stad Delft: Cultuur en maatschappij van 1572 tot 1667*, ed. Leeuw Spander (Delft, n.d.), 214–97.

Orange became the martyred political saint of a fledgling commonwealth, a departed father to his citizens, and a memory whose remains became the stuff of acclaim and worship.

The Virgin in the Town Hall: The Fall of Antwerp

Spanish forces were well practiced in the art of reconquest, and the snuffing out of the Revolt in Flanders and Brabant occurred quickly at the hands of Alexander Farnese. If Anjou's inauguration and Orange's death were two pivotal political moments in the aftermath of the repudiation of Philip II, the fall of Antwerp in August 1585 was the master symbol of the cessation of the Revolt in the southern heartlands and the occasion of an exodus of tens of thousands of the region's Calvinists to the cities of Zeeland and Holland and abroad. Unlike Alba's campaigns, Farnese's were remarkably bloodless; in a letter to Granvelle dated April 14, 1584, he openly spoke of the practical benefits of clemency and reconciliation. Cities surrendered to him with terms that restored traditional privileges, dismantled Calvinist regimes, and permitted a leniency period during which Calvinists and other Protestants could alienate property, secure assets, and freely emigrate northward.[52] Once radical Ghent fell on September 17, 1584, and Brussels capitulated on March 10, 1585, Orange's triumphs there in 1577 were but a distant reminder of the halcyon period of the Revolt.[53]

Far more momentous was Antwerp's surrender on August 17, 1585, for since 1566 the key events of this metropolis had come to define the Revolt's flash points. Hogenberg's famous print of the iconoclasm in Antwerp's Onze-Lieve-Vrouwekerk in 1566 was the visual distillation of the wonder year; Alba's citadel and free-standing statue of himself as conqueror described the restoration of Spanish authority and its accompanying militarization of civic space after 1567; and the Spanish Fury of 1576 epitomized the violence of the Army of Flanders against the civic realm. In each of these chapters of Antwerp's history, the Revolt's cultural tropes reverberated: 1566 and the inversion rituals of the Beggars and iconoclasts; 1567–72 and Alba's idolatrous tyranny; 1576 and the domestic and fraternal rhetoric of the civic Patriots.

Farnese's siege was a new opportunity for Antwerp and the Revolt—it could replay on a grander scale the heroism of the cities that had rebuffed the Army of Flanders in the

---

52. The best account of Farnese's reconquest is Van der Essen, *Alexandre Farnèse*, esp. vol. 4, which principally concerns the fall of Antwerp. On Antwerp's siege and capture, see the snapshot overview in C. E. H. J. Verhoef, *De val van Antwerpen in 1585* (Antwerp, 1985), and Alfons K. L. Thijs, *Van Geuzenstad tot katholiek bolwerk: Maatschappelijke betekenis van de kerk in contrareformatorisch Antwerpen* (Turnhout, 1990), esp. 33–34. The text of the August 17 capitulation of Antwerp is in Bor, *Oorsprongk*, 2:610–13. Farnese's letter to Granvelle is in *Corr. Granvelle*, 11:18–20.

53. Van der Essen, *Alexandre Farnèse*, 4:8–14 on Ghent, and 4:44 on Brussels. For Farnese's campaigns, and his overall strategy of controlling the Scheldt and its estuaries, see Parker, *Dutch Revolt*, 213–15.

1570s. After all, the other two Calvinist regimes, Ghent and Brussels, were now defeated, and Antwerp, the Low Countries' civic powerhouse, was the last great southern holdout. Antwerp could make easy analogy to Leiden's heroic resistance during 1573–74, so much so that like Leideners, Antwerp's magistrates tried to foil the Spanish by flooding the surrounding plains by opening dikes. But Antwerp's situation in 1584–85 was particularly vulnerable. Its siege had begun in July 1584, just after Orange's death, and the city was without its prince father. Orange's tireless right-hand man, Philips van Marnix, Lord of St. Aldegonde, had agreed to serve as Antwerp's outside mayor in 1583, but the city was boxed in; Farnese had effectively blocked its relief by States troops by building a bridge 2,400 feet across the Scheldt. Not only was Antwerp surrounded and its navigational routes cut off, internal divisions tore at the civic fabric. The Calvinist regime had effectively managed the civic realm, but the half of the city's population of eighty thousand who remained Catholic were angry over the curtailment of their faith and the abjuration of their king.[54]

As it turned out, the siege of Antwerp was no reprise of Leiden's success, and the city's fall ended the heroic long decade of the Patriots' glory. The capitulation of Antwerp on August 17, 1585 was an almost familiar exercise in Burgundian triumph and Catholic reconsecration. Before Antwerp's surrender, careful negotiations between its town council, guildsmen in the Broad Council, and Marnix, on the one side, and Farnese and his advisors, on the other side, encountered two sticking points: the city's animus against the refurbishment of the hated citadel and the question of religious freedom for Calvinists and other Protestant groups.[55] For all his Calvinist stridency, Marnix's years of work as a diplomat for Orange had resulted in a mature political pragmatism, particularly after the Anjou fiasco. As Antwerp's outside mayor, he worked hard to mollify intransigence among the heavily Calvinist guilds, in particular to advocate reconciliation with Farnese. The end result was a compromise. Antwerp failed in its effort to prevent the citadel's restoration—no doubt painful since its use by Orange between 1577 and 1583 had been a great triumph over Alba's legacy of spatial supervision. The city was saddled with a hefty indemnity of 400,000 florins. But Farnese confirmed Antwerp's beloved privileges and offered Calvinists and other Protestants four years to either embrace Catholicism or emigrate, leading to the exodus of forty thousand of its citizens.[56]

Antwerp's surrender inspired yet another entry ceremony, more a celebration of martial valor and of Catholic renewal than a true Blijde Inkomst, a constitutional investiture.[57]

---

54. J. Andriessen, "De katholieken te Antwerpen, 1577–1585," *Bijdragen tot de Geschiedenis* 70 (1987): 61–75.

55. On the negotiations, see Van der Essen, *Alexandre Farnèse*, 4:112–32; Prims, *Geschiedenis van Antwerpen*, 19:213; and Bor, *Oorsprongk*, 2:610.

56. Thijs, *Van Geuzenstad tot katholiek bolwerk*, 33; for the text of the capitulation, see Bor, *Oorsprongk*, 2:610–13.

57. Curiously, no official account of the entry was issued. For its description, see Thijs, *Van Geuzenstad*

Farnese's weary troops had withstood a hard winter on the water-logged plains surrounding the city before Antwerp's capitulation, and celebrated heartily with drinking, dancing, and rough music on the tops of inundated dikes and Farnese's great bridge. The victorious military commander opted, however, for the gravitas of a solemn welcome. Farnese entered Antwerp on August 27 riding on horseback from his camp at Beveren and accompanied by a handsome train of southern royalist noblemen, with Philippe de Croy, the Duke of Aarschot, the most prominent, but also the Prince of Chimay, and Philip, Count of Egmont, one of the sons of Lamoral, Count of Egmont, who been involved in Antwerp's affairs since the Spanish Fury of 1576. As he wound his way to the Onze-Lieve-Vrouwekerk to expunge its Calvinist stain with a Catholic mass and a sonorous Te Deum, Farnese paused to give all thanks for his good fortune to the Virgin Mary, and listened to greetings at the Keizerpoort from the Maiden of Antwerp. At this same gate just a few years earlier, in 1582, Anjou had witnessed the Maiden as a tableau on a wagon. Farnese's parallel passage into the city, however, presented the Maiden as a little girl, an in-the-flesh innocent youngster, who handed him the keys to the city, which Farnese, unlike Anjou, did not return, but rather affixed to his collar of the Order of the Golden Fleece.[58]

Both the Maiden as a sweetly deferential girl and the city keys hanging off the master signifier of Burgundian chivalric eliteness speak to the theme of peaceful submission that Farnese's entry cultivated. As such, the entry was completely the opposite of Anjou's, where civic boosterism had prevailed. Deepening the motif of homage, a series of tableaux and classical triumphal arches of conquerors and mythological strongmen greeted Farnese inside the city: Alexander the Great, Caesar, Mars, and Hercules were among them. On the Meirbrugge, the Genoese merchants had commissioned a victory column. The art historian Luc Smolderen attributes the column to Jacques Jonghelinck, the artist who had executed Alba's Antwerp statue years before.[59] Its symbolic timbre was obvious enough: atop the column stood Alexander the Great in military regalia, right hand raised and left hand wielding a baton, not unlike the pose Alba struck in Jonghelinck's notorious free-standing statue. On the statue's pedestal were sculpted two bound captives, generic references to defeat.[60]

Farnese's entry as conqueror-hero concluded with the Te Deum performed at the Onze-

---

tot katholiek bolwerk, 34; Van der Essen, Alexandre Farnèse, 4:141; Prims, Geschiedenis van Antwerpen, 19:217–18; and Bor, Oorsprongk, 2:622.

58. Van der Essen, Alexandre Farnèse, 4:141.

59. Smolderen, Jacques Jonghelinck, 149–51, and A. Eerns, "Literarische Archivalia voor Antwerpen," Bijdgragen tot de Geschiedenis 24 (1933): 279. The column was briefly mentioned by a number of early historians of the Revolt, including Van Meteren.

60. Basic iconographic analysis is in Smolderen, Jacques Jonghelinck, 150, and Eerns, "Literarische Archivalia voor Antwerpen." The column also bore a basic band in relief that identified it as a work in honor of Farnese. Besides Hogenberg's inclusion of the column, however dwarfed, in an illustration of Farnese's entry, the artwork is seen on a medal struck later, which confirms the inclusion of two bound captives on both sides of the pedestal.

Lieve-Vrouwekerk with the bishop of Antwerp present to direct the happy occasion. According to Bor, the church was hurriedly refurbished after Antwerp's surrender with "decorated images, altars, and paintings," a first step in its return to the Catholic fold.[61] Here too the public message could not have been more direct: Antwerp is Catholic once again, and the Calvinist interludes and the two bouts of iconoclasm—the riotous 1566 events and the orderly removal of images in 1581—are blotted out. Following this mass at Onze-Lieve-Vrouwekerk, Farnese retreated to the citadel, while his officers celebrated their victory with a banquet held at the town hall. Farnese's entry had constituted a spatial mapping of royalist renewal. He began at the imperial Keizerpoort, most famously associated with the 1549 entry of Charles V and the young Philip; he attended a Te Deum and mass at the sacred center of Antwerp, the Onze-Lieve-Vrouwekerk; and he concluded the day at Alba's citadel, itself rededicated to its original use as a Spanish fortress.

The motifs of Farnese's triumph, Catholic renewal and political submission, capitalized on well-tested religious and political metaphors of sovereign power in the sixteenth-century Netherlands, and together they neatly culminated in a small act of great importance to the city's political culture. On July 8, 1586, almost a year after the siege of Antwerp had been lifted, a Marian confraternity replaced the statue of Brabo in the central façade of Antwerp's great town hall with one of the Virgin Mary.[62] To remove the statue of Silvius Brabo, the mythic Roman slayer of the giant Druon Antigoon and the symbol of Antwerp's civic pride, in favor of a new one of the Virgin Mary in the center niche of the town hall's central façade was no small matter. Brabo's statue had been part of a sculptural program for the central façade of the town hall when it was finished in the spring of 1566, the heady days of the wonder year and of the ascendancy of the Beggars. Throughout the Revolt, Brabo, like the town hall for which he did symbolic work, served as a beacon of local rights and pride, and his figure had survived the assault on the building during the 1576 Spanish Fury, to become an enduring testament to the civic aspirations of Antwerp after the town hall's restoration in 1581. It was directly beneath his statue, to take one example, that Anjou had sworn publicly to uphold Brabant's privileges as its new duke.

The Virgin Mary, on the other hand, was Farnese's source of inspiration, invoked in thanksgiving as he took Antwerp for the Spanish. She was also, of course, the reference point for Antwerp's iconoclasm of 1566, the great Assumption Day procession of the veneration to her in the eponymous Onze-Lieve-Vrouwekerk, the lightening rod of that turmoil. Her displacement of Brabo in 1586 at the town hall was a public affirmation of a new era for post-Revolt Antwerp, when Catholic revitalization accompanied civic restoration —and the rebuilding of a war-weary community in general. As tens of thousands of

61. Bor, *Oorsprongk*, 2:622.
62. Prims, *Geschiedenis van Antwerpen*, 19:217–18, and on the iconographical and figural program of the town hall's exterior façade see Bevers, *Das Rathaus von Antwerpen*, 41–81; on the statue of the Virgin Mary, see Thijs, *Van Geuzenstad tot katholiek bolwerk*, 107.

Antwerp's Calvinist citizens streamed north over the next four years, reducing its population by about half, the Virgin Mary at the town hall stood for an emerging period of baroque magnificence and civic realignment. In a small but no less important way, the Virgin represented the new political fortunes of Spanish Brabant and Flanders, just as Orange's mausoleum in the Nieuwe Kerk in Delft, completed in 1623, became a shrine to the United Provinces. Twin devotions of a fractured fatherland, Antwerp's Virgin in the town hall and Orange's tomb in Delft's church were symbolic hallmarks of the Revolt's political culture and the future it spawned in the seventeenth-century Spanish Low Countries and the Dutch Republic. The importance of both was enhanced by their internal contradictions. Antwerp's town hall, completed during the wonder year and restored after the trauma of the Spanish Fury during a Calvinist regime, temple of urban rights and privileges, was now graced with Farnese's Virgin Mary, redolent of Spanish authority. Delft's once Catholic Nieuwe Kerk, by contrast, white-washed and redirected to the Reformed cause, boasted its newest relic: the father of the fatherland, an image and cult object for the Calvinist *beeldenstormers*. Both memorials to the sacrifices and accomplishments of the Spanish loyalists and Patriots were also tangible signifiers that Dutch rebels had to confront the reality of a Netherlands with yawning divisions. A king had been abjured, but thanks to Farnese and loyalist allies, his authority had been reclaimed in some of the most important territories, Brabant and Flanders above all. The prince-hero Orange had been lost and instantly sanctified. But his dynastic heirs and fellow rebels were left uncertain about the direction of the Revolt now that the heroic era of resistance had come to an abrupt close and internal divisions among regents, urban magistrates, and Calvinist *predikanten* (ministers) already setting in.

EPILOGUE

Antwerp's fall was bitter blow to the cause of the Du[tch] one felt its loss more acutely than its outside mayor, P[hilips] Lord of St. Aldegonde. Marnix's career was itself a [...] volt and Orange's cause. Born in Brussels to the lower nobility, he and hi[s ...] early converts to Calvinism, and both spent time studying at the new Un[iversity ...] The brothers were back in Brussels when trouble came to a head in 15[66, ...] prompt to sign the Compromise. Jan died at the battle of Oosterweel in [...] short-lived Calvinist military campaign begun that winter, and Philips fl[ed ...] fore Alba's arrival, where he wound up in the service of the Calvinist e[lector ...] By that time, he had penned his apology for Netherlands iconoclasm a[nd his] more famous 1569 satire, *The Beehive of the Roman Church*. In 1571 Marni[x ...] service and soon emerged as the prince's most valuable propagand[ist,] diplomat, and ambassador. Among the highpoints of Marnix's public c[areer ap]pearance before the delegates from Holland's rebellious towns and no[bles] on July 15, 1572, to advocate for Orange as their *stadholder*; his capture b[y Spanish and] imprisonment in Utrecht during 1573; and his subsequent diplomatic [service to] Orange after his release, including overseeing the negotiations betwee[n the gen]eral and the Duke of Anjou. Embarrassed by the failure of Anjou's rule [, Marnix was] prodded by Orange to assume the position of outside mayor of Antwer[p at a crit]ical juncture in the Revolt's and the city's history.[1]

As it turned out, Marnix's reluctance to accept the office was prescie[nt. He had to con]front both the tribulations of the siege of Antwerp, and when there see[med no re]lief for the city, the consequences of his decision to advocate surrende[r in the] summer of 1585. In the aftermath of Antwerp's fall, critics charged tha[t ...]

---

1. The best introduction to Marnix, Lord of St. Aldegonde are his edited writing[s. See ...]gen, *Philips van Marnix van St. Aldegonde*. See also Henk Duits and Ton van Strien, eds., [...] *Studies over leven en werk van Philips van Marnix van Sint Aldegonde* (Hilversum, 2001), ar[nd ...] *Marnix van St. Aldegonde: Groote figuren uit ons verleden* (Utrecht, 1939).

too quick to concede Antwerp to Farnese, and some even accused him of treason. Stung by the invective, Marnix poured out his sorrow, frustration, and hope for the future in a remarkable letter to his cousin Adolf van Meetkerke on October 24, 1585.[2] His tone was doleful, even bitter, his pessimism relieved by his hope that God would inspire Farnese and the Spanish king to clemency. The Revolt was in dire peril, he wrote. Orange had been "a leader of great authority, singular wisdom, admirable humanity, extreme patience and incomparable dexterity," but since his death, "we are in every respect weaker than our enemies: their authority is well grounded and stable, resting on the title of the great and puissant king, whereas our authority is not only floating on the waves of the populace, it is also almost completely ineffective."

The once-pugnacious Calvinist was wearied by years of war, by disappointments like the failure of Orange's policy of religious peace and Anjou's treachery, and by a perception that his compatriots were fickle in their political commitments. After all, Antwerpeners, like so many other Netherlanders, were urban folk, merchants above all, and when tested to their limits, they could easily opt for self-interest over greater moral commitments, for the lure of money and the practice of commerce over absolute allegiance to the Patriots' fight for liberty and the Reformed faith. He continued:

> On our side, I do not know whether we have a commander at all, or whether some shadow of authority remains with the governors, whether the soldiers and the men-at-arms have preserved some notion of obedience, or whether the people have kept some vestige of zeal either for religion or for liberty. War is horror to them, peace is what they long for above all; trade and private profit is their aim, and their hope lies in a change of government; consequently, no one among them will put his shoulder to the preservation of the present state.

Under these circumstances Marnix concluded that it was prudent to opt for peace over arms; rebellion had brought nothing but headaches and sorrow. Better to trust in God's handiwork and in the clemency of rulers, since persistence in rebellion against tyrants could reap nothing but horror, as proved by the violence the Israelites suffered at the hands of Nebuchadnezzar, the kings of Persia, Alexander the Great, and even the Romans.[3] The States General might have abjured Philip II, but the civic realm of the Netherlands was still a political weakling compared to his power.

The tone of Marnix's letter has much to do with the need to justify his decision to surrender Antwerp. But it is also an honest appraisal of the political situation he found him-

2. The letter is reproduced in Bor, *Oorsprongk*, 2 615–19, and Van Toorenenbergen, *Philips van Marnix van St. Aldegonde*, 3:61–74. An abbreviated English translation by Gillian Lewis is available at http://dutchrevolt.leidenuniv.nl/English/Sources%20English/15851024.htm (no. 42).

3. Bor, *Oorsprongk*, 2:616–17.

self in, when "humiliation" at the hands of the Spanish "conquerors" was inevitable. The tensions between civic and regional privilege and dynastic lordship central to questions of power since the fifteenth-century Burgundian period had reached a breaking point during the Revolt. But in the end the rejected king had retained his commanding prestige, even if he had lost his sovereignty over the rebellious provinces.[4] It would be easy to infer from Marnix's letter that by 1585 a political movement that began optimistically, even stridently, with the Beggars and the iconoclasts in 1566 had come to a sputtering end, and that the future's best hope was in prayer, patience, and retreat. But such was not the case, and Marnix himself, after years of quiet study in his castle in West Souburg, Zeeland, emerged in 1590 to lend his political skills to decipher encrypted letters to his government, staying moderately active in public life again until his death eight years later.

The year 1585 did, however, signal a new era in the Revolt of the Netherlands. Most of Brabant, Flanders, and the Walloon provinces returned to Spanish authority and embraced the Catholic Counter-Reformation, and though cities were ravaged, this was no period of cultural or political stagnation, but rather one of baroque redirection under the archducal couple Albert and Isabella. Holland, Zeeland, and the other United Provinces of Utrecht, Friesland, Guelders, Overijssel, and Groningen, by contrast, evolved toward a commonwealth, with the 1579 Union of Utrecht as its constitutional kernel. But even they were not yet ready to dispense with lordship altogether. Having signed the Treaty of Nonsuch with Queen Elizabeth of England on August 20, 1585, they accepted her favorite, Robert Dudley, Earl of Leicester, as governor general after attempts to entice Henry III of France and the English queen herself to assume governorship went nowhere.[5] Leicester's office-taking was a far cry from the inaugural hoopla put on for Anjou in 1582. Orange's capable son Maurits, in a military counteroffensive against the Spanish in the 1590s, regained some important territory, including Breda in northern Brabant, and was appointed *stadholder* of Zeeland and Holland. Maurits of Nassau's title was an effective check on Leicester's authority, a sign of the readiness of the Estates of Holland, and the States General as a whole, not only to assert their authority, but to govern. Still, Leicester's arrival in Vlissingen on December 20, 1585, began a series of triumphal entries that culminated with his welcome by the Estates during a spectacular torch-lit nighttime entry in The Hague on January 6 of the new year.[6]

The United Provinces were in the early stages of its Golden Age, dominated by the great cities, by the advocate of the Estates of Holland, Johan van Oldenbarnevelt, and by Mau-

---

4. Ibid., 2:619.

5. Koenigsberger, *Monarchies, States Generals and Parliaments*, 305–11; F. G. Oosterhoff, *Leicester and the Netherlands, 1586–1587* (Utrecht, 1988), esp. 61–66; and A. Th. van Deursen, *Maurits van Nassau, 1567–1625: De winnaar die faalde* (Amsterdam, 2000).

6. A full review of Leicester's ceremonial entries, based on printed and archival accounts, is in R. C. Strong and J. A. van Dorsten, *Leicester's Triumph* (London, 1964).

rits of Nassau, who inherited the princely charisma of the House of Orange. Leicester's ascendancy was brief: he soon quarreled with the urban patricians who dominated the Estates of Holland, and his favoring of popular Calvinist preachers and their more entrenched evangelicalism only widened the gulf between himself and the traditional political elite of Holland.[7] By the end of 1587, Leicester abandoned the Netherlands. While the United Provinces did not officially proclaim itself a republic, the commonwealth had begun. It was characterized by a swell in population, the ascendancy of Amsterdam, a political rhetoric of popular sovereignty and republicanism, and the political reality of a maritime empire and colonial ambitions.[8] As an emerging world power, the United Provinces quickly generated its own political iconography and canonical histories of the Revolt. Its first great historians, the duo of Pieter Bor and Emanuel van Meteren, set the groundwork with their accounts, which first appeared in 1595 and 1599, respectively. Their work, along with that of Everhard van Reyd in the early seventeenth century, was indispensable for such later patriotic exercises as P. C. Hooft's 1642 *Nederlandsche Historiën* and Jan Wagenaar's tellingly named *Vaderlandsche Historie (History of the Fatherland)*, which appeared between 1749 and 1759 in twenty-one volumes.[9]

As the seven United Provinces moved in a new direction, the commonwealth's political indebtedness to the pivotal decades of the Revolt in the sixteenth century was unquestionable. The cultural ingredients of the Dutch Revolt were distinctly hybrid, birthed during the crisis of Habsburg political authority in the 1560s, but indebted in timbre and quality to the political idioms of the late-medieval Burgundian Netherlands. Beggars, iconoclasts, and civic patriots were more than simply convenient tropes; they did heavy duty as enabling concepts for a larger set of cultural attachments and political aspirations by rebels in the Netherlands. While they had discursive power—as metaphors of opposition and as markers of religious and political belief—they also had material, social reality, describing the ways opponents of Philip II's religious and political policies in the Netherlands identified themselves. In the public realm, they encompassed a body of political rituals that gave the Revolt its vernacular profile. In most instances, these formal enactments were similarly indebted to older cultural modes: the themes of inversion and protest for the Beggars and iconoclasts, that of urban particularism for the civic patriots, and the whole body of Burgundian state ritual for the representation of political authority by Orange, the States General, and their heirs. The rebels who struggled against Philip

---

7. Calvinist enthusiasm for Leicester was evident during his January 12, 1586, entry into Leiden, where the Flemish Calvinist exile community praised him as a prince delivered by God to rescue the Netherlands from idol worshippers; see Strong and Van Dorsten, *Leicester's Triumph*, 61.

8. Oosterhoff, *Leicster and the Netherlands*, and on Amsterdam's growth and built environment, see Marjolein 't Hart, "The Glorious City: Monumentalism and Public Space in Seventeenth-Century Amsterdam," in *Urban Achievement in Early Modern Europe*, 128–50.

9. Janssen, "A 'Trias Historica' on the Revolt of the Netherlands."

II's government in Brussels breathed fresh life into these ritual prescriptions and, in the process, shaped a new political culture with one foot in the late-medieval past and the other in the emerging seventeenth century.

This book began with Charles the Bold's realization that princely acclaim in the Low Countries had to square with civic ambition, that a French coronation ritual like the *sacre* was impossible for Burgundian rulers and their Habsburg heirs no matter how much they embellished their public persona. Sovereignty in the Low Countries was neither indivisible nor an exercise in monarchical triumph, but rather a type of lordship contractually obliged to territorial Estates and civic prerogatives. Philip the Good, Charles the Bold, and their successors spent nearly a century burnishing princely ritual, drawing aggressively on sacred, classical, monarchical, and imperial motifs as they implemented an increasingly supervised urban public realm. But once Philip II departed the Low Countries in 1559, a yawning vacuum of lordly authority and its symbolic representation opened up, just when movements of dissent were confronting public authority. The Beggars spoofed royal policy through rites of inversion, an elite exercise that was overshadowed by the radicalism of the iconoclastic riots, whose own variety of inversion both laid claim to the Beggars' rhetoric and damaged this aristocratic movement by tainting it with the sin of Calvinist excess. In no small measure, iconoclasm shattered the representational universe of the Burgundian lords by overturning images and spaces of sacred power, and by exposing Catholic images and rites of devotion as mere heaps of material, void of sacrality. Alba's restoration primed royal authority and its representation, but with such authoritarianism and ritual self-aggrandizement that Netherlanders in revolt found common cause in an otherwise calcified division between Catholics and Calvinists and other Protestants. Critics decried Alba as a usurper of royal authority and an idolatrous tyrant, holding him responsible for the depredations of the Army of Flanders. The tensions that coursed through Burgundian political culture between the princely and the civic, between monarchical ambition and regional power, surged anew. Alba was interpreted as a tyrant unparalleled in Low Country history, and his opposition was hailed as the guardians and defenders of a revitalized civic ethos.

Orange emerged as the hero defender of a *patria* in peril, a fatherland evoked uneasily in a set of territories that knew no unity, nor even a common nomenclature of geography, ethnicity, or political identity. As the Patriots mined the rich political vocabulary of civic virtue, they drew on age-old traditions of urban dissent and joined them to newer invocations of liberty indebted to classical republican thought. Theirs was a civic republicanism, however, gleaned less from learned treatises than from the stuff of popular politics, forged from the heroic lore evolving out of the brutal sieges and sacks that Dutch cities underwent in the 1570s. In the process, Orange became the symbolic repository of the Revolt's aspirations and cultural vocabulary, edified as father, fraternal brother, prince, and fellow Patriot. He was the only figure in the Revolt able to bridge the gap between the princely and the civic that had so bedeviled the late-medieval and early modern rulers who were his superiors. He had Burgundian élan, princely stature, and all the cultural hallmarks of elite power, and yet he was a fellow Patriot, one of five brothers who fought on behalf of fatherland and the rights and privileges of the territories and cities. That he was studded with princely and fraternal attributes—*pater patriae* and *bon patriot*—and hailed in triumphal entries between 1577 and 1580 as a political savior, made it nearly impossible for any of Philip II's replacements, including Orange's own favorite, the Duke of Anjou, to inherit the charisma of authority he had assumed. Orange had gone far in managing the tension between the royal and the republican, even though he never disputed hereditary lordship. The protean quality that so infuriated his critics—part court dignitary, part urban populist, once Catholic turned ambiguous Calvinist fighting for freedom of conscience—was precisely what made him an appealing political figure, even though his successes were partial at best. With his death, the tension between monarchical authority dispersed in the various titles of lordship in the Netherlands, and civic and provincial regionalism was never again so skillfully balanced. In the end, the conflict between princely authority and regional and civic prerogatives proved intractable, and the *patria* of the Patriots' political idealism fractured between a royalist Spanish Netherlands and the commonwealth of the United Provinces, as the reality of the pluralism, regionalism, and particularism of the Low Countries asserted itself once again.

Bibliographic Note

Like the Dutch Revolt itself, historiography about it is sprawling. Three separate assessments offer the best introduction to this scholarship. J. W. Smit's 1960 "The Present Position of Studies Regarding the Revolt of the Netherlands," reprinted in P. A. M. Geurts and A. E. M. Janssen, eds., *Geschiedschrijving in Nederland: Studies over de historiografie van de Nieuwe Tijd*, 2 vols. (The Hague, 1981), 2:42–54 treats the decline of attention to the Revolt by the mid-twentieth century; S. Groenveld, "Beeldvorming en realiteit: Geschiedschrijving en achtergronden van de Nederlandse Opstand tegen Filips II," in *Geschiedschrijving in Nederland*, 2:55–84 assesses the boom of economic and social history after Smit's survey. An updated appraisal that stresses plural causation and the Revolt as an endemic civil war is Henk van Nierop's "Alva's Throne: Making Sense of the Revolt of the Netherlands," in *The Origins and Development of the Dutch Revolt*, ed. Graham Darby (London, 2001), 29–47.

The first comprehensive histories of the Dutch Revolt were written by its contemporaries: Emanuel van Meteren, Pieter Bor, and Everhard van Reyd. For an assessment of their writings, see A. E. M. Janssen, "A 'Trias Historica' on the Revolt of the Netherlands: Emanuel van Meteren, Pieter Bor, and Everhard van Reyd as Exponents of Contemporary History," in *Clio's Mirror: Historiography in Britain and the Netherlands*, Papers Delivered to the Eighth Anglo-Dutch Historical Conference, ed. A. C. Duke and C. A. Tamse (Zutphen, 1983), 8:9–30. The first part of Pieter Bor's history of the Revolt was published in 1595 and treated the period from 1555 to 1567. See *Oorspronck, begin ende aenvang der Nederlantscher oorlogen, beroerten ende Borgerlijcke oneenicheyden. Warachtighe ende Historische beschrijvinge. Door Pieter Bor Christiaensoon, Notaris* (Utrecht, 1595). Between 1679 and 1684, a four-volume folio edition of Bor's work was published in Amsterdam for the period between 1555 and 1600. In 1599 the first Dutch version of Van Meteren's work appeared, published in Delft as Emanuel van Meteren, *Belgische ofte Nederlantsche historie van onsen tijden* (Delft, 1599). Earlier German versions had appeared in 1593 and 1596. In 1633 Everhard van Reyd published the first edition of his *Oorspronck ende voortganck vande Nederlantsche oorloghen* for the period 1566–1601.

The nineteenth century witnessed a great swell of nationalist interest in the Revolt. For the classics, see Robert Fruin, *Verspreide geschriften*, 10 vols. (The Hague, 1900–05), esp. 1:266–449: "Het voorspel van den tachtigjarigen oorlog"; John Lothrop Motley, *The Rise of the Dutch Republic*, 3 vols. (New York, 1856), followed by his *History of the United Provinces*, 4 vols. (New York, 1860–67); P. J. Blok, *Geschiedenis van het Nederlandsche Volk*, 4 vols. (Groningen, 1892–1908); Johannes van Vloten, *Nederlands Opstand tegen Spanje in zijn beginselen, aard en strekking geschetst, 1564–67* (Haarlem, 1856). Key twentieth-century reevaluations include, for the southern provinces, Henri Pirenne, *Histoire de Belgique*, 7 vols. (Brussels, 1922–32), vols. 3–4; vols. 1 and 2 of Pieter Geyl, *Geschiedenis van de Nederlandse stam*, 6 vols. (Amsterdam–Antwerp, 1961–62; orig., 3 vols., 1930–37), published in English as *The Revolt of the Netherlands, 1555–1609* (London, 1932); J. J. Woltjer, *Friesland in Hervormingstijd* (Leiden, 1962); and H. A. Enno van Gelder, *Van Beeldenstorm tot Pacificatie* (Amsterdam and Brussels, 1964). More recent evaluations include Geoffrey Parker, *The Dutch Revolt* (Ithaca, 1977), an interpretation of the Revolt in the context of the larger concerns of Habsburg Spain; Jonathan I. Israel, *The Dutch Republic: Its Rise, Greatness, and Fall, 1477–1806* (Oxford, 1995); James Tracy, *The Founding of the Dutch Republic: War, Finance, and Politics in Holland, 1572–1588* (New York, 2008); the selected essays of J. J. Woltjer, *Tussen vrijheidsstrijd en burgeroorlog: De Nederlandse Opstand, 1555–1580* (Amsterdam, 1994); Anton van der Lem, *De opstand in de Nederlanden (1555–1609)* (Utrecht, 1995), an updated, interpretive survey; and Henk van Nierop, *Het Verraad van het Noorderkwartier: Oorlog, terreur en recht in de Nederlandse Opstand* (Amsterdam, 1999), on the internal divisions and violence in the Revolt. See also the topical essays in Graham Darby, ed., *The Origins and Development of the Dutch Revolt* (London, 2001).

For the political theory of the Dutch Revolt, see the relevant essays by Ernst H. Kossmann and the editors' introduction in Frank Ankersmit and Wessel Krul, eds., *Geschiedenis is als een olifant: Een keuze uit het werk van E. H. Kossmann*, (Amsterdam, 2005), and Martin van Gelderen, *The Political Thought of the Dutch Revolt, 1555–1590*, (Cambridge, 1992). A valuable selection in English of the Revolt's corpus of pamphlets is in E. H. Kossmann and A. F. Mellink, eds., *Texts concerning the Revolt of the Netherlands* (Cambridge, 1974).

For the Dutch Revolt in the comparative context of early modern European upheavals, see Perez Zagorin, *Rebels and Rulers, 1500–1660*, 2 vols. (Cambridge, 1982), where the Dutch Revolt is reviewed in 1:87–129. H. A. Enno van Gelder was the first to see the links between the civil wars in France and events in the Netherlands in "Een historiese vergelijking: De Nederlandse Opstand en de Franse godsdienstoorlogen," in *Verslag van de algemeene vergadering der leden van het Historisch Genootschap* (Utrecht, 1930): 21–42. The parallels and differences are explored in P. Benedict, et al., eds., *Reformation, Revolt and Civil War in France and the Netherlands, 1555–85* (Amsterdam, 1999).

The University of Leiden's website, http://dutchrevolt.leidenuniv.nl, provides primary sources, secondary literature, bibliographic references, and topical subject entries concerning the Revolt and is an essential reference tool for scholars and students.

Index

Aalst, 222, 243, 246
Aarschot, Duke of (Philippe de Croy): and civic political privileges, 289–290; and Council of State, 76, 246; and Farnese reconquest, 325; and Order of the Beggars, 82, 84; and Spanish military depredations, 221, 258; and States General, 263, 264; and William of Orange Joyous Entry rituals, 286
Aartsbergen, 121
Abjuration of 1581, 2–4, 5, 300, 307–310
Address and Opening to Make a Good, Blessed and General Peace in the Netherlands, 208, 209
Adolf (Duke of Gueldre), 118
Adolph of Nassau, 188, 275, 276, 277, 279
Adoration of the Lineage of Nebuchadnezzar (Aartsen), 122, 123
Aelst, Pieter Coecke van, 39
Aertsen, Pieter, 122, 123, 207–208, 309
Afflighem, Abbey of, 58
Aire, 113
Alba, Duke of (Fernando Alvarez de Toledo). See Alba's policies
Alba's policies, 167–211; Alba's arrival, 167–168; Alba's recall, 204, 208, 211; Antwerp statue, 198–203, 205, 206–207, 208–209, 325; and Calvinist dissent, 170, 182; citadel construction, 191–198, 250; Council of Troubles, 175, 181–183, 184; Egmont/Hornes executions, 181, 183–189, 190, 191, 208, 210; military depredations, 174–181; overview, 168–169; and Pacification of Ghent, 209–210; and popular commentary, 61, 62, 168, 169, 170–171, 188–189, 200n, 204–211; and royal patent, 173–174, 185; sack of Mechelen (1572), 222, 226–232, 236; sack of Naarden (1572), 222, 232, 233–234, 235, 236; sack of Zutphen (1572), 222, 232–234, 236; siege of Alkmaar, 226, 233, 236, 239–240; siege of Haarlem, 222, 226, 229, 233, 236–239, 244, 275; siege of Leiden, 226, 233, 236, 240–243, 279–280; taxes, 173, 181, 203; and William of Orange as symbol, 212–213, 278, 293, 297, 298. See also Orangist armed revolt
Algoet, Anthonis, 97, 129–130
Alkmaar: Calvinist dissent, 86; siege of (1573), 226, 233, 236, 239–240; and William of Orange as symbol, 281
Alvarez de Toledo, Fernando. See Alba's policies
amende honorable ritual, 14, 27–28, 35, 36, 151, 205
Americas, Spanish actions in, 231–232, 233
Amsterdam: and Alba's policies, 182; Alteratie (1578), 264, 295; Calvinist dissent, 67, 86; iconoclastic riots, 111, 218; noble dissent, 84; and Orangist armed revolt, 218, 220; and United Provinces, 331; William of Orange Joyous Entry ritual, 280, 295–298
Anabaptism, 46, 52, 67, 114, 141, 152, 167. See also Protestantism; Protestants, persecution of
animal imagery, 304–306
Anjou, Duke of (Valois, François de). See Anjou lordship
Anjou lordship: and Abjuration of 1581, 307; Antwerp coup attempt, 316–317, 319; and Calvinism, 311–312; and Catholicism, 315–316; and civic republicanism, 310, 315; and civic-sovereign tension, 310–311, 318; and condemnations of Philip II, 300–301, 303; and Dutch Revolt divisions, 4, 296; end of, 318; and Jan of Nassau, 291; and Joyous Entry rituals, 311–313, 314–315, 317; and popular commentary, 282; and William of Orange as symbol, 263
Anne of Saxony, 52, 277–278
annus mirabilis (1566), 53, 54. See also iconoclastic riots (1566)

"Antiapology" (Cornejo), 300
anticlerical violence, 217, 218
Antwerp, 133–143; and abdication of Charles V, 2; Alba statue, 198–203, 205, 206–207, 208–209, 325; and Anjou lordship, 303, 312–313, 314–317, 319; Army of Flanders mutiny (1574), 243–244, 245; Burgundian era uprisings, 13; Burgundian regulatory campaign, 41, 44; Calvinist dissent, 67, 75, 142–143; citadel, 192–198, 247, 248, 250, 252, 269, 271–272; citadel dismantling, 265, 266, 268–269, 270, 271; and ecclesiastical system, 137, 192; economic life, 133–134; Farnese reconquest, 323–327, 328–330; iconoclastic riots, 90–91, 111, 119, 125, 143–148, 164, 167, 313; Joyous Entry rituals, 37–38; multiconfessionalism, 166–167; noble dissent, 84, 88; political life, 134–135; political realignment, 291; popular devotions, 44, 125, 138–140, 142, 143–146, 148, 163–164; population, 5; Protestantism, 46, 97, 141–142; religious institutions, 135–138; state ritual, 42–43; town hall, 244–245, 251–254, 313–314; Virgin Mary statue, 326–327; and William of Orange Joyous Entry rituals, 284, 286, 290. *See also* sack of Antwerp
Apocalypse imagery, 170, 171, 260–261
Apology (William of Orange), 296, 299–300, 301, 302
Arborio di Gattinara, Mercurino, 42
Arentsz., Jan, 86
armed revolts. *See* Orangist armed revolt
Armentières, 67
Army of Flanders. *See* Spanish military depredations
Arnèke, 109
Arras, 295
arrow imagery, 64–65
artisans: and Calvinist dissent, 73, 74; and iconoclastic riots, 92–93, 99, 102–103, 106–107, 156
Artois, 3–4, 5, 101–102
Asseliers, J. van, 296
Assumption Day procession (Antwerp). *See* Onze-Lieve-Vrouw (Assumption Day) devotion
Assumption Day procession (Ghent), 44, 151, 161, 164
Assumption Day procession (Ypres), 125, 128, 130, 163–164
Augsburg, Treaty of (1548), 48
Augustinian cloister (Baillieul), 103–104
Augustinian cloister (Brielen), 130
Augustinian cloister (Ghent), 159
Augustinians, 103–104, 127, 131, 159, 178

Back, Claeys de, 121
Backhouse, Marcel, 102
Baert, Mathieu, 113
Baillieul, 67–68, 75, 100–101, 103–104
ballads: and Alba's policies, 184, 188–189, 204; and Amsterdam, 295 n; and Calvinist dissent, 70–71; and citadel dismantling, 268; and iconoclastic riots, 99; and noble dissent, 61–62; and persecution of Protestants, 75; and Spanish military depredations, 221–222, 236–237, 240, 246, 250–251, 258; and William of Orange as symbol, 275–276. *See also* popular commentary
Barre, Pasquier de la, 68, 87, 115
Bart, Mathieu, 117
Bateman, Gilles, 110
Baudelet, Michel, 87
Baudouin, François, 274
Bautkin, Lieven, 42
Bavière, Anne de, 118
Beaupré, monastery of, 117
Beethoven, Ludwig van, 185
Beggars, Order of the, 80–84; and Alba's policies, 168, 169, 170–171, 172–173, 190, 202, 211; and Amsterdam, 295 n; and Antwerp, 142; and Calvinist dissent, 87, 88; and festive behavior, 110–111; founding of, 53, 80–81; and iconoclastic riots, 94, 99, 100, 117, 159, 160, 163, 170–172; and popular commentary, 61. *See also* Patriots; Sea Beggars; Wood Beggars
Beggar's Songs, 61–62
begging, regulation of, 45, 47
Beke, Hans van, 111
Benedictine monastery (Ghent), 158, 164
Benedictines, 158, 164, 194
Benzoni, Girolamo, 231–232
Berg, Count van den, 220
Berkijn, 108
Berlaymont, Charles de, 79–80, 182, 246
Berlaymont, Gilles de (Baron of Hierges), 265
Béthune, 265
Betrijin, Geerard, 144
Beutterich, Petrus, 310–311
Beveren, 104
Bevers, Holm, 251
Beza, Théodore, 69
Biblical imagery: Apocalypse, 170, 171, 260–261; and Burgundian era lordship, 35–36, 48; and Calvinist dissent, 70; and Egmont/Hornes executions, 185; and iconoclastic riots, 122; Nebuchadnezzar, 122, 123, 203, 207–208, 210, 309, 312;

and Spanish military depredations, 224; and William of Orange, 225, 261–262, 276, 277, 284, 286–287, 292
Biesius, Nicolaus, 215
Blaere, Mathys, 121
Blancheteste, Isabeau, 113
Blas, Bertrand Le, 115–116
Blijde Inkomst. *See* Joyous Entry rituals
Blois, Louis de (Lord of Treslong), 268
Bodin, Jean, 6, 316
Boeschepe, 97
Bogaerde, Goris vanden, 154
Boisot, Louis de, 241
Boone, Marc, 195 n
Bor, Pieter: on iconoclastic riots, 93; on Orangist armed revolt, 217; on sack of Antwerp, 245, 255–256, 257; on sack of Naarden, 233–234, 235; on siege of Leiden, 241; on Spanish military depredations, 222, 223, 229–230, 233–234; on United Provinces, 331; on William of Orange as symbol, 281
Bossu, Count of (Maximilien de Henin), 219, 220
Boulogne, 25
Boulton, D'Acry J. D., 30
Bourgondië, Adolf van, 155
Bousse, Artus, 156
Brabant: and abdication of Charles V, 2; and Anjou lordship, 318; begging regulation, 45; Burgundian era uprisings, 13; Calvinist regimes, 215, 264, 281; and Council of State coup (1576), 247; and ecclesiastical system, 58; Joyous Entry rituals, 32; and Spanish military depredations, 246–247; and William of Orange as symbol, 280. *See also specific towns*
Brabo, Silvius, 251, 326
Bray, Guy de, 71, 72
Brederode, Hendrik van: and Alba's policies, 181; and Antwerp, 142; and Calvinist dissent, 88, 143; and Compromise of the Nobility, 78, 79, 80; death of, 200, 273; and festive behavior, 111; and Holland, 218; and the League, 63; and Order of the Beggars, 84, 88, 142
Brevíssima Relación de la Destrucción de las Indias (Las Casas), 231
Brielen, 130
Brimeu, Guy de, 194
broadsheets. *See* popular commentary
Broxeele, 108
Bruegel, Pieter, 134
Bruegel, Pieter the Younger, 211

Bruges, 24, 33, 34–36, 37, 95–96, 307
Brully, Pierre, 67
Brussels: abdication of Charles V, 1–2, 48–49; and Alba's policies, 174; civic political privileges, 2 n; Egmont/Hornes executions, 183, 185–188; Farnese reconquest, 323, 324; funeral of Charles V, 50; Joyous Entry rituals, 36; persecution of Protestants, 58; popular devotions, 24, 77; and Spanish military depredations, 176; William of Orange Joyous Entry ritual, 280, 281–288
Bry, Theodore de, 213, 260–262, 302
Burgundian era lordship, 12–49; and abdication of Charles V, 1–2, 3, 4, 48–49, 50–51; and Abjuration of 1581, 309; and Alba's policies, 174; and Anjou lordship, 311, 318; and civic-sovereign tension, 1, 16–17, 20, 47–48; and coronation of Louis XI, 12–13; and fatherland, 279; and Joyous Entry rituals, 31–39, 174; and Liège votive statue, 17; and Margaret of Parma, 56; and military depredations, 223–224, 225–226; and monarchical ambitions, 19–20, 29; and Order of the Golden Fleece, 28–31, 48, 49; and Protestantism, 20, 52–53; and regional interaction, 21–22; and state ritual, 1–2, 3, 4, 18–21, 28, 30–31, 40, 42, 48–49; and territorial acquisitions, 17–18; and William of Orange as symbol, 303; and William of Orange funeral, 320, 321. *See also* Burgundian era sacred representations; Burgundian era uprisings; Burgundian regulatory campaign
Burgundian era sacred representations, 22–28; and abdication of Charles V, 48; and Calvinist dissent, 52, 54; and iconoclastic riots, 93, 103–104, 119–120, 122, 124; and Joyous Entry rituals, 33–34, 35; and Liège votive statue, 17; and Order of the Golden Fleece, 29, 30–31; and popular devotions, 22–28; and regulatory campaign, 40, 43
Burgundian era uprisings: and *amende honorable* ritual, 27–28, 35, 36; Ghent (1432–1438), 34; Ghent (1467), 13, 191, 194; Ghent (1539), 44, 149–152, 153, 156, 158, 162–163, 164, 195, 267; and iconoclastic riots, 149–152, 153, 156, 158, 162–163, 164, 165; and Joyous Entry rituals, 34–35, 36; and sack of Liège, 14–16, 194, 224, 225–226
Burgundian regulatory campaign, 38–48; and begging, 45, 47; and Calvinist dissent, 74; and citadel construction, 194; and civic-sovereign tension, 47–48; and festive behavior, 41, 43–45, 47–48, 108, 109; and imperial imagery, 41–42; and Joyous Entry rituals, 38–39, 42; and Protestantism, 40, 45–46; and state ritual, 40, 42–43

Buysscheure, 113
Buzere, Jacob de, 97, 98, 99, 101, 103, 129–130

Caenen, Lodewyck, 113
Calvinism: and Anjou lordship, 311–312; Calvinist regimes (1577–1578), 215, 264, 281, 288–289, 290, 295; and civic political privileges, 290; and Farnese reconquest, 323, 324, 326; growth of, 52, 67–68, 96–97, 152; and iconoclastic riots, 94, 122, 123, 147, 158; and Leicester rule, 331; and Union of Utrecht, 264; and William of Orange, 225; and William of Orange as symbol, 291; and William of Orange Joyous Entry rituals, 288–289. See also Calvinist dissent (1559–1566); Dutch Revolt divisions; Protestantism
Calvinist dissent (1559–1566), 66–74, 85–89; and Alba's policies, 170, 182; Antwerp, 67, 75, 142–143; Fabricius martyrdom, 75, 142; and funeral of Charles V, 51–52; Ghent, 67, 85, 152–155, 158; hedge sermons, 71–72, 85–87, 88, 142–143, 152–153, 154, 158; overview, 54; and popular devotions, 68, 74, 129; and psalm singing, 69–71, 73, 74; and social grievances, 87–88; and Spanish military depredations, 180–181; Tournai march (1561), 68–69, 70–71; Valenciennes *maubruslez* (1562), 72–74; Westkwartier, 97–98. See also iconoclastic riots
Calvin, John, 67, 69, 122
Cambrai, 58
Cambrai, Treaty of (1529), 42–43
Campene, Cornelis van, 116–117, 155
Campi, Bartolomeo, 195
cannibalism, 235, 242
Carmelite cloister (Ghent), 159
Carmelite cloister (Ypres), 130
carnivalesque: and Army of Flanders mutinies, 245; and iconoclastic riots, 92, 106, 110, 112, 149, 156; and noble dissent, 63, 66, 80, 89. See also festive behavior; inversion motifs
Caroline Concession (Ghent) (1540), 151, 153, 154
Carthusians, 137, 158
Casas, Bartholomé de Las, 231, 233
Cassel, 113
Catagna, Giovanni Battista, 200
Cateau-Cambrésis, Treaty of (1557), 55
cathedral (Liège), 14–15
ceremonialism. See state ritual
ceremony. See state ritual
chanteries. See psalm singing
Charles V (Holy Roman Emperor): abdication of (1555), 1–2, 3, 4, 48–49, 50–51; and Alba's policies, 168; and Burgundian regulatory campaign, 39–40, 41, 109; and citadel construction, 191, 194, 265; on civic-sovereign tension, 1; death of, 49; funeral of, 50–51, 55, 320–321; and Joyous Entry rituals, 37, 38, 39, 296; and Protestantism, 40, 46; statue of, 201; and uprisings, 44, 150–152, 158, 267
Charles the Bold (Duke of Burgundy): and Burgundian era sacred representations, 24–25, 27; and civic-sovereign tension, 1, 33; and coronation of Louis XI, 12, 13; death of, 28; and Joyous Entry rituals, 36, 42; marriage of, 18; monarchical ambitions of, 19–20; and state ritual, 19, 42; and uprisings, 14–16, 191, 194, 224, 225–226
Charlotte de Bourbon, 269, 271, 299
Chartreaux Church (Tournai), 115, 119
Chastelain, Steven, 131
Chastellain, Georges, 17
children, 111–112, 117, 131, 160, 238
Chimay, Prince of, 286, 290, 325
chivalric orders. See Golden Fleece, Order of the
Chronicle of Antwerp, 143, 145
Church of Our Lady (Pamele), 119
Church of Saint Donation (Bruges), 33
Circumcision devotion (Antwerp), 138, 142, 164
Cistercians, 137
citadels: construction of, 191–198, 250; dismantling of, 264–269, 270, 271, 281, 289
citizen figure, 8
civic political privileges, 5; and abdication of Charles V, 2n; and Alba's policies, 182, 205, 231; and Anjou lordship, 315; Antwerp, 134–135, 313–314; and citadel dismantling, 267; Ghent, 150, 151–152, 289–290, 291; and Joyous Entry rituals, 32, 283, 284; Liège, 14; and Spanish military depredations, 223, 231; and William of Orange as symbol, 284, 285, 294. See also civic republicanism
civic republicanism, 1; and Abjuration of 1581, 3; and Anjou lordship, 310, 315; and citadel dismantling, 265, 266, 268, 269, 270; and citizen figure, 8; and domestic imagery, 224; and Orangist armed revolt, 219; and Order of the Beggars, 168; and popular commentary, 304–306; and popular devotions, 129; and regional interaction, 21–22; and sack of Antwerp, 251; and Spanish military depredations, 215–216, 224–225, 239, 241, 251; and William of Orange as symbol, 263, 272, 284, 285, 303. See also civic political privileges; civic-sovereign tension
civic-sovereign tension: and Alba's policies, 174; and *amende honorable* ritual, 35, 36; and Anjou

lordship, 310–311, 318; and Burgundian era lordship, 1, 16–17, 20, 47–48; and Burgundian regulatory campaign, 47–48; and ecclesiastical system, 22; and Joyous Entry rituals, 32; and strength of civic sphere, 6, 8; and William of Orange as symbol, 332–333. *See also* Burgundian era uprisings; civic republicanism
classical imagery: and Alba statue, 198; and Burgundian era lordship, 32, 37, 38, 42, 283, 284; and noble dissent, 64; and Spanish military depredations, 224
Clercq, Gilles de, 274
Clough, Richard, 50, 144, 146
Clyte, Gadifer vander, 113
Cock, Hieronymus, 135, 136, 194, 196, 197
commemorative *livrets*: and Burgundian era lordship, 20, 38–39; and funeral of Charles V, 51, 52; and popular devotions, 140; and William of Orange Joyous Entry rituals, 281–283, 286, 295–296
Committee of Eighteen (Brussels), 281, 282
Committee of Eighteen (Ghent), 288–289, 290
Compromise of the Nobility, 53, 76–80, 121, 142, 169, 184, 186
confraternities: Compromise of the Nobility, 53, 76–80, 121, 142, 169, 184, 186; the League, 62–66, 80, 110, 184; and popular devotions, 24, 25, 128, 139, 140; and regional interaction, 21–22. *See also* Golden Fleece, Order of the; rhetoricians
Confraternity of Notre Dame, 24, 25
Cornejo, Pedro, 300
Corpus Christi procession (Antwerp), 44, 139, 142, 164
Coudenberg Palace (Brussels), 1–2, 3, 48, 50, 77, 78, 174
Council of Eighteen (Antwerp), 291
Council of State: and abdication of Charles V, 2; and Calvinist regimes (1577–1578), 281; coup (1576), 247, 280; and ecclesiastical system, 58; and Margaret of Parma, 56; and noble dissent, 76; and Spanish military depredations, 221, 246–247; and William of Orange, 272
Council of Troubles, 175, 181–183, 184. *See also* Alba's policies
Counter-Reformation, 330
Crespin, Jean, 115, 183
Crew, Phyllis Mack, 98
Crone, François van der, 112
Croy, Philippe de. *See* Aarschot, Duke of
Culemborg, Count of (Floris van Pallant), 80, 86, 88, 113, 121, 189–190

Dambruyne, Johan, 149, 157
Damman, Ghilein, 71
Dartois, François, 118–119
d'Assonleville, Christoffel, 172
Dathenus, Pieter, 97, 129
Daubicy, Quintin, 72
David imagery, 70, 276
d'Avila, Sancho, 246, 248, 256, 266
Davis, Natalie, 114
Davison, William, 282, 283
Death of Don Juan, 208, 210
Decavele, Johan, 96
Defense and True Declaration of the Things Lately Done in the Low Country (Marnix), 210, 230, 231, 232
De foelice et infoelici republica (Goethals), 225
Delft, 27, 218, 220, 320–322
Delmotte, Marcel, 157, 158
Den Briel, 203–204, 216, 217, 218n
Deutecum, Johannes van, 51, 52, 320, 321
Deutecum, Lucas van, 51, 52, 320, 321
devotional processions. *See* popular devotions
d'Herde, Lieven, 163
Dierickx, Jan, 158
Dierickx, M., 58n
Diest, 176
Dijon, 33, 34, 36
dissent (1559–1566). *See* Calvinist dissent (1559–1566); noble dissent (1559–1566)
domestic imagery: and sack of Antwerp, 245, 252, 254–256, 257, 268, 272; and sack of Mechelen, 229; and Spanish military depredations, 223–224, 229, 231; and William of Orange as symbol, 225, 262, 269, 271–272, 276, 277–278, 279, 280, 281, 287. *See also* fatherland; rape
Dominican cloister (Ghent), 156, 158, 160, 161, 164
Dominicans, 27, 77, 127, 137, 156, 158, 160, 161
Donc, Maarten, 312
Douai, 295
drinking, 109–110, 131, 162. *See also* festive behavior
Druck, Jan de, 108
Duffel, 88
Duke, Alastair, 11
Dutch Revolt divisions, 303, 306–307; and Abjuration of 1581, 3–4, 5; and Anjou lordship, 4, 296; and States General, 263–264; and Union of Utrecht, 294–295; and William of Orange as symbol, 287–288, 294–295, 319–320
Duym, Jacob, 242

ecclesiastical system: and Alba's policies, 175; and Antwerp, 137, 192; and Burgundian era lordship, 22; and noble dissent, 57–59; and Ypres, 126
economic issues: and Army of Flanders mutinies, 244; and Calvinist dissent, 98, 152–153; and iconoclastic riots, 94, 99, 116, 126, 132, 155, 162, 164–165; and Spanish military depredations, 223
Edict of Proscription (1580), 296, 298–299
Eecke parish church, 108
Egmont, Count of (Lamoral): and Alba's policies, 174; and Calvinist dissent, 88; and citadel construction, 193; and ecclesiastical system, 58–59; execution of, 181, 183–189, 190, 191, 208, 210; and iconoclastic riots, 100, 103, 108, 130, 166, 184; and the League, 62–63, 64; and multiconfessionalism, 167; and persecution of Protestants, 54; and Segovia Woods letters, 76
Egmont, Count of (Philip), 248, 249, 325
Ekelsbeke, 101, 109, 113
Emmanuel-Erneste: *Dialogue of Two Persons on the State of the Netherlands* (Prouninck), 301
Enghien, 176
England, 29, 67, 288, 330, 331
Enkhuizen, 67, 218n, 219, 220, 281
Entrée Joyeuse. *See* Joyous Entry rituals
Erasmus, Desiderius, 46, 104
Esschen, Johan van den, 46
Estaires, 109
Everaert, Cornelius, 60
Exaltation of the True Cross procession (Tournai), 68, 70
exemplary punishment. *See* Council of Troubles; Protestants, persecution of

Fabricius, Christoffel, 75, 142
Fadrique Álvarez de Toledo, Don (4th Duke of Alba), 168, 179, 233, 236, 237, 240, 264
family imagery. *See* domestic imagery; fatherland
Farnese reconquest, 316, 318, 319, 323–327, 328–330
fatherland: and Orangist armed revolt, 169; and Spanish military depredations, 242, 258–259; and United Provinces, 331; and William of Orange as symbol, 212, 219, 225, 272, 276, 277, 278, 279–280, 290, 293, 294. *See also* Low Countries political identity
Fauveau, Simon, 72–74
festive behavior: and Alba's policies, 176–177; and Burgundian regulatory campaign, 41, 43–45, 47–48, 108, 109; and iconoclastic riots, 103, 108, 109–111; and noble dissent, 110–111
field sermons. *See* hedge sermons
Flanders: and Anjou lordship, 318; begging regulation, 45; Calvinist dissent, 68; Calvinist regimes, 215, 264, 281; reconciliation with Spain, 3–4, 5; and Spanish military depredations, 246. *See also* Westkwartier; *specific towns*
Fleurbaix, 182
Fleurquin, Pasquier, 147
Fontenelle, abbey of, 118
foxtail imagery, 66
France, 53, 57, 69, 114, 220, 256n
Franciscans, 63, 127, 128, 131, 137, 283
Francken, Ambrosius, 234
Frederick III (Holy Roman Emperor), 19
Freedberg, David, 159
French Revolution, 301–302
Friesland, 121, 232, 264, 295
Frisius, Johannes Arcerius, 238
Fruytiers, Jan, 225, 235n, 241–242, 275

Gascoigne, George, 249, 251–252
Geertruidenberg, 263
Gelderen, Martin van, 277
Gelderland, 232, 264, 295. *See also specific towns*
Geldorp, Hendrik, 279
gender: and arrow imagery, 65; and citadel dismantling, 268; and iconoclastic riots, 102, 111, 112, 146, 148; and Margaret of Parma, 61, 65; and Spanish military depredations, 254–255. *See also* women
George, Saint, 15, 16
Gérard, Balthasar, 319, 320
Germany, 40, 53, 57, 61, 67
Ghent: Burgundian era Joyous Entry rituals, 36; and Burgundian regulatory campaign, 44–45; Calvinist dissent, 67, 85, 152–155, 158; Calvinist regime, 215, 281, 288–289, 290; citadel construction, 191, 194–195; citadel dismantling, 265, 266–267, 289; civic political privileges, 150, 151–152, 289–290, 291; economic life, 149; Farnese reconquest, 323, 324; Ghent war (1452–1453), 27, 36; iconoclastic riots, 111, 116–117, 118, 119, 120, 121, 125, 148–149, 155–163, 164–165; Joyous Entry rituals, 33; multiconfessionalism, 167; persecution of Protestants, 114, 152; political realignment, 288–289; popular devotions, 44, 151, 161, 164; Protestantism, 46, 152, 288–289; and Spanish military depredations, 176, 177–181, 215,

229, 267; state ritual, 42–43; uprising (1467), 13, 191, 194; uprising (1539), 44, 149–152, 153, 156, 158, 162–163, 164, 195, 267; uprisings (1432–1438), 34; William of Orange Joyous Entry ritual, 280, 288–294
Ghent, Pacification of. *See* Pacification of Ghent
Gherstecooren, Jan, 104–105
Gheyn, Jacques de, I, 269
Gijverinkhove, 104–105, 121
Glymes, Jean de, Marquis de Berghes, 73
Goetghebuer, Claude, 157, 158
Goethals, Frans, 215, 225
Goethe, Johann Wolfgang von, 185
Golden Fleece, Order of the: and abdication of Charles V, 2, 48–49; and Alba's policies, 183, 185, 186, 187; and Burgundian era lordship, 28–31, 33; and citadel construction, 193; and funeral of Charles V, 50; and iconoclastic riots, 119, 146; and Order of the Beggars, 81
Goltzius, Hendrik, 320–321
Gombault, Jacques, 87–88
Gómez de Silva, Ruy, 173
Gracht, François van der, 118
grain riots. *See* economic issues
Granvelle, Antoine Perrenot de: and abdication of Charles V, 4; and citadel construction, 193; and ecclesiastical system, 57, 58, 59, 192; and foxtail imagery, 66 n; and iconoclastic riots, 116; and the League, 62–64, 65–66; and Margaret of Parma, 55–56; and noble dissent, 53; and popular commentary, 59, 60, 61–62; recall of, 65–66, 75, 212; and Spanish military depredations, 223, 238
Grapheus, Cornelius, 39
Gregory XIII (Pope), 260, 261
Gresham, Thomas, 144
Groningen, 91, 265
Guicciardini, Lodovico, 133–134, 138, 176, 198
guild banners, 27
Guilgot, Jehan, 190

Haarlem: Calvinist dissent, 86; and ecclesiastical system, 58; siege of (1573), 222, 226, 229, 233, 236–239, 244, 275; and William of Orange as symbol, 281
Haecht, Godevaert van: on Alba statue, 198–199, 203; on Calvinist dissent, 143; on Egmont/Hornes executions, 188; on fatherland, 169; on iconoclastic riots, 144, 145; on popular devotions, 142; and William of Orange, 192, 275

Haemstede, Adriaen van, 51–52, 183
Hague, The, 86, 121
Hainault, 3–4, 5, 25, 247, 295
Halle, 25, 26
handbills. *See* popular commentary
Hasselaer, Kenau Simonsdochter, 238–239, 266
Havré, Marquis of, 248, 249
Haze, Pieter de, 97
hedge sermons, 71–72, 85–87, 88, 142–143, 152–153, 154, 158
Heere, Jan de, 162, 290
Heere, Lucas de, 288, 289, 290, 294
Heilige Kerst, Church of (Ghent), 151
Hembyze, Jan van, 267, 290, 294–295
Hende, Jacob van, 105, 106
Hendrik of Nassau, 241, 279
Henin, Maximilien de (Count of Bossu), 219, 220
Henrickszoon, Gerrit, 297
Henricxzone, Gillis, 107
heresy placards. *See* Protestants, persecution of
heresy. *See* Protestantism; Protestants, persecution of
Hernighem, Augustijn van, 132
's-Hertogenbosch: Alba's policies, 182; civic political privileges, 2 n; and ecclesiastical system, 58; iconoclastic riots, 107, 109, 110, 111, 113; political life, 135
Hessels, André, 314
Heyndricks, Pieter, 275
Heyndrix, Jan, 154
Historia del mondo nuovo (Benzoni), 231–232
Hogenberg, Frans: on abdication of Charles V, 2, 3; on Egmont/Hornes executions, 189, 190; on Farnese reconquest, 325 n; on iconoclastic riots, 146, 147; on noble dissent, 78, 79; on sack of Antwerp, 253, 254, 255; on sack of Mechelen, 229, 230, 232, 239; on sack of Naarden, 233, 234; on Spanish military depredations, 223, 233
Holland: and Anjou lordship, 296, 318; begging regulation, 45; Calvinist dissent, 67, 86; and civic republicanism, 3; and Orangist armed revolt, 203–204, 218–220; and Pacification of Ghent, 209, 214, 220; Spanish military depredations, 215, 232, 233, 243; Union of Utrecht, 264, 295, 330; and William of Orange as symbol, 280, 281, 321; William of Orange stadholdership, 272, 318. *See also specific towns*
Holy Blood procession (Bruges), 24
Hondschoote, 67, 75, 95, 104, 121, 130, 131
Hooft, Pieter Cornelisz, 209, 235, 255–256, 331

Hoogstade, 104, 121
Hoogstraten, Count of (Antoine de Lalaing), 108, 181, 184
Hoorn, 86, 281
Hornes, Count of (Philip de Montmorency): and ecclesiastical system, 58–59; execution of, 181, 183–189, 190, 191, 208, 210; and iconoclastic riots, 108; and the League, 62–63; and multiconfessionalism, 167
Horst, Daniel, 64–65, 205, 260
Hortensius, Lambertus, 233, 234
household imperiled. *See* domestic imagery
Houwaert, Jan Baptist, 281–283, 286
Hovius, Mathias, 228
Huguenots, 114, 220, 274
Huizinga, Johan, 18, 186
Hulst, 113
humanists: and Burgundian regulatory campaign, 44; and civic republicanism, 215; and Joyous Entry rituals, 37, 38–39; and popular devotions, 25; and Protestantism, 46
Hunt, Lynn, 301

iconoclastic riots (1566), 90–124, 125–126, 163–165; and Alba statue, 202, 208; Antwerp, 90–91, 111, 119, 125, 143–148, 164, 167, 313; behavioral forms of, 92, 106, 108, 109–111, 112, 149, 156, 162; and Burgundian era sacred representations, 93, 103–104, 119–120, 122, 124; and Burgundian era uprisings, 149–152, 153, 156, 158, 162–163, 164, 165; and Calvinism, 94, 122, 123, 147, 158; and children, 111–112, 117; and citadel construction, 191–192; during Alba's rule, 204; and economic issues, 94, 99, 116, 126, 132, 155, 162, 164–165; and Egmont/Hornes executions, 184; and gender, 102, 111, 112, 146, 148; Ghent, 111, 116–117, 118, 119, 120, 121, 125, 148–149, 155–163, 164–165; and inversion motifs, 104, 107–109, 112–114, 158; and Order of the Beggars, 94, 99, 100, 117, 159, 160, 163, 170–172; and persecution of Protestants, 96, 103, 114–116, 117, 126, 130, 158, 159–161; political motivations for, 116–120, 149; and popular devotions, 125, 127–130, 132, 143–144, 145–146, 163–164; and public authority, 120–124, 156; scholarly readings of, 92–95; social profiles of iconoclasts, 102–103, 104–107, 131, 147–148, 156–158, 163; spread of, 90–91, 100–102; Steenvoorde beginnings, 98–99; Utrecht, 265; Ypres, 102, 111, 112, 121, 125, 129–132, 163–164. *See also* Alba's policies

iconoclastic riots (1570s–1580s), 313; and Orangist armed revolt, 204, 216–219; and William of Orange Joyous Entry rituals, 292, 295
imagery: Alba satires, 205–207; and Alba statue, 200–202, 205, 206–207, 208–209, 325; Antwerp town hall, 251; Antwerp Virgin Mary statue, 326–327; Biblical metaphors, 35–36, 276, 277, 286–287, 292; Liège votive statue, 15–16, 17; manly woman legend, 238–239; Nebuchadnezzar, 122, 123, 203, 207–208, 210, 309, 312; Onze-Lieve-Vrouw devotion allegory, 140; rape, 234–235; Sennacherib, 261–262; sweeping up (*schoonmaakactie*), 170, 171. *See also* Biblical imagery; domestic imagery; popular commentary; William of Orange as symbol
image worship, critiques of: and Anjou lordship, 312; and iconoclastic riots (1566), 93, 99, 101, 104, 106, 115, 116, 122, 148, 156, 158, 159, 161. *See also* iconoclastic riots
imperial motifs, 37–38, 41–42, 283, 284
Inquisition: Burgundian era, 46; and ecclesiastical system, 58; and the League, 64; and popular commentary, 60, 75, 206–207; Titelmans, 74–75. *See also* Protestants, persecution of
inversion motifs: and Alba's policies, 175; and iconoclastic riots, 104, 107–109, 112–114, 158; and noble/Calvinist dissent, 54, 81; and Spanish military depredations, 245. *See also* carnivalesque
Isabel of Portugal, 28

Jacobsz. Reael, Laurens, 86, 111
Jacobsz., Wouter, 217, 218, 229, 258
Jan of Nassau, 291, 311–312, 321
Janssen, Gerard, 249
Jaureguy, Jean, 316
Jemmingen, 201, 217
Jenichen, Balthasar, 276
Joanna of Castile, 36
Jonghe, Johan Junius de, 22, 236
Jonghelinck, Jacques, 199, 200–201, 325
Joseph imagery, 287
Joshua imagery, 276, 277
Joyous Entry rituals: and Alba's policies, 174; and Anjou lordship, 311–313, 314–315, 317; and Burgundian era lordship, 31–39, 174; and Burgundian regulatory campaign, 38–39, 42; and Farnese reconquest, 324–326; and Leicester rule, 330; and noble dissent, 77. *See also* William of Orange Joyous Entry rituals
Juan de Austria, Don: and Antwerp, 268, 269; ap-

pointment of, 247; death of, 208, 210, 264; discrediting of, 263–264, 280; and Joyous Entry rituals, 283; and Pacification of Ghent, 220, 221, 258; and William of Orange as symbol, 280, 287
Judas Maccabeus imagery, 292
Junius, Francis, 74
Junius, Franciscus, 158
Justification of the Prince of Orange (William of Orange), 273–274, 279, 299
Justinus van Nassau, 321

Keizerpoort (Ghent): and Anjou lordship, 314; and citadel construction, 196; and Farnese reconquest, 325, 326; and iconoclastic riots, 120, 149, 163; and Spanish military depredations, 177
Kerchove, Anthonis vanden, 107
Kethulle, François van de (Lord of Ryhove), 290
Keyle, John, 142–143
Kipling, Gordon, 36
Knights of the Garter, 29
Kortrijk, Hans van, 150–151
Kossmann, Ernst, 215
Kunzle, David, 224

Laet, Hans de, 140
Lalaing, Antoine de (Count of Hoogstraten), 108, 181, 184
Lalaing, Georges de (Count of Rennenberg), 264
Laloux, Jehan, 115
Lament over the Desolation of the Netherlands, 234–235
Languet, Hubert, 274
Lannoot, Jan, 97
Lannoy, Jean de, 71
Lavantie, 109, 117
League, the, 63–66, 80, 110, 184
Lecuppre-Desjardin, Elodie, 24
Ledringhem, 101, 108–109
Ledringhem parish church, 101, 108
Leemput, Catrijn van, 266, 268
Leese, Antonie van, 253, 254
Leeuwarden, 121
Leicester, Earl of (Robert Dudley), 330, 331
Leiden: iconoclastic riots, 218; and Orangist armed revolt, 226; siege of (1574), 226, 233, 236, 240–243, 279–280
Leken Wechwyser, Der (Veluanus), 99
Leoni, Leone, 201
Lestrem, 182
Lichtervelde, Colard van, 131

Liège: Burgundian era uprisings, 13–16, 224, 225–226; citadel construction, 194; sack of (1468), 14–16, 194, 224, 225–226
Lier, 176
Lille, 24, 141, 265
Limburg, 5, 113
Lipsius, Justus, 25, 26, 28
literacy, 5, 46
livrets. See commemorative *livrets*
Livy, 223
Lixalde, Francisco de, 254
Loo, 121
looting: Burgundian era, 14–15, 225–226; and iconoclastic riots, 107, 112. *See also* Spanish military depredations
Louis XI (King of France), 12
Louis de Bourbon (bishop of Liège), 14, 15
Louis of Nassau, 88, 188, 200, 220, 240, 241, 279
Low Countries map, 7
Low Countries political identity: and Burgundian regulatory campaign, 48; and Burgundian territorial acquisitions, 17–18; and Order of the Golden Fleece, 30; and regional interaction, 21–22. *See also* fatherland
Loyet, Gérard, 15, 16, 19–20
Lutheranism, 46, 52, 67, 152, 159, 167. *See also* Protestantism
Luxemburg, 5
Luyken, Jan, 256, 257

Macs, Jan, 110
Maillart, Philip, 72–74
Maistres, Jean des, 147
manly woman legend, 238–239
Mansfeld, Count of, 65–66
Marche, Olivier de la, 14–15, 17, 31
Marchi, Francesco de, 193–194
Marck, William de la, II (Lord of Lumey), 203–204, 216
Margaret of Parma: and Alba's policies, 174–175; and Calvinist dissent, 152, 153; and citadel construction, 191–192, 193; and Egmont/Hornes executions, 184; and iconoclastic riots, 107–108, 118, 166, 167; and the League, 64; and noble dissent, 54, 55–56, 59, 78, 82; and persecution of Protestants, 72, 73, 75, 80; and popular commentary, 60–62
Margaret of York, 18
Marian devotions. *See* popular devotions
Marnef, Guido, 141, 147

Marnix, Philips van (Lord of St. Aldegonde): and Alba's policies, 210–211; and Farnese reconquest, 324, 328–330; and iconoclastic riots, 100, 122, 148, 166; life of, 328; and Spanish military depredations, 230, 231, 232; and William of Orange as symbol, 275
Marot, Clément, 69
Mary of Hungary, 8, 31, 150
Massacre of the Innocents (Bruegel), 211
Matte, Sebastian, 97, 98–99, 101, 121, 130
Matthias, Archduke of Austria, 221, 263, 264, 282, 283, 287
Maurits of Nassau, 321, 330–331
Mechelen: and Abjuration of 1581, 307; Burgundian era uprisings, 13; and ecclesiastical system, 57, 58; iconoclastic riots, 113; Joyous Entry rituals, 34; sack of (1572), 222, 226–232, 236
Medemblik, 281
Medivil, Miguel de, 174, 175
Mendoza, Bernardino de, 233, 248
Merode, Bernard van, 227
Merville, 109
Meteren, Emanuel van, 93, 222, 223, 233, 245, 279, 331
Micron, Marten, 272
Middelburg, 58
Mirror of Spanish Tyranny in the Netherlands, 232 n
Mirror of Spanish Tyranny, The (Las Casas), 231
Moded, Herman, 145
Molinet, Jean, 17
Mons, 220
Montano, Arias, 200–201
Montmorency, Philip de. *See* Hornes, Count of
Mook, 241, 279
Morbecque, Jean de, 113
Moreel, Philips, 90, 92, 94
Morillon, Maximilian, 77, 88, 142, 227, 321–322
Motley, Lothrop, 229, 256
multiconfessionalism: and Anjou lordship, 315–316; Antwerp, 141–142; Counter-Reformation, 330; and noble dissent, 53–54, 59; and William of Orange, 166–167, 272–273, 294. *See also* Calvinist dissent; Protestantism
Münster, Peace of (1648), 191

Naarden, sack of (1572), 222, 232, 233–234, 235, 236
Namur, 5
Navarase, Juan de, 248–249
Nebuchadnezzar imagery, 122, 123, 203, 207–208, 210, 309, 312

Nederlandsche Historiën (Hooft), 331
Netherlands Anthem of Commemoration (Valerius), 70
New Beggars' Song Book, A, 184
Nice, Treaty of (1538), 45
Nierop, Henk van, 80
Nieuwe Kerk (Delft), 321, 327
Nieuwenaar, Count, 233
Nigri, Filips, 137
nobility: and iconoclastic riots, 120–121; power of, 56–57. *See also* noble dissent (1559–1566)
noble dissent (1559–1566), 53–66, 76–84, 88–89; and Alba's policies, 183–184, 186, 202; Compromise of the Nobility, 53, 76–80, 121, 142, 169, 184, 186; and departure of Philip II, 54–55; and ecclesiastical system, 57–59; and festive behavior, 110–111; and iconoclastic riots, 94, 99, 100, 117, 159, 160, 163, 170–171; and Inquisition, 74–75; the League, 62–66, 80, 110, 184; and Margaret of Parma, 54, 55–56, 59, 78, 82; and noble power, 56–57; and persecution of Protestants, 53–54, 55, 57, 64–65, 76, 79, 80; and popular commentary, 59–62; and Segovia Woods letters, 76, 88. *See also* Beggars, Order of the
Noircarmes, Baron of (Philip of St. Aldegonde), 175, 182
Nonesuch, Treaty of (1585), 330
Nonnenbosch, nunnery of (Zonnebeke), 127, 130
Norbertines, 137
Notre Dame de Boulogne, 25, 27, 28
Notre Dame de Halle, 25, 26, 27, 28, 82
Noyelles, Jehanne de, 131
Noyelles, Pontus de (Lord of Bourse), 269
Noyen, Jacques van, 193

Oberstein, Otto, 248, 249
official commemorations. *See* commemorative livrets
Old Church (Delft), 27
Oldenbarnevelt, Johan van, 330
ommegangs. See popular devotions
Ommelanden, 264, 295
Onghena, Jan, 157, 158
Onghena, Lieven, 155, 157, 158
On Shunning of the Unlawful Rites of the Ungodly and Preserving the Purity of the Christian Religion (Calvin), 122
Onze-Lieve-Vrouw (Assumption Day) devotion (Antwerp), 125, 139–140, 143–146, 148, 163–164
Onze-Lieve-Vrouwekerk (Antwerp): and Burgundian regulatory campaign, 44; Calvinist control

of, 313; and citadel construction, 193; and Farnese reconquest, 325–326; and iconoclastic riots, 119, 144–148, 164; importance of, 135–136, 137; and Order of the Golden Fleece, 30–31; and popular devotions, 125, 138, 139, 140, 143; and state ritual, 43
Onze-Lieve-Vrouwekerk (Ghent), 161–162
Onze-Lieve-Vrouwekerk (Ypres), 130
Onze-Lieve-Vrouw op 't Stocxken popular devotion (Antwerp). *See* Our Lady of the Pole devotion
Onze-Lieve-Vrouw popular devotion (Ypres). *See* Tuin Virgin devotion (Ypres)
Orange, William of. *See* William of Orange
Orangist armed revolt, 216–220, 246; and Alba statue, 200; Den Briel invasion, 203–204, 216, 217; and Egmont/Hornes executions, 188; and fatherland, 169; and iconoclasm, 204, 216–219; and Pacification of Ghent, 220; Sea Beggars, 200, 203–204, 216–217, 219–220, 235 n, 241, 275; and siege of Leiden, 240–241; soldiers' conduct, 226; and Spanish military depredations, 232; and William of Orange as symbol, 273, 274–275, 276
Order of the Beggars. *See* Beggars, Order of the
Order of the Compromise (Compromise of the Nobility), 53, 76–80, 121, 142, 169, 184, 186
Order of the Golden Fleece. *See* Golden Fleece, Order of the
Ortelius, Abraham, 144
Oude, Hans Collaert van, 234
Oudenaarde, 107, 108, 119, 151
Our Lady chapel (Pamele), 107
Our Lady of the Pole devotion (Antwerp), 138, 139, 145
Our Lady of the Seven Sorrows cult (Delft), 27
Our Lady of the Seven Sorrows procession (Brussels), 24, 77
Our Lady procession (Lille), 24
Our Lady procession (Tournai), 23–24, 68
Oustlandt, Vincent, 109
Overijssel, 232
Overveen, 86

Pacification of Ghent (1576): and Alba's policies, 209–210; and citadel dismantling, 265, 266; and civic political privileges, 289; and Dutch Revolt divisions, 264; and Spanish military depredations, 209–210, 214, 220–221, 247, 257–258; and Union of Utrecht, 295; and William of Orange as symbol, 293
Paciotto, Francesco, 193–194, 195

Pallant, Floris van (Count of Culemborg), 80, 86, 88, 113, 121, 189–190
Pamele, 107, 119
pamphlets. *See* popular commentary
Parker, Geoffrey, 243
Parma, Duke of (Alexander Farnese), 316, 318, 319, 323
Patriots: and Alba statue, 202–203; and civic republicanism, 224–225; origins of, 170; and popular commentary, 304–306; and Spanish military depredations, 224–225, 226, 236, 236–237, 238; and William of Orange as symbol, 262–263, 277–278. *See also* Beggars, Order of the
Pauli, Theodoricus (Thierry Pauwels), 224
Payen, Pontus, 66 n, 80, 81, 118, 174, 287
Pays de l'Alleu, 101–102, 109, 118, 182
peasant rebellions, 96
Peeterzone, Leonard, 107
Perrenot, Frédéric (Lord of Champagney), 248, 249
Perron (Liège statue), 15
persecution of Protestants. *See* Protestants, persecution of
Peyt, Jacob, 96
Philip II (King of Spain): and abdication of Charles V, 2, 49, 50–51; Abjuration of 1581, 2–4, 5, 300, 307–310; and Alba's policies, 173, 185, 204; condemnations of, 299–303, 307–308, 309–310; departure from the Low Countries of, 54–55; and ecclesiastical system, 57–58; Edict of Proscription, 296, 298–299; and funeral of Charles V, 50, 51, 55; and iconoclastic riots, 91, 103, 166, 167; and Joyous Entry rituals, 38, 39, 174; and noble dissent, 53, 76, 88; and Pacification of Ghent, 209; and persecution of Protestants, 55, 73, 76; and popular commentary, 171, 172, 261–262; and Protestantism, 52–53; Segovia Woods letters, 76, 88; and Spanish military depredations, 223, 225, 236, 246; and William of Orange as symbol, 260, 261, 293, 294, 296
Philip of Bailleul, 78–79, 80
Philip the Bold (Duke of Burgundy), 25, 33, 279
Philip the Good (Duke of Burgundy): and Burgundian era sacred representations, 24, 25, 27; and civic-sovereign tension, 17; and coronation of Louis XI, 12, 13; and Joyous Entry rituals, 34–36; and nobility, 56; and Order of the Golden Fleece, 28, 29, 30; and regional interaction, 21–22; and uprisings, 14, 34–35
Pien, Lieven, 150
Pius V (Pope), 61, 62, 200

Plakkaat van Verlatinghe. *See* Abjuration of 1581
Plantin, Christopher, 51, 134, 312–313, 314, 315, 320
political culture model, 6n, 8n
Political Education, 307–308, 309–310, 312
political identity. *See* Low Countries political identity
Poll, J. van de, 209
Pollmann, Judith, 114–115
poorter (citizen) figure, 8
Poperinge, 101
popular commentary: and Abjuration of 1581, 307–308, 309–310; and Alba's policies, 61, 62, 168, 169, 170–171, 188–189, 200n, 204–211; animal imagery, 304–306; and Anjou lordship, 282; and arrow imagery, 64–65; and citadel dismantling, 268, 269, 270; and civic republicanism, 304–306; and condemnations of Philip II, 302, 309–310; and Dutch Revolt divisions, 306; and Egmont/Hornes executions, 184, 188–189, 208, 210; and noble dissent, 59–62; and Orangist armed revolt, 274–275, 276; and Pacification of Ghent, 209; and persecution of Protestants, 60, 75, 206–207; and sack of Antwerp, 213, 222, 250–251, 252–254; and sack of Mechelen, 226, 229, 230; and sieges, 236–237, 240, 241; and soldiers' conduct, 214–215, 246, 258; and Spanish military depredations, 214–215, 221–223, 226, 229, 236–237, 240, 241, 246; and William of Orange as symbol, 168, 206, 222, 260–262, 274–280, 281–283, 287
popular devotions: and Alba's policies, 179; Antwerp, 44, 125, 138–140, 142, 143–146, 148, 163–164; and Burgundian era sacred representations, 22–28; and Burgundian regulatory campaign, 41, 44; and Calvinist dissent, 68, 74, 129; Ghent, 44, 151, 161, 164; and iconoclastic riots, 125, 127–130, 132, 143–144, 145–146, 163–164; and noble dissent, 77, 82
Pottre, Jan de, 282
Pragmatic Sanction (1549), 48, 49, 247
Premonstratian abbey (Drongen), 162
Prestz-aux-Nonnains, Abbey of, 87
Priest, Sexton and Weaver, 99
prints. *See* popular commentary
Privy Council, 2, 56
Protestantism: and Burgundian era lordship, 20, 52–53; and Burgundian regulatory campaign, 40, 45–46; and Farnese reconquest, 323; Ghent, 46, 152, 288–289. *See also* Calvinist dissent; multiconfessionalism; Protestants, persecution of

Protestants, persecution of: and Alba's policies, 181, 206–207; Antwerp, 137–138, 141; Burgundian era origins, 40; and Burgundian regulatory campaign, 46, 47; and Calvinist dissent, 67, 68, 69, 72–73, 73, 75, 142; and ecclesiastical system, 58; and funeral of Charles V, 51–52; Ghent, 114, 152; and iconoclastic riots, 96, 103, 114–116, 117, 126, 130, 158, 159–161; and the League, 64; and noble dissent, 53–54, 55, 57, 64–65, 76, 79, 80; and popular commentary, 60, 75, 206–207; Saint Bartholomew's Day Massacre (1572), 220; and Spanish military depredations, 179–180; and Titelmans, 74–75
Prouninck, Gerard, 301
psalm singing, 69–71, 73, 74. *See also* Calvinist dissent
Puys, Remy du, 38

Rade, Gillis vanden, 295, 297
Raephorst, Herbert van, 121
rape: and sack of Antwerp, 252, 254–255, 268; and sack of Mechelen, 228, 230–231; and sack of Naarden, 233, 234–235; and siege of Haarlem, 238; and Spanish military depredations, 223, 224, 228, 230–231, 233, 234, 235, 238, 258
Redeghem, Jan van (Lord of Liedekercke), 268–269
rederijkerskamers, 21–22
Reformation. *See* Protestantism
Reformed faith. *See* Calvinism; Calvinist dissent (1559–1566)
regional interaction, 21–22, 23
Renard, Simon, 66n
Requesens, Luis de, 204, 208, 231, 240, 243–244, 245, 246, 258, 278
Reyd, Everhard van, 331
rhetoricians: and Burgundian regulatory campaign, 45; and Calvinist dissent, 69; and civic sphere, 6; and iconoclastic riots, 99; and Joyous Entry rituals, 37; and Lutheranism, 152; and noble dissent, 60, 63–64; and popular devotions, 128, 140; and regional interaction, 21–22; and William of Orange as symbol, 275, 281, 282, 283, 286–287, 292–294, 297–298
Richardot, Jean, 227
Riethoven, Maarten van, 98, 126, 186
Ripperda, Wigbolt, 237
Roda, Gerónimo de, 246, 247, 268
Roermond, 58, 218n
Rooigem, 158
Rowen, Herbert, 215

Ruyant, Jean, 115–116
Rykers, Hans, 148

sack of Antwerp (1576), 243, 244–258; background of, 245–248; and citadel dismantling, 266, 267, 268; effects of, 257–258; and Pacification of Ghent, 214, 247, 257–258; and popular commentary, 213, 222, 250–251, 252–254; and town hall, 244–245, 251–254, 313–314; wedding violation, 245, 255–256, 257, 272
sacks. *See* Spanish military depredations
Saint Anthony devotions, 103–104
Saint Bartholomew's Day Massacre (1572), 220, 256n
Saint Bavo, Cathedral of (Ghent), 45, 116, 118, 119, 125, 156, 158, 177, 194
Saint Bavo's Abbey (Ghent), 118, 151, 194
Saint Clare, cloister of, 130–131
Saint Gudule's Church (Brussels), 50, 187–188
Saint Jacob's parish church (Ghent), 111, 118, 292
Saint Jacob's parish church (Ypres), 131
Saint Jean, Abbey of (Valenciennes), 71
Saint John's Cathedral (s'-Hertogenbosch), 107, 113
Saint John's Church (Antwerp), 136, 194
Saint John's Church (Ghent), 33, 40, 151
Saint Joris's Church (Antwerp), 136
Saint Lawrence chapel (Steenvoorde), 90, 91, 98–99, 103
Saint Lawrence feast day, 98–99, 103
Saint Lieven procession (Ghent), 13, 44, 151, 162, 194, 195n
Saint Martin's collegiate church (Ypres), 127, 130
Saint Martin's parish church (Ypres), 126, 128
Saint Michael's Abbey (Antwerp), 137, 138, 193, 195
Saint Nicholas parish church (Ghent), 159, 160
Saint Paul's Church (Valenciennes), 119
Saint Peter's Abbey (Ghent), 120, 158, 161–162, 164
Saint Peter's Church (Ghent), 156, 164
Saint Peter's Church (Ypres), 111, 126
Saint Quentin Church (Tournai), 118
Saint-Vaast, Pierre de, 147
Saint Walburgis' Church (Antwerp), 136
Salamon, Vincent, 120
Salle-Le-Comte palace (Valenciennes), 118–119
San Lorenzo de El Escorial, 103
Schilling, Heinz, 6
Schoorman, Jan, 290
Schuere, Nicasius van der, 85
schuttersgilden (shooting guilds), 21–22, 64, 65, 120, 121

Scribner, Robert, 104, 114
Sea Beggars, 200, 203–204, 216–217, 219–220, 235n, 241, 275
Segovia Woods letters, 76, 88
Seigneury of Saint Peter (Ghent), 44
Sennacherib imagery, 261–262
shooting guilds (*schuttersgilden*), 21–22, 64, 65, 120, 121
Short Distinction between Godly and Idolatrous Images (Donc), 312
sieges. *See* Spanish military depredations
Simons, Walter, 22
Sinte-Katherine op de Berg Sinai (Antwerp), 137
Sint-Jan, 130–131
Smedt, Lieven de, 157, 180
Smet, Jan de. *See* Fabricius, Christoffel
Smolderen, Luc, 201, 325
Sohier, Jehan, 118
Song of the Hicks, 102–103
Sonoy, Diederik, 240
South Berkijn parish church, 108
Spanish Fury. *See* sack of Antwerp
Spanish military depredations, 213–216, 220–259; and Alba's policies, 174–181; Burgundian era, 223–224, 225–226; and Calvinist dissent, 180–181; and church violations, 177, 178, 180, 227–228, 229, 256; and civic republicanism, 215–216, 224–225, 239, 241, 251; and fatherland, 242, 258–259; and manly woman legend, 238–239; mutinies, 214, 236, 237, 243–244, 245, 248–249; and Pacification of Ghent, 209–210, 214, 220–221, 247, 257–258; and persecution of Protestants, 179–180; and popular commentary, 214–215, 221–223, 226, 229, 236–237, 240, 241, 246; sack of Liège (1468), 14–16, 194, 224, 225–226; sack of Mechelen (1572), 222, 226–232, 236; sack of Naarden (1572), 222, 232, 233–234, 235, 236; sack of Zutphen (1572), 222, 232–234, 236; siege of Alkmaar, 226, 233, 236, 239–240; siege of Haarlem, 222, 226, 229, 233, 236–239, 244, 275; siege of Leiden, 226, 233, 236, 240–243, 279–280; soldiers' conduct, 176, 178–179, 213–215, 258; and Spanish actions in the Americas, 231–232, 233. *See also* Farnese reconquest; sack of Antwerp
Spiritualism, 67
St. Aldegonde, Lord (Philips van Marnix). *See* Marnix, Philips van
St. Aldegonde, Philip of (Baron of Noircarmes), 175, 182

state ritual: abdication of Charles V, 1–2, 3, 4, 48–49; and Burgundian era lordship, 1–2, 3, 4, 18–21, 28, 30–31, 40, 42, 48–49; and Burgundian regulatory campaign, 40, 42–43; and departure of Philip II, 55; and Egmont/Hornes executions, 186; funeral of Charles V, 50–51, 55, 320–321; funeral of William of Orange, 320–323; and Order of the Golden Fleece, 30–31, 48, 49. *See also* Joyous Entry rituals

States General: and abdication of Charles V, 1, 4, 48; and Abjuration of 1581, 4, 307, 308; and Anjou lordship, 4, 296, 300–301, 316–317, 318; and citadel dismantling, 267; and Council of State coup (1576), 247; divisions in, 263–264; and funeral of William of Orange, 321; and the League, 64; and nobility, 56–57; and Orangist armed revolt, 221; and Pacification of Ghent, 209, 214, 220, 247, 257–258; and Union of Utrecht, 295; and William of Orange, 263, 264, 281; and William of Orange Joyous Entry rituals, 286

Steenvoorde, 90, 91, 98–99, 103
Steenwerck parish church, 100
Stop Rooting in My Garden, Spanish Pigs, 304–306
St. Paul and St. Peter, festival of (Antwerp), 44
Strada, Famiano, 63
Suis, Cornelius, 86
Suys, Cornelis, 121
Swart, Koenraad, 278, 299
syncretism, 18, 29, 38

tableaux vivants: and Anjou lordship, 314–315; and Farnese reconquest, 325; and William of Orange Joyous Entry rituals, 284, 285, 286–287, 291–294, 297
Tacitus, 223
Tahoen, Mathieu, 113
Tanis, James, 205, 260
Tassis, Rogier van, 193
Tavernier, Hans, 131
Templars chapel (Ghent), 155, 156, 157, 158, 159
Tenth Penny tax, 173, 181
Ten Walle (Ghent), 40
textile industry, 95–96, 126, 132
Titelmans, Pieter: and Antwerp, 142; and Calvinist dissent, 72; and iconoclastic riots, 103, 126, 130, 161; and noble dissent, 74–75; and Westkwartier, 96
Tournai: Alba's policies, 183; Calvinist dissent, 67, 68–69, 70–71, 72, 87–88; citadel, 192; iconoclastic riots, 111, 115–116, 118, 119; multiconfessionalism, 167; persecution of Protestants, 115–116, 141; popular devotions, 23–24, 68
town hall (Antwerp), 244–245, 251–254, 313–314
Treslong, Willem Blois van, 216, 217
Trier meeting (1473), 19
True Patriot to the Good Patriots, The (Beutterich), 310–311
Tuin Virgin devotion (Ypres), 125, 127–132, 163–164
Turnhout, 111

Ulloa, Alonso, 188
Union of Arras (1579), 295, 316
Union of Utrecht (1579), 264, 295, 330
United Provinces, 1, 330–331
Utrecht: Alba's policies, 182; and Anjou lordship, 296; citadel construction, 191; citadel dismantling, 265, 266, 281; civic political privileges, 2 n; and ecclesiastical system, 58; iconoclastic riots, 265; and Spanish military depredations, 180, 266; Union of Utrecht, 264, 295, 330; and William of Orange as symbol, 280, 281; William of Orange *stadholder* appointment, 265–266

Vaderlandsche Historie (Wagenaar), 331
Vaernewijck, Marcus van: on Alba's policies, 186; on Calvinist dissent, 85–86, 152–153, 154; on iconoclastic riots, 111, 116, 119, 120, 155, 156–157, 159, 160, 161, 162; on persecution of Protestants, 114, 206–207; on popular devotions, 104; on Spanish military depredations, 177–180, 229, 258
Valdez, Francisco de, 241
Valenciennes: Alba's policies, 182; Calvinist dissent, 66–67, 68, 71, 72–74, 86; citadel construction, 192; citadel dismantling, 265; iconoclastic riots, 118–119, 121; persecution of Protestants, 141
Valerius, Adriaan, 70
Valois, François de (Duke of Anjou). *See* Anjou lordship
Valois, Jeanne de, 118
Van Deursen, A. Th., 299
Vargas, Juan de, 182, 208, 210, 220
Vásquez, Alonso, 176–177, 239
Velde, Frans van den, 162
Velden, Hugo van der, 15, 24
Veluanus, Johannes Anastasius, 99
Venthie, 111–112, 113, 182
Verdickt, Gilles, 51
Vervoort, Hans, 111

Veurne, 101
Viglius, Joachim van Aytta van Zuychem, 56, 57, 59, 68
Vilain, Maximilien (Lord of Rassenghein), 175
Villiers, Pierre Loyseleur de, 314, 320
Virgin procession (Tournai). *See* Our Lady procession (Tournai)
visual satire. *See* popular commentary
Vlissingen, 204, 219–220, 271, 330
Voet, Hendrik, 46
Vos, Maarten de, 269, 270
Vredenburg Citadel (Utrecht), 180, 191, 265, 266, 281
Vries, Hans Vredeman de, 314
Vroede, Gislus, 187

Waerde, Griete van der, 131
Wagenaar, Jan, 331
Wandel, Lee Palmer, 104
Wars of Flanders and France, The (Vásquez), 176
Wassenaar, 121
Wastepatte, Mahieu, 112
Watou, 90, 94
Werchin, Pierre de, 115
Werf, Pieter Andriaanszoon van der, 242
Wesenbeke, Jacob van, 60, 79, 111, 144, 252–253, 273–274
Westkwartier, 67–68, 71, 95–98. *See also* iconoclastic riots (1566)
Westoutre, 113
Wierix, Hieronymus, 171, 172, 269, 270
Wilde, Marx de, 111
"Wilhelmus," 275–276, 286, 293
Willem-Lodewijk, Count of Nassau-Dillenburg, 321
Willem, Philips, 188, 260, 262, 279, 302
William of Orange: and abdication of Charles V, 2; abduction of son, 188, 260, 262, 279, 302; and Alba's arrival, 169; and Alba statue, 201, 203; and Anjou lordship, 263, 301, 316, 317, 318, 319; and Antwerp, 192–193; and Antwerp citadel, 269, 270; *Apology*, 296, 299–300, 301, 302; assassination attempt (1582), 316; and Calvinist dissent, 88, 143; and Calvinist regimes (1577–1578), 281, 288–289, 290; and citadel dismantling, 267; and civic political privileges, 289, 290, 291; and civic republicanism, 310; and Council of State, 272; and Council of State coup (1576), 280; criticism of Alba's policies, 207–208; death of, 225, 319, 320; and Dutch Revolt divisions, 306; and ecclesiastical system, 58–59; Edict of Proscription, 296, 298–299; and Egmont/Hornes executions, 187, 188; exile of, 181, 189, 273, 287; funeral of, 320–323; and funeral of Charles V, 50, 51, 321; and iconoclastic riots, 100, 108, 146, 166, 204; illness of, 241, 279–280; *Justification of the Prince of Orange*, 273–274, 279, 299; and the League, 62–63; and Marnix, 328; marriages of, 52, 277–278, 299–300; and multiconfessionalism, 166–167; and Order of the Beggars, 169; and Order of the Golden Fleece, 31; and Pacification of Ghent, 220; and Protestantism, 52, 212, 272–274, 291; and sack of Antwerp, 248; and sack of Mechelen, 227, 228, 231; and Segovia Woods letters, 76, 88; and siege of Alkmaar, 240; and Spanish military depredations, 215, 222, 227, 228, 231, 240, 241, 258, 279–280; stadholderships, 265–266, 272, 278, 318; and States General, 263, 264, 281; and Union of Utrecht, 295. *See also* Orangist armed revolt; William of Orange as symbol
William of Orange as symbol, 260–263; and Alba's policies, 212–213, 278, 293, 297, 298; and Alba's recall, 211; and Anjou lordship, 263; Apocalypse imagery, 260–261; and assassination, 320; and Biblical imagery, 292; and Burgundian era lordship, 303; and civic republicanism, 263, 272, 284, 285, 303; and civic-sovereign tension, 332–333; and condemnations of Philip II, 301, 302–303; and domestic imagery, 225, 262, 269, 271–272, 276, 277–278, 279, 280, 281, 287; and Dutch Revolt divisions, 287–288, 294–295, 319–320; and fatherland, 212, 219, 225, 272, 276, 277, 278, 279–280, 290, 293, 294; and funeral, 320–323; and Orangist armed revolt, 273, 274–275, 276; and popular commentary, 168, 206, 222, 260–262, 274–280, 281–283, 287; and Protestantism, 212, 272–274, 291; Sennacherib imagery, 261–262; and Spanish military depredations, 212–213. *See also* William of Orange Joyous Entry rituals
William of Orange Joyous Entry rituals, 263, 274, 280–294; Amsterdam, 280, 295–298; Brussels, 280, 281–288; and civic political privileges, 32; Ghent, 280, 288–294
Williams, Roger, 195, 204
Winsum, 91
women: and citadel dismantling, 266; and iconoclastic riots, 111, 112, 131; manly woman legend, 238–239; and sieges, 238–239, 241–242. *See also* domestic imagery; rape

wonderjaar. *See annus mirabilis* (1566); iconoclastic riots (1566)
Wood Beggars, 218
Wormhoudt, 113

Ypres: Calvinist dissent, 67, 98, 129; economic life, 126; iconoclastic riots, 102, 111, 112, 121, 125, 129–132, 163–164; popular devotions, 125, 127–130, 163–164; religious institutions, 126–127; textile industry, 95–96

Zayas, Gabriel de, 208
Zeeland: and Anjou lordship, 296, 318; and civic republicanism, 3; and Orangist armed revolt, 203–204, 219–220; and Pacification of Ghent, 209, 214, 220; Spanish military depredations, 215, 232; Union of Utrecht, 264, 295, 330; William of Orange stadholdership, 272, 318. *See also specific towns*
Zegers van Wassenhove, Ghilein, 121
Zierikzee, 246
Zonnebeke, 127, 130
Zutphen: and Orangist armed revolt, 220; sack of (1572), 222, 232–234, 236
Zuylen van Nijvelt, Willem van, 121
Zyndt, Mathis, 276

www.ingramcontent.com/pod-product-compliance
Lightning Source LLC
Chambersburg PA
CBHW060418300426
44111CB00018B/2887